PROFESSIONAL ALFRESCO®

Continues

▶ PART V APPENDICES *(ONLINE ONLY)*

PROFESSIONAL

Alfresco®

PROFESSIONAL
Alfresco®
PRACTICAL SOLUTIONS FOR ENTERPRISE CONTENT MANAGEMENT

David Caruana
John Newton
Michael Farman
Michael G. Uzquiano
Kevin Roast

Wiley Publishing, Inc.

Professional Alfresco®

Wiley Publishing, Inc.
Professional Alfresco®
Published by
Wiley Publishing, Inc.
10475 Crosspoint Boulevard
Indianapolis, IN 46256
www.wiley.com

Published simultaneously in Canada

ISBN: 978-0-470-57104-0

Manufactured in the United States of America

10 9 8 7 6 5 4 3 2 1

For general information on our other products and services please contact our Customer Care Department within the United States at (877) 762-2974, outside the United States at (317) 572-3993 or fax (317) 572-4002.

Wiley also publishes its books in a variety of electronic formats. Some content that appears in print may not be available in electronic books.

Library of Congress Control Number: 2010921243

To Karen and Matthew for allowing the time.

–David Caruana

For my wife Loveday, my kids Michael and Helena, and all the dedicated people at Alfresco.

–John Newton

For Virgina, William, and James. I told you I was busy.

–Michael Farman

For Jarmi — with whom the cold Chicago winters are fun . . . and even kind of warm.

–Michael G. Uzquiano

For my wife Lyn for putting up with my computer obsessions, and for my two "little bears" Benjamin and Alexander.

–Kevin Roast

ABOUT THE AUTHORS

DAVID CARUANA is Chief Architect and a founding engineer of Alfresco Software, where he is responsible for overall product architecture and design, and has developed many of the core capabilities of Alfresco, such as content modeling, workflow, Web scripts, and CMIS. With over 15 years of experience in the ECM industry, David has previously led product development at Documentum, where he created Web Development Kit, and Oracle, where he developed several content repositories. David is a member of the JSR 283 (Content Repository for Java Technology API Version 2.0) Expert Group and the OASIS Content Management Interoperability Services (CMIS) Technical Committee. He is also active on the Spring Surf and Apache Chemistry open source projects.

JOHN NEWTON, CTO and Chairman of Alfresco, has spent the last 25 years building information management software. In 1990, he co-founded Documentum, the enterprise content management company acquired by EMC, with Howard Shao. John started his career in databases as one of the original engineers at Ingres, the relational database company, and ultimately ran the database development group. John was also one of the first entrepreneurs in residence in Europe at Benchmark Capital. In addition to the Alfresco board, John serves on the board of AIIM, the ECM industry group, and the London International Festival of Theatre. John graduated with a degree in Electrical Engineering and Computer Science from the University of California at Berkeley in 1981.

John blogs on content management, open source, and whatever he feels like on `http://newton.typepad.com`.

MICHAEL FARMAN has over 20 years experience in the content management industry. He started working at Interleaf, specializing in large-scale publishing, and was one of the early employees at Documentum, initially focusing on the pharmaceutical industry and the drug submission process. Mike spent over ten years at Documentum, where he worked in a variety of technical roles and vertical industries. Mike was an early employee at Alfresco, working in almost every department over the past five years, then settling in his current role as Director of Product Management.

MICHAEL G. UZQUIANO is the Director of Web Platform Tools for Alfresco Software, where he has led the development of Alfresco Surf and Web Studio for scriptable Web delivery and visual layout. He is also the head of the Spring Surf Project — a formal Spring Framework extension. With over 12 years of experience in the ECM industry, Michael previously pioneered product and service efforts at Trilogy Software, Epicentric, and Vignette.

Michael holds a Master's Degree of Management from Northwestern University's Kellogg Graduate School of Management. He also holds Bachelor and Master of Science degrees in Electrical Engineering from Cornell University.

KEVIN ROAST is a founding developer of the Alfresco platform and principal developer of the Alfresco Surf Web Framework. He has over 10 years of experience in the software industry and was previously a leading developer at Documentum. Kevin's expertise is in developing and performance-tuning enterprise-scale application platforms, as well as designing and implementing user interfaces based on innovative technology. Kevin is also a contributor to various open source projects.

ABOUT THE ALFRESCO PROJECT EDITOR

BRIANA WHERRY, the Alfresco Information manager, has spent the past 20 years specializing in building new teams, designing processes, and embracing new technologies to deliver innovative documentation solutions to a global audience. Briana has a long working history with the changing face of technical writing, starting out her career with SGML, moving to HTML, and mostly recently adopting DITA. When Briana joined Alfresco in 2007, she was faced with the double challenge of building a new team and implementing DITA in an agile, open source development environment. Briana is a senior member of the Society for Technical Communication (STC), and a member of the OASIS DITA Adoption Committee.

ABOUT THE TECHNICAL EDITOR

DR. PAUL HOLMES-HIGGIN is VP of Engineering, with responsibility for managing Alfresco's research and development team and ensuring both innovation and quality are delivered in Alfresco's software. Paul has over 20 years of experience managing teams in collaborative research and development, both in open source and proprietary software organizations. His expertise covers Knowledge-based Expert Systems, Neural Networks, Information Extraction and Multilingual Natural Language Processing. Paul has a PhD in Artificial Intelligence from the University of Surrey.

CREDITS

EXECUTIVE EDITOR
Robert Elliott

PROJECT EDITOR
Kelly Talbot

ALFRESCO PROJECT EDITOR
Briana Wherry

TECHNICAL EDITOR
Paul Holmes-Higgin

PRODUCTION EDITOR
Daniel Scribner

COPY EDITOR
Christopher Jones

EDITORIAL DIRECTOR
Robyn B. Siesky

EDITORIAL MANAGER
Mary Beth Wakefield

MARKETING MANAGER
Ashley Zurcher

PRODUCTION MANAGER
Tim Tate

VICE PRESIDENT AND EXECUTIVE GROUP PUBLISHER
Richard Swadley

VICE PRESIDENT AND EXECUTIVE PUBLISHER
Barry Pruett

ASSOCIATE PUBLISHER
Jim Minatel

PROJECT COORDINATOR, COVER
Lynsey Stanford

PROOFREADER
Candace English

INDEXER
Ron Strauss

COVER DESIGNER
Michael E. Trent

COVER IMAGE
© Roberto Caucino

ACKNOWLEDGMENTS

WHILE THERE ARE FIVE AUTHORS LISTED ON THE FRONT COVER, producing *Professional Alfresco* has been a huge team effort.

We would like to thank all of the Alfresco Engineering team, particularly Gavin Cornwell, Andrew Hind, Brian Remmington, Nicholas Smith, David Ward, Roy Wetherall, and Erik Winlof, for their insight and technical know-how in the creation of the Alfresco system, and the writing and review of this book. Additional thanks to the many members of the Engineering team who took on the additional burden of driving the Alfresco 3.2 release that was delivered during the writing of *Professional Alfresco*.

We want to provide a very special thanks to Paul Holmes-Higgin, Vice President of Engineering, for his role as technical editor for *Professional Alfresco*. Paul's assistance was invaluable as he ensured that the overall approach was right and the detail was accurate.

We also want to give a very big thank you and appreciation to the Alfresco Documentation team. Without Briana Wherry and her documentation and project management skills, this book would not have happened. Additional big thanks go to Janys Kobernick and Kathryn MacLean, who have done an incredible job of turning our developer-speak into readable English.

And finally, we want to thank the Alfresco customers, partners, and community around the globe for your guidance, feedback, and support through the years. This book is for you.

CONTENTS

INTRODUCTION

In 2005, we felt that the time was right for an open source content management system to challenge the enterprise software landscape. With over 20 years of content management experience, we created Alfresco as a platform for enterprise-scale content management to manage, distribute, and access critical business content, including web sites, office documents, records, images, and rich media. We chose to take an open source approach because we wanted to create Alfresco in a way that was accessible, open, and encouraged community participation.

Professional Alfresco is an in-depth introduction to the Alfresco CMS by the people who built it. It provides you with an overview of Alfresco, its core capabilities and architecture, and the methods to extend it with its RESTful interfaces and lightweight scripting with Alfresco Share as a starting point. This book will help you understand the value of content in your application and show you how to build content-rich applications or web sites that integrate with your enterprise environment or web presence. With detailed guidance and best practices, you will be able to control the exponential growth of content in your organization.

As the creators of Alfresco, we also wanted to give you an understanding of why we have made the choices we have and to demonstrate that this is a powerful and rich yet simple platform for creating content applications. We hope that this will inspire you to join the community of developers using, extending, building new applications, and contributing to Alfresco.

WHO THIS BOOK IS FOR

Professional Alfresco has been created to provide professional developers, system integrators, and architects with the information and guidance they need to implement the Alfresco CMS in an enterprise organization, extending the Alfresco Share application, and integrating Alfresco CMS into existing applications or web sites.

The Alfresco CMS was designed and built using Java, but detailed knowledge of Java development is not required to benefit from this book or to create applications incorporating Alfresco features. Alfresco makes extensive use of popular Web 2.0 techniques, including scripting and RESTful interfaces, to simplify development and improve interoperability.

CTOs, CIOs, IT managers, and IT professionals will be able to use Part I, "Getting to Know Alfresco," to understand what Alfresco is, how it can be used in their business, and the many ways Alfresco Share can be extended to meet specific business requirements. Additionally, Part II, "Getting Technical with Alfresco," will provide you with an overview of the Alfresco environment, including content modeling, authentication and security, and business process design. Chapter 17 will provide you with an introduction of how Alfresco can be integrated with your application or web site.

Application developers with experience in scripting will be able to make use of Part III, "Extending Alfresco with RESTful Services," which includes a range of JavaScript and FreeMarker examples.

Part IV, "Extending Share," will lead you through the steps necessary to build a sample Knowledge Base application using Alfresco Share.

WHAT THIS BOOK COVERS

Since Alfresco is both an application and a programming platform, any book on Alfresco could be much larger than this. We have chosen to focus on the tools most widely used to build content applications and extend Alfresco for this book. These include Web scripts for accessing the Content Application Server and Spring Surf for building Web applications and extending the Share application: All as a framework for building your content application. In doing so, we assume the latest versions of Alfresco from version 3.2 onwards. However, you may find the examples applicable to other versions as well, particularly for Web scripts.

This book covers the topics needed for you to build content applications with Alfresco, to extend Alfresco and the Share application, and to integrate Alfresco into your application or web site. To do this, we give you grounding in Alfresco by providing an overview of Alfresco and its architecture as well as the use cases for which Alfresco is most applicable. We also provide guidance in setting up your Alfresco environment, along with assistance in configuration, security, setting up content models, and workflow.

As with many rich platforms, there are many ways to develop applications with Alfresco, and we concentrate on those that are easiest and most applicable to certain tasks. There is a strong emphasis on Web scripts, the RESTful framework for using and building APIs for content services. You are also introduced to some of the non-programming ways of extending Alfresco, such as rules and actions and metadata modeling and forms configuration.

We also cover the Spring Surf web runtime platform and the role that it plays in building and extending the Alfresco Share application. Once you learn the fundamentals of Surf, you can then extend the Share application with metadata, forms, menus, and other extensions. All this is tied together and provided in the context of an example Knowledge Base application, a typical use for the Alfresco system.

Finally, you will see how Alfresco can be used to extend your application or web site in the patterns that are found in many of the integrations that add content-rich capabilities by accessing or including the Alfresco system.

HOW THIS BOOK IS STRUCTURED

Professional Alfresco is organized into the following parts:

Part I, "Getting to Know Alfresco," introduces you to what Alfresco is, its place in the open source software market, and the business benefits that make Alfresco so widely applicable.

Part II, "Getting Technical with Alfresco," includes a full set of architectural diagrams, providing the reader with both a high-level overview of Alfresco and details on its components, services, and security, explaining how they work together.

Part III, "Extending Alfresco with RESTful Services," explains how to extend Alfresco with web scripts, allowing you to extend the Alfresco data model and deliver custom functionality.

Part IV, "Extending Share," shows you how these extensions can then be tightly integrated with Alfresco core functionality by extending the end-user interface, as demonstrated through the creation of a Knowledge Base sample application with different levels of complexity.

Finally, the book discusses patterns of content management integration with Alfresco as a component of other applications, such as IBM Lotus Quickr and Drupal.

WHAT YOU NEED TO USE THIS BOOK

There are many examples given in this book, all of which can be followed on a standard laptop or server that provides the minimum specification for running an instance of Alfresco. The Alfresco server can run on a range of operating systems, including Microsoft Windows, Linux, Sun Solaris, and Mac OS X. Likewise, a range of different databases can be used, including MySQL, PostgreSQL, Oracle, Microsoft SQLServer, DB2, and Ingres. The Alfresco web applications can be deployed in a number of different Application Servers, including JBoss, Tomcat, Weblogic, and Websphere.

The minimum hardware requirements for a single instance of Alfresco are 2GB RAM and 1GB hard disk.

Throughout the book it is assumed Microsoft Windows is being used, simply for convenience and not any emotional or commercial preference. Also, the book assumes a standard installation of Alfresco is performed through the full installation wizard, which means that Tomcat and MySQL are being used. This is reflected in all the examples.

CONVENTIONS

To help you get the most from the text and keep track of what's happening, we've used a number of conventions throughout the book.

Boxes with a warning icon like this one hold important, not-to-be forgotten information that is directly relevant to the surrounding text.

The pencil icon indicates notes, tips, hints, tricks, or asides to the current discussion.

As for styles in the text:

- We *italicize* new terms and important words when we introduce them.
- We show keyboard strokes like this: Ctrl+A.

- We show file names, URLs, and code within the text like so: `persistence.properties`.
- We present code in two different ways:

```
We use a monofont type with no highlighting for most code examples.
We use bold to emphasize code that's particularly important in the present
context or to show changes from a previous code snippet.
```

SOURCE CODE

As you work through the examples in this book, you can use the source code files that accompany the book. The source code used in this book is available for download at `www.wrox.com`. When at the site, simply locate the book's title (use the Search box or one of the title lists) and click the Download Code link on the book's detail page to obtain all the source code for the book. Code that is included on the Web site is highlighted by the following icon:

Listings include the filename in the title. If it is just a code snippet, you'll find the filename in a code note such as this:

code snippet filename

Because many books have similar titles, you may find it easiest to search by ISBN. This book's ISBN is 978-0-470-57104-0.

Once you download the code, just decompress it with your favorite compression tool. Alternately, you can go to the main Wrox code download page at `www.wrox.com/dynamic/books/download.aspx` to see the code available for this book and all other Wrox books.

ERRATA

We make every effort to ensure that there are no errors in the text or in the code. However, no one is perfect, and mistakes do occur. If you find an error in one of our books, like a spelling mistake or faulty piece of code, we would be very grateful for your feedback. By sending in errata you may save another reader hours of frustration and at the same time you will be helping us provide even higher-quality information.

To find the errata page for this book, go to `http://www.wrox.com` and locate the title using the Search box or one of the title lists. Then, on the book details page, click the Book Errata link. On this page you can view all errata that has been submitted for this book and posted by

Wrox editors. A complete book list, including links to each book's errata, is also available at www.wrox.com/misc-pages/booklist.shtml.

If you don't spot "your" error on the Book Errata page, go to www.wrox.com/contact/techsupport.shtml and complete the form there to send us the error you have found. We'll check the information and, if appropriate, post a message to the book's errata page and fix the problem in subsequent editions of the book.

P2P.WROX.COM

For author and peer discussion, join the P2P forums at p2p.wrox.com. The forums are a Web-based system for you to post messages relating to Wrox books and related technologies and interact with other readers and technology users. The forums offer a subscription feature to e-mail you topics of interest of your choosing when new posts are made to the forums. Wrox authors, editors, other industry experts, and your fellow readers are present on these forums.

At http://p2p.wrox.com you will find a number of different forums that will help you not only as you read this book, but also as you develop your own applications. To join the forums, just follow these steps:

1. Go to p2p.wrox.com and click the Register link.
2. Read the terms of use and click Agree.
3. Complete the required information to join, as well as any optional information you wish to provide, and click Submit.
4. You will receive an e-mail with information describing how to verify your account and complete the joining process.

You can read messages in the forums without joining P2P, but in order to post your own messages, you must join.

Once you join, you can post new messages and respond to messages other users post. You can read messages at any time on the Web. If you would like to have new messages from a particular forum e-mailed to you, click the Subscribe to This Forum icon by the forum name in the forum listing.

For more information about how to use the Wrox P2P, be sure to read the P2P FAQs for answers to questions about how the forum software works, as well as many common questions specific to P2P and Wrox books. To read the FAQs, click the FAQ link on any P2P page.

PART I
Getting to Know Alfresco

1

Introducing Alfresco

WHAT'S IN THIS CHAPTER?

- Understanding Alfresco and its uses
- Looking at the origins of Alfresco and its place in the ECM industry
- Using Alfresco in different scenarios
- Considering factors when implementing an Alfresco content application
- Exploring the importance of open source and community for Alfresco

Alfresco is an open source Enterprise Content Management (ECM) system. It was originally created in 2005 by a team from Documentum, including its co-founder, as an open source alternative to proprietary vendors in the $4 billion ECM market.

Alfresco manages all the content within your enterprise: documents, images, photos, Web pages, records, XML documents, or any other unstructured or semi-structured file. What makes Alfresco stand out are the services and controls that manage this content and features, such as metadata management, version control, lifecycle management, workflow, search, associations to other content, tagging, commenting, and much more. This allows you to find the content you are looking for in the mountain of information accumulating in enterprises and to ensure that it is accurate. It also enables you to present and publish information through the Web or any other channel appropriate to allow users to access that information.

For the End User

For end users, Alfresco appears as a suite of applications or extensions to their existing tools that manages their content. Alfresco exposes itself as though it were a shared drive to replace networked shared disk drives that have no organizational, search, or control mechanisms in place. Alfresco can replace networked shared drives with a store that organizes and controls information and provides a portal interface for searching and browsing content. By emulating the

SharePoint protocol, Alfresco also helps users manage their office documents from within Microsoft Office by using the tools in the Office Suite designed to be used for Microsoft SharePoint. More importantly, Alfresco provides an out-of-the-box suite of applications to browse, search, manage, and collaborate on content in the repository. These applications include document management, Web content management, content collaboration, records management, and email integration. These applications can supplement and can be supplemented by new applications developed on the Alfresco platform.

For the Business

For the business, Alfresco is designed to support the content requirements of a number of business-critical processes and uses. The document management tools, applications, and interfaces support general office work, search, and discovery. The workflow management capabilities support numerous business processes, including case management and review and approval. The collaboration applications and services support the collaborative development of information and knowledge in the creation and refinement of content and documents. The scalable Web content management services support the delivery and deployment of content from the enterprise to its customers. The records management capability provides an affordable means to capture and preserve records based upon government-approved standards. The standards-based platform also provides access to applications that use these standards, such as publishing, image, and email management.

For the Developer

For the developer, Alfresco provides a full-featured, scalable repository and content management platform to simplify the development of the content-centric applications. Based on content management and Internet standards, Alfresco exposes the content management capabilities as services that can be accessed from REST-based or SOAP-based Web services, the new OASIS Content Management Interoperability Services (CMIS) standard Web-based services, or the PHP programming language. It can also be incorporated directly into a Java-based application with core Java services. In addition, Alfresco incorporates lightweight scripting languages that can access these services and provide a lightweight-programming model when speed of development is important. These services provide patterns similar to those used with databases, repositories, or user interface components, but have been extended for the unique challenges of content-centric applications (such as full text search and hierarchical content structures). Being open source, the platform is transparent, and the developer can peer into the internal repository patterns. Alfresco also provides a framework application that delivers much of what end users need, but can be extended by the developer for unique application logic and a customized user interface through Surf, CMIS, Web scripts, and Core Services.

For the IT Organization

For the IT organization, Alfresco provides a low-cost alternative to closed-source, proprietary systems from IBM, EMC, Open Text, Oracle, and Microsoft. Alfresco fits within the enterprise IT governance standards by working with virtually any database, application server, operating system, and system-monitoring infrastructure. By being a 100 percent Java application, the system is portable to virtually any hardware. A multi-tenant capability built into the core applications allows the IT organization to provision virtual instances of Alfresco systems on-demand and maximize the use of existing hardware. The Alfresco system's small size also means that it works well within existing virtualization platforms such as VMware and Xen. Alfresco can also be configured into clusters with built-in redundancy to provide high availability and disaster recovery. Most importantly, Alfresco's open source and open standards approach means that users are not locked into a proprietary platform.

WHAT IS ENTERPRISE CONTENT MANAGEMENT?

According to the Association for Information and Image Management (AIIM) — the leading professional group devoted to ECM — Enterprise Content Management is the collection of strategies, methods, and tools used to capture, manage, store, preserve, and deliver content and documents related to organizational processes. ECM systems use a repository, a number of different applications, and application development platforms to enable this control, access, and delivery of content. Content can be any unstructured information, such as documents, Web pages, images, video, records, or simple files. (Unstructured information refers to computerized information that does not have a data model. The term distinguishes such information from data stored in fielded form in databases or semantically tagged in documents.) The ECM system manages the content and its lifecycle the way a database management system manages data in a database.

An ECM system manages the actual digital binary of the content, the metadata that describes its context, associations with other content, its place and classification in the repository, and the indexes for finding and accessing the content. Just as important, the ECM system manages the processes and lifecycles of the content to ensure that this information is correct. The ECM system manages the workflows for capturing, storing, and distributing content, as well as the lifecycle for how long content will be retained and what happens after that retention period.

According to the research group Forrester, there are five main application areas of ECM: document management, Web content management, records management, image management, and digital asset management. These areas of content management have similar requirements of storage, organization, access, and processing, but each has a different organizational focus and different end users.

- Document management tends to deal with the capture, editing, and distribution of office documents and files.
- Web content management organizes an enterprise's Web site, Web pages, and Web publishing processes.
- Records management deals with the long-term archival or disposal of important documents and records as well as any compliance or regulatory action.
- Image management may deal with documents or records, but handles content in the form of scanned images. Image management manages the process of scanning, quality control, metadata capture, and storage.
- Digital asset management is used primarily by creative and marketing professionals to handle the capture, creation, and editing of photos, videos, and illustrations.

By managing content in an ECM system, organizations are generally able to reduce costs of manual processing, increase the accuracy of information, and aid the search and discovery of important documents and information. Some of the benefits of using an ECM system include:

- Reduction of paper handling and error-prone manual processes
- Reduction of paper storage
- Reduction of lost documents
- Faster access to information
- Improved online experience for customers
- Online access to information that was formerly available only on paper, microfilm, or microfiche
- Improved control over documents and document-oriented processes
- Streamlining of time-consuming business processes
- Security over document access and modification
- Improved tracking and monitoring with the ability to identify bottlenecks and modify the system to improve efficiency

The Origins of ECM

The ECM market started in the late 1980s with image management vendors like FileNet (now owned by IBM) and in the early 1990s with electronic document management such as Documentum (now owned by EMC). Document management married the then–relatively new relational database systems with electronic file management, integration with scanning equipment, and workflow management tools. These companies built platforms to develop applications for managing electronic documents in the emerging client-server enterprise application space and enterprise systems that were large in both scale and price. In the mid 1990s, as the Internet became important, Web content management vendors, such as Interwoven and Vignette, entered into the Web space adjacent to document management.

With the collapse of the dot com bubble in 2001, healthier companies started to acquire smaller players with overlapping functionality. As document management and Web content management vendors started to compete with each other and acquire new technologies, such as archival and records management, the ECM market was born. It was in this period that Microsoft entered with SharePoint. With the intervening years, there are now fewer, but much larger, companies in the growing ECM space. The ECM market is now estimated to be $4 billion according to the analyst firm Gartner.

Enter Alfresco

In 2005, Alfresco started using the open source development and distribution model to spread ECM globally. This enabled them to address underserved parts of the market where existing ECM systems were either too expensive or too complex. At the time, existing ECM vendors put more effort into consolidating disparate product sets than creating new technology, resulting in more difficult development, deployment, and usability, which adversely impacted scalability and performance of these systems. Older technology design, built with no reusable components, meant that these systems were very large, incurred a high overhead for managing information and storing data, and were very expensive to develop and maintain, which affected the cost of the systems. Extending these systems became a major integration problem and applications built upon these systems could cost as much as ten times the sale cost of the core repository and system.

Alfresco built a different kind of system using open source development and incorporating open source components, such as Spring, Lucene, Hibernate, jBPM, FreeMarker, and POI. The Alfresco system incorporated the major applications of ECM — document, image, Web content, record, and digital asset management — but in an easier, more deployable package.

By adopting appropriate open standards, Alfresco generally fits in any enterprise environment. Alfresco's Content Application Server provides a platform for developing content applications in a number of different development styles suitable for the programming task at hand. By being scalable, Alfresco can adapt from small departmental solutions to large-scale Internet solutions.

The end result is a system that is lightweight, flexible, and easy to deploy, with a powerful set of development interfaces. Alfresco recently exceeded 2 million downloads of the ECM system with a large and growing community. Using the professional open source model, Alfresco now has over 1,000 enterprise customers.

ALFRESCO OVERVIEW

The Alfresco system in many ways looks similar to other ECM systems. (See Figure 1-1.) At the core is a repository supported by a server that persists content, metadata, associations, and full text indexes. There is a set of programming interfaces that support multiple languages and protocols upon which developers can create custom applications and solutions. Out of the box applications provide standard solutions such as document management, records management, and Web content management.

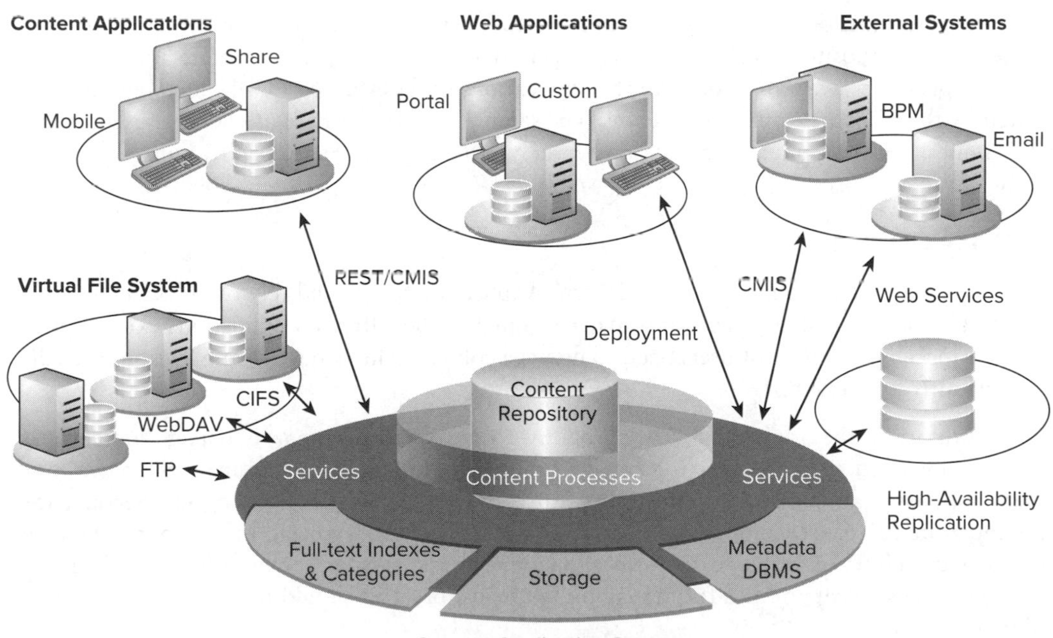

FIGURE 1-1

However, because Alfresco has been created relatively recently compared to other ECM systems, it has been able to take advantage of a more modern architecture. The Alfresco system has grown organically as an entirely Java application, which means that it runs on virtually any system that can run Java Enterprise Edition. At the core is the Spring platform, which provides Alfresco the ability to modularize functionality such as versioning, security, and rules, among other things. Alfresco makes liberal use of scripting to simplify adding new functionality and developing new programming interfaces. This portion of the architecture is known as *Web scripts* and can be used for both data and presentation services. Alfresco has kept the architecture lightweight to make it easy to both download and install and to be able to take advantage of new packaging and deployment options such as in the Cloud.

The Content Application Server and the Repository

At the heart of the Alfresco system is the Content Application Server, which manages and maintains the Content Repository. The repository is comparable to a database except that it holds more than data. The binary streams of content are stored in the repository and the associated full-text indexes are maintained by the Lucene indexes. The actual binary streams of the content are stored in files managed in the repository, although these files are for internal use only and do not reflect what you might see through the shared drive interfaces. The repository also holds the associations among content items, classifications, and the folder/file structure. The folder/file structure is maintained in the database and is not reflected in the internal file storage structure.

Lucene is an open source full-text retrieval engine that is part of the Apache project.

The Content Application Server is responsible for the business logic for the control, access, and update of content in the repository. The Content Application Server allows you to execute applications either as Web scripts or as Java extensions. All the applications of the Alfresco ECM suite are built upon and executed by the Content Application Server. The sample Knowledge Base application used later in this book is built using the Content Application Server and the Alfresco Share application.

Alfresco Applications

Alfresco applications are built upon the Content Application Server and rely on the Content Application Server to persist, access, query, and manage content. The Alfresco applications exist to provide the basic capabilities that most users need to manage content. The two main applications are Alfresco Share and Alfresco Explorer.

Alfresco Explorer is the original application built with the Alfresco system to manage content. Alfresco Explorer allows you to browse the repository, set up rules and actions, and manage content and its metadata, associations, and classifications. Alfresco Explorer was built using JavaServer Faces and is integrated into the Content Application Server. It is currently being phased out in favor of Alfresco Share. However, many extensions and language packs have been built for Alfresco Explorer. It also has extensive capabilities for managing the repository and should be considered a system administrator tool.

Alfresco Share is the next-generation user interface built entirely with the Alfresco Web script technology and can be used to extend the application. Alfresco Share provides content management capabilities with simple user interfaces, providing users with tools to search and browse the repository; content as thumbnails and associated metadata; previews using Flash renditions of content; and a set of collaboration tools such as Wikis, Discussions, and Blogs. Alfresco Share is also the foundation for Alfresco records management. Alfresco Share is organized as a set of sites that can be used as a meeting place for collaboration.

Most importantly, Alfresco Share is an extensible application foundation that can be extended to create vertical applications for certain vertical industries or specialist domains. Records management is a good example of this. The sample Knowledge Base application created in this book also relies on the Alfresco Share core content management capabilities. There is no need to reinvent the content management interfaces of Alfresco Share in order to provide the general-purpose content controls for your end users.

The Alfresco Web Tier and Surf

Alfresco provides ECM capabilities as data services, user interfaces, and user applications. The user interface capabilities are provided by applications and application components using Alfresco's Web tier, Surf, originally developed as a faster way to develop content applications using scripting and REST architecture. Surf uses Web scripts heavily to build user interface components and to access information from the Content Application Server. In 2009, Alfresco contributed Surf as a project to the Spring community where it can be used in conjunction with other Spring Web-tier components, such as Spring MVC, Spring Webflow, and Grails.

Web scripts were developed as part of Alfresco version 2.0 to introduce REST-based development in Alfresco. Web scripts are described in Chapters 8 through 11 and rely heavily on the Web 2.0 style of scripting: interpretive execution of small code pieces that can be configured at runtime. This allows the system to be very adaptable and speeds development of new capabilities. Prototyping is very popular in this environment. If performance is an issue, then Java can be used, but the Web script infrastructure can accommodate Java beans as easily as JavaScript. Web scripts add little overhead but provide a great deal of flexibility and development productivity. Web scripts in the Web tier make it possible to quickly build user interface components with Surf or simple HTML, and deploy them as Alfresco Share components, portlets, or other Web platforms such as Google Gadgets.

Alfresco Programming Models

In order to build an application using the Alfresco Content Application Server, you have the choice of a number of programming models. The simplest model for non-programmers is to use out-of-the-box components of the Alfresco Share application and to use the Rules and Actions model, a set of conditions and actions to take on content, based on those conditions. Rules and actions can be defined using a wizard and can perform such actions as convert content, move content, or execute a simple JavaScript snippet. The sample Knowledge Base application uses rules and actions to do basic processing of content entered into the Knowledge Base.

For more sophisticated processing that doesn't require complex programming, you can use Web scripts. In fact, the Alfresco CMIS implementation and Lotus Quickr integrations were built using Web scripts. By using JavaScript to build these data services, it is easy to create new services in the Alfresco system. If you need to build new user interfaces or extensions to the Alfresco Share application, then you can also use Web scripts by using a Web templating language like FreeMarker. Most of the Alfresco Share application was built using Web scripts. Chapters 8 through 11 show you how to build Web scripts.

If you wish to or need to use Java to build applications or extend Alfresco Share, you can use the many tools associated with Java that were used to build the Alfresco system. Surf, the Web runtime framework contributed by Alfresco to the Spring project, is covered in Chapters 12 through 16 for both extending the Share application and building your own Web applications. Because Share was built using Surf, it is possible to build your own extensions as a combination of Java programming and Web scripts, or with Java alone. You can also use Java to access or even replace whole pieces of Alfresco, Content Application Server, or Alfresco Share by using the Spring platform. This is not covered in this book, but you can use the source code as an example for rewriting pieces and using Spring beans and configuration to extend or replace functionality in Alfresco.

Finally, if you wish to write applications that use Alfresco but are portable to other ECM systems, then you can use Content Management Interoperability Services (CMIS), the OASIS standard for accessing content repositories (including Alfresco, EMC Documentum, IBM FileNet, and Microsoft SharePoint, among others). The sample Knowledge Base application uses some examples of CMIS to show you how you can build portable applications.

CONTENT APPLICATIONS

Alfresco can be used to build most ECM applications. These are the applications in which enterprises use content to engage customers, partners, and employees. These applications are content-rich and their business processes tend to focus on the creation, management, delivery, access, and use of content. Aside from the major applications of document, image, records, digital asset, and Web content management, there are a number of specific applications and use cases that add value to the enterprise and reduce both cost and waste. The following applications are typical of ECM and are ones that Alfresco is particularly adept at supporting.

The Alfresco applications can often be used as the foundation for these application use cases. By applying the programming models previously discussed, you can extend these applications or build your own applications using Alfresco.

Knowledge Management

Knowledge management is the capture of knowledge (from employees in an organization or customers who use their products) and the provision of that knowledge in a form that others can use. Content tends to be the best and most reusable container of knowledge in sharing that knowledge with others. This book uses a knowledge management sample application as the basis for demonstrating how to extend Alfresco and build your own applications.

Document Management

Document management is one of the oldest ECM applications and represents over a quarter of the ECM industry. Document management is used to manage and share office documents and also to incorporate the business processes of creation, review, approval, and distribution of documents. It can be industry- or role-specific (such as management of contracts, proposals, specifications. and procedures), while still using a lot of generic capabilities. Therefore, applications like Alfresco Share and Explorer are good foundations for building document management applications.

Shared Drive Replacement

A more basic form of document management is the replacement of shared drives in the enterprise with a content repository that provides easy access points to content. Shared drives are simple to use because users don't need to be trained and all applications work with them; however, they make a mess of organization, cause a regulatory headache when information is uncontrolled and undiscovered, and are impossible to search in order to find information in terabytes of storage. Because Alfresco supports the protocol used by shared drives, Common Internet File System (CIFS), the repository appears to be a shared drive. With rules, actions, and extensions, you can build complete document management applications that are transparent to the user while getting the content under control and enabling it to be searched.

Enterprise Portals and Intranets

Corporate portals or intranets are used to communicate with employees and keep them abreast of news and developments in the enterprise. While part of enterprise portals are focused on reporting and analyzing data, a large portion of portals are devoted to content and documents. Although folder hierarchies may be an easy way to organize information for a portal, classifications and metadata are often a better way to target information in the portal to end users. Thus, there are elements of document management and business process for delivering into the portal; however, the presentation of lists of content and navigation through classifications may require programming portlets using Web scripts or Java. Portlets provided as part of the Alfresco platform can supplement this development with standardized navigation, search, and content presentation.

Web Content Management

Web content management is about managing Web sites, managing the content that goes into Web sites (such as HTML and images), and managing the processes of building, testing, and deploying Web sites and content. While Alfresco can be used for simple Web sites, it is frequently used for creating Web sites that are Web applications, particularly those developed using Java. Some examples of these Web sites publish a lot of information from multiple sources and integrate e-commerce and back-office systems. Surf is a good platform for creating these types of Web applications and Web sites, and the examples used in this book can be helpful for you to develop them.

Information Publishing

Information publishing is a specialized form of Web content management. It involves the real-time publishing of content from different sources to the Web site and the deployment of that content to the Web farm for Internet access. This can take the form of digital assets such as articles, written internally or syndicated from other sources, or photos. Alfresco is used by many media companies to combine this content and publish it to their Web sites. This straight-through publishing of information requires both strong content control and performance to aggregate and push out the content. Alfresco is well suited to this type of Web content management.

Records Management

Records management is used to control important information that needs to be retained for extended periods of time. You would use records management over document management in regulated or compliant environments, such as in managing governmental information or personnel records, or where information may be audited. Alfresco has been certified to the U.S. Government 5015.2 records standard and is useful for controlling retention and review periods, providing specialized security, and determining whether the records are archived or destroyed after a specified period of time. However, no two records repositories are the same and although Alfresco records management provides a good foundation, you may want to provide additional functionality through configuration or customization. At the very least, you will need to configure the file plan specific to the department deploying records management.

Collaborative Content Development

Many knowledge-oriented business processes rely on content as the container of information captured and developed as part of the creative process. Collaborative work such as new product development, sales proposal preparation, or strategic planning more often than not have a document of some sort (a Word document, a PowerPoint presentation, or an Excel spreadsheet) that represents the fruit of the effort. Sometimes the content is the purpose of the collaboration, such as the creation of a report or a book like the one you are reading right now. Alfresco was used to manage the development of this book, and it is a good example of collaborative content management. Alfresco and Alfresco Share are useful tools in collaborative content management that aids knowledge work. Alfresco Share also provides a good platform to build specialized tools and extensions that may help either with collaboration or with handling content in the collaborative and creative processes.

Case Management

Case Management is the handling of information related to a case, such as an insurance claim, an investigation, or personnel processing. Because of Alfresco's document management capabilities, folder structure, classification schemes, and workflow, it is well suited to managing cases and distributing work in handling cases. Alfresco incorporates the jBPM business process engine from JBoss and can handle sophisticated workflows and queue management. Alfresco has built a content-oriented task model that aggregates all the resources required to perform specific tasks within the case handling process.

ALFRESCO AND YOUR ENVIRONMENT

Alfresco is applicable for most ECM requirements. It is currently deployed in some of the largest organizations in the world, spanning finance, high technology, manufacturing, and government. It has been used by small, medium, and large businesses at the departmental level, enterprise-wide, and across the Internet. Depending on what type of content application you want to create or deploy, Alfresco can be used and configured to meet the requirements of those applications.

In order to make sure that Alfresco meets your needs and can be an effective content platform and content management system, you should evaluate your environment, your target solution, and which tools are best suited to meet your solution.

What to Consider

Although Alfresco can scale from small solutions to enterprise-wide infrastructure, it is important to make sure that Alfresco is configured in the right way and that the solution has been programmed with the most appropriate tools and interfaces. Here are some of the areas that you should consider when developing your content application.

The Audience

The Alfresco system has tools for broad usage and for sophisticated users of content management. By fitting within the user's environment, such as the file system, Microsoft Office, or email, Alfresco can provide services invisibly to a broad range of end users. Alfresco also integrates with enterprise portals and applications where users access content as part of another solution or application. In addition, there are interfaces that allow users to configure powerful rules and workflows without programming. By determining who your audience is and where they need to access content, you can choose the right deployment choices for Alfresco.

Chapter 2 discusses the tools available for presenting content management to the end user. The sample Knowledge Base application uses several different tools to show how you can use interfaces as simple as a shared drive, as well as more sophisticated knowledge-processing tools. Chapter 17 presents you with the patterns of how Alfresco can integrate with other applications.

The Number of Users

After you've downloaded Alfresco from the Alfresco Web site, the system is capable of easily handling dozens of users. However, if you wish to deploy to an entire enterprise, you may want to consider options of clustering and distribution. Chapter 2 shows you different configurations and the impact on development. Alfresco can run as part of a single application or in a multi-tier environment clustered with many machines.

The Architecture

Is this application standalone or part of a broader content infrastructure? If content is reused between applications, you should consider a remote repository from your application and application server. If absolute performance is important, perhaps it makes sense to integrate your application, repository, and database as a single application. If you are in a distributed environment or parts of your content architecture are geographically distributed, consider either federation or synchronization options. Understanding your architecture will be key.

The Level of Configuration or Customization

Analyze how your application will be deployed, how it will be used, and how long you can expect to use it in order to determine whether you want to build a new application, customize one of the existing Alfresco applications, or simply configure the out-of-the-box applications. Configuration can be very powerful, especially in configuring rules and actions or in adding out-of-the-box components. If you choose to customize, you have the option of scripting using Web scripts, thus avoiding heavyweight development. Alternatively, you can develop using a full Java environment using your favorite IDE. Customization can take the form of customizing the Alfresco application or the Content Application Server itself. The sample Knowledge Base application will show you how to do all of these.

The Enterprise IT Environment

The Alfresco system and applications are written in Java and Java-based technologies to ensure that they are as portable as possible. They are quite possibly the most portable ECM systems available. In addition, Alfresco incorporates Hibernate and iBATIS open source database abstraction layers to allow it to be ported to a number of different database management systems. By using the Spring platform, Alfresco can integrate different caching technologies and security and authentication systems. Alfresco is designed to support different languages as well, allowing you to develop using Java, PHP, .NET, or virtually any language that supports REST-based or Web services–oriented programming.

Thus, practically any IT environment can be supported, but operating system, database, language, and security should be considered when developing and deploying your application. The *Installing and Configuring Alfresco* guide on the Alfresco wiki will give you guidance on how to configure for different databases and authentication mechanisms. Chapter 17 provides advice on how Alfresco can be integrated with other applications.

The Support Requirements

Alfresco is open source, so it can be used for free. If you are a small organization or small independent software developer, this can be a great option for using content management without the expense of a large ECM system. However, if you wish to deploy your application in a production environment, you may wish to use the Enterprise version of Alfresco, which provides you with support and prompt bug fixing. Also, if you are running with proprietary databases or operating systems, then the Enterprise version provides configurations on certified platforms that include different operating systems and databases such as Oracle or Sybase. You should consider how you build and deploy your application and determine what your support requirements are based upon these activities. The more mission-critical or the more integrated into the enterprise, the more you may need the Enterprise version.

WHAT IS PROFESSIONAL OPEN SOURCE SOFTWARE?

Alfresco's ECM capabilities are available as open source. If you are a content management developer who has worked with proprietary platforms, you may not be familiar with the implications of open source, nor with the advantages or disadvantages for the products.

Much of the early development of what is now known as open source started with the GNU project by Richard Stallman in the early 1980s to create development tools that emulated Unix but did not require a license from a vendor. Stallman labeled this "Free Software" and felt that the freedom to use this software was paramount. In the mid 1990s Linus Torvalds created a completely open and free Unix-based operating system called Linux under the same license terms as GNU. The Linux movement created a whole genre of software that became known as *open source*. In 1999, IBM backed the Linux operating system and the open source movement in general and thereby gave credence and momentum to open source.

In the early part of the 2000s, entrepreneurs created enterprise software businesses based upon open source and employed a professional open source business model. The database system MySQL, originally developed in the early 1990s, used the GNU GPL (General Public License) to distribute their software. They did this using a dual-license business model that distributed the software under GPL and commercial licenses. Shortly after this, JBoss built and licensed its application server under the more liberal LGPL (Lesser/Library General Public License). JBoss and others raised venture capital and thrived in a down economy, proving the value of distribution via the open source model and developing business through selling support and services.

Why Use Open Source?

Open source is a revolution in business models and a means of production rather than anything technological. It is underpinned by three main principles:

- Opening intellectual property and the transparency approach spreads faster than concealing intellectual property and builds a bigger market.
- Sharing intellectual property will grow that intellectual property faster.
- Reusing other people's intellectual property stops wasting time re-inventing the wheel.

This change in business model has led to companies using open source as their preferred distribution model, including Alfresco. These advantages include:

- Broad distribution of product through Internet download
- The ability of users to try the product before buying, eliminating much of the sales and demand generation activities of ordinary enterprise software
- Much broader testing and code review of products in the beta and product phases of development
- Word-of-mouth marketing and open source meet-ups, reducing the cost of marketing
- Lower cost of development through use of other open source components and contributions from the many extensions that users create
- Bug fixes from users who end up fixing problems themselves

The benefits to the user and business community also are clear:

- Users are not locked into a proprietary platform and they are free to use the open source version of the product.
- The vendors providing these products are the support source upon which users and businesses can rely if they need fixes, advice, warranty, or indemnity.
- The open source vendors are held more accountable than the proprietary vendors, since there is always the possibility to switch back to the free version.
- Users could see the source code and make the minor changes they want without waiting for the next release or even change wholesale parts of the product.
- Because of the lower cost and economies of scale of open source distribution, the lower cost of product is passed on to the consumers of services.
- The transparency of open source means that there is greater visibility of changes coming and of what bugs already exist.
- Through the community and transparency aspects of open source, the users play a more intimate role in the development of the products, with a greater influence on product direction.

There are lots of open source programs and projects out there, and some of them are terrible. However, open source works well when software is a commodity and you cannot tell one piece of software from another, such as word processors, Web browsers, and operating systems. When software is a commodity, you are paying only for a brand where the company receives money without improving or innovating the product. Professional open source works well when enterprise software is commoditized. Alfresco was created because of the increasing difficulty in distinguishing one ECM system from another, and open source can allow the community to move Alfresco beyond the others.

Open source development is painted as chaotic and unreliable by proprietary vendors, but in reality it is just as controlled as any other project. There are project leads who make decisions (and have the final decision on what goes in or out) and no more than a handful of people developing the open source project. Sometimes these developers can come from more than one company. With open source this works fairly seamlessly because there are no secrets or intellectual property to hide. There can, however, be much more testing involved than with ordinary software. In most successful open source projects, you can have hundreds of people downloading the software and testing it out and sometimes even providing fixes because they can see and repair the source code.

In order to make this process work and to build a sustainable open source community, somebody must pay for it. Usually an open source company is in markets directly adjacent to the software, such as system integration. By supporting Linux, IBM makes its money selling hardware that runs Linux and selling consulting services to build solutions for customers. IBM has a huge patent portfolio, but they make twice as much money selling hardware and services around open source as they make from licenses from their patents.

Alfresco Software is building a sustainable business and thus a sustainable open source community by selling technical support on the Alfresco system. Not everyone wants or needs support, but it isn't necessary for everyone to want it. With over 2 million downloads, a small percentage of users who need support in a product environment, especially in the Global 2000, is sufficient to support the community, the project, and the company. By participating in the large enterprise content management market, Alfresco has sufficient scale to continue growing and to service the open source community and product.

Alfresco and the Community

Because Alfresco has built its development processes and its business model on open source, the Alfresco community is extremely important. The process of scoping the product, tracking development, and delivering the product is open and is what distinguishes it from proprietary content management vendors. All the source code is available from the Subversion repository; documentation is available and developed from the wiki; forums provide feedback on plans, bugs, and features; and all the bugs and project plans are available in JIRA through the Internet. You can expect Alfresco to be open about how they build and release product. They won't be perfect, but they believe this transparency holds them accountable to provide a better product for you.

The great thing about open source is you don't re-invent the wheel. If someone has created a piece of code, then others can share it. Ideally, if a community member stumbles across a bug in that code, there is enough information in the code to fix it. If there isn't enough information, then someone else can provide missing documentation. Pitching in and sharing helps save time and effort.

The community has already contributed to Alfresco in many ways. Some code and functionality contributions have helped distinguish Alfresco as a product. Contributed bug fixes allow Alfresco engineers to concentrate on new functionality. Community translations of the user interface enable access to Alfresco around the world. Alfresco has already been translated into more languages than some major products will ever see. Integrations and solutions have been a particularly rich vein of sharing. More experienced users and developers have been extremely helpful in assisting new users in the forums.

If you do develop a solution or can contribute, please take the time to share, as it not only helps Alfresco, but also assists users like you. If you have a solution or translation based on Alfresco, contribute it to the Forge. If you have a bug fix, contribute it through JIRA. If you have time to help others or you see a question that you can answer in the forums, please do, and others will return the favor.

2

Architecture

WHAT'S IN THIS CHAPTER?

- Understanding the Content Application Server and its embedded content repository
- Learning about the Alfresco Web Application Framework, including Spring Surf and Web scripts
- Exploring deployment options
- Integrating with the enterprise infrastructure

Alfresco, the product, has grown rapidly since its inception and therefore offers an extensive set of technologies and building blocks for implementing an ECM solution. You can use this chapter as a map for navigating your way through Alfresco and as assistance for choosing the correct approach to solving your business problems.

GUIDING PRINCIPLES

When Alfresco started in early 2005, the founding engineers were very fortunate to begin with a clean slate, which is a rare position for software development teams these days. Many of the engineers had previous experience building content management systems, so it was an ideal opportunity to step back and think deeply about how to approach building a product to support modern-day ECM requirements. Before diving into designing Alfresco, the engineers first set out the following architecture principles, which are still in use today.

Supporting ECM Requirements

Enterprise Content Management (ECM) covers a broad range of applications, including Document Management (DM), Web Content Management (WCM), Records Management (RM), Digital Asset Management (DAM), and Search. The Alfresco architecture is driven by the need to support the requirements of all these applications, resulting in a coherent solution where content and management processes are not forced into silos. Alfresco recognizes that each of these disciplines has unique and overlapping characteristics, so the design of each Alfresco capability is not done in isolation but in the context of the whole system. Failure to support the requirements of ECM is not an option.

Simple, Simple, Simple

Complexity is a barrier to entry. Many ECM deployments do not reach their full potential due to complexities enforced on developers, IT, and users of the solution. Alfresco aims to be as simple as possible to develop against, customize, deploy, and use. The simplest and probably most widely deployed ECM solution is the shared document drive. The Alfresco architecture is driven by the desire to be as simple as a shared drive.

Scaling to the Enterprise

Content is everywhere and growing at an alarming rate. This is why every service and feature of Alfresco is designed up front to scale: scale in terms of size of data set, processing power, and number of users.

A Modular Approach

Unlike many ECM systems, the Alfresco architecture takes a modular approach. Alfresco recognizes that solutions often require a pick and mix of ECM features; therefore, the architecture promotes a system where capabilities are bundled into modules whose implementation may be replaced if required, or not included at all. Cross-cutting concerns are encapsulated through Aspect-Oriented Programming (AOP) techniques. This allows for fine-tuning and optimization of an ECM solution.

Incorporating Best-of-Breed Libraries

Where possible, Alfresco incorporates best-of-breed third-party libraries. The open source nature of Alfresco lends itself to integrating with the wealth of available open source libraries. This is done whenever it is more profitable to integrate than build or whenever expertise is better provided in another project rather than in-house. This approach allowed Alfresco to efficiently build an ECM suite, innovate in multiple areas, and react quickly to market demands.

Environment Independence

ECM is often not the complete solution; it is part of a whole. Alfresco ECM, therefore, does not dictate the environment upon which it depends. You can choose which operating system, database, application server, browser, and authentication system to use when deploying Alfresco. ECM is less about the application and more about the services embedded within an application. You can choose how to package Alfresco — for example, as a Web application, an embedded library, or a portlet.

A Solid Core

The heart of Alfresco ECM is implemented in Java. This decision was driven by the wealth of available Java libraries, monitoring tools, and enterprise integrations. Just as importantly, Java is a trusted runtime for many enterprises wishing to deploy applications in their data centers. Each Alfresco capability is implemented as a black-box Java service tested independently and tuned appropriately.

Scriptable Extensions

There is no single solution for all ECM problems. Alfresco recognizes that its solid core, although very comprehensive, cannot solve all ECM needs. Extensions will always need to be created for custom solutions and there are many custom solutions versus the single Alfresco core. Therefore, Alfresco extension points are developed using JVM-based scripting languages, allowing a much wider pool of developers to build extensions versus those that can contribute to the Alfresco core. Extensions are packaged entities, allowing for the growth of a library of third-party reusable extensions.

A Standards-Based Approach

The Alfresco architecture always complies with standards where applicable and advantageous. Primary concerns are to reduce lock-in, improve integration possibilities, and hook into the ecosystems built around the chosen standards.

An Architecture of Participation

Finally, and most importantly, the Alfresco architecture promotes a system designed for community contribution. In particular, the architecture principles of a solid core, modularity, standards compliance, simplicity of development, and scriptable extensions encourage contribution of plug-ins and custom ECM solutions. Participation complements the open source approach to the development of Alfresco and fosters growth of the Alfresco community. As the community grows, the quality of self-service improves, as well as the quality of feedback to Alfresco. This, in turn, enhances Alfresco and creates the ultimate feedback loop.

A HIGH-LEVEL OVERVIEW

There are many ways to slice and deploy Alfresco; however, most deployments follow a general pattern. Ultimately, Alfresco is used to implement an ECM solution such as DM, WCM, RM, and DAM; across those solutions may also be elements of Collaboration and Search (as shown in Figure 2-1). The solutions are typically split between clients and server, where clients offer users a user interface to the solution, and the server provides content management services and storage. It is common for a solution to offer multiple clients against a shared server, where each client is tailored for the environment in which it is to be used.

Alfresco offers two primary Web-based clients: *Alfresco Explorer* and *Alfresco Share*. Alfresco Explorer has been offered since the initial release of Alfresco. A power-user client, it exposes all features of the Alfresco Content Application Server. Alfresco Explorer is implemented using Java Server Faces (JSF) and is highly customizable, but it is only deployable as part of the Alfresco Content Application Server.

Alfresco Share is a recent offering, focusing on the collaboration aspects of content management and streamlining the user experience by introducing features such as Web previews, tagging, and social networks. The central concept of Alfresco Share is the notion of a site: a place where users collaborate on the production of content and publish content. It is implemented using Spring Surf and is customizable without knowledge of JSF. Alfresco Share can also be deployed to its own tier separate from the Alfresco Content Application Server and, ultimately, managed through the Alfresco WCM solution. Over time, Alfresco Share will support all the features of Alfresco Explorer.

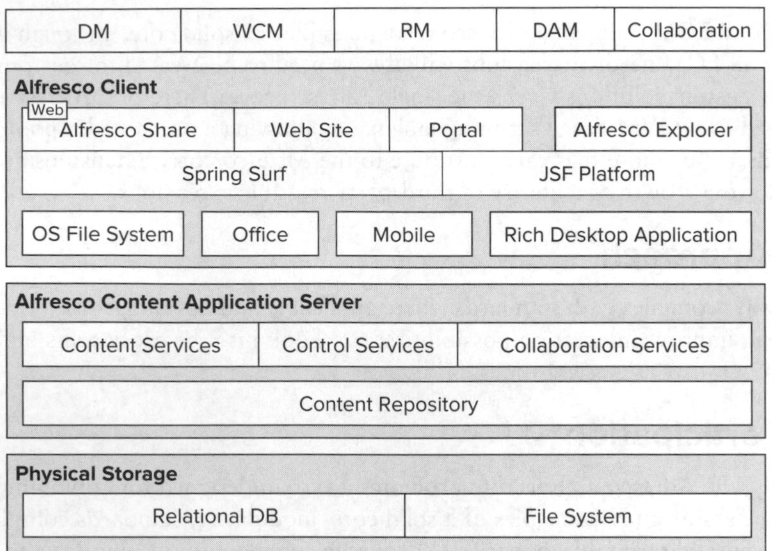

FIGURE 2-1

Of course, Alfresco is not available only through its Web clients. To drive user adoption, clients exist for portals (via JSR-168 portlets), mobile platforms (such as Apple iPhone), Microsoft Office, and the desktop (for example, through Flex and Microsoft .NET).

A client that is often overlooked is the folder drive of the operating system. This is probably one of the most common homegrown ECM solutions where users share documents through a network drive. Using JLAN technology, which Alfresco acquired, Alfresco can look and act just like a folder drive. JLAN is the only Java server-side implementation of the CIFS protocol. With this technology, users interact with Alfresco just as they do any other normal file drive, except the content is now stored and managed in the Alfresco Content Application Server.

The Alfresco Content Application Server comprises a content repository and value-added services for building ECM solutions. Within the last few years, the content repository has been defined by the following standards:

- CMIS (Content Management Interoperability Services)
- JCR (Java Content Repository / JSR-170/286)

These standards provide a specification for content definition and storage, retrieval of content, versioning, and permissions. Alfresco's content repository complies with both standards, providing a highly reliable, scalable, and efficient implementation. Content stored in Alfresco is, by default, placed into a combination of RDBMS (relational database management system) and file system. Due to the support of standards-based interfaces, there is no risk of content repository lock-in.

Even though standards efforts have gone a long way to define the core building blocks for ECM, there is still a gap between the features provided by the content repository and the requirements of a typical ECM solution. The Alfresco Content Application Server provides the following categories of services built upon the content repository:

- Content services (for example, transformation, tagging, metadata extraction)
- Control services (for example, workflow, records management, change sets)
- Collaboration services (for example, social graph, activities, wiki)

Clients communicate with the Alfresco Content Application Server and its services through numerous supported protocols. Programmatic access is offered through HTTP and SOAP, while application access is offered through CIFS, FTP, WebDAV, IMAP, and Microsoft SharePoint protocols.

The Alfresco installer provides an out-of-the-box prepackaged deployment where the Alfresco Content Application Server (with embedded Alfresco Explorer) and Alfresco Share are deployed as distinct Web applications inside Apache Tomcat and configured for use with MySQL.

THE ALFRESCO CONTENT APPLICATION SERVER

The primary responsibility of the server is to provide a comprehensive set of services for use in building ECM solutions. In many respects, the server is just a black box where you place and manage content. Just like an RDBMS, the Alfresco Content Application Server exposes a set of remote public interfaces for allowing a client to communicate with it (as shown in Figure 2-2).

The remote public interfaces are the only part of the server visible to the client. There are two types: *Remote APIs* allow programmatic interaction with services of the server and *Protocol bindings* map those same services for use by a protocol-compliant client.

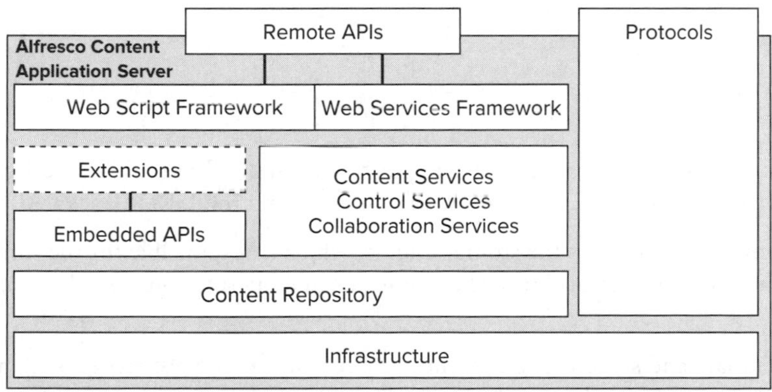

FIGURE 2-2

Internally, the server comprises several layers. The foundation is a set of infrastructure concerns such as configuration, authentication, permissions, and transactions that cut across all capabilities.

Infrastructure also shields the server from being tied to any specific environmental implementation, such as transaction managers or caching mechanisms.

The Alfresco standards-based content repository is then built upon this infrastructure, which itself is the building block for content, control, and collaboration services. Each capability of the content repository and content services is individually bundled as a module with its own in-process interface and implementation. Modules are bound together by the infrastructure through their interfaces.

You can deploy extensions to the Alfresco Content Application Server to extend or override its capabilities. Their implementation may use the in-process interfaces offered by the content repository and content services.

The Content Repository

As already stated, two standards (CMIS and JCR) define what services a content repository should provide. These include (as shown in Figure 2-3):

- Definition of content structure (modeling)
- Creation, modification, and deletion of content, associated metadata, and relationships
- Query of content
- Access control on content (permissions)
- Versioning of content
- Content renditions
- Locking
- Events
- Audits
- Import/Export
- Multilingual
- Rules/Actions

The Alfresco content repository provides a comprehensive implementation of all of these services and exposes each of them through an Alfresco API, CMIS protocol bindings, and the JSR-170 Java API.

At the core of the Alfresco content repository is the storage engine, which is responsible for the storage and retrieval of content, metadata, and relationships. The storage engine operates on the following constructs:

- **Nodes** — Provide metadata and structure to content. A node can support properties, such as author, and relate to other nodes such as folder hierarchy and annotations. Parent to child relationships are treated specially.
- **Content** — The content to record, such as a Microsoft Word document or an XML fragment.

Content models are registered with the content repository to constrain the structure of nodes and the relationships between them, as well as to constrain property values.

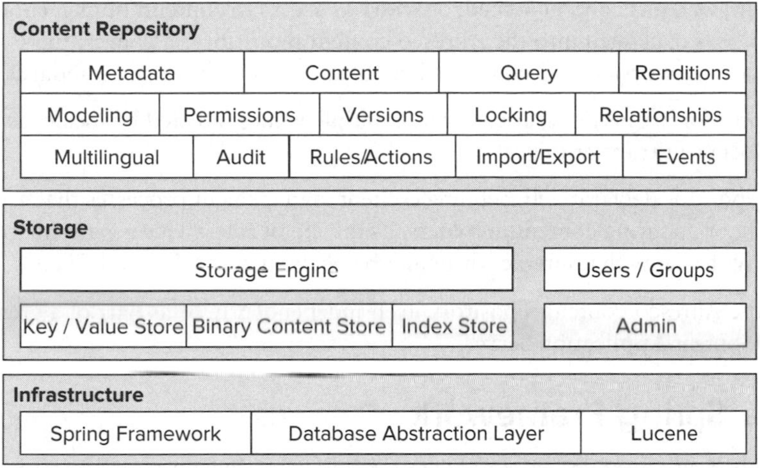

FIGURE 2-3

The storage engine also exposes query capabilities provided by a custom query engine built on Apache Lucene that supports the following search constructs:

- Metadata filtering
- Path matching
- Full text search
- Any combination of the above

The query engine and storage engines are hooked into the transaction and permission support of the infrastructure, thus offering consistent views and permission access. Several query languages are exposed (as shown in Figure 2-4), including native Lucene, XPath, Alfresco FTS (Full Text Search), and CMIS Query Language (with embedded Alfresco FTS).

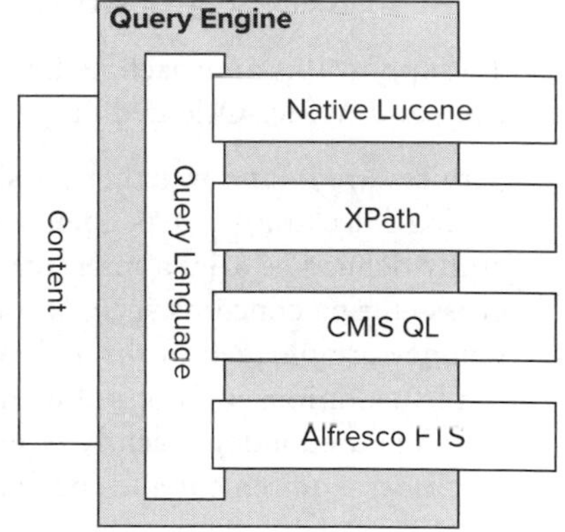

FIGURE 2-4

By default, Alfresco stores nodes in an RDBMS while content is stored in the file system. Using a database immediately brings in the benefits of databases that have been developed over many years, such as transaction support, scaling, and administration capabilities. Alfresco uses a database abstraction layer for interacting with the database, which isolates the storage engine from variations in SQL dialect. This eases the database porting effort, allowing the certification of Alfresco against all the prominent RDBMS implementations. Content is stored in the file system to allow for very large content, random access, streaming, and options for different storage devices. Updates to content are always translated to append operations in the file system. This allows for transaction consistency between database and file system.

Content Repository Services are all built upon the storage and query engines. As with the engines, the same infrastructure is shared. The concept of users and groups is introduced into these services, such as recording the author of content, who has content locked, or who has access to content. Implementation of the standards-defined services is packaged into the Alfresco content repository; however, there are two services, also provided, that are worth mentioning outside of the content-repository standards:

- **Multilingual** — Support for properties that can store multiple values indexed by locale, as well as support for document translations.
- **Rules/Actions** — Support for declaratively defining content management processes that are triggered when adding or updating content in folders. Think email rules. This is particularly powerful when used with clients that interact through protocols such as CIFS and FTP.

You can bundle and deploy the Alfresco content repository itself independently or as part of a greater bundle, such as the Alfresco Content Application Server.

Modularity through a Spring Framework

Looking inside Alfresco reveals a very modular system. Every moving part is encapsulated as a service, where each service provides an external face in a formally defined interface and has one or more black-box implementations. The system is designed this way to allow for:

- Pick and mix of services for building an ECM solution
- Reimplementation of individual services
- Multiple implementations of a service, where the appropriate implementation is chosen based on the context within which the solution is executed
- A pattern for extending Alfresco (at design and runtime)
- Easier testing of services

To support this approach, Alfresco employed the Spring framework for its factory, Dependency Injection, and Aspect-Oriented Programming capabilities.

Services are bound together (as shown in Figure 2-5) through their interfaces and configured using Spring's declarative Dependency Injection. An important point here is that a service interface is literally defined as a Java interface. For services that form the internal embedded API for extensions, cross-cutting concerns such as transaction demarcation, access control, auditing, logging, and multi-tenancy are plugged in through Spring AOP behind the service interface. This means that service implementations are not polluted with these concerns. It also means the cross-cutting concerns may be configured independently or even switched off across the server if, for example, performance is the top-most requirement and the feature is not necessary.

Multiple services are aggregated into an Alfresco subsystem where a subsystem represents a complete coherent capability of the Alfresco server, such as authentication, transformation, and protocols. As a unit, subsystems have their own lifecycle where they may be shut down and restarted while the Alfresco server is running. This is useful to disable aspects of the server, or reconfigure parts of it, such as how LDAP synchronization is mapped. Each subsystem supports its own administration interface that is accessible through property files or JMX.

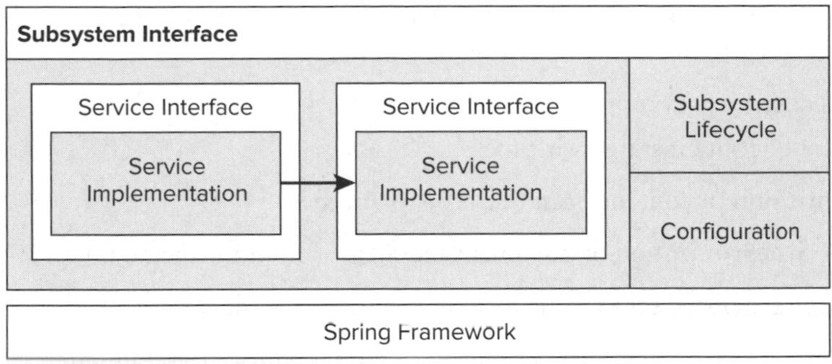

FIGURE 2-5

Content Services

The Alfresco Content Application Server is more than just a content repository. A significant addition is the set of extended high-value services split into the following categories (as shown in Figure 2-6):

- **Content** — Advanced content management capabilities
- **Control** — Encapsulation of processes
- **Collaboration** — Integration of content into social networks

Whereas a content repository provides a very horizontal general set of capabilities, the purpose of these services is to provide focused building blocks to support the requirements of the various disciplines of content management, such as document management, Web content management, and records management. All of these services are implemented on top of the content repository, follow the modular patterns already described, and share the same infrastructure foundation.

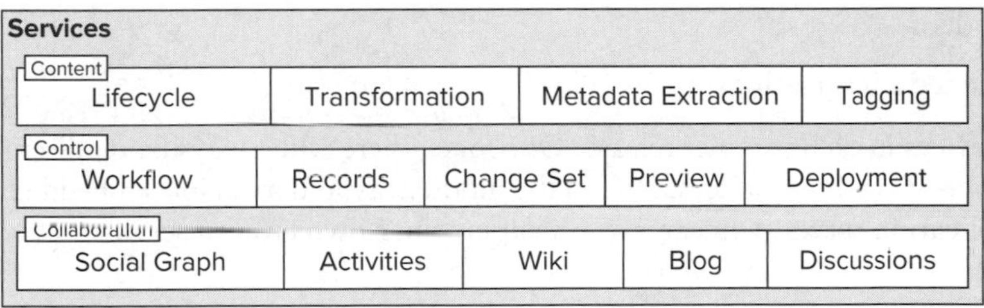

FIGURE 2-6

Something that might seem obvious but not appreciated is that Alfresco can provide a uniform and integrated set of services for all disciplines of content management. Often, ECM architectures are grown through acquisition and combine distinct systems, perhaps each with their own repository. This is not the case with Alfresco, which allows the use of services in isolation or with each other.

Although content management disciplines may seem discrete, there is actually a lot of overlap in their requirements and ECM solutions often require a mix of those disciplines anyway.

In summary, the advanced content services comprise the following:

- **Lifecycle** — Management of content state over time
- **Transformation** — Conversion of content from one type to another
- **Metadata Extraction** — Synchronization of document metadata with node metadata
- **Tagging** — Arbitrary user-generated tags versus formally defined classifications

Control services encapsulate processes through which content flows and comprise the following:

- **Workflow** — Structured process that include a sequence of connected steps, often involving human interactions through allocation of tasks
- **Records** — File plans, record types, retention and archival policies, disposition, and reporting, all certified to the DOD 5015.2 standard
- **Change Set** — Working area for making safe content modifications
- **Preview** — Viewing of content as it should be before publishing
- Deployment: Publishing of content from one environment to another

Collaboration services integrate the production and publishing of content into social networks:

- **Social Graph** — Represents people and their relationship to each other, either directly or indirectly through groups or teams
- **Activities** — Continuous personalized feed of activities performed by others in the social graph or by Alfresco
- **Wiki** — Easy creation and editing of interlinked Web pages
- **Blog** — Log of regularly maintained entries of commentary, events, and other material, such as documents and videos
- **Discussions** — Threaded conversations

Alfresco continues to add services in each product release. Of course, there will always be requirements that are not fulfilled by the out-of-the-box services. Due to the modularity and available embedded API of the Alfresco Content Application Server, you can always deploy your own custom services.

Protocols

To assist the adoption and ease of use of Alfresco, the Alfresco Content Application Server supports many folder- and document-based protocols. This allows you to access and manage content held within the content repository using client tools you may already be familiar with. In fact, some users may not even know they are using Alfresco, although the content they produce or consume has been through a process managed by Alfresco.

All the protocol bindings expose folders and documents held in the Alfresco content repository. This means a client tool accessing the repository using the protocol can navigate through folders, examine properties, and read content. Most protocols also permit updates, allowing a client tool to modify the folder structure, create and update documents, and write content. Some protocols go even further and allow interaction with capabilities such as version histories, search, and tasks.

Internally, the protocol bindings interact with the Content Repository Services (as shown in Figure 2-7), which encapsulate the behavior of working with folders and files. This ensures a consistent view and update approach across all client tools interacting with the Alfresco Content Application Server.

An important feature is Rules and Actions, *which allows the declarative definition of what happens to content when added to a folder or updated. Interaction through a protocol also adheres to those rules, meaning Alfresco can manage sophisticated processes of which the user of the client tool is completely unaware. For example, you can set up a rule to transform documents that are placed into a specific folder to PDF. This rule is triggered whenever you add a document to that folder using any of the available protocols.*

An Alfresco subsystem for file servers allows configuration and lifecycle management for each of the protocols either through property files or JMX.

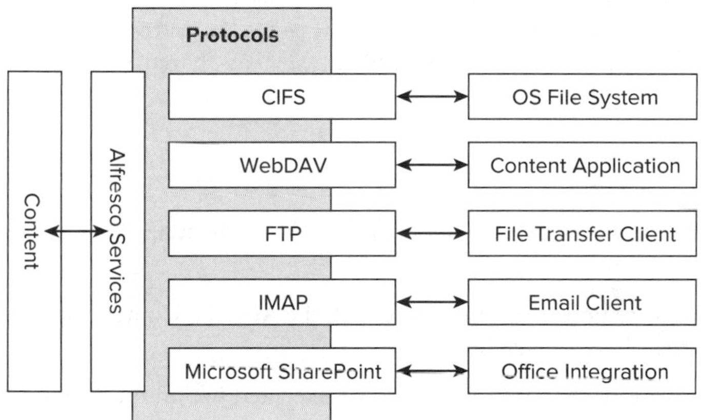

FIGURE 2-7

Here are the supported protocols:

- **CIFS** (Common Internet File System) is a protocol that allows the projection of Alfresco as a native shared file drive. Any client that can read and write to file drives can read and write to Alfresco, allowing the commonly used shared file drive to be replaced with an ECM system without users even knowing. Alfresco acquired the only Java-based CIFS server implementation, known as *JLAN*.
- **WebDAV** (Web-based Distributed Authoring and Versioning) is a set of extensions to HTTP that lets you manage files collaboratively on Web servers. It has strong support for authoring

scenarios such as locking, metadata, and versioning. Many content production tools, such as the Microsoft Office suite, support WebDAV. Additionally, there are tools for mounting a WebDAV server as a network drive.

- **FTP** (File Transfer Protocol) is a standard network protocol for exchanging and manipulating files over a network. This protocol is particularly useful for bulk loading folders and files into the Alfresco content repository.
- **IMAP** (Internet Message Access Protocol) is a prevalent standard for allowing email access on a remote mail server. Alfresco presents itself as a mail server, allowing clients such as Microsoft Outlook, Apple Mail, and Thunderbird to connect to and interact with folders and files held within the Alfresco content repository. Three modes of operation are supported:
  - **Archive** — Allows the storage of emails in the Alfresco content repository simply by using drag/drop and copy/paste from the IMAP client.
  - **Virtual** — Folders and files held in the Alfresco content repository are exposed as emails within the IMAP client with the ability to view metadata and trigger actions using links embedded in the email body.
  - **Mixed** — A combination of the above.
- **Microsoft SharePoint** protocol support enables Alfresco to act as a SharePoint server, creating tight integration with the Microsoft Office suite. This allows a user who is familiar with the Microsoft task pane to view and act upon documents held within the Alfresco content repository. The collaborative features of Microsoft SharePoint, such as Shared Workspace, are all mapped to Alfresco Share site capabilities.

APIs

The Alfresco Content Application Server exposes two flavors of API, each of which has been designed for a specific type of client:

- **Remote API** — Used by clients to remotely communicate with the Alfresco Content Application Server — specifically, to treat it as a black box
- **Embedded API** — Used by extensions that are registered and executed within the Alfresco Content Application Server

The Remote API

The Remote API is the API primarily used when building ECM solutions against the Alfresco Content Application Server. Actually, two styles of Remote API are exposed (as shown in Figure 2-8):

- **Web services** — SOAP-based service-oriented interfaces
- **RESTful** — HTTP-based resource-oriented interfaces

Alfresco first introduced its Web services API in version 1.0 of its product. It covers many of the core services that the Alfresco Content Application Server provides; however, as demand for SOAP-based interfaces has started to diminish, Alfresco is putting less emphasis on this particular API. One advantage of the Web services API is that there are many tools for building client bindings, covering all of the common environments and programming languages. You can remotely interact with the Alfresco Content Application Server through this interface from anywhere, such as Java, Microsoft .NET, PHP, and Adobe Flex. To ensure such compatibility, behind the scenes Alfresco embeds the Apache CXF engine and performs thorough integration testing. The Web services API also lends itself to orchestration through third-party business process engines, allowing the integration of content services into a wider business process.

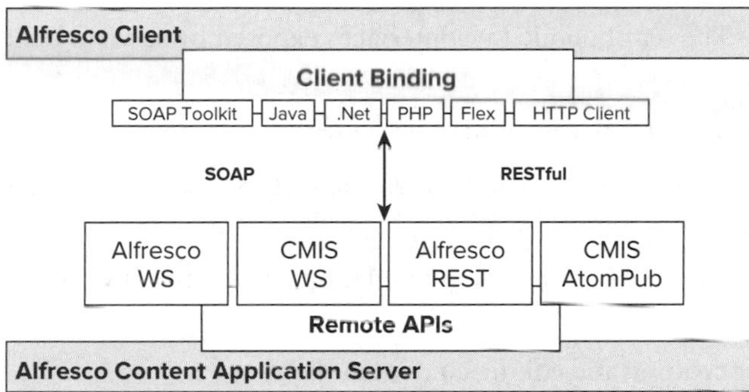

FIGURE 2-8

So, if Alfresco is putting less emphasis on its Web services API, what should be used instead? Alfresco introduced its RESTful API in version 2.1 of its product and has since been expanding its scope to cover all services of the Alfresco Content Application Server. Developers tend to prefer the style of this API due to its natural alignment with the way the Web works. If you have an HTTP client then you can communicate with Alfresco, which covers almost every environment and programming language. Other attractions include the ease of use with AJAX-oriented Web clients. Alfresco Share, a Spring Surf–based client, remotely communicates with the Alfresco Content Application Server exclusively through its RESTful API. Behind the scenes, Alfresco embeds Spring Web scripts (contributed by Alfresco) for developing its RESTful API.

The Web services and RESTful APIs provided by Alfresco, although comprehensive, are proprietary APIs. A client implemented against these APIs can only execute against Alfresco, therefore locking out content that may reside in a content repository of another vendor. This issue has been the plague of the ECM industry for many years and is the reason for the introduction of CMIS.

CMIS provides a standardized set of services for working with content repositories. CMIS is not language-specific, it does not dictate how a content repository works, and it does not seek to incorporate every feature of every content repository. Instead, the goal is to define a set of common services for working with content repositories, both Web service (SOAP)– and RESTful–based.

Alfresco provides an implementation of CMIS Web service and RESTful bindings, as well as a CMIS client API for use in Spring Surf and other environments.

CMIS is important, as it provides a focal point for developers to collaborate on, one which is not locked in to any particular content management repository, allowing the growth of tools, utilities, and clients for ECM solutions. Further detail on CMIS is provided in Chapter 4.

The Embedded API

The Embedded API is the API used when developing extensions to the Alfresco Content Application Server. Extensions, which are deployed into the server, are often dependent on existing services provided by the server. Therefore, developers of extensions use the Embedded API to gain access to those services.

The Embedded API comes in several forms, where each form is structured for a particular need or kind of extension (as shown in Figure 2-9):

- **Alfresco Java Foundation API** — The set of public Java interfaces exposed by services built into the Alfresco Content Application Server
- **JCR** — Standard (JSR-170) set of Java interfaces for interacting with the content repository
- **JavaScript API** — An object-oriented view of the Java Foundation API specifically tailored for use in JavaScript
- **FreeMarker API** — An object-oriented view of the Java Foundation API specifically tailored for use in FreeMarker templates
- **Content Definition** — An API for creating and editing content models
- **Workflow Definition** — An API for defining business processes

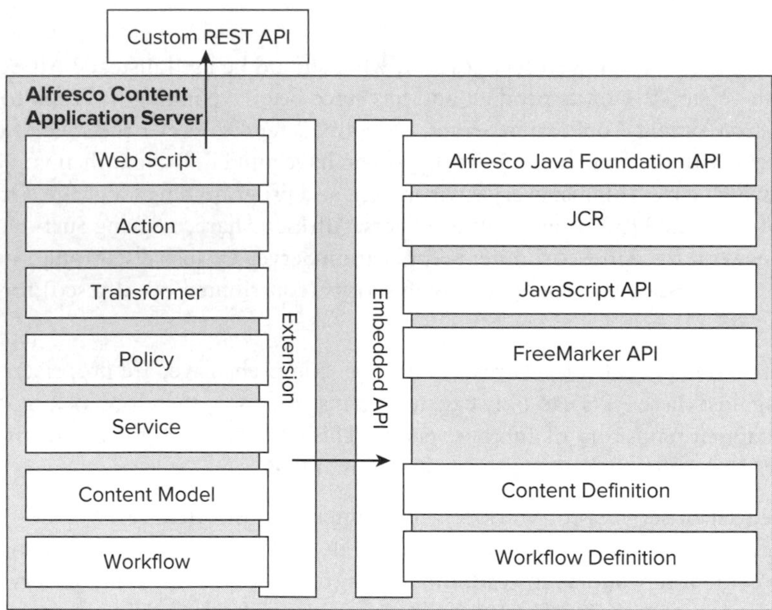

FIGURE 2-9

This allows the following kinds of extension to be developed, some of which require Java knowledge while others may be scripted:

- **Web Script** — Definition and implementation of a RESTful API
- **Action** — Encapsulates a process primarily used with rules

- **Transformer** — Converts content from one format to another
- **Policy** — Event handler registered against an event
- **Service** — Encapsulates a set of related features
- **Content Model** — Definition of types, aspects, and their relationships
- **Workflow** — A business process

Web scripts are an interesting extension as they allow you to define your own custom RESTful API: that is, define your own Remote API for clients to interact with the Alfresco Content Application Server. A Web script implementation may use any of the Embedded APIs, such as the Java Foundation API, JCR, JavaScript, and FreeMarker, for its implementation. Developing your own Remote API is very useful for the following scenarios:

- Exposing new extension services deployed into the Alfresco Content Application Server to remote clients
- Providing alternate batching or transaction demarcation of existing services
- Creating a façade for integration with a third-party tool, such as a Forms engine

In fact, Web scripts have been used for a variety of solutions that were not originally considered when the Web Script Framework was designed, solutions encouraged by the simplicity of implementing a Web script using familiar scripting and MVC approaches. They are a popular extension for the Alfresco Content Application Server.

There is one other use case for the Embedded API. An application or client can directly embed the Alfresco Content Application Server to inherit its suite of content services (as shown in Figure 2-10). As stated before, the infrastructure of the server means it can be deployed into a number of environments, not just as a Web application.

Essentially, the Alfresco Content Application Server is treated as a library, where any of its services, including the content repository, can be chosen independently or mixed to provide a custom solution. The server can scale down as well as up.

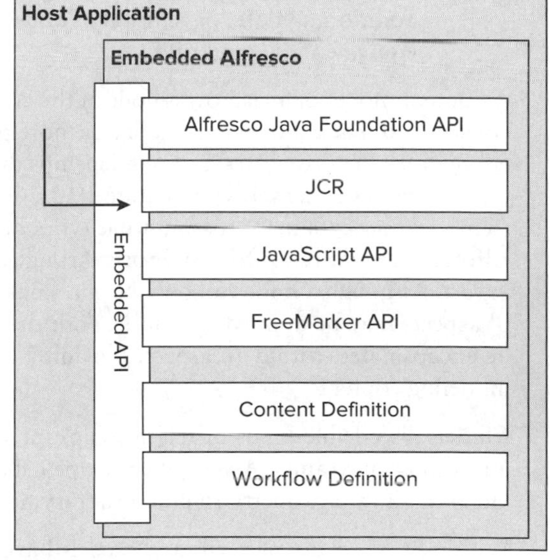

FIGURE 2-10

CONTENT MODELING

The Alfresco content repository takes a simplistic approach to representing content and its relationships. A small number of reusable data structures are defined, which allows sophisticated content models to be built up. It also allows the implementation of the content repository to support different physical storage engines depending on requirements such as read versus write performance.

At the core is hierarchical node support. Nodes are entities that can represent anything you want stored in the repository. Each node is uniquely identified and is a container for any number of named properties, where property values can be of any data type, single or multi-valued. Nodes are related to each other through relationships. A special kind of relationship called parent/child exists to represent a hierarchy of nodes where child nodes cannot outlive their parent. You can also create arbitrary relationships between nodes and define different types of nodes and relationships.

Logically, the repository is split into multiple stores where each store contains its own hierarchy of nodes. Nodes can represent anything, but common ECM representations include folders, documents, XML fragments, renditions, collaboration sites, and people (as shown in Figure 2-11).

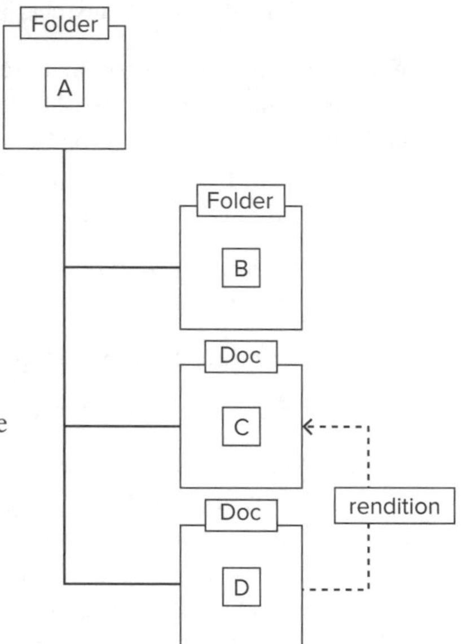

FIGURE 2-11

The Alfresco content repository provides services for reading, querying, and maintaining nodes. Events are fired on changes, allowing for processes to be triggered. In particular, the content repository provides the following capabilities based on events:

- **Policies** — Event handlers registered for specific kinds of node events for either all nodes or nodes of a specific type
- **Rules** — Declarative definition of processes based on addition, update, or removal of nodes (for example, the equivalent of email rules)

A content model defines how a node in the content repository is constrained. Each model defines one or more types, where a type enumerates the properties and relationships that a node of that type can support (as shown in Figure 2-12). Often, it is necessary to model concepts that cross multiple types of node, which the Alfresco content repository supports through the notion of an *aspect*. Although a node can only be of a single type, any number of aspects may be applied to a node. Both data and process can be encapsulated within an aspect, providing a flexible tool for modeling content.

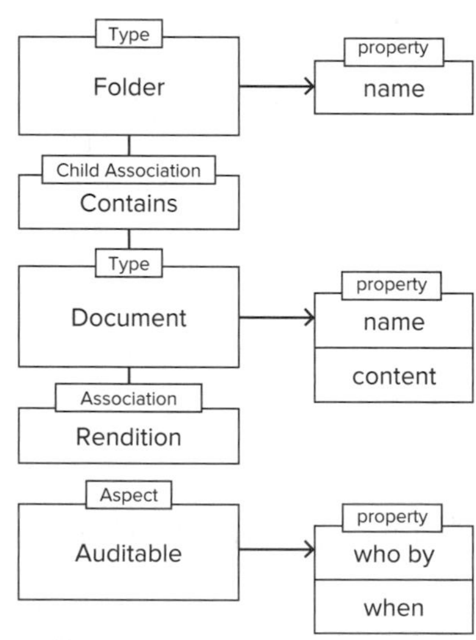

FIGURE 2-12

Models also define kinds of relationships, property data types, and value constraints. A special data type called content is provided to allow a property to hold arbitrary, length binary data.

Within ECM, many patterns and models have emerged and/or been standardized for managing content. The Alfresco Content Application Server comes with many pre-defined models, such as:

- Folder/Document hierarchy
- Dublin Core
- Wiki
- Blogs

- Discussions
- Collaboration Sites
- DOD 5015.2

All of these models are expressed in the content metamodel (as shown in Figure 2-13), which maps neatly to both the CMIS domain model and JCR node-type model.

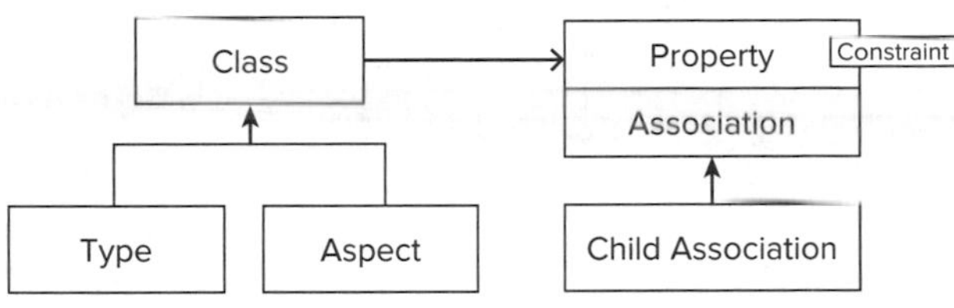

FIGURE 2-13

You can define new models for specific ECM use cases, either from scratch or by inheriting definitions from existing models.

THE ALFRESCO WEB APPLICATION FRAMEWORK

It's time to change direction and focus on the Alfresco Web Application Framework. Alfresco Share and all new Web applications from Alfresco are now built on Spring Surf, a Web application framework contributed by Alfresco. This provides the typical features of a framework of this kind but with one very important design goal: to support the needs of Web content management, where the authoring, review, and publishing of Web site content is just as important as how to develop the Web site.

At the heart of Spring Surf is a site, assembly framework (as shown in Figure 2-14) that bundles a full site construction object model and toolkit for building Web sites and applications. Its features are

- **Site Dispatcher** — Allows you to easily create pages and link them to the overall navigation of the Web site. It also allows you to build pages in a way that promotes reusability so that components do not need to be built more than once.
- **Templates** — Allows you to define a page layout once and then reuse it across a large set of pages. You can develop pages using FreeMarker, JSP, HTML, or Java.
- **UI Library** — Reusable UI components that can be bound into regions (or slots) within your page or template. They consist of back-end application logic and front-end presentation code.
- **Pages** — Allows for pages to be rendered in multiple formats, such as print format, PDF, or mobile device.
- **AJAX support** — Integration with YUI Library.
- **Forms** — Rich Forms engine for rendering and collecting data.

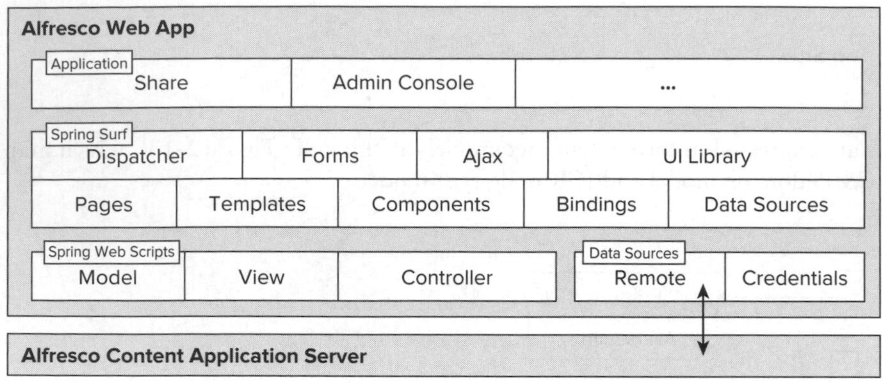

FIGURE 2-14

Spring Surf embeds Spring Web scripts, allowing Surf component developers to use the same techniques that were used when building Alfresco Content Application Server RESTful APIs, taking advantage of scripting languages and a simple MVC approach.

Often, a Spring Surf Web site requires access to and management of content held within the Application Content Server, such as to support user-generated content, dynamic site artifacts, personalized presentation, and tagging. To support this, Spring Surf provides the following integration services:

- **Remote** — Encapsulates any number of data sources with out-of-the-box support for the Alfresco Content Application Server
- **Credentials** — Manages user authentication with out-of-the-box support for the Alfresco Content Application Server

By design, Spring Surf works hand-in-hand with Alfresco Web Content Management and provides virtualized content retrieval, preview, and test support for user sandboxes and Web projects. Applications built with Spring Surf can be deployed from Alfresco Web project spaces to production servers. To help facilitate this, Spring Surf uses a lightweight XML-driven model to represent all site artifacts, such as pages, templates, themes, and chrome. This means a Spring Surf site itself can be managed with Alfresco services such as change sets, preview, and deployment. In addition, an embedded API (as shown in Figure 2-15) is provided to support programmatic control of the same artifacts.

The XML and file-based nature of Spring Surf sites lends itself to being managed in Alfresco WCM (as shown in Figure 2-16), which offers features such as:

- Safe editing of all Spring Surf artifacts, including the ability to snapshot your site and roll it backward in time
- Review and Approve workflow of Spring Surf site changes
- Preview of site changes
- Deployment of site changes to test or production servers

By offering the Surf Web application framework to Spring, it is envisioned that the community will build many more components, thus enhancing the richness of the framework. In conjunction with the

CMIS client API, Spring Surf provides an open, community-backed stack for implementing Web-based content-enabled applications.

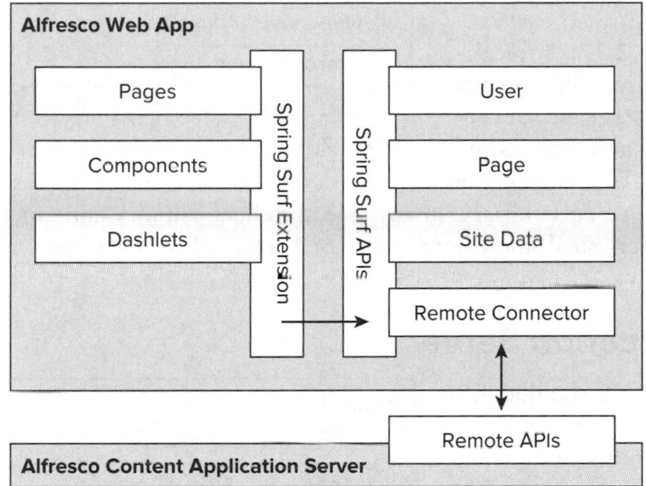

FIGURE 2-15

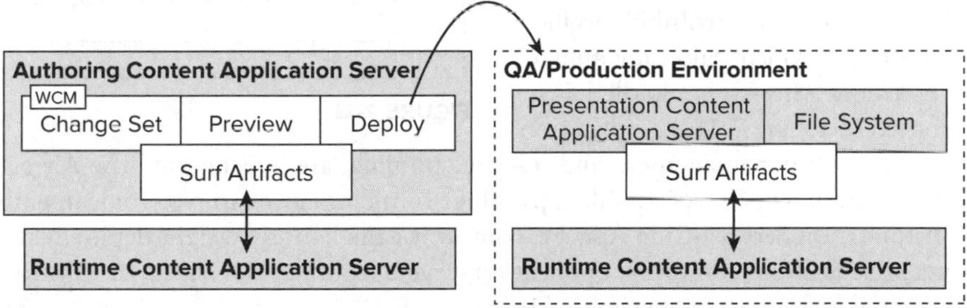

FIGURE 2-16

DEPLOYMENT OPTIONS

As stated at the beginning of this chapter, one of the primary architectural guiding principles is to offer choice to the developer on how they can package Alfresco and to offer choice to those who deploy Alfresco, so they can make appropriate trade-offs to suit their requirements.

Alfresco's modular design and infrastructure foundation provide a platform for allowing Alfresco to be deployed in many different forms and topologies. In particular, the infrastructure foundation protects Alfresco from the environment within which it executes, allowing the choice of components such as operating system, database, application server, Web browser, and authentication system.

It's time to investigate each of the deployment options, starting with the simplest deployment for supporting the smallest footprint and progressing towards the most sophisticated deployments to support large-scale systems. Alfresco is designed to scale down as well as up.

Embedded Alfresco

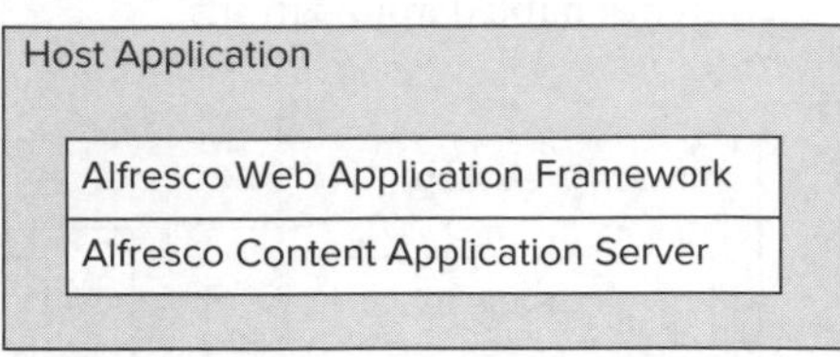

FIGURE 2-17

An embedded Alfresco is contained directly within a host, where the host communicates with Alfresco through its embedded API, meaning the host and Alfresco reside in the same process (as shown in Figure 2-17). Typical hosts include content-rich client applications that require content-oriented storage, retrieval, and services, but can also include hosts such as test harnesses and samples. A client may choose to embed the Alfresco Web Application Framework or Alfresco Content Application Server, or both, treating Alfresco as a third-party library. In any case, the client can pick and mix the services of Alfresco to embed, allowing very small-footprint versions of Alfresco. The host is responsible for the startup and shutdown of Alfresco.

The Alfresco Content Application Server

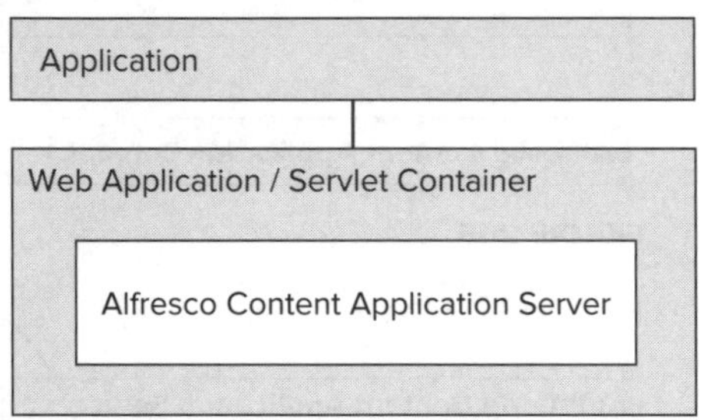

FIGURE 2-18

An Alfresco Content Application Server is a stand-alone server capable of servicing requests over remote protocols. A single server can support any number of different applications and clients where new applications may be arbitrarily added. Clients communicate with Alfresco through its Remote API and Protocol bindings, although a server may be configured to omit or prohibit specific access points. This type of deployment takes advantage of an application server where Alfresco is bundled as a Web application (as shown in Figure 2-18). Application server features, such as transaction management and resource pooling, are injected into the Alfresco infrastructure foundation, allowing Alfresco to take advantage of them. For example, you can embed the Alfresco Content Application Server inside Apache Tomcat for the lightest-weight deployment, as well as inside Java Enterprise Edition–compliant application servers from JBoss, Oracle, or IBM to take advantage of advanced capabilities such as distributed transactions.

Clustered Alfresco

To support large-scale systems, Alfresco may be clustered, where multiple Alfresco servers are set up to work with each other, allowing client requests to be fulfilled across a number of processors (as shown in Figure 2-19). Both the Alfresco Web Application Framework and Alfresco Content Application Server can be clustered, allowing each tier to scale out independently.

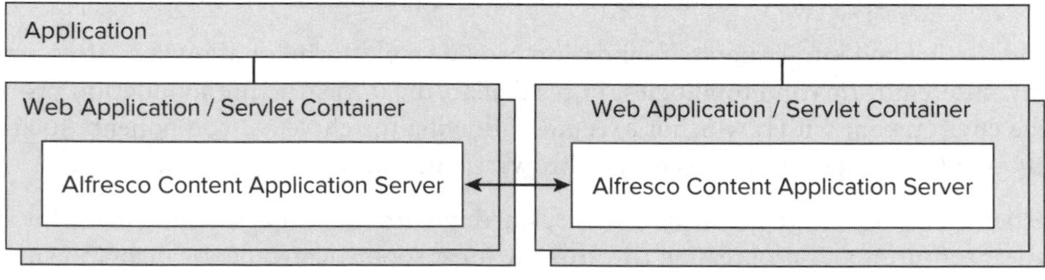

FIGURE 2-19

Each node of a clustered Alfresco Content Application Server shares the same content repository store, although the store itself may be replicated across the nodes, if required. Caches and search indexes are also distributed, meaning that a clustered content application server looks and acts like a single content application server. Typically, a load balancer is placed in front of the clustered Alfresco Content Application Server to distribute requests across the nodes.

This setup also supports Cloud deployments. In fact, Alfresco provides images and tools for easily deploying a clustered Alfresco Content Application Server across multiple Amazon EC2 virtual nodes.

The Backup Server

This is a special case of the clustered deployment where, in case of failure, an application can switch to a backup version of the deployed stack. Depending upon configuration, the backup version may be available immediately on failure (known as *hot backup*) or shortly after failure, following some configuration changes (known as *warm backup*). One of the nodes in the cluster is designated the master, which supports the live application, while the other node is designated the slave, which keeps itself replicated with the master (as shown in Figure 2-20). The slave remains read-only until the point of switchover.

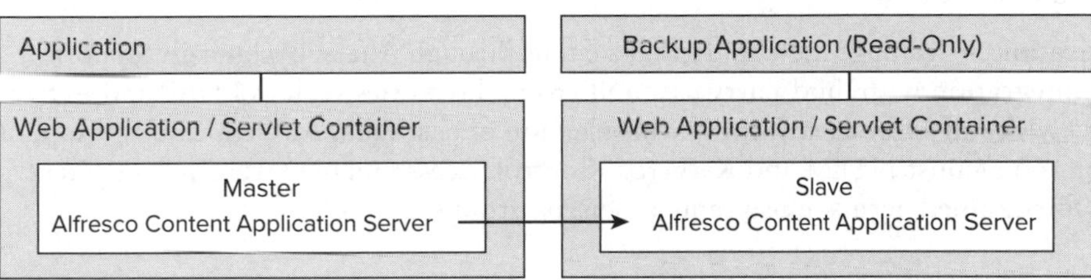

FIGURE 2-20

Multitenancy

Multitenancy allows a single Alfresco Content Application Server (clustered or not) to support multiple tenants, where a tenant such as a customer, company, or organization believes they are the only user of the server as they connect to a logical partition (as shown in Figure 2-21). Physically, all tenants share the same infrastructure, such as deployed nodes in a cluster and content, repository storage. However, data maintained by one tenant cannot be read or manipulated by another tenant.

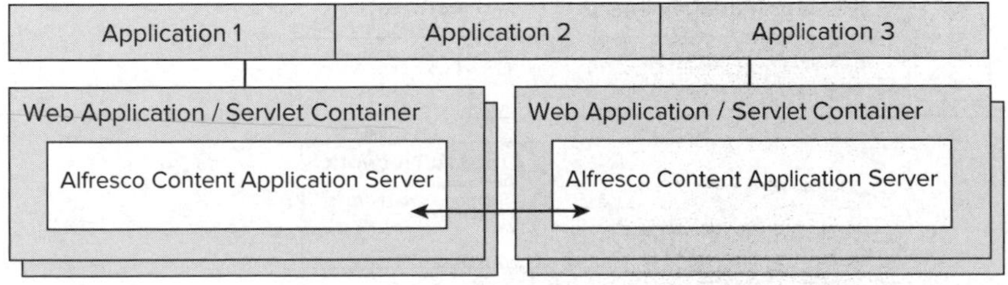

FIGURE 2-21

A deployment of this type eases administration and reduces the cost associated with maintaining many different applications and user bases, in particular when upgrading core services or performing backups, as this only needs to be done once for all tenants.

Alfresco provides administration tools for managing tenants, including the creation of tenants at runtime. In conjunction with clustering, multitenancy provides an ideal deployment option for the cloud.

THE ENTERPRISE INFRASTRUCTURE

It is not always easy to understand what *enterprise class* or *enterprise scale* means, but Alfresco, by design, inherently supports the following capabilities that can be categorized under the enterprise umbrella (as shown in Figure 2-22).

- **Environment agnostic** — Choose your stack, including operating system, database, application server, and Web browser.
- **Standards compliant** — Interoperate with other parts of the software stack and reuse compliant tools. Alfresco supports standards such as JSR-168 (Portlet API), JSR-170 (JCR API), CMIS, and OpenSearch.
- **Authentication** — Manage users and groups either through Alfresco's built-in support or through integration with third-party user and group directories such as LDAP and Active Directory with full and incremental synchronization of user data. Authenticate and support single sign-on against NTLM and Kerberos. Control access and management of content through fine-grained permissions granted to users, groups, and roles.

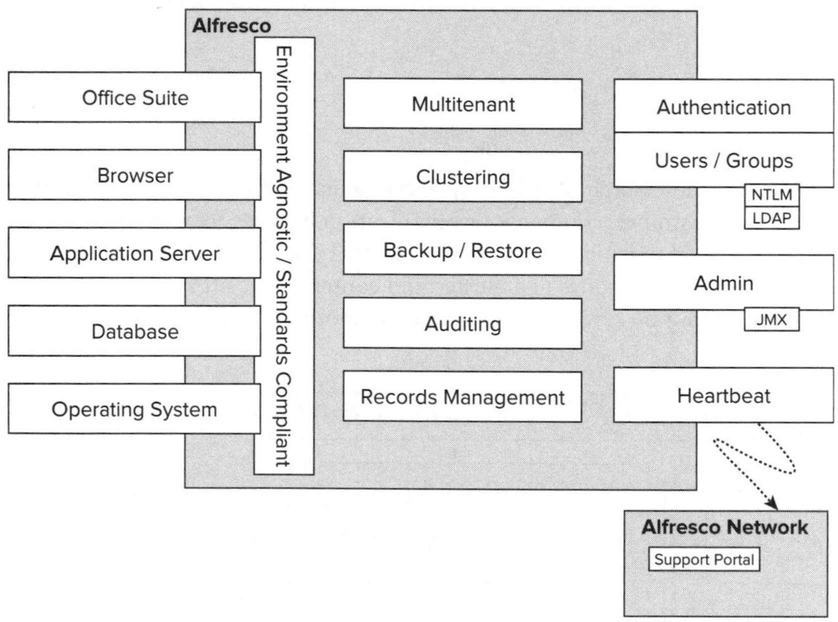

FIGURE 2-22

- **Administration** — Administer all aspects of Alfresco through property files or JMX, including the reconfiguration, startup, and shutdown of subsystems at runtime.
- **Clustering** — Add nodes to an Alfresco cluster and distribute content storage to support large numbers of documents and users.
- **Backup/Restore** — Set up Alfresco topologies that incorporate redundancy or master/slave nodes for warm and hot backup.
- **Audit** — Configurable record of actions performed through Alfresco or by users of Alfresco, stored in the database in a form that is simple for third-party reporting tools to consume.
- **Records management** — File plans, record types, retention and archival policies, disposition, and reporting, all certified to the DOD 5015.2 standard.
- **Alfresco Network** — Alfresco Network is a support portal for registered Alfresco Enterprise users. The Alfresco Content Application Server offers a heartbeat where it periodically sends a record of its health to Alfresco Network for subsequent reporting and pre-emptive care.

3

Setting Up an Alfresco Environment

WHAT'S IN THIS CHAPTER?

- Installing and configuring Alfresco
- Extending Alfresco
- Debugging installations and extensions

There are quite a few things to consider when setting up your Alfresco environment. Obviously, Alfresco first needs to be installed and configured. There are also a number of extensions that can be deployed for configuring Spring, using Web scripts, customizing Share, and more. In addition, there are several considerations for how to handle JavaScript and caches.

INSTALLING ALFRESCO

To follow and implement the examples introduced throughout this book, you must have a version of Alfresco installed and running. The examples in the book presume an environment based on Microsoft Windows with a MySQL database; however, all the techniques explained are similar on all platforms.

There are several ways to install Alfresco on any of the major operating systems. For detailed step-by-step and platform-specific instructions, please refer to the *Installing and Configuring Alfresco* guide on the Alfresco wiki. Alternatively, if you have an Enterprise subscription, you can download the guide from the Alfresco Network at `http://network.alfresco.com`. This book describes the installation using the Alfresco installation wizard.

Running the Alfresco Installation Wizard

The quickest and easiest way to install Alfresco is to run the Alfresco installation wizard for the target platform. This sets up all the required third-party software, configures your environment correctly, and provides a mechanism to start and stop the Alfresco server. It also includes scripts to apply any optional modules you may be interested in leveraging, such as Records Management.

The installation wizard has a default set of installation options, but you can choose to install a subset of these if all are not required. The optional components include WCM, SharePoint protocol support, an embedded MySQL database, OpenOffice, and the Java development kit (JDK). If any of these components are already installed, then selecting the *custom* install step in the installation wizard will allow you to choose what to install. The wizard will prompt you for the location of these existing components, if necessary.

Throughout this book, the install location in the Alfresco installation wizard is referred to as installLocation. *If the defaults are selected, this is* `C:\Alfresco`.

After a successful installation, the *installLocation* will contain the aforementioned scripts and the following folders:

- **alf_data** — Binary content files and full text indexes
- **amps** — Alfresco extensions (AMP files)
- **bin** — Executable programs used by Alfresco
- **extras** — Additional utilities
- **ImageMagick** — Programs used for image manipulation
- **install_extension** — Configuration files used by the installer
- **licenses** — License files
- **mysql** — Optional database
- **OpenOffice.org** — Optional Office document manipulation
- **Tomcat** — Web server that contains the Alfresco and Share applications
- **virtual-tomcat** — optional web server for WCM previewing
- **wcm** — Optional WCM components

There are multiple installation packages available for Alfresco, so if you already have a Web application server installed, such as Tomcat or JBoss AS, then you can choose to get an appropriate installation package. The different installation packages and their installation instructions are available for download from Alfresco. For the purposes of this book, we will assume that the default installation wizard has been used with the default options.

Once installed, you can start the Alfresco server using the alf_start script in the *installLocation*. The server will take a few seconds to start and you can see progress in the log console.

Repository Configuration

When the repository starts, it loads properties files by default. These include:

- *installLocation*/tomcat/webapps/alfresco/WEB-INF/classes/alfresco/repository.properties
- *installLocation*/tomcat/webapps/alfresco/WEB-INF/classes/alfresco/domain/hibernate-cfg.properties
- All the properties files within the subfolders of *installLocation*/tomcat/webapps/alfresco/WEB-INF/classes/alfresco/subsystems
- *installLocation*/tomcat/shared/classes/alfresco-global.properties

The Alfresco installation wizard creates the `alfresco-global.properties` file and populates it with the values provided during installation. As the `alfresco-global.properties` file is loaded last, you can override any properties that appear in any of the previously loaded properties files.

For example, to disable the FTP server, you can override the `ftp.enabled` property from *installLocation*/tomcat/webapps/alfresco/WEB-INF/classes/alfresco/subsystems/fileservers/default/file-servers.properties. This is accomplished by adding the line `ftp.enabled=false` to*installLocation*/tomcat/shared/classes/alfresco-global.properties.

The most important property the Alfresco installation wizard sets is `dir.root`. This property defines the location of the alf_data folder. Alfresco uses a relational database to hold most of its data, such as metadata, folder structures, and versioning information. The content itself and the full-text indexes are stored on the file system in folders within the alf_data folder.

The contents of the contentstore and lucene-indexes folders must remain synchronized with the database; otherwise, you will see the following error at startup: `The indexes are not synchronized with the database.`

When Alfresco is set up without the installation wizard, not overriding `dir.root` is a common mistake. The default value is `./alf_data`. This means that Alfresco looks for the alf_data folder in the location where the server was started and creates a new empty folder if it cannot find the folder. This is worth remembering whenever you delete a database, because if the database data is cleared, so must the contents in the folders lucene-indexes and contentstore within alf_data.

The *Installing and Configuring Alfresco* guide provides explanations of all the other properties in `alfresco-global.properties` as well as examples of other common configuration scenarios.

DEPLOYING EXTENSIONS

You can use several methods to extend Alfresco with new functionality and change the behaviors of existing functionality beyond those exposed through properties files. The recommended way is to use the provided extension mechanism, which takes the form of the folder *installLocation*/tomcat/shared/classes.

The advantage of this is that the extension files are outside the standard Alfresco Web application (alfresco.war), so the out-of-the-box Alfresco files do not need to be modified, making it upgrade-friendly. This means that you can install a newer alfresco.war file and the same extensions still function without changes or any further action.

There are two extension folders in an installed Alfresco system: one for the repository and one for the Share application. By default, the Alfresco installation wizard uses one Tomcat instance for both the repository and Web tiers so both folders (*installLocation*/tomcat/shared/classes/alfresco/extension and *installLocation*/tomcat/shared/classes/alfresco/web-extension) are in the same location. However, you can use two separate Tomcat instances or even two separate machines, in which case *installLocation*/tomcat/shared/classes/alfresco would only contain the relevant folder for that tier.

The messages folder in *installLocation*/tomcat/shared/classes/alfresco is for language files for the repository tier. The repository automatically loads properties files placed in this location, allowing different languages to be displayed in the user interface. There are many language packs available for Alfresco and this messages folder is where they need to be placed to be used.

You can apply various types of extensions; the type determines the required location of the files within the extension folder. Extension categories discussed in the following sections are:

- Spring configuration
- Web script
- Web tier configuration
- Share customization

Spring Configuration Extensions

The Spring context loaded by the repository provides an extension mechanism in the form of a wildcard import of any Spring context file ending with *-context.xml*. The Alfresco installation wizard includes several sample Spring configuration files in *installLocation*/tomcat/shared/classes/alfresco/extension. For example, to enable the custom content model, remove the *.sample* suffix from the file custom-model-context.xml.sample.

To provide your own Spring configuration, simply place your file in the folder *installLocation*/tomcat/shared/classes/alfresco/extension. As with any Spring configuration changes, you must restart the server for the changes to take effect.

Web Script Extensions

While the process of creating a Web script is detailed in Chapter 9, this section explains where you can place the Web script files.

You can place repository Web script files under *installLocation*/tomcat/shared/classes/alfresco/extension/templates/webscripts. You can use any arbitrary folder structure beneath this location with the exception of org/alfresco, which is reserved for Alfresco use.

You can also place repository Web scripts within the repository itself in the space /Company Home/Data Dictionary/Web Scripts Extensions. Files in this location supersede those in *installLocation*/tomcat/shared/classes/alfresco/extension/templates/webscripts. This lets you edit the file from any location, providing an upgrade-friendly approach, as no changes are required when you upgrade the WAR file. The only disadvantage of using this approach is that the `runAs` feature of the Web script engine is not supported when the files are located in the repository.

You can also use these two locations to override Web scripts provided by Alfresco. For example, placing a file with the same name in the relevant folder structure will override the out-of-the-box file of the same name.

Whenever you make any changes to a Web script or add a new Web script, you will need to refresh the Web script service. Using the following URL will display the Web scripts currently available in your server. There is also a Refresh Web Scripts button you can click to force a refresh. The URL depends on your install, but by default it will be:

```
http://localhost:8080/alfresco/service/index
```

Web Tier Configuration Extensions

You can configure various aspects of the Web tier — for example, the appearance of forms and debugging options. These configuration files should be provided as extensions and placed in the folder *installLocation*/tomcat/shared/classes/alfresco/web-extension.

The Share application is built upon the Surf platform, which itself provides an extension point in the form of the file web framework-config-custom.xml.

Placing this file in the web-extension folder will make it load as part of the application. However, as all Surf-based applications load this file, problems can occur if you place any application-specific configuration in this file. To resolve this potential issue, all Surf-based applications can supply an application-specific custom configuration file. In the Share application, a custom configuration file share-config-custom.xml is available for this.

The advantage of providing configuration in this way is that the files are not cached by the application server's classloader. This lets you use the Refresh Web Scripts feature already described to reload the configuration files.

Share Customization Extensions

The process of creating various Share customizations is explained in Chapters 14 through 16. This section explains where the files are located.

As Share is running on the Web tier, most extension files are placed in various hierarchies under the folder *installLocation*/tomcat/shared/classes/alfresco/web-extension. However, there are a few exceptions; Web assets, CSS files, and images must be available on a file system accessible to the application server. You must place these files somewhere within *installLocation*/tomcat/webapps.

Following the principle of locating files in an upgrade-friendly location, do not use the folder *installLocation*/tomcat/webapps/share, as it will be deleted when a new or updated WAR file is deployed. When using Tomcat, the recommended location is within the folder *installLocation*/tomcat/webapps/ROOT. The ROOT folder in Tomcat, as the name suggests, represents the root context of the application server — for example, `http://localhost:8080`. As this is separate from the Alfresco Web applications, you can update the files independently. Once again, no changes are required for extensions to continue to work.

In cases where using the ROOT context of the application server is not viable, the best option is to package the extension as an Alfresco Module Package (AMP) file, which is further explained in the "Packaging Extension Files" section.

Packaging Extension Files

Depending on the complexity of the extension, there may well be several files. In the case of a Records Management module, there could be hundreds! This may be fine if there is only one extension, but once there are files of two or three extensions, things could get quite messy and complex. This may also require a mechanism for distributing the extension, especially if it is being shared with the community. For these scenarios, Alfresco provides AMP files.

An AMP file is essentially a ZIP file with a pre-determined internal folder structure and, at its minimum, a single required configuration file. An AMP file is applied to a WAR file, which is then redeployed to the application server. This makes the extension appear as part of the Alfresco Web application; for example, all the files are within *installLocation*/tomcat/webapps/alfresco or *installLocation*/tomcat/webapps/share. The repository also maintains a registry of the installed modules and their version, enabling the modules to be upgraded independently of the WAR file.

There are some disadvantages, though, as discussed in previous sections of this chapter. As this means the files are all loaded by the application server's main classloader, you lose the ability to reload configuration files. In addition, since the AMP construction, WAR integration, and deployment are not conducive to a streamlined development cycle, you should use AMP files only for completed extensions.

You will be creating an AMP file of the Knowledge Base application created from samples throughout this book.

DEBUGGING TIPS

The following sections provide some tips and tricks for developing extensions.

Server-Side JavaScript Logging

Alfresco uses the RhinoScript engine to run programs written in JavaScript within the Alfresco server (in contrast to running client JavaScript in the Web browser for the user interface). This server-side JavaScript engine gives the developer access to Alfresco objects and processes through JavaScript programs that are simpler to write than Java, as well as easier to debug since the code is interpreted rather than compiled. Better still, these JavaScript program files can be managed as documents in the Alfresco Content Application Server and executed dynamically.

All JavaScript files being executed in the RhinoScript JavaScript engine have a `logger` root object available to them. The `logger` object exposes two methods: `isLoggingEnabled()` and`log()`. As with log4j, the `isLoggingEnabled()` method determines whether logging is turned on. The `log()` method outputs the provided string to the application server console and the alfresco.log file. The following code shows the typical usage for the `logger` object:

```
if (logger.isLoggingEnabled())
   logger.log("Output some useful information to the console");
```

To turn on JavaScript debugging, set the log4j level for the ScriptLogger class to `debug` in the file *installLocation*/tomcat/webapps/alfresco/WEB-INF/classes/log4j.properties (on the repository or Web tier). For example:

```
log4j.logger.org.alfresco.repo.jscript.ScriptLogger=debug
```

Server-Side JavaScript Debugging

JavaScript files executed in the RhinoScript JavaScript engine (as previously described) can be debugged in a similar manner to any popular IDE. You can use a couple of methods to enable the JavaScript debugger. The first approach enables the debugger to appear every time the server starts, and the second approach allows you to enable it when required.

- To enable the debugger to appear when the server starts, set the log4j level for the class to `on` for the appropriate tier, as follows:
    - For the repository tier, add the following line to *installLocation*/tomcat/webapps/alfresco/WEB-INF/classes/log4j.properties:

      ```
      log4j.logger.org.alfresco.repo.web.scripts.AlfrescoRhinoScript
      Debugger=on
      ```

    - For the Web tier, add the following line to *installLocation*/tomcat/webapps/share/WEB-INF/classes/log4j.properties:

      ```
      log4j.logger.org.alfresco.web.scripts.AlfrescoScriptDebugger=on
      ```

- To enable the JavaScript debugger on an ad hoc basis, use the JavaScript debugger Web script for the appropriate tier, and then click the Enable button to launch the debugger.
    - For the repository tier, go to `http://localhost:8080/alfresco/service/api/javascript/debugger`
    - For the Web tier, go to `http://localhost:8080/share/service/api/javascript/debugger`

  A GUI appears, allowing you to set breakpoints in the scripts being executed.

Client-Side JavaScript Logging and Debugging

By default, client-side JavaScript is minimized for performance reasons. However, this is not ideal for development, as the JavaScript in utilities such as Firebug for Firefox show the source file as one very long line of text. To make Share use the full version, you can turn on client-side debugging through the file web-framework-config-custom.xml.

To turn on client-side debugging, create the file *installLocation*/tomcat/shared/classes/alfresco/web-extension/web-framework-config-custom.xml, and add the following:

```
<alfresco-config>
<config replace="true">
<flags>
<client-debug>true</client-debug>
</flags>
</config>
</alfresco-config>
```

This also enables a `log4javascript` utility written by Tim Down (`http://log4javascript.org`) embedded in Share that provides logging capabilities to client-side JavaScript. To see the log window, press ***Ctrl, Ctrl, Shift, Shift***. To make the logger window appear on every page load, add *<client-debug-autologging>false</client-debug-autologging>* to the file web-framework-config-custom.xml. For example:

```
<alfresco-config>
<config replace="true">
<flags>
<client-debug>true</client-debug>
<client-debug-autologging>false</client-debug-autologging>
</flags>
</config>
</alfresco-config>
```

Disabling Caching

By default, there are several caches in place to aid performance; however, during development these caches prevent changes to source files from taking effect. JavaScript files are compiled so they do not need to be continually interpreted. You can turn this feature off with a custom Spring configuration file. This file can be called anything as long as it has the *-content.xml* suffix.

In this example, create the file custom-web-framework-application-context.xml in the folder *installLocation*/tomcat/shared/classes/alfresco/web-extension, and type the following:

```
<?xml version='1.0' encoding='UTF-8'?>
<!DOCTYPE beans PUBLIC '-//SPRING//DTD BEAN//EN'
'http://www.springframework.org/dtd/spring-beans.dtd'>
<beans>
<bean id="webframework.webscripts.scriptprocessor"
class="org.alfresco.web.scripts.PresentationScriptProcessor">
<property name="searchPath" ref="webframework.searchpath" />
<property name="compile"><value>false</value></property>
</bean>
<bean id="webframework.scriptprocessor"
class="org.alfresco.web.scripts.PresentationScriptProcessor">
<property name="searchPath" ref="webframework.templates.searchpath" />
<property name="compile"><value>false</value></property>
</bean>
</beans>
```

The application server's main classloader caches files, including files included in FreeMarker templates. While this is a desired feature in a production environment, this is not the case during development.

To disable caching of included folders, set the log4j level for the `PresentationScriptProcessor` and `RhinoScriptProcessor` classes to `debug` by adding the following lines to the file *installLocation*/tomcat/webapps/share/WEB-INF/classes/log4j.properties:

```
log4j.logger.org.alfresco.web.scripts.PresentationScriptProcessor=debug
log4j.logger.org.alfresco.repo.jscript.RhinoScriptProcessor=debug
```

PART II
Getting Technical with Alfresco

Services

WHAT'S IN THIS CHAPTER?

- Introducing the Content Repository Services
- Understanding the existing Content, Control, and Collaboration Services
- Using and extending services
- Developing your own services
- Introducing Content Management Interoperability Services
- Understanding CMIS concepts
- Using CMIS with Alfresco

The Alfresco server provides capabilities for capturing, managing, and collaborating on content using services. These services form the basis of the functionality provided by any Alfresco implementation.

Services address the core use cases for content management applications, including the logical organization of content, file management, version control, and security. In addition, services support the control of content through workflow and process management, and social and collaborative applications.

Alfresco exposes services at various levels, including Java, scripting, REST, and Web services, as well as through client interfaces such as Explorer and Share. Some services are considered internal; others are public. For example, the Java-level services are internal services. The majority of these are accessible through other public interfaces, including the public APIs, client applications, and CMIS.

The services are divided into two main categories: *Content Repository Services* and *Content Application Services*.

CONTENT REPOSITORY SERVICES

The Content Repository Services, written in Java, are the fundamental services for working with content. The following describes the out-of-the-box services for organizing and managing content, controlling versions, recording changes and updates, enforcing security, modeling content types, and searching for information in the repository.

File and Folder Management

Services are provided to support the management of the nodes used to model files and folders in the repository. The services provide methods to create and update nodes and define the relationships between them.

The operations supported by the File Folders service include:

- **Create** — Creates nodes, sets property values, creates associations between nodes.
- **Read** — Reads node properties and content, reads and navigates node associations.
- **Update** — Updates the properties and content of nodes.
- **Delete** — Deletes nodes. If the archive store is enabled, the node is not deleted, but is moved from its current node to the archive node store. From there, they can then be restored or purged.

Versioning and Check Out/Check In

Alfresco's version management is designed to manage versions of individual content nodes. To enable the versioning behavior, the *versionable* aspect must be applied to the node.

The Versioning services include the following capabilities:

- **Create Version** — Creates a new version of the referenced node, which is placed at the end of the appropriate version history. If the node has no version history, one is created and this version is considered the initial version.
- **Version History** — Gets the version history that relates to the referenced node.
- **Get Current Version** — Gets the current version for a referenced node.
- **Revert** — Reverts the state of a referenced node to that of a previous node.
- **Restore Version** — Restores a previously deleted node from a version in its version history.
- **Delete Version History** — Deletes the version history for a versioned node.

Each version has a version number, which is allocated on a sequential basis and follows a similar strategy to Concurrent Versions System (CVS) version numbering. Generally, this version number is only used internally; the version label is used publicly to identify the version.

The version label is calculated from the version number and gives, within the scope of the version history, a unique label for the version. This label is placed in the *versionable* aspect to indicate the related current version for a node.

You can customize the generation of the version label by creating a version label policy behavior and registering it in place of the default version label policy. This gives applications flexibility to determine their own version-labeling policies. The default version label policy uses the 1.1, 1.2 style of progressive version labels, moving to 2.0 if the version is considered a major change. This is indicated in the version metadata to which the version label policy has access.

Check Out and Check In services are provided to control updates to document and prevent unwanted overwrites. When you check out a document, the document is locked, thus preventing other users writing changes to it. Alfresco uses an exclusive locking model that allows only one user to have a particular document checked out (locked) at any time. The user or application can unlock the document by either checking in the document or canceling the checkout.

You can use Check Out and Check In with or without versioning. If versioning is not enabled on a node (the *versionable* aspect is not present on the node), the check in overwrites the existing node and releases the lock unless the `keepCheckedOut` flag is used. With versioning enabled on the node, a new version is always created.

Auditing

The Audit service provides a configurable record of actions and events. The information is stored in a database in a form that is designed to be simple for third-party reporting tools to consume.

The capabilities provided by the Audit service include:

- Auditing of virtually any system event (user- and system-triggered)
- Metadata change auditing, including before and after values
- Audit data stored in database-indexed tables according to the type of data

Authentication, Authorities, and Permissions

A number of services are provided to support creating and updating user and group (authorities) information, authenticating users, and defining the actions that users can perform against nodes.

These services are:

- **Authority Service** — Provides capabilities to support creating and deleting authorities, querying authorities, and managing zones
- **Permission Service** — Provides methods for reading, setting and deleting permissions for nodes, querying permissions, and evaluating permissions for a user against nodes
- **Person Service** — Provides methods for looking up people from user names, and for creating, deleting, and altering user information

See Chapter 6 for more detail on these services.

Modeling

The content repository uses the repository Data Dictionary to manage definitions for content models such as folders, files, and metadata schemes. The content models are registered with the content repository to constrain the structure of nodes and the relationships between them, as well as to constrain property values. A Dictionary service is provided to allow access to the content models and provide a range of methods for querying and inspecting the model definitions.

See Chapter 5 for detailed information on working with content models.

Search

The Search service provides methods for querying the repository and returning a filtered collection of nodes based on the user's permission. A number of search languages are available, including the following:

- **Lucene** — Based on Apache Lucene, provides any combination of metadata, path, and full-text search using the Lucene query syntax. This includes the ability to search for terms and/or phrases in properties and content, paths, types, aspects, and ranges.
- **XPath** — Supports simple path-based contextual navigation against the node service based on version 1 of the XPath specification.
- **Alfresco Full Text** — Provides a comprehensive, language independent full text search capability.
- **CMIS QL** — Supports all CMIS QL (except `join between Types`) standard. The Alfresco Full Text Search language can also be embedded in the CMIS QL `contains()` predicate.

See the "Content Management Interoperability Services" section later in this chapter for more detail on CMIS and CMIS QL.

CONTENT APPLICATION SERVICES

Content Application Services extend the repository services to provide the extended capabilities required for rich content and collaborative applications. These can be further categorized as Content, Control, and Collaboration services.

Content Services

Content services provide advanced content management capabilities to automate tasks, handle format conversions, automatically extract content metadata, and generate thumbnails and proxies.

Rules and Actions

Rules and actions automatically trigger behavior when certain defined conditions are met. A standard set of conditions and actions is provided that can be further extended using scripts and custom actions.

Transformation

Transformation services provide the ability to convert content between different file formats, such as generating PDF files from Microsoft Office formats and converting between a large range of image formats. The Transformation service is designed to be extensible, allowing the use of additional transformers.

Metadata Extraction

This service automatically extracts metadata information from inbound and/or updated content, and updates the corresponding node properties with the metadata values.

Thumbnailing

This service creates a thumbnail of a given content property for a node. A number of different standard types of thumbnails can be generated, including Flash Web previews and image thumbnails (small and medium-sized). The Thumbnailing service makes use of the specific transformations available via the Transformation service.

Control Services

Control services provide the ability to manage workflow, Web projects, sandboxes, and assets.

Workflow

Workflow services are provided to manage business processes around content using user-assigned tasks, automated steps, and flow control. The underlying workflow engine uses the embedded JBoss jBPM Workflow engine, which is encapsulated within a Workflow service that provides a standard interface to the underlying workflow engine itself. Workflow definitions are used to define process templates, a number of which are provided out of box. You can also define additional process definitions (see Chapter 7).

Web Projects

Web content management applications use Web projects to store Web content related to a Web site, Web application, and other types of managed Web property. The key use case is where multiple artifacts must be managed together through the concept of change sets – collections of related assets that must be managed as a whole.

The Web Projects service provides a set of methods for creating and managing Web project instances to support Web applications. These services are accessible from both the JavaScript and RESTful layers.

Sandboxes

Within a Web project, sandboxes provide users with an isolated working area in which to make changes to the Web content without affecting the view of the data by other users. Workflow is then used to manage a controlled submission process for publishing the changes to the production Web property.

The Sandbox services provide methods for creating, reading, modifying, and deleting content in a sandbox, and for submitting content from the sandbox for review, approval, and publishing.

Assets

Assets are the individual items of content being managed within a Web project sandbox. Methods include the ability to list all the assets, inspect their properties, and submit collections of changes in the form of a change set for review and publishing.

Collaboration Services

Collaboration services provide the ability to manage sites, user and group membership, activities, tagging, and comments.

Sites

Sites are a key concept within Alfresco Share for managing documents, wiki pages, blog posts, discussions, and other collaborative content relating to teams, projects, communities of interest, and other types of collaborative sites. The Sites service itself provides management capabilities for creating, updating, and deleting sites.

Invite

The Invite service is used to maintain the user and group membership for sites. The service is responsible for sending invite notices to users and managing the acceptance or rejection status for particular invites.

Activity

Alfresco Share uses activities to track a range of changes, updates, events, and actions, allowing users to be aware of what is being changed, and where, by whom, and when the changes occurred. The Activity service provides facilities for posting events and generating feeds for Share sites.

Tagging

Tags are keywords or terms assigned to a piece of information, including documents, blogs, wiki pages, and calendar events. The Tagging service provides methods and properties to add, remove, use information, and search by tags.

Commenting

Comments are modeled as separate content items that are associated with the relevant node through child associations. The Commenting service provides a RESTful API for managing comments against nodes and provides methods to get existing comments, post new comments, and delete comments.

See Chapter 5 for more information on modeling and associations.

HOW SERVICES ARE BUILT

Most services are built using three tiers: core Java, a Public Script service, and a RESTful API (see Figure 4-1). In some cases, services may be implemented using just one or two of the layers. For example, some low-level services are only available at the core Java level, in which case they may be used as a component of a higher-level service.

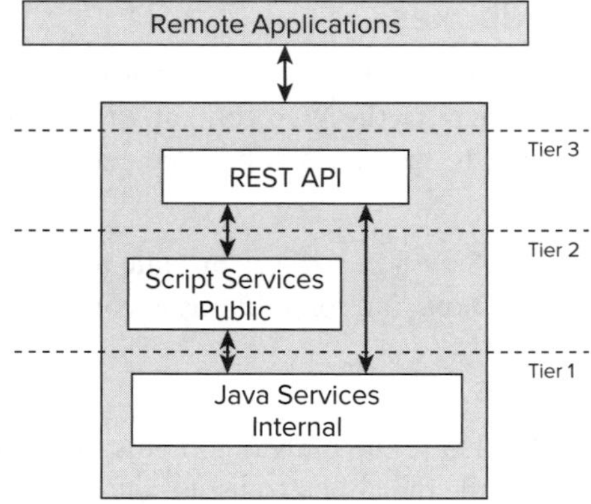

FIGURE 4-1

Generally, each tier has the following characteristics:

➤ **Tier 1 — Embedded Java API** — The Embedded Java API is a low-level, stateless API implemented in Java. It encapsulates all the functionality provided by the service and is typically a collection of fine-grained, stateless methods. It is considered an internal API only suitable for core Java developers. All other interfaces are built on top of these APIs. Examples include the FileFolderService, SearchService, and AuthenticationService.

➤ **Tier 2 — JavaScript API** — The JavaScript API provides an object-based interface on top of the Embedded Java API. It is designed to provide a developer-friendly interface to the capabilities provided by the server. Example methods available include `createNode`, `createAssociation`, `setPermission`, and `query`.

Scripts can be used to implement independent behaviors in the form of actions and are used to provide the backing behavior for Web scripts when implementing the RESTful APIs.

- **Tier 3 — RESTful API** — The RESTful APIs are designed around resources and data to provide a remote, URL-based API. As they are URL-based, they can be called from virtually any language. Although they are typically built on top of the Public Script services, they can also be implemented directly on the Java API. Examples include the Sites service and Tagging service, both of which are implemented on top of associated Script services.

USING SERVICES

As services are core to the Alfresco Content Application Server, they are used by all applications working against the server, including the Explorer and Share clients, Virtual File System interfaces such as CIFS and WebDAV, and the APIs. The APIs fall into two main categories: those available directly against the server (embedded APIs) and those that run on a separate tier (remote APIs). Developers use these APIs as appropriate to access and extend the out-of-the-box services.

Embedded APIs

Embedded APIs are used by custom extensions executed directly against the Content Application Server. There are three main embedded APIs: the Alfresco Java Foundation API, the JavaScript API, and the Template API.

- **Alfresco Java Foundation API** — Provides a collection of public Java Interfaces to the services provided by the server.
- **JavaScript API** — Provides an object-oriented view of the Java Foundation API with comprehensive access to the core services.
- **Template API** — A read-only API designed to render output such as HTML, XML, JSON, and text using the FreeMarker template engine; the Template API uses an object-oriented view of the content repository in combination with templates to generate the output.

The JavaScript and Template APIs are the key building blocks for Web scripts, which are used to develop the RESTful APIs.

The following code samples illustrate usage of the embedded APIs.

The following example uses the Java API to create new content:

Available for download on Wrox.com

```
/**
 * Creates a new content node setting the content provided.
 *
 * @param  parent   the parent node reference
 * @param  name     the name of the newly created content object
 * @param  text     the content text to be set on the newly created node
 * @return NodeRef  node reference to the newly created content node
 *
private NodeRef createContentNode(NodeRef parent, String name, String text)
    {
        // Create a map to contain the values of the properties of the node
        Map<QName, Serializable> props = new HashMap<QName, Serializable>(1);
        props.put(ContentModel.PROP_NAME, name);
```

```
        // use the node service to create a new node
        NodeRef node = this.nodeService.createNode(
                    parent,
                    ContentModel.ASSOC_CONTAINS,
                    QName.createQName(NamespaceService.CONTENT_MODEL_1_0_URI, name),
                    ContentModel.TYPE_CONTENT,
                    props).getChildRef();

        // Use the content service to set the content onto the newly created node
        ContentWriter writer = this.contentService.getWriter(node,
        ContentModel.PROP_CONTENT, true);
        writer.setMimetype(MimetypeMap.MIMETYPE_TEXT_PLAIN);
        writer.setEncoding("UTF-8");
        writer.putContent(text);

        // Return a node reference to the newly created node
        return node;
    }
```

Code Snippet: createContentNode.java

This example uses the Java API and the NodeService and ContentService to create a content node including both content and metadata. It takes a nodeRef of the folder that will contain the node, a string to be used for the nodes name, and a string containing the content. A map of the metadata data values is then created, which is passed as a parameter to the NodeServer that creates the node itself. The content is written to the node using the ContentService and finally the node reference for the newly created node is returned.

This second example uses the JavaScript API to create new content:

Available for download on Wrox.com

```
// create file in the user's home folder
var doc = userhome.createFile("myDoc.txt");
doc.content = "This is some content.";
doc.save();
```

Code Snippet: createfile.js

In this example a new document called `myDoc.txt` is created in the home space of the current user. The content for the new document is set to `doc.content` and the document is saved to commit our changes.

The final example uses the Template API to display all the properties for a given document:

Available for download on Wrox.com

```
<table>
 <#-- Get a list of all the property names for the document -->
 <#assign props = document.properties?keys>
 <#list props as t>
    <#-- If the property exists -->
    <#if document.properties[t]?exists>
       <#-- If it is a date, format it accordingly-->
       <#if document.properties[t]?is_date>
```

```
            <tr><td>${t} = ${document.properties[t]?date}</td></tr>
            <#-- If it is a boolean, format it accordingly-->
            <#elseif document.properties[t]?is_boolean>
            <tr><td>${t} = ${document.properties[t]?string("yes", "no")}</td></tr>

            <#-- Otherwise treat it as a string -->
            <#else>
            <tr><td>${t} = ${document.properties[t]}</td></tr>
            </#if>
        </#if>
    </#list>
    </table>
```

Code Snippet: documentProperties.ftl

The template iterates over all the properties for a node called document and renders the values as appropriate for the data types returned.

Remote APIs

There are several remote APIs available, allowing clients connecting from a separate tier to communicate with the Alfresco Content Application Server. These are based on Web services, and RESTful and CMIS protocols. The remote APIs are designed to be language agnostic, allowing development against these APIs using a range of development languages, including Java, PHP, Ruby, .NET, and many more.

- **Web services:** An object-oriented API using SOAP and supporting a range of content services, including authentication, query, node creation and update, access control, and actions.
- **REST:** HTTP-based resource-oriented interfaces used by the Surf framework and Alfresco Share.
- **CMIS:** The CMIS standard defines Web services and REST-based bindings for working with CMIS-compliant repositories.

The following is an example of calling a RESTful API to retrieve the list of tags for a document:

```
http://localhost:8080/alfresco/service/api/node/workspace/SpacesStore/
97526d57-d1ce-4578-931d-0cc48ff23602/tags
```

This will retrieve all the tags for the node with the node reference workspace://SpacesStore/97526d57-d1ce-4578-931d-0cc48ff23602 in the body of the HTTP response, formatted in JSON. For example:

```
{
   "data" : ["tagOne", "tagTwo"]
}
```

Configuring and Extending Existing Services

Alfresco uses the Spring framework to implement an extremely modular architecture. Services are bound together through their interfaces and configured using Spring's declarative Dependency Injection. This allows existing services to be configured, extended, and replaced, and new services to be introduced.

The specific details vary from service to service. For example, it is possible to define new transformers by extending the `baseContentTransformer`. This defines how the new transformer is invoked, the source and target MIME types it supports, and the transformer's availability. This is done through configuration that extends the existing service. The underlying service itself does not need to be modified and no additional code is required.

The following example shows the Spring configuration required to extended the out-of-the-box `RuntimeExecutableContentTransformer`. This is a standard transformer that is able to execute system executables. An example of a command line transformation program is HTML Tidy (`http://tidy.sourceforge.net/`), which can transform HTML documents into XHTML documents.

Available for download on Wrox.com

```
<?xml version='1.0' encoding='UTF-8'?>
<!DOCTYPE beans PUBLIC '-//SPRING//DTD BEAN//EN' 'http://www.springframework.org/
dtd/spring-beans.dtd'>

<beans>
   <bean id="transformer.Tidy.XHTML" class="org.alfresco.repo.content.transform.
   RuntimeExecutableContentTransformer" parent="baseContentTransformer">
      <property name="checkCommand">
         <bean class="org.alfresco.util.exec.RuntimeExec">
            <property name="commandMap">
                <map>
                    <entry key=".*">
                        <value>tidy -help</value>
                    </entry>
                </map>
            </property>
            <property name="errorCodes">
               <value>2</value>
            </property>
         </bean>
      </property>
      <property name="transformCommand">
         <bean class="org.alfresco.util.exec.RuntimeExec">
            <property name="commandMap">
                <map>
                    <entry key="Linux">
                        <value>tidy -asxhtml -o '${target}' '${source}'</value>
                    </entry>
                    <entry key="Windows.*">
                        <value>tidy -asxhtml -o "${target}" "${source}"</value>
                    </entry>
                </map>
            </property>
            <property name="errorCodes">
               <value>2</value>
            </property>
         </bean>
      </property>
      <property name="explicitTransformations">
```

```
        <list>
           <bean class="org.alfresco.repo.content.transform.
           ExplictTransformationDetails" >
               <property name="sourceMimetype"><value>text/html</value></property>
               <property name="targetMimetype"><value>application/xhtml+xml
               </value></property>
           </bean>
        </list>
     </property>
  </bean>
</beans>
```

Code snippet: tidyTransformer.xml

The actual transformation command used is defined in the `transformCommand` property. The transformation mechanism performs substitutions of the variables `${source}` and `${target}`, which are the full file paths of the source and target files for the transformation. For example:

```
tidy -asxhtml -o "${target}" "${source}"
```

The transformer comes with an optional feature, `checkCommand`, which is executed by the `init` method. If an error occurs during execution of this command, which cannot take any parameters, then the transformer is flagged as `not available`. When not available, the `getReliability` method will always return 0.0; otherwise it is assumed that the transformation command will be successful. The reliability of the transformation is used by the transformation registry to select the most appropriate transformer for a given transformation. The transformer remains directly usable — you can directly select it as an action to perform.

External utilities stick to a rough convention regarding the return codes. In this case, `tidy` returns a code value 2. The `errorCodes` property defines a comma separated list of values indicating failure; the default is "1, 2".

The final piece of configuration defines the MIME types that this transformer supports via the `explicitTransformations` property. In this case, the transformer supports a source MIME type of `text/html` and a target MIME type of `application/xhtml+xml`.

This example illustrates how to extend an existing service via configuration only: it has been possible to add a new transformer without any code changes. To complete the example, additional configuration is needed to expose the new transformer via the client interfaces or as a repository action. See Chapter 14 for more details.

Building a Simple Service

The following section walks through an example of building a new service by showing the high-level interfaces for each tier of the service. To simply the example, the full detail of some of the methods will not be shown.

This example can be considered as a new content application service built on the Content Repository Services.

The example service provides a counter with methods for creating, listing, incrementing, decrementing, and resetting integer counter instances and their values. The counter can be used to persist how many times a particular event has occurred. For example, to generate a unique reference number for a document, the counter can be used to generate an integer that can be used as the basis of the reference number.

The service will implemented using the three tier approach described earlier in this chapter. Java will be used to provide underlying methods in Tier 1; the JavaScript API is used for Tier 2 to provide higher-level methods, allowing the counter to be called via repository actions and exposed via Tier 3 as the new RESTful counter API.

Example Counter Service: Tier 1 – Java Service Layer

The following code outline shows Tier 1 of the Counter service.

Java Service Layer

```
public interface CounterService
// Low level services for creating and updating counters.
{
    public enum CounterOperation { INC, DEC };

    // Create a counter and set the initial value.
    // Returns the counter id.
    String createCounter(int initialValue);

    // Get the value of a counter.
    int getCounterValue(counterId);

    // Update the counter value by a given step.  The counter operation
    // is provided.
    int updateCounterValue(String counterId, CounterOperation operation, int step);

    // Delete the counter.
    int deleteCounter();
}
```

The Java Service Layer outline implements the low-level Java methods for the counter. It includes methods for creating counters, getting counters by ID, updating counter values, and resetting counter values. These methods will use other services (not shown) from the Internal Java API to create the underlying repository objects used to persist the counters.

Example Counter Service: Tier 2 – JavaScript API

To allow the Java service to be used outside of Java, such as for a repository action or as a RESTful API, access is provided via Tier 2, the JavaScript API layer.

JavaScript API

```
// Create counter.  Initial value and default step are optional parameters.
// Returns the created counter object
function createCounter(initialValue=1, defaultStep=1);

// Get counter.
// Returns the counter object
function getCounter(counterId);

Counter
{
   var id;
   var defaultStep;
   var value;

   function increment(value=0);

   function decrement(value=0);

   function delete();
}
```

The `createCounter` script outline implements higher-level methods on top of the Tier 1 Java service. It includes a function to get instances of a counter by ID and functions to increment, decrement, and reset the counter value. This script will be callable via the Tier 3 RESTful API that follows.

Example Counter Service: Tier 3 – RESTful API

The Service layer exposes the script layer as two resource URIs working against counter collections and counter instances. The first resource returns a *counter collection*, which a list of all the available counters and is also used to create new counter instances. The second resource is *counter*, which is used to manipulate the value of a particular counter instance.

Resource: Counter Collection

```
Method: GET /alfresco/counters
   Description: Returns a list of counters

   Example output:

   {
      "counters":
      {
         "counter0":
         {
            "id" : "counter0",
            "value" : 12,
            "url" : "/counters/counter0"
         },

 "counter1":
```

```
        {
            "id" : "counter1",
            "value" : 3,
            "url" : "/counters/counter1"
        }
    }
}
```

The counter collection resource is called using a simple HTTP GET method against the /alfresco/counters URI. It provides a platform- and language-independent interface to get a list of counters. The response is formatted using JSON and the calling application can parse the JSON response to get the list of counters as appropriate.

```
Method: POST /alfresco/counters
Description: Creates a new counter

Example input:
{
    "id" : "counter2",
    "initialValue" : 0,
    "defaultStep" : 1
}

Example output:

{
    "id" : "counter2",
    "value" : 0,
    "url" : "/counters/counter2"
}
```

Calling the counter collection resource using an HTTP POST method creates a new counter instance. The body of the post method uses a JSON-formatted payload that includes the ID for the new counter, the `initialValue`, and also the default value (`defaultStep`) used to increment or decrement the counter.

Resource: Counter

```
Method: GET /alfresco/counters/{counter-id}
Description: Gets the current value for a counter

Example output:

{
    "id" : "counter2",
    "value" : 0,
    "url" : "/counters/counter2"
}
```

The counter resource is used to read and update the values for a particular counter. As with the counter collection, the behavior is based on the HTTP request method used to call the resource. In this example the URI is being called using an HTTP GET, which returns the current value as a JSON response for the `counter-id` identified at the end of the URI request.

```
Method - POST /alfresco/counters/{counter-id}
Description: Increments or decrements a counter's value according to the passed
in step value.

Example input:

{
   "step" : 1
}

Example output where existing value is 11:

{
   "id" : "counter0",
   "value" : 12,
   "url" : "/counters/counter0"
}
```

Calling the counter resource with POST increments or decrements the counter according to the step value passed in via the request BODY. If no BODY is provided, the default step value will be used. It returns a JSON response including the new counter value.

```
Method - DELETE /alfresco/counters/{counter-id}
Description: Deletes the counter
```

The final method is used to delete the counter by calling the counter with an HTTP DELETE method. Note that in this case, there is no response in the HTTP body. A 204 status code would be returned in the HTTP header to indicate the delete had been successful.

You now have a set of RESTful APIs that provide simple, URI-addressable and platform-independent services to manage and inspect your counters.

CONTENT MANAGEMENT INTEROPERABILITY SERVICES (CMIS)

In September 2008, Microsoft, IBM, EMC, Alfresco, BEA (now Oracle), and SAP submitted the Content Management Interoperability Services (CMIS) specification to OASIS to become a standard. The goal of CMIS is to access any content management systems that implement CMIS, such as Microsoft SharePoint, IBM FileNet, EMC Documentum, and Alfresco, in a standardized and interoperable way. This allows the ECM industry to create a new ecosystem around content management. CMIS is designed to enable new classes of cross-repository applications in areas such as eDiscovery, publishing, collaboration, and information access. CMIS also strives to create a common understanding of content query, content properties and types, type inheritance, and common content operations; however, CMIS is not designed to expose all capabilities of a repository or expose administration or management functions.

CMIS provides a level of portability that allows you to build applications that are not locked into any content management system and to future-proof those applications. CMIS provides a rich set of functionality, yet is capable of handling a wide variety of content management systems. CMIS provides a set of content services for managing content metadata, versioning, folder containment, associations, and binary transfer. In addition, CMIS provides a query language based upon SQL querying content, its metadata, and context.

After a lot of development and public review, 2010 shows the emergence of CMIS as a full-fledged standard.

Figure 4-2 shows a high-level overview of CMIS.

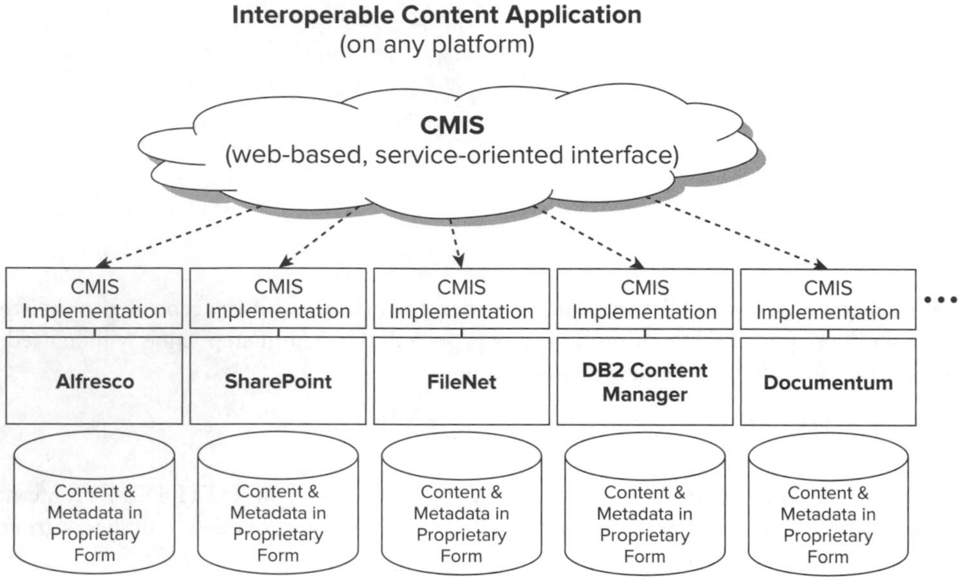

FIGURE 4-2

CMIS Requirements

Many large organizations today run multiple Enterprise content management systems, each with millions of dollars of implementation and integration on top of those systems that are specific to each underlying repository. Yet each system usually remains a silo of information that does not share content. In addition, an application built to a system cannot be used on another system. The lack of integration and interoperability means that organizations using multiple systems cannot get a consistent view of information. This creates substantial operational and compliance risks in that content cannot be found and consistently managed. The challenge is even greater for independent application vendors who create content management application solutions. Supporting more than one content management system can be a very expensive proposition.

CMIS promises to be a standard that provides interoperability where others have not. CMIS focuses on a few use cases and on being able to map to existing systems rather than specify how those systems should work. It is particularly important for CMIS to work with major ECM systems with a large installed base of users and content. CMIS is designed to be language-independent and uses Web protocols to access the repositories. CMIS supports both SOAP and REST through the AtomPub protocol.

Atom Publishing Protocol, or AtomPub, is an IETF standard for creating and updating Web resources. It is a REST-based protocol and is very flexible in extending the metadata it handles. The OASIS CMIS committee chose this protocol as the basis for its REST-based APIs.

CMIS does a good job of mapping data modeling, query capabilities, and content functionality of basic content services of these underlying systems. Despite the relative commonality of these systems, the CMIS Technical Committee has tried to ensure that the functionality exposed can actually be implemented.

The core use cases targeted by CMIS are:

- **Collaborative content creation:** Collaborative content creation allows users to work collaboratively to create one or more documents or Web pages.
- **Portal access of ECM systems:** Portals with CMIS provide an aggregated interface to viewing content from multiple sources.
- **Mashups of content in Web sites:** Web sites using CMIS can create composite applications that mash up or integrate data and functionality from one or more repositories.
- **Portable search against multiple repositories:** Search interfaces in CMIS support a consistent way for search engines to index and access content from a content repository.

These core use cases drove requirements around query, authentication, security, versioning, change logs, and basic content operations.

Some of the applications not directly addressed by CMIS but that the Technical Committee intended to be built on CMIS are:

- **Workflow and Business Process Management** — Business processes frequently have content attached and CMIS is a good way to ensure accurate versions of content are attached, such as contracts or invoices.
- **Archival** — As the archive stores information as part of an ECM system, applications can be archive-independent by using CMIS.
- **Compound or virtual document publishing** — There aren't specifically publishing functions for compound documents. However, publishing applications can manipulate and access compound or virtual documents, which can be modeled using CMIS relationships.
- **eDiscovery** — Applications to discover content in many different repositories can create a federated view of what documents are discoverable using CMIS to access many different repositories in a consistent way.

Core Concepts of CMIS

At the root of the CMIS model and services is a repository, which is an instance of the content management system and its store of metadata, content, and indexes. The repository is the end point to which all requests are directed. In the RESTful model, it is the root path of the resources being addressed in CMIS. The repository is capable of describing itself and its capabilities.

The core CMIS object model (see Figure 4-3) is not very different from the Alfresco object model minus the support of aspects. Like Alfresco, CMIS supports object types that define properties associated with each type. Each object has an object type, properties defined by that object type, and an object ID that uniquely identifies that object. Object types support inheritance and are sub-typed as Document object types and Folder object types. Document object types may have content streams to store and access binary data. Object types may also be related through Relationship object types.

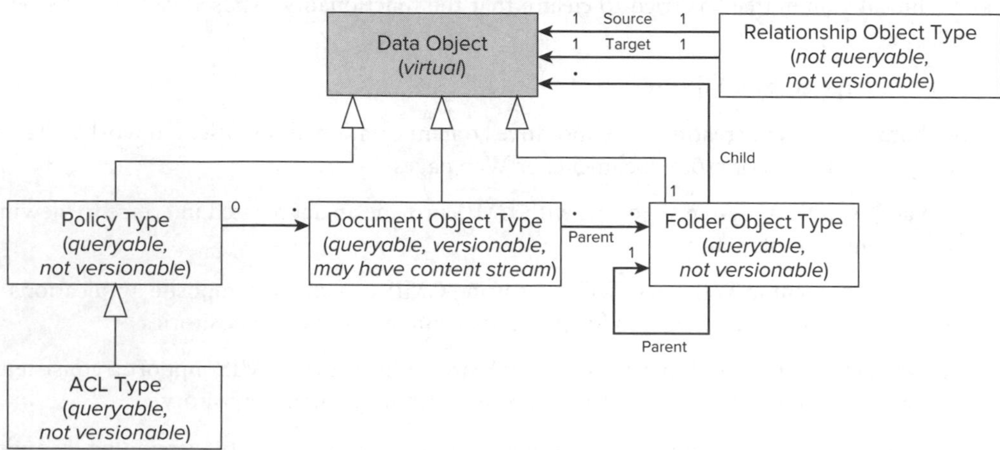

FIGURE 4-3

A Policy object represents an administrative policy that can be enforced by a repository, such as a retention management policy. An Access Control List (ACL) is a type of Policy object. CMIS allows applications to create or apply ACLs. The Alfresco repository also uses Policy objects to apply aspects.

Document objects have properties and content streams for accessing the binary information that is the document, properties that may be multi-valued, and versions (see Figure 4-4). Document objects

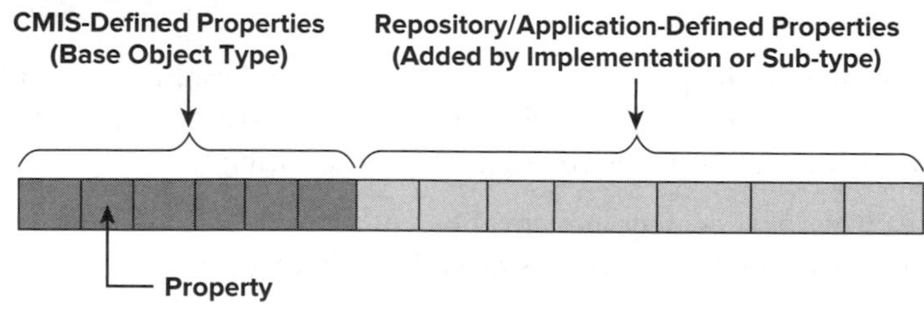

FIGURE 4-4

can also have Renditions that represent alternate file types of the document. Only one Rendition type, a Thumbnail, is well defined.

Versioning in CMIS (see Figure 4-5) makes it relatively simple to encompass the various versioning models of different CMIS implementations. Each version is a separate object with its own object ID. For a given object ID, you can retrieve the specific version, the current version, or all versions of the object, as well as delete specific or all versions of a Document object. Document versions are accessed as a set of Document objects organized on the timestamp of the object. CMIS does not provide a history graph.

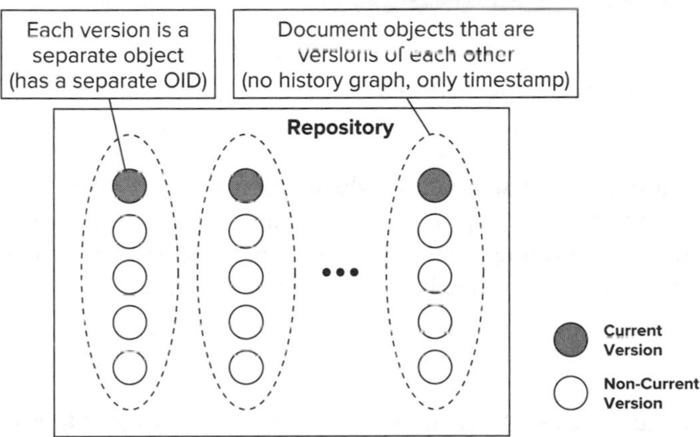

FIGURE 4-5

Document objects live in a folder hierarchy (see Figure 4-6). As in Alfresco, a folder can exist in another folder to create the hierarchy. The relationship between folder and document is *many-to-many* if the repository supports multifiling, allowing a document to appear in more than one folder. Otherwise, it is *one-to-many*.

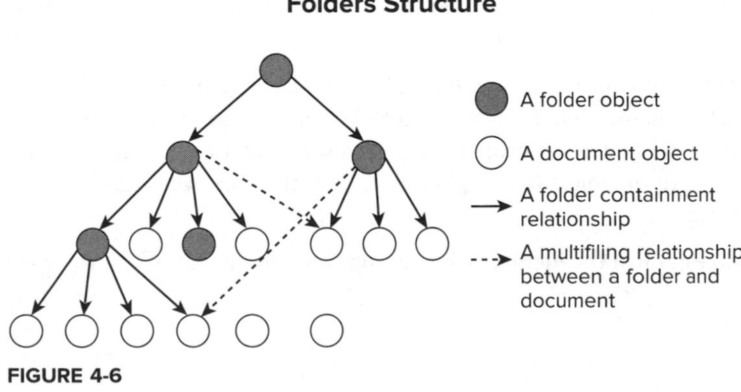

FIGURE 4-6

A query in CMIS is based upon SQL-92 and should be familiar if you have used a relational database system like MySQL. The query itself is read-only and presents no data manipulation capabilities. The syntax consists of the following clauses:

- `SELECT` with a target list
- `FROM` with the object types being queried
- `JOIN` to perform a join between object types
- `WHERE` with the predicate
- `IN` and `ANY` to query multivalue properties
- `CONTAINS` to specify a full-text qualification
- `IN_FOLDER` and `IN_TREE` to search within a folder hierarchy
- `ORDERBY` to sort the results

The CMIS query maps the object type into a relational structure where object type approximates a table, the object approximates a row, and the property approximates a column that can be multivalued. The actual binary content can be queried using a full-text query and folder path information using the `in_folder` and `in_tree` functions. A query can also be paged for user interface presentation.

CMIS Services

CMIS Services comprise Repository Change services, Navigation services, Object services, Multifiling (Folder) services, Discovery (Query) services, Versioning services, Relationship services, Policy services, and ACL services. You can access these services equally using SOAP or AtomPub, depending on your preferred architectural style. This book uses AtomPub and the RESTful style as an example of how to use CMIS with Alfresco.

- **Repository services** discover available repositories and get the capabilities of these repositories. They also provide some basic Data Dictionary information of what types are available in the repository.
- **Navigation services** let you navigate the repository by accessing the folder tree and traversing the folder/child hierarchy. These services can be used to get both children and parents of an object.
- **Object services** provide the basic CRUD (Create, Read, Update, Delete) and Control services on any object, including Document, Folder, Policy, and Relationship objects. For Document objects, this includes setting and getting of properties, policies, and content streams. Object services retrieve objects by path or object ID. Applications may also discover what actions users are allowed to perform.
- **Multifiling services** let you establish the hierarchy by adding or removing an object to or from a folder.

- **Discovery services** provide Query and Change services. Discovery services accept the SQL-like query described earlier and provide a means of paging the results of the query.
- **Change services** let you discover what content has changed since the last time checked, as specified by a special token. Change services can be used for external search indexing and replication services.
- **Versioning services** control concurrent operation of the Object services by providing Check In and Check Out services. Version services also provide version histories for objects that are versioned.
- **Relationship services** create, manage, and access relationships or associations between objects as well as allow an application to traverse those associations.
- **Policy services** apply policies on document objects. Policies are free-form objects and can be used by implementations for security, record, or control policies.
- **ACL services** are used to create, manage, and access Access Control Lists to control who can perform what operation on an object.

Obviously, each CMIS service can become quite an involved topic in its own right. For a complete catalog of services, please see the CMIS specification on the OASIS Web site at `www.oasis-open.org/committees/tc_home.php?wg_abbrev=cmis`.

Using CMIS with Alfresco

The Alfresco implementation is a thorough implementation of CMIS and has been the basis for many CMIS applications. Most applications that use CMIS with Alfresco use the AtomPub protocol over the SOAP protocol; however, some applications that have a strong Web services framework, like SAP and Tibco, use SOAP instead. In this book, examples are presented using the AtomPub protocol.

If you are programming CMIS applications in Java, you can use the Apache Abdera libraries, which were built to handle AtomPub. Abdera provides both client and server implementations of the Atom Publish and Subscribe protocols. You can find Apache Abdera at `http://abdera.apache.org`.

To use CMIS with PHP, it is best to use one of the PHP Web frameworks such as Drupal or Joomla. The Drupal interface was built by Optaros and Acquia and can be found at `http://drupal.org/project/cmis`.

CMIS is a good choice for building applications or application integrations against Alfresco when you wish to make the application portable to other systems; however, you will need to use Web scripts instead to:

- Use or query aspects or access properties in aspects
- Add or manage workflows
- Apply actions or rules

- Perform any records management operations
- Work with Web content management
- Perform any management or administrative task, such as user or group management, or indexing control

You can also integrate Web scripts with the AtomPub protocol of CMIS.

For more information on using CMIS with Alfresco, including new Java bindings, visit `http://cmis.alfresco.com`. To access the CMIS specification, visit `www.oasis-open.org/committees/cmis`.

5

Content Modeling

WHAT'S IN THIS CHAPTER?

- Defining a content model to represent your business domain
- Registering your content model with the Alfresco content repository
- Interacting with your content model via JavaScript
- Understanding how a content model relates to the CMIS Data Model

Content modeling is a fundamental building block of the Alfresco content repository that provides a foundation for structuring content and working with content. It is an important concept to grasp, as nearly all solutions built with Alfresco require some form of content modeling.

The purpose of content modeling is to specify how nodes stored in the content repository are constrained. This imposes a formal structure on nodes that can be understood and enforced by an ECM application.

The storage engine of the content repository employs an uncomplicated data structure for recording entities, metadata, and relationships. The data structure is a tree of nodes where each node supports one or more properties whose values may be of any data type and either single- or multi-valued. A node has at least one parent (except for the root node, which has no parent) and may contain one or more child nodes. Nodes may also be related through arbitrary peer relationships. Although a straightforward data structure, its inherent simplicity allows the development of complex content constructs.

Content modeling puts the following constraints on the data structure:

- A node must be of a given kind.
- A node must carry an enumerated set of properties.
- A property must be of a given data type.
- A value must be within a defined set of values.
- A node must be related to other nodes in a particular way.

These constraints allow the definition of (or modeling of) entities within the ECM domain. For example, many ECM applications are built around the notion of folders and documents (as show in Figure 5-1). It is content modeling that adds meaning to the node data structure.

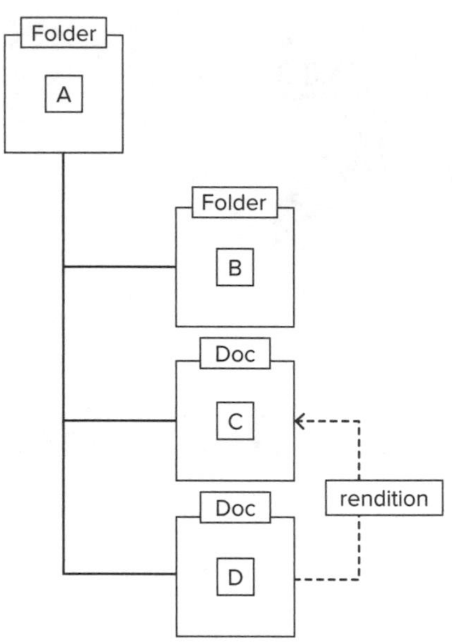

FIGURE 5-1

Out of the box, Alfresco comes prepackaged with several content models for support of the common or standardized aspects of ECM, especially for Document and Records Management. You can accomplish a lot with just these models, but if you want to break beyond the classic file system, you'll need to roll up your sleeves and get modeling to support the specific needs of your ECM solution.

MODELING IN CONTEXT

Content modeling is really all about metadata (that is, data describing data). But one man's metadata is another man's data, so it can very quickly become confusing when discussing content models.

To put content modeling in context, Alfresco talks in terms of the four-layer metadata model, as shown in Figure 5-2.

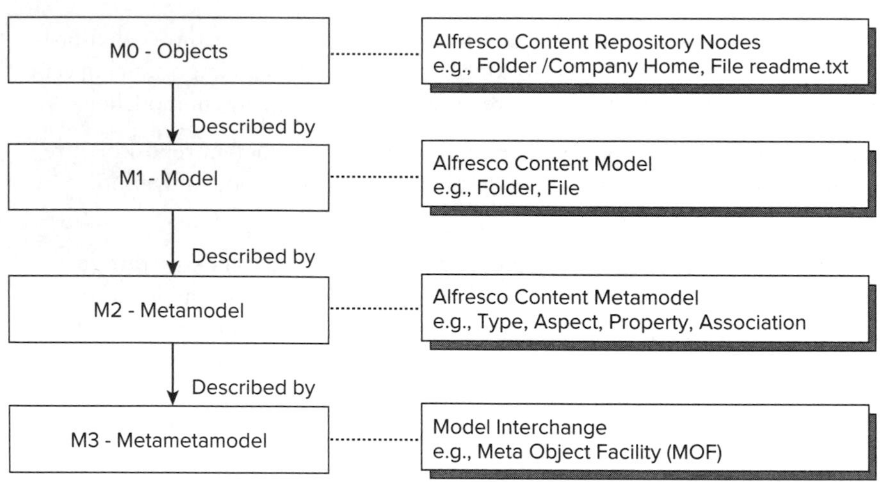

FIGURE 5-2

The first layer, M0, represents the nodes, properties, and relationships held in the Alfresco content repository. These entities are managed through the various Content Repository Services, such as the File Folder service or CMIS (Content Management Interoperability Services).

The next layer, M1, is a content model that defines a set of related definitions to constrain the nodes in layer M0. Many content models may be registered with the content repository.

A content model is itself described by the next layer, M2, the content metamodel. Although this chapter is titled "Content Modeling," the majority of the chapter really focuses on the content metamodel, as this is how you express your new content models. If you do not understand the content metamodel, you cannot define a content model. There are already some standardized content metamodels: the CMIS Data Model and JSR-170 Node Type model. This chapter also explains how the content metamodel maps to these standards.

Finally, there is the most abstract layer, M3, the content metametamodel that supports the conversion of content models expressed in one content metamodel to another, such as from the CMIS Data Model to JCR Node Types. Out of the box, Alfresco does not provide a definition of the content metametamodel or a conversion tool, but there are third-party tools that specialize in this area.

So, in summary, you'll be learning all about the Alfresco content metamodel (M2), in order to define one or more content models (M1), to constrain the structure of your nodes (M0) held in your content repository.

DEPLOYING A CONTENT MODEL

A content model is defined in its entirety as a single XML document, which must comply with the content metamodel XSD schema provided by the Alfresco content repository. Each model contains a set of related and coherent definitions, and is deployed as a unit.

Several content models may be deployed to the content repository, and definitions in one content model may depend on definitions in another content model, allowing for the sharing of definitions.

There are two approaches to deploying a content model into the content repository: *bootstrap* and *dynamic*.

The bootstrap approach involves modifying Alfresco content repository XML configuration files in order to register the content model such that on startup of the content repository, the content model is read, validated, and registered. A repository component called the Dictionary Bootstrap is responsible for loading a specified list of content models and registering them with the content repository. To register new content models, it is necessary either to modify the content model list of an existing Dictionary Bootstrap component or to define a new Dictionary Bootstrap component. For encapsulated modular extensions, it is recommended to define a new Dictionary Bootstrap component. Content model .xml files are placed in the classpath.

A Dictionary Bootstrap component is defined using the following snippet of Spring framework XML:

Available for download on Wrox.com

```
<bean id="kbmodel.extension.dictionaryBootstrap" parent="dictionaryModelBootstrap"
    depends-on="dictionaryBoot strap">
  <property name="models">
    <list>
      <value>alfresco/extension/kbModel.xml</value>
    </list>
  </property>
</bean>
```

Code snippet kbModel-model-context.xml

This snippet must be added to an Alfresco extension context XML file following the usual Alfresco customization conventions. Content models provided out of the box by Alfresco are all registered this way.

For a default installation of Alfresco, extension context XML files are placed into installLocation/tomcat/shared/classes/alfresco/extension.

Remember, with the bootstrap approach, changes to model definitions through the content-model XML file are only registered after restarting the content repository. This can lead to long development and test cycles, so the bootstrap approach should only be used once the model is baked.

For this reason, an alternate dynamic approach to deploying a content model is provided, allowing the registration and updates to content models without the need to restart the content repository to pick up the changes. Instead of placing content model XML files into the classpath, they are placed in the content repository itself under the folder

```
Company Home/Data Dictionary/Models
```

The easiest tool for this is Alfresco Explorer, which provides full access to the Alfresco content repository Data Dictionary folder. Upon creating or uploading a content model XML file, the model, by default, will not be active. To activate a model (that is, to auto-register it with the content repository), select the View Details option for the XML file and then select the Modify icon on the Properties pane. On the Modify Content Properties page, enable the Model Active checkbox.

To update a content model, simply edit its XML and save via Alfresco Explorer. If the model is active, the content repository will automatically register the changes with the content repository on save. If the content model XML file is checked out, the working copy will be ignored until it is checked in.

To deactivate a model, select the View Details option for the content model XML file and then select the Modify icon on the Properties pane. On the Modify Content Properties page, disable the Model Active checkbox. To remove a content model completely, simply delete the content model XML file.

There are restrictions on what changes can be made to a content model XML file and when a content model XML file can be deleted. Only incremental additions — changes that do not require modifications to existing data in the content repository — are allowed. The content model can be deleted only if it is not used by any data in the content repository.

THE CONTENT METAMODEL EXPLAINED

Now that you know how to register and deploy a content model XML file to the content repository, it is time to discover how to define a content model itself, which is expressed in terms of the content metamodel.

The content metamodel (as shown in Figure 5-3) is as follows:

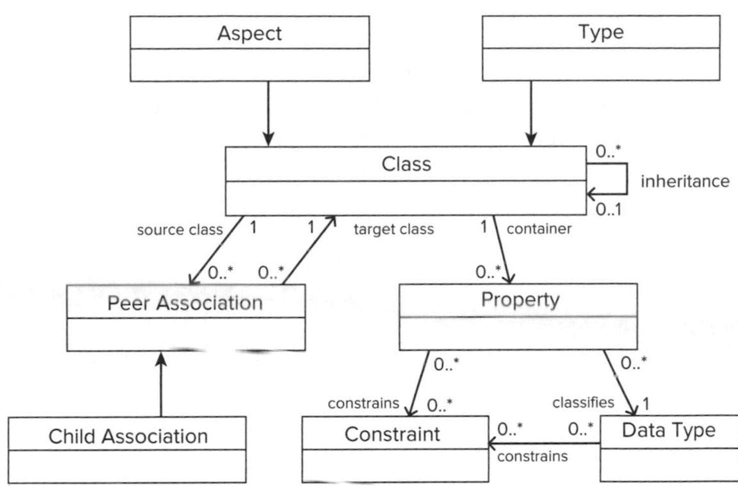

FIGURE 5-3

At the heart of the content metamodel is a *type*. A type is just like a type or class in an object-oriented model. It represents objects in the real world with support for properties and the ability to inherit the definition of a parent type. *Properties* are named items of metadata associated with the type, where each property is of a given data type. *Constraints* can be applied to restrict the values of a property.

Relationships between types are modeled with *associations*, of which there are two types: *child associations* and *peer associations*. Child associations provide the ability to model compositions where the parent effectively owns the children and, therefore, operations like delete will propagate through to the children, just like a cascade delete in a relational database. Peer associations, on the other hand, define a relationship between two objects where neither object is superior to the other.

A concept that may not be so well understood is an *aspect*. The closest equivalent in the object-oriented world is the notion of multiple inheritance, where a type may inherit features from more than one parent type. In Alfresco, an aspect supports the same capabilities as a type, meaning it supports properties, and may be related to and may inherit the definition of a parent aspect. On the surface, aspects seem very similar to types, but there is one important distinguishing feature, which is that aspects may be shared across types. In other words, aspects allow *cross-cutting* of the content model, which is the sharing of property and association definitions by attaching them to multiple types. This is the content metamodel equivalent of multiple inheritance.

Content models constrain the structure of nodes held in the content repository. It is worth highlighting how nodes are tied to a content model. Each node, on creation, is given a type. The type may change over time, as long as the new type is compatible with the old type; however, a node is only ever of one type at any given time. In contrast, a node may be attached to one or more aspects. On creation, a node inherits the aspects attached to its type, as defined by the content model (at design time). But aspects go one step further. At runtime, it is possible to adjust the aspects attached to a node. This is a powerful feature, which allows content held in the content repository to be loosely constrained and for content to dynamically inherit features and capabilities.

The Metamodel XML Schema

The content metamodel is formally described by an XML-schema document. When in doubt about how to express a content model or understand the full capabilities of the content metamodel, it is highly recommended to interrogate the XML schema, as it provides the definitive description of the content metamodel.

The latest content metamodel XSD schema can always be located at `http://svn.alfresco.com/repos/alfresco-open-mirror/alfresco/HEAD/root/projects/repository/config/alfresco/model/modelSchema.xsd`

The target namespace of the content metamodel XML schema is

```
www.alfresco.org/model/dictionary/1.0
```

Enough of the theory: It's time to learn how to define a content model using each of the content metamodel capabilities.

The Model Header

Each content model starts with a model header, which provides an introduction to the model, composed of description, author, publication date, and version number. All parts of the model introduction are optional.

Available for download on Wrox.com

```
<xs:element name="model">
  <xs:attributeGroup ref="name" />
  ...
  <xs:complexType>
    <xs:sequence>
      <xs:element name="description" type="string"maxOccurs="1" minOccurs="0" />
      <xs:element name="author" type="string"maxOccurs="1" minOccurs="0" />
      <xs:element name="published" type="date"maxOccurs="1" minOccurs="0" />
      <xs:element name="version" type="string"maxOccurs="1" minOccurs="0" />
      ...
    </xs:sequence>
    ...
  </xs:complexType>
  ...
  <xs:attributeGroup name="name">
    <xs:attribute name="name" type="string" use="required" />
  </xs:attributeGroup>
</xs:element>
```

Code snippet modelSchema.xsd

A content model must be uniquely named within a given content repository. To assist with the definition of unique names across all content repositories, the content metamodel supports the notion of a namespace.

Model Namespaces

Namespaces provide a mechanism for specifying globally unique names for definitions within content models. A namespace is composed of a *URI* (a unique string often prefixed with an HTTP address associated with the author) and a *Prefix* (a shorthand code for the URI). Alfresco has defined several namespaces for the models provided out of the box with the content repository. The prefix for those namespace URIs is `www.alfresco.org`.

To associate a name with a namespace, it is only necessary to prefix the name with the relevant namespace prefix. For example, if the namespace URI `http://example.org/contentmodels` and associated prefix *ex* are defined, then the name *ex:customtype* means that *customtype* is a name defined within the namespace `http://example.org/contentmodels`.

Each content model must define at least one namespace for the names defined in that content model.

Available for download on Wrox.com

```
<xs:element name="model">
  ...
  <xs:element name="namespaces">
    <xs:complexType>
      <xs:sequence>
        <xs:element name="namespace" maxOccurs="unbounded" minOccurs="1">
          <xs:complexType>
            <xs:attributeGroup ref="namespaceDefinition" />
          </xs:complexType>
        </xs:element>
      </xs:sequence>
    </xs:complexType>
  </xs:element>
  ...
  <xs:attributeGroup name="namespaceDefinition">
    <xs:attribute name="uri" type="string" use="required" />
    <xs:attribute name="prefix" type="string" use="required" />
  </xs:attributeGroup>
  ...
</xs:element>
```

Code snippet modelSchema.xsd

Quite often, it is necessary for a content model to refer to definitions that reside in another content model. For example, a type may inherit from a type defined in another content model.

To refer to names defined outside of the content model, it is necessary to import the namespace within which that name is defined. Once imported, the name can be used just as if the content model itself defined it.

Available for download on Wrox.com

```
<xs:element name="model">
  ...
  <xs:element name="imports" maxOccurs="1" minOccurs="0">
    <xs:complexType>
      <xs:sequence>
```

```
            <xs:element name="import" maxOccurs="unbounded" minOccurs="1">
              <xs:complexType>
                <xs:attributeGroup ref="namespaceDefinition" />
              </xs:complexType>
            </xs:element>
          </xs:sequence>
        </xs:complexType>
      </xs:element>
      ...
    </xs:element>
```

Code snippet modelSchema.xsd

On import of a namespace URI, it is possible to remap the namespace prefix defined in the originating content model just in case there are prefix clashes between imported namespaces.

The content repository does not allow a content model to reference names that do not exist.

Types

A content model may define one or more types.

```
<xs:element name="model">
  ...
  <xs:element name="types" maxOccurs="1" minOccurs="0">
    <xs:complexType>
      <xs:sequence>
        <xs:element name="type" type="type" maxOccurs="unbounded" minOccurs="1" />
      </xs:sequence>
    </xs:complexType>
  </xs:element>
  ...
</xs:element>
```

Code snippet modelSchema.xsd

Each type is uniquely named and is optionally labeled with a title and description. A type may declare any number of properties to represent metadata associated with the type and any number of associations to other types.

```
<xs:complexType name="type">
  <xs:complexContent>
    <xs:extension base="class"/>
  </xs:complexContent>
</xs:complexType>

<xs:complexType name="class">
  ...
```

```
<xs:attributeGroup ref="name" />
...
<xs:sequence>
  ...
  <xs:group ref="TextualDescription"/>
  <xs:element name="properties" maxOccurs="1" minOccurs="0">
    <xs:complexType>
      <xs:sequence>
        <xs:element name="property" type="property"maxOccurs="unbounded"
        minOccurs="0" />
      </xs:sequence>
    </xs:complexType>
  </xs:element>

  <xs:element name="associations" maxOccurs="1" minOccurs="0">
    <xs:complexType>
      <xs:sequence>
        <xs:element name="association" type="association"
        maxOccurs="unbounded" />
      </xs:sequence>
    </xs:complexType>
  </xs:element>
  ...
</xs:sequence>
</xs:complexType>

<xs:group name="TextualDescription">
  <xs:sequence>
    <xs:element name="title" type="string" maxOccurs="1" minOccurs="0" />
    <xs:element name="description" type="string" maxOccurs="1" minOccurs="0" />
  </xs:sequence>
</xs:group>
```

Code snippet modelSchema.xsd

You may have observed that the schema definition of a type is simply a derivation of the schema definition named *class*. The reason for this will become apparent when the definition of an aspect is discussed.

The final feature of a type definition is to allow control over whether nodes of that type are archived when deleted.

Available for download on Wrox.com

```
<xs:complexType name="class">
  ...
  <xs:element name="archive" type="boolean" maxOccurs="1" minOccurs="0" />
  ...
</xs:complexType>
```

Code snippet modelSchema.xsd

Archived nodes may be restored just like the recycle bin of many operating systems.

Properties

Each property must be uniquely named and is optionally labeled with a title and description.

Available for download on Wrox.com

```
<xs:complexType name="property">
  <xs:attributeGroup ref="name" />
  <xs:sequence>
    <xs:group ref="TextualDescription" />
    <xs:element name="type" type="string" />
    <xs:element name="mandatory" maxOccurs="1" minOccurs="0" type="mandatoryDef" />
    <xs:element name="multiple" type="boolean" maxOccurs="1" minOccurs="0" />
    <xs:element name="default" type="anyType" maxOccurs="1" minOccurs="0" />
    <xs:element name="index" maxOccurs="1" minOccurs="0">
      <xs:complexType>
        <xs:sequence>
          <xs:element name="atomic" type="boolean" maxOccurs="1" minOccurs="0" />
          <xs:element name="stored" type="boolean" maxOccurs="1" minOccurs="0" />
          <xs:element name="tokenised" maxOccurs="1" minOccurs="0" >
            <xs:simpleType>
              <xs:restriction base="string">
                <xs:enumeration value="true"/>
                <xs:enumeration value="false"/>
                <xs:enumeration value="both"/>
              </xs:restriction>
            </xs:simpleType>
          </xs:element>
        </xs:sequence>
        <xs:attribute name="enabled" type="boolean" use="required" />
      </xs:complexType>
    </xs:element>
  </xs:sequence>
</xs:complexType>

<xs:complexType name="mandatoryDef" mixed="true">
  <xs:attribute name="enforced" use="optional" type="boolean"/>
</xs:complexType>
```

Code snippet modelSchema.xsd

The only feature of a property that must be specified is its data type, of which the content repository supports a wide variety. Each data type is named, and the commonly used data types out of the box are:

- **`d:text`** — A text value, a character string
- **`d:mltext`** — A multilingual text value where many localized representations of the text value may be held
- **`d:content`** — An arbitrarily long text or binary stream
- **`d:int`** — An integer value (java.lang.Integer equivalent)
- **`d:long`** — A long value (java.lang.Long equivalent)

- **`d:float`** — A float value (java.lang.Float equivalent)
- **`d:double`** — A double value (java.lang.Double equivalent)
- **`d:date`** — A date value (java.lang.Date equivalent)
- **`d:datetime`** — A date and time value (java.lang.Date equivalent)
- **`d:boolean`** — A boolean value (java.lang.Boolean equivalent)
- **`d:any`** — Any value, regardless of type

With the basics defined, it is possible to fine-tune the definition of a property. By default a property supports a single value, but this may be changed to support multiple values via the `multiple` element. Multiple values are rendered as lists in the various Alfresco APIs.

A value can also be mandated on creation of a node via the `mandatory` element. That is, a transaction will not commit unless all mandatory values have been provided for nodes modified within that transaction. There are actually two forms of mandatory: *enforced* and *relaxed*. Enforced is as described but relaxed gives finer control over when mandatory values must be provided. A transaction will still commit if a relaxed mandatory value has not been specified; however, the node with the missing value will be marked as incomplete (via the `sys:incomplete` aspect). This is important, as not all content creation processes (for example, via many of the protocols supported by Alfresco) provide the ability to set property values. Custom solutions can then be configured or built that trigger a business process for collecting the missing values (for example, via workflow user-assigned tasks).

In conjunction with mandating a value, a property definition can also specify a default value that is set automatically by the content repository if the value has not been set at transaction commit time.

To enable the content repository to query on a property value, the property must first be indexed, which is controlled via the `index` element. It is recommended to choose carefully which properties are indexed, as each property will increase the size of the index. Properties may be indexed as part of the transaction commit (known as *atomic* indexing) or indexed in the background. Typically, properties of type `d:content` are background-indexed. Control over how values are tokenized is also possible, such that only the tokenized value is stored in the index, or only the original value is stored in the index, or both. Tokenization is the process used by the query engine for recognizing words and other elements, such as punctuation.

Although the content model provides the ability to specify property definitions, the content repository supports a feature known as a *residual property*, where a value can be set on a node for which there is no associated property definition defined in a content model. This allows for a node to act as a property bag for an arbitrary set of named-value pairs.

Associations

Each association must be uniquely named and is optionally labeled with a title and description.

Available for download on Wrox.com

```
<xs:complexType name="association">
  <xs:attributeGroup ref="name" />
  <xs:sequence>
    <xs:group ref="TextualDescription" />
    <xs:element name="source" maxOccurs="1" minOccurs="0">
```

```
        <xs:complexType>
          <xs:sequence>
            <xs:element name="mandatory" type="boolean"maxOccurs="1" minOccurs="0" />
            <xs:element name="many" type="boolean"maxOccurs="1" minOccurs="0" />
          </xs:sequence>
        </xs:complexType>
      </xs:element>
      <xs:element name="target">
        <xs:complexType>
          <xs:sequence>
            <xs:element name="class" type="string" maxOccurs="1" minOccurs="1" />
            <xs:element name="mandatory" type="mandatoryDef"maxOccurs="1"
            minOccurs="0" />
            <xs:element name="many" type="boolean"maxOccurs="1" minOccurs="0" />
          </xs:sequence>
        </xs:complexType>
      </xs:element>
    </xs:sequence>
  </xs:complexType>
```

Code snippet modelSchema.xsd

Associations are always between two types — a source type and a target type — where the source type is inherently the type that defines the association. The only feature of an association that must be specified is its target type via the `class` element on the target end.

Each end of the association may be fine-tuned by specifying features such as cardinality via the `mandatory` and `many` elements:

- 0 or 1 => mandatory = false and many = false
- 1 => mandatory = true and many = false
- 0 or more => mandatory = false and many = true
- 1 or more => mandatory = true and many = true

As with mandatory properties, both enforced and relaxed modes are supported for the target end, allowing control over whether a transaction can commit or not based on missing associations. In relaxed mode, the incomplete aspect is added to source nodes where associations to target nodes are missing.

Child associations are defined in the same way as peer associations, with a few additional features.

Available for download on Wrox.com

```
<xs:complexType name="childAssociation">
  <xs:complexContent>
    <xs:extension base="association">
      <xs:sequence>
        <xs:element name="duplicate" type="boolean"maxOccurs="1" minOccurs="0" />
```

```
        <xs:element name="propagateTimestamps" type="boolean"maxOccurs="1"
        minOccurs="0" />
      </xs:sequence>
    </xs:extension>
  </xs:complexContent>
</xs:complexType>
```

Code snippet modelSchema.xsd

First, the uniqueness of child-node names within the parent may be specified via the `duplicate` element. If `duplicate` is true, the content repository will not allow the commit of a transaction where duplicate node names are found within a set of children for a given single parent.

Second, the `propagateTimestamps` element allows control over whether the modified timestamp of a parent should be modified if any of its children are modified.

Constraints

Constraints can be defined either standalone, allowing for the reuse of constraints across many properties, or inline, where the constraint is defined specifically for a single property.

```
<xs:complexType name="constraint">
  <xs:attribute name="name" use="optional" type="string" />
  <xs:attribute name="type" type="string" use="optional"/>
  <xs:sequence>
    <xs:element name="parameter" maxOccurs="unbounded" type="namedValue"
    minOccurs="0"/>
  </xs:sequence>
  <xs:attribute name="ref" use="optional" type="string" />
</xs:complexType>

<xs:complexType name="namedValue">
  <xs:attributeGroup ref="name" />
  <xs:choice>
    <xs:element name="value" type="string" maxOccurs="1"minOccurs="0" />
    <xs:element name="list" maxOccurs="1" minOccurs="0">
      <xs:complexType>
        <xs:sequence>
          <xs:element name="value" type="string"maxOccurs="unbounded"
          minOccurs="0"/>
        </xs:sequence>
      </xs:complexType>
    </xs:element>
  </xs:choice>
</xs:complexType>
```

Code snippet modelSchema.xsd

A standalone constraint must specify a unique name and a type. There are several constraint types provided out of the box; the commonly used types are:

- REGEX — Property value matches regular expression.
- LENGTH — Text property value length must reside within minimum and maximum length limits.
- MINMAX — Numeric property value must reside within minimum and maximum range limits.
- LIST — Property value must be one of those specified in the list of values.

Custom constraint types may be developed and registered with the content repository.

Each constraint type is parameterized via zero or more `parameter` elements, where the parameter names are specific to each type:

- REGEX — Expression
- LENGTH — `minLength` and `maxLength`
- MINMAX — `minValue` and `maxValue`
- LIST — `allowedValues` and `caseSensitive`

A content model may define one or more standalone constraints.

```
<xs:element name="model">
  ...
  <xs:element name="constraints" maxOccurs="1" minOccurs="0">
    <xs:complexType>
      <xs:sequence>
        <xs:element name="constraint" type="constraint" maxOccurs="unbounded"
          minOccurs="1" />
      </xs:sequence>
    </xs:complexType>
  </xs:element>
  ...
</xs:element>
```

Code snippet modelSchema.xsd

Each property may support one or more constraints either by referencing an existing standalone constraint definition or defining one inline via the `constraint` element.

```
<xs:complexType name="property">
  ...
  <xs:element name="constraints" maxOccurs="1" minOccurs="0">
```

```
        <xs:complexType>
          <xs:sequence>
            <xs:element name="constraint" type="constraint" maxOccurs="unbounded"
              minOccurs="1" />
          </xs:sequence>
        </xs:complexType>
      </xs:element>
      ...
    </xs:complexType>
```

Code snippet modelSchema.xsd

An existing constraint is referenced via the `ref` element, whose value is the name of the constraint to reference. Otherwise, an inline constraint is defined in the same manner as a standalone constraint.

Inheritance

A type may inherit its definition from another type. What does that actually mean? All features of the parent type are inherited, including property, association, and constraint definitions — except for the parent type name, title, and description.

Available for download on Wrox.com

```
<xs:complexType name="class">
  <xs:sequence>
    ...
    <xs:element name="parent" type="string" maxOccurs="1" minOccurs="0" />
    ...
  </xs:sequence>
</xs:complexType>
```

Code snippet modelSchema.xsd

A type is said to inherit from another type when its `parent` element is populated with the name of the parent type to inherit. The inheriting type is often referred to as the subtype, while its parent is often referred to as the super-type. Inheritance may be nested, so it is possible to inherit from a type which itself inherits from another type.

Subtypes have the freedom to specify further property, association, and constraint definitions in addition to those inherited from its parent. However, in some cases, it is useful to refine a definition inherited from its parent. For example, a parent type may support an optional property, which the subtype wishes to lock down by mandating its value.

It is not possible to refine all inherited definitions, as it would be very easy to define an incoherent content model. For that reason, the content metamodel provides a fixed set of refinements known as property overrides.

```
<xs:complexType name="class">
  ...
  <xs:element name="overrides" maxOccurs="1" minOccurs="0">
    <xs:complexType>
      <xs:sequence>
        <xs:element name="property" type="propertyOverride" minOccurs="1" />
      </xs:sequence>
    </xs:complexType>
  </xs:element>
  ...
</xs:complexType>

<xs:complexType name="propertyOverride">
  <xs:attributeGroup ref="name" />
  <xs:sequence>
    <xs:element name="mandatory" type="boolean" maxOccurs="1" minOccurs="0" />
    <xs:element name="default" type="string" maxOccurs="1" minOccurs="0" />
    <xs:element name="constraints" maxOccurs="1" minOccurs="0">
      <xs:complexType>
        <xs:sequence>
          <xs:element name="constraint" type="constraint" minOccurs="1" />
        </xs:sequence>
      </xs:complexType>
    </xs:element>
  </xs:sequence>
</xs:complexType>
```

Code snippet modelSchema.xsd

Each property override is given the same name as the property it wishes to override from its parent type. The following property features may be overridden:

- **`mandatory`** — A subtype may enforce a property to become mandatory but it cannot relax an existing parent mandatory constraint.
- **`default`** — A subtype may introduce a default value or change an existing parent default value.
- **`constraints`** — Additional constraints may be applied to a parent property, but existing constraints cannot be modified.

Aspects

Aspects allow property and association definitions to be shared across many types of node. This means a cross-cutting feature of an ECM domain model may be encapsulated and applied throughout the rigid part of the model represented by types. It is the equivalent of multiple inheritance.

A node in the content repository must be of a single type, but may be attached to one or more aspects. The aspects are either inherited from its type (as defined in the content model), or can be attached or detached at runtime, allowing a node to dynamically inherit features and capabilities.

Each content model may define one or more aspects.

Available for download on Wrox.com

```
<xs:element name="model">
  ...
  <xs:element name="aspects" maxOccurs="1"minOccurs="0">
    <xs:complexType>
      <xs:sequence>
        <xs:element name="aspect" type="aspect"maxOccurs="unbounded"
        minOccurs="1"/>
      </xs:sequence>
    </xs:complexType>
  </xs:element>
  ...
</xs:element>
```

Code snippet modelSchema.xsd

Aspects support all the same features as types and therefore are defined in the same way as types.

Available for download on Wrox.com

```
<xs:complexType name="aspect">
  <xs:complexContent>
    <xs:extension base="class" />
  </xs:complexContent>
</xs:complexType>
```

Code snippet modelSchema.xsd

You can see that, as with the type definition, an aspect definition is simply a derivation of the schema definition named `class`. This means that an aspect shares all the same features as a class, including property, association, and constraint definitions. Aspects may inherit from parent aspects and support property overrides.

An aspect may be attached to one or more types. Remember, this means that a node created of that type automatically inherits the attached aspects.

Available for download on Wrox.com

```
<xs:complexType name="class">
  ...
  <xs:element name="mandatory-aspects" maxOccurs="1" minOccurs="0">
    <xs:complexType>
      <xs:sequence>
        <xs:element name="aspect" type="string" maxOccurs="unbounded"
        minOccurs="1"/>
      </xs:sequence>
    </xs:complexType>
  </xs:element>
  ...
</xs:complexType>
```

Code snippet modelSchema.xsd

Attaching an aspect simply requires specifying the name of the aspect to attach in the `aspect` element of the source type. You may have noticed this feature is available at the class level, allowing aspects to be attached to other aspects as well as types.

OUT-OF-THE-BOX MODELS

The content repository comprises several content models provided out of the box for specifying the core content types expected of an ECM system. They are expressed in terms of the content metamodel and provide an excellent set of samples on which to base your own custom content models.

The base model upon which all other models depend is the Data Dictionary model (located in the file dictionaryModel.xml), which provides definitions for the fundamental data types, such as `d:text` and `d:boolean`. It exposes the namespace URI `www.alfresco.org/model/dictionary/1.0` with prefix *d*.

Next, the content repository itself depends on a system model (located in the file systemModel.xml), which provides definitions for types used by the implementation of the content repository, such as `sys:base`, `sys:root`, and `sys:reference`. In most cases, it should not be required to refer to definitions in the system model from your own custom models. It exposes the namespace URI `www.alfresco.org/model/system/1.0` with prefix *sys*.

Finally, an ECM domain model (located in the file contentModel.xml) provides definitions for types influenced by the CMIS and JCR standards, such as `cm:folder`, `cm:content`, `cm:versionable`, and `cm:auditable`. All Alfresco Content Application Server services, protocols, and clients are focused on these types. It exposes the namespace `www.alfresco.org/model/content/1.0` with prefix *cm*.

A STEP-BY-STEP CUSTOM MODEL

Now that you have an understanding of the content metamodel, it is time to define a custom model: an uncomplicated model for representing knowledge base articles for the Knowledge Base application.

The Knowledge Base model (as shown in Figure 5-4) utilizes most of the constructs of the content metamodel. The primary entity in the model is the knowledge article, which encapsulates knowledge in a form such as an answer (to a frequently asked question) or a white paper. Articles may relate to each other. Supplementary artifacts, such as software patches and sample code, may be attached to the article.

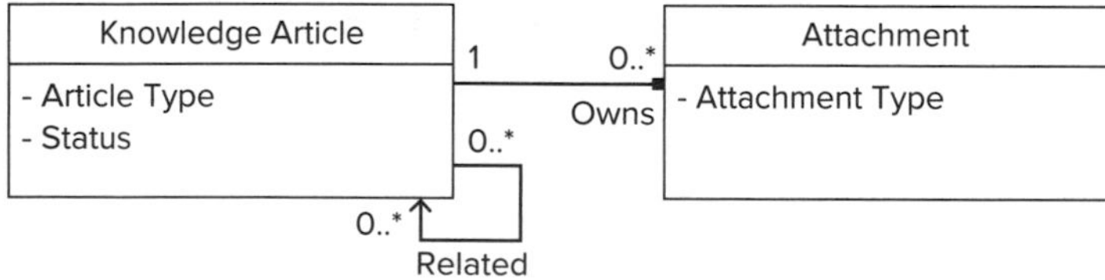

FIGURE 5-4

It has been decided to define a type for the attachment, which inherits from the `cm:content` type defined in the ECM domain model. A single additional property is used to represent the attachment type whose value is constrained to one of Patch, Sample, and Documentation.

An aspect is defined for the article with the intent that any existing content held in the content repository may become an article. The aspect defines an article type property whose value is constrained to one of Article, FAQ, and White Paper. It also includes a status property through the inclusion of a status aspect whose value is constrained to one of Draft, Pending Approval, Current, and Archived.

A child association is ideal for representing the relationship between article and attachment. Attachments are owned by articles and therefore do not outlive their owning article, which child association semantics support. Related articles are peers and one is not superior to the other; thus a peer association is ideal for representing this relationship.

The first step in defining any content model is to set up the model header to introduce the model.

Available for download on Wrox.com

```
<model name="kb:contentmodel" xmlns="http://www.alfresco.org/model/dictionary/1.0">
  <description>Knowledge Base Content Model</description>
  <author>alfresco_professional</author>
  <version>1.0</version>
```

Code snippet kbModel.xml

Model names are scoped by a namespace. In this case, the model name `kb:knowledgebase` uses the namespace prefix *kb*. However, its associated namespace has yet to be defined, which is the next step.

Available for download on Wrox.com

```
<imports>
  <import uri="http://www.alfresco.org/model/dictionary/1.0" prefix="d"/>
  <import uri="http://www.alfresco.org/model/content/1.0" prefix="cm"/>
</imports>

<namespaces>
  <namespace uri="http://www.example.org/knowledgebase" prefix="kb"/>
</namespaces>
```

Code snippet kbModel.xml

As well as defining a new namespace, two out-of-the-box content models (the Data Dictionary and ECM domain model) are imported.

It is now possible to start defining the features of the model. First, standalone constraints are defined to restrict the values of attachment type, status, and article type, which are ideally constrained through the `LIST` constraint.

Available for download on Wrox.com

```
<constraints>
  <constraint name="kb:attachmenttype_constraint" type="LIST">
    <parameter name="allowedValues">
      <list>
        <value>Patch</value>
        <value>Sample</value>
        <value>Documentation</value>
      </list>
    </parameter>
  </constraint>
  <constraint name="kb:status_constraint" type="LIST">
    <parameter name="allowedValues">
      <list>
        <value>Draft</value>
        <value>Pending Approval</value>
        <value>Current</value>
        <value>Archived</value>
      </list>
    </parameter>
  </constraint>
  <constraint name="kb:articletype_constraint" type="LIST">
    <parameter name="allowedValues">
      <list>
        <value>Any</value>
        <value>Article</value>
        <value>FAQ</value>
        <value>White Paper</value>
      </list>
    </parameter>
  </constraint>
</constraints>
```

Code snippet kbModel.xml

Everything is now set up to define the attachment type with its single property, whose data type is `d:text` and whose value is constrained through the standalone constraint `kb:attachmenttypelist` defined earlier in the model. For completeness, a default value is also specified.

Available for download on Wrox.com

```
<types>
  <type name="kb:attachment">
    <title>Attachment</title>
    <parent>cm:content</parent>
    <properties>
      <property name="kb:attachmenttype">
        <title>Attachment Type</title>
        <type>d:text</type>
        <default>Sample</default>
        <constraints>
          <constraint ref="kb:attachmenttype_constraint" />
        </constraints>
```

```
        </property>
      </properties>
    </type>
  </types>
```

Code snippet kbModel.xml

Through namespace prefixes, references to imported definitions are simply made, such as to the `d:text` data type and `cm:content` type. The article aspect is defined in a similar manner to the attachment type, only this time an inline constraint is specified for its property.

```
<aspects>
  <aspect name="kb:article">
    <title>Knowledge Base Article</title>
    <properties>
      <property name="kb:articletype">
        <title>Article Type</title>
        <type>d:text</type>
        <default>Article</default>
        <constraints>
          <constraint type="LIST">
            <parameter name="allowedValues">
              <list>
                <value>Any</value>
                <value>Article</value>
                <value>FAQ</value>
                <value>White Paper</value>
              </list>
            </parameter>
          </constraint>
        </constraints>
      </property>
    </properties>
    ...
```

Code snippet kbModel.xml

Associations are between a source and target class. In this case, the article aspect will represent the source and therefore provide the association definitions.

```
    ...
    <associations>
      <child-association name="kb:artifacts">
        <target>
          <class>kb:attachment</class>
          <mandatory>false</mandatory>
          <many>true</many>
        </target>
```

```
          <duplicate>true</duplicate>
        </child-association>
        <association name="kb:related">
          <title>Related Articles</title>
          <source>
            <mandatory>false</mandatory>
            <many>true</many>
          </source>
          <target>
            <class>kb:article</class>
            <mandatory>false</mandatory>
            <many>true</many>
          </target>
        </association>
      </associations>
    </aspect>
  </aspects>
```

Code snippet kbModel.xml

Finally, the model is closed.

```
</model>
```

Code snippet kbModel.xml

The preceding XML may be saved to a file on the Java classpath for registration by a Dictionary Bootstrap component at repository startup time or saved as a file in the content repository folder Company Home/Data Dictionary/Models for dynamic registration.

CREATING CONTENT WITH JAVASCRIPT

With the example content model defined, it is now possible to create articles within the content repository that adhere to the model. The best way to demonstrate this is to develop some JavaScript code that uses the Alfresco JavaScript API to create knowledge articles.

1. You first need to log in to Alfresco Explorer.
   a. Type the following in your Web browser, and log in with the user name `admin` and password `admin` if requested:

      ```
      http://localhost:8080/alfresco
      ```

   b. Navigate to Company Home > Data Dictionary > Scripts.
2. Now create a JavaScript file.

a. In the Create menu, click Create Content.

b. Enter the name for the JavaScript in the Name field, such as:

   kb.js

c. In the Content Type list, select Plain Text.

d. Click Next.

e. Type the following in the Enter Content box:

Available for download on Wrox.com

```
var article = companyhome.createNode("article", "cm:content");
article.addAspect("kb:article");

article.properties["cm:name"] = "How to Create Content Models";
article.properties["kb:articletype"] = "FAQ";

article.properties["wordcount"] = 7000;
article.content = "The attached tutorial provides an overview of how to...";
article.save();

var attachment = article.createNode("attachment", "kb:attachment",
"kb:artifacts");
attachment.properties["cm:name"] = "Content Modeling Tutorial";
attachment.properties["kb:attachmenttype"] = "Documentation";
attachment.content = "Content modeling is a fundamental building block...";
attachment.save();

var relatedarticle = companyhome.createNode("relatedarticle", "cm:content");
relatedarticle.addAspect("kb:article");
relatedarticle.properties["cm:name"] = "Model Schema Reference";
article.createAssociation(relatedarticle, "kb:related");
relatedarticle.save();
```

Code snippet kb.js

f. Click Next.

g. Click Finish.

h. Click OK.

3. Next, execute the JavaScript.

   a. In the More Actions menu, click View Details.

   b. Click Run Action.

   c. In the Select Action list, select Execute a script.

   d. Click the Set Values and Add button.

   e. In the Select a Script to Execute list, select `kb.js`.

   f. Click OK.
   g. Click Finish.
   h. Click Close.
4. Finally, it's time to test.
   a. Navigate to Company Home.
   b. If you see two content items, one named How To Create Content Model and the other named Model Schema Reference, your JavaScript is working.

It's time to take a deeper look at the JavaScript code and how the Alfresco JavaScript API is used. The first step is to create a node of a given type from the model and then attach an aspect from the model at runtime. All nodes have a parent (except for the system root node), so implicit child association is created between the new node and its chosen parent. By default, the JavaScript `createNode` method creates a `cm:contains` child association as defined in the ECM domain model. Access to the content repository Company Home folder is provided, so your article can be created as a child of this folder.

Available for download on Wrox.com

```
var article = companyhome.createNode("article", "cm:content");
article.addAspect("kb:article");
```

Code snippet kb.js

With the node created, it is possible to set property values for property definitions as specified by the types and aspects from the model. Note that some of the properties, such as `cm:name`, are inherited. Default values are applied to properties that have not been set.

Available for download on Wrox.com

```
article.properties["cm:name"] = "How to Create Content Models";
article.properties["kb:articletype"] = "FAQ";
```

Code snippet kb.js

Remember, it is also possible to set properties that do not have an associated property definition, known as *residual properties*.

Available for download on Wrox.com

```
article.properties["wordcount"] = 7000;
```

Code snippet kb.js

Properties of type `d:content` are treated specially by the JavaScript API, which provides support for setting those values either from a content stream or a string.

Available for download on Wrox.com

```
article.content = "The attached tutorial provides an overview of how to...";
```

Code snippet kb.js

When creating a child node, you may override the default `cm:contains` child association by specifying the name of the custom child association to use.

Available for download on Wrox.com

```
var attachment = article.createNode("attachment", "kb:attachment", "kb:artifacts");
attachment.properties["cm:name"] = "Content Modeling Tutorial";
attachment.properties["kb:attachmenttype"] = "Documentation";
attachment.content = "Content modeling is a fundamental building block...";
```

Code snippet kb.js

Peer associations between nodes may be established via the JavaScript `createAssocation` method. The target node and association name are specified.

Available for download on Wrox.com

```
var relatedarticle = companyhome.createNode("relatedarticle", "cm:content");
relatedarticle.addAspect("kb:article");
relatedarticle.properties["cm:name"] = "Model Schema Reference";
article.createAssociation(relatedarticle, "kb:related");
```

Code snippet kb.js

Finally, the nodes are saved and the transaction is committed. If any of the property values happen to violate an associated constraint and the constraint is enforced, the transaction will not commit, meaning an error is raised. Otherwise, the transaction commits and the nodes are persisted in the content repository.

MODEL LOCALIZATION

Every type, aspect, property, association, constraint, and data type defined within a model has a title and description. Both of these values are provided in the model XML file but only one language may be supported: the language of the values specified in the XML file.

To support localization of a model, it is possible to augment the model XML values with locale-specific values. This is achieved by registering a standard Java resource bundle for each language variant of a model.

You may be asking why you need to localize content-model values. Often, it is required to render user interfaces that are driven from the content model, such as a property sheet that displays a grid of property name and value.

The content models provided out of the box are all augmented with a default (for US English) Java resource bundle. The following is an extract from the resource bundle for the ECM domain model:

```
cm_contentmodel.description=Alfresco Content Domain Model
cm_contentmodel.type.cm_object.title=Object
cm_contentmodel.type.cm_object.description=Base Content Domain Object
cm_contentmodel.property.cm_name.title=Name
cm_contentmodel.property.cm_name.description=Name

cm_contentmodel.type.cm_folder.title=Folder
cm_contentmodel.type.cm_folder.description=Folder
cm_contentmodel.association.cm_contains.title=Contains
cm_contentmodel.association.cm_contains.description=Contains
```

Resource bundles are composed of many key/value pairs. For content models, the keys are structured as follows:

```
<model_prefix>_<model_name>.[title|description]
```

or

```
<model_prefix>_<model_name>.<feature>.<feature_prefix>_<feature_name>.
[title|description]
```

Where:

- `model_prefix` is the model namespace prefix.
- `model_name` is the model name.
- `feature` is one of type, aspect, property, association, constraint, or data type.
- `feature_prefix` is the namespace prefix of the feature definition name.
- `feature_name` is the feature definition name.

Content model resource bundles must be registered with their associated content model. If you remember back to how to register a content model, there are two approaches: *bootstrap* and *dynamic*. The same applies for content model resource bundles.

In the bootstrap case, the Dictionary Bootstrap component supports the additional `labels` property, which allows for a list of resource bundle files (located in the classpath) to be specified. The Alfresco content repository must be restarted in order for the resource bundle to be registered.

```
<bean id="kbmodel.extension.dictionaryBootstrap" parent="dictionaryModelBootstrap"
    depends-on="dictionaryBootstrap">
  ...
  <property name="labels">
    <list>
      <value>alfresco/extension/kbModel.properties</value>
    </list>
  </property>
  ...
</bean>
```

In the dynamic case, the resource bundle file is placed into the content repository folder

```
Company Home/Data Dictionary/Messages
```

Again, Alfresco Explorer is the best tool for uploading and editing resource bundles in this folder.

THE RELATIONSHIP TO CMIS

CMIS defines a data model, which encapsulates the core concepts found in most content repositories. Alfresco provides an implementation of the CMIS bindings, and as part of the implementation maps the Alfresco content metamodel to the CMIS domain model. This allows content models defined in Alfresco to be exposed and manipulated via CMIS.

The CMIS data model (as shown in Figure 5-5) is summarized as follows:

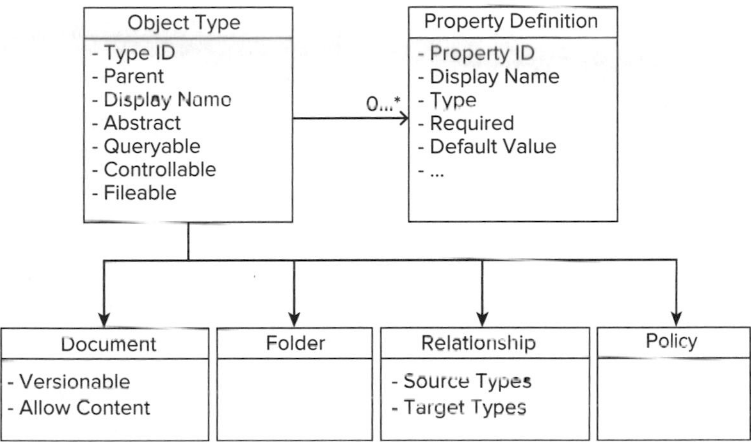

FIGURE 5-5

The core of the domain model allows for the definition of object types with associated properties. Types are identified by their type ID and may inherit their definition from a parent type. Features of a type include whether they can be queried by the CMIS query language, filed into multiple folders, and controlled via permissions. Features of a property include its data type, whether a value is required, and a default value if one is not explicitly provided.

You may be thinking that these features are familiar, and the Alfresco content modeling capabilities described in this chapter are indeed very similar. This is a good thing and makes it possible to map between the CMIS data model and the Alfresco content metamodel with little loss of information.

The Alfresco content metamodel is mapped to the CMIS data model as follows:

- **Type** — Maps to CMIS Object Type
- **Property** — Maps to CMIS Property Definition
- **Peer Association** — Maps to CMIS Relationship

You may be wondering how child associations are mapped. The obvious approach is to also map them to CMIS Relationship, but CMIS has special built-in support for hierarchies through CMIS Folder and CMIS Document. So, Alfresco maps its out-of-the-box types `cm:folder` and `cm:content` (as defined in the Alfresco ECM domain model) to CMIS Folder and CMIS Document, respectively. A folder may contain a mixture of documents and folders, allowing for a hierarchy of documents to be built. Through this, CMIS supports an implicit notion of parent to child, to which Alfresco maps its child association. Subtypes of `cm:folder` and `cm:content` are exposed as subtypes of CMIS Folder and Document, respectively.

CMIS does not explicitly support the notion of an aspect. However, it does provide a CMIS Policy, which represents an administrative policy that can be enforced by the content repository. Alfresco maps each aspect defined in a content model to a CMIS Policy.

Services offered by CMIS allow the discovery of type definitions and the ability to create objects of a given type, similar to those of the Alfresco JavaScript API.

Authentication and Security

WHAT'S IN THIS CHAPTER?

- Configuring authentication
- Working with users, groups, and zones
- Configuring security
- Implementing permissions
- Implementing the ACEGI Spring security framework and services

This chapter discusses the authentication and security functionality built into Alfresco for user and group management, user authentication, permissions, and access control. In addition, this chapter provides instructions on how you can customize Alfresco for your own user base and needs using configurable modules for LDAP, NTLM, Kerberos, and other commonly used authentication protocols.

ALFRESCO AUTHENTICATION

The first time you access a vanilla Alfresco installation through the Alfresco Explorer Web client, Alfresco identifies you as a guest user. You can identify yourself as another user by clicking the Login link and entering a new user name and password in the Login window. If you log in with the credentials of a user with administrator privileges (Alfresco uses `admin` as the default user name and password), you can use the Administration Console to create additional users and assign them passwords.

In this out-of-the-box setup, you can manage the user base and their passwords manually from within Alfresco, and unauthenticated users still have limited access as the guest user.

From here, there are a number of common customizations you might want to make to scale up to the needs of a larger enterprise. For example, you might want to:

- Disable unauthenticated guest access

- Enable automatic sign-on using operating system credentials or a single sign-on (SSO) server to remove the need for a Login page
- Delegate authentication responsibility to a central directory server to remove the need to set up users manually in the Administration Console

You will learn how to achieve these different levels of customization in various examples presented later in this chapter. To more fully understand the examples, you will first look at an overview of the Alfresco authentication subsystems.

Authentication Subsystems

The Alfresco authentication and identity management functionality is provided by a set of configurable software modules called *subsystems*. An authentication subsystem provides the following functions to Alfresco:

- Password-based authentication for Web browsing, Microsoft SharePoint protocol, FTP, and WebDAV
- CIFS and NFS file system authentication
- Web browser, Microsoft SharePoint protocol, and WebDAV single sign-on (SSO)
- User registry export (the automatic population of the Alfresco user and authority database)

Authentication Subsystem Types

A number of alternative authentication subsystem types exist for the most commonly used authentication protocols. These are each identified by a unique type name and summarized in Table 6-1.

TABLE 6-1: Authentication Subsystem Types

TYPE	DESCRIPTION	SINGLE SIGN-ON (SSO)	CIFS AUTHENTICATION	USER REGISTRY EXPORT?
`alfrescoNtlm`	Native Alfresco authentication	Yes, NTLM	Yes	No
`ldap`	Authentication and user registry export through the LDAP protocol (for example, OpenLDAP)	No	No	Yes
`ldap-ad`	Authentication and user registry export from Active Directory through the LDAP protocol	No	No	Yes
`passthru`	Authentication through a Windows domain server	Yes, NTLM	Yes	No
`kerberos`	Authentication through a Kerberos realm	Yes, SPNEGO	Yes	No
`external`	Authentication through an external SSO mechanism	Yes	No	No

The following sections show how these subsystem types enable you to tie Alfresco to some of the most widely used authentication infrastructures.

The Authentication Chain

It is very likely that at least one of the authentication subsystem types previously discussed will allow you to integrate Alfresco with one of the authentication servers in use in your enterprise. However, integrating Alfresco with just one of these systems may not be enough. For various reasons, you might want to mix and match multiple authentication protocols against a collection of servers.

That is why Alfresco has a built-in authentication chain. In simple terms, this is a priority-ordered list of authentication subsystem instances. A subsystem instance is a configuration of one of the subsystem types. Each subsystem instance has:

- A type
- A unique name that makes it distinguishable from other instances of the same type
- A set of property values provided by user configuration

The following sections demonstrate the authentication chain in use.

Authentication Configuration Examples

The examples in this section demonstrate how to express various authentication configuration requirements in subsystem instances in the authentication chain. They also explain how the authentication chain integrates the functions of multiple subsystem instances into a more powerful conglomerate, letting you cater for even the most complex authentication scenarios. All the examples adopt the following structured approach:

1. Decide the authentication chain composition (required subsystem types, instance names, order of precedence) and express this in alfresco-global.properties.
2. For each subsystem instance:
    a. Locate the properties files for its subsystem type. These define the configurable properties for that subsystem type and their default values.
    b. Create a folder named after the subsystem instance under the alfresco extension folders.
    c. Copy the properties files into your new folder.
    d. Edit the properties files to record the desired configuration of the subsystem instance.

Example 1: Customizing alfrescoNtlm

An authentication chain containing a single subsystem instance of type `alfrescoNtlm` provides the Alfresco default authentication behavior. This means that Alfresco performs all user account management and password validation. As implied by the type name, `alfrescoNtlm` subsystem instances support automatic sign-on to internal Alfresco accounts through the NTLM protocol. But you do not have to use NTLM at all; in fact, it is turned off by default.

This example shows how to achieve two of the basic customizations using an instance of `alfrescoNtlm`:

- Disabling unauthenticated guest access
- Enabling automatic sign-on

Authentication Chain Composition

The first task is to declare your customized authentication chain to Alfresco. To do so, you must edit the configuration file alfresco-global.properties. In a default Alfresco installation, this is located in the following path:

<*installLocation*>\shared\classes\alfresco-global.properties

You are still only relying on the internal capabilities of Alfresco, so you only need one `alfrescoNtlm` subsystem instance in your authentication chain. In this case, the subsystem instance name is `alfinst`. The name you choose does not really matter, as long as it is meaningful to you and unique within the authentication chain.

In alfresco-global.properties, add the following line:

```
authentication.chain=alfinst:alfrescoNtlm
```

Here you can see that the `authentication.chain` property declares the authentication chain to Alfresco. Its value is a comma-separated list of authentication chain instances. Each instance is declared by an instance name, followed by a colon, and then followed by the subsystem type.

Configuring the Instance

Now you will create the property files to configure your subsystem instance. First, you must create an appropriately named directory in the Alfresco extension location.

```
mkdir <installLocation>\shared\classes\alfresco\extension\subsystems\
Authentication\alfrescoNtlm\alfinst

cd /d <installLocation>\shared\classes\alfresco\extension\subsystems\
Authentication\alfrescoNtlm\alfinst
```

Like other Alfresco configurations, the subsystem instance configuration lives in a directory below alfresco/extension in the application server's classpath. Below this path, subsystem configuration is further organized by category, type, and instance name. A subsystem category is a broad categorization given to a set of subsystem types. All authentication subsystem types have the category `Authentication`*. To be precise, the configuration for a particular subsystem instance of category* `sc`*, type* `st`*, and name* `sn` *should be under a path* `alfresco/extension/subsystems/sc/st/sn`*.*

Now you will source the properties files that define the configurable properties of your instance.

```
copy <installLocation>\webapps\alfresco\WEB-INF\classes\alfresco\subsystems\
Authentication\alfrescoNtlm\*.properties
```

As you can see, the default properties for a subsystem of category `sc`, type `st`, and name `sn` are under `alfresco/subsystems/sc/st/*.properties` in the Alfresco WAR file.

Never edit the properties files in the WAR file or under the Tomcat webapps directory. Always create your own copies in the extension classpath as shown in this example. Otherwise, any customizations you make would be lost whenever you upgraded Alfresco.

Two separate properties files appear in your alfinst directory after running one of the previous commands. These are:

- alfresco-authentication.properties
- ntlm-filter.properties

This demonstrates how the properties of a subsystem may be spread across multiple properties files. The number of files and their names do not matter, as long as they end with the suffix *.properties*. For the `alfrescoNtlm` subsystem type, alfresco-authentication.properties contains properties relating to core authentication capabilities, whereas ntlm-filter.properties groups together those relating to automatic sign-on.

Now you are set to configure your `alfinst` authentication subsystem instance.

To disable unauthenticated guest access, open the alfresco-authentication.properties file from the alfinst directory in a text editor and locate the following line:

```
alfresco.authentication.allowGuestLogin=true
```

Edit this line to disable guest access; for example:

```
alfresco.authentication.allowGuestLogin=false
```

To activate NTLM-based single sign-on (SSO), open the ntlm-filter.properties file from the alfinst directory in a text editor, and locate the following line:

```
ntlm.authentication.sso.enabled=false
```

Edit this line to enable SSO; for example:

```
ntlm.authentication.sso.enabled=true
```

Putting It in Action

Start or restart the Alfresco server. If you enter the Alfresco Explorer URL `http://localhost:8080/alfresco/` in your browser, you should find that the guest home page does not appear, as this has been disabled. Instead, a browser authentication window appears. Although you enabled NTLM-based sign-on, this happens because your browser cannot log you in automatically as there is not yet an account in Alfresco whose credentials match your operating system credentials.

To remedy this, log in as the admin user (using `admin` as the user name and password). Use the Administration Console link at the top of the home page, and create a user with a user name and password that matches those of your operating system account. Close and restart your browser and try accessing Alfresco again. If your browser supports NTLM and its security settings allow, it will automatically log you in using your operating system account name.

This rather simplistic demonstration of SSO still involved the manual creation of users in Alfresco and the duplication of password information in two systems. To achieve truly enterprise-grade authentication, you will have to use some of the different subsystem types, as demonstrated in Example 2.

Example 2: The ldap-ad Subsystem

This example addresses the more advanced goal of delegating authentication responsibility to a centralized directory server. Most organizations maintain their user database in a directory server supporting the LDAP protocol, such as Active Directory or OpenLDAP. When integrated with an LDAP server, Alfresco can delegate both the password checking and account setup to the LDAP server, thus opening up Alfresco to your entire enterprise. This avoids the need for an administrator to manually set up user accounts or to store passwords outside of the directory server.

To integrate Alfresco with a directory server, you simply need to include an instance of the `ldap` or `ldap-ad` subsystem types in the authentication chain. Both subsystem types offer exactly the same capabilities and should work with virtually any directory server supporting the LDAP protocol. Their only differences are the default values configured for their attributes. The `ldap` type is preconfigured with defaults appropriate for OpenLDAP, whereas `ldap-ad` is preconfigured with defaults appropriate for Active Directory.

This example uses an Active Directory server and therefore will configure in an instance of the `ldap-ad` subsystem.

Authentication Chain Composition

You have two choices in this scenario. You can replace or add to the authentication chain.

- **Replace the authentication chain.**

  You could remove `alfinst` from the previous example and instead add an instance of `ldap-ad`. This would hand over all authentication responsibility to Active Directory and would mean that the built-in accounts, such as admin and guest, could not be used.

  In this scenario, it would be important to configure at least one user who exists in Active Directory as an administrator and enable the guest account in Active Directory if guest access were required. Furthermore, because `ldap-ad` cannot support CIFS authentication (as it requires an MD5 password hash exchange), it would rule out use of the CIFS server for all users and the CIFS server would be disabled.

- **Add to the authentication chain.**

  You could instead supplement the existing capabilities of `alfinst` by inserting an `ldap-ad` instance before or after `alfinst` in the chain. This means that you could use the built-in accounts alongside those accounts in the directory server. Furthermore, the built-in accounts could access Alfresco through the CIFS server, since `alfrescoNtlm` is able to drive CIFS authentication.

In this scenario, where you chose to position your `ldap-ad` instance in the chain determines how overlaps or collisions between user accounts are resolved. If an admin account existed in both Alfresco and Active Directory, then admin would be Alfresco if `alfinst` came first, or Active Directory if the `ldap-ad` instance came first.

This example uses the second option to append an instance of `ldap-ad` to the authentication chain. This instance name is `ldap1` and is declared by changing the `authentication.chain` property in alfresco-global.properties as follows:

```
authentication.chain=alfinst:alfrescoNtlm,ldap1:ldap-ad
```

Configuring the Instances

First, you will undo a previous modification to `alfinst` and disable NTLM-based SSO. This is done because the `ldap-ad` and `ldap` subsystem types cannot participate in the NTLM handshake; therefore, leaving SSO enabled would prevent any of the Active Directory users from logging in. You will see how to get around this in the next example.

For now, disable SSO by opening the ntlm-filter.properties file in the alfinst directory in a text editor, and editing the property `ntlm.authentication.sso.enabled` as follows:

```
ntlm.authentication.sso.enabled=false
```

Next, create the properties files to configure `ldap1`:

```
mkdir <installLocation>\shared\classes\alfresco\extension\subsystems\
Authentication\ldap-ad\ldap1

cd /d <installLocation>\shared\classes\alfresco\extension\subsystems\
Authentication\ldap-ad\ldap1

copy <installLocation>\webapps\alfresco\WEB-INF\classes\alfresco\subsystems\
Authentication\ldap-ad\*.properties
```

A single file called ldap-ad-authentication.properties now appears in your ldap1 directory. You can now edit this file to define your LDAP setup.

When you open ldap-ad-authentication.properties, the large number of configurable properties may alarm you. This demonstrates the flexibility of the Alfresco LDAP infrastructure. Luckily, because `ldap-ad` already has sensible defaults configured for a typical Active Directory setup, there are only a few edits you must make to tailor the subsystem instance to your needs.

The following lines show the set of properties you will typically need to edit and how you might set them for a domain controller for a fictitious domain called *domain.com*.

```
ldap.authentication.allowGuestLogin=false
ldap.authentication.userNameFormat=%s@domain.com
ldap.authentication.java.naming.provider.url=ldap://domaincontroller.domain.com:389

ldap.authentication.defaultAdministratorUserNames=Administrator,alfresco
ldap.synchronization.java.naming.security.principal=alfresco@domain.com
ldap.synchronization.java.naming.security.credentials=secret
ldap.synchronization.groupSearchBase=ou=Security Groups,ou=Alfresco\
,dc=domain,dc=com

ldap.synchronization.userSearchBase=ou=User Accounts,ou=Alfresco,dc=domain,dc=com
```

Here is a brief description of the settings that have been changed:

- **ldap.authentication.allowGuestLogin** — Enables/disables unauthenticated access to Alfresco.
- **ldap.authentication.userNameFormat** — A template that defines how Alfresco user IDs are expanded into Active Directory User Principal Names (UPNs) containing a placeholder `%s`, which stands for the unexpanded user ID. A UPN generally consists of the user's account ID followed by an `@` sign and then the domain's UPN suffix. You can check the appropriate UPN suffix for your domain by connecting to the directory with an LDAP browser, browsing to a user account, and looking at the value of the `userPrincipalName` attribute.
- **ldap.authentication.java.naming.provider.url** — An LDAP URL containing the host name and LDAP port number (usually 389) of your Active Directory server.
- **ldap.authentication.defaultAdministratorUserNames** — A list of user IDs who should be given Alfresco administrator privileges by default. Another administrator can include more users as administrators by adding those users to the ALFRESCO_ADMINISTRATORS group.
- **ldap.synchronization.java.naming.security.principal** — The UPN for an account with privileges to see all users and groups. This account is used by Alfresco to retrieve the details of all users and groups in the directory so that it can synchronize its internal user and authority database. Passwords are never compromised and remain in the directory server.
- **ldap.synchronization.java.naming.security.credentials** — The password for the previous account.
- **ldap.synchronization.groupSearchBase** — The Distinguished Name (DN) of the Organizational Unit (OU) below which security groups can be found. You can determine the appropriate DN by browsing to security groups in an LDAP browser.
- **ldap.synchronization.userSearchBase** — The Distinguished name (DN) of the Organizational Unit (OU) below which user accounts can be found. You can determine the appropriate DN by browsing to user accounts in an LDAP browser.

Putting It in Action

Restart the Alfresco server. If you watch the output from Tomcat in alfresco.log in the installation directory, you will eventually see lines similar to the following:

```
13:01:31,225 INFO
[org.alfresco.repo.management.subsystems.ChildApplicationContextFactory]
Starting 'Synchronization' subsystem, ID: [Synchronization, default]


...


13:01:49,084 INFO
[org.alfresco.repo.security.sync.ChainingUserRegistrySynchronizer]
Finished synchronizing users and groups with user registry 'ldap1'
```

```
13:01:49,084 INFO
[org.alfresco.repo.security.sync.ChainingUserRegistrySynchronizer]
177 user(s) and 19 group(s) processed

13:01:49,131 INFO
[org.alfresco.repo.management.subsystems.ChildApplicationContextFactory]
Startup of 'Synchronization' subsystem, ID: [Synchronization, default] complete
```

What you are seeing is output is from the `Synchronization` subsystem. This is another Alfresco subsystem responsible for synchronizing the Alfresco internal user and authority database with all user registries in the authentication chain. Since the authentication chain now provides a user registry, the `Synchronization` subsystem has some work to do when Alfresco starts up.

From the previous logs, notice that the `Synchronization` subsystem automatically created 177 users and 19 groups using attributes, such as email address and group memberships, retrieved from Active Directory through an LDAP query. This has eliminated a lot of work for the admin user!

The Synchronization subsystem uses an incremental timestamp-based synchronization strategy, meaning that it only queries for changes since the last synchronization run. So after the first startup, further synchronization runs can be almost instantaneous. Because synchronization runs are also triggered by a scheduled nightly job, whenever an unknown user successfully authenticates you should find that Alfresco stays synchronized with hardly any effort.

Now, if you enter the Alfresco Explorer URL `http://localhost:8080/alfresco/`into your browser, you can log in using the ID and password of any of the Active Directory users.

Passwords are validated through an LDAP bind operation on Active Directory in real time. Passwords for Active Directory users are not stored locally.

If you navigate to a user profile, notice that attributes such as email address were populated automatically from Active Directory.

You are somewhat closer now to the ideal of delegating authentication responsibility to Active Directory, but you still do not have the automatic sign-on and CIFS browsing capabilities that internal Alfresco users enjoyed in the first example. Is there anything more you can do? The next example demonstrates this.

Example 3: The passthru Subsystem

In Example 2, you saw that the authentication capabilities offered by the `ldap-ad` subsystem type were not capable of supporting CIFS and NTLM authentication. Instead, you had to settle for form-based login for all users, and only Alfresco internal users could access CIFS. This is the compromise you would have to make if the directory server did not support any other authentication protocol. But for Active Directory, which also supports NTLM and Kerberos authentication, you can overcome this limitation by using either the `passthru` or the `kerberos` subsystem types.

As `passthru` is simpler to set up, this is the one used for this example. The `passthru` subsystem supports SSO, CIFS, and password authentication against a Windows domain server using the NTLM v1 protocol. Many prefer Kerberos for its enhanced security and you should certainly consider it as an alternative.

Authentication Chain Composition

Append an instance of `passthru` to the authentication chain for this example. Call the instance `passthru1` and declare it by changing the `authentication.chain` property in alfresco-global.properties as follows:

```
authentication.chain=alfinst:alfrescoNtlm,ldap1:ldap-ad,passthru1:passthru
```

Configuring the Instances

First, ensure that CIFS authentication is no longer targeted at your internal `alfrescoNtlm` subsystem instance, `alfinst`.

Open the alfresco-authentication.properties file in the alfinst directory in a text editor, and edit the `alfresco.authentication.authenticateCIFS` property as follows:

```
alfresco.authentication.authenticateCIFS=false
```

Functions such as NTLM SSO and CIFS authentication can only be targeted at a single subsystem instance in the authentication chain. This is a restriction imposed by the authentication protocols themselves. For this reason, Alfresco targets these "direct" authentication functions at the first member of the authentication chain that has them enabled. By disabling CIFS in `alfinst` earlier, `passthru1` has a chance to handle CIFS authentication for its larger user base. SSO is also left disabled in `alfinst`, which means that you can enable it in `passthru1`.

Next, stop `ldap1` from performing authentication. You can leave that to `passthru1`, which will be authenticating against the same server using more secure protocols. This leaves the `ldap1` user registry export capabilities active, which you still rely on for account synchronization.

Edit the `ldap.authentication.active` property in the ldap-ad-authentication.properties file located in your ldap1 directory as follows:

```
ldap.authentication.active=false
```

Finally, create the properties files to configure `passthru1`.

```
mkdir <installLocation>\shared\classes\alfresco\extension\subsystems\
Authentication\passthru\passthru1
```

```
cd /d <installLocation>\shared\classes\alfresco\extension\subsystems\
Authentication\passthru\passthru1

copy <installLocation>\webapps\alfresco\WEB-INF\classes\alfresco\subsystems\
Authentication\passthru\*.properties
```

After running the previous commands, two separate properties files should appear in your passthru1 directory. These are:

- passthru-authentication-context.properties
- ntlm-filter.properties

Using a similar distinction to the `alfrescoNtlm` subsystem type, passthru-authentication-context.properties contains properties relating to core authentication capabilities, whereas ntlm-filter.properties groups those properties relating to automatic sign-on. Unlike the `alfrescoNtlm` subsystem type, SSO is enabled by default in `passthru` subsystems so there is no need to edit ntlm-filter.properties.

The following lines show the set of properties you typically need to edit and how they might be set for a domain controller for the fictitious domain *domain.com.*

```
passthru.authentication.servers=DOMAIN\\domaincontroller.domain.com\
,domaincontroller.com
passthru.authentication.domain=# Leave blank
passthru.authentication.guestAccess=false
passthru.authentication.defaultAdministratorUserNames=Administrator,alfresco
```

Here is a brief description of the settings that have changed:

- **`passthru.authentication.servers`** — A comma-separated list of domain controller host names, each prefixed by the name of the domain they correspond to and a double backslash. The last member of the list is a host name without a domain prefix, and this host will be used when a client does not include a domain name in an authentication request.
- **`passthru.authentication.domain`** — This property is a less-reliable alternative to passthru.authentication.servers and should be left empty.
- **`passthru.authentication.defaultAdministratorUserNames`** — A list of user IDs who should be given Alfresco administrator privileges by default. Additional users can be made administrators by another administrator if they add those users to the ALFRESCO_ADMINISTRATORS group.

Putting It in Action

Restart the Alfresco server. The main differences to notice from last time are:

- All Active Directory users can point their browser to the Alfresco server and be signed on automatically. In Internet Explorer, this requires adding the Alfresco server to the Local Intranet security zone.
- All Active Directory users can access Alfresco as a CIFS file system using their Active Directory credentials.

These examples have demonstrated the flexibility and power of an Alfresco authentication chain. You can combine the strengths of a variety of different authentication protocols and keep the Alfresco user database synchronized almost transparently.

ALFRESCO SECURITY

Authentication is concerned with validating that a user or principal is who or what they claim to be. Alfresco normally refers to users. A user's credentials can take many forms and can be validated in a number ways (for example, a password validated against an LDAP directory, or a Kerberos ticket validated against a Microsoft Active Directory Server).

Alfresco includes an internal, password-based, authentication implementation; the support to integrate with many external authentication environments; the option to write your own authentication integration; and the ability to use several of these options simultaneously. Alfresco can integrate with LDAP, Microsoft Active Directory Server, the Java Authentication and Authorization Service (JAAS), Kerberos, and NTLM. A user ID can also be presented as an HTML attribute over HTTPS to integrate with Web-based single sign-on solutions.

Authorization determines what operations an authenticated user is allowed to perform. There are many authorization models. Popular ones include Role Based Access Control (RBAC), UNIX-style Access Control Lists (ACLs) and extended ACLs, Windows-style ACLs, and many more. Authorization requirements for the management of records are more detailed and include additional requirements (for example, enforcing access based on security clearance or record state).

Alfresco authorization is based on UNIX-extended ACLs. Each node in the repository has an ACL that is used to assign permissions to users and groups. Operations, such as creating a new node, describe what permissions are required to carry out the operation. ACLs are then used to determine if a given user may execute the operation based on the permissions that have been assigned directly to the user or indirectly through a group. An operation in Alfresco is invoking a method on a public service bean. For example, creating a user's home folder requires invoking methods on several public services; to create the folder, set permissions, disable permission inheritance, and so on. Each public service method invocation will check that the user is allowed to execute the method.

By convention, public service beans are the beans whose names start with capital letters, such as the `NodeService`. You configure the security requirements for public service beans in XML. A given method on a particular service may be available to all users, all users in a specified group, all users with a specified role, or users who have particular permissions on specified arguments to the method or its return value. In addition, for methods that return collections or arrays, their content may be filtered based on user permissions. If the authorization requirements for a method call are not met, the method call will fail and it will throw an `AccessDeniedException`. Non-public beans, such as `nodeService`, do not enforce security; use these only when the enforcement of authorization is not required.

Permission assignments are made in Access Control Lists (ACLs), which are lists of Access Control Entries (ACEs). An ACE associates an authority (group or user) with a permission or set of permissions, and defines whether the permission is denied or allowed for the authority. Every node has a related ACL. When you create a node, it automatically inherits an ACL from its parent. You can alter this behavior after node creation by breaking inheritance or modifying the ACL.

The XML configuration for permissions also defines a context-free ACL for ACEs that apply to all nodes. For example, you could use this to assign everyone `Read` access to all nodes regardless of what individual ACLs any node has set. (See the "Permissions" section in this chapter for more details on how to modify the permission model.)

```
<!-- Extension to alfresco\model\permissionDefinitions.xml -->
<globalPermission permission="Read" authority="GROUP_EVERYONE" />
```

Code snippet GlobalRead.xml

A check that a user has Read permission for a node is done in two stages. First, the context-free ACL is checked to see if it allows access. If not, the ACL assigned or inherited by the node is checked. A user may be allowed to perform an operation because of permissions assigned to the context-free ACL, assigned to the node's ACL, inherited by the node from its parent, or a combination of all three.

AUTHORITIES

Authorities are people (or persons) or groups. A group may contain people or other groups as members. The authorities assigned to a user at any time are the `userName` from their associated `Person` node, all of the groups of which the user is a direct or indirect member, and any appropriate dynamic authorities. Dynamic authorities are used for internal roles.

People and Users

When logging in, Alfresco validates the user's identifier and password. Alfresco employs the user's identifier to look up the appropriate person details for the user, using the `userName` property on the `Person` type. You can configure this look-up to be case-sensitive or case-insensitive. The `userName` property on the matching `Person` node is used as the actual user authority; it may differ in case from the user identifier presented to the authentication system. After the `Person` node look-up, Alfresco is case-sensitive when matching authorities to permissions, group membership, roles, and for all other authorization tests.

Any user who authenticates by any mechanism must have an associated person node in Alfresco. Person nodes may be:

- Explicitly created
- Created on demand with some default entries
- Created from LDAP synchronization

Person nodes are explicitly created when using the administration pages of the Alfresco Explorer and Alfresco Share Web clients to manage users.

By default, person nodes will be auto-created if not present. If an external authentication system is configured, such as NTLM, when any user authenticates, an appropriate person node may not exist. If a person node does not exist and auto-creation is enabled, a person node will then be created using the identifier exactly as presented by the user and validated by the authentication system. The auto-created

`Person` node's `userName` will have the same case as typed by the user. LDAP synchronization will create person nodes with the `userName` as provided from the LDAP server.

It is possible that LDAP synchronization can change the `userName` associated with a `Person` node. For example, this can happen with a system that uses NTLM authentication and LDAP synchronization, creates person nodes on demand, and uses case-insensitive authentication. For example, Andy could log in as "Andy" and the associated `Person` node would be created with the `userName` "Andy." Later, the LDAP synchronization runs and changes the `userName` to "andy." From version 3.2, changes to `Person` node `userNames` will cause updates to other related data in Alfresco, such as ACL assignment.

Groups

Groups are collections of authorities with a name and display name. As such, groups may include other groups or people. You may include a group in one or more other groups, as long as this inclusion does not create any cyclic relationships.

Zones

All person and group nodes are in one or more zones. You can use zones for any partitioning of authorities. For example, Alfresco synchronization uses zones to record from which LDAP server users and groups have been synchronized. Zones have been used to hide some groups that provide Role Based Access Control (RBAC) role-like functionality from the administration pages of the Alfresco Explorer and Alfresco Share Web clients. Examples of hidden groups are the *roles* used in Alfresco Share and Records Management (RM). Only users and groups in the default zone are shown for normal group and user selection on the group administration pages. Zones cannot be managed from the administration pages of the Alfresco Explorer and Alfresco Share Web clients.

Zones are intended to have a tree structure defined by naming convention. Zones are grouped into two areas: Application-related zones and authentication-related zones.

Within a zone, a group is considered to be a root group if it is not contained by another group in the same zone.

Figure 6-1 shows the model used for persisting people, groups, and zones in Alfresco. Each person is represented by a `Person` node and groups are represented by an `AuthorityContainer`, which can be used for other authority groupings, such as roles. `AuthorityContainer` and `Person` are sub-classes of `Authority` and as such can be in any number of `Zones`.

Application-Related Zones

Application-related zones, other than the default, are used to hide groups that implement RBAC like roles. Application zones, by convention, start with APP. and include the following:

- APP.DEFAULT is for person and group nodes to be found by a normal search. If no zone is specified for a person or group node they will be a member of this default zone.
- APP.SHARE is for hidden authorities related to Alfresco Share.
- APP.RM will be added for authorities related to RM.

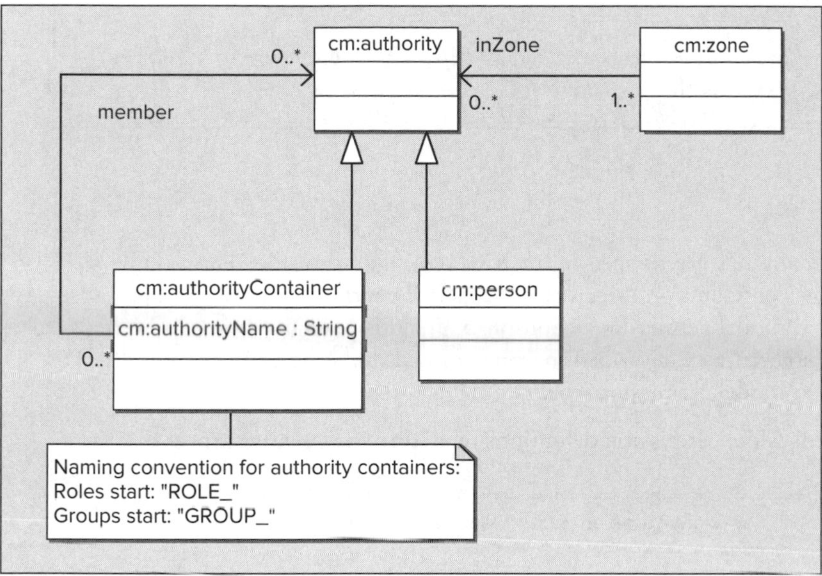

FIGURE 6-1

Authentication-Related Zones

Zones are also used to record the primary source of person and group information. They may be held within Alfresco or some external source. While authorities can be in many zones, it makes sense for an authority to be in only one authentication-related zone.

- AUTH.ALF is for authorities defined within Alfresco and not synchronized from an external source. This is the default zone for authentication.
- AUTH.EXT.<ID> is for authorities defined externally, such as in LDAP.

Dynamic Authorities and Roles

Alfresco uses some custom roles. To implement a custom role, you create a dynamic authority for that role and assign global permissions to it. The Alfresco internal roles have not been assigned any object-specific rights. The internal roles are as follows:

- ROLE_ADMINISTRATOR is assigned to the default administrators for the configured authentication mechanisms or members of the administration groups defined on the `AuthorityServiceImpl` bean. This role has all rights.
- ROLE_OWNER is assigned to the owner of a node. If there is no explicit owner, this role is assigned to the creator. This role has all rights on the owned node.
- ROLE_LOCK_OWNER is assigned to the owner of the lock on a locked node. This supports a lock owner's right to check in, cancel a checkout, or unlock the node.

The Alfresco Web clients support the assignment of permissions only to the owner role. You can use such things as the Java API and scripting to make other assignments.

Hierarchical and zoned roles may be added to Alfresco in the future to avoid the hidden group implementation for true roles.

PERMISSIONS

Permissions and their groupings are defined in an XML configuration file. The default file is found in the distribution configuration directory as <*installLocation*>\tomcat\webapps\alfresco\WEB-INF\classes\alfresco\model\permissionDefinitions.xml. This configuration can be replaced or extended and has a structure as described in <*installLocation*>\tomcat\webapps\alfresco\WEB-INF\classes\alfresco\model\permissionSchema.dtd.

The following example uses the permission definitions related to the `Ownable` aspect.

Available for download on Wrox.com

```
<!-- ============================================== -->
  <!-- Permissions associated with the Ownable aspect -->
  <!-- ============================================== -->

  <permissionSet type="cm:ownable" expose="selected">

    <!-- Permission control to allow ownership of node to be taken from others -->
    <permissionGroup name="TakeOwnership" requiresType="false" expose="false">
      <includePermissionGroup permissionGroup="SetOwner" type="cm:ownable" />
    </permissionGroup>

    <permissionGroup name="SetOwner" requiresType="false" expose="false"/>

    <!-- The low level permission to control setting the owner of a node -->
    <permission name="_SetOwner" expose="false" requiresType="false">
      <grantedToGroup permissionGroup="SetOwner" />
      <requiredPermission on="node" type="sys:base" name="_WriteProperties" />
    </permission>

  </permissionSet>
```

Code snippet OwnablePermissions.xml

As you can see in the preceding code, permissions and permission groups are defined in a permission set, which is a sub-element of the permissions root element. A permission set is associated with a type or aspect and applies only to that type and sub-types, or aspect and sub-aspects.

A permission has a name. By convention, the names of permissions start with an underscore character. They may be exposed in the administration pages of the Alfresco Explorer and Alfresco Share Web clients but, by convention, are not. A permission, in its definition, may be granted to any number of permission groups. This means that those permission groups will include the permission. The permission may require that the type or aspect specified on the permission set be present on the node. If a permission is associated with an aspect and the `requiresType` property is set to true, then if that aspect is not applied to a node, the permission does not apply to that node either. If an aspect-related permission definition has the `requiresType` property set to false, the permission applies to any node, even if the aspect has not been applied to the node.

An aspect can be applied at any time and there are no restrictions as to which aspects can be applied to a type. A permission may also require other permissions be tested on the same node, its children, or its parent. In the preceding example, `_SetOwner` requires `_WriteProperties`. This means you cannot set ownership on a node if you are not allowed to write to its properties. You can also use this to check that all children can be deleted before deleting a folder, or to enforce that you can read only the nodes for which you can read all the parents; neither are normally required in Alfresco. The configuration to do this is present in the standard configuration file but is commented out. The `_DeleteNode` permission definition (as shown in the following DeleteNode.xml code snippet) is an example. If permission A requires permission B and this requirement is implied (by setting the `implies` attribute of the `requiredPermission` element to true), assigning an authority permission A will also give them permission B (as opposed to checking they have permission B).

Available for download on Wrox.com

```
<permission name="_DeleteNode" expose="false" >
  <grantedToGroup permissionGroup="DeleteNode" />
  <!-- Commented out parent permission check ...
  <requiredPermission on="parent" name="_ReadChildren" implies="false"/>
  <requiredPermission on="parent" name="_DeleteChildren" implies="false"/>
  <requiredPermission on="node" name="_DeleteChildren" implies="false"/>
   -->
  <!-- Recursive delete check on children -->
  <!--  <requiredPermission on="children" name="_DeleteNode" implies="false"/>  -->
</permission>
```

Code snippet _DeleteNode.xml

Permissions are normally hidden inside permission groups. Permission groups are made up of permissions and other permission groups. By convention, each permission has a related permission group. Permission groups can then be combined to make other permission groups. As for permissions, a permission group may be exposed by the administration pages of the Alfresco Explorer and Alfresco Share Web clients and may require the presence of a type or aspect to apply to a particular node. In addition, a permission group may allow full control, which grants all permissions and permission groups. As a type or aspect may extend another, a permission group defined for a type or aspect can extend one defined for one of its parent types and be assigned more permissions, include more permission groups, or change what is exposed in the administration pages of the Alfresco Explorer and Alfresco Share Web clients.

It is unusual to extend or change the default permission model unless you are adding your own types, aspects, and related public services or you wish to make minor modifications to the existing behavior. The following code snippets show how to extend and replace the default permission model.

Available for download on Wrox.com

```
<bean id='permissionsModelDAO'
class="org.alfresco.repo.security.permissions.impl.model.PermissionModel">
        <property name="model">
<-- <value>alfresco/model/permissionDefinitions.xml</value> -->
<value>alfresco/extension/permissionDefinitions.xml</value>
        </property>
        <property name="nodeService">
            <ref bean="nodeService" />
        </property>
```

```
        <property name="dictionaryService">
            <ref bean="dictionaryService" />
        </property>
    </bean>
```

Code Snippet ReplacePermissionModel.xml

The preceding code example shows how to replace the default permission model with one located in the alfresco/extension directory. The following code snippet shows how to extend the existing model.

Available for download on Wrox.com

```
<bean id="extendPermissionModel" parent="permissionModelBootstrap">
  <property name="model" value="alfresco/extension/permissionModelExtension.xml" />
</bean>
```

Code Snippet ExtendPermissionModel.xml

ACCESS CONTROL LISTS

An Access Control List (ACL) is an ordered list of Access Control Entries (ACEs). An ACE associates a single authority to a single permission group or permission, and states whether the permission is to be allowed or denied. All nodes have an associated ACL. There is one special, context-free, ACL defined in the XML configuration to support global permissions. An ACL specifies if it should inherit ACEs from a parent ACL. The parent ACL is associated with the primary parent node. When a new node is created it automatically inherits all ACEs defined on the parent within which it is created. Linking a node to a secondary parent has no effect on ACE inheritance; the node will continue to inherit permission changes from its primary parent (defined when it was first created).

By default, ACL inheritance is always from the primary parent. The underlying design and implementation does not mandate this. ACL inheritance does not have to follow the parent-child relationship. It is possible to change this through the Java API but not via the administration pages of the Alfresco Explorer and Alfresco Share Web clients.

There are several types of ACL defined in `ACLType`. The main types are:

- `DEFINING`
- `SHARED`
- `FIXED`
- `GLOBAL`

A node will be associated with an ACL. It will have a `DEFINING` ACL if any ACE has been set on the node. `DEFINING` ACLs include any ACEs inherited from the node's primary parent and above, if inheritance is enabled. All `DEFINING` ACLs are associated with one `SHARED` ACL. This `SHARED` ACL includes all the ACEs that are inherited from the `DEFINING` ACL. If the primary children of a node with a `DEFINING` ACL do not themselves have any specific ACEs defined, then they can be assigned the related

SHARED ACL. For the primary children of a node with a SHARED ACL that also have no specific ACEs set, they can use the same SHARED ACL. A single SHARED ACL can be associated with many nodes. When a DEFINING ACL is updated, it will cascade-update any related ACLs via the ACL relationships rather than walk the node structure. If a DEFINING ACL inherits ACEs, then these will come from the SHARED ACL related to another DEFINING ACL.

ACLs and nodes have two linked tree structures. See the example in Figure 6-2, the ACL descriptions in Table 6-2, and the discussion in the section titled "An ACL Example."

FIXED ACLs are not associated with a node but found by name. A node ACL could be defined to inherit from a fixed ACL. A GLOBAL ACL is a special case of a FIXED ACL with a well-known name. It will be used to hold the global ACE currently defined in XML.

ACEs comprise an authority, a permission, and a deny/allow flag. They are ordered in an ACL.

ACL Ordering and Evaluation

The ACEs within an ACL are ordered and contain positional information reflecting how an ACE was inherited. DEFINING ACLs have entries at even positions; SHARED ACLs have entries at odd positions. For a DEFINING ACL, any ACEs defined for that ACL have position 0, any inherited from the parent ACL have position 2, and so on. For a SHARED ACL, ACEs defined on the ACL from which it inherits will have position 1.

When Alfresco makes permission checks, ACEs are considered in order, with the lowest position first. Deny entries take precedence over allow entries at the same position. The default configuration is that "any allow allows." Once a deny entry is found for a specific authority and permission combination, any matching ACE, at a higher position from further up the inheritance chain, is denied. A deny for one authority does not deny an assignment for a different authority. If a group is denied Read permission, a person who is a member of that group can still be assigned Read permission via another group or directly via their person userName. However, if an authority is granted Read (made up of ReadContent and ReadProperties) and the same authority denied ReadContent, they will just be granted ReadProperties permission. The administration pages of the Alfresco Explorer and Alfresco Share Web clients do not expose deny.

You can alter the configuration to support "any deny denies."

An ACL Example

This example relates a tree of nodes to two corresponding trees of ACLs, all shown in Figure 6-2. The nodes in the node tree are identified by number and are shown filled in black if they have any ACEs set, or white/clear if not. Primary child relationships are drawn as black lines and secondary child relationships as dashed lines. ACLs in the ACL trees are identified by letter, DEFINING ACLs are shown filled in black, and SHARED ALCs are shown as clear. Under each node on the node tree, the related ACL is referenced.

Table 6-2 describes the ACEs in each ACL and their position.

ACL A, and any ACL that inherits from it, allows Read for everyone (All) unless permissions are subsequently denied for everyone (All). If ACL A is changed, all the ACLs that inherit from ACL A in the ACL tree will reflect this change. In the example, nodes 1–12 would be affected by such a change. Nodes 13 and 14 would not inherit the change due to the definition of ACL G.

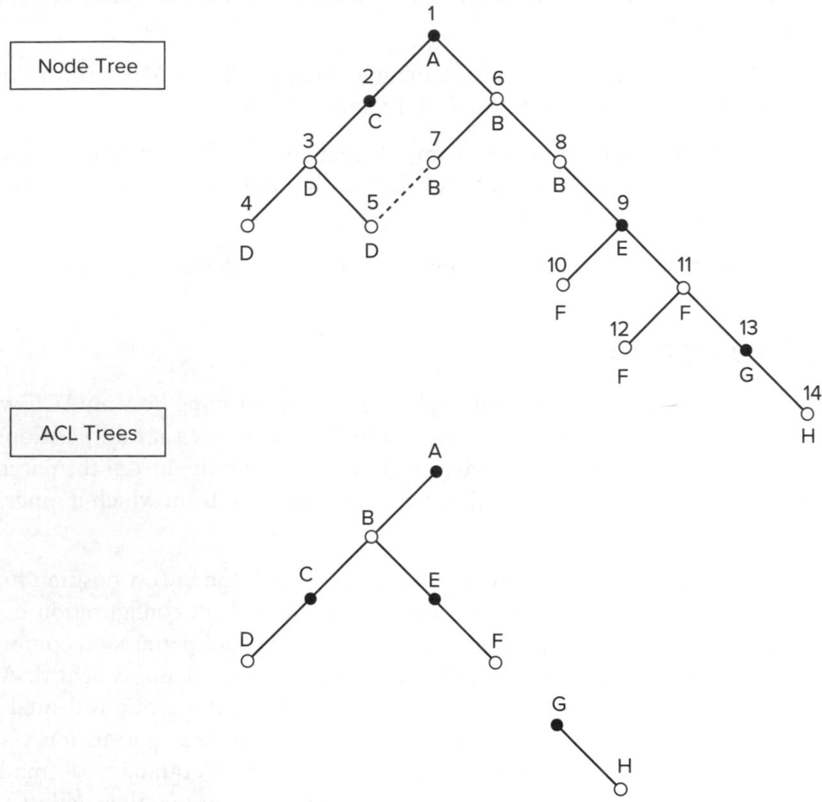

FIGURE 6-2

ACL C adds Contributor and Editor permissions for any authority in GROUP_A.

The GROUP_ prefix is normally hidden by the administration pages of the Alfresco Explorer and Alfresco Share Web clients.

Anyone in GROUP_A can edit existing content or create new content. The owner ACE means that anyone who creates content then has full rights to it. The ACE assignment for owner is not normally required, as all rights are given to node owners in the context-free ACL defined in the default permission configuration.

ACL E adds some specific user ACEs in addition to those defined in ACL A. As an example, it allows Bob `Write` but also denies `WriteContent`. `Write` is made up of `WriteContent` and `WriteProperties`. Bob will only be allowed `WriteProperties`.

TABLE 6-2: ACL Formats

ACL FORMAT	AUTHORITY	PERMISSION	ALLOW/ DENY	POSITION
ACL A (DEFINING, no inheritance)	All	Read	Allow	0
ACL B (SHARED, inherits from ACL A)	All	Read	Allow	1
ACL C (DEFINING, inherits from ACL B)	All	Read	Allow	2
	ROLE_OWNER	All	Allow	0
	GROUP_A	Write	Allow	0
	GROUP_A	CreateChildren	Allow	0
ACL D (SHARED, inherits from ACL C)	All	Read	Allow	3
	ROLE_OWNER	All	Allow	1
	GROUP_A	Write	Allow	1
	GROUP_A	CreateChildren	Allow	1
ACL E (DEFINING, inherits from ACL B)	All	Read	Allow	2
	Andy	All	Allow	0
	Bob	Write	Allow	0
	Bob	WriteContent	Deny	0
ACL F (SHARED, inherits from ACL E)	All	Read	Allow	3
	Andy	All	Allow	1
	Bob	Write	Allow	1
	Bob	WriteContent	Deny	1
ACL G (DEFINING, no inheritance)	Bob	All	Allow	0
ACL H (SHARED, inherits from ACL G)	Bob	All	Allow	1

ACL G does not inherit and starts a new ACL tree unaffected by any other ACL tree unless an inheritance link is subsequently made.

If a new node were created beneath node 13 or 14, it would inherit ACL H. If a new node were created beneath nodes 1, 6, 7, or 8, it would inherit ACL B.

If a node that has a shared ACL has an ACE set, a new defining ACL and a related shared ACL are inserted in the ACL tree. If a defining ACL has all its position-0 ACEs removed, it still remains a defining ACL: There is no automatic cleanup of no-op defining ACLs.

PUBLIC SERVICES

Security is enforced around public services. Web services, Web scripts, Alfresco Explorer and Alfresco Share Web clients, CIFS, WebDAV, FTP, CMIS, and more all use public services, so include security enforcement. Public services are defined in <*installLocation*>\tomcat\webapps\alfresco\WEB-INF\classes\alfresco\public-services-context.xml.

Access control allows or prevents users or processes acting on behalf of a user from executing service methods on a particular object by checking if the current user, or any of the authorities granted to the current user, has a particular permission or permission group, or that the user has a particular authority.

For example, on the `NodeService` bean, the `readProperties` method checks that the current user has `Read` permission for the node before invoking the method and returning the node's properties. On the `SearchService` query method, the results are restricted to return only the nodes for which a user has `Read` permission.

Configuration

Security is enforced in the Spring configuration by defining proxies for each internal service implementation and adding a method interceptor to enforce security for each public service proxy. These interceptors also have other roles discussed elsewhere. When a method is called on a public service, the security interceptor is called before the method it wraps. At this stage, the interceptor can examine the function arguments to the method and check that the user has the appropriate rights for each argument in order to invoke the method. For example, a method `delete(NodeRef nodeRef)` exists on the node service. The security interceptor can see the `nodeRef` argument before the underlying `delete(...)` method is called. If configured correctly, the interceptor could check that the current user has `Delete` permission for the node. If they do not have the permission, a security exception is raised. If all the entry criteria are met, the method goes ahead.

In a similar manner, after a method has executed, the interceptor can examine the returned object and decide if it should return it to the caller. For example, a search method could return a list of nodes. The security interceptor could filter this list for only those nodes for which the current user has `Read` permission.

It is also possible to configure a method so that it can be called by all users, only by users with the admin role, or only by specific users or groups. This can also be enforced by the security method interceptor.

Access control interceptor definitions for public services are included in <*installLocation*>\tomcat\webapps\alfresco\WEB-INF\classes\alfresco\public-services-security-context.xml along with any other supporting beans. This configuration file also defines the location from which the permission model is loaded. The interceptors are wired up to the public services in <*installLocation*>\tomcat\webapps\alfresco\WEB-INF\classes\alfresco\public-services-context.xml. The public services are the only Spring beans to have access control.

Defining Method-Level Security

The beans required to support Spring ACEGI-based security around method invocation are defined in <*installLocation*>\tomcat\webapps\alfresco\WEB-INF\classes\alfresco\

public-services-security-context.xml. This configures two Alfresco-specific beans: A voter that can authorize method execution based on the permissions granted to the current user for specific arguments to the method, and an after-invocation provider to apply security to objects returned by methods. Method access is defined in the normal ACEGI manner with some additions.

For the following information detailing pre-conditions and post-conditions, these factors are all relevant:

- **<authority>** — Represents an authority (user name or group)
- <#> — Represents a method argument index
- **<permission>** — Represents the string representation of a permission

Pre conditions take one of the following forms:

- **ACL_METHOD.<authority>** — Restricts access to the method to those with the given authority in Alfresco. This could be a user name or group. *Dynamic authorities are not supported.*
- **ACL_NODE.<#>.<permission>** — Restricts access control to users who have the specified permission for the node at the identified argument. If the argument is a `NodeRef`, it will be used; if it is a `StoreRef`, the root node for the store will be used; if it is a `ChildAssociationRef`, the child node will be used.
- **ACL_PARENT.<#>.<permission>** — Restricts access control to users who have the specified permission for the parent of the node on the identified argument. If the argument is a `NodeRef`, the parent of the node will be used; if it is a `ChildAssociationRef`, the parent node will be used.
- **ROLE_...** — Checks for an authority starting with ROLE_
- **GROUP_...** — Checks for an authority starting with GROUP_

If more than one ACL_NODE.<#>.<permission>, ACL_PARENT.<#>.<permission>, or ACL_METHOD.<permission> entry is present, then *all* of the ACL_NODE and ACL_PARENT permissions must be present as well as *any one* of the ACL_METHOD restrictions, if present, for the method to execute.

Post-conditions take the forms:

- **AFTER_ACL_NODE.<permission>** — Similar to ACL_NODE.<#>.<permission> but the restriction applies to the return argument
- **AFTER_ACL_PARENT.<permission>** — Similar to ACL_PARENT.<#>.<permission> but the restriction applies to the return argument

The support return types are:

- `StoreRef`
- `ChildAssociationRef`
- Collections of `StoreRef`, `NodeRef`, `ChildAssociationRef`, and `FileInfo`
- `FileInfo`

- NodeRef
- Arrays of StoreRef, NodeRef, ChildAssociationRef, and FileInfo
- PagingLuceneResultSet
- QueryEngineResults
- ResultSet

The post-conditions will create access denied exceptions for return types such as NodeRef, StoreRef, ChildAssociationRef, and FileInfo. For collections, arrays, and result sets, their members will be filtered based on the access conditions applied to each member.

Continuing the example from the permissions defined for the Ownable aspect, the definition for the security interceptor for the related OwnableService is shown in the following code snippet.

Available for download on Wrox.com

```
<bean id="OwnableService_security"
  class="org.alfresco.repo.security.permissions.impl.acegi.
  MethodSecurityInterceptor">
    <property name="authenticationManager"><ref bean="authenticationManager"/>
    </property>
    <property name="accessDecisionManager"><ref local="accessDecisionManager"/>
    </property>
    <property name="afterInvocationManager"><ref local="afterInvocationManager"/>
    </property>
    <property name="objectDefinitionSource">
      <value>
      org.alfresco.service.cmr.security.OwnableService.getOwner=
      ACL_NODE.0.sys:base.ReadProperties
    org.alfresco.service.cmr.security.OwnableService.setOwner=
    ACL_NODE.0.cm:ownable.SetOwner
     org.alfresco.service.cmr.security.OwnableService.takeOwnership=
     ACL_NODE.0.cm:ownable.TakeOwnership
      org.alfresco.service.cmr.security.OwnableService.hasOwner=
      ACL_NODE.0.sys:base.ReadProperties
      org.alfresco.service.cmr.security.OwnableService.*=ACL_DENY
      </value>
    </property>
</bean>
```

Code Snippet OwnableServiceSecurity.xml

Here, security for the four methods on the OwnableService is defined. To invoke the OwnableService getOwner() method on a node, the invoker must have permission to read the properties of the target node. To set the owner of a node, a user must have been explicitly assigned the SetOwner permission or have all rights to the node. A user may have all rights to a node via the context-free ACL or be assigned a permission which grants all permission or includes SetOwner. With the default configuration, a user will own any node they create and therefore be able to give ownership to anyone else and possibly not have the right to take ownership back.

The last entry catches and denies access for any other method calls other than those listed. If any additional methods were added to this service and no security configuration explicitly defined for the new methods, these methods would always deny access.

MODIFYING ACCESS CONTROL

Modifying access control may involve:

- Changing the definition of existing security interceptors to check for different conditions
- Adding new public services and related security interceptors
- Defining new types and aspects and their related permissions
- Adding new definitions to the security interceptor by implementing an ACEGI `AccessDecisionVoter` and/or `AfterInvocationProvider` (in extreme cases)

A few constraints and design patterns should be observed when modifying access control. Permissions apply to the node as whole. In particular, the same `Read` rights apply to all properties and content. You should check that methods can be executed and not that a user has a particular permission. The access control restrictions for a public service method may change. Follow the design pattern to implement RBAC roles.

When modifying access control, do not try to split `ReadProperties` and `ReadContent`. This does not make sense for search. A node and all of its properties, including content, are indexed as one entity. Splitting the evaluation of access for content and properties is not possible. Search would have to apply both criteria so as to not leak information. Other services, such as `copy`, may not behave as expected or may produce nodes in an odd state.

Permissions are assigned at the node level, not at the attribute level. Again, this makes sense with the search capabilities. Search results need to reflect what the user performing the search can see. It makes sense that all properties have the same `Read` access as the node, as nodes are indexed for searching and individual properties are not Applying `Read` ACLs at the property level would require a change to the indexing implementation or a complex post analysis to work out how nodes were found by the search. If not, the values of properties could be deduced by how a readable node was found from a search on restricted properties.

Fine-grain attribute permissions could be implemented by using child nodes to partition metadata. Queries would have to be done in parts and joined by hand, as there is no native support for SQL-like join.

Check that method execution is allowed; do not check that the user has a fixed permission. Rather than checking for `Read` permission in code, check that the appropriate method can be called using the `PublicServiceAccessService` bean. This avoids hard-coding to a specific permission implementation and is essential if you intend to mix records management and the content repository. In any case, the access restrictions for public service methods may change. The `PublicServiceAccessService` bean allows you to test if any public service method can be invoked successfully with a given set of arguments. It checks all the entry criteria for the method and, assuming these have not changed, the method can be called successfully. The method call may still fail if the conditions for the returned object are not met or some security configuration has changed, such as an ACE has been removed, a user has been removed from a group, or the method has failed for a non-authorization reason.

If you are coming from an RBAC background, Alfresco has roles in the RBAC sense only for limited internal use. To implement RBAC in Alfresco, use zoned groups. These groups will not appear in the administration pages of the Alfresco Explorer and Alfresco Share Web clients as normal groups (unless you also add them to the APP.DEFAULT zone) but can be used to assign users and groups to *roles*. This approach has been taken in Alfresco to support roles in Alfresco Share and records management. Here is how RBAC terminology maps to Alfresco: Operations map to method calls on public service beans; objects map to method arguments, including nodes (folders, documents, and so on). Users and permissions/privileges map directly. Alfresco allows the assignment of permissions to users or groups.

By default, the owner of an object can manage any aspect of its ACL. Users with `ChangePermissions` rights for a node can also change its ACL. If users have the ability to alter the ACL associated with an object, they can allow other users to do the same. There is no restriction on the permissions they may assign. The Alfresco model supports liberal discretionary access control with multi-level grant. A user who can grant access can pass on this right without any restriction. In addition, anyone who can change permissions can carry out the revocation of rights: it is not restricted to the original granter. Normally, when someone can perform an operation you would not expect it is because they own the node and therefore have all permissions for that node.

ACCESS CONTROL EXTENSION

The access control model described so far is used for all nodes in the content repository *except* those related to the Records Management extension. Records Management is used as an example here to outline how to extend access control.

The Records Management authorization is based on a fixed set of capabilities that are part of the DOD 5015.2 specification. These capabilities describe records management operations for which there is not a direct mapping to an Alfresco public service method call. There are separate Records Management implementations of the ACEGI `AccessDecisionVoter` and `AfterInvocationProvider` interfaces to support this mapping. The `AccessDecisionVoter` allows or denies access on method entry. The `AfterInvocationProvider` allows or denies access based on the method return value; it can also alter the return value. All Records Management nodes carry a marker aspect (an aspect that defines no properties or associations). If this marker is present, the default voter will abstain; if this marker is absent, the Records Management voter will abstain.

Public services are protected for Records Management in the same manner as already described but with two sets of configuration: one for each of the two different implementations. It is more complex to map the Records Management capabilities and caveats (for example, security clearance) to public service method calls and to enforce the restrictions. For example, the node service `updateProperties` method has to incorporate the idea of updating declared and undeclared records, allow updates to selected properties, and restrict access to some properties that should be updated only as part of state management. The Records Management voter has additional Records Management hard-coded policies to protect the public services in order to encapsulate the logic for this and related use cases.

In Records Management, normal users cannot pass on their rights to other users.

IMPLEMENTATION AND SERVICES

There are four key services involved in access control: the `PersonService`, the `AuthorityService`; the `PermissionService`, and the `OwnableService`. The `PersonService` and the `AuthorityService` are responsible for managing authorities. The `PermissionService` is responsible for managing ACLs and ACEs and for checking if a user has been assigned a permission for a particular node. The `OwnableService` manages object ownership and is used in evaluation the dynamic `ROLE_OWNER` authority.

The protection of public services methods is implemented using Spring method interceptors defined as part of the related ACEGI 0.8.2 security package. The Alfresco implementation adds new implementations of the ACEGI interfaces `AccessDecisionVoter` and `AfterInvocationProvider`, which support the configuration elements that have already been described (for example, ACL_NODE.<#>.<permission>). These extension classes make use of the four key services.

The Person Service

The `PersonService` interface is the API by which nodes of the person type, as defined in <*installLocation*>\tomcat\webapps\alfresco\WEB-INF\classes\alfresco\model\contentModel.xml, should be accessed.

The `PersonService` is responsible for all of the following:

- Obtaining a reference to the `Person` node for a given user name
- Determining if a person entry exists for a user
- Potentially creating missing people entries with default settings on demand
- Supplying a list of mutable properties for each person
- Creating, deleting, and altering personal information

The beans to support the `PersonService` and its configuration can be found in <*installLocation*>\tomcat\webapps\alfresco\WEB-INF\classes\alfresco\authentication-services-context.xml. The principle configuration options are around how people are created on demand if users are managed via NTLM or some other external user repository.

The Authority Service

The `AuthorityService` is responsible for:

- Creating and deleting authorities
- Querying for authorities
- Structuring authorities into hierarchies
- Supporting queries for membership
- Finding all the authorities that apply to the current authenticated user
- Determining if the current authenticated user has admin rights
- Managing zones and the assignment of authorities to zones

The authority service does not support user authentication or user management. This is done by the `AuthenticationService`. `Person` nodes are managed via the `PersonService`.

The default implementation allows a list of group names to define both administration groups and guest groups. Each authentication component defines its own default administrative user(s), which can also be set explicitly. The default service is defined in *<installLocation>*\tomcat\webapps\alfresco\WEB-INF\classes\alfresco\authority-services-context.xml.

The Permission Service

The `PermissionService` is responsible for all of the following:

- Providing well-known permissions and authorities
- Providing an API to read, set, and delete permissions for a node
- Providing an API to query, enable, and disable permission inheritance for a node
- Determining if the current, authenticated user has a permission for a node

The `PermissionService` interface defines constants for well-known permissions and authorities.

The default implementation coordinates implementations of two service provider interfaces: a `ModelDAO` and a `PermissionsDAO`. A permission is simply a name scoped by the fully qualified name of the type or aspect to which it applies. The beans are defined and configured in *<installLocation>*\tomcat\webapps\alfresco\WEB-INF\classes\alfresco\public-services-security-context.xml. This file also contains the configuration for security enforcement.

The `ModelDAO` interface defines an API to access a permissions model. The default permission model is in XML and defines permission sets, and their related permission groups and permissions. Global permissions are part of the permission model. There may be more than one permission model defined in XML; they are in practice merged into one permission model. A module can extend the permission model.

The available permissions are defined in the permission model. This is defined in *<installLocation>*\tomcat\webapps\alfresco\WEB-INF\classes\alfresco\model\permissionDefinitions.xml. This configuration is loaded in a bean definition in *<installLocation>*\tomcat\webapps\alfresco\WEB-INF\classes\alfresco\public-services-security-context.xml. This file also defines global permissions. The definition file is read once at application start-up. If you make changes to this file, you will have to restart the repository in order to apply the changes.

The Ownable Service

The idea of file ownership is present in both UNIX and Windows. In Alfresco, the repository has the concept of node ownership. This ownership is optional and is implemented as an aspect.

The owner of a node may have specific ACLs granted to them. Ownership is implemented as the dynamic authority, `ROLE_OWNER`, and is evaluated in the context of each node for which an authorization request is made. The `Ownable` aspect, if present, defines a node's owner by storing a `userName`; if the `Ownable` aspect is not present, the creator is used as the default owner. If the `userName` of the current user matches, including case, the `userName` stored as the owner of the node, the current user will be granted all permissions assigned to the authority `ROLE_OWNER`.

The `OwnableService` is responsible for all of the following:

- Determining the owner of a node
- Setting the owner of a node
- Determining if a node has an owner
- Allowing the current user to take ownership of a node

The `OwnableService` is supported by an `Ownable` aspect defined in <*installLocation*>\tomcat\webapps\alfresco\WEB-INF\classes\alfresco\model\contentModel.xml.

There are permissions and permission groups associated with the `Ownable` aspect in the permission model and related access controls applied to the methods on the public `OwnableService`.

7

Business Process Management

WHAT'S IN THIS CHAPTER?

- Introducing workflow in Alfresco
- Defining a workflow
- Creating a process definition
- Creating tasks based on the task model
- Customizing the workflow behavior
- Configuring the Explorer user interface

This chapter describes how to create and deploy workflows in Alfresco. It discusses core Business Process Management workflow concepts, including process definitions, how the JBoss Business Process Engine (jBPM) interprets processes, and task models. It also shows you how to configure the behavior of the workflow and customize Alfresco Explorer to view and edit tasks. To illustrate the workflow creation and deployment process, this chapter uses a simple Review and Approve workflow example.

INTRODUCTION TO WORKFLOW IN ALFRESCO

Alfresco implements workflow through several modular, loosely coupled components (as shown in Figure 7-1).

The core components of Alfresco workflows are the workflow engine and the workflow service. The *workflow engine* is the underlying workflow implementation and is responsible for executing workflows, managing tasks, and managing process definitions. The *workflow service* is responsible for encapsulating the workflow engine, meaning all access to Alfresco workflows is made through the workflow service. This ensures that Alfresco workflows and services that use Alfresco workflows remain agnostic to the underlying implementation. Though the underlying workflow service API is written in Java, a JavaScript API is also available. For further information on the JavaScript Workflow API, see Online Appendix D.

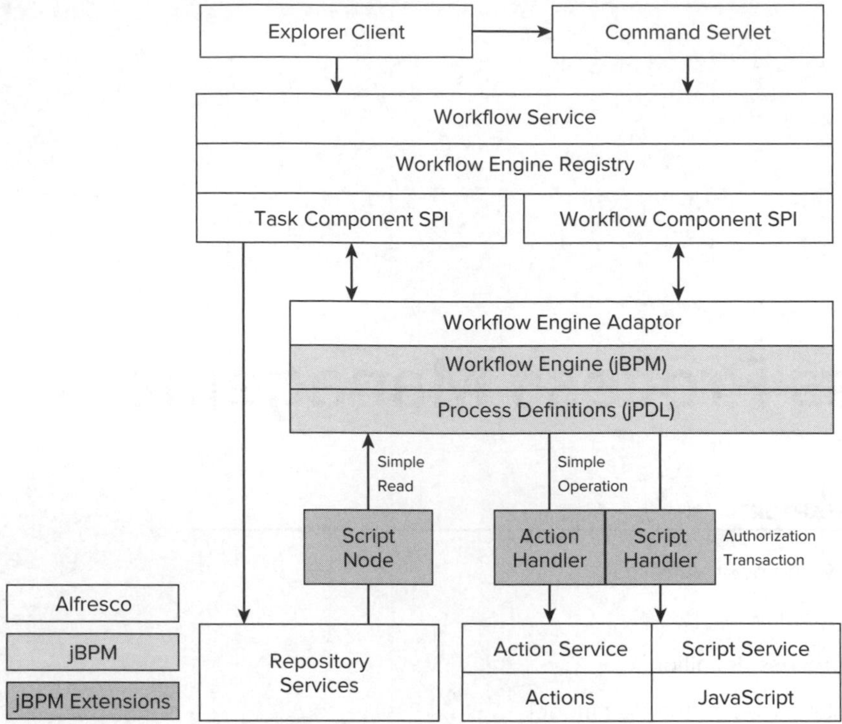

FIGURE 7-1

Each implementation of a workflow engine must have a workflow engine adapter specified for it. This adapter effectively maps workflow service calls onto the workflow engine. Out of the box, Alfresco provides a JBoss Business Process Management (jBPM) adapter and supports jBPM as its default workflow engine. Alfresco makes use of many of the extension points provided by jBPM to offer additional functionality, such as enhanced scripting capabilities and custom actions.

The workflow service uses several other components in Alfresco. For example, the repository services are used to create and store metadata associated with tasks, taking advantage of the Alfresco content modeling capabilities. The Explorer Web client is also used to provide an out-of-the-box user interface for creating and managing workflows and tasks.

How jBPM Interprets and Implements a Process

The JBoss jBPM engine is the default engine used by Alfresco to power its workflow functionality. It is responsible for interpreting the process definitions that are registered with it, and creating and executing instances of those process definitions – the actual processes – when requested. jBPM provides the environment in which processes run and it provides each process with a common set of services that allows the process to do its work.

Each process that runs inside the engine follows a path that is laid out for it by its associated process definition. Each process is related to just one process definition and each process definition describes the steps that are involved in the process: how one step moves on to the next step, what occurs during each step, and so on.

You can find the full user guide for jBPM at `http://docs.jboss.com/jbpm/v3.3/userguide`, but you can review its core features here.

Nodes and Transitions

In jBPM, a process definition comprises a set of nodes joined together with transitions. For the more mathematically minded, a process definition describes a directed graph of nodes with transitions forming the edges of the graph. There are a number of different types of node that can be used in a process definition. It's worth spending a little time here to look at each type.

The first type of node that all process definitions must include is the *start-state*. As the name suggests, when the jBPM engine starts a new process using a given process definition, the start state of that process definition is the state that the process enters initially. Every executable process definition has precisely one start-state node.

At the other end of each process are one or more *end-state* nodes. An end-state node indicates to jBPM that the process has finished. Where a process branches (or *forks*), an end-state node marks the end of each branch.

As hinted at in the previous paragraph, it is possible to cause a process to fork in to two or more branches by using a *fork* node. This has the effect of spawning a new thread of execution for each branch. Subsequently, a *join* node can be used to bring different branches back together again. There are many possible uses for this forking and joining functionality. For example, if an organization is producing a new brochure then it may want the design review to be carried out in parallel with the proofreading. Once both tasks are successfully completed, the brochure can be published. Forking the process allows the parallel tasks to happen, and then joining the parallel branches together again ensures that both are complete prior to entering the publishing activity.

It is often desirable to be able to define rules that dictate which path a particular process should follow. For example, one may wish to use a more rigorous review stage if a document has been flagged as "commercially sensitive" or perhaps take a different path depending on the outcome of a design review. In jBPM, these kinds of choices are modeled using *decision* nodes. A decision node will normally have more than one transition leaving it, and there are two ways in which the process definition can specify which transition is to be taken. The first approach is to define conditions on each of the transitions. In this case, when executing the decision node, jBPM will evaluate the conditions of each transition in turn and will follow the first transition that returns true (or the default transition if none returns true). The second approach is to define an expression on the decision node that returns the name of the transition that should be followed.

The final types of nodes to look at are also the most widely used: *state* and *task-node*. When a process enters a state node it simply waits to be told when to move on. This type of node is typically used when the process needs to wait for another system to do some work before continuing. This other system is expected to notify jBPM when it has finished, thus releasing the process to carry on. Nodes of type task-node are similar to state nodes except that they cause a task to be created and assigned to one or more users of the workflow system. For example, the nodes representing the design review and proofreading activities mentioned earlier are likely to be of the type task-node, with the tasks being assigned to the relevant people. In this case, the person to whom the task has been assigned is responsible for telling jBPM when the task has been completed, and jBPM will then continue executing the process.

Figure 7-2 illustrates a process that includes an example of each type of node.

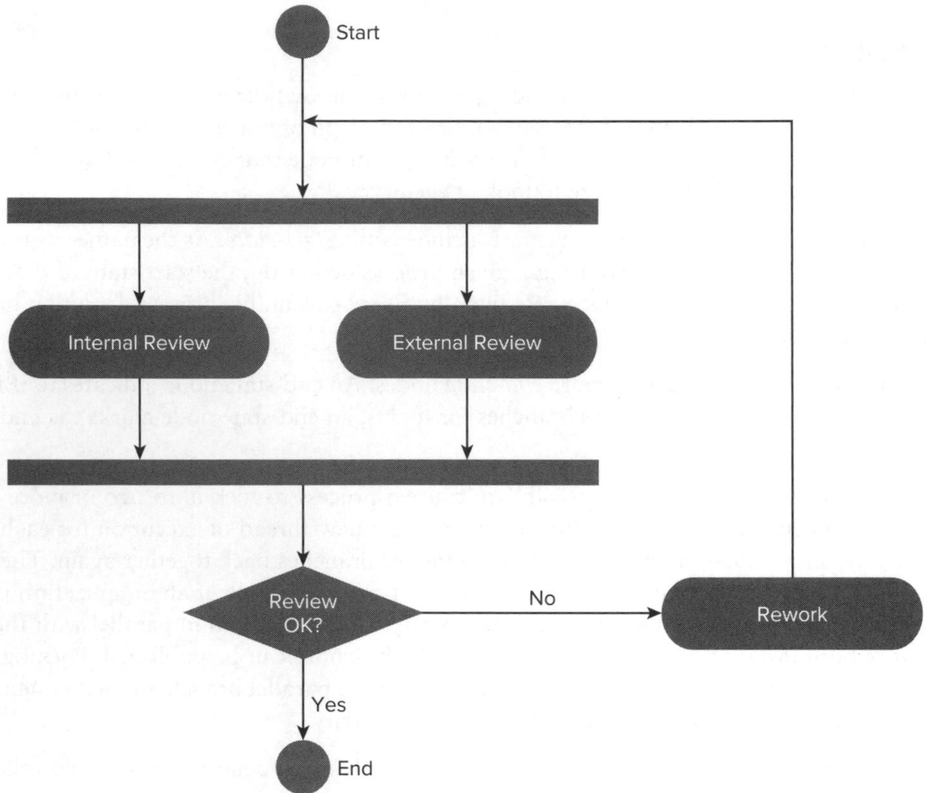

FIGURE 7-2

This process starts and then immediately forks into the Internal Review and External Review nodes. The Internal Review node represents a human activity undertaken by a user who is known to the workflow engine and would, therefore, be modeled as a node of type task-node – when this node starts executing, a task is added to the assigned user's task list. Conversely, the activity represented by the External Review node is undertaken by someone unknown to the workflow engine – perhaps an email is sent to that person with the document attached when this node is executed – so this node is modeled as a plain state node.

Once complete, both the Internal Review and External Review nodes transition into a join node that waits for both branches to reach it. Once this happens, the transition that leads to the Check Review node is followed. The Check Review node is responsible for deciding whether the process can complete or whether some rework is required. Unsurprisingly, this task is best modeled with a decision node. Perhaps, in this case, this node expects a couple of Boolean variables to have been defined, such as `internalReviewSuccessful` and `externalReviewSuccessful`, and decides which transition to follow by examining their values. Presumably in this particular case, if either the internal review or external review was unsuccessful, then the transition leading to the Rework node is followed. This is most likely to be a task-node node that adds a task to the original author's task list.

The following XML code snippet illustrates how such a process definition may be described using jPDL.

```
<?xml version="1.0" encoding="UTF-8"?>
<process-definition name="document-review">

  <start-state>
    <transition to="review fork" />
  </start-state>

  <fork name="review fork">
    <transition name="internal" to="internal review" />
    <transition name="external" to="external review" />
  </fork>

  <task-node name="internal review">
    <task name="review task">
      <assignment actor-id="brian" />
    </task>
    <transition to="review join" />
  </task-node>

  <state name="external review">
    <transition to="review join" />
  </state>

  <join name="review join">
    <transition to="review decision" />
  </join>

  <decision name="review decision">
    <transition to="rework"
      condition="#{!internalReviewSuccessful || !externalReviewSuccessful}" />
    <transition to="end" />
  </decision>

  <task-node name="rework">
    <task name="rework task">
      <assignment actor-id="colin" />
    </task>
    <transition to="review fork" />
  </task-node>

  <end-state name="end" />

</process-definition>
```

Actions and Events

In jBPM, an action is a piece of code that can be executed when certain events occur in a process. For example, it is possible to specify that a particular action should be executed when a given transition is followed, or when the process enters or leaves a node, or when a task is created. Out of the box, jBPM allows actions to be coded in Java or in a scripting language called BeanShell (see `www.beanshell.org`). In Alfresco, there is a hybrid option: a Java class named `AlfrescoJavaScript` that allows you to supply a script written against the Alfresco JavaScript API. That will be discussed in more detail later in this chapter.

In the example introduced in the previous section, you may decide that you'd like to email the document being reviewed to the external reviewer when the External Review node is entered. Of course, there is more than one way of achieving this, but for the sake of this example, there is a class named `EmailDocToReviewer` that performs the required functionality. To cause jBPM to execute an instance of this class at the appropriate point in the process, you modify the way that the External Review node is defined in the previous process definition to add in the event handler:

```
<state name="external review">
  <event type="node-enter">
    <action class="com.example.jbpm.EmailDocToReviewer" />
  </event>
  <transition to="review join" />
</state>
```

These actions will be discussed in more detail later on in this chapter.

Tasks, Swimlanes, and Timers

If you look closely at the example process definition, you will see that each of the two task-nodes defines a "task." This tells jBPM to create a new task and to assign it to someone. There are a few ways of indicating to whom the task should be assigned, such as identifying the user by name (as is the case here), writing an expression that resolves the user, or writing a custom assignment handler in Java. Another option is to use is a *swimlane*.

A swimlane identifies a role in a process. It is particularly useful when a process definition defines a number of tasks that should all be carried out by the same user. All such tasks are placed in the same swimlane and the swimlane determines to which user those tasks are assigned. By default, while running a single process, the person who is assigned the first task in a given swimlane will be assigned any other tasks that are in the same swimlane.

Since the example process definition isn't very complex, there isn't much need for swimlanes but, for completeness, here is how one might modify the process definition to use a swimlane for the reviewer:

```
<?xml version="1.0" encoding="UTF-8"?>
<process-definition name="document-review">

  <swimlane name="reviewer">
    <assignment actor-id="brian" />
  </swimlane>

  <start-state>
    <transition to="review fork" />
  </start-state>
  ...
  <task-node name="internal review">
    <task name="review task" swimlane="reviewer" />
```

```
    <transition to="review join" />
  </task-node>
  ...
</process-definition>
```

Timers are another useful feature supported by jBPM. Any number of timers can be placed within any node or task, and each one specifies the time at which it should trigger. In addition, a timer definition may identify a transition that is to be followed, an action to execute, and a repeat interval. All of these optional attributes take effect when the timer first triggers.

For example, if you want to send an email reminder to the internal reviewer every other day until the review is complete, then you could modify the "internal review" task-node in your process definition to look something like this:

```
<task-node name="internal review">
  <task name="review task" swimlane="reviewer">
    <timer name="internal review timer" duedate="2 business days" repeat="yes">
      <action class="com.example.jbpm.SendReviewReminder" />
    </timer>
  </task>
  <transition to="review join" />
</task-node>
```

Note that the previous code snippet assumes that the functionality needed to send out the email reminder has been written as a Java class. This makes the example compact but, in reality, you may choose to use Alfresco's JavaScript API instead. It's also worth pointing out the expression used for the timer's due date: "2 business days." jBPM expects the format of the due date to be `[<basedate> +/-] <duration>` where the optional `basedate` can be any expression that resolves to a `Date` or `Calendar` object and `duration` has the form `<quantity> [business] <unit>` where `quantity` is a number and `unit` can be one of second(s), minute(s), hour(s), day(s), week(s), month(s), or year(s). If no base date is provided, then the time starts from the moment the timer is created (when the internal review task starts, in this case). The optional word "business" in the duration causes only business hours to be used when calculating the trigger time.

Super-States and Sub-Processes

The final concepts in this overview of jBPM are those of super-states and sub-processes. These are fairly advanced concepts. Though it may well be that you'll never feel the need to use them, it's worth mentioning them for the sake of completeness.

A *super-state* is used to group a set of nodes together, introducing a hierarchical structure to the process definition. A common usage is to separate the process definition into phases where each phase is composed of more than one task or state. In the example already presented in this section, you may choose to introduce a review phase that encompasses all the nodes that relate to reviewing the document. This is also a good opportunity to take a look at the process definition with all the changes so far:

```
<?xml version="1.0" encoding="UTF-8"?>
<process-definition name="document-review">

  <swimlane name="reviewer">
    <assignment actor-id="brian" />
  </swimlane>
```

```
  <start-state>
    <transition to="review" />
  </start-state>

  <super-state name="review">

    <fork name="review fork">
      <transition name="internal" to="internal review" />
      <transition name="external" to="external review" />
    </fork>

    <task-node name="internal review">
      <task name="review task" swimlane="reviewer">
        <timer name="internal review timer" duedate="2 business days" repeat="yes">
          <action class="com.example.jbpm.SendReviewReminder" />
        </timer>
      </task>
      <transition to="review join" />
    </task-node>

    <state name="external review">
      <event type="node-enter">
        <action class="com.example.jbpm.EmailDocToReviewer" />
      </event>
      <transition to="review join" />
    </state>

    <join name="review join">
      <transition to="../review decision" />
    </join>

  </super-state>

  <decision name="review decision">
    <transition to="rework"
      condition="#{!internalReviewSuccessful || !externalReviewSuccessful}" />
    <transition to="end" />
  </decision>

  <task-node name="rework">
    <task name="rework task">
      <assignment actor-id="colin" />
    </task>
    <transition to="review fork" />
  </task-node>

  <end-state name="end" />

</process-definition>
```

You have now wrapped the fork, internal review, external review, and join in a super-state named "review." The start state now transitions directly to the new super-state, which causes jBPM to start executing the first node in the super-state (the fork). An alternative to this would have been to transition explicitly to the fork by changing the transition from the start state to be `review/review fork`. The process definition later emerges from the super-state when transitioning out of "review join." Note the way that this is done: specifying the target node with `../review decision`. This is interpreted by jBPM as "transition to the node named 'review decision' that is one level up the state hierarchy."

jBPM allows one process to "spawn" another process with the concept of *sub-processes*. If, for example, you have a mini-process that is used in the context of a number of other different processes, then this way of composing process definitions may be useful to you. Inserting a node of type "process-state" into your process definition causes jBPM to execute a new instance of the specified process definition when a process reaches that node. In the example, you may want to define a sub-process named "process-document" that is executed before the review occurs. Perhaps this extracts metadata from the document, auto-classifies it, and generates a new rendition of it.

To include this sub-process in the process definition, insert a "process-state" node and adjust the start state so that it transitions to this new node:

```
<process-definition name="document-review">
  ...
  <start-state>
    <transition to="process" />
  </start-state>

  <process-state name="process">
    <sub-process name="process-document" />
    <transition to="review" />
  </process-state>
  ...
</process-definition>
```

That's all there is to it. It's also possible to pass variables from the parent process into the sub-process, optionally allowing the sub-process to modify their values such that the new values are returned to the parent process.

DEFINING A WORKFLOW IN ALFRESCO

To add a new workflow to Alfresco, you must create and deploy a *workflow definition*. Figure 7-3 shows how the various components of a workflow definition interact with components in the workflow service.

A workflow definition comprises a *process definition*, a *task model*, and some *user interface configuration*. All three of these components are necessary to build a workflow.

- **Process definition:** Specifies the workflow process, defining what human tasks and automated processes to execute, and flow control.
- **Task model:** Provides a description of each task in a workflow by defining the various attributes associated with that task. A UI component can use this description to automatically generate a user interface suitable for displaying task information, as well as to initialize a newly created task instance.

- **UI configuration:** Allows for customization of the UI component that is used for presenting workflow-related information to the user and taking inputs from the user. The Alfresco Explorer Web client allows customization of the property sheets used to display task information. It also uses resource bundles to customize the text that displays. In particular, resource bundles allow the customization of the language used to display information about a workflow or task.

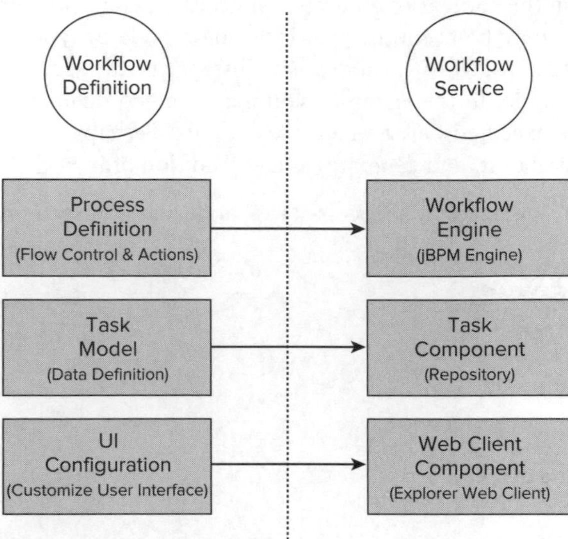

FIGURE 7-3

The following sections describe how to create and deploy a workflow definition. This includes

1. Creating the process definition
2. Creating the task model
3. Customizing the behavior
4. Configuring the user interface (Explorer Web client)

Throughout the chapter, the simple Review and Approve process workflow example shown in Figure 7-4 will be used to illustrate how to create and deploy a workflow.

The key steps in this classic workflow are:

1. The initiator submits a document and assigns it to a Reviewer in **Start Workflow**.
2. The reviewer reviews the document and either approves or rejects it in **Review Document**.
3. The initiator is informed of the outcome of the review through an email, which is sent when the workflow reaches **Complete Review**.
4. The initiator completes the review process in **Complete Review**, ending the workflow.

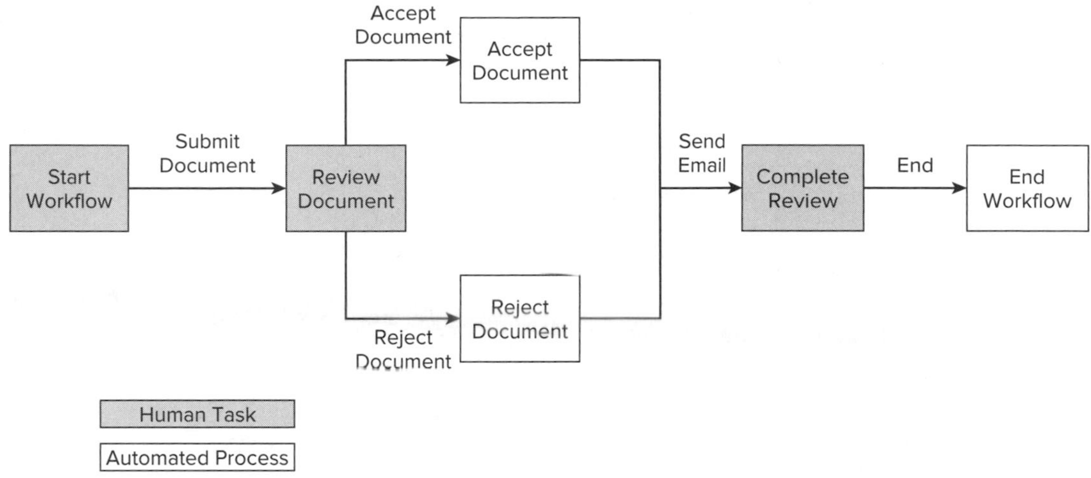

FIGURE 7-4

CREATING THE PROCESS DEFINITION

Since Alfresco uses jBPM as its underlying workflow implementation, process definitions must be specified using the jBPM domain-specific language, jPDL.

> *Although not used in creating this process definition, you can also use the JBoss jBPM Process Designer, which is a graphical tool for developing jPDL process definitions. For full details on defining process definitions using jPDL, see the jBPM jPDL User Guide at* `http://docs.jboss.com/jbpm/v3.3/userguide/`.

The following jPDL process definition describes the Review and Approve workflow example. For now, only an outline or skeleton definition is provided. This definition does not assign the various roles (swimlanes) to users nor does it define any automated behavior, such as sending emails. These elements will be added in the next section.

Available for download on Wrox.com

```
<?xml version="1.0" encoding="UTF-8"?>

<process-definition xmlns="urn:jbpm.org:jpdl-3.1" name="wf:myReviewAndApprove">

   <swimlane name="initiator" />

   <swimlane name="reviewer" />

   <start-state name="start">
      <task name="wf:mySubmitReviewTask" swimlane="initiator" />
      <transition name="" to="review" />
   </start-state>
```

```
    <task-node name="review">
       <task name="wf:myReviewTask" swimlane="reviewer" />
       <transition name="approve" to="approve" />
       <transition name="reject" to="reject" />
    </task-node>

    <node name="approve">
       <transition to="completed" />
    </node>

    <node name="reject">
       <transition to="completed" />
    </node>

    <task-node name="completed">
       <task name="wf:myCompleteReviewTask" swimlane="initiator" />
       <transition name="" to="end" />
    </task-node>

    <end-state name="end" />

</process-definition>
```

Code snippet my_outline_review_and_approve_processdefinition.xml

This code snippet is a structured outline for building the example workflow illustrated in Figure 7-4. It defines a process definition with the name wf:myReviewAndApprove. Two `<swimlane>` tags define the major roles in the workflow: the Initiator and the Reviewer. The `<node>`, `<task-node>`, `<start-state>`, and `<end-state>` tags define the different states depicted in Figure 7-4. The connection between states is defined by the various `<transition>` tags.

Note that some of the states include `<task>` tags. These are states that require human interaction and the `<task>` tags represent the human actions to be performed. The name attributes on these `<task>` tags and the `<process-definition>` tag are used as keys to reference the task and process definition components within Alfresco. This is described in more detail in "The Task Model" section.

Deploying a Process Definition

To use the process definition, you must first deploy it into jBPM. This can be done either when the Alfresco server starts up (through configuration) or through hot deployment to a running Alfresco server.

Configuring the Alfresco Server

The Alfresco server can automatically deploy the workflow on startup when configured to do so. To configure Alfresco to deploy a custom workflow definition, you must include a Spring bean in the Spring configuration to extend `workflowDeployer`. Consider the following example:

```
<?xml version="1.0" encoding="UTF-8"?>
<!DOCTYPE beans PUBLIC
'-//SPRING//DTD BEAN//EN' 'http://www.springframework.org/dtd/spring-beans.dtd'>

<beans>

   <bean id="myworkflows.workflowBootstrap" parent="workflowDeployer">
      <property name="workflowDefinitions">
         <list>
            <props>
               <prop key="engineId">jbpm</prop>
               <prop key="location">
alfresco/extension/workflow/my_outline_review_and_approve_processdefinition.xml
               </prop>
               <prop key="mimetype">text/xml</prop>
               <prop key="redeploy">true</prop>
            </props>
         </list>
      </property>
   </bean>
</beans>
```

Code snippet myWorkflowBootstrap-outline-context.xml

The Spring XML configuration file must be placed in the folder *installLocation*\tomcat\shared\classes\alfresco\extension\ and its name must end with -context.xml (such as myWorkflowBootstrap-context.xml). This allows Alfresco to automatically load this configuration when the server starts.

Each process definition to be deployed must include one `<props>` element and the following specified properties:

- **engineId** — ID for the workflow engine being used. This will normally be *jbpm*.
- **Location** — Classpath location of the process definition jPDL file. The standard extension mechanism places this file in the following location. *installLocation*\tomcat\shared\classes\alfresco\extension\workflow\[*my_review_and_approve_processdefinition.xml*].
- **MIME type** — Type of the process definition file (for example, a jPDL XML file is *text/xml*); a process archive file is *application/zip*.
- **Redeploy** — Boolean value that determines whether the process definition is redeployed on server startup, resulting in a new version being created. When developing new definitions, set this value to true to see modifications on the server. In a production environment, set this value to false.

Hot-Deploying a Process Definition

Using the workflow console, you can deploy a process definition directly onto a running Alfresco server. You do not need to restart the server.

With Administrator credentials, you can access the workflow console through the Explorer Web client at the following URL:

```
http://localhost:8080/alfresco/faces/jsp/admin/workflow-console.jsp
```

On the workflow console, type the following command to deploy a process definition:

```
deploy <process definition file class path location>
```

In the Review and Approve example, the process definition file location is *installLocation*\shared\classes\alfresco\workflow\my_outline_review_and_approve_processdefinition.xml, so the command is:

```
deploy alfresco/extension/workflow/review_processdefinition.xml
```

Testing the Deployment

After deploying a process definition either through configuration or using hot deployment, check that the process definition has been successfully deployed to the Alfresco server. To do so, perform the following steps:

- Start the Alfresco server.
- Connect to the Explorer Web client (on a typical installation, the URL will be `http://localhost:8080/alfresco`) and log in.
- Browse to some content (you may have to add content if none exists).
- Click the down arrow next to the content and select Start Advanced Workflow.

You should now see the Start Advanced Workflow Wizard listing all available workflows. If you have successfully deployed your process definition, it will be included in this list. For example, if you have just deployed the example process definition you should see three workflow options (as shown in Figure 7-5).

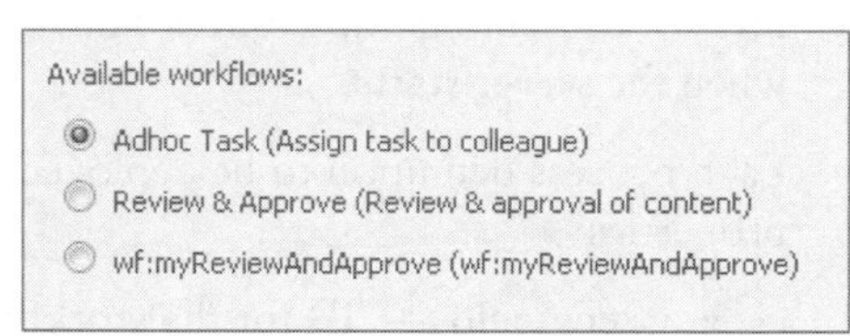

FIGURE 7-5

Note that in addition to the example workflow wf:myReviewAndApprove, there is a workflow called Review & Approve. This is Alfresco's built-in workflow for reviewing content and should not be confused with the example. Do not start the workflow at this point, as the workflow is only partially defined and will cause errors.

Try deploying the example process definition now. Use the Spring configuration method to deploy the outline process definition. Call the process definition **my_review_and_approve_processdefinition.xml**. Then check that the process definition was deployed successfully.

THE TASK MODEL

A task model specifies task definitions and associates them with `<task>` elements defined in process definitions. A task definition describes which attributes (task variables) are associated with a given task. The Explorer Web client uses these task definitions to generate property forms, allowing you to view or edit the task attributes. Figure 7-6 demonstrates the relationship between a task model, its task definitions, and their task variables using the Review and Approve workflow tasks.

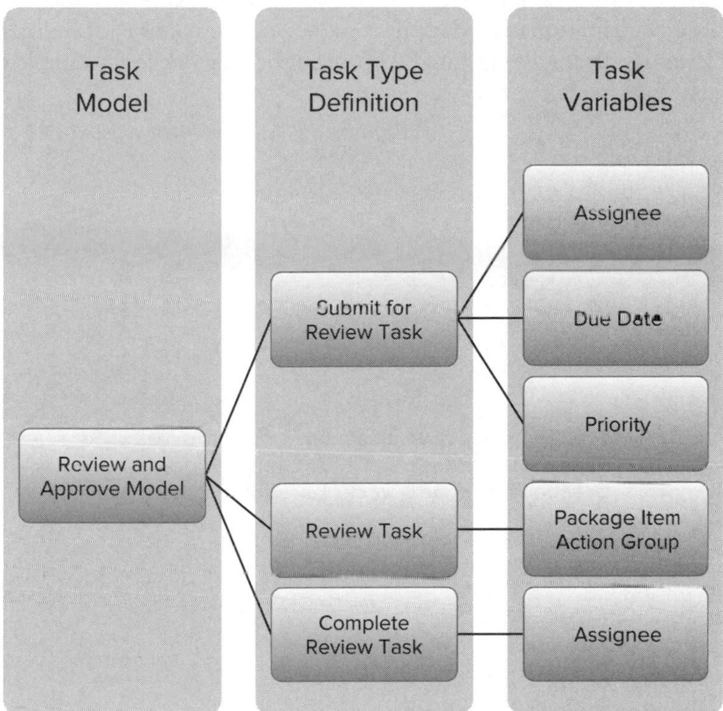

FIGURE 7-6

The task definition also controls access to the *workflow package*, a special repository space created when a workflow starts that contains all the content associated with that workflow. The task definition specifies how the task assignee can access the package and the items stored within it.

This section describes how to create a task model and associate task definitions with tasks in a process definition. It also describes the common task model, which defines the base types and aspects used in workflows, including the types upon which all task definitions are based.

Creating a Task Model

A task model is simply a content model and each task definition is a type definition. All the features available in content modeling are also available in task modeling, including property data types, constraints, and default values. For more information on Content Modeling, refer to Chapter 5. If there is commonality across the tasks, you can use subtyping or aspects to encapsulate the shared features. The different attributes of a task are modeled as properties and associations on the task definition.

The task model is defined just like any other content model, using XML. As well as importing the dictionary model, the task model imports the common task model (`uri = "http://www.alfresco.org/model/bpm/1.0"`) containing several useful predefined types and aspects that may be inherited by custom task definitions.

When creating custom task definitions, you must ensure the name of the `<type>` element for the task definition exactly matches the name of the task specified in the process definition. This is because Alfresco uses these names to link the task definition to the relevant task in the process definition. It is also important to ensure the custom task definition extends either `bpm:workflowTask` or `bpm:startTask`. The following code shows the task model for the Review and Approve process workflow example that you have been exploring throughout this chapter.

Available for download on Wrox.com

```
<?xml version="1.0" encoding="UTF-8"?>

<model name="wf:myReviewAndApproveModel"
xmlns="http://www.alfresco.org/model/dictionary/1.0">

   <description>Example Review And Approve Task Model</description>
   <author>Alfresco</author>
   <version>1.0</version>

   <imports>
      <import uri="http://www.alfresco.org/model/dictionary/1.0" prefix="d" />
      <import uri="http://www.alfresco.org/model/bpm/1.0" prefix="bpm" />
      <import uri="http://www.alfresco.org/model/workflow/1.0" prefix="wf" />
   </imports>

   <types>

      <type name="wf:mySubmitReviewTask">
         <parent>bpm:startTask</parent>
         <mandatory-aspects>
            <aspect>bpm:assignee</aspect>
         </mandatory-aspects>
      </type>

      <type name="wf:myReviewTask">
         <parent>bpm:workflowTask</parent>
         <overrides>
            <property name="bpm:packageItemActionGroup">
               <default>edit_package_item_actions</default>
            </property>
         </overrides>
      </type>

      <type name="wf:myCompleteReviewTask">
         <parent>bpm:workflowTask</parent>
         <mandatory-aspects>
            <aspect>bpm:assignee</aspect>
         </mandatory-aspects>
      </type>

   </types>

</model>
```

Code snippet myReviewAndApproveModel.xml

Store this example code snippet in *installLocation*\tomcat\shared\classes\alfresco\extension\workflow.

The key elements to note in the previous code snippet are the three `<type>` tags that define task types. The first of these, wf:mySubmitReviewTask, defines the task responsible for starting the workflow, assigning a reviewer, and submitting a document for review. The next type, wf:myReviewTask, defines the task for reviewing the document and deciding to accept or reject it. The final type, wf:myCompleteTask, defines the task that informs the initiator of the outcome of the review and then ends the review workflow.

The Common Task Model

The common task model is a pre-registered content model that defines the base types and aspects used in workflows. The model is located under WEB-INF\classes\alfresco\model\ in the file bpmModel.xml.

The two most important types defined in this model are the *base workflow task definition* (`bpm:workflowTask`) and the *base start task definition* (`bpm:startTask`). All other task definitions must extend one of these types. Furthermore, if no type definition is specified for a task, it is automatically assigned to one of these types. The common task model also defines several aspects that are useful in assigning roles to people or groups.

Workflow Task Definitions

All task definitions extend the base workflow task definition (`bpm:workflowTask`). The base workflow task definition has several attributes that are inherited by all other task definitions, as follows:

Base Task Attributes

NAME	TYPE	MANDATORY	DESCRIPTION
bpm:taskId	d:long	Yes	The task identifier
bpm:description	d:text	No	The task description
bpm:startDate	d:date	No	The date the task started
bpm:completionDate	d:date	No	The date the task was completed
bpm:dueDate	d:date	No	The date the task was due to be completed
bpm:status	d:text	Yes	Task status (default is "Not Yet Started")
bpm:priority	d:int	Yes	Task priority (defaults to 2)
bpm:percentComplete	d:int	Yes	Measure of task completion as a percentage

continues

Base Task Attributes *(continued)*

NAME	TYPE	MANDATORY	DESCRIPTION
bpm:comment	d:text	No	Notes on the task
bpm:pooledActors	sys.base	No	A list of users who may be assigned to this task
cm:owner	d:text	No	The task owner (assignee)
bpm:context	d:noderef	No	The folder or content on which the workflow was started
bpm:outcome	d:text	No	The outcome of the task (transition ID)
bpm:completedItems	d:noderef	No	A set of the completed items in the package
bpm:packageActionGroup	d:text	No	Allowed actions to perform on package
bpm:packageItemActionGroup	d:text	No	Allowed actions to perform on items within the package
bpm:package	bpm:workflowPackage	Yes	A container holding content involved in the workflow

The Start Task

The start task is defined within the `<start-state>` of a process definition. All start task definitions must inherit from the base start task (`bpm:startTask`), which in turn inherits from the base workflow task definition. In addition to the attributes inherited from the base workflow task definition, all start task definitions also inherit the following attributes:

Start Task Attributes

NAME	TYPE	MANDATORY	DESCRIPTION
bpm:workflowDescription	d:text	No	A description of the workflow
bpm:workflowDueDate	d:date	No	The date the workflow is due to be completed
bpm:workflowPriority	d:int	No	The priority of the workflow (defaults to 2)

The start task is often used to collect the initializing parameters needed to start a workflow. For instance, the review workflow example uses the start task to specify who will review the article. The start task is automatically assigned to the initiator of the workflow when that workflow starts.

Assignment Aspects

Tasks are frequently used as a way of assigning workflow roles (for example, swimlanes) to participants (people or groups). This is most commonly done through the start task, but such assignments can be made at any point in a workflow. To facilitate these assignments, a set of predefined aspects is provided:

Assignment Aspects

ASPECT	TYPE OF PARTICIPANT
bpm:assignee	A single person
bpm:assignees	One or more people
bpm:groupAssignee	A single group
bpm:groupAssignees	One or more groups

Applying any of these aspects to a task definition as a mandatory aspect automatically adds a component to the task property form on the Explorer Web client. This enables the initiator to easily assign workflow roles to people or groups. Looking at the start task definition for the Review and Approve workflow example, notice that it expects an assignment of a single person to a role (the reviewer in this case).

```
<type name="wf:mySubmitReviewTask">
   <parent>bpm:startTask</parent>
   <mandatory-aspects>
      <aspect>bpm:assignee</aspect>
   </mandatory-aspects>
</type>
```

Workflow Package Actions

Many of the attributes defined in the base workflow task definition relate to a *package*. A package is a space within the Alfresco repository dedicated to storing content associated with the workflow instance. Not only does the task have a reference to the package; it also has properties that define access rights to the package for that task through the package action group property (`bpm: packageActionGroup`) and the package item action group property (`bpm: packageItemActionGroup`).

The Explorer Web client uses action groups to specify access rights to the package and its contents. Several out-of-the-box action groups are defined in the web-client-config-workflow-actions.xml file in WEB-INF\classes\alfresco/. These are:

- read_package_item_actions
- edit_package_item_actions
- remove_package_item_actions
- edit_and_remove_package_item_actions
- add_package_item_actions
- start_package_item_actions

Setting the default value of the package item action group to one of these action groups (or a custom action group) alters what actions the Explorer Web client makes available to the user during that task. If the default value is explicitly set to be empty, then no actions are possible.

The base workflow task definition specifies an empty default for the package action group and specifies read_package_item_actions as the default for the package item action group. These defaults are inherited by custom workflow task definitions unless they explicitly override these properties. The base start task overrides these properties, having add_package_item_actions as the default package item action group and start_package_item_actions as the default package action group.

Referring back to the example task model, you can see that the review task definition overrides the package item action groups default and sets it to edit_package_item_actions so that the reviewer can edit the article during the review process.

```
<type name="wf:myReviewTask">
   <parent>bpm:workflowTask</parent>
   <overrides>
      <property name="bpm:packageItemActionGroup">
         <default>edit_package_item_actions</default>
      </property>
   </overrides>
</type>
```

Accessing Task Attributes

You can access all the attributes specified on a task definition from within the process definition. The majority of these attributes are exposed as task variables. However, a colon (:) is not a legal character in task variable names. Instead, the namespace prefix is followed by an underscore(_). Thus, the task definition attribute `bpm:assignee` would be available as the task variable *bpm_assignee*.

A number of attributes on the base workflow task do not relate to task variables, but instead relate to specific properties on the jBPM task instance object. These are described as follows:

Special Task Attribute Mappings

TASK ATTRIBUTE	jBPM PROPERTY
bpm:taskId	`taskInstance.id`
bpm:description	`taskInstance.description`
bpm:startDate	`taskInstance.start`
bpm:dueDate	`taskInstance.dueDate`
bpm:completionDate	`taskInstance.end`
bpm:priority	`taskInstance.priority`
bpm:comment	`taskInstance.comments.get(0).message`
cm:created	`taskInstance.create`
cm:owner	`taskInstance.actorId`

Deploying the Task Model

As with the process definition, you must deploy the task model onto the Alfresco server before you can use it. To do so, modify the same (or similar) Spring bean used to deploy the process definition (remember that the bean must extend `workflowDeployer`). Add a new `<property>` element with the name *models* as shown in the following code snippet. Inside this element, add a `<list>` element containing one or more `<value>` elements. Each of these values should specify the location of a task model file. If correctly configured, the task model will automatically deploy when the Alfresco server starts.

```
<bean id="myworkflows.workflowBootstrap" parent="workflowDeployer">
   <property name="workflowDefinitions">
      ...
   </property>
   <property name="models">
      <list>
         <!-- Task Model associated with above process definition -->
         <value>alfresco/extension/workflow/myReviewAndApproveModel.xml
         </value>
      </list>
   </property>
</bean>
```

Deploy the task model file myReviewAndApprove.xml now by adding the `models` property to your `workflowDeployer` Spring bean. Once the task model has been deployed, check that the Alfresco server starts and that the workflow is still in the list of available workflows on the Start Advanced Workflow Wizard. At this stage, the workflow definition is still only partially defined, so do not start the workflow.

CUSTOMIZING BEHAVIOR

While the process definition defines the flow of a process, it can also define custom behavior for a process. This might include adding business logic to control the flow of the process, executing some external action (such as sending an email), or assigning a task to a specific user. The jPDL language provides a variety of extension points for implementing custom behavior, including support of BeanShell scripts, `ActionHandlers`, and `AssignmentHandlers`. For full details on how to use these extension points, refer to the jBPM jPDL User Guide at `http://docs.jboss.com/jbpm/v3.3/userguide/`.

Alfresco makes use of these extension points to implement its own `AssignmentHandler` and several useful `ActionHandlers`. Using the Review and Approve example to illustrate how these components are used, the initiator must assign a reviewer to review the document. Also, once the review task is complete, an email is automatically sent to the initiator informing him of the outcome of the review. The Review and Approve process definition has been modified to implement this behavior. The updated listing is shown in the following code snippet. The main differences to note are the addition of assignments, events, actions, scripts, and variables. These components will be explained in detail in the following sections.

Deploy the updated process definition now. To do so, delete the old my_review_and_approve_processdefinition.xml file and replace it with the updated listing that follows. Remember that the `redeploy` property specified on the `workflowDeployer` Spring bean must be set to true for the new process definition to be deployed. If you deployed the first process definition using hot deployment you will need to either redeploy using the workflow console using the "deploy" command or add your process definition to the `workflowDeployer` Spring bean.

```
<?xml version="1.0" encoding="UTF-8"?>
<process-definition xmlns="urn:jbpm.org:jpdl-3.1" name="wf:myReviewAndApprove">

   <swimlane name="initiator" />

   <swimlane name="reviewer">
      <assignment class="org.alfresco.repo.workflow.jbpm.AlfrescoAssignment">
         <actor>#{bpm_assignee}</actor>
      </assignment>
   </swimlane>

   <start-state name="start">
      <task name="wf:mySubmitReviewTask" swimlane="initiator" />
      <transition name="" to="review" />
   </start-state>

   <task-node name="review">
      <task name="wf:myReviewTask" swimlane="reviewer" />
      <transition name="approve" to="approve" />
      <transition name="reject" to="reject" />
   </task-node>

   <node name="approve">
      <event type="node-enter">
         <script>
            <variable name="reviewResult" access="write" />
            <expression>
               reviewResult = "approved";
            </expression>
         </script>
      </event>
      <transition to="completed" />
   </node>

   <node name="reject">
      <event type="node-enter">
         <script>
            <variable name="reviewResult" access="write" />
            <expression>
               reviewResult = "rejected";
            </expression>
         </script>
      </event>
      <transition to="completed" />
   </node>

   <task-node name="completed">
      <event type="node-enter">
         <action class="org.alfresco.repo.workflow.jbpm.AlfrescoJavaScript">
            <script>
```

```
                var mail = actions.create("mail");
                mail.parameters.to =
                   initiator.properties["cm:email"];
                mail.parameters.subject =
                   "Review Task " + bpm_workflowDescription;
                mail.parameters.from
                =bpm_assignee.properties["cm:email"];
                mail.parameters.text=
                   "The article has been " + reviewResult + ".";
                mail.execute(bpm_package);
             </script>
          </action>
       </event>
       <task name="wf:myCompleteReviewTask" swimlane="initiator" />
       <transition name="" to="end" />
    </task-node>

    <end-state name="end" />

 </process-definition>
```

Code snippet my_review_and_approve_processdefinition.xml

Process Variables

The jBPM engine keeps track of data associated with a workflow instance as *process variables*. Process variables are represented as name-value pairs and persisted as part of the process state. jBPM and Alfresco automatically create several process variables, but you can also define your own variables.

By default, these variables effectively have global scope. It is possible, however, to scope a variable to a specific token, making it accessible by only that token. Tokens are how jBPM keeps track of the execution state of an active workflow instance. Every workflow starts with a single root token; however, more child tokens are spawned every time the process forks. When the process reaches a join, these child tokens are merged back into their parent token.

Many process variables have a data type defined by an Alfresco content model. For some of the simpler types this can be directly translated into a BeanShell type (for example, `d:text` can be represented as a string). Types that are more complex are represented using the `ScriptNode` class, described in Online Appendix D.

Alfresco provides several out-of-the-box process variables that are always available, as follows:

Default Process Variables

VARIABLE NAME	TYPE	DESCRIPTION
initiator	cm:person Node	The person who initiated the workflow instance
Initiatorhome	cm:space Node	The home folder of the initiator
Companyhome	cm:space Node	The company home folder
Cancelled	Boolean	Indicates whether or not the workflow has been cancelled

Once the start-task is complete, several more properties become available:

Start-Task Process Variables

VARIABLE NAME	TYPE	DESCRIPTION
bpm_workflowDescription	String	A description of the workflow instance
bpm_workflowDueDate	Date	The date by which the workflow should be completed
bpm_workflowPriority	int	The priority of the workflow
bpm_package	bpm:workflowPackage Node	A container holding all the content associated with this workflow
bpm_context	cm:folder Node	A reference to the folder in which the workflow was initiated

To demonstrate process variables in action, the following code snippet defines a variable *reviewResult* and sets it to either *accepted* or *rejected* depending on which path the process execution takes. The variable is set using BeanShell scripts.

```
<node name="approve">
   <event type="node-enter">
      <script>
         <variable name="reviewResult" access="write" />
         <expression>
            reviewResult = "approved";
         </expression>
      </script>
   </event>
   <transition to="completed" />
</node>

<node name="reject">
   <event type="node-enter">
      <script>
         <variable name="reviewResult" access="write" />
         <expression>
            reviewResult = "rejected";
         </expression>
      </script>
   </event>
   <transition to="completed" />
</node>
```

Assigning Tasks and Swimlanes

You can assign tasks and swimlanes to a user by specifying an `<assignment>` element inside the task or swimlane to be assigned. In Alfresco workflows, you should use the `AlfrescoAssignment` class to reference users by user name from the `Person` service. To do this, add the following attribute and value:

```
class="org.alfresco.repo.workflow.jbpm.AlfrescoAssignment"
```

The assignment must contain an <actor> element specifying the user name of the user to be assigned. You can also assign a task or swimlane to a group of actors by simply replacing the <actor> element with a <pooledactors> element, and specifying the list of user names to be assigned.

The initiator swimlane is a special case that does not require an explicit assignment. If no assignment is specified for this swimlane, it is automatically assigned to the user who initiated the workflow instance.

Continuing the review workflow example, the reviewer swimlane is now assigned using the process variable *bpm_assignee*. This variable is typically used to specify swimlane and task assignments and is usually set by the initiator when the workflow is started.

```
<swimlane name="reviewer">
<assignment class="org.alfresco.repo.workflow.jbpm.AlfrescoAssignment">
<actor>#{bpm_assignee}</actor>
</assignment>
</swimlane>
```

The Alfresco JavaScript Action

The Alfresco JavaScript action lets you embed custom JavaScript into process definitions in much the same way that you can embed BeanShell scripts. To do so, simply add an <action> element with the following attribute:

```
class="org.alfresco.repo.workflow.jbpm.AlfrescoJavaScript"
```

Inside the <action> element, include a <script> element that defines the JavaScript to execute. As with the BeanShell script definitions, this <script> element may optionally contain <variable> elements and an <expression> element if you want to limit access to process and task variables.

The Alfresco JavaScript action exposes the full power of the Alfresco JavaScript API, giving access to several useful services and helper classes. The Alfresco JavaScript action also allows you to run the script as a specific user. To do so, include a <runas> element under <action> and specify a user name as the text body of the element, as follows:

```
<action class="org.alfresco.repo.workflow.jbpm.AlfrescoJavaScript">
   <runas>admin</runas>
   <script> ...some script... </script>
</action>
```

The Review and Approve workflow example can have behavior added that will send an email to the author once an article is either approved or rejected. The text of the email is dependent upon the process variable *example_reviewResult*. The ActionService is used to send the email.

```
<action class="org.alfresco.repo.workflow.jbpm.AlfrescoJavaScript">
   <script>
      var mail = actions.create("mail");
      mail.parameters.to =
         initiator.properties["cm:email"];
      mail.parameters.subject =
```

```
            "Review Task " + bpm_workflowDescription;
         mail.parameters.from =      bpm_assignee.properties["cm:email"];
         mail.parameters.text =
            "The article has been " + example_reviewResult + ".";
         mail.execute(bpm_package);
      </script>
   </action>
```

The ForEachFork Action

For some workflow scenarios, it is necessary to support a fork where the number of paths is only known at runtime, as in a parallel review process where the review task is allocated to an arbitrary number of people for review.

A `ForEachFork` action supports this functionality, whose behavior is similar to a `for` loop in Java. An array or collection is supplied to the action, creating one subtoken per element in the array or collection and assigning a different process variable to each subtoken representing one element in the array or collection. Each subtoken is then processed in parallel until it reaches a join node or the end-state. Join nodes merge the subtokens back together just as they would for a standard fork node.

The `ForEachFork` action takes two parameters, both specified as elements directly under the `<action>` element. The `<foreach>` parameter specifies the array or collection over which the action iterates. The `<var>` parameter specifies the name given to the process variable used to hold the individual elements of the array or collection. The action is specified inside a `<node>`.

The following code snippet demonstrates how you might use the `ForEachFork` action as part of a parallel review process where each member of a group, named wf_reviewGroup, reviews an article. An array containing each member of wf_reviewGroup is created using the method `people.getMembers`. This array is then passed to the `ForEachFork` action as the `<foreach>` parameter. A task is created for each member of the array with the *reviewer* variable set to that member. Finally, a join node merges all the subtokens back together once all group members have reviewed the article.

```
<node name="forEach">
   <action class="org.alfresco.repo.workflow.jbpm.ForEachFork">
      <foreach>#{people.getMembers(wf_reviewGroup)}</foreach>
      <var>reviewer</var>
   </action>
   <transition name="review" to="review" />
</node>

<task-node name="review">
   <task name="wf:reviewTask">
      <assignment class="org.alfresco.repo.workflow.jbpm.AlfrescoAssignment">
         <actor>#{reviewer}</actor>
      </assignment>
   </task>
   <transition name="reject" to="merge" />
   <transition name="approve" to="merge" />
</task-node>

<join name="merge">
   <transition to="completed" />
</join>
```

CONFIGURING THE EXPLORER WEB CLIENT

The Alfresco Explorer Web client provides a customizable graphical interface that allows you to view and edit the tasks assigned to you. The primary component of this interface is a task property page that displays your task properties and associations and allows you to edit some of them. Customization of the Explorer Web client is achieved through resource bundles and property sheet configuration as described in the following sections.

Resource Bundles

Resource bundles allow customization of text on the user interface without the need to alter the underlying models, such as the process definition and task model. They are particularly useful for rendering user interfaces in different languages dependent on the locale of the user. A resource bundle is simply a set of name-value pairs where the name is a logical key representing some UI component and the value is the actual label to display.

Creating a Resource Bundle

Alfresco uses standard Java resource bundles to support localization of the workflow user interface. Alfresco supports title and description definitions for all types defined within the task model, as well as four types associated with workflows. These are described in the following sections.

Task Model Types

Since the task model is simply a content model, you can specify all the types and properties defined in the task model using the standard Data Dictionary localization keys. The task model itself has the following keys:

```
<model prefix>_<model name>.title
<model prefix>_<workflow name>.description
```

`<model prefix>` refers to the prefix used in the task model name and `<model name>` is the local name used in the task model name. For example, the review workflow example uses the following task model keys:

```
wf_myReviewAndApproveModel.title
wf_myReviewAndApproveModel.description
```

The various elements defined in the task model can also be linked to a resource bundle. These include task types, properties, associations, and aspects. To specify a key for an element within a task model, use the following format:

```
<model prefix>_<model name>.{<element>.<element prefix>_<element name>}.title
<model prefix>_<model name>.{<element>.<element prefix>_<element name>}.description
```

Here, `<element>` refers to the type of element being specified (for example, type, aspect, property, and so on). `<element prefix>` and `<element name>` refer to the prefix and local name of the element name. Note that the section in curly braces ({}) can be repeated multiple times to reference elements several layers deep (for example, elements that are not immediate children of the `<model>` element). A simple example would be the task definition for `submitReviewTask`:

```
wf_myReviewAndApproveModel.type.wf_mySubmitReviewTask.title
wf_myReviewAndApproveModel.type.wf_mySubmitReviewTask.description
```

A more complex example defining the bpm:status property on submitReviewTask would be:

```
example_reviewModel.type.example_submitReviewTask.property.bpm_status.title
example_reviewModel.type.example_submitReviewTask.property.bpm_status.description
```

Workflow Definition

The workflow definition can have a title and a description associated with it. The key for each of these follows the format:

```
<prefix>_<workflow name>.workflow.title
<prefix>_<workflow name>.workflow.description
```

<prefix> refers to the prefix used in the process definition name and <workflow name> is the local name used in the process definition name. For example, the review workflow example uses the following keys:

```
wf_myReviewAndApprove.workflow.title
wf_myReviewAndApprove.workflow.description
```

Workflow Node

Each workflow node can have an associated title and description. The key format is:

```
<prefix>_<workflow name>.node.<node name>.title
<prefix>_<workflow name>.node.<node name>.description
```

<node name> refers to the name of the node being described. For example, the keys for the start-state node (called "start") of the review workflow example are:

```
wf_myReviewAndApprove.node.start.title
wf_myReviewAndApprove.node.start.description
```

Workflow Transitions

Each workflow transition can have a title and a description. The keys are defined with the following format:

```
<prefix>_<workflow name>.node.<node name>.transition.<transition name>.title
<prefix>_<workflow name>.node.<node name>.transition.<transition name>.description
```

<transition name> is the name of the <transition> element in the specified node. The "approve" transition of the "review" node would have the keys:

```
wf_myReviewAndApprove.node.review.transition.approve.title
wf_myReviewAndApprove.node.review.transition.approve.description
```

Workflow Tasks

Each task in a workflow can have a title and a description. The keys are defined as follows:

```
<workflow prefix>_<workflow name>.task.<task prefix>_<task name>.title
<workflow prefix>_<workflow name>.task.<task prefix>_<task name>.description
```

Here, <workflow prefix> and <workflow name> refer to the process definition name, while <task prefix> and <task name> refer to the task name. The keys for submitReviewTask in the example are:

```
wf_myReviewAndApprove.task.wf_myCompletedTask.title
wf_myReviewAndApprove.task.wf_myCompletedTask.description
```

Resource Bundle Example

The following shows the full listing of `review-messages.properties`, a resource bundle for the review workflow example. Resource bundles are stored in *installLocation*\tomcat\shared\classes\alfresco\messages.

Available for download on Wrox.com

```
# Review & Approve Workflow
wf_myReviewAndApprove.workflow.title = My Review & Approve
wf_myReviewAndApprove.workflow.description = Review & approval of an article

# Review & Approve Task Definitions
wf_myReviewAndApproveModel.title = My Review And Approve Model
wf_myReviewAndApproveModel.description =
Model for Review And Approve workflow.
wf_myReviewAndApproveModel.type.wf_mySubmitReviewTask.title =
Submit Article
wf_myReviewAndApproveModel.type.wf_mySubmitReviewTask.description =
Submit article for review.
wf_myReviewAndApproveModel.type.wf_myReviewTask.title = Review Article
wf_myReviewAndApproveModel.type.wf_myReviewTask.description =
Review article and Approve or Reject it.
wf_myReviewAndApproveModel.type.wf_myCompleteReviewTask.title = Review Completed
wf_myReviewAndApproveModel.type.wf_myCompleteReviewTask.description =
The review process is complete.

# Review & Approve Process Definitions
wf_myReviewAndApprove.node.start.title = Start
wf_myReviewAndApprove.node.start.description = Start
wf_myReviewAndApprove.node.review.title=Review
wf_myReviewAndApprove.node.review.description=Review
wf_myReviewAndApprove.node.review.transition.reject.title=Reject
wf_myReviewAndApprove.node.review.transition.reject.description=Reject
wf_myReviewAndApprove.node.review.transition.approve.title=Approve
wf_myReviewAndApprove.node.review.transition.approve.description=Approve
wf_myReviewAndApprove.node.rejected.title=Rejected
wf_myReviewAndApprove.node.rejected.description=Rejected
wf_myReviewAndApprove.node.approved.title=Approved
wf_myReviewAndApprove.node.approved.description=Approved
wf_myReviewAndApprove.node.completed.title=Completed
wf_myReviewAndApprove.node.completed.description=Completed
wf_myReviewAndApprove.task.wf_myCompletedTask.title=Completed
wf_myReviewAndApprove.task.wf_myCompletedTask.description=Completed
wf_myReviewAndApprove.node.end.title=End
wf_myReviewAndApprove.node.end.description=End
```

Code snippet my_review_and_approve_messages.properties

Store this example code snippet in *installLocation*\tomcat\shared\classes\alfresco\extension\.

Deploying Resource Bundles

A `workflowDeployer` Spring bean is used to deploy the resource bundles, just as it is used to deploy the process definition and task model. A `labels` property must be added to the `workflowDeployer` bean. This property element contains a `<list>` of `<value>` elements specifying the location of the resource bundle file on the classpath, as shown in the following code snippet. Note that the file location specified omits the .properties suffix from the resource bundle file name. For example, the following code snippet specifies the path to the file my_review_and_approve_messages.properties. If configured correctly the resource bundle is deployed into the Alfresco server.

Available for download on Wrox.com

```
<bean id="myworkflows.workflowBootstrap" parent="workflowDeployer">
   <property name="workflowDefinitions">
      ...
   </property>
   <property name="models">
      ...
   </property>
   <property name="labels">
      <list>
         <!-- Resource Bundle associated with above process definition -->
         <value>alfresco/messages/my_review_and_approve_messages</value>
      </list>
   </property>
</bean>
```

Code snippet myWorkflowBootstrap-final-context.xml

Now try deploying the resource bundle my_review_and_approve_messages.properties by adding a `labels` property to the `workflowDeployer` Spring bean. Once deployed, start the Alfresco server and navigate to the Start Advanced Workflow Wizard. If you deployed the resource bundle correctly, the name and description of the workflow will match the text in the bundle. The wizard will appear as in Figure 7-7.

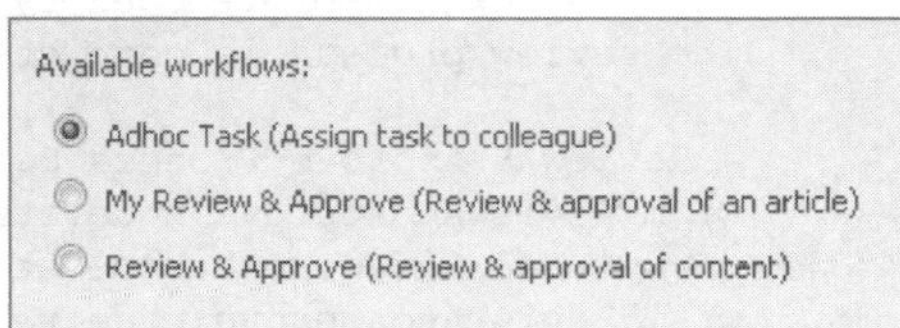

FIGURE 7-7

Configuring Task Property Pages

The Explorer Web client can auto-generate a task property page from the metadata defined in the task definition; however, you will normally want to customize this page. To do so, specify a Web client configuration in the file web-client-config-custom.xml in the folder *installLocation*\tomcat\shared\classes\alfresco\extension\. The following code snippet shows how to configure the tasks in the Review and Approve workflow example.

Available for download on Wrox.com

```
<config evaluator="node-type" condition="wf:mySubmitReviewTask" replace="true">
   <property-sheet>
      <separator name="sep1" display-label-id="general"
         component-generator="HeaderSeparatorGenerator" />
      <show-property name="bpm:workflowDescription"
         component-generator="TextAreaGenerator" />
      <show-property name="bpm:workflowPriority" />
      <show-property name="bpm:workflowDueDate" />
      <separator name="sep2" display-label-id="users_and_roles"
         component-generator="HeaderSeparatorGenerator" />
      <show-association name="bpm:assignee" />
```

```
      </property-sheet>
   </config>

   <config evaluator="node-type" condition="wf:myReviewTask" replace="true">
      <property-sheet>
         <separator name="sep1" display-label-id="general"
            component-generator="HeaderSeparatorGenerator" />
         <show-property name="bpm:taskId" />
         <show-property name="bpm:description"
         component-generator="TextAreaGenerator" read-only="true" />
         <show-property name="bpm:dueDate" read-only="true" />
         <show-property name="bpm:priority" read-only="true" />
         <show-property name="bpm:status" />
      </property-sheet>
```

</config>Code snippet web-client-config-custom.xml

Add this code snippet to the web-client-config-custom.xml file in the installLocation *\tomcat\alfresco\extension\ folder directly under the root <alfresco-config> element.*

Each task property sheet has a defined `<config>` element under the root `<alfresco-config>` element. The `evaluator` and `condition` attributes link `<config>` to a specific task. The `evaluator` must be set to `node-type` and the `condition` to the task name (including prefix). `<config>` should also specify a `replace` attribute set to true.

Each `<config>` element contains a `<property-sheet>` element. This element contains configuration for all the components to be displayed in the task property sheet. The order in which these components are listed in the configuration file determines the order in which they will appear on the screen in the task property sheet (seen in Figure 7-8).

Figure 7-8 shows the property sheet for the task `wf:mySubmitReviewTask`. Notice that inside the `<property-sheet>` element there are six elements that match up to the six components on the task property sheet user interface.

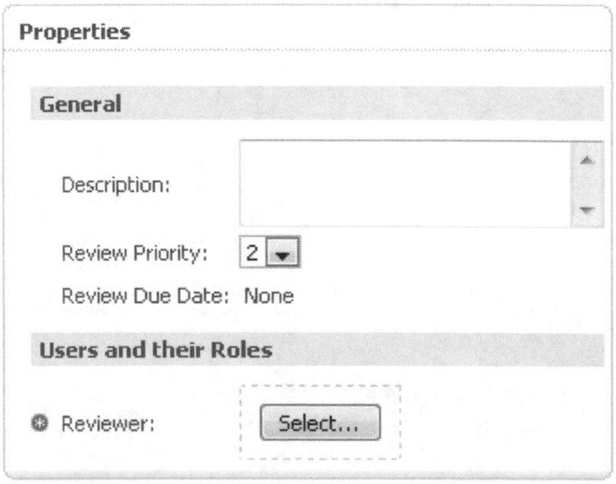

The `<separator>` element is used for adding labels or whitespace to the property sheet. In this case, the separator was used to add two headings. You can set the text in a separator using the `display-label-id` attribute, while the `component-generator` attribute determines what kind of separator component is created.

The `<show-property>` element is used to display attributes on the task definition. The `name` attribute should match the name of the attribute to be displayed. A read-only flag can be set to true to prevent users from editing the value; by default it is set to false.

FIGURE 7-8

The `component-generator` can be explicitly set to specify the type of component used to display the attribute. If no component generator is specified, the property sheet uses the type definition to deduce a sensible default component type to use. The different assignee properties (`bpm:assignee`, `bpm:groupAssignee`, and so on) all have special UI components associated with them to facilitate assigning people and groups to tasks.

Try configuring the task property sheets for the Review and Approve workflow example by adding the preceding code snippet to web-client-config-custom.xml. Once this is done, restart the Alfresco server, then go to the Start Advanced Workflow Wizard and start the My Review And Approve workflow. If the configuration was correct, the Workflow Options page of the wizard should resemble Figure 7-8. If you assign the workflow to yourself, you can then see the task in the My Alfresco dashboard in Alfresco Explorer.

PART III
Extending Alfresco with RESTful Services

8

Introducing Web Scripts

WHAT'S IN THIS CHAPTER?

- Understanding Web scripts
- Developing a Hello World Web script
- Exploring pre-built Web scripts
- Invoking Web scripts
- Working with client limitations

Alfresco Web scripts provide a unique way to programmatically interact with the Alfresco Content Application Server. Unlike other interfaces exposed by Alfresco, Web scripts offer a RESTful API for the content residing in the content repository. REST (Representational State Transfer) is an architectural style of which the Web architecture is the most prominent example, one based on HTTP requests and responses, URIs (Uniform Resource Identifiers), and document types.

The most exciting feature of Alfresco Web scripts is that they allow you to implement your own RESTful API. You do not need tooling or Java knowledge to create Web scripts; you simply need your favorite text editor or the Alfresco Explorer Web client: No compilation, generators, server restarts, or complex installs are required. This approach to developing an Alfresco API means that Web scripts offer many advantages over existing technologies, such as SOAP, including ease and speed of development, and flexibility in API design.

By focusing on the RESTful architectural style and ease of development, Web scripts allow you to simply build your own custom URI-identified and HTTP-accessible content management Web services backed by the Alfresco Content Application Server. It's like having an HTTP server with a built-in content repository allowing clients to easily access, manage, and cross-link content via a tailored RESTful interface designed specifically for the application requirements. It's this combination that has made Web scripts the first choice for integrating content-rich clients with the Alfresco Content Application Server.

Before diving into the technical details of Web scripts, it's a good idea to explore the architectural background that has made Web scripts so popular today. Alfresco Web scripts, introduced in 2006, brought together the worlds of content repository and the Web. There's a blindingly obvious synergy between the two.

Consider the Web: It's one huge single collection of interrelated documents. Physically, the documents are located in many machines and, in many data centers across the globe, stored and managed with many types of software. And yet, to the user, in a browser it's just one huge collection of information with easy-to-click links. This logical simplicity is all due to the underpinnings of the Web: HTTP, URIs, and HTML (and other types of documents, such as XML).

So, what does this have to do with Enterprise Content Management (ECM) repositories? ECM repositories are containers for important documents that are at the heart of enterprises. However, ECM repositories have traditionally provided proprietary access points, therefore restricting potential use of those documents. This is made worse when ECM repositories multiply within the enterprise. Those proprietary access points make it difficult to link documents between repositories.

Unlike the way that users on their home computers can access the world's collection of documents using just a browser, it can't be quite that easy within the enterprise. Here's why: Traditional ECM repository interfaces are Application Programming Interfaces (APIs), a collection of programmer methods for interacting with the repository where documents are often accessed by some kind of repository-specific identifier. These APIs are barriers to accessing the documents held within the repository: You can't get to the documents unless you have a tool that can speak to the API. This style of interface is broadly known as Remote Procedure Call (RPC). It turns out that RPC is not particularly suited to providing the capabilities of the Web, where distribution and uniform access of content is key. The Web underpinnings of HTTP, URIs, and media types follow the style known as REST, where procedure calls are no longer central. Instead, we have uniquely identified resources (for example, document, feed, stock price, person) via URIs, representations of those resources (for example, HTML, Atom, JSON) containing links to other resources, and a small, well-defined uniform interface for access (for example, HTTP GET, POST, PUT, and DELETE). So, until ECM repositories become RESTful, it will be difficult to write applications and services that can access all ECM-managed content distributed across the enterprise. Think back to the Web. The very essence of a uniform interface gave birth to Google (a search for the world's documents), Digg (a rating system for the world's documents), and Delicious (a bookmarking and categorization system for the world's documents). Within the enterprise, content-oriented services, such as Transformation, Encryption, Workflow, Entitlement, and Deployment, can flourish with a uniform interface.

Web scripts provide RESTful access to content held within your Alfresco content repository. This allows you to place controls on your content to manage it and, at the same time, provide uniform access for a wide variety of client applications and services, such as a browser, portal, search engine, or custom application. Because of the inherent distributed nature of this interface, all Alfresco content repositories within the enterprise can resemble one logical collection of inter-related documents, just like the Web. And as with any other Web citizen, you can apply Web technologies such as caching, authentication, proxies, and negotiation to your repository resources.

With Web scripts, you can either build your own RESTful interface using lightweight scripting technologies (such as JavaScript and FreeMarker), allowing you to arbitrarily map any content in the repository to resources on the Web, or you can use prebuilt out-of-the-box Web scripts that already encapsulate many of the mappings. In fact, Alfresco's CMIS (Content Management Interoperability Services) AtomPub binding is implemented as a series of Web scripts.

Since 2006, Web scripts have proven themselves exceedingly useful, being utilized in several solutions, including:

- Integrating Alfresco with third-party systems
- Providing feeds
- Developing data services
- Developing UI services such as portlets
- Customizing search
- Acting as a backend to client tools such as Orbeon Forms
- Integrating with Microsoft Office
- Developing Facebook applications
- Building UI components in Alfresco Surf

TYPES OF WEB SCRIPTS

A Web script is simply a service bound to a URI that responds to HTTP methods such as GET, POST, PUT, and DELETE. While using the same underlying code, there are broadly two kinds of Web scripts: data Web scripts and presentation Web scripts (as shown in Figure 8-1).

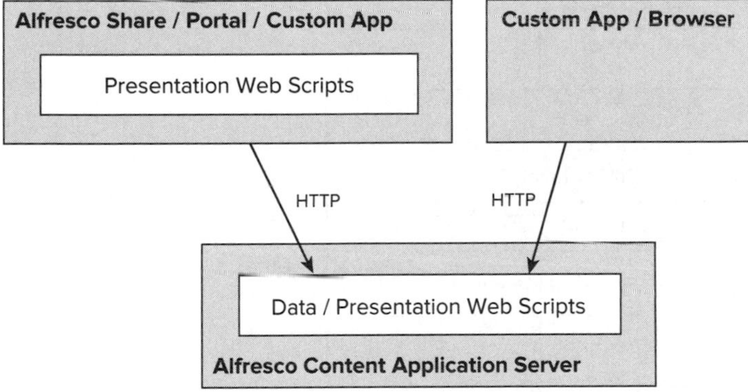

FIGURE 8-1

Data Web Scripts

Data Web scripts encapsulate access and modification of content/data held in the content repository; therefore, they are provided and exposed only by the Alfresco Content Application Server. Data Web scripts provide a server interface for client applications to query, retrieve, update, and perform processes, typically using request and response formats such as XML and JSON.

Presentation Web Scripts

Presentation Web scripts allow you to build user interfaces such as a dashlet for Alfresco Explorer or Alfresco Share, a portlet for a JSR-168 portal, a UI component within Alfresco Surf, a Web site, or a custom application. They typically render HTML (and perhaps include browser-hosted JavaScript). Unlike data Web scripts, presentation Web scripts may be hosted in the Alfresco Content Application Server or in a separate presentation server. When hosted separately, presentation Web scripts in the presentation server interact with data Web scripts in the Alfresco Content Application Server via HTTP (as shown in Figure 8-1).

THE WEB SCRIPT FRAMEWORK

As a developer, you may call existing Web scripts that have already been created or create your own Web scripts for scenarios that have not yet been catered for. For example, you can create your own Web script to expose a RESTful interface onto a custom content repository extension.

If you're familiar with the Model View Controller (MVC) design pattern, then you'll be familiar with how to create a Web script. Alfresco designed its Web Script Framework according to this pattern (as shown in Figure 8-2). Within the Alfresco community, the Web Script Framework is sometimes referred to as MVC for the Web.

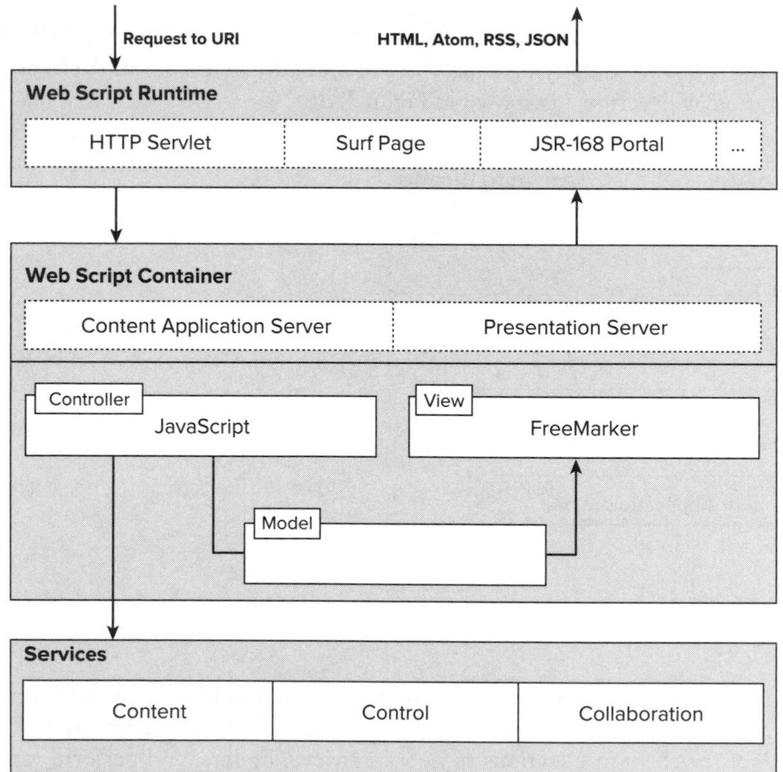

FIGURE 8-2

One of the primary design goals of the Web Script Framework is to make it as simple as possible to create a Web script using technologies that are familiar to a broad base of developers, such as scripting and template languages. Therefore, each Web script comprises only the following components:

- **A description document** — This describes the URI and HTTP method that will initiate the Web script. For example, the Web script is given a short name and description, along with authentication and transactional needs. URI bindings are described as URI templates.
- **An optional controller script** — Written in JavaScript, this will do the actual work. For example, the script may query the Alfresco content repository to build a set of data items, known as a *model*, to render in the response; or for URIs that intend to modify the repository (hopefully, PUT, POST, and DELETE method bindings), the script may update the Alfresco repository. The JavaScript has access to the URI query string, Alfresco Content Application Services, and content repository data entry points.
- **One or more FreeMarker response templates** — Known as *views*, these will render output in the correct format for your specific needs (for example, HTML, Atom, XML, RSS, JSON, CSV, or any combination of these). The HTTP response is rendered via one of the supplied templates, where the chosen template is based on the required response content type or status outcome. The template has access to the URI query string, common repository data entry points, and any data items built by the optional controller script.

Each of the different components (description document, controller scripts, and templates) is a simple text file that is placed into the Alfresco Content Application Server. To simplify registration of the files, the Web Script Framework employs convention over configuration, where each of the file names adheres to a file-naming convention as defined by the Web Script Framework. For example, all description document file names must end with `.desc.xml`. This allows the Web Script Framework to automatically find and register all created Web scripts. (How to create a Web script is discussed fully in Chapter 9.)

In some cases, a Web script may fall back to Java or rely on advanced Web Script Framework features where scripting alone cannot support the requirements of the Web script. This is unusual, but useful on those rare occasions. (Advanced implementations are discussed in more detail in Chapter 10 and Java-backed implementations are discussed further in Chapter 11.)

The components of a Web script are only of concern to the developer who created the Web script. That is, they are implementation and private details that do not need to be known by those who just wish to use the Web script. Users of a Web script only interact through the Web script interface, which comprises its URI, HTTP method, and request/response document types. All of these are described in the Web script description document as defined by the creator of the Web script.

HELLO WORLD WEB SCRIPT

It's time to dive in and build a Web script. This is the best way to gain an understanding of the Web Script Framework and appreciate how simple it is to develop your own Web script.

As is customary, we'll start with a Hello World example that is simple enough to build and execute within a few minutes. This example will consist of one Web script description document and one FreeMarker response template, both created via Alfresco Explorer.

Okay, let's get started.

1. You first need to log in to Alfresco Explorer.

   a. Type the following in your Web browser, and log in with the user name `admin` and password `admin` if requested:

      ```
      http://localhost:8080/alfresco
      ```

   b. Navigate to Company Home > Data Dictionary > Web Scripts Extensions.

2. Create a Web script description document for your Hello World example.

   a. In the Create menu, click Create Content.

   b. Enter the name for the Web script in the Name field, as follows:

      ```
      hello.get.desc.xml
      ```

   c. In the Content Type list, select XML.

   d. Click Next.

   e. Type the following in the Enter Content box:

Available for download on Wrox.com

```
<webscript>
  <shortname>Hello</shortname>
  <description>Polite greeting</description>
  <url>/hello</url>
</webscript>
```

hello.get.desc.xml

   f. Click Next.

   g. Click Finish.

   h. Click OK.

3. Next create a Web script response template to render the Hello World greeting.

   a. In the Create menu, click Create Content.

   b. Enter the name in the Name field, such as:

      ```
      hello.get.html.ftl
      ```

   c. In the Content Type list, select Plain Text.

   d. Click Next.

   e. Type the following in the Enter Content box:

Available for download on Wrox.com

```
Hello World
```

hello.get.html.ftl

   f. Click Next.

   g. Click Finish.
   h. Click OK.
4. Now register the Hello World Web script with Alfresco.
   a. Type the following in your Web browser, and log in with the user name `admin` and password `admin` if requested:

      ```
      http://localhost:8080/alfresco/service/index
      ```

   b. Click Refresh Web Scripts. You'll see a message indicating there is one additional Web script.
5. Finally, it's time to test.
   a. Type the following in your Web browser:

      ```
      http://localhost:8080/alfresco/service/hello
      ```

   b. If you see a Hello World message, your Web script is working.

The URL typed into your Web browser caused the Alfresco Web Script Framework to kick into action. It's triggered whenever a URL starting with `/alfresco/service` is invoked. First, the Web Script Framework determines which Web script to invoke by matching the remainder of the URL and the HTTP method of the HTTP request (in this case, a GET request from the Web browser) to the appropriate registered Web script descriptor, if one matches. The Hello World Web script is matched to the URL `/hello` as defined by its Web script descriptor file named `hello.get.desc.xml`.

Having found a Web script, the Web Script Framework executes it by first invoking its controller script, if one exists, and then invoking its response template to render an HTTP response. The simple Hello World example does not consist of a controller script and does not define a default kind of response to render, so the Web Script Framework assumes an HTML response is to be rendered and locates the FreeMarker template named `hello.get.html.ftl`. The template renders an HTML response back to the Web browser, which in turn displays `Hello World`.

LISTING ALREADY-BUILT WEB SCRIPTS

Our Hello World example demonstrates how to create the simplest of Web scripts, but there are plenty of pre-built Web scripts provided out of the box for you to reuse. In fact, before you go ahead and spend time developing a new Web script, you should always check to see if one already exists that supports your requirements or is near enough. This can save you a lot of time.

So, how do you establish what's already available? The Web Script Framework keeps an index of all Web scripts registered in your Alfresco Content Application Server. In your Web browser, type the following URI and, if requested, log in with the user name `admin` and password `admin` to display an HTML page of the index:

```
http://localhost:8080/alfresco/service/index
```

The index contains an entry for each registered Web script and provides several ways to navigate through them. It's not unusual for hundreds of Web scripts to be registered, so the index organizes Web scripts by their URI, Web script package, and Web script family to ease navigation and to help you find an appropriate Web script for reuse. A Web script package is a collection of related Web scripts, such as those for integrating with Microsoft Office or those providing the CMIS AtomPub binding. A Web script family identifies Web scripts of a similar kind, such as portlets and Share dashlets. Think of families as a way of tagging or categorizing Web scripts.

For each Web script, a full description is given, including its URIs for invocation. For the curious, it's also possible to drill down into the implementation of the Web script, allowing you to see its descriptor, controller script, and response template components. This can be very useful as a learning resource or as the basis for a copy/paste approach to creating new Web scripts.

One of the most useful uses of the index is to determine if a Web script actually exists. When invoking a Web script URI, the Web Script Framework may respond with a Not Found error. This can be due to an incorrectly formed URI or because the Web script is not registered at all. To determine which, navigate the index to see if the Web Script Framework knows of it. To locate the Hello World example, visit the Web script index (as shown in Figure 8-3) and select the Browse by Web Script URI link. Use the Web browser search feature to locate `/hello` within the page. Once found, click the `/hello` link to display the full description of the Hello World Web script.

FIGURE 8-3

You may have noticed that the Web script index URI starts with `/alfresco/service`. That's correct; the Web script index is itself just another Web script. In fact, the index is a series of Web scripts, each providing a different navigation of the index at the following URIs:

```
http://localhost:8080/alfresco/service/index/uri/
```

```
http://localhost:8080/alfresco/service/index/package/
```

In addition, the Web script index provides some administration of Web scripts, in particular for those who develop new Web scripts. As seen earlier in this chapter when creating the Hello World example, the index provides a Refresh Web Scripts button that asks the Web Script Framework to find all Web scripts it can and register them with Alfresco. If there happens to be an issue with the registration of a Web script, the index also provides a list of Web scripts that failed registration, along with the reason for failing.

As you'll notice from the Web script index, Alfresco provides hundreds of pre-built, out-of-the-box Web scripts with the Alfresco Content Application Server. These Web scripts offer a rich interface for interacting with the server, covering all sorts of capabilities, such as:

- Alfresco API for interacting with all of the features of the Alfresco Content Application Server, such as tagging, activities, and site management
- CMIS (Content Management Interoperability Services) for standards-based access to the Alfresco content repository
- OpenSearch for keyword searching of the Alfresco content repository
- Office Integration for hosting in Microsoft Office

Alfresco Spring Surf also provides pre-built presentation Web scripts for hosting inside or outside the Alfresco Content Application Server, such as:

- Portlets for hosting in any JSR-168 portal, such as Inbox and My Checked-Out Documents
- Alfresco Share dashlets for exposing capabilities in personal and site dashboards

It is always worth browsing the list of available pre-built Web scripts before developing your own, as there is a good chance that something already exists to suit your needs. The Alfresco Share application communicates with the Alfresco Content Application Server exclusively via Web scripts, and this alone is a rich a set of Web scripts to explore.

WHERE CAN I INVOKE A WEB SCRIPT?

You have seen from the Hello World example that a Web script can be invoked from a Web browser. This is a common client for Web scripts, as many content-rich applications are Web applications. The Web browser also provides an easy and convenient client for testing Web scripts while developing them.

However, the Web browser is not the exclusive client from which to invoke a Web script. Any client capable of sending HTTP requests and receiving HTTP responses may be used. A good example is the cURL client, which has full support for the HTTP protocol and is often used for testing the various capabilities of Web scripts. (cURL is discussed in more detail in the next section.)

Although a client may use HTTP directly to invoke Web scripts, the Web Script Framework also provides many helpers for invoking Web scripts from environments that do not know HTTP. This allows the invocation of a Web script using a mechanism that is natural to the calling environment and to the developer who knows the calling environment. For example, helpers are provided that allow the following clients to naturally invoke Web scripts:

- **Alfresco Surf** — Allows the invocation of a Web script as if it were a Surf component; for example, to create a Share dashlet

- **JSR-168 portal** — Allows the invocation of a Web script as if it were a JSR-168 portlet
- **JSF page** — Allows the invocation of a Web script as if it were a tag library

A carefully developed Web script may be used from multiple environments without the need to change its implementation. For example, a Web script for displaying your Alfresco checked-out documents may be used standalone directly in a Web browser, as a portlet in a JSR-168 portal, or as a dashlet in Alfresco Share.

Using cURL Instead of a Web Browser

When exploring or developing Web scripts, a Web browser can be limiting as a client. For example, it cannot perform any HTTP method other than GET without coding. An alternative client that's worth becoming familiar with is cURL (`http://curl.haxx.se/`), which is a command line tool that supports common protocols such as FTP and HTTP. If you are using Linux or Mac OS X, you can install cURL through apt-get or MacPorts. If you are running Microsoft Windows, cURL may be installed through Cygwin.

Once cURL is installed, you can invoke your Hello World example. Type the following in your command line:

```
curl "http://localhost:8080/alfresco/service/hello"
```

This informs cURL to invoke the URL defined by your Hello World Web script, which returns:

```
Hello World
```

It's worth becoming familiar with cURL, as it is an invaluable Web script debugging and testing tool. cURL will be explored further as you learn more about Web scripts.

RESTClient (`http://code.google.com/p/rest-client/`), a Java application for testing RESTful Web services, is also worth investigating for testing your Web scripts.

AUTHENTICATING

The Hello World example may be invoked without first authenticating; that is, without specifying a user name and password to identify you. When interacting with the Alfresco Content Application Server this is rare, as in most cases access to or management of content in the content repository is restricted to particular people or groups of people.

To support restricted access, a Web script can specify its authentication requirements. There are four levels of required authentication:

- **None** — The Web script does not require any authentication to be invoked.
- **Guest** — The Web script may be invoked by a guest user of the Alfresco Content Application Server.

- **User** — The Web script must be invoked by a named user known to the Alfresco Content Application Server.
- **Admin** — The Web script must be invoked by a named user who is an administrator of the Alfresco Content Application Server.

An authenticated Web script has access to all the services of the Alfresco Content Application Server and thus can perform any operation, although it still adheres to the permissions of the authenticated user.

Creating the Hello User Web Script

Now it is time to make a slightly more interesting Hello World example named Hello User that requires authenticated access and responds with a personalized greeting.

1. You first need to log in to Alfresco Explorer.
   a. Type the following in your Web browser, and log in with the user name `admin` and password `admin` if requested:

      ```
      http://localhost:8080/alfresco
      ```

   b. Navigate to Company Home > Data Dictionary > Web Scripts Extensions.
2. Create a Web script description document for the Hello User example.
   a. In the Create menu, click Create Content.
   b. Enter the name for the Web script in the Name field, such as:

      ```
      hellouser.get.desc.xml
      ```

   c. In the Content Type list, select XML.
   d. Click Next.
   e. Type the following in the Enter Content box:

Available for download on Wrox.com

```
<webscript>
  <shortname>Hello User</shortname>
  <description>Personalized greeting</description>
  <url>/hellouser</url>
  <authentication>user</authentication>
  <negotiate accept="text/html">html</negotiate>
  <negotiate accept="application/json">json</negotiate>
</webscript>
```

hellouser.get.desc.xml

   f. Click Next.
   g. Click Finish.
   h. Click OK.

3. Next create a Web script response template to render your Hello User greeting.

   a. In the Create menu, click Create Content.

   b. Enter the name in the Name field, such as:

      ```
      hellouser.get.html.ftl
      ```

   c. In the Content Type list, select Plain Text.

   d. Click Next.

   e. Type the following in the Enter Content box:

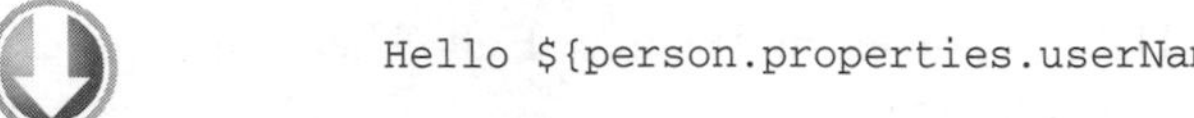

```
Hello ${person.properties.userName}
```

Available for download on Wrox.com

hellouser.get.html.ftl

   f. Click Next.

   g. Click Finish.

   h. Click OK.

4. Now register the Hello User Web script with Alfresco.

   a. Type the following in your Web browser, and log in with the user name `admin` and password `admin` if requested:

      ```
      http://localhost:8080/alfresco/service/index
      ```

   b. Click Refresh Web Scripts. You'll see a message indicating there is one additional Web script.

5. Finally, it's time to test.

   a. Type the following in your Web browser, and log in with the user name `admin` and password `admin` if requested:

      ```
      http://localhost:8080/alfresco/service/hellouser
      ```

   b. If you see a Hello admin message, your Web script is working.

The Hello User Web script required user-level authentication in its `hellouser.get.desc.xml` descriptor file. This indicated to the Web Script Framework that prior to invoking the Web script, a user has to first log in. By default, the Web Script Framework initiates the login process through HTTP Basic authentication, which informs the Web browser to display a login box for the user to enter their user name and password. Upon successful authentication, which is performed by the Alfresco Content Application Server, the Web script is invoked. Otherwise, the process stops and the invocation of the Web script fails.

Having found the `hellouser.get.html.ftl` response template, the Web Script Framework renders its result back to the Web browser. The template, which is now running as an authenticated user, has access to special Alfresco Content Application Server objects. In this case, the template renders the name of the authenticated user through the object `${person.properties.userName}`.

HTTP Basic authentication is a method designed to allow a Web browser or other client program to provide credentials in the form of a user name and password when making an HTTP request.

Specifying User Identity

There are several options for specifying the user with which to invoke a Web script: HTTP Basic authentication, Alfresco Ticket, or as a Guest.

HTTP Basic authentication allows you to specify your user name and password within an HTTP request. A request to a Web script can include the user name and password of the Alfresco user to authenticate as, meaning the client does not have to ask for them. The cURL client supports this feature. Type the following in your command line:

```
curl -uadmin:admin "http://localhost:8080/alfresco/service/hellouser"
```

This informs cURL to invoke the URL defined by your Hello User Web script as the user admin, which returns:

```
Hello admin
```

When comparing this to invoking the Hello User Web script through the Web browser, you can see that the cURL client did not subsequently ask for the user name and password, whereas the Web browser did.

Upon successful authentication, a client may remember that the current session is authenticated, thus requiring the authentication process to be initiated only once. For example, if you've already logged in using the current Web browser session, you won't be asked to log in again.

The next option is to specify an Alfresco Ticket instead of an explicit user name and password. A ticket represents a pre-authenticated user who has already performed the login process. Tickets can be programmatically established via the pre-built Login Web script. To log in, type the following in your command line:

```
curl "http://localhost:8080/alfresco/service/api/login?u=admin&pw=admin"
```

This informs cURL to invoke the URL defined by the Login Web script, which returns XML similar to the following:

```
<?xml version="1.0" encoding="UTF-8"?>
<ticket>TICKET_0a748bc2543f2b271dc4cb9955c11a042cad72cd</ticket>
```

With a ticket established, it's possible to invoke other Web scripts with that ticket, indicating to the Web Script Framework to execute the Web script as the user represented by the ticket. This is achieved by adding the following URL query parameter to the Web script URL:

```
alf_ticket=<ticket>
```

To execute the Hello User Web script with a ticket, type the following in your command line, substituting the ticket with the value returned from your Web script login:

```
curl "http://localhost:8080/alfresco/service/
hellouser?alf_ticket=TICKET_0a748bc2543f2b271dc4cb9955c11a042cad72cd"
```

The final option is to specify that a Web script be executed as an Alfresco guest. Guests are not named users, so do not need to log in; however, they may be restricted in what they can see or do in the Alfresco content repository. Guest invocation is achieved by adding the following URL query parameter to the Web script URL:

```
guest=true
```

Remember, guests can only invoke Web scripts that require Guest authentication; they cannot invoke User or Admin required Web scripts. To invoke the Hello User Web script as guest, type the following in your command line:

```
curl "http://localhost:8080/alfresco/service/hellouser?guest=true"
```

You might expect this to respond with a polite greeting, but instead you'll receive a 401 error message stating that the Hello User Web script requires user authentication and a guest has attempted access.

Custom Client Authentication

When Web scripts are invoked from a client environment such as a JSR-168 portal or Alfresco Share, the Web Script Framework provides special support for authentication. The reason for this is that these clients provide their own login mechanism, which the Web Script Framework plugs into.

Imagine you're using the Alfresco checked-out documents Web script as a JSR-168 portlet configured into your portal. When you launch the portal, the portal itself will ask you to log in. The Web script needs to know who is authenticated, so the Web Script Framework communicates with the portal to determine the currently authenticated user. When the Web script is rendered in the portal page, the Web script is invoked as the portal user.

Behind the scenes, the Web Script Framework chooses the most appropriate option for specifying the user identity, either HTTP Basic authentication, ticket, or guest when invoking the Web script. The same mechanism is used for Alfresco Share.

RESPONSE FORMATS

The Hello World example has so far returned only HTML. While this is fine for rendering a user interface, it's not so good for a data Web script that needs to return a format that is machine-readable, such as JSON.

JSON, short for JavaScript Object Notation, is a lightweight data interchange format, often used for transmitting structured data over a network connection.

A Web script may offer multiple response formats, where each format is supported by its own response template. Clients that invoke the Web script either rely on the default response format or can explicitly ask for a specific response format.

Adding a Response Format to the Hello User Web Script

Now add another response format to your Hello User Web script that returns the greeting in JSON format.

1. You first need to log in to Alfresco Explorer.
   a. Type the following in your Web browser, and log in with the user name `admin` and password `admin` if requested:

      ```
      http://localhost:8080/alfresco
      ```

   b. Navigate to Company Home > Data Dictionary > Web Scripts Extensions.
2. Create a new Web script response template to render your Hello User greeting in JSON.
   a. In the Create menu, click Create Content.
   b. Enter the name in the Name field, such as:

      ```
      hellouser.get.json.ftl
      ```

   c. In the Content Type list, select Plain Text.
   d. Click Next.
   e. Type the following in the Enter Content box:

      ```
      {greeting: "hello", user: "${person.properties.userName}"}
      ```

      hellouser.get.json.ftl

   f. Click Next.
   g. Click Finish.
   h. Click OK.
3. Now re-register the Hello User Web script with Alfresco.
   a. Type the following in your command line, and log in with the user name `admin` and password `admin` if requested:

      ```
      http://localhost:8080/alfresco/service/index
      ```

   b. Click Refresh Web Scripts.
4. Finally, it's time to test.
   a. Type the following in your command line:

      ```
      curl -uadmin:admin "http://localhost:8080/alfresco/service/hellouser.json"
      ```

   b. If you see a `{greeting: "hello", user: "admin"}` message, your Web script is working.

Selecting a Response Format

There are several ways for a client to explicitly select a response format: URL extension, URL query parameter, and Accept header.

The URL extension approach simply requires the URL to end with the format of the response to select:

```
<webscript url>.<format>
```

As you've seen already with your Hello User Web script, type one of the following statements in your command line to explicitly select either HTML or JSON:

```
curl -uadmin:admin "http://localhost:8080/alfresco/service/hellouser.json"
curl -uadmin:admin "http://localhost:8080/alfresco/service/hellouser.html"
```

Sometimes, it's not possible for a Web script URL to support the format extension approach, as the URL may naturally end with an extension anyway. For example, Web script URL paths that refer to folder and file names in the content repository already have the extension inherited from the file name. For these scenarios, it's possible to explicitly select the response format via the URL query parameter:

```
<webscript url>?format=<format>
```

To explicitly select the response format for the Hello User Web script using the URL query parameter, type one of the following statements in your command line:

```
curl -uadmin:admin "http://localhost:8080/alfresco/service/hellouser?format=json"
curl -uadmin:admin "http://localhost:8080/alfresco/service/hellouser?format=html"
```

What exactly are these formats? Each format actually maps to a MIME type, which is set on the HTTP response, allowing a client to process or render the response appropriately. The Web Script Framework provides a registry of formats where the commonly used MIME types are mapped as follows:

- html => text/html
- text => text/plain
- xml => text/xml
- atom => application/atom+xml
- rss => application/rss+xml
- json => application/json

Another approach to selecting a response format is to use the HTTP Accept header, as defined by RFC 2616 section 14. A client uses an Accept header to specify a prioritized list of preferred MIME types for the response. When the Web Script Framework accepts an HTTP request with an Accept header, it responds with the response format that most closely matches the highest-priority preference.

RFC 2616 (`www.ietf.org/rfc/rfc2616.txt`) is the specification for the Hypertext Transfer Protocol – HTTP/1.1.

Web browsers typically provide an Accept header on all their HTTP requests, but most HTTP clients offer some way of specifying an Accept header. For example, using cURL, the following command line specifies an Accept header when invoking the Hello User Web script:

```
curl -uadmin:admin -H "Accept: text/html"
"http://localhost:8080/alfresco/service/hellouser"
```

If a client does not explicitly request a specific response format, the Web script uses its predefined default response format.

ANATOMY OF A WEB SCRIPT URI

Web scripts are invoked through their defined URIs, but what exactly is the structure of a Web script URI? Luckily, every Web script URI follows the same form, so it's worth spending some time understanding how they are constructed. This will help you formulate URIs when developing your own Web scripts, as well as ease the calling of existing pre-built Web scripts.

A Web script URI is of the form:

```
http[s]://<host>:<port>/[<contextPath>/]/<servicePath>[/<scriptPath>]
[?<scriptArgs>]
```

The `host`, `port`, and `contextPath` are all predefined by where the Alfresco Content Application Server is installed. By default, the `contextPath` is `alfresco`, although the person who installed Alfresco may have changed this.

The Web Script Framework is mapped to `servicePath`. All Alfresco Content Application Server URL requests that start with `/<contextPath>/<servicePath>` trigger the Web Script Framework into action on the assumption that a Web script is to be invoked. By default, there are two variations of `servicePath` that are acceptable: `/service` and an abbreviated version `/s`.

Your Hello User Web script may be invoked through both of the following URIs:

```
curl -uadmin:admin "http://localhost:8080/alfresco/service/hellouser"
curl -uadmin:admin "http://localhost:8080/alfresco/s/hellouser"
```

The `scriptPath` identifies the Web script to invoke and is defined by the Web script itself. It must be unique within an Alfresco Content Application Server. In fact, duplicate URIs will result in a Web script registration failure and one of the URIs will have to be adjusted before successful registration. A `scriptPath` can be as simple or as complex as required and may consist of many path segments. For example, the CMIS Web script URI to retrieve children of a folder residing in the content repository contains the folder path. The following command line retrieves the children of the Data Dictionary folder as an Atom feed:

```
curl -uadmin:admin "http://localhost:8080/alfresco/s/cmis/p/Data%20Dictionary/
children"
```

Finally, a Web script URI may support query parameters as defined by the Web script to control its behavior. For example, the CMIS Web script to retrieve folder children can be restricted to return only documents, filtering out folders:

```
curl -uadmin:admin "http://localhost:8080/alfresco/s/cmis/p/Data%20Dictionary/
children?types=documents"
```

Remember, there are some query parameters that apply to all Web script invocations, such as `alf_ticket` and `format`, which may be mixed with Web script–specific parameters.

```
curl -uadmin:admin "http://localhost:8080/alfresco/s/cmis/p/Data%20Dictionary/
children?types=documents&format=atomfeed"
```

When in doubt about how to construct a URI for a given Web script, always consult its Web script descriptor file, which you can find via the Web script index.

WORKING WITH CLIENT LIMITATIONS

It's an unfortunate reality that not all HTTP clients are equivalent in their capabilities. Many clients have limitations that mean certain HTTP features are not supported. Rather than dismiss those clients and reduce the scope of where Web scripts may be invoked, the Web Script Framework provides helpers for working around those limitations.

Tunneling HTTP Methods

Not all clients can issue all HTTP methods. In the most severe case, a client may be restricted to GET and POST only. In this situation, the Web Script Framework provides a mechanism for tunneling any HTTP method through a POST method. This is achieved by setting an override header named `X-HTTP-Method-Override` on the HTTP request whose value is the method name to invoke.

For example, to invoke the Hello World Web script through an HTTP POST but inform the Web Script Framework to really perform a GET, type the following command line:

```
curl -d "" -H "X-HTTP-Method-Override:GET" http://localhost:8080/alfresco/s/hello
```

cURL's `-d` parameter informs cURL to perform an HTTP POST. The complete cURL manual is found at `http://curl.haxx.se/docs/manual.html`.

In really unfortunate circumstances, some clients do not even support HTTP headers; therefore, the Web Script Framework also supports a query parameter named `alf_method` for representing the method to override. Type the following in your command line for the equivalent of the override header, but expressed as a query parameter:

```
curl -d "" http://localhost:8080/alfresco/s/hello?alf_method=GET
```

Tunneling HTTP methods is a last resort that should only be used when no other workaround is available. Each HTTP method has its own characteristics, such as how it's cached, which HTTP clients and intermediaries expect. When tunneling these methods through HTTP POST, those expectations can no longer be met.

If both the override header and query parameter are specified in the HTTP request, then the header takes precedence over the query parameter.

Method overrides are also supported when issuing HTTP GET requests through the `alf_method` query parameter. This is particularly useful for testing some non-GET methods via the Web browser.

Forcing Success Response Status

Not all clients can gracefully handle non-success HTTP response codes, such as the Adobe Flash runtime player, which is the runtime for Adobe Flex applications.

In this situation, Web scripts provide a mechanism to force an HTTP response to indicate success in its response header; however, the response body will still represent the content as if a non-success status had occurred, allowing a client to interrogate error codes and messages, if provided by the Web script.

To force success, the `alf-force-success-response` header is set on the HTTP request whose value is always set to true. For example, to force a success response status for a request to retrieve children of a folder that does not exist, type the following in your command line:

```
curl -uadmin:admin -v -H "alf-force-success-response:true"
"http://localhost:8080/alfresco/s/cmis/p/doesnotexist"
```

Although the response status code is 200 (which means Success), the body of the response will still represent a failure and include details such as the real status code (in this case, 404, which means Not Found) and an error message.

JSON Callbacks

Web scripts that provide JSON responses are often invoked directly from within a Web browser via the `XMLHttpRequest` object. This is a technique popularly known as AJAX. For security reasons, solutions like these may run into cross-domain issues, a restriction that requires you to proxy your requests on the server side. Typically, to work around these issues, public services, such as Yahoo! JSON Services, provide a callback mechanism.

A full description of the JSON callback mechanism can be found at `http://developer.yahoo.com/common/json.html#callbackparam` *on the Yahoo! Developer Network.*

Web scripts also provide this mechanism, which wraps the JSON response text in parentheses and a function name of your choosing. A callback is invoked by adding the following URL query parameter to the Web script request:

```
alf_callback=<function>
```

The `function` parameter specifies the name of a client-side JavaScript function to invoke.

Now create a simple HTML page that invokes the Hello User Web script with a callback that displays the JSON response in an alert box:

1. You first need to create the HTML page.
   a. Create a file named `callback.html` on your machine's local file system.

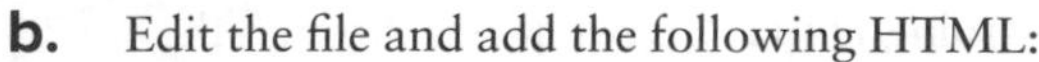

b. Edit the file and add the following HTML:

Available for download on Wrox.com

```
<html>
<body>
<script>
// callback function to display greeting
function showGreeting(res) {alert(res.greeting + ' ' + res.user);}
// invoke web script hello user web script
var script = document.createElement('SCRIPT');
script.type = 'text/javascript';
script.src = 'http://localhost:8080/alfresco/s/hellouser.json?alf_callback=
showGreeting';
document.body.appendChild(script);
</script>
</body>
</html>
```

callback.html

2. Next, it's time to test the callback.

a. Open the `callback.html` file in your Web browser, and log in with the user name `admin` and password `admin` if requested.

b. If you see an alert box displaying `hello admin`, your callback is working.

The easiest way to understand the callback example is to invoke your Hello User Web script directly and interrogate the response. Type the following in your command line, which mimics the Web script invocation made in the `callback.html` file:

```
curl -uadmin:admin "http://localhost:8080/alfresco/s/hellouser.json?alf_callback=
showGreeting"
```

The response is:

```
showGreeting({greeting: "hello", user: "admin"})
```

This is simply the vanilla Hello User Web script response passed as an argument to the function named `showGreeting` as defined by the `alf_callback` query parameter. The full response is treated as JavaScript by the Web browser, which executes it.

CACHING

An important consideration when developing any application is that it meets its performance requirements, even as user demand grows. An application built on Web scripts has the ability to introduce caching to support these demands.

The Web Script Framework does not invent its own caching approach, but instead relies on the caching protocol defined by HTTP. Each Web script specifies how it is to be cached, which the Web Script Framework translates into appropriate HTTP headers when it is invoked. A third-party HTTP cache that is deployed as part of the application then caches the Web script response.

It is often necessary to cache the retrieval of content streams of documents residing in the Alfresco content repository as these can be large in size. One way to handle this situation (as shown in

Figure 8-4) is to put an HTTP cache proxy between the Alfresco Content Application Server and the client (for example, a Web browser).

There is a Web script that you can use for retrieving the content stream of a document residing in the content repository. This Web script is CMIS-compliant, supports HTTP caching requirements, and, best of all, is available out of the box. With the HTTP cache proxy installed, the content responses are cached intelligently and the cache is only updated when the content is updated in the content repository. This setup will also cache all other responses from Web scripts that indicate how they are to be cached.

Web script caching is described in greater detail in Chapter 10.

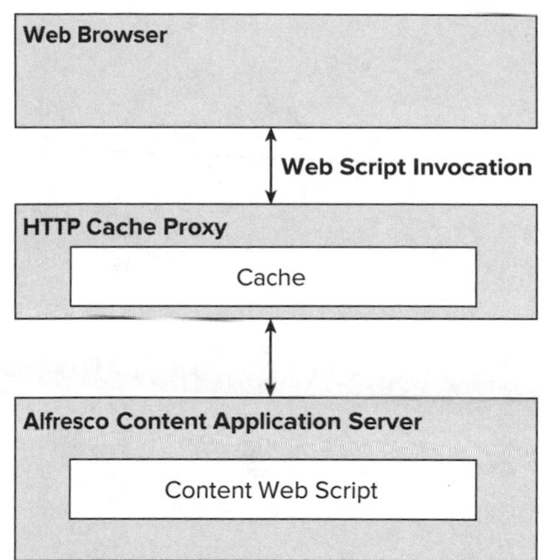

FIGURE 8-4

How to Create a Web Script

WHAT'S IN THIS CHAPTER?

- Understanding Web script components
- Developing a Folder Listing Web script
- Accessing Alfresco services
- Debugging Web scripts
- Creating the Knowledge Base Search Web script

In this chapter you'll discover how to create your own Web scripts. The Web Script Framework is designed with the developer in mind, aiming to make it as easy and quick as possible to create new Web scripts in order to construct a RESTful interface to the Alfresco Content Application Server.

Web scripts are implemented using lightweight scripting languages such as JavaScript and FreeMarker, so their development is not restricted to only those who know the Java language. One of the key advantages of using scripting languages is that minimal tooling is required. An example of this is that there is no need to compile or package a Web script implementation. This simplicity also removes the need for a complex development environment. In fact, Web scripts can be built using only a basic text editor or even just the Alfresco Explorer client.

Scripting also brings immediacy to the development of Web scripts by removing the painful steps of compilation and packaging. It is possible to quickly turn around implementation changes, which can be seen and tested just by refreshing your Web browser. This mode of development has become very attractive to the Alfresco community, making Web scripts a preferred approach to interacting with, integrating with, and extending Alfresco.

To develop a Web script, you'll need to understand the following technologies:

- XML for expressing the Web script description
- JavaScript for writing the Web script logic
- FreeMarker for rendering the Web script response

This chapter will take you step-by-step through the development process of a Web script. You will first build a Web script that provides the ability to list the contents of a folder in the Alfresco content repository: that is, the equivalent of the `dir` command in Microsoft Windows, or `ls` in Linux or Mac OS X. Along the way, you'll be introduced to the features of the Web Script Framework, so that by the end you'll be knowledgeable enough to tackle the development of the back-end search capability of the Knowledge Base sample application. Don't panic; you'll step through that one too.

Now you can get started.

COMPONENTS OF A WEB SCRIPT

Before you start writing code, it's worth stepping back and taking a high-level view of how a Web script is constructed. A Web script is comprised of the following components (as shown in Figure 9-1): a description document, a controller script, and one or more response templates (which are MVC views).

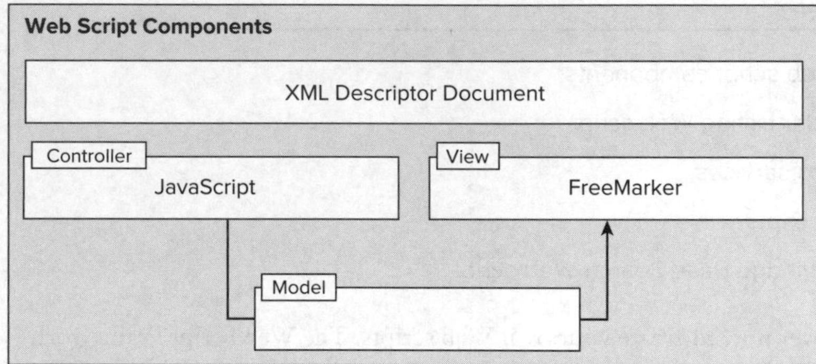

FIGURE 9-1

The description document, expressed in XML, describes the Web script — in particular its URI and HTTP method binding. It's also used to configure some of the Web script behavior, such as its authentication and transactional needs.

The controller script, written in JavaScript, is where the actual logic of the Web script is contained. For example, the JavaScript may query or perform actions against content residing in the Alfresco content repository. The output of the JavaScript is a model (a set of data) to render in the Web script response. Context such as the URI used to invoke the Web script and the currently authenticated user is available to the JavaScript.

The response template, written in FreeMarker, renders the output for the response in the requested format, such as HTML, XML, or JSON. Access to the model generated by the controller script is provided, as well as the same context available to invoke the Web script.

Each component is implemented in its own file. The Web Script Framework dictates where the files are to be located and also how they are named. This allows the framework to automatically locate and register Web scripts without you having to tell the framework where they are. This is an approach commonly known as convention over configuration, and is one that the Web Script Framework employs often to ease development of Web scripts.

So, where do you place Web script component files? You actually have two choices: in the file system within the Java classpath, or in the Alfresco content repository. The Web Script Framework searches for Web scripts in the following order:

- In the content repository under the folder `/Company Home/Data Dictionary/Web Scripts Extensions`
- In the content repository under the folder `/Company Home/Data Dictionary/Web Scripts`
- In the classpath under the folder `/alfresco/extension/templates/webscripts`
- In the classpath under the folder `/alfresco/templates/webscripts`

Placing Web scripts in the classpath allows you to package them and deploy them with other extensions that make up your solution. It means they can be installed using standard Alfresco tools without the extra step of uploading them into the content repository; however, the ability to edit them while developing them may not be as convenient as if they were located in the Alfresco content repository, where they can be easily edited using Alfresco Explorer or Share. Web scripts located in the content repository may also be exported and imported using the ACP (Alfresco Content Package) mechanism.

For a default installation of Alfresco, the classpath is located at installLocation*/tomcat/shared/classes/alfresco/extension.*

It's worth considering that a single Alfresco Content Application Server may contain hundreds of Web scripts, each implemented with multiple files. To assist the management of all these Web scripts, the Web Script Framework allows you to organize Web script component files into a hierarchical folder or package structure. If you're familiar with Java, you'll see that it's very similar to Java's package construct. Typically, the package name follows the reverse domain name pattern. For example, Alfresco's Web scripts are all located in a folder named `org/alfresco`, which is reserved by Alfresco.

As you go through the rest of this chapter, the naming convention for each of the Web script component files will become clear.

CREATING A DESCRIPTION DOCUMENT

It's time to get started on the Folder Listing Web script, which will mimic the behavior of the `dir` command in Microsoft Windows or `ls` in Linux and Mac OS X. Given a folder path, the Web script will list the contents of that folder in the Alfresco content repository either in abbreviated or verbose form, depending on a user-provided flag.

First, create a Web script description document for the Folder Listing Web script.

1. You first need to log in to Alfresco Explorer.

   a. Type the following in your Web browser, and log in with the user name `admin` and password `admin` if requested:

      ```
      http://localhost:8080/alfresco
      ```

   b. Navigate to Company Home > Data Dictionary > Web Scripts Extensions.

2. Create a folder to represent the top-level package structure.

   a. In the Create menu, click Create Space.

   b. Enter the name for the folder in the Name field, such as:

      ```
      org
      ```

   c. Click Create Space.

3. Next, create a sub-package.

   a. Navigate to Company Home > Data Dictionary > Web Scripts Extensions > org.

   b. In the Create menu, click Create Space.

   c. Enter the name for the folder in the Name field, such as:

      ```
      example
      ```

   d. Click Create Space.

4. Now create a Web script description document for the Folder Listing example.

   a. In the Create menu, click Create Content.

   b. Enter the name for the Web script in the Name field, such as:

      ```
      dir.get.desc.xml
      ```

   c. In the Content Type list, select XML.

   d. Click Next.

   e. Type the following in the Enter Content box:

Available for download on Wrox.com

```
<webscript>
  <shortname>Folder Listing Utility</shortname>
  <description>Sample demonstrating the listing of folder
  contents</description>
  <url>/dir/{folderpath}?verbose={verbose?}</url>
  <format default="html">extension</format>
  <authentication>user</authentication>
</webscript>
```

Code snippet dir.get.desc.xml

   f. Click Next.

   g. Click Finish.

   h. Click OK.

The first thing to note is that you now have a Web script package named `/org/example`. This is where you will place all of your component files for the Folder Listing Web script. In fact, you have already placed the description document there, which is named `dir.get.desc.xml`.

Component file naming is important and must adhere to the naming conventions defined by the Web Script Framework. Web script description document file names are structured as follows:

```
<web script id>.<http method>.desc.xml
```

The `<web script id>` identifies the Web script and must be unique within a Web script package. Therefore, a Web script is uniquely identified by its Web script package and Web script ID. Your Folder Listing Web script is uniquely identified as:

```
/org/example/dir
```

The `<http method>` specifies which HTTP method will initiate the Web script. Typically, this is GET, but other common methods include POST, PUT, and DELETE. There isn't actually a restriction on the method name but, in reality, most HTTP clients will only know of these four methods. Your Folder Listing Web script will only query the Alfresco content repository, so it is bound to the HTTP GET method.

Finally, all description document file names must end with `.desc.xml`, which indicates to the Web Script Framework the file is actually a description document that defines a Web script.

Now take a look at the description document, which is expressed in XML. All Web script descriptors have a root `<webscript>` element within which everything is defined.

The `<shortname>` and `<description>` elements provide human-readable titles for the Web script. These can be seen in Web script documentation and the Web script index located at:

```
http://localhost:8080/alfresco/service/
```

Your Folder Listing Web script defines the following short name and description:

Available for download on Wrox.com

```
...
<shortname>Folder Listing Utility</shortname>
<description>Sample demonstrating the listing of folder contents</description>
...
```

Code snippet dir.get.desc.xml

As the Folder Listing Web script queries the Alfresco content repository, it is necessary to ensure that only authenticated users have access. This means the Web script will only return folder contents that the authenticated user has permission to see. The `<authentication>` element specifies the level of required authentication to access the Web script, of which the following levels are available:

- **None** — The Web script does not require any authentication to be invoked.
- **Guest** — The Web script may be invoked by a guest user of the Alfresco Content Application Server.
- **User** — The Web script must be invoked by a named user known to the Alfresco Content Application Server.

➤ **Admin** — The Web script must be invoked by a named user who is an administrator of the Alfresco Content Application Server.

Your Folder Listing Web script defines the following level of authentication:

Available for download on Wrox.com

```
...
<authentication>user</authentication>
...
```

Code snippet dir.get.desc.xml

Next, define one of the most important parts of the Web script definition: the URI to which the Web script is bound. Your Folder Listing Web script is mapped to the URI `/dir`, but it is also necessary to decide how to pass arguments to the Web script: that is, how to define the folder to list and the flag to determine if an abbreviated or verbose listing is returned.

There are two options for passing arguments through the URI: as part of the URI path or as a query parameter. Which option you choose mostly depends on your style preference. Often, though, arguments that represent identifiers such as user ID are good candidates for the URI path, while arguments that represent switches for changing the behavior of the Web script are good candidates for query parameters.

Your Folder Listing Web script chooses to specify the folder as part of the URI path and the verbose flag as a query parameter:

Available for download on Wrox.com

```
...
<url>/dir/{folderpath}?verbose={verbose?}</url>
...
```

Code snippet dir.get.desc.xml

Note that the URI is expressed as a URI template, which is a URI containing placeholders; that is, slots for specifying arguments. URI templates are described in much greater detail later in this chapter, but for now the `{folderpath}` token represents where the folder path should be placed and the `{verbose?}` token represents the flag.

Although your Web script only defines a single URI, it is possible to declare multiple URIs.

You now need to decide how to render the list of folder contents. Your example will provide both a human-readable HTML format, allowing access from a Web browser, and a JSON format, providing a machine-readable format for other clients to parse.

JSON, short for JavaScript Object Notation, is a lightweight data interchange format that is often used for transmitting structured data over a network connection.

The <format> element of the Web script description document allows a Web script to specify (through the default attribute) which response format is returned if a client does not explicitly request a format. In some cases, the returned format may not be known until the Web script is invoked with its arguments, in which case a default value of "" must be set.

The means by which a client can request a format is also specified by the <format> element through its value, which may be one of the following: extension, argument, or any.

A value of extension allows a client to request the format through an extension on the URL, where the extension is the name of the format. If this value were chosen, your Folder Listing URL for returning JSON would be constructed as follows:

```
/dir/<folderpath>.json?verbose=true
```

A value of argument allows a client to request the format through a query parameter on the URL. This is useful for cases where the URL path naturally ends in an extension, such as if the path represents a document name in the Alfresco content repository. If this value were chosen, your Folder Listing URL for returning JSON would be constructed as follows:

```
/dir/<folderpath>?format=json&verbose=true
```

A value of any allows a client to request the format through either of the above.

Your Folder Listing Web script specifies a default format of HTML and expects a client to request the format through the URL-extension approach:

```
...
<format default="html">extension</format>
...
```

It is possible to exclude the <format> section from the descriptor document altogether, in which case the Web Script Framework defaults to returning HTML and allows a client to request a format through any approach.

URI Templates

While you have seen an example of a URI template as defined by your Folder Listing Web script, it is worth spending some time taking a deeper look at what exactly a URI template is and how expressive it can be for defining complex Web script URIs.

A URI template is simply a URI containing tokens that may be substituted with actual values. Tokens may represent values to query parameters or values within the URI path, where the syntax for expressing a token is {<token name>}.

An example of specifying a URI with two query parameters — one named 'a' and the other named 'b' — follows:

```
/add?a={a}&amp;b={b}
```

The query parameter delimiter '&' must be expressed as '&' in Web script descriptor documents, as '&' has special meaning within XML.

A client can generate the URI for invoking this Web script when given the URI template and values for 'a' and 'b'. For example, if 'a' is set to '1' and 'b' is set to '2', the resulting URI is:

```
/add?a=1&b=2
```

Query parameter tokens can indicate that the parameter is optional through the convention of appending a '?' to the token name. For example, to indicate that the query parameter 'b' is optional, the URI template becomes:

```
/add?a={a}&amp;b={b?}
```

Although parameters may be marked as optional, it is only a convention and the Web Script Framework does not enforce mandatory query parameters. This responsibility is given to the Web script developer.

An example of specifying a URI path with embedded tokens — one named 'user' and the other named 'profilekind' — follows:

```
/user/{user}/profile/{profilekind}
```

Any URI that matches the URI template will invoke the Web script that defines it. But what does it mean to match? A match is made when:

- All static parts of the URI template match the URI
- All tokens within the URI template have been given values by the URI

For example, the following URIs match:

```
/user/joe/profile/public
/user/fred/profile/full
```

But the following URIs do not match:

```
/user/profile/public
/user/joe/profile
```

The value of a token in a URI path may itself consist of multiple path segments. For example, the following URI specifies the user value `joe/smith` and matches the previous URI template:

```
/user/joe/smith/profile/public
```

When a URI request is made, the Web Script Framework locates the associated Web script by finding the closest matching URI template for the URI. For example, consider that two Web scripts each define their own similar URIs:

- Web script A defines the URI template: `/a/b`
- Web script B defines the URI template `/a/{z}`

The URI `/a/b` will invoke Web script A, while the URI `/a/c` will invoke Web script B. Matching of static parts of the URI template takes precedence over matching a token value.

Finally, the same token name may appear multiple times in a single URI template. Although very rare, it's worth knowing the implications of matching to a Web script. Consider the following URI template where the 'user' token is specified twice:

```
/user/{user}/profile/{user}
```

For a match to occur, the value provided for each same-named token must be the same. The following URI matches:

```
/user/joe/profile/joe
```

But the following URI does not match:

```
/user/joe/profile/fred
```

Web script developers have access to the value provided for each token in both the controller script and response template.

Remember, if you get stuck defining your own URI template, there are plenty of examples provided by out-of-the-box Web scripts, which you can browse through the Web script index.

CREATING A CONTROLLER SCRIPT

Having described the Folder Listing Web script through its description document, it's now time to implement its behavior by developing a controller script in the JavaScript language. In this case, the controller will simply establish the folder to list from the invoked URI and query the Alfresco content repository for that folder, ensuring error conditions are catered for.

You can now create the controller script.

1. You first need to log in to Alfresco Explorer.
    a. Type the following in your Web browser, and log in with the user name `admin` and password `admin` if requested:

    ```
    http://localhost:8080/alfresco
    ```

    b. Navigate to Company Home > Data Dictionary > Web Scripts Extensions > org > example.
2. Create a Web script controller script for your Folder Listing example.
    a. In the Create menu, click Create Content.
    b. Enter the name for the Web script in the Name field as follows:

    ```
    dir.get.js
    ```

    c. In the Content Type list, select Plain Text.
    d. Click Next.
    e. Type the following in the Enter Content box:

Available for download on Wrox.com

```
// extract folder listing arguments from URI
var verbose = (args.verbose == "true" ? true : false);
var folderpath = url.templateArgs.folderpath;

// search for folder within Alfresco content repository
var folder = roothome.childByNamePath(folderpath);
```

```
// validate that folder has been found
if (folder == undefined || !folder.isContainer) {
   status.code = 404;
   status.message = "Folder " + folderpath + " not found.";
   status.redirect = true;
}

// construct model for response template to render
model.verbose = verbose;
model.folder = folder;
```

Code snippet dir.get.js

f. Click Next.

g. Click Finish.

h. Click OK.

The first thing to note is the component script file name `dir.get.js`, which adheres to the naming convention defined by the Web Script Framework. Controller script file names are structured as follows:

```
<web script id>.<http method>.js
```

The `<web script id>` identifies the Web script and must be the same as the Web script ID defined in the file name of the associated Web script description document. The `<http method>` specifies which HTTP method will initiate the Web script and again must be the same as the associated Web script description document.

Finally, all controller script file names must end with `.js`. This indicates to the Web Script Framework that the file is indeed a controller script.

Your Folder Listing example now consists of the following two component files:

```
/org/example/dir.get.desc.xml
/org/example/dir.get.js
```

The Web Script Framework knows that both of these files are related to the same Web script, as they share Web script package, Web script ID, and HTTP method.

Parsing the Web Script URI

A Web script is invoked when a URI is requested that matches one of the URI templates defined by the Web script. It is often necessary for the Web script to gain access to the requested URI to allow it to extract arguments that may have been passed in as URI query parameters or embedded as values in the URI path.

Your Folder Listing Web script defines the following URI template with one URI-path token and one query parameter token:

```
<uri>/dir/{folderpath}?verbose={verbose?}</uri>
```

To extract the values provided for the {folderpath} and {verbose} tokens, your Folder Listing controller script uses the following JavaScript:

Available for download on Wrox.com

```
...
var verbose = (args.verbose == "true" ? true : false);
var folderpath = url.templateArgs.folderpath;
...
```

Code snippet dir.get.js

The args root object is a special object provided by the Web Script Framework to all controller scripts. It represents a map of the URI query-parameter values indexed by their name. In this case, the controller script is extracting the verbose query parameter. If the query parameter is not specified on the URI, the returned value is null.

Web script root objects are globally named values and services provided by the Web Script Framework to the Web script controller and response templates.

The url.templateArgs root object is another special object provided by the Web Script Framework. It represents a map of all values provided for tokens in the URI path, indexed by token name. In this case, the controller script is extracting the value for the folderpath token. URI-path values are never null.

Imagine a client has made the following URI request:

```
/dir/Company%20Home?verbose=true
```

The resulting value of verbose is true and the value of folderpath is Company Home.

Calling Alfresco Services

Controller scripts have access to services provided by the Alfresco Content Application Server. This allows a Web script to query or perform operations against content residing in the Alfresco content repository. Services are exposed as root objects and each service provides its own application programming interface (API) to program against.

Your Folder Listing Web script simply needs to retrieve the folder value provided on the URI, identified by the {folderpath} token:

Available for download on Wrox.com

```
...
var folder = roothome.childByNamePath(folderpath);
...
```

Code snippet dir.get.js

The `roothome` root object is a special object provided by the Web Script Framework, which represents the root folder in the Alfresco content repository. From this object, it is possible to navigate through the content repository folder hierarchy or find sub-folders by name. Your controller script finds a sub-folder using the folder name provided in the URI.

There are many other root objects available to controller scripts:

- **`args`** — A map of query parameter values indexed by query parameter name.
- **`argsM`** — A map of multi-valued query parameters, where each key is an argument name and each value is an array containing all respective argument values, even if only one is supplied.
- **`headers`** — A map of request header values indexed by header name.
- **`headersM`** — A map of multi-valued request headers, where each key is a header name and each value is an array containing all respective header values, even if only one is supplied.
- **`url`** — Provides access to the Web script URI, or parts of the URI, that triggered the Web script. See the "Complex Root Objects Reference" section at the end of this chapter for more details.
- **`guest`** — A Boolean indicating if the Web script is executing as a "Guest" user.
- **`webscript`** — A description of the Web script currently being executed. See the "Complex Root Objects Reference" section at the end of this chapter for more details.
- **`server`** — A description of the Web script container hosting the Web script. See the "Complex Root Objects Reference" section at the end of this chapter for more details.

When executing a Web script as an authenticated user, the controller script also has access to the following Alfresco services.

- **`roothome`** — The repository root folder
- **`companyhome`** — The company home folder
- **`person`** — The person node of the currently authenticated user
- **`userhome`** — The user home folder
- **`people`** — A service for accessing people and groups registered with the Alfresco Content Application Server
- **`search`** — A service for querying and searching the content repository
- **`actions`** — A service for invoking Alfresco Actions
- **`classification`** — A service for navigating and managing categories
- **`workflow`** — A service for starting workflows and managing in-flight workflows

Remember, the out-of-the-box, pre-built Web scripts provide plenty of examples demonstrating how to use the root objects provided to controller scripts.

Setting the Response Status Code

A Web script uses a response status code to inform the calling client of its execution outcome. Status codes may be used for the following scenarios:

- To inform the client of an error situation. For example, an item is not found in the Alfresco content repository.
- To inform the client of an occurrence of an event. For example, a new item has been created.
- To instruct the client to perform a follow-up request. For example, to ask for user name and password credentials.
- To inform the client of success.

Your Folder Listing Web script validates that the provided folder path actually exists in the Alfresco content repository using the following JavaScript in the controller script:

Available for download on Wrox.com

```
...
if (folder == undefined || !folder.isContainer) {
   status.code = 404;
   status.message = "Folder " + folderpath + " not found.";
   status.redirect = true;
}
...
```

Code snippet dir.get.js

The `status` root object is a special object provided to all controller scripts by the Web Script Framework. It allows a Web script to specify the response status code along with an associated status message. Typically, the value of the status code is set to a standard HTTP status code.

The list of HTTP status codes and their meaning can be found at `www.w3.org/Protocols/rfc2616/rfc2616-sec10.html`.

It is useful when reporting error status codes to provide additional information about the error in the response, such as the cause of the error. To support this, the Web Script Framework allows for a custom status response template to be rendered, but this happens only if the `status.redirect` value is set to true. A default status response template is provided by the Web Script Framework, which renders everything known about the status, so it's not necessary to develop your own; however, later in this chapter, you will discover how to create a custom status response template.

If the value of `status.redirect` is set to `false`, the status code is set on the response, but the response template for the requested format is rendered anyway.

Constructing the Model

One of the responsibilities of the controller script is to create a model for subsequent rendering by a response template. A model is a map of values indexed by their name, which can be read from and written to by the controller script.

Your Folder Listing Web script adds the verbose flag and retrieved folder to the model:

```
...
model.verbose = verbose;
model.folder = folder;
...
```

Code snippet dir.get.js

The `model` root object is provided to the controller script by the Web Script Framework. All items added to the model are available to the response template.

CREATING A RESPONSE TEMPLATE

The final stage of Web script execution is to render a response back to the initiating client in the most appropriate format based on the client's preference. A response template written in the FreeMarker language is responsible for rendering each format provided by the Web script.

Your Folder Listing Web script provides two responses: one in HTML for rendering to a Web browser and one in JSON for consumption by other clients. The response will list all the documents and folders contained within the folder retrieved by the controller script, as specified in the Folder Listing Web script URL. For now, focus on creating the HTML response template.

1. You first need to log in to Alfresco Explorer.
   a. Type the following in your Web browser, and log in with the user name `admin` and password `admin` if requested:

      ```
      http://localhost:8080/alfresco
      ```

   b. Navigate to Company Home > Data Dictionary > Web Scripts Extensions > org > example.
2. Create a Web script response template for your Folder Listing example.
   a. In the Create menu, click Create Content.
   b. Enter the name for the Web script in the Name field as follows:

      ```
      dir.get.html.ftl
      ```

   c. In the Content Type list, select Plain Text.
   d. Click Next.
   e. Type the following in the Enter Content box:

Available for download on Wrox.com

```
<html>
  <head>
    <title>Folder ${folder.displayPath}/${folder.name}</title>
  </head>
  <body>
     Alfresco ${server.edition} Edition v${server.version} : dir
    <p>
    Contents of folder ${folder.displayPath}/${folder.name}
    <p>
    <table>
    <#list folder.children as child>
       <tr>
           <td><#if child.isContainer>d</#if></td>
           <#if verbose>
              <td>${child.properties.modifier}</td>
              <td><#if child.isDocument>
                 ${child.properties.content.size}</#if></td>
              <td>${child.properties.modified?date}</td>
           </#if>
           <td>${child.name}</td>
       </tr>
    </#list>
    </table>
  </body>
</html>
```

Code snippet dir.get.html.ftl

f. Click Next.

g. Click Finish.

h. Click OK.

The first thing to note is the component script file name `dir.get.html.ftl`, which adheres to the naming convention defined by the Web Script Framework. Response template file names are structured as follows:

```
<web script id>.<http method>.<format>.ftl
```

The `<web script id>` identifies the Web script and must be the same as the Web script ID defined in the file name of the associated Web script description document. The `<http method>` specifies which HTTP method will initiate the Web script and again must be the same as the associated Web script description document.

The format rendered by the response template is represented by `<format>`, the Web Script Framework abbreviation for a MIME type, for which the following common formats are defined as follows:

- `html` maps to text/html.
- `text` maps to text/plain.
- `xml` maps to text/xml.
- `atom` maps to application/atom+xml.

- `atomentry` maps to application/atom+xml;type=entry.
- `atomfeed` maps to application/atom+xml;type=feed.
- `rss` maps to application/rss+xml.
- `json` maps to application/json.
- `opensearchdescription` maps to application/opensearchdescription+xml.
- `mediawiki` maps to MediaWiki markup as text/plain.
- `portlet` maps to text/html (where HTML excludes header and footer markup).
- `fbml` maps to text/html.
- `php` maps to text/html.
- `js` maps to text/javascript.
- `calendar` maps to text/calendar.

Finally, all response template file names must end with `.ftl`. This indicates to the Web Script Framework that the file is indeed a response template.

Your Folder Listing example now consists of the following three component files:

```
/org/example/dir.get.desc.xml
/org/example/dir.get.js
/org/example/dir.get.html.ftl
```

The Web Script Framework knows that all of these files are related to the same Web script, as they share Web script package, Web script ID, and HTTP method.

Accessing the Model

Response templates have access to the model created by the controller script. Each named value added to the model is accessible as a template root object by its respective model name.

Your Folder Listing controller script placed two values into the model: one named `folder`, a folder object, and the other named `verbose`, a Boolean. Your response template uses these two values to drive the rendered output on the response:

Available for download on Wrox.com

```
 ...
Contents of folder ${folder.displayPath}/${folder.name}
 ...
<#list folder.children as child>
 ...
  <#if verbose>
    ...
  </#if>
</#list>
 ...
```

Code snippet dir.get.html.ftl

The `folder` object is used to render properties of the folder and to iterate through its children while the `verbose` flag is used to determine if extra detail should be output.

Accessing Alfresco Services

As well as model root objects, response templates have access to services provided by the Alfresco Content Application Server. This allows a response template to directly query or navigate parts of the content repository or access the context within which the Web script is executing, such as the currently authenticated user.

It must be noted that although response templates can perform their own logic, this should not be encouraged. Web script logic is better implemented in controller scripts, allowing the response template to focus only on rendering the output. This allows the easy creation of multiple response templates, as logic does not have to be duplicated in each. It also means logic is encapsulated in one place, so changes to logic are centralized.

Your Folder Listing Web script first renders details about the Alfresco Content Application Server:

Available for download on Wrox.com

```
...
Alfresco ${server.edition} Edition v${server.version} : dir
...
```

Code snippet dir.get.html.ftl

The `server` root object is a special object provided by the Web Script Framework, which represents the server within which the Web script is executing. In this case, the response template simply accesses properties of the server.

There are many other root objects available to response templates:

- **`args`** — A map of query parameter values indexed by query parameter name.
- **`argsM`** — A map of multi-valued query parameters, where each key is an argument name and each value is an array containing all respective argument values, even if only one is supplied.
- **`headers`** — A map of request header values indexed by header name.
- **`headersM`** — A map of multi-valued request headers, where each key is a header name and each value is an array containing all respective header values, even if only one is supplied.
- **`url`** — Provides access to the Web script URI, or parts of the URI, that triggered the Web script. See the "Complex Root Objects Reference" section at the end of this chapter for more details.
- **`guest`** — A Boolean indicating whether the Web script is executing as a "Guest" user.
- **`webscript`** — A description of the Web script currently being executed. See the "Complex Root Objects Reference" section at the end of this chapter for more details.

- `server`: A description of the Web script container hosting the Web script. See the "Complex Root Objects Reference" section at the end of this chapter for more details.
- `date`: The date and time the Web script was invoked.

When executing a Web script as an authenticated user, the controller script also has access to the following Alfresco services:

- **`roothome`** — The repository root folder
- **`companyhome`** — The company home folder
- **`person`** — The person node of the currently authenticated user
- **`userhome`** — The user home folder

Remember that the out-of-the-box, pre-built Web scripts provide plenty of examples demonstrating how to use the root objects provided to response templates.

FreeMarker Methods

The FreeMarker template language supports the notion of a method. A method encapsulates an action to perform on a set of input parameters and may return an output value. Although FreeMarker provides many methods of its own, it also allows the registration of custom methods. The Web Script Framework takes advantage of this to provide the following methods specifically for developers of Web script response templates:

- **`absurl(url)`** — Returns an absolute URL representation of the passed URL. Useful when rendering links within Atom (and similar formats).
- **`xmldate(date)`** — Returns an ISO8601-formatted result of the passed date. Useful when rendering dates within XML.
- **`scripturl(queryString)`** — Returns a URL that references this Web script. The passed `queryString` is added to the URL. System arguments such as guest and format are automatically added. Note that this method is particularly useful for protection against the runtime environment within which the Web script is executing. In some environments, such as a Portal, the URL may be encoded.
- **`clienturlfunction(funcName)`** — Generates a client-side JavaScript function that can generate a URL back to this Web script.
- **`argreplace(argString, argName, argValue, ...)`** — Replaces the specified `argName` with `argValue` or adds `argName` if it does not exist in `argString`.
- `encodeuri(uriString)`: Encodes the string into URL-safe form.

The out-of-the-box, pre-built Web scripts provide plenty of examples demonstrating how to use these methods. Imagine, though, you need to output the complete URL that was used to invoke a Web script. This is achieved using:

```
${absurl(url.full)}
```

The `url` root object represents the URL used to invoke the Web script. Access to the URL path, including its query parameters, is provided by the property named `full`; however, the URL scheme and authority are not included. To render a full URL, including scheme and authority, the `absurl` method is used.

REGISTERING AND TESTING

Congratulations. You now have a complete Folder Listing Web script implementation. Now begins the fun of testing.

1. You first need to register the Folder Listing Web script with Alfresco.

   a. Type the following in your Web browser, and log in with the user name `admin` and password `admin` if requested:

      ```
      http://localhost:8080/alfresco/service/index
      ```

   b. Click Refresh Web Scripts. You'll see a message indicating there is one additional Web script.

2. Perform your first test.

   a. Type the following in your Web browser, and log in with the user name `admin` and password `admin` if requested:

      ```
      http://localhost:8080/alfresco/service/dir/Company%20Home
      ```

   b. If you see the contents of the Company Home folder listed, your Web script is working.

3. Next, check the verbose flag.

   a. Type the following in your Web browser:

      ```
      http://localhost:8080/alfresco/service/dir/Company%20Home?verbose=true
      ```

   b. If you see the contents of the Company Home folder listed in verbose form, your Web script is working.

4. Finally, check the error handling of a folder that does not exist:

   a. Type the following in your Web browser:

      ```
      http://localhost:8080/alfresco/service/dir/doesnotexist
      ```

   b. If you see an error page detailing a 404 status response, your Web script is working.

When testing status response codes, it is useful to test with the cURL client, as this gives you access to the status code sent on the HTTP response. For example, to repeat the 'folder does not exist' test with cURL, type the following in your command line:

```
curl -uadmin:admin -v "http://localhost:8080/alfresco/service/dir/doesnotexist"
```

The returned response is similar to the following, where the 404 status code is explicitly logged:

```
* About to connect() to localhost port 8080 (#0)
*   Trying ::1... connected
* Connected to localhost (::1) port 8080 (#0)
* Server auth using Basic with user 'admin'
> GET /alfresco/service/dir/doesnotexist HTTP/1.1
> Authorization: Basic YWRtaW46YWRtaW4=
> Host: localhost:8080
> Accept: */*
>
< HTTP/1.1 404 Not Found
```

```
< Server: Apache-Coyote/1.1
< Cache-Control: no-cache
< Pragma: no-cache
< Content-Type: text/html;charset=UTF-8
< Content-Length: 1487
< Date: Tue, 26 Jan 2010 10:28:28 GMT
```

Each time a Web script component file is modified, the Web script will need to be re-registered via the Web script index page.

Debugging a Controller Script

At some point during the development of a Web script, you may hit an issue for which the solution is not obvious. In this case, it is really useful to be able to step through the controller script code line by line to pinpoint the cause of the issue.

The Alfresco Content Application Server provides a built-in JavaScript Debugger (as shown in Figure 9-2) that can be applied to Web scripts.

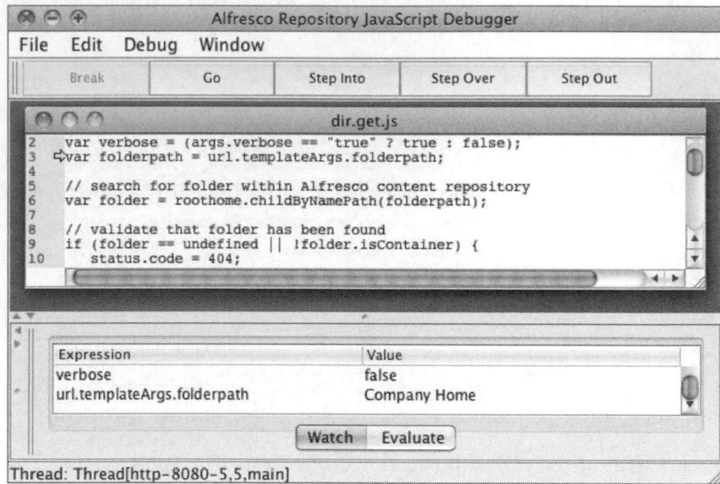

FIGURE 9-2

Step through the controller script of your Folder Listing Web script:

1. You first need to enable the JavaScript Debugger.

    a. Type the following in your Web browser, and log in with the user name `admin` and password `admin` if requested:

    ```
    http://localhost:8080/alfresco/service/index
    ```

    b. Click the Refresh Web Scripts link to ensure the Web Script Framework has cleared its caches, which is required for the JavaScript Debugger.

   c. Click the List Web Scripts link.

   d. Click the Alfresco JavaScript Debugger link.

   e. Click the Enable button, which launches the JavaScript Debugger in a separate window.

2. Now invoke the Folder Listing Web script.

   a. Type the following in your Web browser, and log in with the user name `admin` and password `admin` if requested:

   ```
   http://localhost:8080/alfresco/service/dir/Company%20Home
   ```

   b. If you see the Folder Listing controller script inside the JavaScript Debugger window, you're ready to debug.

3. Next, debug the controller script.

   a. Click the Step Over button in the JavaScript Debugger to execute the currently highlighted line.

   b. Interrogate the value of the `verbose` variable by typing the following in the Expression window of the JavaScript Debugger:

   ```
   verbose
   ```

   c. Interrogate the value of the `{folderpath}` token by typing the following in the Expression window of the JavaScript Debugger:

   ```
   url.templateArgs.folderpath
   ```

4. Finally, continue Web script execution.

   a. Click the Go button in the JavaScript Debugger.

   b. If you see the output of the Folder Listing Web script in the Web browser, you have successfully used the JavaScript Debugger.

Remember, the JavaScript Debugger is an extremely useful tool for diagnosing the cause of issues. It is also really useful for stepping through other people's controller scripts to learn how they've implemented capabilities and how they've utilized Alfresco's services.

MULTIPLE RESPONSE TEMPLATES

A Web script may support multiple response formats to allow it to be used by a variety of clients. For example, a Web script may render an HTML response for human consumption in a Web browser and render a JSON response for machine consumption by other clients.

So far, your Folder Listing Web script only renders HTML. Now you can add support for JSON:

1. You first need to log in to Alfresco Explorer.

   a. Type the following in your Web browser, and log in with the user name `admin` and password `admin` if requested:

   ```
   http://localhost:8080/alfresco
   ```

   b. Navigate to Company Home > Data Dictionary > Web Scripts Extensions > org > example.

2. Create a JSON response template for your Folder Listing example.

   a. In the Create menu, click Create Content.

   b. Enter the name for the Web script in the Name field as follows:

      `dir.get.json.ftl`

   c. In the Content Type list, select Plain Text.

   d. Click Next.

   e. Type the following in the Enter Content box:

```
{
  "server" : "Alfresco ${server.edition} Edition v${server.version}",
  "folder" :
  {
    "path" : "${folder.displayPath}",
    "name" : "${folder.name}"
  },
  "children" : [
    <#list folder.children as child>
    {
        "isfolder" : <#if child.isContainer>true<#else>false</#if>,
        <#if verbose>
        "modifier" : "${child.properties.modifier}",
        "size" : <#if child.isDocument>
          ${child.properties.content.size?c}<#else>null</#if>,
        "modified" : "${child.properties.modified?date}",
        </#if>
        "name" : "${child.name}"
    }<#if child_has_next>,</#if>
  </#list>
  ]
}
```

Code snippet dir.get.json.ftl

   f. Click Next.

   g. Click Finish.

3. Next, re-register the Web script.

   a. Type the following in your Web browser, and log in with the user name `admin` and password `admin` if requested:

      `http://localhost:8080/alfresco/service/index`

   b. Click Refresh Web Scripts. You will see a message indicating all Web scripts have been refreshed.

4. Finally, it's time to test.

   a. Type the following in your command line:

   ```
   curl -uadmin:admin "http://localhost:8080/alfresco/service/dir/
   Company%20Home.json"
   ```

   b. If you see the contents of the Company Home folder, your response template is working.

Each Web script can support an unlimited number of response templates; however, there can only be one response template for each format. This is enforced by the naming convention for response templates as described in the section "Creating a Response Template".

Your Folder Listing Web script now supports two formats: HTML and JSON. You have seen what happens when the client requests a specific format and the Web script successfully returns the folder contents, but what happens if there is an error?

Type the following in your command line to request the contents of a folder that does not exist in JSON format:

```
curl -uadmin:admin
"http://localhost:8080/alfresco/service/dir/doesnotexist.json"
```

The Web script responds with an error response, but in JSON format, as the client requested.

Whenever you change a Web script implementation, including the addition and removal of response templates, you must re-register the Web script via the Web script index.

Response Status Code Templates

Response status code templates allow a Web script to render a custom response for a given status code. This is useful for providing unique information about a status code or to render a custom human-readable interface.

Your Folder Listing Web script returns a 404 (Not Found) status code if the requested folder does not exist in the content repository. By default, the Web script responds with a generic response that provides details about the status, including its descriptive message. This is useful for diagnosis but may not necessarily be consumable by the typical user of the Web script.

Add a custom response status code template that renders a human-readable message when the folder cannot be found:

1. You first need to log in to Alfresco Explorer.

   a. Type the following in your Web browser, and log in with the user name `admin` and password `admin` if requested:

   ```
   http://localhost:8080/alfresco
   ```

   b. Navigate to Company Home > Data Dictionary > Web Scripts Extensions > org > example.

2. Create the response status code template.

   a. In the Create menu, click Create Content.

   b. Enter the name for the Web script in the Name field, such as:

   ```
   dir.get.html.404.ftl
   ```

   c. In the Content Type list, select Plain Text.

   d. Click Next.

   e. Type the following in the Enter Content box:

```
<html>
   <body>
     Alfresco ${server.edition} Edition v${server.version} : dir
     <p>
     Folder <b>${url.templateArgs.folderpath}</b> not found.
   </body>
</html>
```

Code snippet dir.get.html.404.ftl

   f. Click Next.

   g. Click Finish.

3. Next, re-register the Web script.

   a. Type the following in your Web browser, and log in with the user name `admin` and password `admin` if requested:

   ```
   http://localhost:8080/alfresco/service/index
   ```

   b. Click Refresh Web Scripts. You'll see a message indicating all Web scripts have been refreshed.

4. Finally, it's time to test.

   a. Type the following in your Web browser:

   ```
   http://localhost:8080/alfresco/service/dir/doesnotexist
   ```

   b. If you see the custom message, your response status code template is working.

As with all Web script component files, response status code template file names adhere to a naming convention as defined by the Web Script Framework. The appropriate response status code template is searched for in the following order:

1. A template located in the same folder as the Web script description document for rendering a specific status code response, which adheres to the naming convention:

   ```
   <web script id>.<http method>.<format>.<status code>.ftl
   ```

2. A template located in the same folder as the Web script description document for rendering a response of any status code, which adheres to the naming convention:

```
<web script id>.<http method>.<format>.status.ftl
```

3. A package-level template located in the package of the Web script. If the template is not found, it is searched for in the parent package hierarchy, up to the root package for rendering a specific status code; it adheres to the naming convention:

```
<format>.<status code>.ftl
```

4. A package-level template located in the package of the Web script. If the template is not found, it is searched for in the parent package hierarchy, up to the root package for rendering a response of any status code; it adheres to the naming convention:

```
<format>.status.ftl
```

5. A template located in the root package for rendering an HTML response for the specific status code, which adheres to the naming convention:

```
<status code>.ftl
```

6. A template located in the root package for rendering an HTML response of any status code, which adheres to the naming convention:

```
status.ftl
```

Response status code templates have access to the same root objects as normal Web script response templates, with the exception that the default templates `<code>.ftl` and `status.ftl` only have access to the root objects `url`, `status`, `server`, and `date`.

When developing Web scripts, a useful tip is to leave the implementation of response status code templates until the end, as the templates are not essential to the Web scripts' execution. Testing can take place without custom response status code templates, as the Web Script Framework will always eventually find the default template `status.ftl` in the root package.

As with all other response templates, the addition and removal of a response status code template requires the Web script to be re-registered.

STEP-BY-STEP: KNOWLEDGE BASE SEARCH WEB SCRIPT

It is time to build your Web script for supporting the Knowledge Base sample application. The Web script in question provides the back-end search capability for querying Knowledge Base articles within a knowledge base. Knowledge articles are identified by their attached knowledge article aspect and located in the document library of a Knowledge Base site in Alfresco Share. The knowledge article aspect is discussed in detail as part of content modeling in Chapter 5.

The Knowledge Base Search Web script searches the Alfresco content repository for Knowledge Base articles within a specified Alfresco Share site using the Alfresco FTS (Full Text Search) query language. It returns a JSON-formatted response containing the found articles.

You can now get started.

1. You first need to log in to Alfresco Explorer.
   a. Type the following in your Web browser, and log in with the user name `admin` and password `admin` if requested:

      `http://localhost:8080/alfresco`

   b. Navigate to Company Home > Data Dictionary > Web Scripts Extensions.
2. Create a folder to represent the top-level package structure. You may skip this step if the `org` space already exists.
   a. In the Create menu, click Create Space.
   b. Enter the name for the folder in the Name field, such as:

      `org`

   c. Click Create Space.
3. Next, create a sub-package. You may skip this step if the `example` space already exists.
   a. Navigate to Company Home > Data Dictionary > Web Scripts Extensions > org.
   b. In the Create menu, click Create Space.
   c. Enter the name for the folder in the Name field, such as:

      `example`
4. You can now create a Web script description document for your Knowledge Base Search.
   a. In the Create menu, click Create Content.
   b. Enter the name for the Web script in the Name field, as follows:

      `kb-search.get.desc.xml`

   c. In the Content Type list, select XML.
   d. Click Next.
   e. Type the following in the Enter Content box:

```
<webscript>
   <shortname>Knowledge Base Search</shortname>
   <description>Searches for knowledge base articles</description>
   <url>/slingshot/knowledgebase/search/site/{site}?maxResults={maxResults?}
</url>
   <format default="json">argument</format>
   <authentication>user</authentication>
</webscript>
```

Code snippet kb-search.get.desc.xml

   f. Click Next.
   g. Click Finish.
   h. Click OK.

5. Next, create a controller script for your Knowledge Base Search Web script.

   a. In the Create menu, click Create Content.

   b. Enter the name in the Name field, such as:

      kb-search.get.js

   c. In the Content Type list, select Plain Text.

   d. Click Next.

   e. Type the following in the Enter Content box:

Available for download on Wrox.com

```
/**
 * KnowledgeBase Search Component
 *
 * Inputs:
 *   mandatory: siteId = site ID to search in
 *   optional:  maxResults = max items to return.
 *
 * Outputs:
 *   data.items/data.error - object containing list of search results
 */

/**
 * Search constants
 */
const DEFAULT_MAX_RESULTS = 500;
const SITES_SPACE_QNAME_PATH = "/app:company_home/st:sites/";

/**
 * Performs a search for knowledge base articles in a site
 *
 * @method doSearch
 * @param siteId {string} The site to search in
 * @param maxResults {int} Maximum number of results to return
 * @return {array} Articles matching the query
 */
function doSearch(siteId, maxResults)
{
   // The initial template
   var alfQuery =
     'ASPECT:"{http://www.alfresco.org/model/knowledgebase/1.0}article"' +
     ' AND PATH:"' + SITES_SPACE_QNAME_PATH + '/cm:' + siteId +
     '/cm:documentLibrary//*"' +
     ' AND NOT TYPE:"{http://www.alfresco.org/model/content/1.0}thumbnail"' +
     ' AND NOT TYPE:"{http://www.alfresco.org/model/content/1.0}folder"';

   // Perform fts-alfresco language query for articles
   var queryDef = {
      query: alfQuery,
      language: "fts-alfresco",
      page: {maxItems: maxResults},
      templates: []
   };
```

```
   // Get article nodes
   var nodes = search.query(queryDef),
      articles = [],
      item;

   // Turn nodes into article objects
   for (var i = 0, j = nodes.length; i < j; i++)
   {
      // Create core object
      node = nodes[i];
      item =
      {
         nodeRef: node.nodeRef.toString(),
         type: node.typeShort,
         name: node.name,
         title: node.properties["cm:title"],
         description: node.properties["cm:description"],
         modifiedOn: node.properties["cm:modified"],
         modifiedByUser: node.properties["cm:modifier"],
         createdOn: node.properties["cm:created"],
         createdByUser: node.properties["cm:creator"],
         author: node.properties["cm:author"],
         nodeDBID: node.properties["sys:node-dbid"],
         properties: {}
      };

      // Calculate display names for users
      var person = people.getPerson(item.modifiedByUser);
      item.modifiedBy = (person != null ? (person.properties.firstName +
        " " + person.properties.lastName) : item.modifiedByUser);
      person = people.getPerson(item.createdByUser);
      item.createdBy = (person != null ? (person.properties.firstName +
        " " + person.properties.lastName) : item.createdByUser);

      // Add the Article namespace properties
      for (var k in node.properties)
      {
         if (k.match("^{http://www.alfresco.org/model/knowledgebase/1.0}")==
           "{http://www.alfresco.org/model/knowledgebase/1.0}")
         {
            item.properties["kb_" + k.split('}')[1]] = node.properties[k];
         }
      }
      articles.push(item);
   }

   return articles;
}

/**
 * The WebScript bootstrap method
 *
 * @method main
 */
```

```
function main()
{
   // Gather webscript parameters
   var siteId = url.templateArgs.site;
   var maxResults = (args.maxResults !== null) ? parseInt(args.maxResults) :
     DEFAULT_MAX_RESULTS;

   // Perform search
   var articles = doSearch(siteId, maxResults);

   // Generate model from results
   model.data = {
      items: articles
   };
}

main();
```

Code snippet kb-search.get.js

f. Click Next.

g. Click Finish.

h. Click OK.

6. Create a response template for your Knowledge Base Search Web script.

   a. In the Create menu, click Create Content.

   b. Enter the name in the Name field, such as:

      kb-search.get.json.ftl

   c. In the Content Type list, select Plain Text.

   d. Click Next.

   e. Type the following in the Enter Content box:

Available for download on Wrox.com

```
<#escape x as jsonUtils.encodeJSONString(x)>
{
   "items":
   [
      <#list data.items as item>
      {
         "nodeRef": "${item.nodeRef}",
         "type": "${item.type}",
         "name": "${item.name}",
         "title": "${item.title!''}",
         "description": "${item.description!''}",
         "modifiedOn": "${xmldate(item.modifiedOn)}",
         "modifiedByUser": "${item.modifiedByUser}",
         "modifiedBy": "${item.modifiedBy}",
         "createdOn": "${xmldate(item.createdOn)}",
         "createdByUser": "${item.createdByUser}",
```

```
                "createdBy": "${item.createdBy}",
                "author": "${item.author!''}",
                "nodeDBID": "${item.nodeDBID}",
                "properties":
                {
                <#assign first=true>
                <#list item.properties?keys as k>
                   <#if item.properties[k]??>
                      <#if !first>,<#else><#assign first=false></#if>"${k}":
                         <#assign prop = item.properties[k]>
                         <#if prop?is_date>"${xmldate(prop)}"
                         <#elseif prop?is_boolean>${prop?string("true", "false")}
                         <#elseif prop?is_enumerable>[
                            <#list prop as p>
                               "${p}"<#if p_has_next>, </#if>
                            </#list>]
                         <#elseif prop?is_number>${prop?c}
                         <#else>"${prop}"
                      </#if>
                   </#if>
                </#list>
                }
             }<#if item_has_next>,</#if>
             </#list>
          ]
       }
       </#escape>
```

Code snippet kb-search.get.json.ftl

7. Now register the Knowledge Base Search Web script with Alfresco.

   a. Type the following in your Web browser, and log in with the user name `admin` and password `admin` if requested:

   `http://localhost:8080/alfresco/service/index`

   b. Click Refresh Web Scripts. You'll see a message indicating there is one additional Web script.

How Does Knowledge Base Search Work?

Authentication is required, as the Web script needs to query the Alfresco content repository.

The Knowledge Base site to search is passed in as a value within the Web script URI path through the `{site}` token. An Alfresco FTS (Full Text Search) query statement is constructed, which searches within the content repository path that represents the document library of the specified site:

`/app:company_home/st:sites/cm:{site}/cm:documentLibrary`

The query also filters results to knowledge articles by selecting only items that have the knowledge article aspect attached.

Having constructed the query statement, the query is executed through the `search` root object where the result set is optionally constrained to a maximum number of items, as specified by the `{maxResults}` URI query parameter.

Each row of the result set is converted to a knowledge-article item whose properties are fully calculated where necessary, such as the calculation of the author's full name. The converted result set is placed into the Web script model with the name `data`.

A default JSON response format is specified in the Web script descriptor, for which a single response template is provided. Each knowledge article item in the `data` model is visited and rendered into JSON. To ensure valid JSON is generated, the template utilizes the FreeMarker escape capability in conjunction with the Web script JSON encoding helper named `jsonUtils.encodeJSONString()`.

Testing Knowledge Base Search

You can't test the Knowledge Base Search Web script unless there are some knowledge articles to search for. To create knowledge articles you will develop another Web script, which first constructs an Alfresco Share site with a document library and then adds a knowledge article into the document library. The Web script may be executed repeatedly to create further knowledge articles.

1. You first need to log in to Alfresco Explorer.
   a. Type the following in your Web browser, and log in with the user name `admin` and password `admin` if requested:

      ```
      http://localhost:8080/alfresco
      ```

   b. Navigate to Company Home > Data Dictionary > Web Scripts Extensions.
2. Create a folder to represent the top-level package structure. You may skip this step if the `org` space already exists.
   a. In the Create menu, click Create Space.
   b. Enter the name for the folder in the Name field, such as:

      ```
      org
      ```

   c. Click Create Space.
3. Next, create a sub-package. You may skip this step if the `example` space already exists.
   a. Navigate to Company Home > Data Dictionary > Web Scripts Extensions > org.
   b. In the Create menu, click Create Space.
   c. Enter the name for the folder in the Name field, such as:

      ```
      example
      ```

4. You can now create a description document for your Create Knowledge Base Web script.
   a. In the Create menu, click Create Content.
   b. Enter the name for the Web script in the Name field, as follows:

      ```
      kb-create.get.desc.xml
      ```

   c. In the Content Type list, select XML.
   d. Click Next.
   e. Type the following in the Enter Content box:

Available for download on Wrox.com

```
<webscript>
   <shortname>Create Knowledge Base</shortname>
   <description>Create knowledge base article for testing</description>
   <url>/slingshot/knowledgebase/create</url>
   <authentication>user</authentication>
</webscript>
```

Code snippet kb-create.get.desc.xml

   f. Click Next.
   g. Click Finish.
   h. Click OK.

5. Next, create a controller script for your Knowledge Base Create Web script.
   a. In the Create menu, click Create Content.
   b. Enter the name in the Name field, such as:

      `kb-create.get.js`

   c. In the Content Type list, select Plain Text.
   d. Click Next.
   e. Type the following in the Enter Content box:

Available for download on Wrox.com

```
// establish site with document library
var doclib = null;
var site = siteService.getSite("kbtest");
if (site == null) {
   site = siteService.createSite(null, "kbtest", "KB Search Test",
     "KB Search Test", siteService.PUBLIC_SITE);
   doclib = site.createContainer("documentLibrary");
   site.save();
   doclib.save();
} else {
   doclib = site.getContainer("documentLibrary");
}

// create knowledge article
var article = doclib.createNode("article", "cm:content");
article.addAspect("kb:article");
article.properties["cm:name"] = "article" + doclib.children.length;
article.properties["kb:articletype"] = "FAQ";
article.content = "The attached tutorial...";
article.save();

// create model
model.article = article;
```

Code snippet kb-create.get.js

f. Click Next.

g. Click Finish.

h. Click OK.

6. Create a response template for your Knowledge Base Create Web script.

   a. In the Create menu, click Create Content.

   b. Enter the name in the Name field, such as:

      `kb-create.get.html.ftl`

   c. In the Content Type list, select Plain Text.

   d. Click Next.

   e. Type the following in the Enter Content box:

```
Created ${article.name} within site 'kbtest'.
```

Code snippet kb-create.get.json.ftl

7. Now register the Knowledge Base Create Web script with Alfresco.

   a. Type the following in your Web browser, and log in with the user name `admin` and password `admin` if requested:

      `http://localhost:8080/alfresco/service/index`

   b. Click Refresh Web Scripts. You'll see a message indicating there is one additional Web script.

You can now create some test data for the Knowledge Base Search Web script. Type the following in your command line to create the Alfresco Share site named *kbtest* and an initial knowledge article:

```
curl -uadmin:admin
"http://localhost:8080/alfresco/service/slingshot/knowledgebase/
create"
```

If successful, the response is:

```
Created article1 within site 'kbtest'.
```

You may repeat the command to create further knowledge articles.

With data created, it is finally time to test the Knowledge Base Search Web script. Type the following in your command line:

```
curl -uadmin:admin
"http://localhost:8080/alfresco/service/slingshot/knowledgebase/
search/site/kbtest"
```

If successful, the response is similar to the following, where each knowledge article is represented in JSON.

```
{
  "items":
  [
    {
      "nodeRef":
        "workspace:\/\/SpacesStore\/1016b656-6288-4e17-be30-787138d1693b",
      "type": "cm:content",
      "name": "How to Create Content Models",
      "title": "",
      "description": "",
      "modifiedOn": "2010-01-29T10:57:59.608Z",
      "modifiedByUser": "admin",
      "modifiedBy": "Administrator ",
      "createdOn": "2010-01-29T10:57:59.451Z",
      "createdByUser": "admin",
      "createdBy": "Administrator",
      "author": "",
      "nodeDBID": "614",
      "properties":
        {
          "kb_articletype": "FAQ",
          "kb_status": "Draft"
        }
    }
  ]
}
```


You've now completed your first set of Web scripts that interact with the Alfresco Content Application Server. You'll see how they are used in Chapters 14–16, which go through the exercise of building the Knowledge Base application in Alfresco Share.

COMPLEX ROOT OBJECTS REFERENCE

There are many root objects available to Web scripts. Most are just scalars whose value can be read and potentially updated; however, some root objects are more complex and have structures of their own. This reference details those complex root objects.

url

`url` is a root object providing access to the URL (or parts of the URL) that triggered the Web script. Access to the URL parts is via the following properties on the `url` object:

- **`context`** — (read-only string) Alfresco context path.
- **`serviceContext`** — (read-only string) Alfresco service context path.
- **`service`** — (read-only string) Web script path.
- **`full`** — (read-only string) Web script URI with query parameters.

- **`templateArgs`** — (read-only map) A map of substituted token values (within the URI path) indexed by token name.
- **`args`** — (read-only map) Web script URI query parameters.
- **`match`** — (read-only string) The part of the Web script URI that matched the Web script URI template.
- **`extension`** — (read-only string) The part of the Web script URL that extends beyond the match path (if there is no extension, an empty string is returned).

For example, imagine a Web script URI template of:

```
/user/{userid}
```

When the following URI is requested:

```
/alfresco/service/user/fred?profile=full&format=html
```

The `url` root object returns:

- `url.context` => /alfresco
- `url.serviceContext` => /alfresco/service
- `url.service` => /alfresco/service/user/fred
- `url.full` => /alfresco/service/user/fred?profile=full&format=html
- `url.args` => profile=full&format=html
- `url.templateArgs.userid` => fred
- `url.match` => /user/
- `url.extension` => fred

status

The `status` object represents a response status. The following properties allow for access to the status or the setting of a new status.

- **`code`** — (read/write int) Status code; this is primarily an HTTP status code, but can be any number.
- **`codeName`** — (read-only string) Human-readable status code name.
- **`codeDescription`** — (read-only string) Human-readable status code description.
- **`message`** — (read/write string) The status message.
- **`redirect`** — (read/write Boolean) Indicates whether to redirect to a status-specific response template.
- **`exception`** — (read/write java.lang.Exception) The exception, if any, that has caused this status.

- **location** — (read/write string) The absolute URI to which the client should resubmit a request; this is often used with 3xx redirect status codes.

cache

The cache object allows control over how the Web script response is cached. Caching is controlled via the following properties.

- **neverCache** — (read/write Boolean) Controls whether Web script response should be cached at all; true means never cache. If not set, the default value is specified by the cache control section of the Web script definition.
- **isPublic** — (read/write Boolean) Controls whether Web script response should be cached by public caches. If not set, the default value is specified by the cache control section of the Web script definition.
- **mustRevalidate** — (read/write Boolean) Controls whether cache must revalidate its version of the Web script response to ensure freshness. If not set, the default value is specified by the cache control section of the Web script definition.
- **maxAge** — (read/write long) Specifies the maximum amount of time (in seconds, relative to the time of request) that the response will be considered fresh. If not set, the default value is null.
- **lastModified** — (read/write date) Specifies the time that the content of the response last changed. If not set, the default value is null.
- **ETag** — (read/write string) Specifies a unique identifier that changes each time the content of the response changes. If not set, the default value is null. This is useful for indicating to a client cache when content has changed.

format

The format object represents the chosen format of the rendered response. The format is interrogated via the following properties.

- **Name** — (read-only string) Format name
- **Mimetype** — (read-only string) MIME type associated with format

webscript

The webscript object provides metadata describing the Web script currently being executed. Web script metadata is accessed via the following properties of the webscript object.

- **id** — (read-only string) The Web script identifier
- **shortName** — (read-only string) The Web script short name
- **description** — (read-only string) The Web script description
- **defaultFormat** — (read-only string) The default response format if none is explicitly specified in the Web script URI

- **formatStyle** — (read-only string) The accepted ways of specifying the format in the Web script URI
- **URIs** — (read-only string array) URI templates
- **method** — (read-only string) HTTP method
- **requiredAuthentication** — (read-only string) Required level of authentication
- **requiredTransaction** — (read-only string) Required level of transaction
- **storePath** — (read-only string) The path of the persistent store where the Web script is stored
- **scriptPath** — (read-only string) The path (within `storePath`) of Web script implementation files
- **descPath** — (read-only string) The path (within `storePath`) of the Web script description document

server

The `server` object provides metadata describing the host Alfresco server within which the Web script is currently being executed. Server metadata is accessed via the following properties of the server object.

- **versionMajor** — (read-only string) Server major version number; for example 1.2.3
- **versionMinor** — (read-only string) Server minor version number; for example 1.2.3
- **versionRevision** — (read-only string) Server revision number; for example 1.2.3
- **versionLabel** — (read-only string) Server version label; for example, Dev
- **versionBuild** — (read-only string) Server build number; for example, build-1
- **version** — (read-only string) Server version; for example, major.minor.revision (label)
- **edition** — (read-only string) Server edition; for example, Enterprise
- **schema** — (read-only string) Server schema; for example, 10

10

Advanced Web Scripts

WHAT'S IN THIS CHAPTER?

- Internationalizing Web scripts
- Configuring Web scripts
- Processing complex HTTP requests
- Caching Web scripts
- Setting advanced Descriptor options

The primary design goal of the Web Script Framework is to ensure that simple Web scripts are easy to develop, but advanced Web scripts are still possible. Advanced Web scripts support features such as rendering outputs in multiple languages, exposing and adhering to configuration options, and handling HTML form uploads.

This chapter explores the finer details of the Web Script Framework that allow the development of such advanced features.

INTERNATIONALIZATION

Internationalization (often abbreviated to I18N) is an important consideration when developing any piece of software, and this includes developing a Web script. For human-readable Web script responses it is often necessary to render the output in the preferred language of the user or the preferred language of the client. This means that human-readable text cannot be placed directly in the Web script response template. Therefore, the Web Script Framework employs the common practice of allowing text to be placed into resource bundles, where a resource bundle exists for each supported language.

This is easily demonstrated by creating a simple Web script that renders an HTML message.

1. You first need to log in to Alfresco Explorer.
   a. Type the following in your Web browser, and log in with the user name `admin` and password `admin` if requested:

      ```
      http://localhost:8080/alfresco
      ```

   b. Navigate to Company Home > Data Dictionary > Web Scripts Extensions.
2. Create a folder to represent the top-level package structure. You may skip this step if the `org` space already exists.
   a. In the Create menu, click Create Space.
   b. Enter the name for the folder in the Name field, such as:

      ```
      org
      ```

   c. Click Create Space.
3. Next, create a sub-package. You may skip this step if the `example` space already exists.
   a. Navigate to Company Home > Data Dictionary > Web Scripts Extensions > org.
   b. In the Create menu, click Create Space.
   c. Enter the name for the folder in the Name field, such as:

      ```
      example
      ```

   d. Navigate to Company Home > Data Dictionary > Web Scripts Extensions > org > example.
4. You can now create a Web script description document for your I18N sample.
   a. In the Create menu, click Create Content.
   b. Enter the name for the Web script in the Name field, as follows:

      ```
      i18n.get.desc.xml
      ```

   c. In the Content Type list, select XML.
   d. Click Next.
   e. Type the following in the Enter Content box:

Available for download on Wrox.com

```
<webscript>
   <shortname>I18N Sample</shortname>
   <description>Internationalization Sample</description>
   <url>/i18n</url>
</webscript>
```

Code snippet i18n.get.desc.xml

   f. Click Next.
   g. Click Finish.
   h. Click OK.

5. Create a default message bundle for your I18N sample.

   a. In the Create menu, click Create Content.

   b. Enter the name in the Name field, such as:

      ```
      i18n.get.properties
      ```

   c. In the Content Type list, select Plain Text.

   d. Click Next.

   e. Type the following in the Enter Content box:

```
greeting=Hello
farewell=Goodbye
```

Code snippet i18n.get.properties

6. Next, create a response template for your I18N sample.

   a. In the Create menu, click Create Content.

   b. Enter the name in the Name field, such as:

      ```
      i18n.get.html.ftl
      ```

   c. In the Content Type list, select Plain Text.

   d. Click Next.

   e. Type the following in the Enter Content box:

```
${msg("greeting")}. ${msg("farewell")}.
```

Code snippet i18n.get.html.ftl

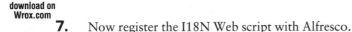

7. Now register the I18N Web script with Alfresco.

   a. Type the following in your Web browser, and log in with the user name `admin` and password `admin` if requested:

      ```
      http://localhost:8080/alfresco/service/index
      ```

   b. Click Refresh Web Scripts. You'll see a message indicating there is one additional Web script.

The Web script response template uses the `msg` method to render text whose value is taken from the resource bundle associated with the required language. Resource bundles contain one or more messages, each identified by a name; this is the name passed to the `msg` method. The example refers to the messages `greeting` and `farewell`.

Each resource bundle adheres to the naming convention defined by the Web Script Framework. Resource bundle file names are structured as follows:

```
<web script id>.<http method>[_<locale>].properties
```

The `<web script id>` identifies the Web script and must be the same as the Web script ID defined in the file name of the associated Web script description document. The `<http method>` specifies which HTTP method will initiate the Web script and again must be the same as the associated Web script description document.

The optional `<locale>` identifies the language for which this resource bundle applies. If not specified, the resource bundle is treated as the fallback set of values if no other relevant resource bundle for the required language can be found.

Finally, all resource bundle file names must end with `.properties`. This indicates to the Web Script Framework that the file is indeed a resource bundle.

You can now test your response template to ensure it is rendering values from the default resource bundle. To do this, type the following in your command line:

```
curl "http://localhost:8080/alfresco/service/i18n"
```

The response is:

```
Hello. Goodbye.
```

Now add another resource bundle for the German language.

1. You first need to log in to Alfresco Explorer.
   a. Type the following in your Web browser, and log in with the user name `admin` and password `admin` if requested:

      ```
      http://localhost:8080/alfresco
      ```

   b. Navigate to Company Home > Data Dictionary > Web Scripts Extensions > org > example.
2. You can now create a German resource bundle for your I18N sample.
   a. In the Create menu, click Create Content.
   b. Enter the name for the Web script in the Name field, as follows:

      ```
      i18n.get_de.properties
      ```

   c. In the Content Type list, select Plain Text.
   d. Click Next.
   e. Type the following in the Enter Content box:

Available for download on Wrox.com

```
greeting=Guten Tag
farewell=Auf Wiedersehen
```

Code snippet i18n.get_de.properties

   f. Click Next.
   g. Click Finish.
   h. Click OK.

3. Now re-register the I18N Web script with Alfresco.

   a. Type the following in your Web browser, and log in with the user name `admin` and password `admin` if requested:

   ```
   http://localhost:8080/alfresco/service/index
   ```

   b. Click Refresh Web Scripts.

This time you have created a resource bundle for the German language as identified by the locale of `de`. Locales are specified as follows:

```
<language>[_<country>][_<variant>]
```

The language argument is a valid ISO language code, which is a lowercase, two-letter code as defined by ISO-639. The optional country argument is a valid ISO country code, which is an uppercase, two-letter code as defined by ISO-3166. Finally, the optional variant argument is a vendor-or Web browser–specific code.

The full list of language and country codes can be found at `www.ics.uci.edu/pub/ietf/http/related/iso639.txt` *and* `www.chemie.fu-berlin.de/diverse/doc/ISO_3166.html`.

You can now test your response template to ensure it is rendering values from the German resource bundle. To do this, type the following in your command line:

```
curl -H "Accept-Language: de" "http://localhost:8080/alfresco/service/i18n"
```

This results in the following response:

```
Guten Tag. Auf Wiedersehen.
```

A client specifies its preferred language through the HTTP header named `Accept-Language`, which the Web Script Framework adheres to.

A complete definition of the HTTP Accept-Language header can be found at `www.w3.org/Protocols/rfc2616/rfc2616-sec14.html`.

CONFIGURATION

When developing a Web script, it is sometimes convenient to implement capabilities that provide some flexibility in how they behave. The Web Script Framework supports this by allowing each Web script to carry a configuration file, which the Web script can interrogate in order to alter its behavior.

This is easily demonstrated by creating a Web script whose response is driven by a configuration file.

1. You first need to log in to Alfresco Explorer.
    a. Type the following in your Web browser, and log in with the user name `admin` and password `admin` if requested:

       ```
       http://localhost:8080/alfresco
       ```

    b. Navigate to Company Home > Data Dictionary > Web Scripts Extensions.
2. Create a folder to represent the top-level package structure. You may skip this step if the *org* space already exists.
    a. In the Create menu, click Create Space.
    b. Enter the name for the folder in the Name field, such as:

       ```
       org
       ```

    c. Click Create Space.
3. Next, create a sub-package. You may skip this step if the *example* space already exists.
    a. Navigate to Company Home > Data Dictionary > Web Scripts Extensions > org.
    b. In the Create menu, click Create Space.
    c. Enter the name for the folder in the Name field, such as:

       ```
       example
       ```

    d. Navigate to Company Home > Data Dictionary > Web Scripts Extensions > org > example.
4. You can now create a Web script description document for your configuration sample.
    a. In the Create menu, click Create Content.
    b. Enter the name for the Web script in the Name field, as follows:

       ```
       configuration.get.desc.xml
       ```

    c. In the Content Type list, select XML.
    d. Click Next.
    e. Type the following in the Enter Content box:

Available for download on Wrox.com

```
<webscript>
  <shortname>Configuration Sample</shortname>
  <description>Response driven from configuration</description>
  <url>/config</url>
  <authentication>user</authentication>
</webscript>
```

Code snippet configuration.get.desc.xml

f. Click Next.
g. Click Finish.
h. Click OK.

5. Create a configuration file for your configuration sample.
   a. In the Create menu, click Create Content.
   b. Enter the name in the Name field, such as:

      configuration.get.config.xml

   c. In the Content Type list, select XML.
   d. Click Next.
   e. Type the following in the Enter Content box:

```
<greeting>
  <text>Hello</text>
  <repeat>3</repeat>
</greeting>
```

Code snippet configuration.get.config.xml

6. Next, create a controller script for your configuration sample.
   a. In the Create menu, click Create Content.
   b. Enter the name in the Name field, such as:

      configuration.get.js

   c. In the Content Type list, select Plain Text.
   d. Click Next.
   e. Type the following in the Enter Content box:

```
var greeting = new XML(config.script);
model.repeat = parseInt(greeting.repeat);
```

Code snippet configuration.get.js

7. Create a response template for your configuration sample.
   a. In the Create menu, click Create Content.
   b. Enter the name in the Name field, such as:

      configuration.get.html.ftl

   c. In the Content Type list, select Plain Text.
   d. Click Next.

e. Type the following in the Enter Content box:

Available for download on Wrox.com

```
<#list 1..repeat as i>
  ${config.script.greeting.text}
</#list>
```

Code snippet configuration.get.html.ftl

8. Now register the Web script with Alfresco.

   a. Type the following in your Web browser, and log in with the user name `admin` and password `admin` if requested:

   ```
   http://localhost:8080/alfresco/service/index
   ```

   b. Click Refresh Web Scripts.

The first thing to note is the configuration file name `configuration.get.config.xml`, which adheres to the naming convention defined by the Web Script Framework. Configuration file names are structured as follows:

```
<web script id>.<http method>.config.xml
```

The `<web script id>` identifies the Web script and must be the same as the Web script ID defined in the file name of the associated Web script description document. The `<http method>` specifies which HTTP method will initiate the Web script and again must be the same as the associated Web script description document.

Finally, all configuration file names must end with `.config.xml`. This indicates to the Web Script Framework that the file is indeed a configuration file.

Configuration is expressed as any valid XML. In your sample, you specify the greeting text to render and the number of times to repeat the greeting.

Controller scripts access the configuration XML through the root object named `config.script`. Additionally, E4X, a JavaScript XML API, is used to traverse the XML structure and extract values.

Available for download on Wrox.com

```
...
var greeting = new XML(config.script);
model.repeat = greeting.repeat;
...
```

Code snippet configuration.get.js

Your sample extracts the number of times to repeat the greeting from the configuration XML and places the value into the Web script model with the name `repeat`.

An explanation of how to process XML with E4X can be found at `https://developer.mozilla.org/En/E4X/Processing_XML_with_E4X`.

Response templates also have access to the configuration XML through the `script.config` root object. The FreeMarker language supports the traversal of XML, thus allowing response templates to directly extract values from the configuration.

Available for download on Wrox.com

```
...
${config.script.greeting.text}
...
```

Code snippet configuration.get.html.ftl

Your sample response template simply extracts the greeting text from the configuration XML and renders it.

A complete guide to processing XML with the FreeMarker language can be found at `http://freemarker.org/docs/xgui.html`.

You can now test your configuration sample by typing the following in your command line:

```
curl -uadmin:admin "http://localhost:8080/alfresco/service/config"
```

This responds with:

```
Hello
Hello
Hello
```

Configuration is altered by modifying the configuration XML file, or by creating a new configuration file of the same name in a Web script location that's earlier in the Web Script Framework search path (as described in Chapter 9).

CONTENT NEGOTIATION

Content negotiation is a mechanism defined in the HTTP specification that makes it possible to serve different versions of a document at a given URI, so that a client can specify which version best fits its capabilities. The classic example is for a Web browser to use this mechanism to specify which type of image is preferred, such as GIF or PNG, for display purposes.

As defined in RFC 2616 section 14, a client uses an Accept header to specify a prioritized list of preferred MIME types for the response. When the Web Script Framework receives an HTTP request with an Accept header, it responds with the Web script response format that most closely matches the highest-priority MIME type preference.

RFC 2616 (`www.ietf.org/rfc/rfc2616.txt`) is the specification for the Hypertext Transfer Protocol – HTTP/1.1.

By default, content negotiation is disabled; however, each Web script may enable content negotiation by declaring its requirements in its descriptor document. This simply involves mapping an incoming Accept header MIME type preference to one of its response formats.

This is best demonstrated by creating a Web script whose response format may be driven by the HTTP Accept header.

1. You first need to log in to Alfresco Explorer.
   a. Type the following in your Web browser, and log in with the user name `admin` and password `admin` if requested:

      ```
      http://localhost:8080/alfresco
      ```

   b. Navigate to Company Home > Data Dictionary > Web Scripts Extensions.
2. Create a folder to represent the top-level package structure. You may skip this step if the *org* space already exists.
   a. In the Create menu, click Create Space.
   b. Enter the name for the folder in the Name field, such as:

      ```
      org
      ```

   c. Click Create Space.
3. Next, create a sub-package. You may skip this step if the *example* space already exists.
   a. Navigate to Company Home > Data Dictionary > Web Scripts Extensions > org.
   b. In the Create menu, click Create Space.
   c. Enter the name for the folder in the Name field, such as:

      ```
      example
      ```

   d. Navigate to Company Home > Data Dictionary > Web Scripts Extensions > org > example.
4. You can now create a Web script description document for your content negotiation sample.
   a. In the Create menu, click Create Content.
   b. Enter the name for the Web script in the Name field, as follows:

      ```
      negotiate.get.desc.xml
      ```

   c. In the Content Type list, select XML.
   d. Click Next.
   e. Type the following in the Enter Content box:

Available for download on Wrox.com

```
<webscript>
  <shortname>Negotiation Sample</shortname>
  <description>Response format driven by content negotiation</description>
```

```
  <url>/negotiate</url>
  <negotiate accept="text/html">html</negotiate>
  <negotiate accept="application/json">json</negotiate>
</webscript>
```

Code snippet negotiate.get.desc.xml

f. Click Next.

g. Click Finish.

h. Click OK.

5. Create an HTML response template for your content negotiation sample.

a. In the Create menu, click Create Content.

b. Enter the name in the Name field, such as:

```
negotiate.get.html.ftl
```

c. In the Content Type list, select Plain Text.

d. Click Next.

e. Type the following in the Enter Content box:

Available for download on Wrox.com

```
<html><body>HTML response.</body></html>
```

Code snippet negotiate.get.html.ftl

6. Next, create a JSON response template for your content negotiation sample.

a. In the Create menu, click Create Content.

b. Enter the name in the Name field, such as:

```
negotiate.get.json.ftl
```

c. In the Content Type list, select Plain Text.

d. Click Next.

e. Type the following in the Enter Content box:

Available for download on Wrox.com

```
{"response": "json"}
```

Code snippet negotiate.get.json.ftl

7. Now register the Web script with Alfresco.

a. Type the following in your Web browser, and log in with the user name `admin` and password `admin` if requested:

```
http://localhost:8080/alfresco/service/index
```

b. Click Refresh Web Scripts.

Content negotiation is declared by listing the mappings between an incoming preferred MIME type and a Web script response format. In your sample, the HTML and JSON response formats are mapped to the `text/html` and `application/json` MIME types, respectively:

Available for download on Wrox.com

```
...
<negotiate accept="text/html">html</negotiate>
<negotiate accept="application/json">json</negotiate>
...
```

Code snippet negotiate.get.desc.xml

You can now test that your sample Web script responds appropriately to content negotiation. First, explicitly request JSON by typing the following in your command line:

```
curl -H "Accept: application/json" "http://localhost:8080/alfresco/service/
negotiate"
```

The response is:

```
{"response": "json"}
```

Next, you can test to ensure the best response format is chosen. To do this, type the following in your command line:

```
curl -H "Accept: text/xml,text/*" "http://localhost:8080/alfresco/service/
negotiate"
```

This time the response is:

```
<html><body>HTML response.</body></html>
```

Your sample Web script does not provide an XML response format so cannot respond to the preferred `text/xml` MIME type; however, it can respond with the HTML response format that matches the second preference of `text/*`.

MULTIPART FORM PROCESSING

It is common for applications to utilize HTML forms to create and update data and, in particular, for content applications to use forms to upload files from the user's local file system. HTML forms allow data to be submitted in one of two content types: URL-encoded (`application-x-www-form-urlencoded`) and multipart form data (`multipart/form-data`).

URL-encoded submissions can be handled by Web scripts in the same manner as other requests, where the Web script can parse the URI to extract the form data. However, the URL-encoded approach is inefficient for sending large quantities of binary data or text containing non-ASCII characters.

To submit forms containing files, non-ASCII, and binary data, the multipart form data content type must be used; however, this type of request is not as simple to parse for the server. Given the common requirement to submit files to the Alfresco content repository, the Web Script Framework provides

data submissions by hiding the complexity of request
.

-form content types can be found at
orms.html#h-17.13.4.

tipart/form-data form submits, you will create two
ws the selection of a file along with title and description,
o the Alfresco content repository.

lorer

rowser, and log in with the user name admin and pass-

o

ata Dictionary > Web Scripts Extensions.

l package structure. You may skip this step if the *org*

ace.

Name field, such as:

this step if the *example* space already exists.

Dictionary > Web Scripts Extensions > org.

ce.

Name field, such as:

examp

d. Navigate to Company Home > Data Dictionary > Web Scripts Extensions > org > example.

4. You can now create a Web script description document for your form.

a. In the Create menu, click Create Content.

b. Enter the name for the Web script in the Name field, as follows:

```
multipart.get.desc.xml
```

c. In the Content Type list, select XML.

d. Click Next.

e. Type the following in the Enter Content box:

Available for download on Wrox.com

```
<webscript>
  <shortname>File Upload Sample</shortname>
  <description>Form to upload file.</description>
  <url>/multipart</url>
  <authentication>user</authentication>
</webscript>
```

Code snippet multipart.get.desc.xml

f. Click Next.

g. Click Finish.

h. Click OK.

5. Create an HTML response template for your form.

a. In the Create menu, click Create Content.

b. Enter the name in the Name field, such as:

`multipart.get.html.ftl`

c. In the Content Type list, select Plain Text.

d. Click Next.

e. Type the following in the Enter Content box:

Available for download on Wrox.com

```
<html>
<body>
  <form action="${url.service}" method="post" enctype="multipart/form-data">
    File: <input type="file" name="file"><br>
    Title: <input name="title"><br>
    Description: <input name="description"><br>
    <input type="submit" name="submit" value="Upload">
  </form>
</body>
</html>
```

Code snippet multipart.get.html.ftl

6. Now create a Web script description document for your upload Web script.

a. In the Create menu, click Create Content.

b. Enter the name in the Name field, such as:

`multipart.post.desc.xml`

c. In the Content Type list, select XML.

d. Click Next.

e. Type the following in the Enter Content box:

Available for download on Wrox.com

```
<webscript>
  <shortname>File Upload Sample</shortname>
  <description>Handling of multipart/form-data requests.</description>
  <url>/multipart</url>
  <authentication>user</authentication>
</webscript>
```

Code snippet multipart.post.desc.xml

7. Create a controller script for your upload Web script.

   a. In the Create menu, click Create Content.

   b. Enter the name in the Name field, such as:

   ```
   multipart.post.js
   ```

   c. In the Content Type list, select Plain Text.

   d. Click Next.

   e. Type the following in the Enter Content box:

Available for download on Wrox.com

```
// extract file attributes
var title = args.title;
var description = args.description;

// extract file
var file = null;
for each (field in formdata.fields)
{
  if (field.name == "file" && field.isFile)
  {
    file = field;
  }
}

// ensure file has been uploaded
if (file.filename == "")
{
  status.code = 400;
  status.message = "Uploaded file cannot be located";
  status.redirect = true;
}
else
{
  // create document in company home from uploaded file
  upload = companyhome.createFile(file.filename) ;
  upload.properties.content.guessMimetype(file.filename);
  upload.properties.content.write(file.content);
  upload.properties.title = title;
```

```
      upload.properties.description = description;
      upload.save();

      // setup model for response template
      model.upload = upload;
   }
```

Code snippet multipart.post.js

8. Next, create a response template for your upload Web script.
   a. In the Create menu, click Create Content.
   b. Enter the name in the Name field, such as:

      `multipart.post.html.ftl`

   c. In the Content Type list, select Plain Text.
   d. Click Next.
   e. Type the following in the Enter Content box:

```
<html>
<body>
  Uploaded ${upload.name} of size ${upload.properties.content.size}.
</body>
</html>
```

Code snippet multipart.post.html.ftl

9. Now register the Web scripts with Alfresco.
   a. Type the following in your Web browser, and log in with the user name `admin` and password `admin` if requested:

      `http://localhost:8080/alfresco/service/index`

   b. Click Refresh Web Scripts. You'll see a message indicating there are two additional Web scripts.

Your sample form consists of only three input fields, where one is of type `file`. The form posts its content to the action URI as identified by the root object `url.service`, which for this sample is `/multipart` and specifies the `multipart/form-data` content type.

```
...
<form action="${url.service}" method="post" enctype="multipart/form-data">
...
```

Code snippet multipart.get.html.ftl

It is important to note that your two Web scripts are mapped to the same URI. However, the form is attached to the HTTP GET method and the upload is attached to the HTTP POST method, which allows your form to post to the same URI as the form itself.

When multipart/form-data is posted to a Web script, the Web Script Framework provides a special root object named formdata. This root object allows access to the posted request through a simple API, hiding the complexities of parsing the request directly. The API provides access to each form field, including its name and value. For form fields of type file, the content of the uploaded file is also provided. To simplify even further, all fields other than those of type file are also added to the root objects args and argsM.

Your upload Web script extracts the form title and description fields from the args root object and locates the uploaded file through the formdata root object.

Available for download on Wrox.com

```
...
var title = args.title;
var description = args.description;

var file = null;
for each (field in formdata.fields)
{
  if (field.name == "file" && field.isFile)
  {
    file = field;
  }
}
...
```

Code snippet multipart.post.js

If a file has been uploaded, the upload Web script creates a new document within the Alfresco content repository under the Company Home folder. The document is named after the file name of the uploaded file and its content is taken from the file content.

Available for download on Wrox.com

```
...
upload = companyhome.createFile(file.filename) ;
upload.properties.content.guessMimetype(file.filename);
upload.properties.content.write(file.content);
...
```

Code snippet multipart.post.js

Finally, the created document is placed into the Web script model, allowing the upload response template to render a message confirming the name and size of the uploaded file.

Available for download on Wrox.com

```
...
model.upload = upload;
...
```

Code snippet multipart.post.js

It's time to test your upload Web script.

1. You first need to launch the upload form.
   a. Type the following in your Web browser, and log in with the user name `admin` and password `admin` if requested:

      ```
      http://localhost:8080/alfresco/service/multipart
      ```

   b. Fill in the file, title, and description fields of the form and click the Upload button.
   c. If you see a confirmation message detailing the name and size of the uploaded file, your Web script is working.
2. Now locate the created document in the Alfresco content repository.
   a. Type the following in your Web browser, and log in with the user name `admin` and password `admin` if requested:

      ```
      http://localhost:8080/alfresco
      ```

   b. Navigate to the Company Home folder and locate the document whose name matches the uploaded file name.
   c. Examine the properties and content of the created document.

The Form Data API

The Form Data API provides direct access to form fields submitted through the `multipart/form-data` content type. When requests of this type are posted to a Web script, the Web Script Framework supplies the root object named `formdata` to the controller script of the Web script.

formdata

`formdata` is the root object that represents the submitted form, which comprises one or more form fields. Access to the form fields is provided through the following API:

- **`hasField(string fieldname)`** — Returns a Boolean indicating the existence of the form field named `fieldname`
- **`fields`** — (read-only) An array of `formfield` objects where each entry represents a field within the form

formfield

The `formfield` object represents a single field within the form, allowing access to the field metadata and content through the following API:

- **`name`** — (read-only string) The name of the field as defined in the form. Note that form fields may not be uniquely named.
- **`isFile`** — (read-only Boolean) Indicates whether the field is of type `file`.
- **`value`** — (read-only string) The value of the field as entered into the form. Fields of type `file` return the file name. File content must be retrieved through `content` instead.

- **`content`** — (read-only `ScriptContent`) The value of the field as entered into the form represented as a `ScriptContent` object whose API is described in Online Appendix D.
- **`mimetype`** — (read-only string) For form fields of type `file`, the MIME type of the content; otherwise, `null`.
- **`filename`** — (read-only string) For form fields of type `file`, the file name of the uploaded file; otherwise, `null`.

REQUEST PROCESSING

When performing an HTTP POST to a Web script, the posted request body often contains content that needs processing by the Web script. To allow access to the request body, the Web Script Framework provides a special root object named `requestbody` that represents the content of the request.

The `requestbody` is a `ScriptContent` object allowing access to the request content either as a string or as a content stream.

`ScriptContent` is an object provided with the JavaScript API, which is described in full in Online Appendix D.

Request processing is best demonstrated by creating a Web script, which simply responds with the content of the HTTP request.

1. You first need to log in to Alfresco Explorer.
   a. Type the following in your Web browser, and log in with the user name `admin` and password `admin` if requested:

      ```
      http://localhost:8080/alfresco
      ```

   b. Navigate to Company Home > Data Dictionary > Web Scripts Extensions.
2. Create a folder to represent the top-level package structure. You may skip this step if the *org* space already exists.
   a. In the Create menu, click Create Space.
   b. Enter the name for the folder in the Name field, such as:

      ```
      org
      ```

   c. Click Create Space.
3. Next, create a sub-package. You may skip this step if the *example* space already exists.
   a. Navigate to Company Home > Data Dictionary > Web Scripts Extensions > org.
   b. In the Create menu, click Create Space.
   c. Enter the name for the folder in the Name field, such as:

      ```
      example
      ```

   d. Navigate to Company Home > Data Dictionary > Web Scripts Extensions > org > example.

4. You can now create a Web script description document for your request body sample.

   a. In the Create menu, click Create Content.

   b. Enter the name for the Web script in the Name field, as follows:

      `requestbody.post.desc.xml`

   c. In the Content Type list, select XML.

   d. Click Next.

   e. Type the following in the Enter Content box:

Available for download on Wrox.com

```
<webscript>
  <shortname>Request Body Sample</shortname>
  <description>Render the request body in the response</description>
  <url>/requestbody</url>
  <authentication>user</authentication>
</webscript>
```

Code snippet requestbody.post.desc.xml

   f. Click Next.

   g. Click Finish.

   h. Click OK.

5. Create a controller script for your request body sample.

   a. In the Create menu, click Create Content.

   b. Enter the name for the Web script in the Name field, as follows:

      `requestbody.post.js`

   c. In the Content Type list, select Plain Text.

   d. Click Next.

   e. Type the following in the Enter Content box:

Available for download on Wrox.com

```
model.requestcontent = requestbody.content;
```

Code snippet requestbody.post.js

   f. Click Next.

   g. Click Finish.

   h. Click OK.

6. Next, create an HTML response template for your request body sample.

   a. In the Create menu, click Create Content.

   b. Enter the name in the Name field, such as:

      `requestbody.post.html.ftl`

c. In the Content Type list, select Plain Text.

d. Click Next.

Available for download on Wrox.com

e. Type the following in the Enter Content box:

```
${requestcontent}
```

Code snippet requestbody.post.html.ftl

7. Now register the Web script with Alfresco.

a. Type the following in your Web browser, and log in with the user name `admin` and password `admin` if requested:

```
http://localhost:8080/alfresco/service/index
```

b. Click Refresh Web Scripts. You'll see a message indicating there is an additional Web script.

Your example consists of just two lines of code. The controller script extracts the request content from the `requestbody` root object and places it into the Web script model under the name `requestcontent`. The response template simply outputs the model value into the response.

You can test this Web script with cURL by typing the following in your command line:

```
curl -uadmin:admin -H "Content-Type: application/json" --data-binary "{\"request\":
\"body\"}" "http://localhost:8080/alfresco/service/requestbody"
```

This posts a request body of `{"request": "body"}` to your Web script, which in turn responds with:

```
{"request": "body"}
```

Often the content posted in a request is structured using data formats such as XML or JSON, which the Web script has to parse. Parser code is generally painful to develop, so the Web Script Framework provides a mechanism known as a Format Reader that parses a request of a given MIME type into an object that represents the request content. The object is then supplied to the controller script, which can interrogate the object to extract request content.

The Web Script Framework provides the following out-of-the-box Format Readers:

- JSON: Parses a request of MIME type `application/json` into a root object named `json`
- Atom Feed: Parses a request of MIME type `application/atom+xml;type=feed` into a root object named `feed` whose type is an Apache Abdera Feed object
- Atom Entry: Parses a request of MIME type `application/atom+xml;type=entry` into a root object named `entry` whose type is an Apache Abdera Entry object
- Atom: Parses a request of MIME type `application/atom+xml` into a root object named either `feed` (Apache Abdera Feed) or `entry` (Apache Abdera Entry), depending on the request content

Apache Abdera is an open source implementation of the Atom Syndication Format (RFC 4287) and the Atom Publishing Protocol (RFC 5023).

You can now extend your request processing Web script example by adding a new controller script that uses the `json` root object provided by the Web Script Framework.

1. You first need to log in to Alfresco Explorer.
   a. Type the following in your Web browser, and log in with the user name `admin` and password `admin` if requested:

   ```
   http://localhost:8080/alfresco
   ```

   b. Navigate to Company Home > Data Dictionary > Web Scripts Extensions > org > example.
2. You can now create the additional controller script document for your request body sample.
   a. In the Create menu, click Create Content.
   b. Enter the name for the Web script in the Name field, as follows:

   ```
   requestbody.post.json.js
   ```

   c. In the Content Type list, select Plain Text.
   d. Click Next.
   e. Type the following in the Enter Content box:

Available for download on Wrox.com

   ```
   model.requestcontent = json.get("request");
   ```

   Code snippet requestbody.post.json.js

   f. Click Next.
   g. Click Finish.
   h. Click OK.
3. Now re-register the Web script with Alfresco.
   a. Type the following in your Web browser, and log in with the user name `admin` and password `admin` if requested:

   ```
   http://localhost:8080/alfresco/service/index
   ```

   b. Click Refresh Web Scripts.

Format Readers are not invoked automatically. You have to ask the Web Script Framework to convert the response and provide the resulting object to the controller script. This is achieved by creating a controller script with an alternate naming convention:

```
<web script id>.<http method>.<format>.js
```

The difference here is that the controller script file name also contains the `<format>` segment, indicating to the Web Script Framework that requests of the specified format are handled by this controller and require the converted root object.

In the example, you create a new controller script named `requestbody.post.json.js` to handle JSON posted requests. This controller now has access to the `json` root object, as provided by the JSON Format Reader, and can extract values directly from the JSON document.

```
...
model.requestcontent = json.get("request");
...
```

Code snippet requestbody.post.json.js

You can test the updated Web script with cURL by typing the following in your command line:

```
curl -uadmin:admin -H "Content-Type: application/json" --data-binary
"{\"request\": \"body\"}" "http://localhost:8080/alfresco/service/requestbody"
```

This posts a request body of `{"request": "body"}` to your Web script, which in turn responds with:

```
body
```

Instead of echoing the complete request as before, the updated controller script extracts the value named `request` from the JSON document and places it into the Web script model, which in this case is the value `body`.

The JSON Object API

The JSON Object API provides the ability to programmatically traverse JSON documents, where the root of the document is either a JSON array or a JSON object.

The Web Script Framework, if instructed, supplies a root object named `json` to the Web script, which is one of the following object types, depending on the root of the JSON document.

JSONArray

The `JSONArray` object type represents an array within a JSON document and provides the following API:

- **`length()`** — (read-only integer) Returns the length of the JSON array
- **`getJSONObject(integer index)`** — Returns the JSON object located in the JSON array at the specified index

JSONObject

The `JSONObject` object type represents an object within a JSON document and provides the following API:

- `get(string name)`: Returns the value of the specified name from the JSON object
- `has(string name)`: Indicates whether the value of the specified name exists within the JSON object

- `isNull(string name)`: Indicates whether the value of the specified name is null within the JSON object
- `getJSONArray(string name)`: Returns a JSONArray object for the array of the specified name within the JSON object

CACHING

A key aspect of HTTP is its ability to support caching of HTTP responses, relieving workload on the HTTP server, which does not have to re-create the HTTP response for every request. From a client perspective this gives a prompt response.

The Web Script Framework complies with HTTP caching, in particular with the notions of Last Modified Time and ETag (a kind of hash), allowing the caching of Web script responses using HTTP-aware caches.

An ETag (entity tag) is a response header and is used to determine change in content at a given URL. Clients and caches use the ETag in subsequent requests to determine with the server if the content needs refreshing.

As a developer of a Web script you may specify its caching requirements, such as how long to keep the response in the cache or how to calculate the hash for the response. It's important to note that the Web Script Framework does not actually perform any caching. Alfresco decided that it is better to rely on one of the many HTTP caches already available, such as Squid (`www.squid-cache.org`), an HTTP caching proxy. Therefore, it is necessary to either embed an HTTP cache in your client or deploy an HTTP-cache proxy in front of the Alfresco Content Application Server to enable caching.

Descriptor Cache Controls

When developing a Web script, it is possible through the Web script descriptor document to specify whether its response is to be cached and, if so, how it is to be cached.

The optional `<cache>` element of the Web script descriptor provides the following cache flags:

- `never` (optional) specifies whether caching should be applied at all. If true, the Web script response should never be cached; otherwise, the Web script response may be cached.
- `public` (optional) specifies whether authenticated responses should be cached in a public cache. If true, the Web script response should never be cached; otherwise, the Web script response may be cached.
- `mustrevalidate` (optional) specifies whether a cache must revalidate its version of the Web script response in order to ensure freshness. If true, the cache must revalidate; otherwise, the cache may revalidate.

For example, the following Web script descriptor specifies that responses may be cached, but never in a public cache as the response requires authentication, and that the cache must revalidate to ensure freshness of the content.

```
<webscript>
  <shortname>Design time cache sample</shortname>
  <url>/cache</url>
  <authentication>user</authentication>
  <cache>
     <never>false</never>
     <public>false</public>
     <mustrevalidate/>
  </cache>
</webscript>
```

Runtime Cache Controls

Some cache controls can be set only during the execution of a Web script, such as setting when the content of the response was last modified. To support this, the Web Script Framework provides a special root object named `cache` to all controller scripts for allowing cache controls to be set at runtime.

The `cache` root object provides the following API:

- **`neverCache`** (read/write Boolean) — Controls whether Web script response should be cached at all; true means never cache. If not set, the default value is specified by the cache control section of the Web script descriptor.
- **`isPublic`** (read/write Boolean) — Controls whether Web script response should be cached by public caches. If not set, the default value is specified by the cache control section of the Web script descriptor.
- **`mustRevalidate`** (read/write Boolean) — Controls whether cache *must* revalidate its version of the Web script response to ensure freshness. If not set, the default value is specified by the cache control section of the Web script descriptor.
- **`maxAge`** (read/write long) — Specifies the maximum amount of time (in seconds, relative to the time of request) that the response will be considered fresh. If not set, the default value is null.
- **`lastModified`** (read/write date) — Specifies the time that the content of the response last changed. If not set, the default value is null.
- **`ETag`** (read/write string) — Specifies a unique identifier that changes each time the content of the response changes. If not set, the default value is null.

Cache controls are best demonstrated by creating a sample Web script which sets the last modified date.

1. You first need to log in to Alfresco Explorer.
   a. Type the following in your Web browser, and log in with the user name `admin` and password `admin` if requested:

      ```
      http://localhost:8080/alfresco
      ```

   b. Navigate to Company Home > Data Dictionary > Web Scripts Extensions.

2. Create a folder to represent the top-level package structure. You may skip this step if the *org* space already exists.

   a. In the Create menu, click Create Space.

   b. Enter the name for the folder in the Name field, such as:

   ```
   org
   ```

   c. Click Create Space.

3. Next, create a sub-package. You may skip this step if the *example* space already exists.

   a. Navigate to Company Home > Data Dictionary > Web Scripts Extensions > org.

   b. In the Create menu, click Create Space.

   c. Enter the name for the folder in the Name field, such as:

   ```
   example
   ```

   d. Navigate to Company Home > Data Dictionary > Web Scripts Extensions > org > example.

4. You can now create a Web script description document for your cache sample.

   a. In the Create menu, click Create Content.

   b. Enter the name for the Web script in the Name field, as follows:

   ```
   cache.get.desc.xml
   ```

   c. In the Content Type list, select XML.

   d. Click Next.

   e. Type the following in the Enter Content box:

```
<webscript>
   <shortname>Cache example</shortname>
   <description>Demonstrate cache controls</description>
   <url>/cache</url>
   <authentication>user</authentication>
   <cache>
     <never>false</never>
     <mustrevalidate/>
   </cache>
</webscript>
```

Code snippet cache.get.desc.xml

   f. Click Next.

   g. Click Finish.

   h. Click OK.

5. Create a controller script for your cache sample.

   a. In the Create menu, click Create Content.

b. Enter the name for the Web script in the Name field, as follows:

```
cache.get.js
```

c. In the Content Type list, select Plain Text.

d. Click Next.

e. Type the following in the Enter Content box:

Available for download on Wrox.com

```
cache.lastModified = new Date();
```

Code snippet cache.get.js

f. Click Next.

g. Click Finish.

h. Click OK.

6. Next, create an HTML response template for your cache sample.

a. In the Create menu, click Create Content.

b. Enter the name in the Name field, such as:

```
cache.get.html.ftl
```

c. In the Content Type list, select Plain Text.

d. Click Next.

e. Type the following in the Enter Content box:

Available for download on Wrox.com

```
Cached response.
```

Code snippet cache.get.html.ftl

7. Now register the Web script with Alfresco.

a. Type the following in your Web browser, and log in with the user name `admin` and password `admin` if requested:

```
http://localhost:8080/alfresco/service/index
```

b. Click Refresh Web Scripts. You'll see a message indicating there is an additional Web script.

Remember, the Web Script Framework does not perform any caching of its own. It ensures correct HTTP headers are transmitted based on the Web script cache controls for an external cache to interpret.

When testing cache controls, it is useful to test with cURL, as this gives you access to the headers sent on the HTTP response. For example, to test your cache sample, type the following in your command line:

```
curl -uadmin:admin -v "http://localhost:8080/alfresco/service/cache"
```

The returned response is similar to the following, where the Cache-Control and Last-Modified headers are present:

```
* About to connect() to localhost port 8080 (#0)
*   Trying ::1... connected
* Connected to localhost (::1) port 8080 (#0)
* Server auth using Basic with user 'admin'
> GET /alfresco/service/cache HTTP/1.1
> Authorization: Basic YWRtaW46YWRtaW4=
> Host: localhost:8080
> Accept: */*
>
< HTTP/1.1 200 OK
< Server: Apache-Coyote/1.1
< Cache-Control:  must-revalidate
< Last-Modified: Tue, 02 Feb 2010 09:07:05 GMT
< Content-Type: text/html;charset=UTF-8
< Content-Length: 16
< Date: Tue, 02 Feb 2010 09:07:05 GMT
```

Caching is an important aspect of Web scripts and is often required in order to support high-load applications such as Internet Web sites backed by the Alfresco Content Application Server. As such, caching should be considered when developing all Web scripts.

ADVANCED DESCRIPTOR OPTIONS

The following Web script descriptor options are not essential, but provide useful capabilities on those rare occasions they are needed.

Lifecycle

The `lifecycle` option allows a Web script developer to indicate the development status of a Web script. Typically, Web scripts start out in a draft state while being developed or tested, are then promoted to production quality for widespread use, and are finally retired at the end of their life.

The following `lifecycle` values are available:

- `none` indicates that this Web script is not part of a lifecycle.
- `sample` indicates that this Web script is a sample and is not intended for production use.
- `draft` indicates that this Web script may be incomplete, experimental, or still subject to change.
- `public_api` indicates that this Web script is part of a public API and should be stable and well tested.
- `draft_public_api` indicates that this Web script is intended to become part of the public API but is incomplete or still subject to change.
- `deprecated` indicates that this Web script should be avoided; it may be removed in future versions of the product.

- `internal` indicates that this Web script is for Alfresco use only; it should not be relied upon between versions and is likely to change.

An example usage of the `lifecycle` option follows:

```
<webscript>
  <shortname>Example Lifecycle Usage</shortname>
  <url>/lifecycle</url>
  <lifecycle>sample</lifecycle>
</webscript>
```

Family

The `family` option allows a Web script developer to categorize their Web scripts. Any value may be assigned to `family` and any number of families may be assigned to the Web script, providing a free-form tagging mechanism. The Web script index provides views for navigating Web scripts by family.

The Web script index is provided at `http://localhost:8080/alfresco/service/` *on the machine on which you installed Alfresco.*

An example usage of the `family` option follows:

```
<webscript>
  <shortname>Example Family Usage</shortname>
  <url>/family</url>
  <family>CMIS</family>
  <family>Dashlet</family>
</webscript>
```

Run As

The Run As option allows a Web script developer to state that the execution of a Web script must run as a particular Alfresco content repository user regardless of who initiated the Web script.

This is useful in scenarios where the behavior of the Web script requires specific permissions to succeed. Due to security concerns, the Run As option is only available for Web script implementations that are placed into the Java classpath.

The user to run as is specified through the `runas` attribute of the `<authentication>` element of the Web script descriptor, as demonstrated in the following:

```
<webscript>
  <shortname>Example Run As Usage</shortname>
  <url>/runas</url>
  <authentication runas="admin">user</authentication>
</webscript>
```

Here the Web script still requires a user to authenticate before execution; however, the Web script executes as the `admin` user. Content repository features such as auditing still reflect the user who initiated the Web script.

11

Java-Backed Web Scripts

WHAT'S IN THIS CHAPTER?

- Understanding Java-backed Web scripts
- Implementing a Java Folder Listing Web script
- Creating a new kind of Web script

In this chapter, you will discover how to develop Java-backed Web scripts, which are Web scripts whose controller implementation is written in Java, rather than JavaScript. You might be wondering why you would need to dive into Java, when JavaScript Web scripts seem to cater to most requirements. Although rare, Java-backed Web scripts are useful when:

- Accessing Alfresco Content Application Services not available via the JavaScript API
- Interacting with systems whose only API is exposed via Java
- Overriding how responses are rendered, such as to stream large content
- Performance is absolutely critical

Unlike scripted Web scripts, Java-backed Web scripts require more tooling for their development. The Java source code has to be compiled, then packaged, and finally deployed to the Alfresco Content Application Server. This means deeper knowledge of the Alfresco architecture is required, such as knowing how Alfresco employs the Spring Framework for registering and binding together Java components.

Although this seems daunting, it's not that different from developing a scripted Web script, especially if you're already familiar with Java. A Java-backed Web script (as shown in Figure 11-1) has a very similar construction to that of a scripted Web script.

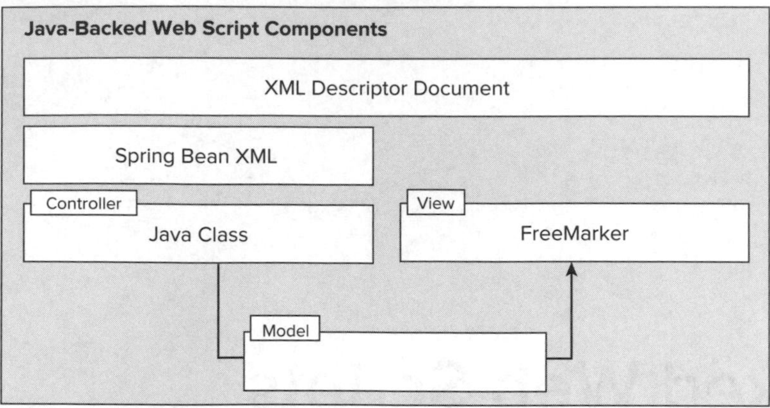

FIGURE 11-1

The primary difference is that a Java class replaces the controller script. It still has the same intent of encapsulating the behavior of the Web script and producing a model for subsequent rendering by a response template. Alfresco is aware of the Java class through Spring Framework configuration, which identifies the Java class as being the behavior for the Web script. All other components are exactly the same as those for scripted Web scripts.

The Spring Framework is an open source application framework for the Java platform best known for providing an Inversion of Control container, Aspect-Oriented Programming, and abstractions for data access and transaction management. Led and sustained by SpringSource, full details of the Spring Framework can be found at `www.springsource.org`.

STEP-BY-STEP: FOLDER LISTING JAVA-BACKED WEB SCRIPT

Java-backed Web scripts are best illustrated by developing an example. In this case, you are going to build the equivalent of the Folder Listing Web script that was introduced in Chapter 9. This Web script mimics the behavior of the 'dir' command in Microsoft Windows, or 'ls' in Linux and Mac OS X.

Although the implementation introduced in this chapter replaces the controller script with Java, the behavior will not change: users will perceive no difference. In fact, it doesn't matter how the Web script is implemented, as the client only interacts with it through HTTP requests and responses. This is very useful as it is sometimes convenient and efficient to build a library of scripted Web scripts exposing a well-defined interface and then, over time, replace their implementation with Java, if requirements such as performance become critical. As long as the interface does not change, the user will not notice.

Get started by first creating the scripted components of your Folder Listing Web script.

1. You first need to log in to Alfresco Explorer.

   a. Type the following in your Web browser, and log in with the user name `admin` and password `admin` if requested:

      ```
      http://localhost:8080/alfresco
      ```

   b. Navigate to Company Home > Data Dictionary > Web Scripts Extensions.

2. Create a folder to represent the top-level package structure. You may skip this step if the `org` space already exists.

   a. In the Create menu, click Create Space.

   b. Enter the name for the folder in the Name field, such as:

      ```
      org
      ```

   c. Click Create Space.

3. Next, create a sub-package. You may skip this step if the `example` space already exists.

   a. Navigate to Company Home > Data Dictionary > Web Scripts Extensions > org.

   b. In the Create menu, click Create Space.

   c. Enter the name for the folder in the Name field, such as:

      ```
      example
      ```

   d. Navigate to Company Home > Data Dictionary > Web Scripts Extensions > org > example.

4. Now create a Web script description document for your Java Folder Listing example.

   a. In the Create menu, click Create Content.

   b. Enter the name for the Web script in the Name field, such as:

      ```
      javadir.get.desc.xml
      ```

   c. In the Content Type list, select XML.

   d. Click Next.

   e. Type the following in the Enter Content box:

Available for download on Wrox.com

```
<webscript>
  <shortname>Folder Listing Utility</shortname>
  <description>Java-backed implementation of listing folder contents
</description>
  <url>/javadir/{folderpath}?verbose={verbose?}</url>
  <authentication>user</authentication>
</webscript>
```

Code snippet javadir.get.desc.xml

   f. Click Next.

   g. Click Finish.

   h. Click OK.

5. Create a Web script response template for your Java Folder Listing example.

   a. In the Create menu, click Create Content.

   b. Enter the name for the Web script in the Name field as follows:

      `javadir.get.html.ftl`

   c. In the Content Type list, select Plain Text.

   d. Click Next.

   e. Type the following in the Enter Content box:

```
<html>
  <head>
    <title>Folder ${folder.displayPath}/${folder.name}</title>
  </head>
  <body>
     Alfresco ${server.edition} Edition v${server.version} : dir
    <p>
    Contents of folder ${folder.displayPath}/${folder.name}
    <p>
    <table>
    <#list folder.children as child>
       <tr>
          <td><#if child.isContainer>d</#if></td>
          <#if verbose>
             <td>${child.properties.modifier}</td>
             <td><#if child.isDocument>
                ${child.properties.content.size}</#if></td>
             <td>${child.properties.modified?date}</td>
          </#if>
          <td>${child.name}</td>
       </tr>
    </#list>
    </table>
  </body>
</html>
```

Code snippet javadir.get.html.ftl

   f. Click Next.

   g. Click Finish.

   h. Click OK.

The Web script description specifies a URI template containing the tokens `{folderpath}` and `{verbose?}`. The `folderpath` token represents the folder to list and the `verbose` URI argument specifies whether a verbose listing is required or not.

The HTML response template renders the contents of the specified folder, taking into account the `verbose` flag. It does this by accessing the Web script model values named `folder` and `verbose`.

You haven't yet completed your Web script, which is still missing its controller. In this case, the controller needs to parse the URI to extract the token values, interact with the Alfresco content repository to locate the specified folder, and populate the model for subsequent rendering by the HTML response template.

It's now time to switch to Java for developing your controller.

1. First, create the Java class for your Folder Listing Web script.

    a. Launch your Java IDE.

    b. Create a Java package whose name is:

    ```
    org.example
    ```

    c. Create a Java class whose name is:

    ```
    JavaDir
    ```

    d. Implement the Java class as follows:

Available for download on Wrox.com

```
package org.example;

import java.util.HashMap;
import java.util.Map;

import org.alfresco.repo.model.Repository;
import org.alfresco.service.cmr.repository.NodeRef;
import org.alfresco.web.scripts.Cache;
import org.alfresco.web.scripts.DeclarativeWebScript;
import org.alfresco.web.scripts.Status;
import org.alfresco.web.scripts.WebScriptException;
import org.alfresco.web.scripts.WebScriptRequest;

public class JavaDir extends DeclarativeWebScript
{
    private Repository repository;

    public void setRepository(Repository repository)
    {
        this.repository = repository;
    }

    protected Map<String, Object> executeImpl(WebScriptRequest req,
        Status status, Cache cache)
    {
        // extract folder listing arguments from URI
        String verboseArg = req.getParameter("verbose");
        Boolean verbose = Boolean.parseBoolean(verboseArg);
        Map<String, String> templateArgs =
          req.getServiceMatch().getTemplateVars();
        String folderPath = templateArgs.get("folderpath");
```

```
            // search for folder within Alfresco content repository
            String nodePath = "workspace/SpacesStore/" + folderPath;
            NodeRef folder = repository.findNodeRef("path", nodePath.split("/"));

            // validate that folder has been found
            if (folder == null)
            {
                throw new WebScriptException(Status.STATUS_NOT_FOUND,
                  "Folder " + folderPath + " not found");
            }

            // construct model for response template to render
            Map<String, Object> model = new HashMap<String, Object>();
            model.put("verbose", verbose);
            model.put("folder", folder);
            return model;
        }
    }
```

Code snippet JavaDir.java

e. Compile the Java class.

f. Place the compiled Java class into the folder `org/example` within the Web application classpath of the Alfresco Content Application Server.

2. Next, create the Spring Framework configuration for registering your Web script Java class.

a. Create an XML file whose name is:

`javadir-context.xml`

b. Register the Java class as follows:

Available for download on Wrox.com

```
<?xml version='1.0' encoding='UTF-8'?>
<!DOCTYPE beans PUBLIC '-//SPRING//DTD BEAN 2.0//EN'
  'http://www.springframework.org/dtd/spring-beans-2.0.dtd'>

<beans>
  <bean id="webscript.org.example.javadir.get"
        class="org.example.JavaDir" parent="webscript">
    <property name="repository" ref="repositoryHelper"/>
  </bean>
</beans>
```

Code snippet javadir-context.xml

c. Place the Spring Framework configuration file into the extension classpath of the Alfresco Content Application Server.

The Java samples in this chapter depend on the following libraries: alfresco-core, alfresco-repository, alfresco-webscript-framework, and dom4j.

For a default installation of Alfresco, the web application classpath is located at installLocation*/tomcat/webapps/alfresco/WEB-INF/classes and the extension classpath is located at* installLocation*/tomcat/shared/classes/alfresco/extension.*

When deploying a Java-backed Web script to the Alfresco Content Application Server, the server must be restarted for it to be fully registered.

You can now test your Java-backed Web script. In your Web browser, type the following:

```
http://localhost:8080/alfresco/service/javadir/Company%20Home?verbose=true
```

If successful, you will see a verbose listing of the contents of the Company Home folder. Externally, this Folder Listing Web script looks and behaves the same as its scripted Web script implementation.

JAVA APPROACH TO WEB SCRIPTS

The Java class for a Java-backed Web script only has to follow one rule, which is that it implements the Java interface:

```
org.alfresco.web.scripts.WebScript
```

This interface defines the following two methods, which must be implemented:

```
/**
 * Gets the Web script Description
 *
 * @return the Web script description
 */
public WebScriptDescription getDescription();

/**
 * Execute the Web script
 *
 * @param req  the Web script request
 * @param res  the Web script response
 */
public void execute(WebScriptRequest req, WebScriptResponse res) throws
IOException;
```

The first method, `getDescription()`, returns a `WebScriptDescription` object, which is a Java representation of the Web script description XML document. The second method, `execute()`, is invoked by the Web Script Framework to initiate the Web script.

Thankfully, the Web Script Framework also provides two Java classes that implement the difficult parts of this interface, which you can extend as a starting point. The simplest helper Java class is named as follows:

```
org.alfresco.web.scripts.AbstractWebScript
```

This helper provides an implementation of `getDescription()` but does not provide any execution assistance, which it delegates to its derived class. This allows a Java-backed Web script to take full control of the execution process, including how output is rendered to the response.

The other helper Java class is named as follows:

```
org.alfresco.web.scripts.DeclarativeWebScript
```

This helper provides an implementation of `getDescription()` and `execute()`. Interestingly, it encapsulates the execution of a scripted Web script, which is:

- Locate an associated controller script written in JavaScript and, if found, execute it.
- Locate an associated response template for the requested format and execute it, passing the model populated by the controller script.

By default, all Web scripts implemented through scripting alone are actually backed by the `DeclarativeWebScript` Java class. There is one special hook point, though, that makes this a very useful class for your own Java-backed Web scripts to extend. Just prior to controller script execution, `DeclarativeWebScript` invokes the template method `executeImpl()`, which it expects derived Java classes to implement.

```
protected Map<String, Object> executeImpl(WebScriptRequest req, Status status,
    Cache cache)
```

This is where the behavior of a custom Java-backed Web script is encapsulated, including the population of the Web script model, which is returned from this method.

Your Java Folder Listing Web script uses `DeclarativeWebScript` for its starting point.

```
...
public class JavaDir extends DeclarativeWebScript
{
  ...
  protected Map<String, Object> executeImpl(WebScriptRequest req, Status status,
      Cache cache)
  {
    ...
    return model;
  }
  ...
}
```

Code snippet JavaDir.java

The model returned from `executeImpl()` is passed to the response template for subsequent rendering. Prior to template rendering, the model may also be accessed and further refined by a controller script, if one happens to be provided for the Web script.

Apart from implementing the `WebScript` interface, there are no other Web script demands on the Java class. You are free to give the Java class any name and place it in any Java package.

Parsing the URI

Your Folder Listing Web script defines the following URI template with one URI-path token and one query parameter token:

```
<uri>/javadir/{folderpath}?verbose={verbose?}</uri>
```

To extract the values provided for the `{folderpath}` and `{verbose}` tokens, the following Java code is used:

Available for download on Wrox.com

```
...
String verboseArg = req.getParameter("verbose");
Boolean verbose = Boolean.parseBoolean(verboseArg);
Map<String, String> templateArgs = req.getServiceMatch().getTemplateVars();
String folderPath = templateArgs.get("folderpath");
...
```

Code snippet JavaDir.java

Access to the request that invoked the Web script is through the `req` parameter of the `executeImpl()` method. This parameter encapsulates everything about the request, including its URI, query parameters, and header values. In particular, the `getParameter()` method of the request provides access to query parameters, which your Web script uses to retrieve the value of the `verbose` flag. If the query parameter is not specified on the URI, the returned value is null.

Access to tokens specified in the URI path is also through the `req` parameter. A map of all URI-path token values indexed by token name is provided by `req.getServiceMatch().getTemplateVars()`. Your Web script uses this map to retrieve the value of the `folderpath` token. URI-path token values are never null.

Imagine a client has made the following URI request:

```
/javadir/Company%20Home?verbose=true
```

The resulting value of `verbose` is `true` and the value of `folderpath` is `Company Home`.

Calling Alfresco Services

As a Java-backed Web script, all services provided by the Alfresco Content Application Server are available for use. In fact, any Java API within the server process, subject to security controls, is accessible.

Access to services is provided through a mechanism known as Dependency Injection (DI). Instead of the Java-backed Web script locating its dependent services, the dependent services are handed to the Web script.

Dependency Injection is a technique for supplying an external dependency to a software component. A full description of this technique can be found at `http://en.wikipedia.org/wiki/Dependency_injection`.

Alfresco employs the Spring Framework for its Dependency Injection capabilities. This means that dependencies are specified in a separate XML configuration file as part of the Java-backed Web script registration. This XML configuration will be covered in more detail later in this chapter.

How are dependent services actually injected? For each dependency, the Java-backed Web script provides a setter method for accepting a reference to the dependent service. The Spring Framework invokes each of the setter methods with the appropriate configured dependency during the initialization of the Java-backed Web script. By the time the Web script is executed, all dependent services are available within the `executeImpl()` method.

Your Folder Listing Web script needs to locate the folder within the Alfresco content repository that is identified by the `folderpath` token. To accomplish this, the Web script injects a `Repository` service that provides some simple content repository access capabilities.

Available for download on Wrox.com

```
...
public class JavaDir extends DeclarativeWebScript
{
    private Repository repository;

    public void setRepository(Repository repository)
    {
        this.repository = repository;
    }

    protected Map<String, Object> executeImpl(WebScriptRequest req,
        Status status, Cache cache)
    {
        ...
        String nodePath = "workspace/SpacesStore/" + folderPath;
        NodeRef folder = repository.findNodeRef("path", nodePath.split("/"));
        ...
    }
}
```

Code snippet JavaDir.java

The `setRepository` method represents the setter method that is called by the Spring Framework. Its implementation simply stores the `Repository` service reference in a member variable of the Java-backed Web script for subsequent access in the `executeImpl()` method.

Setting the Response Status Code

A Web script uses a response status code to inform the calling client of its execution outcome. In Java, exceptions are often used for this and Java-backed Web scripts may follow suit.

Your Folder Listing Web script validates that the provided folder path actually exists in the Alfresco content repository using the following code pattern:

Available for download on Wrox.com

```
...
if (folder == null)
{
   throw new WebScriptException(Status.STATUS_NOT_FOUND,
     "Folder " + folderPath + " not found");
}
...
```

Code snippet JavaDir.java

The WebScriptException class is a special kind of exception supported by the Web Script Framework, which carries a status code and message. Whenever a Web script throws this kind of exception, the Web Script Framework translates it into the equivalent status on the HTTP response.

All other exceptions are caught by the Web Script Framework and translated into the 500 status code, which means an internal error occurred. In all cases, the status response template has access to details such as the status code, status message, and exception call stack.

Throwing an exception is not always ideal, so the Web Script Framework provides another approach to setting the response status code. The executeImpl() method is passed a Status object, which allows the Web script to set the status explicitly.

Your Folder Listing Web script can implement folder validation using the following alternate code:

```
...
if (folder == null)
{
   status.setCode(Status.SC_NOT_FOUND);
   status.setMessage("Folder " + folderPath + " not found");
   status.setRedirect(true);
   return;
}
...
```

One advantage of setting the status explicitly is that the Web script may control whether a status response template is used to render the status through the setRedirect() method.

Exceptions may be handled in a similar manner:

```
...
catch(ConstraintException e)
{
   status.setCode(Status.SC_FORBIDDEN);
   status.setMessage("Cannot create folder");
   status.setException(e);
   status.setRedirect(true);
}
...
```

The setException() method allows the Web script to associate the status with the caught exception.

Constructing the Model

One of the responsibilities of the controller is to create a model for subsequent rendering by a response template. A model is a map of values indexed by name. In Java, the model is simply returned from the `executeImpl()` method as a `Map`.

Your Folder Listing Web script constructs a `HashMap` and places the `verbose` flag and located `folder` into it.

```
...
Map<String, Object> model = new HashMap<String, Object>();
model.put("verbose", verbose);
model.put("folder", folder);
return model;
...
```

Code snippet JavaDir.java

The model is then subsequently available to response templates, which can use the values to render the output. An important point is that values placed into the map by Java are converted to values that are accessible to the FreeMarker template language.

For example, your Java Folder Listing Web script places a `NodeRef` into the model under the name `folder`, which it received from the `Repository` service. A `NodeRef` represents a reference to an object residing in the content repository. The Web Script Framework converts `NodeRefs` into full objects so that FreeMarker templates can easily reference their object properties and methods as demonstrated by your Folder Listing response template:

```
Contents of folder ${folder.displayPath}/${folder.name}
```

Code snippet javadir.get.html.ftl

A Java-backed Web script does not have to create a model. In this case, the `executeImpl()` method can simply return null.

SPRING-FRAMEWORK REGISTRATION

A Java-backed Web script must be registered with the Web Script Framework. This is done through Spring Framework configuration, which supports the notion of a bean: a declaration of a Java class instance.

Each Java-backed Web script is defined by its own bean declaration. For example, your Java Folder Listing Web script is declared as follows:

Available for download on Wrox.com

```
...
<beans>
  ...
  <bean id="webscript.org.example.javadir.get"
      class="org.example.JavaDir" parent="webscript">
    ...
  </bean>
  ...
</beans>
```

Code snippet javadir-context.xml

Spring beans are given a unique identifier through their `id` attribute and construct an instance of the Java class as named through their `class` attribute.

The Web Script Framework uses the following bean `id` naming convention for locating Java-backed Web scripts:

```
webscript.<web script package>.<web script id>.<http method>
```

The `<web script package>`, `<web script id>`, and `<http method>` are used to bind the Java class to the associated Web script. The `class` attribute simply refers to the Java class implementing the Java-backed Web script.

Finally, all Web script bean declarations must have the parent `'webscript'`.

Service Dependencies

The Spring bean is also the place where service dependencies are declared. Your Folder Listing Web script declares a single dependency on the `Repository` service as follows:

Available for download on Wrox.com

```
...
<bean id="webscript.org.example.javadir.get"
    class="org.example.JavaDir" parent="webscript">
  <property name="repository" ref="repositoryHelper"/>
</bean>
...
```

Code snippet javadir-context.xml

Each dependency is represented by a `<property>` element whose `name` attribute identifies the setter method to call and whose `ref` attribute identifies the service to depend on. The `ref` value is actually an ID of another bean. All Alfresco services are declared as beans, so can be injected in this way.

In the example, `repository` maps to the `setRepository()` method and `repositoryHelper` maps to the bean representing the `Repository` service.

Available for download on Wrox.com

```
...
public class JavaDir extends DeclarativeWebScript
{
   ...
   public void setRepository(Repository repository)
   {
      ...
   }
}
```

Code snippet JavaDir.java

Although your example only declares a single dependency, multiple dependencies may be declared. The Spring Framework calls setter methods during the initialization of the Java-backed Web script, so all dependencies are resolved by the time the `executeImpl()` is invoked.

CREATING A NEW KIND OF WEB SCRIPT

On some occasions it is useful to extend the capabilities of the Web Script Framework by introducing a new kind of Web script. This is useful for encapsulating behavior that you wish to reuse across many scripted Web scripts.

This is best demonstrated by developing a new kind of Web script. Your example will encapsulate the logic for finding a node in the content repository given a node path and placing that node into the Web script model. Web scripts of this kind only have to declaratively specify the node path in their Web script description for the model to be automatically populated with the associated node.

Behavior for a new kind of Web script is encapsulated in Java; therefore, you can follow the same steps as for developing a Java-backed Web script.

Time to get started.

1. First, create the Java class for your new kind of Web script.
    a. Launch your Java IDE.
    b. Create a Java package whose name is:

       `org.example`

    c. Create a Java class whose name is:

       `NodeWebScript`

    d. Implement the Java class as follows:

Available for download on Wrox.com

```
package org.example;

import java.io.Serializable;
import java.util.HashMap;
import java.util.Map;
```

```
import org.alfresco.repo.model.Repository;
import org.alfresco.service.cmr.repository.NodeRef;
import org.alfresco.web.scripts.Cache;
import org.alfresco.web.scripts.DeclarativeWebScript;
import org.alfresco.web.scripts.Status;
import org.alfresco.web.scripts.WebScriptException;
import org.alfresco.web.scripts.WebScriptRequest;

public class NodeWebScript extends DeclarativeWebScript
{
    private Repository repository;

    public void setRepository(Repository repository)
    {
        this.repository = repository;
    }

    protected Map<String, Object> executeImpl(WebScriptRequest req,
        Status status, Cache cache)
    {
        // extract node path from description extensions
        Map<String, Serializable> extensions =
          getDescription().getExtensions();
        String path = (String)extensions.get("path");

        // search for folder within Alfresco content repository
        String nodePath = "workspace/SpacesStore/" + path;
        NodeRef node = repository.findNodeRef("path", nodePath.split("/"));

        // validate that node has been found
        if (node == null)
        {
            throw new WebScriptException(Status.STATUS_NOT_FOUND,
              "Path " + path + " not found");
        }

        // construct model for response template to render
        Map<String, Object> model = new HashMap<String, Object>();
        model.put("node", node);
        return model;
    }
}
```

Code snippet NodeWebScript.java

e. Compile the Java class.

f. Place the compiled Java class into the folder `org/example` within the Web application classpath of the Alfresco Content Application Server.

2. Next, create a Java class for extracting the node path configuration for your new kind of Web script.

   a. Create a Java class in the package `org.example` whose name is:

   ```
   NodeWebScriptExtension
   ```

b. Implement the Java class as follows:

Available for download on Wrox.com

```
package org.example;

import java.io.InputStream;
import java.io.Serializable;
import java.util.HashMap;
import java.util.Map;

import org.alfresco.web.scripts.DescriptionExtension;
import org.alfresco.web.scripts.WebScriptException;
import org.dom4j.Document;
import org.dom4j.DocumentException;
import org.dom4j.Element;
import org.dom4j.io.SAXReader;

public class NodeWebScriptExtension implements DescriptionExtension
{
    public Map<String, Serializable> parseExtensions(String serviceDescPath,
        InputStream servicedesc)
    {
        Map<String, Serializable> extensions =
          new HashMap<String, Serializable>();
        SAXReader reader = new SAXReader();
        try
        {
            // extract path value from description document
            Document document = reader.read(servicedesc);
            Element rootElement = document.getRootElement();
            Element pathElement = rootElement.element("path");
            String path = pathElement.getTextTrim();
            extensions.put("path", path);
        }
        catch (DocumentException e)
        {
            throw new WebScriptException("Failed to parse", e);
        }
        return extensions;
    }
}
```

Code snippet NodeWebScriptExtension.java

c. Compile the Java class.

d. Place the compiled Java class into the folder `org/example` within the Web application classpath of the Alfresco Content Application Server.

3. Now create the Spring Framework configuration file for registering your new kind of Web script.

a. Create an XML file whose name is:

```
nodewebscript-context.xml
```

b. Register the Java classes as follows:

Available for download on Wrox.com

```
<?xml version='1.0' encoding='UTF-8'?>
<!DOCTYPE beans PUBLIC '-//SPRING//DTD BEAN 2.0//EN'
'http://www.springframework.org/dtd/spring-beans-2.0.dtd'>

<beans>

  <bean id="webscript.org.example.nodewebscript"
        class="org.example.NodeWebScript" parent="webscript"
        scope="prototype">
    <property name="repository" ref="repositoryHelper"/>
  </bean>

  <bean id="webscriptdesc.org.example.nodewebscript"
        class="org.example.NodeWebScriptExtension"/>

</beans>
```

Code snippet nodewebscript-context.xml

c. Place the Spring Framework configuration into the extension classpath of the Alfresco Content Application Server.

Your example Java class extends `DeclarativeWebScript` just like other Java-backed Web scripts. Its primary purpose is to locate a node in the Alfresco content repository given a node path, which it does using the `Repository` service. The `NodeRef` returned from the `Repository` service is placed into the Web script model under the name `node`.

How does the implementation get hold of the node path? Instead of parsing the URI, the example uses a Web script description extension, which allows custom information to be placed into the Web script description. In this case, the path is to be extracted from a `<path>` element as follows:

```
<webscript>
  ...
  <path>Company Home/Data Dictionary</path>
  ...
</webscript>
```

Extensions to the Web script description are accessed through the `getDescription().getExtensions()` method, which returns a map of extension values indexed by name. Your example extracts the path as follows:

Available for download on Wrox.com

```
...
Map<String, Serializable> extensions = getDescription().getExtensions();
String path = (String)extensions.get("path");
...
```

Code snippet NodeWebScript.java

The extension map still needs to be created from the Web script description XML document. This requires the development of another Java class that implements the following interface:

```
org.alfresco.web.scripts.DescriptionExtension
```

This interface defines the following single method, which must be implemented:

```
/**
 * Parse Web script description extensions
 *
 * @param serviceDescPath  path to service document
 * @param serviceDesc  service document input stream
 * @return extensions mapped by name
 */
public Map<String, Serializable> parseExtensions(String serviceDescPath,
   InputStream servicedesc);
```

An implementation of this interface parses the Web script description document to extract the custom extensions and returns a map of those extensions indexed by name. This is the same map that is returned by `getDescription().getExtensions()`.

Your example extracts the value of the `<path>` element from the Web script description document and places it into the extension map under the name `path`.

```
 ...
// extract path value from description document
Document document = reader.read(servicedesc);
Element rootElement = document.getRootElement();
Element pathElement = rootElement.element("path");
String path = pathElement.getTextTrim();
extensions.put("path", path);
 ...
```

Code snippet NodeWebScriptExtension.java

Finally, both Java classes are registered as Spring beans whose identifiers follow the naming convention defined by the Web Script Framework.

```
 ...
<bean id="webscript.org.example.nodewebscript"
      class="org.example.NodeWebScript" parent="webscript"
      scope="prototype">
  ...
</bean>

<bean id="webscriptdesc.org.example.nodewebscript"
      class="org.example.NodeWebScriptExtension"/>
 ...
```

Code snippet nodewebscript-context.xml

The Web script Java class identifier is structured as follows:

```
webscript.<web script kind id>
```

whereas the Web script description extension Java class identifier is structured as follows:

```
webscriptdesc.<web script kind id>
```

The `<web script kind id>` can be any unique value but both IDs must match each other to be tied together.

Using a New Kind of Web Script

When developing a scripted Web script, it is possible to specify its kind through its Web script description document. If the new kind of Web script supports extensions to the Web script description document, then those must be provided as well. Otherwise, development of the Web script is the same as any other Web script.

You will implement a simple Web script based on the example `NodeWebScript` kind, which simply renders information about the Data Dictionary folder held in the Alfresco content repository.

1. You first need to log in to Alfresco Explorer.
   a. Type the following in your Web browser, and log in with the user name `admin` and password `admin` if requested:

      ```
      http://localhost:8080/alfresco
      ```

   b. Navigate to Company Home > Data Dictionary > Web Scripts Extensions.
2. Create a folder to represent the top-level package structure. You may skip this step if the *org* space already exists.
   a. In the Create menu, click Create Space.
   b. Enter the name for the folder in the Name field, such as:

      ```
      org
      ```

   c. Click Create Space.
3. Next, create a sub-package. You may skip this step if the *example* space already exists.
   a. Navigate to Company Home > Data Dictionary > Web Scripts Extensions > org.
   b. In the Create menu, click Create Space.
   c. Enter the name for the folder in the Name field, such as:

      ```
      example
      ```

   d. Navigate to Company Home > Data Dictionary > Web Scripts Extensions > org > example.
4. You now create a Web script description document for your Data Dictionary information sample.

a. In the Create menu, click Create Content.

b. Enter the name for the Web script in the Name field, as follows:

```
info.get.desc.xml
```

c. In the Content Type list, select XML.

d. Click Next.

e. Type the following in the Enter Content box:

```
<webscript kind="org.example.nodewebscript">
  <shortname>Node Info</shortname>
  <description>Demonstration of Web script Kind</description>
  <url>/info</url>
  <authentication>user</authentication>
  <path>Company Home/Data Dictionary</path>
</webscript>
```

Code snippet info.get.desc.xml

f. Click Next.

g. Click Finish.

h. Click OK.

5. Create a response template for your Data Dictionary information sample.

a. In the Create menu, click Create Content.

b. Enter the name in the Name field, such as:

```
info.get.html.ftl
```

c. In the Content Type list, select Plain Text.

d. Click Next.

e. Type the following in the Enter Content box:

```
${node.name} created on ${node.properties.created?date}
```

Code snippet info.get.html.ftl

f. Click Next.

g. Click Finish.

h. Click OK.

6. Now register the Data Dictionary Information Web script with Alfresco.

a. Type the following in your Web browser, and log in with the user name `admin` and password `admin` if requested:

```
http://localhost:8080/alfresco/service/index
```

   b. Click Refresh Web Scripts. You'll see a message indicating there is one additional Web script.

7. Finally, it's time to test.

   a. Type the following in your Web browser, and log in with the user name `admin` and password `admin` if requested:

   ```
   http://localhost:8080/alfresco/service/info
   ```

   b. If you see a message similar to *Data Dictionary created on Jan 12, 2010*, your Web script is working.

The Web script kind is specified through the `kind` attribute of the `<webscript>` element contained within the Web script description document. Its value is the `<web script kind id>` as defined in the Spring configuration for the new kind of Web script.

In your example, the `NodeWebScript` kind is selected by specifying its identifier of `org.example.nodewebscript`:

```
<webscript kind="org.example.nodewebscript">
  ...
  <path>Company Home/Data Dictionary</path>
  ...
</webscript>
```

Code snippet info.get.desc.xml

As expected by the `NodeWebScript`, the description document also specifies a path to a node in the Alfresco content repository. In the example, you specify the Data Dictionary folder through the custom `<path>` element.

Your example does not provide a controller script, as the `NodeWebScript` Java class already encapsulates the behavior of locating a node given a path and populating the Web script model. In this case, the located node is placed into the Web script model under the name `node`.

```
${node.name} created on ${node.properties.created?date}
```

Code snippet info.get.html.ftl

This means the response template can simply refer to `node` to render the output.

PART IV
Extending Share

12

Understanding the Surf Framework

WHAT'S IN THIS CHAPTER?

- Introducing Spring Surf
- Understanding the general concepts for scriptable Web applications
- Viewing Spring Surf examples

Surf is a scriptable Web framework that powers the presentation-tier rendering capabilities of applications in the Alfresco application suite. These include Alfresco Share, Alfresco Records Management, and both authoring and presentation tools for Alfresco Web Content Management.

This chapter will guide you to an understanding of building Web applications using Spring Surf. It begins by covering some of the essential concepts behind a content-driven design and then moves on to discuss the architecture. It covers Spring Web MVC (Model-View-Controller) and describes how this pattern facilitates the design and delivery of Web pages. The chapter includes code and examples that help to tie all of the concepts together.

The material presented in this chapter is applicable to any Spring Surf application. You could use it to build your own. That said, you're going to use this material starting in Chapter 15 as you extend Alfresco Share.

WHAT IS SURF?

Surf provides a way for you to build user interfaces for your Web applications using server-side scripts and templates. No Java coding, no recompilation, no server restarts, and no heavy lifting.

The result is reduced complexity and lower costs. Surf follows a content-driven approach – everything is content on disk. Scripts and templates are just simple files on disk. You can just open up a text editor and begin making changes to the live site.

Surf is a view composition plug-in for Spring Web MVC. More specifically, Surf is a Spring Framework extension that you can use to build new Spring Framework applications, or you can plug it into existing Spring Web MVC applications in your business. Spring Web MVC provides an elegant separation between the application's model, view, and controller – thus the acronym "MVC." If you wish, you can use Surf side-by-side with other popular Spring Web MVC technologies, including Tiles, Grails, and Web Flow.

Surf provides a simple object model that allows you to define pages, templates, components, themes, and more. It's all just simple XML content on disk. Your Spring application picks up the new files and processes them through your scripts and your templates to produce the view. Scripts are written using server-side JavaScript and Groovy. Templates are written using FreeMarker and PHP.

Using Surf, you can build both *page-centric* and *content-centric* Web sites. Surf provides out-of-the-box support for rendering content delivered through content delivery services, such as CMIS, Atom, and RSS.

Surf provides many features for Web site developers. Among these are:

- **Scripts and templates** — Everything in Surf consists of scripts, templates, or configuration. This means no server restarts and no compilation. Surf developers benefit by faster iteration.
- **Reusability** — Surf's presentation objects, templates, and scripts emphasize reusability. Scoped regions and component bindings allow developers to describe presentation with much less code.
- **Spring Web MVC** — Surf plugs in as a view resolver for Spring Web MVC, which enables Spring application developers to use Surf for all or part of their site's view resolution. Surf renders views on top of annotated controllers and is plug-compatible with Spring Web Flow, Spring Security, Spring Roo, and Spring tag libraries.
- **RESTful scripts and templates** — All page elements and remote interfaces are delivered through a RESTful API. The full feature set of Web scripts is available to Surf applications. You can write new remote interfaces or new portlets with just a script, a template, and a configuration file.
- **Content management** — Surf provides a set of client libraries and out-of-the-box components to streamline interoperability with CMIS content management systems. Enterprise content is easily accessed and presented using Surf components and templates.
- **Two-tier mashup architecture** — Surf is designed to work in a decoupled architecture where the presentation tier is separate from the content services tier. Surf provides credential management and mashup mechanics so that the rendered page can surface content from multiple back-end data providers. These might be CMIS, Atom, SOAP, XML, or JSON feeds. Surf builds pages, serves them, and caches for performance optimization.
- **Production, development, and staging/preview** — Surf can be configured to work in a number of deployment scenarios, including development, preview, or production environments.
- **Development tools** — Surf provides development tools that plug into the SpringSource suite of development tools. These include Eclipse add-ons for SpringSource Tool Suite as well as Spring Roo plug-ins to enable scaffolding and script-driven site generation. Developers can build an entire Web site with just a few commands.

BASIC CONCEPTS

One of the core aspects of Surf is the "no-compile" philosophy. Everything is just content or files on disk. You can change them and they will be picked up by the server right away.

In this section, you'll look more closely at this content and investigate how it is used by Surf to generate user interfaces for your Web site. In doing so, you'll distinguish between semantic and presentation content and describe how Surf's dual-tier architecture provides advantages for both. Finally, you'll look at Spring Web MVC and dig into the details of how Surf plugs in as a view resolver.

Content

Talking about *content* here refers to dynamic information or data that the Web application looks to at runtime to inform its decision about *what to render* or *how to render*. It may change between requests and the Web application is expected to behave accordingly.

Information that comes from a real-time feed (like an RSS feed) would fall into this category. Such content describes *what to render* into the user interface; for example, news articles. However, things like Java code or Spring context files are not dynamic content since they are resolved once (at compile time for Java code and during application context startup for Spring context files). The server must be restarted for any changes to be picked up.

A Spring Surf Web application architect concerns themselves with two kinds of dynamic content: *semantic content* and *presentation content*. Together, these inform Surf of *what* to render as well as *how* to render.

Semantic content consists of documents or files that describe business-generated content. This content is authored, approved, and published. It arrives to the Web site, and it is then the duty of the Web site to figure out what to do with it.

The following items are all examples of semantic content:

- An approved press release for display on the home page
- A Knowledge Base article that has been tagged and appears on several different pages of the Web site
- A product inventory descriptor that includes images, thumbnails, and references to product documentation

You can think of semantic content as information that describes *what* should be rendered. It contains the approved message but it does not contain any formatting information. It is represented in a structured, *pure data* format such as JSON or XML. Consider the following JSON text for a biography:

```
{
  "author": "Pablo Neruda",
  "country": "Chile",
  "image": "pablo_neruda.jpg",
  "description": "Pablo Neruda is adored in South America for his romantic prose.",
  "popular_works": ["Cien sonetos de amor", "Confieso que he vivido"]
}
```

Notice that this doesn't contain any formatting. No HTML tags or other markup. Just simple data. It isn't pretty, to be sure, but it does contain all of the right information – the factual bits that the Web site consumer ultimately wants.

You publish this semantic content to a Web site and then let the Web site managers figure out how they want to display it. You may publish it to more than one Web site. Each Web site manager might choose to display the semantic content differently. You don't really care. All you need to know is that the correct and approved information is being worked with.

Presentation content consists of documents and files that describe presentation configuration for a Web site. Presentation content consists of configuration that informs the Surf rendering engine how the Web page or page component should look and feel.

Presentation content answers questions like:

- Which theme should be used to render the Web site's home page?
- How many articles should I display on the front page?
- Which advertisement should I display in this section of the site for the current user?

You can think of presentation content as information that is specific to the Web site user interface. It answers the question of *how* things should be rendered. A Web site presentation framework (such as Surf) looks to this content to figure out how to do its thing.

Consider the following XML that configures a Surf Web script responsible for rendering a biography to the end user. It tells the Web script to render a link to the full article as well as to show the image of the author. Don't worry about the XML syntax yet – you'll cover that later!

```
<component>
   <url>/content/display/biography</url>
   <properties>
<link-title-to-full-article>true</link-title-to-full-article>
      <show-image>true</show-image>
   </properties>
</component>
```

This XML tells the Web script how to render the biography. The end-to-end rendering flow looks something like what is shown in Figure 12-1.

Figure 12-1 depicts a simple request for a biography of Chile's famous poet. Here is what happens.

1. The browser request arrives to Spring Surf.
2. Surf asks the *content delivery services* for the presentation content that describes what is being requested.
3. The presentation content is handed back as XML.
4. Surf determines the Web script to execute and does so using the configuration specified by the XML.

5. The Web script calls over to the content delivery services and asks for biography data.
6. The biography is returned as JSON.
7. The Web script renders HTML markup to the end user. This HTML contains presentation output (formatting) as well as the semantic data (the biography itself).

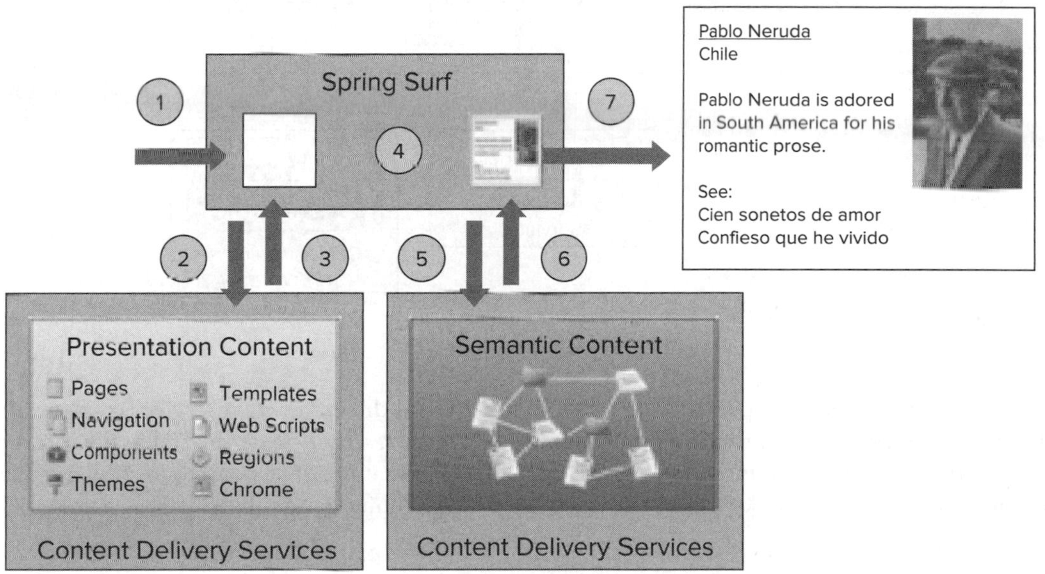

FIGURE 12-1

The Web site user is then presented with the poetic expressions of Pablo Neruda. In the sections that follow, you'll take a closer look at the content delivery services and investigate how the Alfresco Content Application Server can be used to deliver these services for your Spring applications.

Content Delivery Services

Surf connects to content delivery services to provide content retrieval and query for both presentation and semantic content. This means that Surf applications can consist of either a single-tier or dual-tier application, as shown in Figure 12-2.

Figure 12-2 shows three valid configurations for Surf. In the *standalone* configuration on the left-hand side, all of the presentation and semantic content is stored as part of the Surf Web application. It is self-contained and has everything that it needs so that requests can be services entirely from the Web application in the *presentation tier*. This is a perfectly acceptable configuration. Surf imposes no requirements here; it does not require a database, any local persistence, or even a user session.

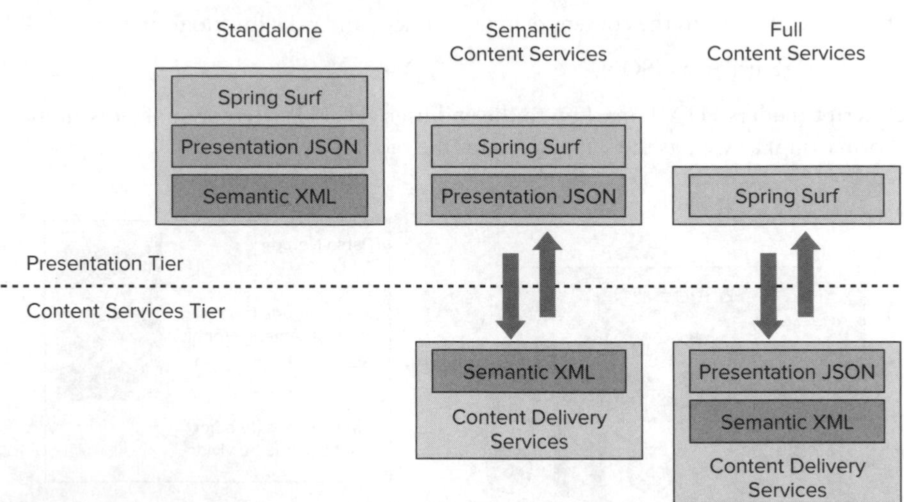

FIGURE 12-2

On the other hand, a far more interesting scenario is shown in the *full content services* configuration on the right-hand side. Here, the Surf application lives in the *presentation tier* but relies upon content delivery services in the *content services tier* to hand it data so that it can respond to incoming requests. This data consists of things like the biography or Web script configuration information.

In this case, Surf provides developers with connector and credential management so that interactions with the content delivery services can be performed on behalf of the end user. Surf provisions connectors to Web script developers so that they can retrieve feeds of data. This data is often represented in either JSON or XML, but it could also be in any number of other formats. Developers work with these feeds and render them back through view templates. Surf focuses on view caching and render performance to minimize the number of remote calls needed on each request.

Surf also has native support for the CMIS standard (Content Management Interoperability Services). CMIS is an industry-adopted API for talking to ECM systems. Alfresco ECM provides the leading open source CMIS implementation, as well as an entire suite of tools around CMIS authoring and delivery. Surf is an ideal presentation technology for CMIS content delivery.

Surf developers benefit from having the option to independently scale out the presentation tier from the content services tier. The presentation tier is primarily developed with the intention of scaling to user load (while providing quick end-user responses), whereas the content services tier scales to content retrieval and query. A single page hit to the Surf application could result in several content services hits, a single hit, or no hits at all. It depends on how you design your application.

Content Applications

In the previous section, you looked at Surf's split-tier architecture and explored some of the advantages of having a separate content services tier built around content standards, such as the Content Management Interoperability Services (CMIS). In this section, you'll explore the big picture about how Surf fits into Alfresco's Content Application vision for Web Content Management.

Surf's intended design pattern is such that it maintains a content-driven and scriptable approach to Web application delivery. As a result of being so content-centric, Surf interoperates very well with Alfresco Web Content Management. Alfresco provides facilities to define, contribute, and manage lifecycle for both semantic and presentation content. It provides a number of very robust WCM capabilities around your content, such as:

- Managed lifecycle from origination to disposition
- Object- or attribute-level authority for users, groups, or roles
- Deployment of content from an approved environment out to all of your Surf applications in the delivery tier
- Rendering of content into alternative delivery formats

Alfresco Web Content Management allows you to define content lifecycle for your Surf application's semantic and presentation content. It allows you to author content in an *authoring environment* and publish that content out for consumption to a *delivery environment*. This is shown in Figure 12-3.

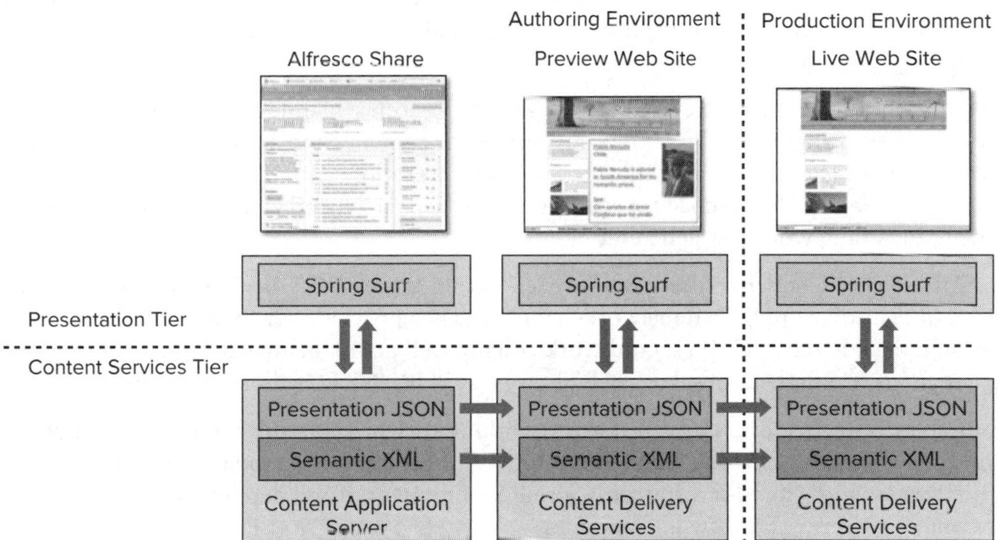

FIGURE 12-3

In the previous section, you looked at a full content services configuration for Surf. This is what you see in Figure 12-3 on the right-hand side. This is your live Web site. All of the content for your site (both semantic and presentation) is retrieved from the live Web site's content delivery services. This Web site runs in the *production environment*. The users of this Web site are actual live Web traffic users. The *production environment* is therefore sized and configured to scale for your live Web traffic needs.

Figure 12-3 also shows the *authoring environment*. The *authoring environment* consists of a preview Web site and Alfresco Share. Alfresco Share is Alfresco's Web interface to the Content Application Server. Alfresco Share is used to author content and save it into the Content Application Server.

The gray arrows along the bottom indicate deployment. Alfresco Web Content Management provides deployment for your Surf presentation objects as well as your semantic content. Content contributors can create content using Alfresco Share and the Alfresco Content Server. They can then instantly preview their content so as to get an idea of how it might look if it were part of the actual Web site.

In Figure 12-3, a contributor has written the biography for Pablo Neruda and then elected to preview it. The content has been published to the content delivery services for the preview Web site. Surf picks up these changes automatically and shows the contributor what the biography looks like in context with the rest of the page. It only shows this on the preview Web site. The live Web site is not affected by the preview.

If the contributor enabled Surf's in-context editing features, they will be able to make changes to the content right on the Web site. If not, they can always make changes to the content within the Content Application Server using Alfresco Share. When they are happy with the content, they can deploy it to the production environment.

You can configure this any number of ways. Figure 12-3 simply serves to illustrate the concept. Deployment transports the content from the Content Application Server to the content delivery services for a Web site. This is usually done for integration testing, quality assurance, preview, and ultimately for delivery to a live Web site.

The Alfresco authoring facilities are ideal for working with both semantic and presentation content. They include Alfresco Share, the Alfresco Forms Service for content contribution, CIFS for desktop and file system interaction, and Microsoft Office/SharePoint integration. Alfresco lets you manage semantic and presentation content object models, permissions, and behaviors, and gives you a rich set of services around them, including workflow and auditing.

While the Alfresco content delivery services are excellent for Spring Surf, they're also not proprietary to Spring Surf. In fact, they are Web framework–agnostic. They provide a CMIS interface to the outside world. As an open standard, CMIS should work equally well across many platforms. You can use CMIS to support Web applications that are built in Java, PHP, .NET, Python, and more.

Spring Surf gives Java developers a head start by working very nicely in this kind of content delivery architecture. Surf provides a strong open source option for getting started today. The Alfresco Content Application Server works hand-in-hand with Spring Surf to manage and deploy both presentation and semantic content to Spring Framework Web sites.

PUTTING IT INTO ACTION

With all of that theoretical stuff behind you, now you can get down into the details of how Surf works. In this section, you'll review the basic ideas behind MVC and then take a closer look at Spring Web MVC. This will set the stage for understanding how the Surf page dispatcher works.

You don't need to type in any code in this section. Just follow along and enjoy. You'll get hands-on experience with the examples in Chapter 14.

Plug-in for the Spring Framework

Surf snaps into the Spring Framework as a view composition plug-in for Spring Web MVC. Spring Web MVC allows developers to build Web applications in a highly configurable way where the view rendering technology can be plugged in and out. The Spring Framework has many plug-in view resolver technologies available for it, including JSP, Tiles, Grails and, of course, Spring Surf. Spring Surf is a formal Spring Extension Project that was developed as a collaboration between Alfresco and SpringSource.

Spring application architects can mix and match these technologies as they see fit. Surf provides a scriptable, no-compile alternative that quickens the pace of building Web applications by allowing for faster iteration and fewer server restarts. Surf provides several tools for developers to help ease this process:

- **The Spring Roo Add-on for Surf** gives developers additional commands that they can use to quickly install, configure, and scaffold Surf applications. With a few simple commands, developers can create new pages and Web scripts for their applications.
- **The SpringSource Tool Suite Plug-in for Surf** gives developers additional wizards and templates for the SpringSource Eclipse-based IDE environment. These wizards let developers configure and build new Surf applications from the ground up.
- **Spring Travel and Spring Petclinic Sample Sites** provide developers with quick-start reference applications that serve as a guide for building Surf applications.

Model-View-Controller

If you are a bit rusty on the Model-View-Controller pattern, this is your chance to brush up. Don't worry; extensive theses have been written on MVC, and you can refer to them if you really need details. This is a high-level refresher so that you can dig in a little deeper.

Imagine an application that receives requests from the outside world. In an MVC application, a *dispatcher* handles these requests for your application and then figures out what to do with them. The dispatcher is responsible for looking at the URL to determine the following:

- Which *controller* to invoke (to set up a *model*)
- Which *view* to invoke (to render the *model*)

It does so in that order. The dispatcher uses mappings (usually URL mappings) to figure out which controllers should be invoked for the incoming URL. It also uses mappings to figure out which view should be invoked to render the response back. This is illustrated in Figure 12-4.

Here is what happens.

1. The request comes in and is handled by the dispatcher. Imagine that the incoming URI is `/hotels`.
2. The dispatcher tries to find a matching controller for this URI.

3. If a controller is found, it is invoked. The controller calls out to some services to retrieve a list of hotels. It creates a model and then places this list of hotels into the model.
4. The dispatcher tries to find a matching view for this URI.
5. If a view is found, it is invoked. The view receives the model and uses it to render HTML markup that displays the list of hotels.
6. The response is sent back to the end user.

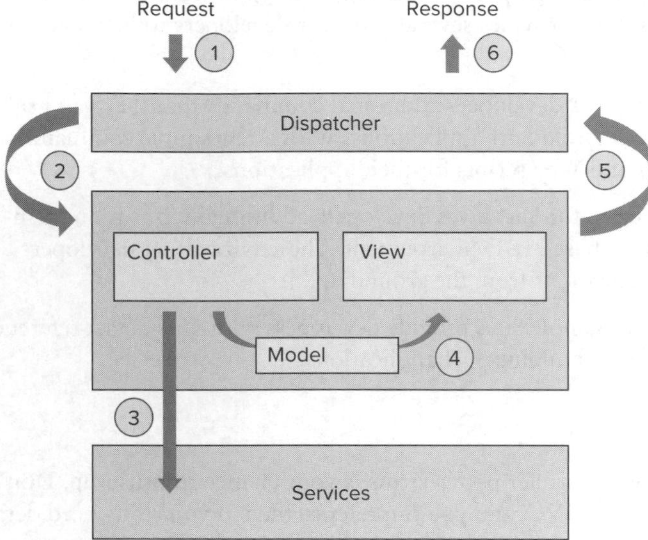

FIGURE 12-4

A controller contains business logic that should run before the response is generated. It can do things like query a database or call out to a service. Its job is to place this data into the model. A view contains rendering logic responsible for building the response that the end user receives. It looks to the data in the model to inform its rendering process.

The main benefit of the MVC pattern is that it makes a nice clear separation between the business logic and the rendering logic. This modularizes your application architecture. It allows you to plug in new views and new controllers. It gains you a lot in terms of reuse; many views can share a single controller, or many controllers can share a single view.

Spring Web MVC

Spring Web MVC is the Model-View-Controller implementation for Spring Framework Web applications. It is based on Spring configuration, where Java beans are used to implement controllers, views, the model, and even the mappings between URIs and handlers. One of the really nice things about

Spring Web MVC is that it is very extensible. You can write your own Java code, plug in new beans, or rewire things through configuration.

The *dispatcher* for a Spring Web MVC application is the dispatcher servlet. The dispatcher servlet is responsible for handling the request and executing the MVC pattern. It tries to identify a controller that will handle the incoming request. A controller is a simple Plain Old Java Object (POJO) registered with the Spring Framework.

In the Spring Framework, the model is just a simple map of named properties. The controller may do some heavy lifting to compute these. Once the controller finishes, it hands the model back to the dispatcher servlet. So far, nothing has been rendered to the end user.

The dispatcher servlet then tries to determine a view that will be used to render the model to the end user. It consults a registry of view resolvers and asks each of them if they can handle the incoming request URI. If a matching view resolver is found, it is used to produce a view object. The view object renders the model to the end user.

Typically, Spring Web MVC application developers focus the majority of their effort writing controllers and views in Java. They then wire them together with Spring configuration XML. This is often a very code-intensive and inflexible effort.

Surf View Resolvers

Surf is a view resolver for your Spring Web MVC application. When you add it into your Spring Web MVC application, the dispatcher servlet will consider Surf's view resolvers just like any other view resolvers. It will ask whether Surf can provide a view object for the incoming request URI.

Unlike the code-intensive approaches, Surf's configuration is driven from presentation content. The Surf view resolver will look to the presentation content to figure out whether a page has been defined for the incoming URI. In fact, Surf knows how to render many types of views. These views are listed in the following table along with the names of the view resolver beans that produced each.

VIEW	VIEW RESOLVER BEAN
Page	`PageViewResolver`
Region of a Page	`RegionViewResolver`
Component on a Page	`ComponentViewResolver`
Content	`ContentViewResolver`
Web Script	`WebScriptViewResolver`

By default, Surf uses a simple URL file name controller to look up and discover what kind of thing is being requested. If the URI describes an object of one of the types listed, it will discover this, look up the object, and then inform the Spring MVC dispatcher that it can produce the view object.

Surf can also be used with custom controllers. Spring developers will frequently write custom controllers to back incoming requests. These controllers are either simple controllers or annotated controllers.

- Simple controllers are Java beans that are wired to the incoming URI via a mapping declaration in a Spring configuration file. The Spring MVC framework looks to its configuration files to figure out which controller bean should handle the incoming URL.
- Annotated controllers are Java beans that use Java Annotations to bind specific methods on the bean to the incoming URL.

Either one is fine. If the controller hands back an explicit ID, the dispatcher servlet will consult Surf's view resolvers to see if they can produce an appropriate view object.

With Surf, you are free to dig in and customize the wiring of the Spring Web MVC configuration. However, in most cases, the out-of-the-box configuration will suit your application just fine.

Examples

You'll walk through a few quick examples now. These are merely simple examples intended to illustrate some of the dispatching mechanics through Spring Web MVC. A little bit of pseudo-code is introduced to help show how things fit together.

You don't have to type anything in. Just see if you can follow along for the basic concepts.

A Surf Page

Imagine that a request arrives to a simple Spring Surf application. For the purposes of this example, imagine that the request takes on the following form:

```
http://localhost:8080/hotels
```

The Spring MVC dispatcher receives this request and tries to find a controller that matches the URI `/hotels`. In this case, it does not find a match. Thus, a controller is not found, nothing is invoked, and a model is not set up. No big deal.

The Spring MVC dispatcher then moves on to the next step. It tries to find a view resolver that can resolve views for the URI `/hotels`. It will walk through the available view resolvers and ask each one if it can handle this URI.

Since this is a very simple Surf application, each of the Surf view resolvers will be interrogated and asked whether they can resolve `/hotels`. The two most interesting resolvers are these:

- `PageViewResolver` checks to see if there is a Surf `Page` object defined that maps to the URL `/hotels`. If so, it produces a `PageView` view object to render the response.
- `WebScriptViewResolver` checks to see if there is a Web script defined that maps to the URL `/hotels`. If so, it produces a `WebScriptView` view object to render the response.

If a `PageView` is produced, Surf will render back the Hotels page. If a `WebScriptView` is produced, Surf will ask the Web script engine to render back the Web script matching the URI `/hotels`.

Suppose you want to have Surf render back a Hotels page. This page will list all of the hotels available on your Web site. You just have to define a page in Surf that maps to the `/hotels` URI. You can do this with a little bit of XML — something like this:

```
<?xml version='1.0' encoding='UTF-8'?>
<page>
   <id>hotels</id>
</page>
```

Easy enough. You'll go into where you place this XML fragment a bit later. However, for now, assume that Surf picks this up. It knows that there is a page object with the URI `/hotels`.

The only other thing you have to do is provide the template to use to render markup to the response. You can do this with a bit of FreeMarker. You can hard-code this for the moment, as shown here:

```
<html>
   <body>
      <table>
         <tr>
            <td>Walton Cottage</td>
            <td>Maidenhead, UK</td>
         </tr>
         <tr>
            <td>Victorian Treasure</td>
            <td>Lodi, WT</td>
         </tr>
      </table>
   </body>
</html>
```

Now when you hit the `/hotels` URI, the dispatcher walks through the view resolvers and settles on the `PageViewResolver` to work its magic. Your page will be rendered to the browser.

Using an Annotated Controller

As previously mentioned, Spring developers write controllers to build the model that your page ultimately uses. Take a look at how this is done.

Imagine that you want the page to display the hotels received from a query to a Hotels service. In other words, you do not want to just hard-code it as you did before. You would like to pull in content from a service that is an expert in all things hotel.

A Spring developer would typically approach this challenge by defining a new controller. With Spring 3.0, you can use annotated controllers to define a RESTful binding for the incoming request. You declare the annotated controller in its own Java bean. The code might look something like this:

```
@Controller
public class HotelsController
{
   privateTravelServicetravelService;
   @Autowired
   publicHotelsController(TravelServicetravelService) {
     this.travelService = travelService;
```

```
    }
    @RequestMapping("/hotels")
    public void getHotels(SearchCriteria criteria, Model model) {
       List<Hotel> hotels = travelService.findHotels(criteria);
       model.addAttribute("hotelList", hotels);
    }
}
```

This Java bean is annotated to inform Spring that it should bind to the incoming URL of `/hotels`. Simple enough. When the Spring MVC dispatcher servlet needs to figure out which controller can handle the incoming URL, it will consult these annotations to find your bean.

As you can see by the code, all of the "heavy lifting" is done inside of the bean. It calls out to the `travelService` to retrieve a list of hotel properties. It then places these into the model and returns it. Thus, unlike in the last example, you're populating the model in the controller.

So far, this is all just Spring Web MVC. How would your Surf template use this model data? You can adjust your Surf template as follows:

```
<html>
   <body>
      <table>
      <#if hotelList?size == 0>
         <tr>
            <td colspan="2">No hotels found</td>
         </tr>
      <#else>
         <#list hotelList as hotel>
         <tr>
            <td>${hotel.name}</td>
            <td>${hotel.address}</td>
         </tr>
         </#list>
      </#if>
      </table>
   </body>
</html>
```

That's all there is to it. You used Spring Web MVC to define your controller. The model generated by the controller is available to your Surf template. You mapped your controller and page to the same `/hotels` URI and let the framework figure stuff out for you.

VIEW COMPOSITION

You just finished looking at a very simple example of a Surf page. It consisted of a little bit of XML configuration and a FreeMarker template. The XML identifies the URI where the page lives. This helps the Surf page view resolver find the page and ultimately find the FreeMarker template to use.

Surf provides a view composition framework that enables much richer user interface definition. In this section, you'll look at how this works. You'll dig into user interface concepts like pages, templates, regions, and components.

Pages

Surf pages are defined using Surf page XML. A page binds to a URI. Surf allows you to render pages by simply passing the URI in the request. You can request a page by using a URL like the ones shown here:

```
http://localhost:8080/surf/<page-id>
```

```
http://localhost:8080/surf?p=<page-id>
```

If Surf finds this page, it will look at the page XML configuration to figure out which template to use to render the output. Each page can have multiple templates keyed by format. A page might have a default template that it uses for HTML output to a browser, but it may have another template configured that it uses for output to a wireless device.

You can request a particular format for a page using URLs like these:

```
http://localhost:8080/surf/<page-id>?f=<format-id>
```

```
http://localhost:8080/surf?p=<page-id>&f=<format-id>
```

This allows you to have different markup for different intended formats (such as for small-display devices or integration purposes).

Surf pages are also locale-aware. This lets you finely adjust your site's pages for different languages and localization needs. When you make a request for a page, Surf will do its best to find a match for your browser's locale. If a locale match cannot be made, Surf will fall back to a specified default locale.

Surf lets you group pages into page types. By requesting a page type, Surf will determine which page to use to satisfy your request. It determines this by looking to your currently configured theme. Themes can override default pages for a given page type. You can request a page type like this:

```
http://localhost:8080/surf/pt/<page-type-id>
```

```
http://localhost:8080/surf?pt=<page-type-id>
```

For example, Surf defines a `login` page type. Your site might have two themes, such as a normal theme and a holiday theme. You may also have two distinct login pages, such as a normal login page and a holiday login page.

When the holiday theme is active, you would like Surf to resort to using the holiday login page. All you have to do is switch the theme for the site. None of the links or URLs change at all. The following URLs, for example, will always take you to the theme's designated login page.

```
http://localhost:8080/surf/pt/login
```

```
http://localhost:8080/surf?pt=login
```

As before, you can request a particular format of the login page type by using a format parameter. Here are two URLs that request the wireless format of the login page type.

```
http://localhost:8080/surf/pt/login?f=wireless
```

```
http://localhost:8080/surf?pt=login&f=wireless
```

Templates and Regions

Once Surf looks at your URI and figures out what you are requesting, it has to go about the process of handling the view. The request may be for a specific page. Or it may be for a content item of type "article." Or it may be for a specific region of the current page (for example, in an AJAX request).

No matter what is being requested, the objective is eventually going to be to produce markup and send it out to the response. The key to making this happen is the template. The template file provides the basic layout of the response to the browser.

The idea for a template is that it is a reusable layout. You can build it once and then apply it to many pages. Each page can then benefit from a common look and feel that was prescribed ahead of time. By later changing the template, a Web designer can affect many pages all at the same time. This lets you achieve a common look and feel and lowers the costs of maintenance.

This is especially meaningful for large Web sites where you may need to manage hundreds, if not thousands, of pages. Or imagine a catalog site with tens of thousands of products. If you had to code each of these pages by hand one at a time, you'd find it very frustrating regardless of whether you used Java, Surf, .NET, or 6510 assembler. Don't try that.

Figure 12-5 shows three pages for a sample Web site. The Web site isn't all that exciting but that is not the point. Take a look at the pages. You'll notice that two of the pages are quite similar. In fact, they have exactly the same page layout. They have four regions on the page, whereas the first page has only three regions. Therefore, you can describe these three pages with two templates. The templates are shown below the pages.

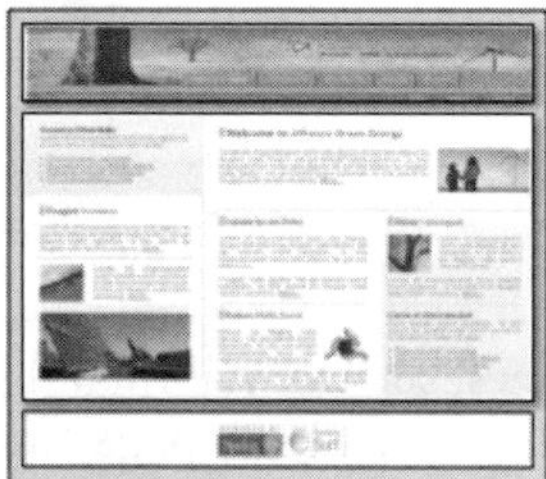

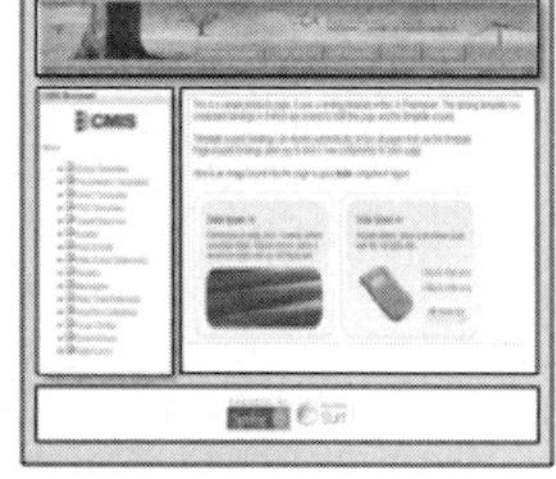

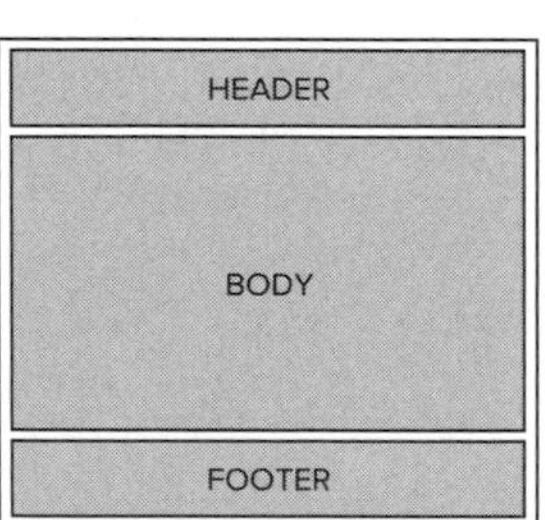

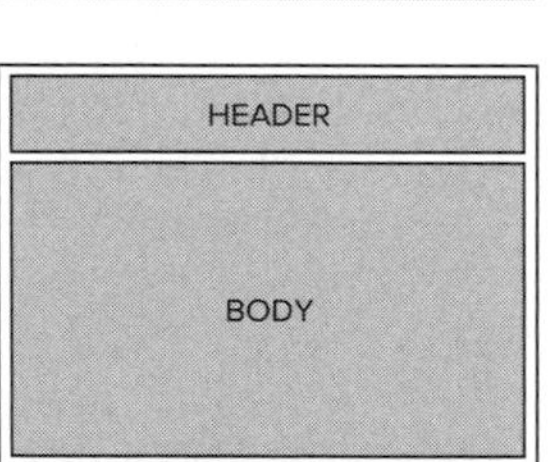

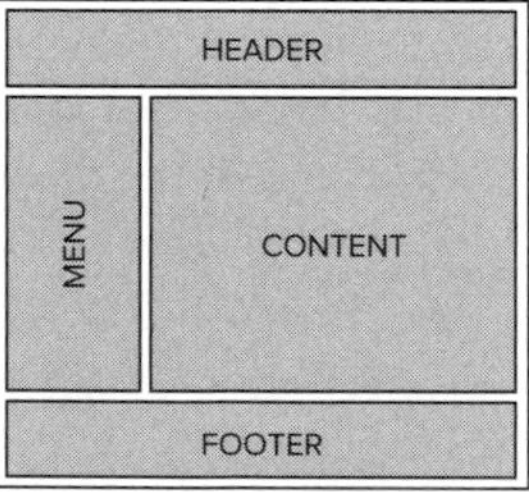

FIGURE 12-5

Notice that the first template defines three regions and gives them some placeholder names (HEADER, BODY, FOOTER). The second template defines four regions and also gives them names (HEADER, MENU, CONTENT, FOOTER). Take a look at the pages again. Notice that the HEADER and FOOTER regions are common across all three pages.

You can define the two templates in Surf and define regions along with region scope to allow reuse across templates. This is illustrated in Figure 12-6.

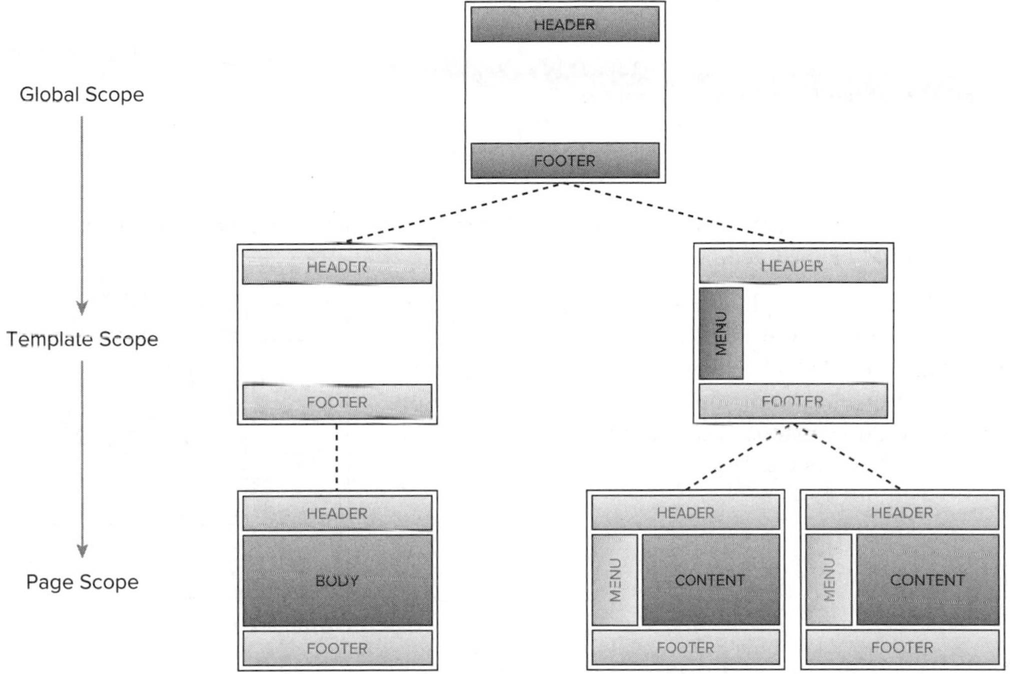

FIGURE 12-6

In Figure 12-6, the notion of region scope is employed so as to define the entire Web site with only two templates and five scoped regions. There are three scopes: *global*, *template* and *page*.

Regions in the global scope only need to be configured one time. Their configuration is then reused by any templates or pages that include them. In this case, the HEADER and FOOTER regions are defined once in the global scope. Their content appears exactly the same on all of the pages of the site.

Regions in the template scope need to be configured once per template. Their configuration is then reused by any pages that use the template. In this case, the MENU region is defined in the template scope for one of the templates (but not the other). Thus, the two pages on the right-hand side that use this template will have the MENU region in common.

Regions in the page scope need to be configured once per page. Their configurations are not reused. Each page needs to configure the region anew. In this case, the BODY and CONTENT regions are in the page scope. As you can see from Figure 12-5, this allows the two right-hand pages to be slightly different (but only in the CONTENT region).

In the previous section you saw how to write templates using FreeMarker. Now you will learn about the region tag. You define regions on a template using the region tag. When you place the region tag onto the template, you have to inform it of what scope it is in (either page, template, or global). The following examples are indicative of how this is done in FreeMarker:

```
Globally scoped header region:
<@region id="header" scope="global" />
Template scoped navigation region:
<@region id="navigation" scope="template" />
Page scoped content region:
<@region id="content" scope="page" />
```

A template defines the basic structure of the rendered view. It then defines regions into which additional presentation should be included.

Figure 12-7 shows an example of the right-hand template that defines four regions: HEADER, MENU, CONTENT, and FOOTER. Some sample code below suggests how you could weave this into a FreeMarker template. It is up to Surf to resolve exactly what should be placed in each of these regions when the template is actually rendered.

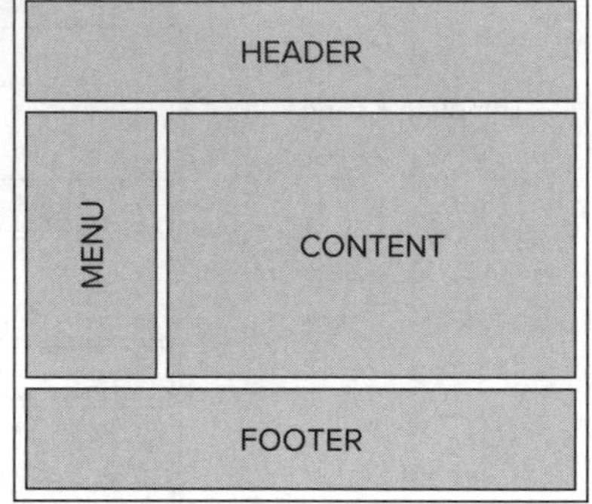

FIGURE 12-7

```
<html>
   <head>
      ${head}
   </head>
   <body>
      <div class="header">
         <@region id="header" scope="global" />
      </div>
      <div class="menu">
         <@region id="menu" scope="template" />
      </div>
      <div class="content">
         <@region id="content" scope="page" />
      </div>
      <div class="footer">
         <@region id="footer" scope="global" />
      </div>
   </body>
</html>
```

When the template is processed, each of its region tags will execute and attempt to look up something that should be included in that location in the template. In other words, the region tag will be replaced by the output of something that is bound into that place in the template.

Components

Surf allows you to bind components to the regions (as shown in Figure 12-8). A component usually associates a region with a Web script. Templates and scoped regions make it possible to reuse Web scripts quite heavily. You can have as many Web scripts as you like, each encapsulating a unique bit of application functionality.

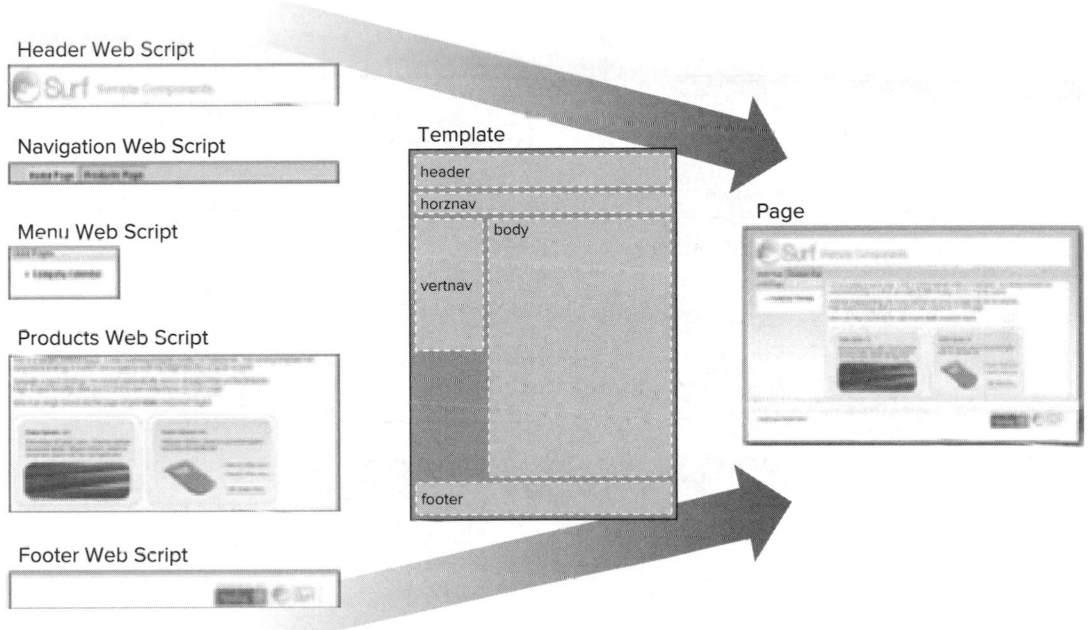

FIGURE 12-8

In Figure 12-8, a template is used to bring several Web scripts together into an overall markup structure. Here you are rendering a page. However, the same concepts apply for any kind of view rendered from Surf using a template.

Surf lets you define regions in various scopes and then resolves these upon request. This makes your site definition efficient and easier to manage by promoting reuse.

Alfresco Share is an example of a Surf application whose pages are constructed through elegant reuse of templates. All three scopes are used. Figure 12-9 provides an example of how this fits together.

You'll explore Alfresco Share in Chapter 13 and then customize it in Chapter 15 by making adjustments to Surf. For now, you should pick up on the general idea. You can make changes to Alfresco Share pages by tweaking FreeMarker templates and Web scripts.

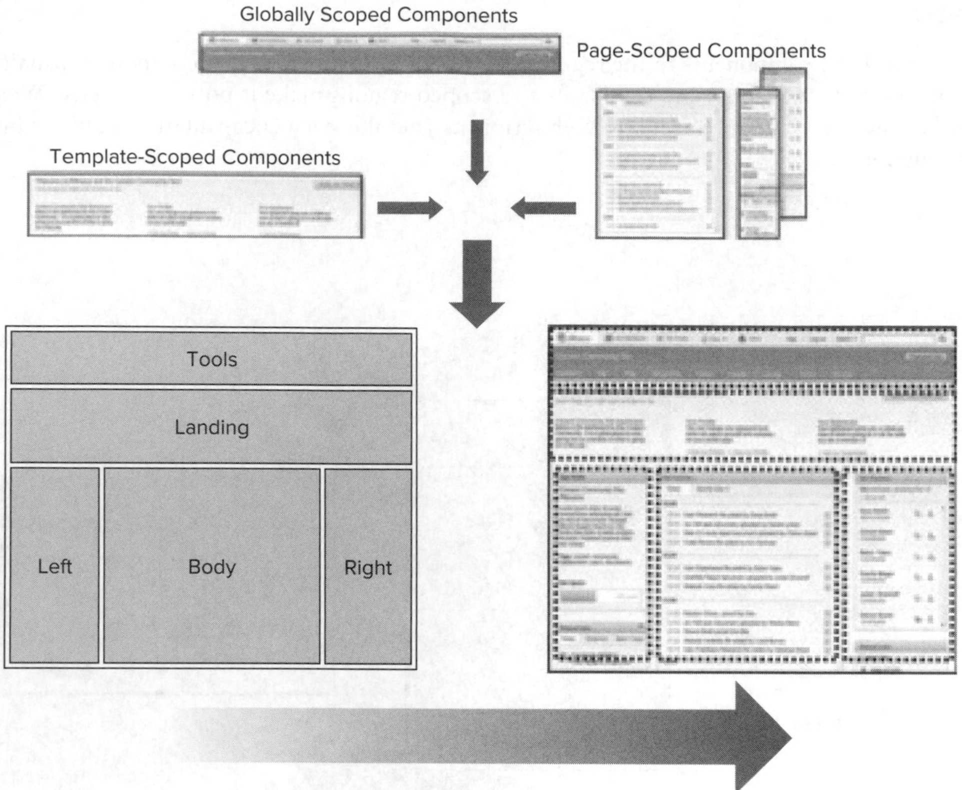

FIGURE 12-9

In Surf, Web scripts are elevated to the role of not only provisioning remote interfaces to your applications, but also of providing your application's presentation logic. These are presentation-tier Web scripts. Surf orchestrates them so that they can all live together on a single view and interoperate against a common request context.

Web script and template developers have many more capabilities at their disposal. They can do things like pre-process controllers to generate markup that should be injected into different parts of a page (for example, the `<head>` of an HTML page). Surf also provides additional Web script and template API root-scoped objects and methods for developers.

The API references for both the Web script and template processors are provided in Online Appendix E.

PRESENTATION CONTENT

In this section, you'll do a quick review of the presentation content that Surf consults when it renders the user interface. As you recall, presentation content consists of templates, scripts, and XML files that Surf can pick up without a server restart.

Surf's presentation content consists of three kinds of files:

- Surf objects
- Templates
- Web scripts

Surf Objects

Surf objects define parts of the Web site and describe how these parts fit together to build the complete Web application structure. Objects describe things like pages, page hierarchy, chrome, or components that are reused across many pages.

Objects are defined in XML files that are generally short in nature. A single Surf application will have many XML files to define its objects. When Surf starts up, it looks for all of these small XML fragments and gathers them together to form a complete registry of all of the objects.

An example of the XML for a `Page` object is shown here:

```
<?xml version='1.0' encoding='UTF-8'?>
<page>
   <id>mypage</id>
   <title>My First Page</title>
   <description>This is an example of the XML for a Page</description>
</page>
```

A Spring project will generally maintain these XML files as part of its project resources. They can reside either under the WEB-INF directory or inside the classpath. Users of Alfresco have the additional option of managing these files inside the Alfresco Content Application Server.

The Alfresco Content Application Server allows these XML files to be individually managed, authorized, and approved as part of a lifecycle process. Once approved, Alfresco makes these files available to the Surf application.

Online Appendix E provides you with a complete breakdown of the Surf objects and the locations where you should place these files if you wish them to be picked up out of the classpath. The appendix provides sample XML that you can use as a reference when you define your own Surf objects.

Here are a few examples of the various presentation objects that Surf provides:

- **Chrome** — Application borders for your regions and components
- **Components** — Binds Web scripts into templates and pages
- **Content Instance** — Points to pages or templates to use when rendering content types (`cm:content` or `my:article`)
- **Page** — A navigable location within the site
- **Page Type** — Indirection to non-navigable locations (for example, a login page)
- **Template Instance** — Configuration for dynamic templates
- **Theme** — Settings that define the site experience

Templates

Templates are transformers that generate markup for the browser to render. For a Web site, this markup is generally HTML. Templates are applied to the current request context or model.

Templates are often files that contain a composite of the output markup and processing tags. The tags execute and generate markup that is injected into the template at the location of the tag. This pattern is common for such template types as FreeMarker, PHP, and XSL.

Surf supports several tags out of the box that are useful to template developers. One commonly used tag is the region tag. The region tag tells the template to look up a component and render its output at the location of the tag.

Here is an example of what a FreeMarker template responsible for rendering a page may look like in Surf:

```
<html>
   <head>
      ${head}
   </head>
   <body>
      <div class="header">
         <@region id="header" />
      </div>
      <div class="body">
         <@region id="body" />
      </div>
   </body>
</html>
```

A Spring project will generally maintain these template files as part of its project resources. They could reside either under the WEB-INF directory or inside the classpath. Users of Alfresco have the additional option of managing these files inside a Content Application Server.

Web Scripts

You looked at Web scripts in depth starting with Chapter 8. By now, you should be familiar with the way that they work. From Surf's perspective, Web scripts are miniature applications that you use to build part or all of the page experience. Surf lets you reuse Web scripts and bind them together into as many pages as you like. They are lightweight scripts, which makes them easy to assemble and deploy.

As you know, Declarative Web scripts implement a Model-View-Controller pattern. They have a single descriptor XML file that informs the Web script dispatcher how to behave. Declarative Web scripts have their own template views and optional scriptable controllers. You write new views by writing new template files. You write new controllers by writing new script files. Your scriptable controllers populate the `model` variable (a map). Your view uses the model during render. It's straight up MVC, right?

Yes, but there is one interesting difference. Surf allows you to merge your Web scripts into the rendering of the overall page. In other words, Surf lets your Web script MVC participate in the overall Spring MVC.

Surf makes sure to provide each Web script with the appropriate context and runtime environment so that it renders in the context of the overall request. The output of each Web script is merged together with the output of the template to form the final markup. This markup is returned from the Spring MVC view as shown in Figure 12-10.

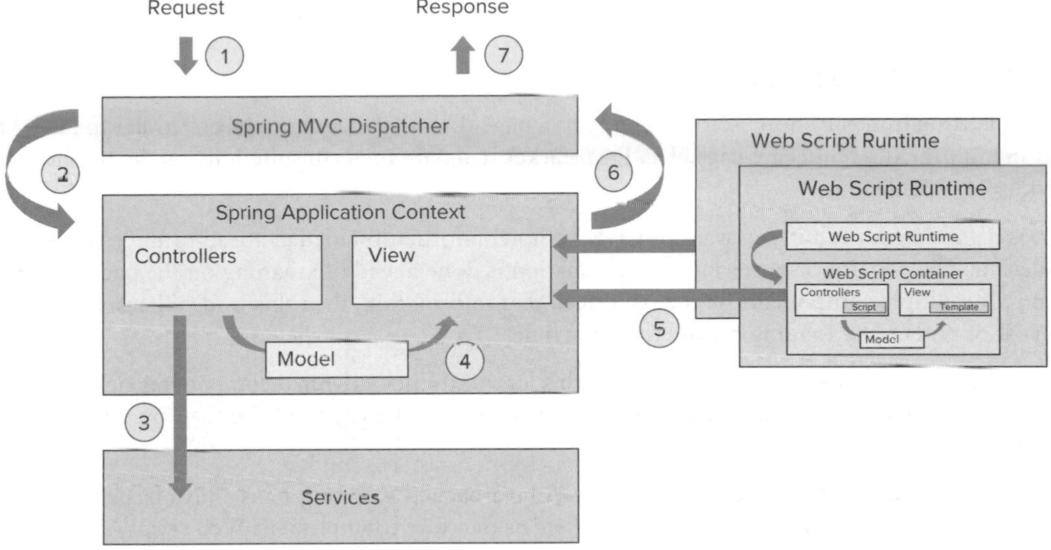

FIGURE 12-10

Figure 12-10 is a modified version of Figure 12-4, with one major adjustment. This is step 5. Rather than produce 100% of the output itself, the rendering template occasionally delegates off to the Web script runtime to do some work. This occurs when the region tags execute. The Web script runtime executes miniature, scriptable MVC processes whose output is then merged into the overall rendition. Surf sets everything up so that the Web script runtime can utilize and take advantage of the full request, user, and page context.

Surf developers build Web scripts to define component implementations that can be accessed either standalone or stitched into an overall page presentation. A component is sometimes thought of as a widget or a gadget – something that you can plug into a Web site on one or more pages. It is a reusable bit of application functionality that participates in the overall page experience.

Web scripts can also be invoked standalone. This means that Web scripts can run entirely outside the context of a page. You can surface components in pop-ups or refresh portions of a Web page via AJAX callbacks. Surf also provides portlet capabilities so that your Web scripts and components can be wrapped up as JSR-268 portlets and dropped into portal servers.

A Spring project will generally maintain Web script files as part of its project resources. They could either reside under the WEB-INF directory or inside the classpath. Users of Alfresco have the additional option of managing these files inside a Content Application Server.

Example

Now you'll build on the example you started earlier. Take your hotel listing page and mix in a Web script. In fact, mix in a Java-backed Web script. This builds on some of the advanced stuff you saw in Chapter 11.

You don't have to type anything in. Just enjoy as you shimmy up your example and make it shine.

A Java-Backed Web Script

In the "Putting It into Action" section, you built a page that used an annotated controller to fetch hotel information for the rendering page. The FreeMarker template then consulted the model to build the markup of hotel listings.

This is a good approach if you want to have the hotel information loaded ahead of the page actually rendering. The penalty of retrieving the information is done ahead of anything on the page even rendering. If multiple components on the page need that information, then this is ideal because it avoids the cost of potentially loading it more than one time.

That said, what if you want to move some of this logic into the individual components on the page? In other words, what if you want the individual Web scripts on the page to have their own Java-backed controllers?

You can do this with a Java-backed Web script. A Java-backed Web script has a Java bean that executes ahead of the Web script's view. You can use them as one way to implement Web script–specific Java controllers.

Look at how this is done. You begin by modifying your template to use a region tag. You looked at region tags when you read about Surf view composition. You do this so as to bind a Web script into the template. It looks something like this:

```
<html>
   <body>
      <@region id="hotels" scope="page" />
   </body>
</html>
```

This declares a page-scoped region with the name *hotels*. You can then develop a Java-backed Web script that retrieves the Hotel list for you and places the result into the model. The Java code would look something like this:

```
public class HotelListingWebScript extends DeclarativeWebScript
{
   privateTravelServicetravelService;
   public void setTravelService(TravelServicetravelService)
   {
      this.travelService = travelService;
   }
   @Override
   protected Map<String, Object>executeImpl(WebScriptRequestreq, Status status)
   {
      Map<String, Object> model = new HashMap<String, Object>(7, 1.0f);
```

```
        model.put("hotelList",  travelService.findHotels());
        return model;
    }
}
```

You then wire this into place with a little Spring configuration. All you then have to do is declare two files.

The Web script descriptor:

hotellisting.get.desc.xml

```
<webscript>
   <shortname>Hotel Listing</shortname>
   <url>/hotel/listing</url>
   <format default="html">argument</format>
   <authentication>none</authentication>
   <transaction>required</transaction>
</webscript>
```

And the view template (written in FreeMarker):

hotellisting.get.html.ftl

```
<table>
   <#if hotelList?size == 0>
   <tr>
      <td colspan="2">No hotels found</td>
   </tr>
   <#else>
   <#list hotelList as hotel>
   <tr>
      <td>${hotel.name}</td>
      <td>${hotel.address}</td>
   </tr>
   </#list>
   </#if>
</table>
```

That's just about it. You now have a reusable Java-backed Web script. All that remains is an empty page-scoped region called *hotels* on your template. You can plug in your new Web script by adding a component binding. Since the region tag defines a region in the page scope, you add a page-scoped component definition, as shown here.

```
<?xml version='1.0' encoding='UTF-8'?>
<component>
   <source-id>hotels</source-id>
   <scope>page</scope>
   <region-id>hotels</region-id>
   <url>/hotel/listing</url>
</component>
```

That's all. By using this approach, you have created a reusable Web script that can be placed into multiple locations in your Web site. It could appear on different pages, in different regions, and in different scopes. The advantage is that the controller is only hit when the Web script is on the page. The disadvantage is that the Java-backed controller isn't as portable as the rest of the Web script files. Moving it from one Surf application to another would require a server restart.

CONNECTORS AND CREDENTIALS

Web script developers often work with remote sources of data. Surf makes it easy for developers to reach out to these information sources and pull together feeds of data.

These data sources might be SOAP or RESTful providers, CMIS repositories, or perhaps completely proprietary in nature. Furthermore, each data source may require a unique set of credentials to be presented in order to work with the data source.

Surf allows you to define *connectors* that are responsible for communicating with *endpoints*. An endpoint is a place where a data source lives. It could be a server in your business residing at an HTTP address. Connectors are used to connect to an endpoint and communicate with it.

Connectors are wired together with *authenticators* so that they can effectively handshake and establish credentials with endpoints. This pattern abstracts away any of the manual management of connection state that developers would otherwise need to perform. Using authenticators, connectors manage user identity and session state to the endpoint. This is automatically managed for the duration of the user session in the Surf application itself.

Connectors and Endpoints

Connectors and endpoints are both defined through simple configuration as part of Surf's remote configuration block. Declaring an endpoint is fairly simple. It may look something like this:

```
<config evaluator="string-compare" condition="Remote">
   <remote>
      <endpoint>
         <id>springsurf</id>
         <name>Spring Surf</name>
         <connector-id>http</connector-id>
         <endpoint-url>http://www.springsurf.org</endpoint-url>
      </endpoint>
   </remote>
</config>
```

This defines an endpoint named `springsurf`. When talking to this endpoint, a connector of type `http` should be used. The data source lives at `www.springsurf.org:8080`. Since nothing else is provided, this is assumed to be an unauthenticated endpoint.

Surf provides a number of out-of-the-box connectors. The `http` connector lets you connect to HTTP or HTTPS endpoints. If you want to assert an identity to the endpoint, you can do that by adjusting the configuration:

```
<config evaluator="string-compare" condition="Remote">
   <remote>
      <endpoint>
         <id>springsurf</id>
         <name>Spring Surf</name>
         <connector-id>http</connector-id>
         <endpoint-url>http://www.springsurf.org</endpoint-url>
         <identity>declared</identity>
         <username>USERNAME</username>
         <password>PASSWORD</password>
```

```
        </endpoint>
    </remote>
</config>
```

For an `http` connector, the credentials are passed through using Basic authentication. The values *USERNAME* and *PASSWORD* are just placeholders – you would want to fill in your own values here.

With an endpoint like this defined, you can now code against the endpoint and use it without having to worry about managing connection state and asserting credentials.

You could use the following Web script controller code to retrieve something from the `springsurf` endpoint:

```
// get a connector to the springsurf endpoint
var connector = remote.connect("springsurf");
// place text file into the model
var txt = connector.get("/sample/helloworld.txt");
model.txt = txt;
```

The `remote` root-scope variable gives you a variety of methods and accessors for working with connectors. When it is used, the connection mechanics are abstracted away and your Web script code becomes highly portable from one environment to another, as well as reusable across many users.

Credentials

Surf provides credential management on behalf of users who access content using connectors. If a connector needs to know which credentials to attach to a given request during an authentication handshake, it can call upon the *credential vault*.

Surf's default credential vault is runtime-only, meaning that it is populated and used at runtime. If you restart the server, the credentials are lost and the user will be required to provide their credentials all over again the next time the connector is used.

Surf also lets you override the credential vault implementation. It provides a number of additional credential vaults out of the box that you can use or base your implementations on. These include a file-system–persistent credential vault and an Alfresco credential vault (where your credentials are stored in an Alfresco-managed file).

To use the credential vault, you simply need to inform the endpoint that its identity is driven from the current user. You can make this change to your endpoint definition:

```
<config evaluator="string-compare" condition="Remote">
    <remote>
        <endpoint>
            <id>springsurf</id>
            <name>Spring Surf</name>
            <connector-id>http</connector-id>
            <endpoint-url>http://www.springsurf.org</endpoint-url>
            <identity>user</identity>
        </endpoint>
    </remote>
</config>
```

Connectors to this endpoint will now look for the user's credentials in the credential vault. If credentials are not found and the endpoint requires authentication, the connection may fail. However, if credentials are available in the vault, they will be applied and the connector will access the endpoint on behalf of the developer without the need for manual login.

Authenticators

Authenticating connectors are connectors that have authenticators plugged into them. An *authenticator* is a class that knows how to perform an authentication handshake with a specific kind of service or application.

For example, consider MediaWiki, which provides a REST-based means for authenticating. You pass in your user credentials and it hands back an HTTP cookie. This cookie must be applied to every subsequent request, as MediaWiki looks to it to inform the application of who is making the request.

Alfresco has a similar REST-based means for authenticating. It is slightly different in that the RESTful parameters are not the same as those of MediaWiki. Furthermore, Alfresco hands back a ticket in an XML return payload. This ticket must be applied to the HTTP headers of every subsequent call so that Alfresco knows who is making the request.

In fact, every application has a slightly different way of handling its authentication. For this reason, Surf makes it easy to write your own authenticators and plug them into your connectors entirely through configuration.

You define authenticators through configuration as well:

```
<authenticator>
   <id>alfresco-ticket</id>
   <name>Alfresco Authenticator</name>
   <description>Alfresco Authenticator</description>
   <class>org.alfresco.connector.AlfrescoAuthenticator</class>
</authenticator>
```

You can then bind them to connectors using configuration. Additionally, you can write your own connectors if you so choose:

```
<connector>
  <id>alfresco</id>
  <name>Alfresco Connector</name>
  <description>Connects to Alfresco using ticket-based authentication</description>
  <class>org.alfresco.connector.AlfrescoConnector</class>
  <authenticator-id>alfresco-ticket</authenticator-id>
</connector>
```

The `alfresco-ticket` authenticator and the `alfresco` connector are both available to Surf developers out of the box. You can use them to connect to an Alfresco instance. All you need to do is define an endpoint that points to an Alfresco instance and uses the `alfresco` connector.

Alfresco connectors use an Alfresco authenticator to perform a handshake ahead of any actual interaction. The handshake establishes who the user is and then sets up the connector session so that subsequent requests contain the appropriate connection information (cookies, request headers, and so forth). The endpoint definition may look like this:

```
<endpoint>
   <id>alfresco</id>
   <name>Alfresco REST API</name>
   <description>Alfresco REST API</description>
   <connector-id>alfresco</connector-id>
   <endpoint-url>http://localhost:8080/alfresco/s</endpoint-url>
   <identity>user</identity>
</endpoint>
```

This endpoint is named *alfresco*. It uses an `alfresco` connector and it will draw credentials from the user's credential vault. This is all defined in configuration.

You could use the *alfresco* endpoint to talk to an Alfresco instance and access its remote API. For example, you may wish to interact with the CMIS API on the Alfresco repository. Here is an example of retrieving XML from the Alfresco CMIS API:

```
// get a connector to the alfresco endpoint
var connector = remote.connect("alfresco");
// place CMIS text onto the model
model.cmis = connector.get("/api/path/workspace/SpacesStore");
```

Web script developers do not need to worry about how to connect to the endpoint or pass along user state. They simply code to the `remote` object.

The Remote API

The `remote` root-scoped object is very useful for connecting to remote services and retrieving data feeds. It abstracts away all the underlying connectivity stuff, and, therefore, remains a fairly easy API to use.

The basic pattern is to use the `remote` object to get a connector to a specific endpoint. Endpoints are identified by endpoint ID. You essentially need to do something like this:

```
var connector = remote.connect(ENDPOINT_ID);
```

You simply fill in *`ENDPOINT_ID`* with the correct value. You now have a connector to the remote service. The connector variable is an object with additional methods describing all of the ways you can work with the endpoint.

The following methods are typically what you will use:

- **`post(uri, body)`** — POSTs content to the given URI
- **`post(uri, body, contentType)`** — POSTs content of the specified type to the given URI
- **`get(uri)`** — GETs content from the given URI
- **`put(uri, body)`** — PUTs content to the given URI
- **`put(uri, body, contentType)`** — PUTs content of the specified type to the given URI
- **`delete(uri)`** — Invokes a URI as a DELETE request

These are the basic HTTP method types that are used to support the essential CRUD (create, read, update, delete) operations of most RESTful services. You can use these to work with services right within your Web scripts.

Example

Now you'll use the Surf remote API to further enhance your hotel listing example. You'll adjust the Java-backed Web Script example from the previous section so that it uses a scriptable controller to access the remote service. This removes the need for Java code and makes your code much more portable!

As before, you don't have to type anything in. Just enjoy as you do a little dance with Surf's remote API. You'll get more hands-on in Chapter 14.

Scriptable Controller

You can also solve the challenge of retrieving a list of hotels from the Travel Service using a purely script-based approach. Declarative Web scripts support scriptable controllers. Spring Surf provides out-of-the-box support for server-side JavaScript, but you can also plug in add-on processors for Groovy and PHP.

You can use Surf's remote API from within a scriptable controller to call out to the Travel Service and acquire the very same information as in the previous example.

Look at how you can do this. Begin by removing the Java-backed Web script. It is very cool and exciting; however, for this example, you want to use a purely scriptable approach. So you remove the Java class and remove the registration of the Java bean from the Spring configuration.

All you need to do then is add one additional file to the Web script:

hotellisting.get.js

```
var connector = remote.connect("travelService");
varjsonString = connector.call("/hotels/find");
model.hotelList = eval(jsonString);
```

This is a JavaScript controller that uses the `remote` variable to pull back content from an endpoint named `travelService`. You assume that the Travel Service lives at this location. You also assume that it speaks JSON. This means that many different Web applications in the business can all talk to this Travel Service and pull back data for use in rendering pages. It is a pure service-oriented architecture.

If you have set up the endpoint as well as any necessary connectors or authenticators, then the `remote` variable will let you open connections and work with services on the other side. In this case, you pull back a JSON object and then work with it via pure JavaScript. Nothing else changes.

The advantage of this approach over the previous one is that it is entirely script-based. This means that the Web script is much more transportable; you can move it from one environment to the next with very little difficulty. It is as easy as copying and pasting a set of files. It is also easy to change and does not require Java development skills.

GETTING INVOLVED

The Spring Surf Extension project is maintained and developed as a collaborative effort between Alfresco Software and SpringSource. Alfresco contributed Surf to SpringSource so as to enable the project to grow and accelerate in a wider developer community. It is available today as a plug-in for Spring MVC 3.x applications under the Apache 2.0 license.

Alfresco continues this investment into the project with the active participation of its core engineering team. At the same time, Alfresco has opened up the project to the Spring developer community and encourages open participation and contribution.

If you would like to learn more about the Spring Surf Project or become involved, you can visit the Spring Surf Project here:

`www.springsurf.org`

From this project page, you can download the latest Spring Surf releases, access documentation, and browse through project information, including build details, technical documentation, and tutorials. It also provides information about how you can check out the code and contribute.

13

Levels of Customization

WHAT'S IN THIS CHAPTER?

- Extending the Alfresco repository
- Extending Alfresco Explorer
- Extending Alfresco Share

The Alfresco product suite provides several out-of-the-box applications that interact with the core Alfresco repository through well-defined interfaces and services. These applications provide interaction with content and business logic from the repository to deliver solutions for Enterprise Content Management (ECM).

The product suite leverages open standards and well-understood service interfaces to provide valuable options for customization and extension. This chapter describes the extension points and focuses on how they are commonly used to build custom integrations and solutions. You will then use some of these hooks in the subsequent chapters to build a custom application on top of Spring Surf and Alfresco Share.

OVERVIEW

The Alfresco repository provides a rich platform for building content applications. It provides scalable storage, extensible services, RESTful interfaces, and a rich content-modeling facility for building your content definitions and content-driven business processes. You can master and maintain these definitions and processes in one single location.

Web applications can use or render the content and access it through any of the many open standards interfaces. This makes it easy and cost-effective for your organization to introduce new applications or scale out existing applications by leveraging a common content infrastructure.

The repository can be clustered or configured standalone so as to support everything from very small to very large throughput.

A small project might consist of no more than a few users hitting the server every once in a while. They might work with Alfresco from their desktop and require no more than basic CIFS integration. In that case, you could set up a single instance of the repository and users could contribute and retrieve content as they pleased.

A larger project might be a real-time Web site with lots of traffic. Each Web site request might in turn make several back-end requests to the Alfresco repository for information – things like the retrieval of articles, images, or personalized user data. In this case, you may elect to cluster the repository so as to ensure not only greater scalability but also higher availability for the content services that back your Web site.

Alfresco provides two out-of-the-box Web applications that make use of the repository and its interfaces: Alfresco Explorer and Alfresco Share. These are fully fledged working ECM applications that perform very well for most purposes. They are preconfigured with most of the common features for both small and large projects. However, most organizations will eventually want to customize and extend these Web applications for their specific project needs.

Alfresco Explorer provides an extensible application for working with documents, records, and Web content. It is built using Java Server Faces (JSF) and provides a navigable experience through the content repository. It features granular access control for the Web client so that you can provision the application for everyone, from administrative users to departmental users, in your business.

Alfresco Share delivers collaborative content management by allowing your users to organize their documents, records, Web content, and activities into projects. It features invitations, notifications, in-context preview, and thumbnails to provide an easy end user experience. Alfresco Share is the primary delivery vehicle for Alfresco document management and records management.

Both of these applications interact with the Alfresco repository; however, they do so in different ways (see Figure 13-1).

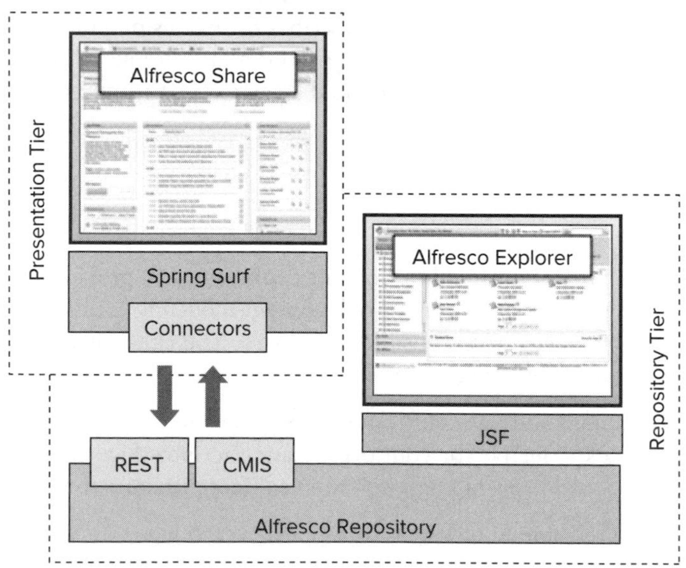

FIGURE 13-1

Alfresco Share runs on a separate tier (a *presentation tier*) and interacts with the Alfresco repository through the Alfresco RESTful interface. Data flows back and forth between Alfresco Share and the repository in formats such as XML and JSON. By having the application on its own tier, IT managers are free to scale out the application independently of the repository.

In contrast, Alfresco Explorer runs on the *repository tier* itself. It interacts with the Alfresco repository's Java service interfaces in process. As such, no marshalling of data occurs. IT managers have to scale out both the repository and the Web client application together as one unit.

Both applications are extensible and provide businesses with the opportunity to extend their features for the needs of their users. Alfresco Share provides a more flexible script-driven framework based on Spring Surf and is the favored direction for future Alfresco applications.

THE ALFRESCO REPOSITORY

When building custom content-driven Web applications, one of the first things to consider is the kind of semantic content your Web application will deal with. Semantic content must be modeled inside the repository. Once it is modeled, you can begin to wrap business logic around the content to provide lifecycle, rendering, and, eventually, publication to a Web site.

Content Models

As discussed in Chapter 5, a content model defines content types, aspects, and constraints. It is defined in an XML file that declares a namespace and all its members. These members belong to the namespace and an associated prefix. For example, the prefix `cm` refers to the formal namespace `www.alfresco.org/model/content/1.0`. You can find a list of namespaces and prefixes at the following wiki page: `http://wiki.alfresco.com/wiki/Alfresco_Namespaces`

A content type has metadata on it, which comprises properties and associations. Properties have names and values (either single or multi-value). Associations define relationships to other content nodes in the repository. Child associations define associations to objects that are considered part of the parent object. When the parent object is deleted, so are the child-associated objects.

Aspects are similar to content types in that they are containers of properties and associations. Aspects are implemented using the Aspect-Oriented Programming (AOP) framework within Spring. Aspects let you define metadata and behavior that cuts across one or more nodes in the repository. You can apply aspects at any time as you see fit. Aspects can be applied arbitrarily to content types as well as content instances.

Both content types and aspects feature inheritance. When a content type or aspect inherits from a parent, it incorporates all the parent's properties, associations, and aspects. If a content type has an aspect applied, the inheriting content type will also have the aspect applied.

A content model can also define one or more constraints. Constraints allow you to ensure the validity of your content ahead of persisting it (for example, when the object is saved). For instance, you may specify a regular expression that must be evaluated against a property to ensure that a property's value is in a valid format.

Content models are defined in an XML file. You bootstrap the XML file into the Alfresco repository using a Spring bean, which is defined in its own XML file (see Figure 13-2). You can define content types, aspects, and constraints as part of a content model using these two XML files that are placed into <*installLocation*>\tomcat\shared\classes\alfresco\extension.

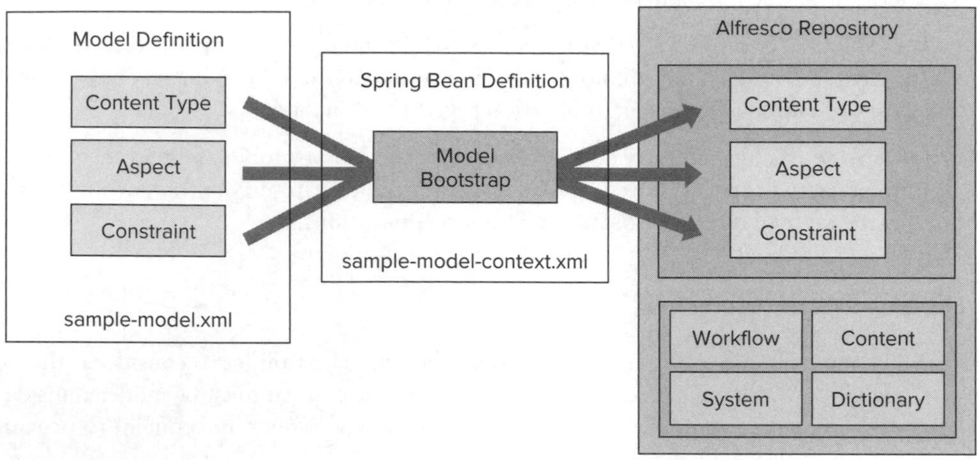

FIGURE 13-2

When Alfresco starts up, it finds the sample-model-context.xml file that declares the Spring bean responsible for bootstrapping the model into the repository model registry. This may appear as follows:

```
<bean id="extension.dictionaryBootstrap" parent="dictionaryModelBootstrap"
depends-on="dictionaryBootstrap">
<property name="models">
<list>
<value>alfresco/extension/sample-model.xml</value>
</list>
</property>
</bean>
```

That's all there is to it. All the things described inside the sample-model.xml file will be available to the repository and accessible to your end users from any of the Alfresco service interfaces.

Content Behavior

One of the most powerful features of the Alfresco repository is the ability to inject behavior into your content. You may want to enforce certain policies on your content or have your own custom business logic execute when a content object is accessed, modified, or saved.

Aspects make this possible. They let you describe additional metadata, such as properties and associations. They also let you override and inject your own handlers for events that occur to the content instance that has the aspect applied. Using aspects, you can *inject* your own business logic as method handlers for events that are raised, such as when a content property is modified.

You can write your own business logic using JavaScript files or Java beans. You then need to register these files or beans with your aspect in the Alfresco repository. The basic registration pattern is shown in Figure 13-3.

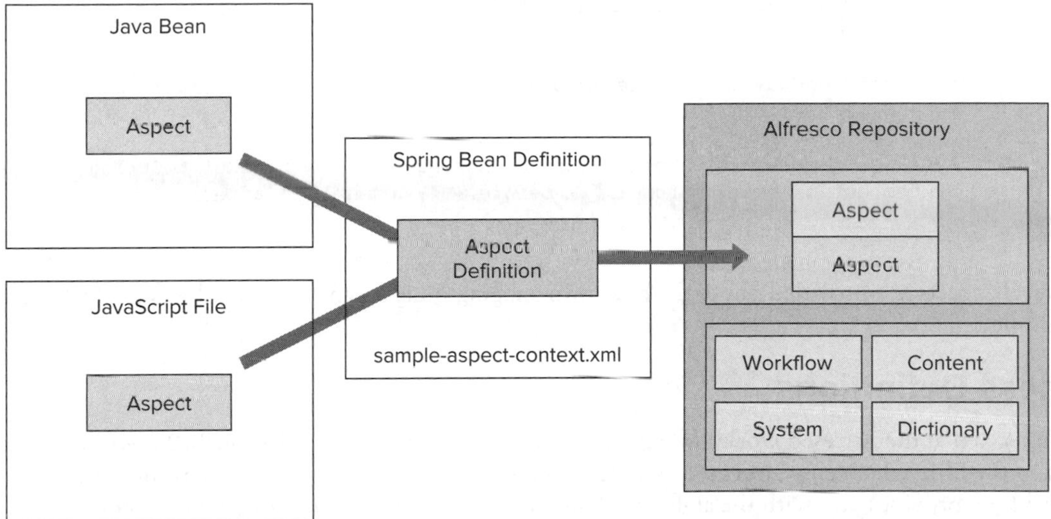

FIGURE 13-3

You can declare the aspect available to the system using a Spring bean that might be defined like this:

```
<bean id="extension.sampleaspect" class="org.alfresco.sample.SampleAspect"
      init-method="init">
  <property name="policyComponent">
    <ref bean="policyComponent" />
  </property>
  <property name="serviceRegistry">
    <ref bean="ServiceRegistry"/>
  </property>
</bean>
```

When the aspect code's `init` method is called, it registers itself with the Alfresco repository using the same namespace as defined in the content model. That way, Alfresco knows how to invoke the aspect's interceptors.

Here is a sample aspect that intercepts the `onUpdateProperties` event and injects its own method to log the event to the Java console or log file. The aspect identifier is `{http://www.alfresco.org/module/sample/1.0}sample`, the same identifier used in the content model to define properties and metadata.

```
public class SampleAspect extends AbstractPolicyServiceBean
  implements NodeServicePolicies.OnUpdatePropertiesPolicy
{
  public void init()
```

```
    {
      this.policyComponent.bindClassBehaviour(
        QName.createQName(NamespaceService.ALFRESCO_URI, "onUpdateProperties"),
        QName.createQName("http://www.alfresco.org/model/sample/1.0", "sample"),
        new JavaBehaviour(this, "onUpdateProperties",
        NotificationFrequency.TRANSACTION_COMMIT));
    }

    public void onUpdateProperties(NodeRef nodeRef, Map<QName, Serializable> before,
      Map<QName, Serializable> after)
    {
      System.out.println("onUpdateProperties heard for " + nodeRef.toString());
      System.out.println("before: " + before + ", after: " + after);
    }
  }
```

Several aspects are provided out of the box for managing things such as content lifecycle, locking, and auditing.

Process Definitions

You looked at the Alfresco workflow engine in Chapter 7. Alfresco provides the jBPM workflow engine out of the box, which empowers solution developers to model business processes around their content. Workflow provides you with the ability to design lifecycle management around your content.

A *process definition* is written in jPDL. A separate Spring bean is then responsible for bootstrapping the process definition into the Alfresco repository at startup. Along with the process definition, the Spring bean can also optionally bootstrap a *workflow content model* as well as any I18N resource bundles (properties files) in support of localization.

This process is illustrated in Figure 13-4 for a sample process definition that defines a content lifecycle.

The lifecycle-workflow-context.xml file defines the Spring bean that bootstraps the three other files into the repository:

Available for download on Wrox.com

```
<?xml version='1.0' encoding='UTF-8'?>
<!DOCTYPE beans PUBLIC '-//SPRING//DTD BEAN//EN' 'http://www.springframework.org/
dtd/spring-beans.dtd'>

<beans>
  <bean id="lifecycle.workflowBootstrap" parent="workflowDeployer">
    <property name="workflowDefinitions">
      <list>
        <props>
          <prop key="engineId">jbpm</prop>
          <prop key="location">
            alfresco/extension/lifecycle_processdefinition.xml
          </prop>
          <prop key="mimetype">text/xml</prop>
          <prop key="redeploy">false</prop>
        </props>
      </list>
    </property>
```

```
        <property name="models">
          <list>
            <value>alfresco/extension/lifecycleModel.xml</value>
          </list>
        </property>
        <property name="labels">
          <list>
            <value>alfresco/extension/lifecycle-messages</value>
          </list>
        </property>
      </bean>
    </beans>
```

Code snippet lifecycle-workflow-context.xml

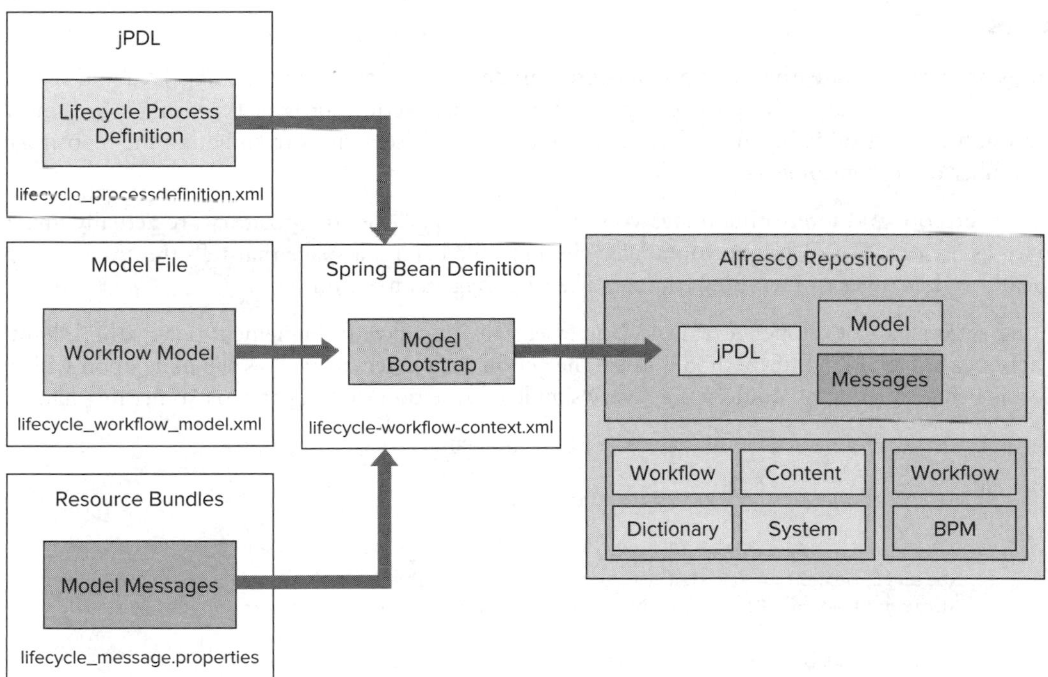

FIGURE 13-4

These files are available from the book's Web site in case you would like to try them in your own Alfresco repository.

Workflow Models

Workflow models allow you to wrap forms and property sheets around your jBPM workflow processes. They inform the Alfresco repository how to map content contained within the in-flight processes to display elements for the end user. This includes mapping end-user input into process variables as well as mapping process variables back into display elements.

You can think of the raw process definition as a graph or a mathematical construct that links together different task nodes via transitions. The in-flight process transitions from node to node either automatically or based on external interaction from an end user. With Alfresco, this external interaction is usually facilitated through forms or workflow wizards.

The workflow content model informs these forms of how to render. It draws from the I18N resource bundles to provision text elements (like labels) that are meaningful for many languages and geographies.

How might you use this? Imagine a scenario where you may want to have multilingual support for your workflow tasks, such as forms automatically localized for Italian versus French. A workflow model makes this possible. It informs Alfresco how to retrieve and persist information from the underlying in-flight process while providing an Italian-localized interface for the Italian users and a French-localized interface for the French users.

Actions

Actions are Spring beans that act upon a content node. You develop actions using Java and register them with the repository through a Spring configuration file. Actions provide the ideal place to put your common, highly reusable business logic. You can then call these actions from within the repository for any number of content objects.

Most of the cool and interesting things you can do with the Alfresco repository are actually implemented as actions. For example, you might wire in a rule behind a space that tells the space to automatically make copies of incoming content. The rule triggers an action.

Writing actions is a developer-level task. You essentially just have to implement one method that tells the action what to do. Your method is given the action parameters as well as the node upon which the action is being called. You could write a very simple copy action that might look something like this:

```
public void executeImpl(Action action, NodeRef node)
{
  if (this.nodeService.exists(node) == true)
  {
    // we take in two parameters
    NodeRef parent = (NodeRef) action.getParameterValue("destination_folder");
    String name = (String) action.getParameterValue("destination_name");

    // association type and associated content name
    QName assocType = (QName) ContentModel.ASSOC_CONTAINS;
    Qname assocName = QName.createQName(ContentModel.CONTENT_MODEL_1_0_URI, name);

    // Create a new copy of the node
    this.copyService.copyAndRename(node, parent, assocType, assocName, true);
  }
}
```

You register your Java bean via Spring configuration. It is then registered with the repository under a specified ID. For the example above, you might select the ID "my-copy-action."

If you have written other Java backing classes for Alfresco (such as aspects, transformers, or other actions), you could reuse this action from within those. You may also reuse it from within any server-side scripting files you may have. Here is an example of JavaScript that copies a document to the Company Home folder by using your custom action:

```
var myCopyAction = actions.create("my-copy-action");
myCopyAction.parameters["destination_folder"] = companyhome;
myCopyAction.parameters["destination_name"] = "Copy of " + document.name;
myCopyAction.execute(document);
```

In addition, you can invoke this action from the user interface directly if you so choose. You can configure Alfresco Explorer and Alfresco Share to participate in providing buttons to trigger actions directly. You will look at some extensions to Alfresco Explorer and Alfresco Share in the coming chapters.

Other Extension Points

The Alfresco repository features many additional extension points that are beyond the scope of this book.

You can define custom transformers that are responsible for converting a document of a source file type to a destination file type. For example, you might plug in a transformer that converts an MPEG video file to an audio output stream. You could then push both of these files to a Web server for delivery.

You can define custom metadata extractors responsible for interrogating the content and pulling out metadata fields. For example, you can write a metadata extractor that extracts values from a custom file format and places it onto Alfresco metadata properties. You can then search on these properties or fire off custom business logic.

You can also define custom template and scripting variables that you can provision to developers who wish to extend the Alfresco repository using server-side JavaScript or FreeMarker.

All these extension points and more can be achieved using the very same pattern shown here. An implementation Spring bean is developed and then declared or bootstrapped through configuration.

ALFRESCO EXPLORER

Alfresco Explorer was the first end user Web application developed by Alfresco. It was designed with the intention of supporting many ECM applications within it, such as Document Management or Web Content Management. It has a flexible and extensible design that affords implementors the opportunity to either customize the existing applications or introduce their own right inside of the Alfresco Explorer application.

The Basics

You typically access Alfresco Explorer using the following URL:

```
http://localhost:8080/alfresco
```

You can then log in using your credentials (see Figure 13-5). The default administrator account has a user name of `admin` and a password of `admin`.

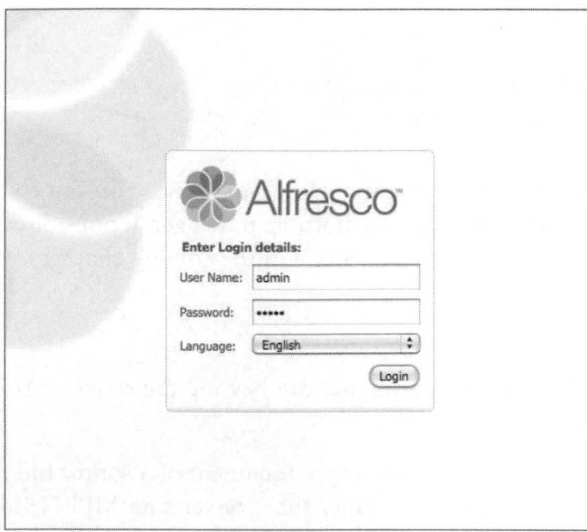

FIGURE 13-5

Once inside Alfresco Explorer, you will see a simple dashboard that serves as a landing page for users (see Figure 13-6). Each user can customize this dashboard to their liking by arranging the out-of-the-box dashlets or custom dashlets that you build using Web scripts.

FIGURE 13-6

Dashboards and dashlets are discussed in more detail in the "Alfresco Share" section later in this chapter.

Clicking on Company Home takes you to the root of the content repository. Here, you will see a navigable view of nodes in the repository.

Nodes consist of spaces and content items:

- A *space* is a node in the repository that has zero or more child nodes inside of it. Spaces are very similar to folders or directories on your computer's desktop. They are assigned the type `cm:folder`. They maintain metadata as well as user access rights.
- A *content item* is a node in the repository that is contained inside of a space. Content items are similar to files on your computer. They hold a content payload in addition to metadata and access rights. They are assigned the type `cm:content`.

Spaces and content items are implemented using Alfresco's content model facilities. Therefore, you can extend their definitions and add in your own business logic. You may wish to add new metadata, bind in content rules, or wire in new behaviors using aspects.

Alfresco Explorer provides default icons for these object types, but you can plug in as many of your own as you like. Figure 13-7 shows an example of a default space and a content item with the extension `ftl`.

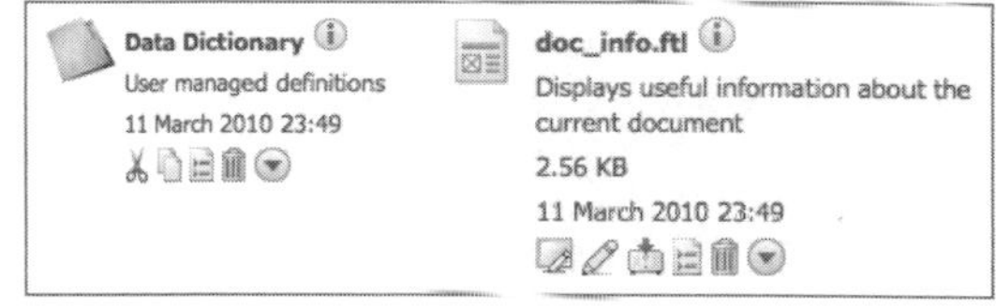

FIGURE 13-7

Alfresco Explorer lets you define the specific actions that users will have available to them when they interact with nodes in the repository. These actions appear as clickable icons next to either the space or the content item, as shown in Figure 13-7, or they can appear along the menu at the top of the page. You can associate different actions to different types of objects. You can also have role-based actions where actions are only available to certain users.

For any given space with Alfresco Explorer, you will have several actions available to you by default for creating new content and new spaces. These actions are available along the top of the page, as shown in Figure 13-8.

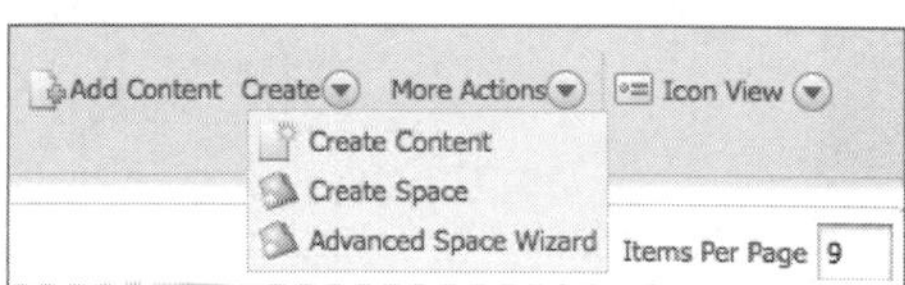

FIGURE 13-8

From this menu, you can upload new content items or perform actions against the current space. You can also create new content items or spaces inside of this space from scratch. The Create Space option brings up the Create Space dialog box (see Figure 13-9). A form is presented for setting the properties of your new space. You can define forms within Alfresco Explorer for all of your custom content types for both spaces and content items. You have complete control over the end-user content contribution experience.

If you create new spaces, they will appear alongside the default spaces shown in Figure 13-6. If you want to see what is inside a space, just click on its icon or its name. This will navigate you into that space. Once there, you can click on the View Details icon to bring up the Details page for your space. Figure 13-10 shows the Details page for the Data Dictionary space.

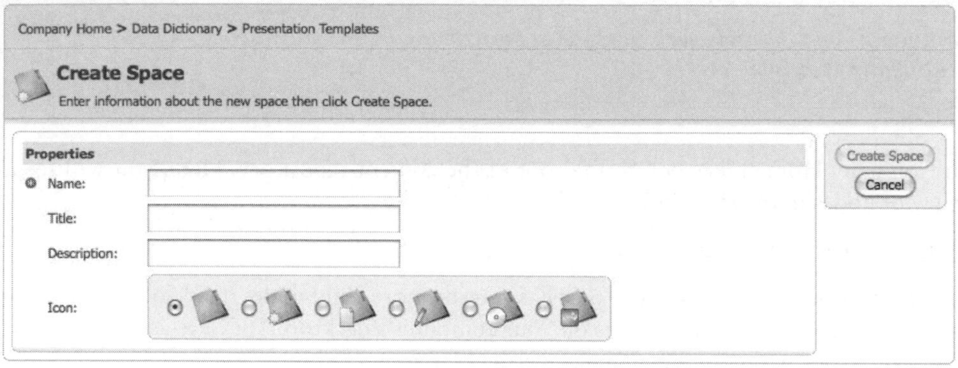

FIGURE 13-9

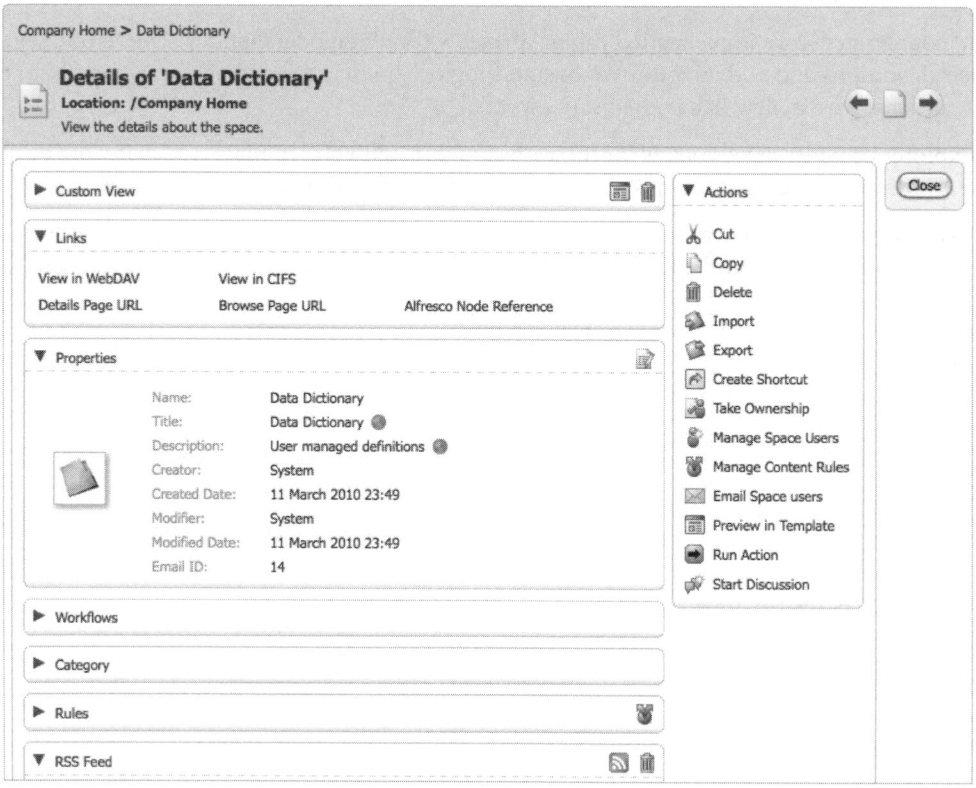

FIGURE 13-10

You can view the properties for any node in the repository, whether it is a space or a content item. On the right side of the page is a list of actions you can perform against this node.

Alfresco Explorer provides many more features and extension points. You will look at some of these as you explore and build out the sample application.

Permissions

Alfresco Explorer provides you with an interface for assigning permissions to nodes in the repository. Permissions themselves are actually a repository-level feature; Alfresco Explorer simply provides an elegant interface for assigning and working with permissions.

You can modify permissions for a space by selecting Manage Space Users in the More Actions menu (see Figure 13-11).

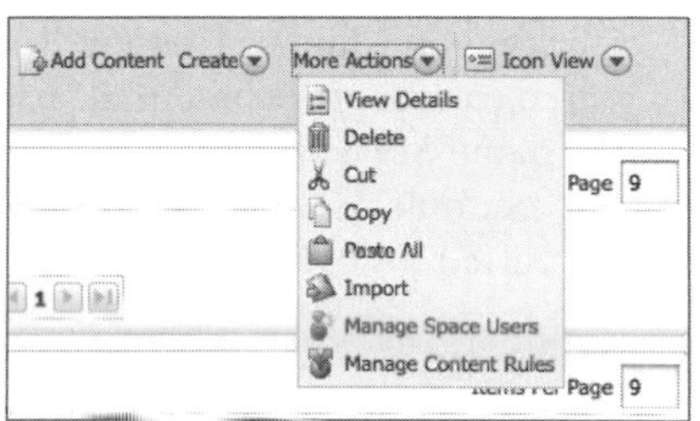

FIGURE 13-11

By clicking on Invite, you begin the process of inviting users or groups of users into the space (see Figure 13-12). You invite users or groups to participate in the space in one or more roles.

Roles are groupings of permissions. When you assign a user or a group to a role against a node, you grant them a set of permissions against that node. Alfresco ships with a number of predefined roles. These roles are described in Chapter 6.

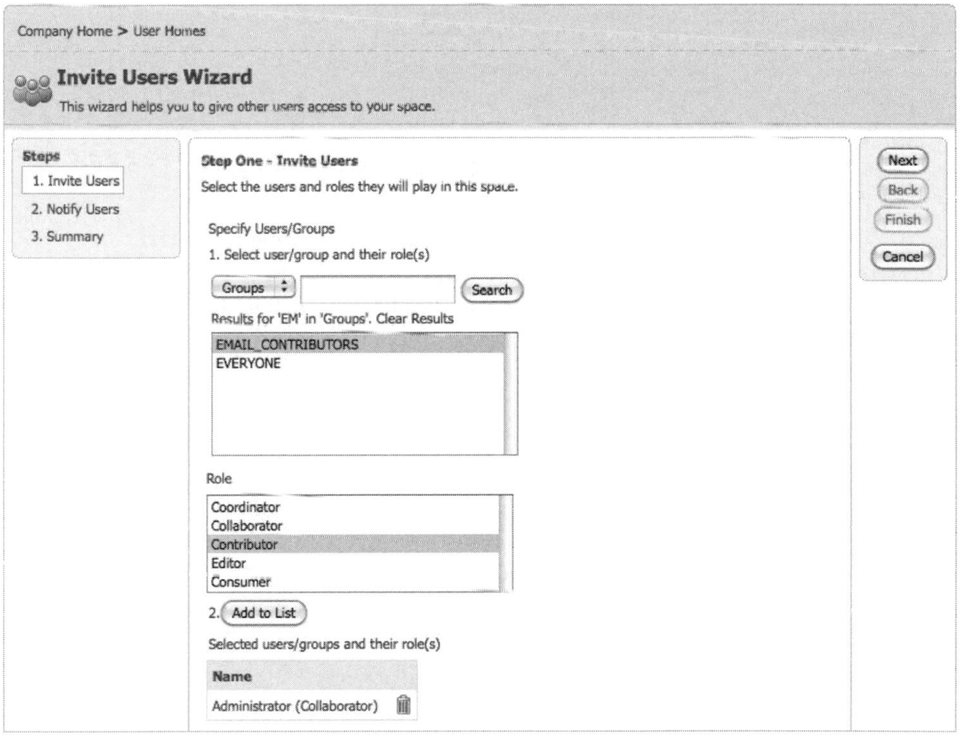

FIGURE 13-12

Rules

Alfresco Explorer provides a convenient way to define repository rules wired into your content spaces. A rule is a bit of business logic configured to trigger when something happens to or with content inside of the space. There are three types of triggers:

- **Inbound:** A content item is newly placed into the space.

- **Update:** A content item is updated within the space.
- **Outbound:** A content item leaves the space either by being moved or by being deleted.

You can define rules directly within the user interface. If you navigate into a space using Alfresco Explorer, you will see several options listed under More Actions (see Figure 13-11).

Clicking on Manage Content Rules brings up the Content Rules page, which lists all the rules currently wired to execute behind that space. As shown in Figure 13-13, three rules are wired into the space with the name *My Sample Space*. These rules will automatically execute when users interact with this space. For example, when a user drops a Word document into this space, the document will automatically be converted to PDF.

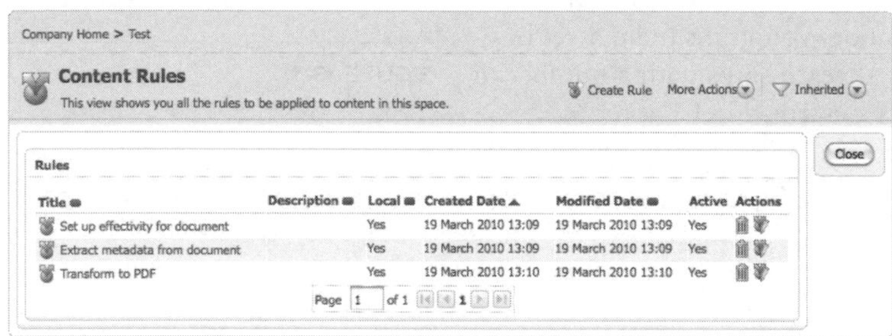

FIGURE 13-13

Let's look at how to set up a new rule. Clicking Create Rule at the top of the Content Rules page lets you create a brand new rule. A preliminary page appears that lets you define the conditions by which your new rule will be fired (see Figure 13-14).

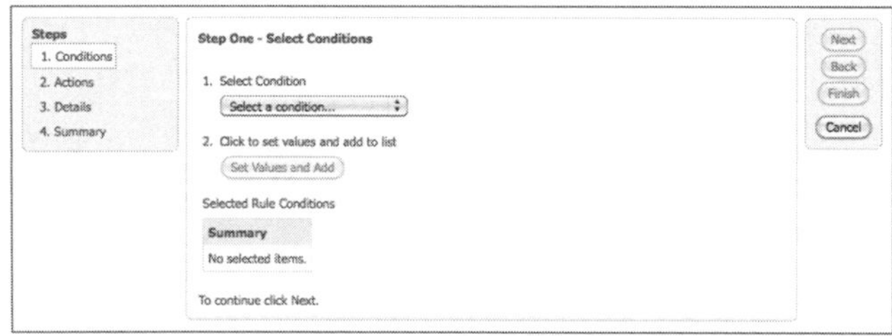

FIGURE 13-14

You can select from many different kinds of conditions, including the following:

- Content items or spaces of a specific type
- Content items that have a specific aspect or title
- Content items that have a specific property value
- Content items of a specific MIME type or categorization

Many more conditions are available. In addition, Alfresco Explorer allows you to plug in your own conditions. Once you have specified a condition, click Next to advance to the next page, where you can define what actions should occur if the condition is satisfied (see Figure 13-15).

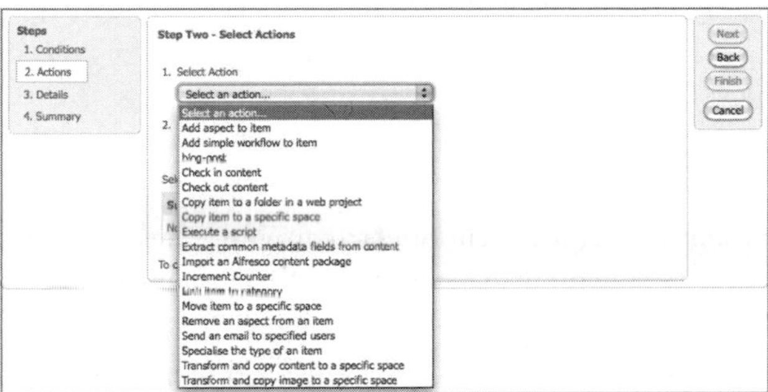

FIGURE 13-15

The actions shown in Figure 13-15 are repository actions. As mentioned previously, you can build your own or choose from the list of actions available out of the box. You can have the rule automatically apply aspects to your content, transform your content, fire off emails about your content, or move it to an entirely different space in the repository. You can have these rules run in the background or execute while the user waits.

Clicking Next takes you to the next step of the wizard, where you define which type of event will trigger the execution of the rule (see Figure 13-16).

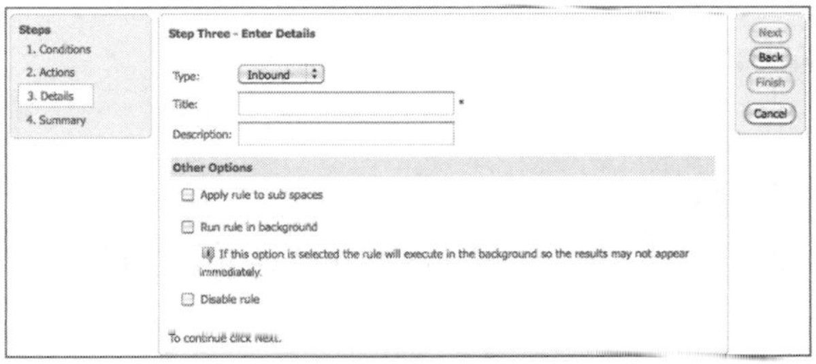

FIGURE 13-16

You might want the rule to trigger when content is added to the folder (*inbound*) or when it is updated within the folder (*update*). Give your rule a name and description, and click Finish to save it.

That's all there is to it. You can be very descriptive with rules and the business logic that they invoke. A single rule can fire off many repository actions and can even execute server-side JavaScript. You are also free to define many different rules, each configured to trigger under slightly different conditions. Rules allow you to implement simple processes on the fly by moving content between spaces while triggering email notifications, metadata updates, and scriptable actions to modify the content-item lifecycle state.

Other Extension Points

Alfresco Explorer features many additional extension points that are beyond the scope of this chapter.

You can add new user interface actions, customize icons, plug in custom templates, and build new behaviors using server-side JavaScript. You will look at some of these in more detail in the chapters that follow.

ALFRESCO SHARE

Alfresco Share provides highly collaborative content management oriented around projects and activities. It represents the Alfresco modern approach to content management, one that brings together social context and notifications around content activities to provide increased productivity.

Alfresco Share essentially inverts the top-down hierarchical approach of Alfresco Explorer by situating the end user inside of a project or task. End users can create project spaces any time they like, invite other users, collaborate on content, and approve and publish content, all while taking full advantage of the rich content modeling, behavior, and lifecycle management of the underlying Alfresco repository.

In addition, Alfresco Share is built and delivered using Spring Surf. Surf provides Alfresco Share with script- and template-driven presentation. This makes it easy to extend Alfresco Share without heavy Java development. Alfresco Share, therefore, becomes an ideal environment for building out your custom content authoring and contribution applications.

Alfresco Share is the main Web application platform for Alfresco document management and records management in Alfresco 3.2.

The Basics

Users typically access Alfresco Share using the following URL:

```
http://localhost:8080/share
```

This directs the browser to the Alfresco Share Web client.

Alfresco Share features an Alfresco authenticator that informs Surf how to authenticate and interact with the Alfresco repository.

On the Login page (see Figure 13-17), you can log in using the same authentication credentials as with the underlying repository and Alfresco Explorer (`admin/admin`).

Once logged in, the current user's dashboard displays (see Figure 13-18). This provides a single place to see all the content and activity touch points for the projects in which the user is involved.

The user dashboard contains a series of *dashlets* arranged onto the page according to a prescribed layout. Each user will have a slightly different preference as to which dashlets are most useful to them. They may also prefer different layouts. For this reason, Alfresco Share lets you configure your user's dashboard layout and preferred dashlets through the Customize Dashboard feature (located in the top-right corner of the dashboard).

FIGURE 13-17

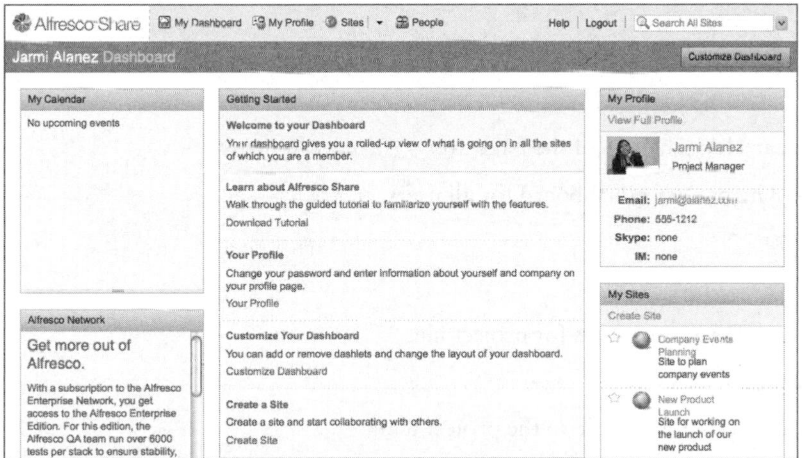

FIGURE 13-18

Users can participate in public projects either by discovering content activities through their dashboard or by searching for sites explicitly. You search for sites by typing the name of the site in the search box on the top right of the page. You then click the search icon to start your search.

Sites may also be marked as private, in which case the user must be explicitly invited. Users can also create new sites using the Create Site Wizard (see Figure 13-19). You launch the Create Site Wizard by clicking on the Create Site link under the My Sites dashlet. The Create Site Wizard will pop up in a modal dialog.

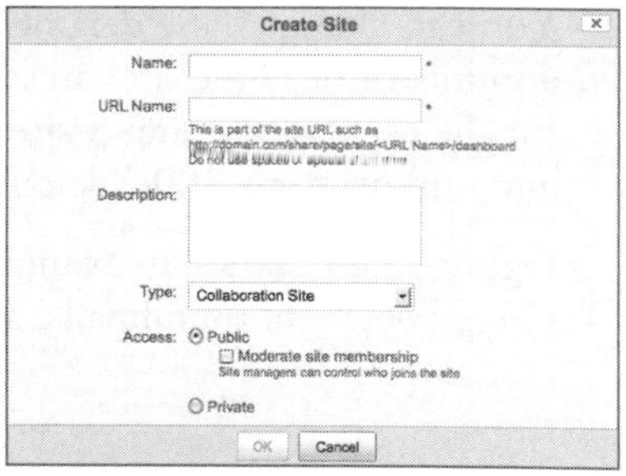

FIGURE 13-19

The wizard creates a new project site preconfigured with a set of default pages that appear along the top of the page. Each page offers collaboration tools around the project. See Figure 13-20 for a sample of how a project might appear.

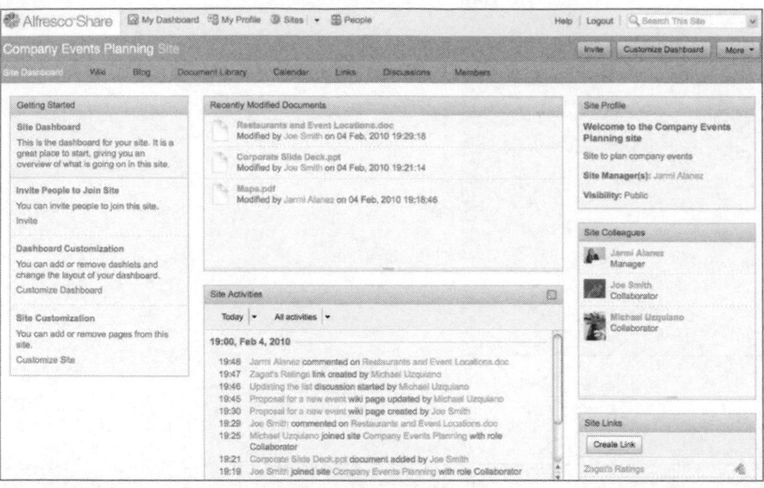

FIGURE 13-20

The default pages that appear along the top of the page are:

- **Site Dashboard** — The project's dashboard for all users
- **Wiki** — Project wiki
- **Blog** — Project blog
- **Document Library** — Document store for project files
- **Calendar** — Project team calendar
- **Links** — Collection of URLs available to the project team
- **Discussions** — Forums for the project team
- **Members** — Ability to invite and assign roles to users and groups

You can change these default pages, add new pages, or even define new types of project sites. The administrator of the site can set up the site dashboard page to offer unique project-specific functionality for the users of the site. A site administrator may, for example, wish to customize the site dashboard and remove some of the default pages or add in their own custom pages and dashlets.

Figure 13-21 shows an example of the Document Library page, one of the default project pages. It offers document thumbnails, a left-hand navigation tree, and in-context document preview.

The site administrator can also add members to the site. All site members take on roles; some may be contributors, others collaborators. When users interact with content in the site, these interactions are tracked as activities. At any point, you can view the list of recent activities for a given site. These are shown in the Site Activities dashlet on your site dashboard (see Figure 13-20).

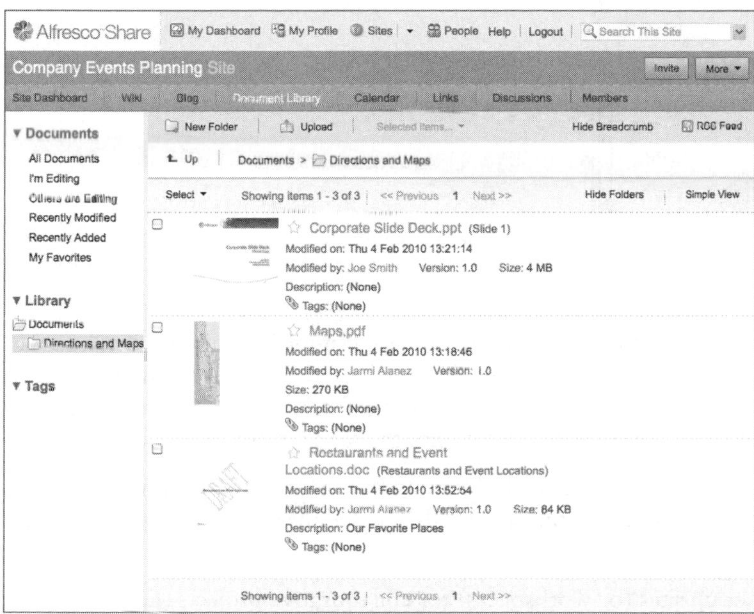

FIGURE 13-21

Dashboards

Alfresco Share provides a user dashboard to which each user has full access and control. The user dashboard is the very first thing that users see when they log into Alfresco Share. It provides a quick view into all the user's touch points within the Alfresco Share content store.

A dashboard consists of dashlets plugged into the dashboard's layout. A dashlet is a miniature view or application that can be snapped into the dashboard. Users can configure the layout of their dashboard, which lets them place their dashlets in a variety of different places.

Figure 13-22 shows an example of a three-column layout with a few dashlets plugged into the columns. The left column has three dashlets assigned to it, whereas the middle and right columns only have a single dashlet each.

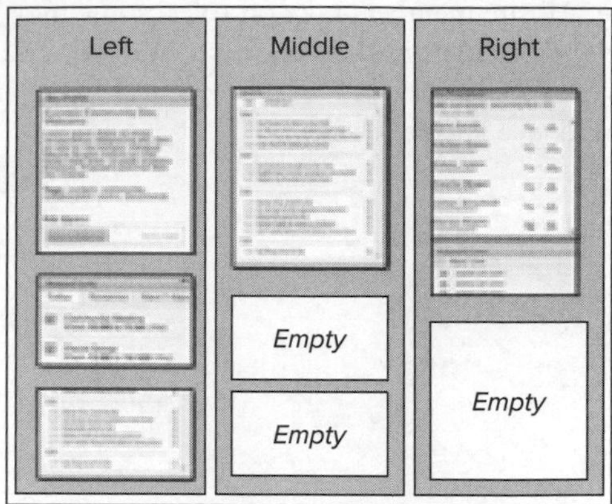

FIGURE 13-22

Alfresco Share allows users to customize their user dashboards by simply clicking on the Configure Dashboard button at the top of their user dashboard page. They can then pick from alternative layouts using the Change Layout button. Alfresco Share comes pre-stocked with a few common and useful layouts. You can also add your own; however, that is beyond the scope of this discussion.

At the bottom of the page, users can discover new dashlets. They can drag and drop them into their dashboard. If you add new custom dashlets to the system, they will appear here for users to select and place onto their user dashboard.

Alfresco Share allows you to set up sites (or workspaces) for collaborative projects. Each site also has a dashboard. Site dashboards behave very similarly to user dashboards, except that site administrators are the ones to configure them, rather than the end user. Site administrators can set site dashboard layout and pre-configure which dashlets are available to their site users.

Dashlets

Dashlets are Web scripts that belong to a specific family. Dashlets that you intend to make available for placement onto the user dashboard should be placed into the `user-dashlet` family. Dashlets that you intend to make available for placement onto a site dashboard should be placed into the `site-dashlet` family. As discussed in the previous section, this can be accomplished by simply dragging the dashlets from the bottom of the page onto the dashboard.

Dashlet Web scripts must provide `GET` handlers. This means you should define a scriptable controller for the HTTP `GET` method, and your template view should output to the HTML format.

If your dashlet is added to a user dashboard or a site dashboard, Alfresco Share will render it in the context of the entire page. You will look at dashlets in more detail in the next chapter.

14

Custom Knowledge Base: Getting Started

WHAT'S IN THIS CHAPTER?

- Defining a content model in the Alfresco repository
- Building a Knowledge Base space template
- Configuring business process rules
- Writing articles in Alfresco Explorer

This chapter guides you through the foundation work required as a first step for building a compelling Knowledge Base application. This chapter focuses on the Alfresco repository and Alfresco Explorer. It walks you through the design and implementation of the content model and content rules required to implement a lifecycle for your Knowledge Base articles.

Familiarity with Chapter 13, which discusses levels of customization and their associated terminology, will be helpful to you in working through this chapter. Subsequent chapters build on the foundation work presented in this chapter. They focus on how to customize Alfresco Share to incorporate your Knowledge Base lifecycle within collaborative projects.

This chapter is structured to provide the following sections:

- **Overview** — A high-level explanation of the concepts and application extension points that you will use in the example. You don't have to type in any of the code in this section; it is simply provided to help guide along the conversation.
- **Installing the Code** — A step-by-step guide to the approach you will need to take in order to install all of the sample code on your own Alfresco installation.
- **Putting It into Action** — A walkthrough of your new extensions. Try them out and see what they do!

At the end of this chapter you will find the source code for the samples. This is only provided for reference. To install the samples, you should download the source files from the book's page at `www.wrox.com` and follow the instructions provided in the section titled "Installing the Code."

OVERVIEW

This section provides an overview of the concepts and product features you'll take advantage of as you build out your Knowledge Base foundation. You'll start by defining your content and content lifecycle. From this you can derive your content model requirements. You'll examine Alfresco Explorer and see some of the extension points that it provides. Finally, you'll look at how you can use space templates and rules in Alfresco Explorer to make things really easy.

You don't have to type in any code in this section. Just read and enjoy!

Content Lifecycle

Your Knowledge Base will consist of articles that are contributed and collaborated upon by an internal team of knowledge experts. External consumers of the articles expect them to contain valid and approved information.

Content contributors can author new articles or work on existing articles using any of the authoring facilities in Alfresco. They can use Alfresco Explorer to navigate the content hierarchy to find and work on articles. Contributors can also use conventional desktop applications, such as Microsoft Word, to open and save files directly against Alfresco through its CIFS interface.

Articles must have a lifecycle state. For example, when an article is first authored, it is assigned with a *draft* status. This simply means that the article's content has not yet been approved. It may require more work before it can be considered complete, or it may be essentially complete and just need someone to sign off on its validity.

The workflow engine is responsible for handling the routing of the article to the appropriate people for sign-off and approval. This process may be instantaneous or take quite a while, even days, depending on the availability of staff to participate in the process. During this time, the article is assigned with a *pending approval* status.

As a positive outcome of this workflow process, the article's status should be modifiable to an approved *current* state. An article with a *current* status is valid and the external consumer audience should be able to retrieve it.

Alternatively, the workflow process may discover a problem with the article. In that case, it sets the article's status back to *draft* and allows the internal staff to continue making modifications.

Figure 14-1 shows an overview of this workflow process.

The Knowledge Base article conforms to this lifecycle. Now you'll look at how you can model your Knowledge Base article using the content modeling facilities of the Alfresco repository.

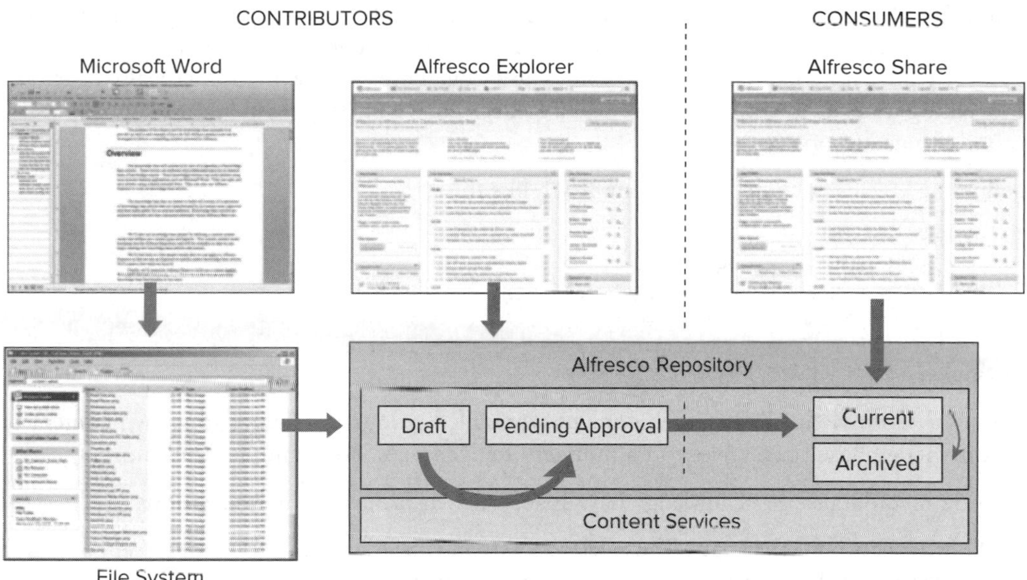

FIGURE 14-1

Content Model

To define a content model for the Knowledge Base metadata, you first determine a namespace URI and a prefix you want to use. While you can use anything you like as long as it is unique, it helps to have a short prefix. This example uses the following:

- **URI** — `http://www.alfresco.org/model/knowledgebase/1.0`
- **Prefix** — `kb`

With this in place, you can reference anything you define in the model by using the simple `kb` prefix. Now you can start defining things inside of the model. You should focus on two primary entities:

- Knowledge Base space
- Knowledge Base article

The next sections look at Knowledge Base spaces and articles in detail.

Knowledge Base Spaces

Your Knowledge Base articles will be authored and managed within a container known as a Knowledge Base *space*. As you saw earlier, a space is an Alfresco container that behaves a lot like a folder. It may even appear like a folder on your desktop (for example, if you are using the Alfresco CIFS desktop integration). However, while it looks like a folder, it may have custom business logic and behavior wired up behind it.

You can define the Knowledge Base space as a content type inside of your content model and extend it from `cm:folder`. The content type `cm:folder` is an out-of-the-box content type provided by the Alfresco repository. By inheriting from `cm:folder`, your Knowledge Base space will automatically be endowed with everything it needs to act and behave like a folder. You can then plug in additional properties and other good things on top.

You define the `kb:space` content type using XML like this:

```
<types>
   <type name="kb:space">
      <title>Knowledge Base Space</title>
      <parent>cm:folder</parent>
   </type>
</types>
```

This defines a "Knowledge Base space" content type called `kb:space`. Having your own content type for the Knowledge Base space gives you a number of advantages. For example, you can:

- Add metadata to the Knowledge Base space (such as properties or associations).
- Plug aspects onto the space. These let you wire in your own Java code to intercept events that occur to the folder (for example, when someone drops content into it).
- Tell Alfresco Explorer, Alfresco Share, or your own custom Web applications to treat this folder uniquely. For instance, you can easily configure Alfresco Explorer to show a different icon for this folder.

This is a good design practice. You may not use all of these advantages right away, but you have a good foundation to do so in the future.

Knowledge Base Articles

A Knowledge Base article is a document submitted by a knowledge expert. It might be a Word document, a PDF, a text file, or even an Excel file. Assume that your knowledge experts are a diverse bunch – you don't want to constrain them with respect to the kinds of files they can submit. After all, Alfresco works very well with any file type you drop in.

You would like to define some metadata to wrap this Knowledge Base article. This additional metadata would let you store things on the document that aren't part of the document's internal representation or binary payload. If that's a little confusing, that's all right. Consider the following example.

Imagine you have a Word document. Your desktop users like to use Word – they're comfortable with it and they have a passion for Bill Gates. So they save their Word documents into Alfresco. At that moment, you can tell Alfresco to wrap metadata around the document. You can have as many properties and associations on this metadata as you would like. You can use that metadata to store things that the end user never sees or has to know about. As far as they are concerned, it is just a Word document.

For example, you may want to store an internal representation of the lifecycle state (such as draft, pending approval, and so on). Or perhaps a field that indicates the type of document (such as article, FAQ, or White Paper). One valid way you might think to do this would be to do as you did in the previous section. You could create another content type, call it `kb:article`, and add metadata to the `kb:article` content type. If you did that, it might appear like this:

```
<types>
   <type name="kb:article">
      <title>Knowledge Base Article</title>
      <parent>cm:content</parent>
      <properties>
         <property name="kb:status">
            <title>Status</title>
            <type>d:text</type>
            <default>Draft</default>
         </property>
         <property name="kb:articletype">
            <title>Article Type</title>
            <type>d:text</type>
            <default>Article</default>
         </property>
      </properties>
   </type>
</types>
```

This snippet declares the `kb:article` content type and gives it two `d:text` properties: `kb:status` and `kb:articletype`. The `kb:status` property tracks the lifecycle status of the Knowledge Base article. The `kb:articletype` property describes the type of article.

This approach would work, but you may eventually discover it to be too constraining. Why? Well, requiring Knowledge Base articles to be typed as `kb:article` means that you will forever require anyone who uses your Knowledge Base to have their content typed as `kb:article`. Since documents can only have one base content type, it is quite restrictive.

If you went with this approach, you would require that any Knowledge Base articles be of either type `kb:article` or another type that extends from `kb:article`. This would then force other third-party applications to consider your Knowledge Base schema ahead of time, which is often very inconvenient. Instead, you could use an approach that does not require rebasing the content instances onto a base type from your schema.

It would be ideal to take an arbitrary content item or document and mark it as a Knowledge Base article. By doing this, the content item would take on the additional metadata (`kb:status` and `kb:articletype`). You could mark any number of content items this way, no matter if they are desktop documents, XML files, or custom object types.

Alfresco makes all of this possible with content aspects. Instead of defining a Knowledge Base article content type, you can define content aspects and then mark up your content using these aspects as you see fit.

Here is what the revised code might look like:

```
<aspects>

   <aspect name="kb:status">
      <title>Status</title>
      <properties>
         <property name="kb:status">
            <title>Status</title>
            <type>d:text</type>
            <default>Draft</default>
```

```
            </property>
         </properties>
      </aspect>

      <aspect name="kb:article">
         <title>Article</title>
         <properties>
            <property name="kb:articletype">
               <title>Article Type</title>
               <type>d:text</type>
               <default>Article</default>
            </property>
         </properties>
         <mandatory-aspects>
            <aspect>kb:status</aspect>
         </mandatory-aspects>
      </aspect>

   </aspects>
```

You have defined `kb:article` as an aspect in the XML fragment previously shown. The `kb:article` aspect has the `kb:articletype` text property on it. It also has a mandatory inclusion of the `kb:status` aspect. The `kb:status` aspect is defined as a separate aspect and defines the `kb:status` text property.

You can now mark content in the Alfresco repository with the `kb:article` aspect. By doing so, the content item will have two aspects applied: `kb:article` and, by implication, `kb:status`. It will therefore have two properties on it: `kb:articletype` and `kb:status`.

Why two aspects? One reason is that it offers a more flexible forward-thinking approach. Imagine that in the near future you need to add support for Knowledge Base videos. You could create a Knowledge Base video aspect called `kb:video`. This aspect would have unique video-related properties on it, but it would like to reuse the same `kb:status` fields that the rest of the Knowledge Base application uses. All you have to do is specify `kb:status` as a mandatory aspect for the new `kb:video` aspect, and away you go.

Constraints

One additional improvement you can introduce is to apply a few constraints to your defined aspect properties. Property constraints allow you to specify checks that must pass before the property value is considered valid and safe for persistence. Constraints fire when the property values change. A content item must have all of its constraints pass before it can be created or saved.

Alfresco provides several default constraint types that you can use in your content model. These include regular-expression evaluators and value lists. Of course, you are also free to write your own constraint implementations. Large projects will use custom constraints to perform complex lookups in third-party databases or services to assert the correctness of property values.

In this case, you can use some of the default out-of-the-box constraints to ensure the validity of any content marked with your aspects. Here, you can declare two constraints that specify the valid values for `kb:status` and `kb:articletype`:

```
<constraints>
   <constraint name="kb:status_constraint" type="LIST">
      <parameter name="allowedValues">
         <list>
            <value>Draft</value>
            <value>Pending Approval</value>
            <value>Current</value>
            <value>Archived</value>
         </list>
      </parameter>
   </constraint>
   <constraint name="kb:articletype_constraint" type="LIST">
      <parameter name="allowedValues">
         <list>
            <value>Any</value>
            <value>Article</value>
            <value>FAQ</value>
            <value>White Paper</value>
         </list>
      </parameter>
   </constraint>
</constraints>
```

These declare the constraints. All you need to do then is tell your properties to use these as property constraints by simply modifying the property declarations on your aspects:

```
<property name="kb:status">
   <title>Status</title>
   <type>d:text</type>
   <default>Draft</default>
   <constraints>
      <constraint ref="kb:status_constraint" />
   </constraints>
</property>
<property name="kb:articletype">
   <title>Article Type</title>
   <type>d:text</type>
   <default>Article</default>
   <constraints>
      <constraint ref="kb:articletype_constraint" />
   </constraints>
</property>
```

That's about it. By putting the content model together, you effectively inform the Alfresco repository how to manage the interaction and persistence of Knowledge Base assets.

Alfresco Explorer Extensions

Alfresco Explorer is an out-of-the-box Web application that provides a useful interface for content contributors. For example, content contributors can use Alfresco Explorer to create new Knowledge Base articles and adjust metadata properties using automatically rendered property sheets.

Alfresco Explorer features a number of configuration options that you can tweak to make it easier to work with your Knowledge Base spaces and articles.

Property Sheets

Alfresco Explorer automatically renders content metadata to the end user for viewing and editing. It generates a property sheet for content in the Knowledge Base. You can tweak this property sheet by informing Alfresco Explorer of properties that exist on the `kb:status` and `kb:article` aspects.

The following code provides this configuration for Alfresco Explorer. It defines how to render property sheets for matching aspect and content-type names. Each property sheet can have zero or more fields that render controls for displaying and editing individual properties of the content model.

```
<config evaluator="aspect-name" condition="kb:article">
   <property-sheet>
      <separator name="sep" display-label="KB Article Properties"
                 component-generator="HeaderSeparatorGenerator"
                 show-in-edit-mode="false"/>
      <show-property name="kb:kbid"  show-in-edit-mode="true"/>
      <show-property name="kb:article_type"  show-in-edit-mode="true"/>
      <show-property name="kb:status" display-label="kb:status"
                     show-in-edit-mode="true"/>
   </property-sheet>
</config>
<config evaluator="aspect-name" condition="kb:status">
   <property-sheet>
      <show-property name="kb:status" display-label="kb:status"/>
   </property-sheet>
</config>
```

Alfresco Explorer will now display your Knowledge Base properties to end users for viewing and editing.

Wizards and Icons

Alfresco Explorer features a number of wizards that let you do things like fire off actions or create new content. These wizards are configurable and you can plug in your Knowledge Base assets straight away.

You can inform Alfresco Explorer to let you create spaces of type `kb:space` by using the following code snippet:

```
<config evaluator="string-compare" condition="Space Wizards">
   <folder-types>
      <type name="kb:space" icon="/images/icons/space-icon-pen.gif" />
   </folder-types>
</config>
```

You can also inform Alfresco Explorer to include your `kb:article` aspect as one of the available aspect options in the Action Wizard. The following code snippet achieves this:

```
<config evaluator="string-compare" condition="Action Wizard">
   <aspects>
      <aspect name="kb:article"/>
   </aspects>
</config>
```

Finally, you may want to adjust the way that Knowledge Base spaces appear in the Alfresco Explorer navigator. You can set up a custom icon for the `kb:space` content type with the following snippet.

```
<config evaluator="string-compare" condition="kb:space icons">
   <icons>
      <icon name="space-icon-pen" path="/images/icons/space-icon-pen.gif" />
   </icons>
</config>
```

Your `kb:space` spaces will now show up with a different icon – a folder superimposed with a pen. This is simply a cosmetic change, but a useful one nonetheless. It will help end users locate the Knowledge Base space. You could also make additional customizations to the Alfresco Explorer configuration file.

Smart Spaces and Scripting

A *space* in the Alfresco repository is fundamentally a container. Users who interact with a space through a CIFS file share will really see nothing more than a folder. For all intents and purposes, they believe they are actually working with content in a folder.

In reality, however, you can make your spaces smart by wiring in business logic behind them. You can tell your spaces how to behave when certain things occur to them or within them. For example, you could tell your spaces to perform specific actions when content is newly placed within. You could tell them to launch workflows, automatically tag content, or fire off emails to notify collaborators of updates and activities.

You can do this because Alfresco provides out-of-the-box event handling for interactions with spaces and content. Alfresco fires events when interactions occur between a user or the environment and a piece of content. These events are like signals that your custom code or scripts can listen for. When they hear these signals, they can react.

The principal hook point for these interactions is achieved using aspects. You have seen aspects throughout this book. Aspects let you catch these signals and then act on them. They provide a code-level interface for intercepting the events and triggering a repository action as a response.

This means that you could write custom aspects to wire in some intense behavior behind your content spaces. This is ideal for developers and for testing. You can write custom handlers along with unit and integration tests.

However, there are many times when you do not need as much rigor. Alfresco makes things easier for non-developers by providing simple user interface tools for applying business logic behind your spaces.

Rules let you describe actions that should be triggered when one or more conditions are met. Rules were discussed in Chapter 13. They are accessible through Alfresco Explorer and appear as shown in Figure 14-2.

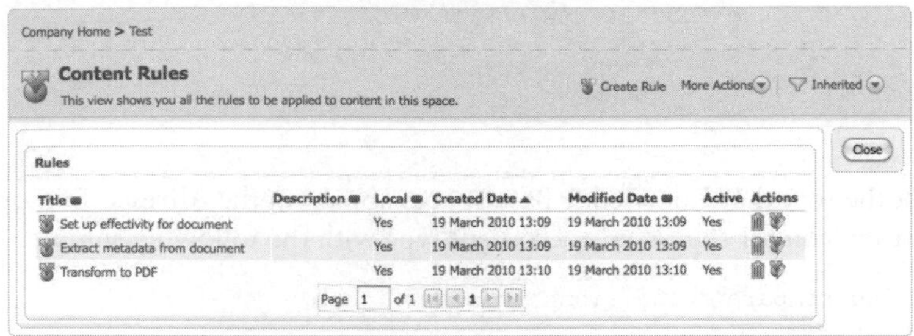

FIGURE 14-2

A rule fires when one or more of its conditions is met. For example, if a rule has a single condition for the content item's `mimetype` property to equal `application/word`, the rule will only trigger for Microsoft Word documents. When a rule triggers, it fires off one or more repository actions that you configure.

For example, you may tell the rule to copy the content item to another place in the repository or you may have it transform the content into another MIME type (such as PDF). A large number of repository actions are available out of the box for you to work with or you can add your own.

Alfresco makes things even easier by letting you create scriptable actions using server-side JavaScript. You can write your own JavaScript files and have them do anything you would like to your content.

JavaScript files can be defined in one of two places:

- A file in the application classpath
- Content in the Data Dictionary

Thus, you really do not have to do any development at all! Using rules and scripting, you can wire custom business logic into your space without the need for any Java code. No compilers, no server restarts.

Space Templates

Using content types, rules, and server-side JavaScript, you can implement a wide variety of custom workspaces. You may have elaborate folder structures or a complex chain of rules established. You may have set up permissions and groups exactly according to the needs of your project or task. It would be ideal if there were an easy way to capture and reuse that work!

Fortunately — you guessed it — there is! Alfresco lets you capture your smart spaces into *space templates*. A space template is a bit like a cookie cutter – you can apply it to any location in the repository and stamp out an exact copy of your entire preconfigured workspace. This includes

- The entire folder structure of your project
- All of the rules on the folders in your project

- All of the permissions on the folders in your project
- All of the server-side JavaScript or FreeMarker templates you have configured for the folders of your project
- Any sample content you have placed in the folders of your project

You'll walk through the creation of a space template when you get to the "Putting It into Action" section. You'll actually build your Knowledge Base space as a space template. That way, you can stamp out Knowledge Base spaces very quickly (and so can anyone else)!

INSTALLING THE CODE

This section provides step-by-step instructions for installing this chapter's code into your Alfresco installation. It assumes that you have downloaded the sample source code from `www.wrox.com`. This is available as a ZIP compressed file.

Inside of the ZIP file, you will find the following folder structure:

```
/chapter14
      /extension
      /scripts
      install_chapter_14.bat
      readme.txt
```

If you've performed a default installation on Windows under the C:\Alfresco directory, you can run the install_chapter_14.bat file to quickly install all of this chapter's sample code in one quick step! If you elect to do so, you can skip ahead to the section titled "Putting It into Action."

Otherwise, follow the manual installation instructions provided here. The sample files are assumed to have been extracted into a location referred to as *<sampleLocation>*. Bear in mind that the path references in this section use a Windows file convention. If you are using a non-Windows box (such as a Linux distribution), you will need to adjust the file paths accordingly.

Please read through the readme.txt file for last-minute updates and tips on installing the sample code.

Stopping the Alfresco Server

Before doing anything else, you should stop the Alfresco server. You can do this either from a command line or through the Windows Start menu (if you used the Windows Installer).

From the command line, type the following:

```
cd <installLocation>
alf_stop.bat
```

This shuts down Alfresco and returns you to the command prompt.

Adding the Knowledge Base Content Model

Begin by introducing the Knowledge Base content model to the Alfresco repository. This informs Alfresco how to deal with your Knowledge Base content types and aspects.

From the following directory:

- <*sampleLocation*>\chapter14\extension

copy the following files:

- kbModel.xml
- kbModel-model-context.xml

to:

- <*installLocation*>\tomcat\shared\classes\alfresco\extension

Adding Alfresco Explorer Configuration

Next, you can plug in your Alfresco Explorer configurations. This enables the additional property sheets, wizards, and icons for your Knowledge Base space content type and Knowledge Base aspects.

From the following directory:

- <*sampleLocation*>\chapter14\extension

copy the following files:

- web-client-config-knowledgebase-config.xml
- web-client-config-knowledgebase-context.xml

to:

- <*installLocation*>\tomcat\shared\classes\alfresco\extension

Adding the Knowledge Base Search Web Script

Finally, install the Knowledge Base Search Web script into the Alfresco repository.

From the following directory:

- <*sampleLocation*>\chapter14\extension\templates\webscripts\org\alfresco\knowledgebase

copy the following files:

- kb-search.get.desc.xml
- kb-search.get.js
- kb-search.get.json.ftl

to:

- *<installLocation>*\tomcat\shared\classes\alfresco\extension\templates\webscripts\org\alfresco\knowledgebase

PUTTING IT INTO ACTION

If you have followed the instructions, you should be ready to try things out.

Starting the Alfresco Server

You can start up the Alfresco server either from a command prompt or through the Windows Start menu (if you used the Windows Installer).

From the command line, type the following:

```
cd <installLocation>
alf_start.bat
```

This starts Alfresco and returns you to the command prompt.

Signing on to Alfresco Explorer

You are going to use Alfresco Explorer to set up the Alfresco Knowledge Base workspace. Follow these instructions:

1. Open a browser and go to Alfresco Explorer. You can access Alfresco Explorer using the following URL: `http://localhost:8080/alfresco`
2. Click the Login link at the top of the page to log in to Alfresco Explorer (see Figure 14-3).

You can use the administrator account with the user name `admin` and password `admin`. Your user dashboard will display once you log in.

FIGURE 14-3

Adding a Script to the Data Dictionary

The Alfresco repository provides a Data Dictionary into which you can place your custom script files. This is the ideal place for you to put your custom server-side JavaScript file.

You want to add a custom JavaScript file that will use the Alfresco Tagging Service to apply tags to your document. Tags are universal throughout the repository and they provide an elegant way to discover relevant information. By applying lifecycle tags to your documents, you simply make it easier for other people to locate knowledge in the Knowledge Base.

1. Click the Company Home link at the top left of the page (see Figure 14-4).

   This takes you to the root space of the repository.

FIGURE 14-4

2. On the left-hand side of the page you will see a Navigator view of the repository. Click the small arrow next to the Data Dictionary space to reveal the subspaces inside the Data Dictionary. You should see something like what is shown in Figure 14-5.
3. Click on Scripts in the Navigator's subspaces. This will take you into the Scripts space. It should look a little like what is shown in Figure 14-6.
4. Click the Add Content link at the top of the page. This brings up the Add Content dialog.
5. Click the Browse button to select the file on disk you want to upload. In this case, upload the following file:

   <*sampleLocation*>\chapter14\scripts\add-and-update-knowledge-base-tags.js
6. In the Other Properties area, clear the check box.
7. Click OK to upload the file.
8. Click OK again to complete the installation. You should then see your file in the Scripts folder along with the rest of the out-of-the-box scripts.

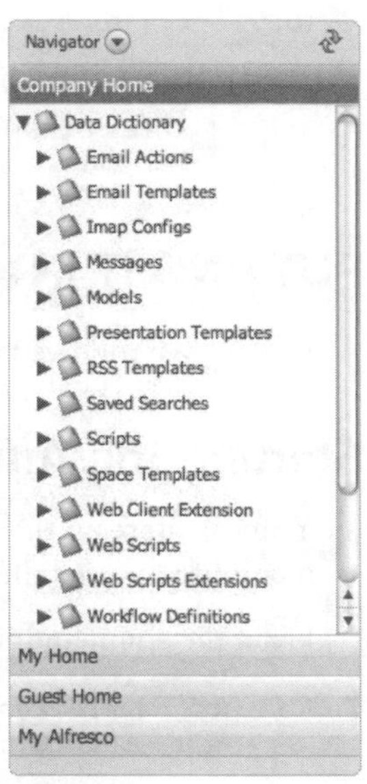

FIGURE 14-5

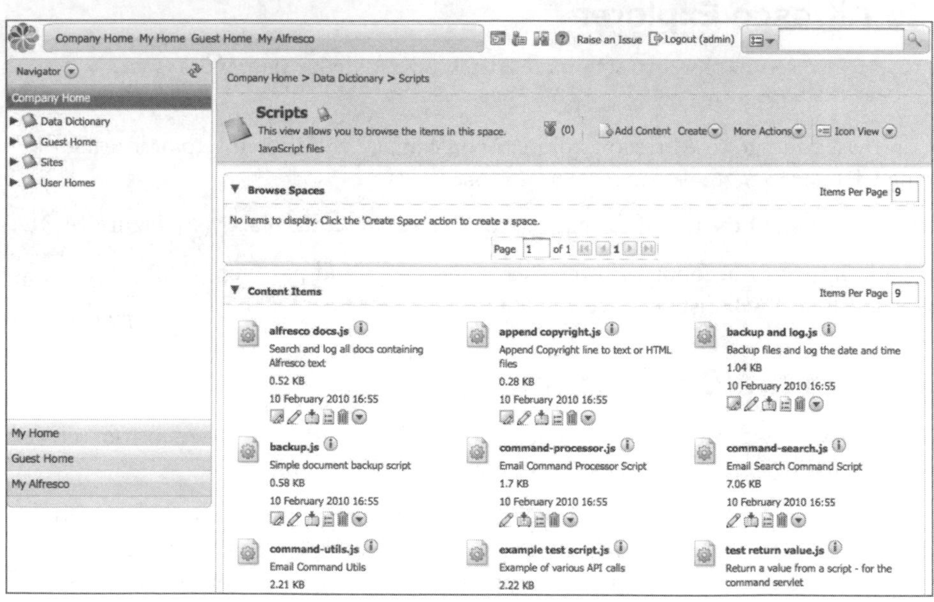

FIGURE 14-6

Creating a Knowledge Base Space Template

Now you'll have some fun. You will create a Knowledge Base *space template* inside of Alfresco Explorer. In doing so, you're creating a "cookie cutter" that you can use to quickly stamp out preconfigured workspaces that implement all of your Knowledge Base functionality.

Creating the Space Template

Follow these instructions to create the Space template:

1. Click the Company Home link at the top left of the page.
2. In the Navigator view on the left-hand side of the page, click the small arrow next to the Data Dictionary space to reveal its subspaces.
3. Click on Space Templates in the Navigator's subspaces. This will take you into the Space Templates space. You should only see one subspace inside, called *Software Engineering Project*.
4. Click the Create menu to display options for content creation and select Advanced Space Wizard from the drop-down list (see Figure 14-7).

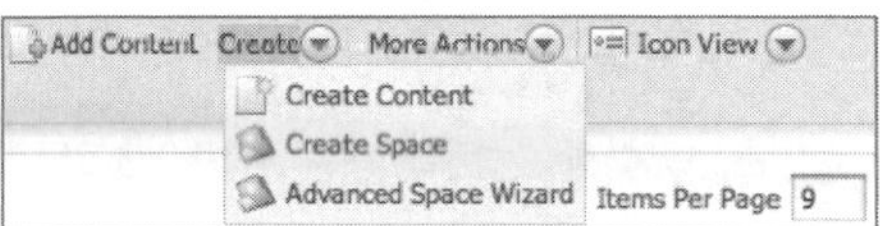

FIGURE 14-7

This brings up the Create Space Wizard that lets you create different kinds of spaces.

5. On the Step One - Starting Space page, choose the From Scratch option and click Next (see Figure 14-8).

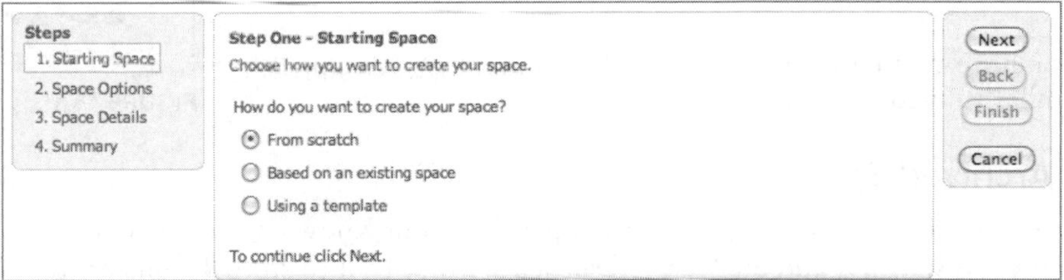

FIGURE 14-8

The next page you see will be titled Step Two – Space Options. This will show you the various kinds of spaces that you can create. Notice there is now an extra icon for a Knowledge Base Space (as shown in Figure 14-9). This is because you configured it to be thus using the Alfresco Explorer configuration file that you provided (web-client-config-knowledgebase-custom.xml).

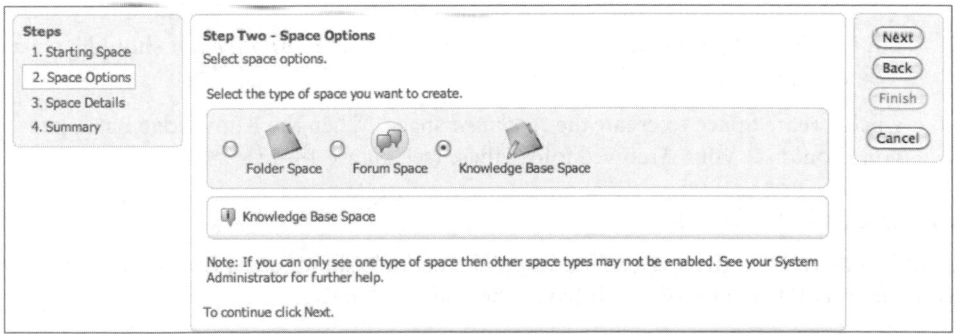

FIGURE 14-9

6. Select the Knowledge Base Space option and click Next.
7. On the Step Three - Space Details page, enter the details about the Knowledge Base space you wish to create (see Figure 14-10), and then click Finish. In this example, you've elected to call the space template "Knowledge Base Project."

Steps
1. Starting Space
2. Space Options
3. Space Details
4. Summary

Step Three - Space Details
Enter information about the space.

Space Details
Name: Knowledge Base Project
Title: Knowledge Base Project
Description:
Icon:

To continue click Next.

Next
Back
Finish
Cancel

FIGURE 14-10

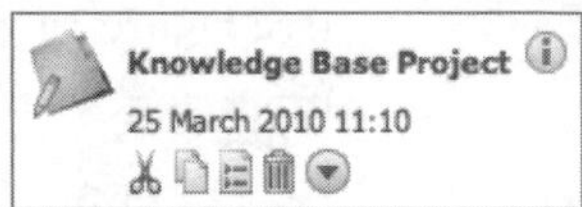

FIGURE 14-11

You have created your Knowledge Base space. It should appear similar to Figure 14-11.

Adding an Archived Space

In the previous section, you created a space template for your Knowledge Base. So far, this space template is empty. Now you'll add an Archived subspace inside of it to store documents that have been moved into an archived lifecycle state.

Follow these instructions:

1. Click on the Knowledge Base Project space template. This will navigate down into the Knowledge Base Project space. It should be empty right now.
2. Click the Create menu to display options for content creation and select Create Space from the list.
3. On the Create Space page, give the new space the name *Archived*. It should have a capital A. You can give it any description you like.
4. Click Create Space to create the *Archived* space. When the Knowledge Base space refreshes, you should see your Archived folder there (see Figure 14-12).

Setting Up Content Rules

Now add some rules to the space. That way, when people stamp out a Knowledge Base space, you can provide them with some pre-wired behavior behind their space.

1. Make sure you are in the Knowledge Base Project template space. You should see the Archived space within it, as shown in Figure 14-12.

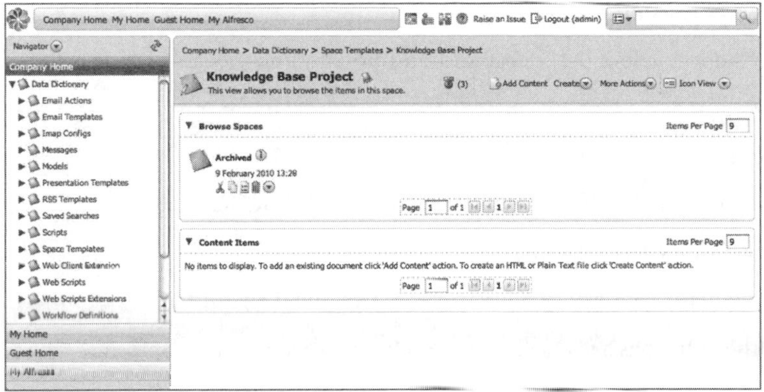

FIGURE 14-12

2. Click More Actions at the top of the page, and select Manage Content Rules from the drop-down list.

This will take you to the Content Rules page where you can see all the rules set up for this space. Currently there shouldn't be any so you will create a few. In fact, you will create three rules.

Rule 1: Apply KB Article Aspect and Tag Draft

The purpose of this rule is to automatically apply the `kb:article` aspect to any document that arrives into the Knowledge Base space. In addition, a server-side JavaScript will be executed that will update all of the tags on the newly arrived content.

1. On the Content Rules page, click the Create Rule link. This opens the Create Rule Wizard that lets you create new rules.
2. On the Step One - Select Conditions page, perform the following:
    a. In the Select a condition list, choose All Items.
    b. Click Add to List.
    c. Click Next.
3. On the Step Two - Select Actions page, perform the following:
    a. In the Select an action list, choose Add aspect to item.
    b. Click Set Values and Add.
    c. In the Set action values list, select Knowledge Base Article.
    d. Click OK.

    You should now see Add aspect 'Knowledge Base Article' appear under Summary in the Selected Rule Actions area. Keep going.
4. On the same page, Step Two – Select Actions, continue by performing the following:
    a. In the Select an action list, choose Execute a script.

  b. Click Set Values and Add.
  c. In the Set action values list, select add-and-update-knowledge-base-tags.js.
  d. Click OK.
  e. Click Next.
5. On the third page, Step 3 – Enter Details, perform the following:
  a. In the Type list, select Inbound.
  b. In the Title field, type *Apply KB Article Aspect and Tag draft*.
  c. In the Other Options area, select the Apply rule to sub spaces option.
  d. Click Finish.

Rule 2: Apply Move Archived Documents to Archived Folder

The purpose of this rule is to automatically move some items into the Archived folder. The items that should be moved are any items where the `kb:status` property value is equal to "Archived."

1. On the Content Rules page, click the Create Rule link to create a new rule.
2. On the Step One - Select Conditions page, perform the following:
  a. In the Select a condition list, select Items with a specific text value in property.
  b. Click Set Values and Add.
  c. In the Property name field, type *kb:status*.
  d. Set the Operation to Equals To.
  e. For the Value field, type *Archived*.
  f. Click OK.
  g. Click Next.
3. On the Step Two – Select Actions page, perform the following:
  a. In the Select an action list, choose Move item to a specific space.
  b. Click Set Values and Add.
  c. Click on the Click here to select a destination link.
  d. Click the Add icon (green + sign) in the same row as Archived. This selects the Archived folder.
  e. Click OK.
  f. Click Next.
4. On the Step 3 – Enter Details page, perform the following:
  a. In the Type list, select Update.

   b. In the Title field, type *Apply Move Archived Documents to Archived Folder*.
   c. In the Other Options area, select the Apply rule to subspaces option.
   d. Click Finish.

Rule 3: Update Status Tag

The purpose of this rule is to automatically execute the server-side JavaScript responsible for updating tags on a document if a document is updated while it is in the Knowledge Base space.

1. Click the Create Rule link to create a new rule.
2. On the Step One - Select Conditions page, perform the following:
   a. In the Select a condition list, select All Items.
   b. Click Add to List.
   c. Click Next.
3. On the Step Two – Select Actions page, perform the following:
   a. In the Select an action list, choose Execute a script.
   b. Click Set Values and Add.
   c. In the Set action values list, select add-and update-knowledge-base-tags.js.
   d. Click OK.
   e. Click Next.
4. On the Step 3 – Enter Details page, perform the following:
   a. In the Type list, select Update.
   b. In the Title field, type *Update Status Tags*.
   c. Select the Apply rule to sub spaces option.
   d. Click Finish.

That's all there is to it. You have created three business rules and wired them in behind your Knowledge Base space template. Now, whenever you work with content inside a Knowledge Base space these rules will be triggered automatically.

Creating a Knowledge Base

Now that you've built your Knowledge Base space template, you can use it to stamp out Knowledge Base workspaces quite easily. You'll create a test space under the Company Home space to see how it works.

Follow these steps:

1. Click the Company Home link at the top left of the page. This takes you to the root folder of the repository.

2. Click the Create menu to display options for content creation, and select the Advanced Space Wizard option from the list. This brings up the Create Space Wizard for creating different kinds of spaces.
3. On the Step One - Starting Space page, choose the Using a template option and click Next.

   The next page you see will be titled Step Two – Space Options. Here, you will see a drop-down list in which all of the space templates appear. Notice that the Knowledge Base Project is available (see Figure 14-13).

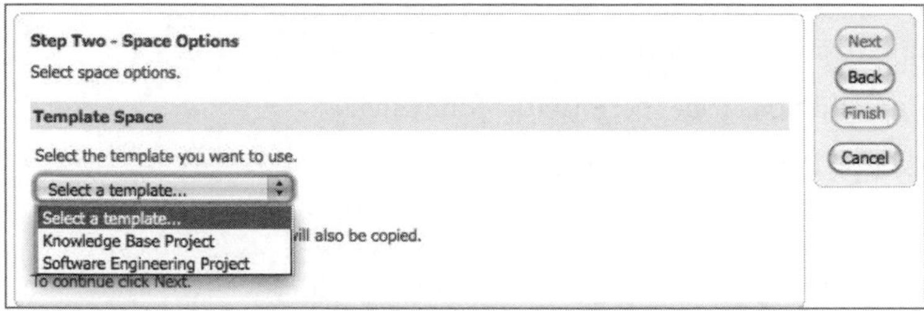

FIGURE 14-13

4. Select Knowledge Base Project from the drop-down list.
5. Click Next.
6. Give your new Knowledge Base space a name, title, and description. You might choose to use the values as shown in Figure 14-14.
7. Click Finish to create the space.

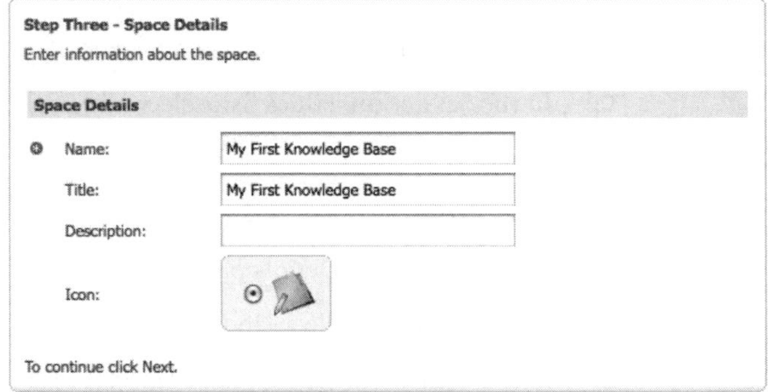

FIGURE 14-14

With that, your new Knowledge Base space is created in the Company Home folder. You should see it appear alongside the other folders, as shown in Figure 14-15.

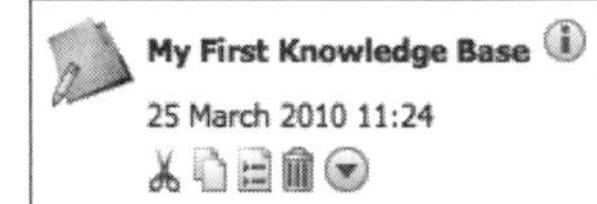

FIGURE 14-15

Contribute a Document

You can now create a Knowledge Base article and contribute it to your new Knowledge Base. You can do this using either Alfresco Explorer or CIFS desktop integration.

Using Alfresco Explorer

You can use Alfresco Explorer to create a Knowledge Base article and contribute it to your new My First Knowledge Base workspace.

1. Browse into the My First Knowledge Base space by clicking on it in Alfresco Explorer.
2. Click the Create menu for content creation options, and select Create Content from the list.

   You will use the Create Content Wizard to create a Knowledge Base article.
3. On the first page of the Create Content Wizard, do the following (see Figure 14-16):
   a. In the Name field, type a name for your Knowledge Base article, such as *Article1.txt*. For this example, make sure it ends in *.txt* so you can treat the article as plain text.
   b. In the Type menu, select Content.
   c. In the Content Type menu, select Plain Text.
   d. In the Other Properties area, clear the check box.
   e. Click Next.

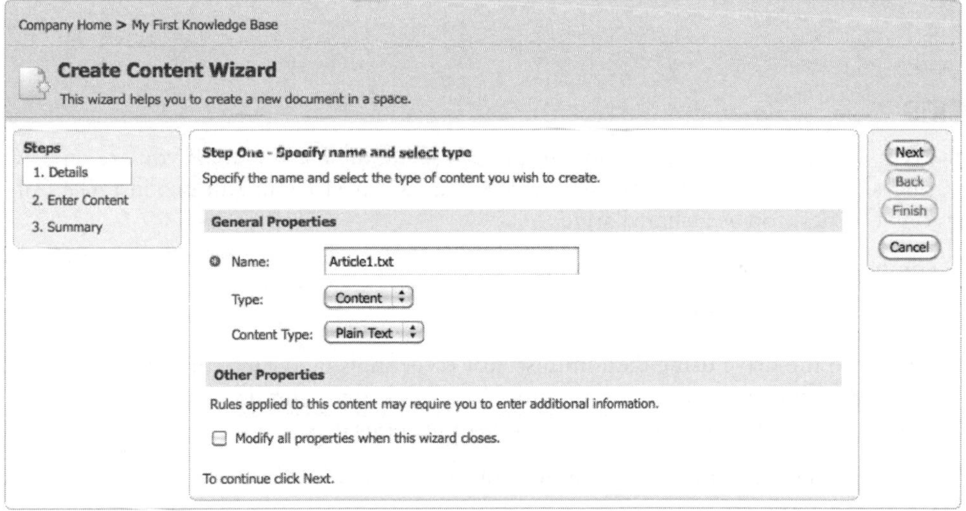

FIGURE 14-16

4. On the second page, titled Step Two- Enter Content, type the following text content:

   A book is a gift you can open again and again.
5. Once you have finished entering your content, click Finish.

Your content has been created. Your space titled My First Knowledge Base should appear similar to what is shown in Figure 14-17.

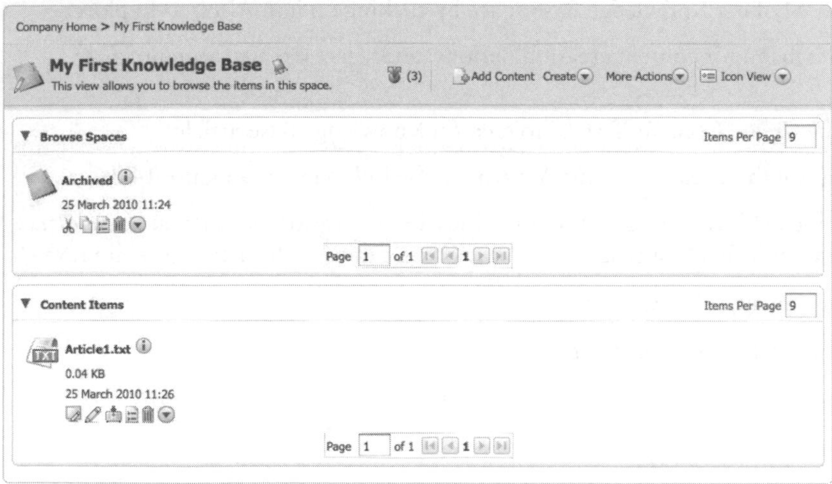

FIGURE 14-17

Using CIFS

Alternatively, you can contribute documents directly using the file system. If you are on a Windows system, this is easy to try out. All you need to do is map a drive to your Alfresco instance. Alfresco then appears on your desktop as a shared drive.

From a command prompt, run the following:

```
net use z: \\<MACHINE_NAME>A
```

You can log in to the drive using the administrator credentials (`admin`/`admin`). Once you do that, you should have a Z: drive mapped to your desktop. You can browse this drive just as you would a normal drive or folder. You can even drag and drop content into this drive.

This means that you use your desktop applications to create documents and save them directly into Alfresco. Feel free to do so!

Editing Your Knowledge Base Article

If you like, you can modify the properties of your Knowledge Base article in Alfresco Explorer.

1. Under the Article1.txt file in your Knowledge Base space, you will see a set of icons. Click the View Details icon. This icon is identified in Figure 14-18.

   You will now see the Details page. The Details page displays a pane that lists all the properties of your content item (see Figure 14-19).

   Notice that your additional `kb:articletype` and `kb:status` properties appear, exactly as you instructed.

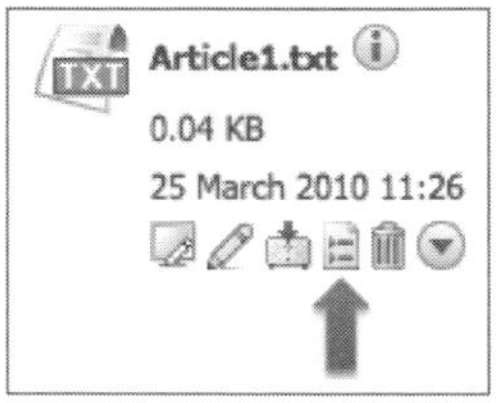

FIGURE 14-18

Properties
Name: Article1.txt
Content Type: Plain Text
Encoding: MacRoman
Title:
Description:
Author:
Size: 0.04 KB
Creator: admin
Created Date: 25 March 2010 11:26
Modifier: admin
Modified Date: 25 March 2010 11:26
Edit Inline: Yes
Email ID: 783
Tags: draft
Article Type: Article
KB Status: Draft

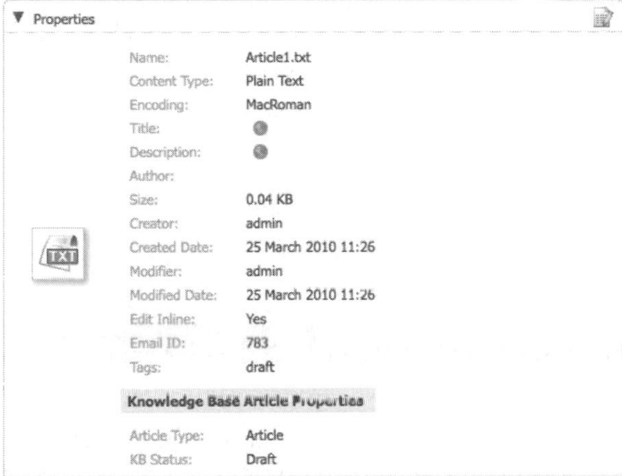

FIGURE 14-19

2. To edit these values, click the Modify icon on the top right of the Properties pane to bring up the Modify Content Properties page (see Figure 14-20).

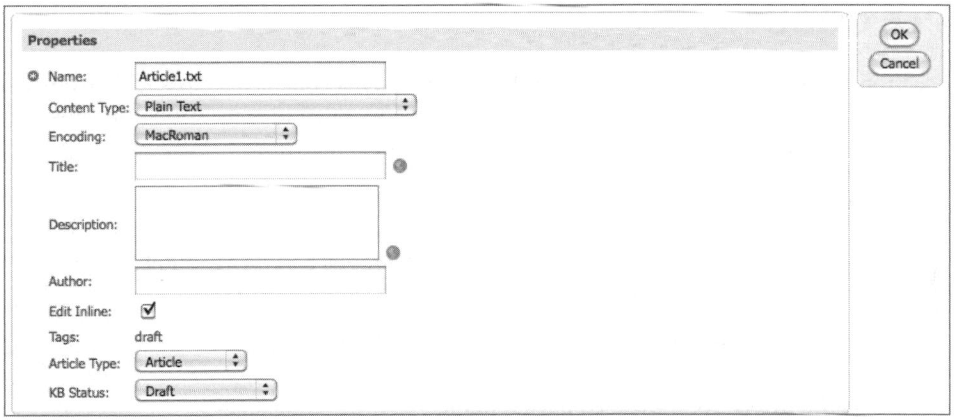

Properties
Name: Article1.txt
Content Type: Plain Text
Encoding: MacRoman
Title:
Description:
Author:
Edit Inline:
Tags: draft
Article Type: Article
KB Status: Draft
OK
Cancel

FIGURE 14-20

You can make any changes you like.

3. Click OK to commit the changes and save your content item.

Seeing It in JSON!

So far, you've used Alfresco Explorer and/or desktop integration via CIFS to create and modify Knowledge Base articles. All of these articles are ultimately stored in the Alfresco repository as pure content objects with metadata, aspects, and content types, exactly as you prescribed.

You can now try fetching this content via HTTP by calling into your custom Knowledge Base Web script. The HTTP interface lets third-party systems or external applications (such as Alfresco Share) interact with your Knowledge Base and interrogate the data inside.

It's pretty simple to try this out. Just do the following:

1. Open a new browser.
2. In the URL field, type the following:
   `http://localhost:8080/alfresco/service/knowledgebase/search`
3. Press Enter.
4. If you are challenged for authentication credentials, just use the user name `admin` and the password `admin`.

If things are working correctly, you should be given back a JSON (JavaScript Object Notation) structure as a bit of text. You might see this show up in your browser or you may be asked to download it. You can simply save it somewhere and then open it inside of a text editor.

The JSON text is pure data. It contains the search results for content in the Knowledge Base. This includes your Article1.txt file. It is pure data – ready for consumption by external applications, including Alfresco Share!

SAMPLE CODE

This section provides sample code used in this chapter. This code is also available from `www.wrox.com`. This is available as a ZIP compressed file. The paths to source files mentioned in this section are relative to the root of the ZIP file.

Alfresco Repository

This section describes the configuration of the Alfresco repository. The following content model files should be placed into this directory:

<*installLocation*>\tomcat\shared\classes\alfresco\extension

Available for download on Wrox.com

Defines the Knowledge Base content model

```
<?xml version="1.0" encoding="UTF-8"?>

<!--                                 -->
<!-- Knowledge Base Content Model -->
<!--                                 -->

<model name="kb:contentmodel" xmlns="http://www.alfresco.org/model/dictionary/1.0">

   <!-- Metadata about the model -->
   <description>Knowledge Base Content Model</description>
```

```
<author>alfresco_professional</author>
<version>1.0</version>

<!-- Imports are required to allow references to definitions in other models -->
<imports>
  <!-- Import Alfresco Dictionary Definitions -->
   <import uri="http://www.alfresco.org/model/dictionary/1.0" prefix="d"/>
   <!-- Import Alfresco Content Domain Model Definitions -->
   <import uri="http://www.alfresco.org/model/content/1.0" prefix="cm"/>
</imports>

<!-- Define the URI and Prefix for this content model -->
<namespaces>
   <namespace uri="http://www.alfresco.org/model/knowledgebase/1.0"
   prefix="kb"/>
</namespaces>

<!-- Define constraints -->
<constraints>

   <!-- Ensures that one of the allowed values is assigned -->
   <constraint name="kb:status_constraint" type="LIST">
      <parameter name="allowedValues">
         <list>
            <value>Draft</value>
            <value>Pending Approval</value>
            <value>Current</value>
            <value>Archived</value>
         </list>
      </parameter>
   </constraint>

   <!-- Ensures that one of the allowed values is assigned -->
   <constraint name="kb:articletype_constraint" type="LIST">
      <parameter name="allowedValues">
         <list>
            <value>Any</value>
            <value>Article</value>
            <value>FAQ</value>
            <value>White Paper</value>
         </list>
      </parameter>
   </constraint>
</constraints>

<!-- Content Types -->
<types>
   <type name="kb:space">
      <title>Knowledge Base Space</title>
      <parent>cm:folder</parent>
   </type>
</types>
```

```
    <!-- Aspects -->
    <aspects>

       <!-- Marks a content item as having status -->
       <aspect name="kb:status">
          <title>Knowledge Base Status</title>
          <properties>

             <!-- Adds a new metadata property to the KB article -->
             <!-- Constrains the value -->
             <property name="kb:status">
                <title>Status</title>
                <type>d:text</type>
                <default>Draft</default>
                <constraints>
                   <constraint ref="kb:status_constraint" />
                </constraints>
             </property>

          </properties>
       </aspect>

       <!-- Marks a content item as a KB Article -->
       <aspect name="kb:article">
          <title>Knowledge Base Article</title>
          <properties>

             <!-- Adds a new metadata property to the KB article -->
             <!-- Constrains the value -->
             <property name="kb:articletype">
                <title>Article Type</title>
                <type>d:text</type>
                <default>Article</default>
                <constraints>
                   <constraint ref="kb:articletype_constraint" />
                </constraints>
             </property>

          </properties>

          <!-- Content with this aspect also receive kb:status aspect -->
          <mandatory-aspects>
             <aspect>kb:status</aspect>
          </mandatory-aspects>
       </aspect>

    </aspects>

 </model>
```

Code snippet extension\kbModel.xml

Available for download on Wrox.com

Bootstraps the Knowledge Base content model into the Alfresco repository

```
<?xml version='1.0' encoding='UTF-8'?>
<!DOCTYPE beans PUBLIC '-//SPRING//DTD BEAN//EN'
'http://www.springframework.org/dtd/spring-beans.dtd'>
<beans>

<!-- Registration of new models -->
<bean id="kbmodel.extension.dictionaryBootstrap"
      parent="dictionaryModelBootstrap"
      depends-on="dictionaryBootstrap">
<property name="models">
<list>
<value>alfresco/extension/kbModel.xml</value>
</list>
</property>
</bean>

</beans>
```

Code snippet extension\kbModel-model-context.xml

Alfresco Explorer

The following files should be placed into this directory:

<installLocation>\tomcat\shared\classes\alfresco\extension

Available for download on Wrox.com

Defines customizations for Alfresco Explorer

```
<alfresco-config>

   <!--  Configuration for the kb:article aspect -->
   <config evaluator="aspect-name" condition="kb:article">

      <!-- Display the kb:article properties -->
      <property-sheet>
         <separator name="sep" display-label="Knowledge Base Article Properties"
                    component-generator="HeaderSeparatorGenerator"
                    show-in-edit-mode="false"/>
         <show-property name="kb:articletype" display-label="Article Type"
                        show-in-edit-mode="true" />
      </property-sheet>

   </config>
```

```
   <!-- Configuration for the kb:status aspect -->
   <config evaluator="aspect-name" condition="kb:status">

      <!-- Display the kb:status property -->
      <property-sheet>
         <show-property name="kb:status" display-label="KB Status"
                        show-in-edit-mode="true" />
      </property-sheet>
   </config>

   <!--  Configures the space wizards -->
   <config evaluator="string-compare" condition="Space Wizards">

      <!-- Allow for the creation of kb:folder instances -->
      <folder-types>
         <type name="kb:space" icon="/images/icons/space-icon-pen.gif" />
      </folder-types>

   </config>

   <!-- Configures the action wizards -->
   <config evaluator="string-compare" condition="Action Wizards">

      <!-- Allow the kb:article aspect to be added and removed -->
      <aspects>
         <aspect name="kb:article"/>
      </aspects>

   </config>

   <!-- Specify icon for the kb:space instances -->
   <config evaluator="string-compare" condition="kb:space icons">
      <icons>
         <icon name="space-icon-pen" path="/images/icons/space-icon-pen.gif" />
      </icons>
   </config>

</alfresco-config>
```

Code snippet extension\web-client-config-knowledgebase-custom.xml

Available for download on Wrox.com

Bootstraps the Alfresco Explorer customizations into Alfresco Explorer

```
<?xml version='1.0' encoding='UTF-8'?>
<!DOCTYPE beans PUBLIC '-//SPRING//DTD BEAN//EN'
'http://www.springframework.org/dtd/spring-beans.dtd'>

<beans>
```

```
<!--  Bootstraps the Web client configuration -->
<bean id="kb.extension.webClientBootstrap"
      class="org.alfresco.web.config.WebClientConfigBootstrap"
      init-method="init">
   <property name="configs">
      <list>
         <value>
            classpath:alfresco/extension/web-client-config-
            knowledgebase-custom.xml
         </value>
      </list>
   </property>
</bean>

</beans>
```

Code snippet extension\web-client-config-knowledgebase-context.xml

Data Dictionary Script

The following file should be copied into the Alfresco repository using Alfresco Explorer and placed in the following path:

/Company Home/Data Dictionary/Scripts

Available for download on Wrox.com

Updates the tags for a content item based on the content item's status

```
if (document.type != "{http://www.alfresco.org/model/content/1.0}thumbnail" &&
document.type != "{http://www.alfresco.org/model/content/1.0}folder")
{
 // All Knowledge Base status ids
 var kbStatusIds = ["draft", "pending", "current", "archived"];

 // Remove all previous status tags so you only have the latest one added
 document.removeTags(kbStatusIds);

 // Add a tag to reflect the status
 switch (document.properties["kb:status"])
 {
case "Draft":
 document.addTag("draft");
 break;

case "Pending Approval":
 document.addTag("pending");
 break;

case "Current":
document.addTag("current");
break;
```

```
case "Archived":
 document.addTag("archived");
 break;

default:
 }

 // Save changes
 document.save();
}
```

Code snippet scripts\add-and-update-knowledge-base-tags.js

Knowledge Base–Search Web Script

The following files should be placed into this directory:

> *<installLocation>*\tomcat\shared\classes\alfresco\extension\templates\webscripts\org\alfresco\knowledgebase

Knowledge Base–search Web script descriptor file

```
<webscript>
   <shortname>Knowledge Base Search</shortname>
   <description>Searches for knowledge base articles</description>
   <url>/knowledgebase/search?maxResults={maxResults?}</url>
   <url>/knowledgebase/search/site/{site}?maxResults={maxResults?}</url>
   <format default="json">argument</format>
   <authentication>user</authentication>
</webscript>
```

Code snippet extension\templates\webscripts\org\alfresco\knowledgebase\kb-search.get.desc.xml

Knowledge Base–search Web script controller

```
/**
 * KnowledgeBase Search Web Script
 *
 * Inputs:
 *   optional:  siteId = site ID to search in
 *   optional:  maxResults = max items to return.
 *
 * Outputs:
 *   data.items/data.error - object containing list of search results
 *
 * If siteId is null, the entire repository will be searched.
 */
/**
```

```
 * Search constants
 */
const DEFAULT_MAX_RESULTS = 500;
const SITES_SPACE_QNAME_PATH = "/app:company_home/st:sites/";

/**
 * Performs a search for knowledge base articles in a site
 *
 * @method doSearch
 * @param siteId {string} The site to search in (or null to search full repository)
 * @param maxResults {int} Maximum number of results to return
 * @return {array} Articles matching the query in the same format that toArticle()
                   method returns
 */
function doSearch(siteId, maxResults)
{
   // The initial template
   var alfQuery='ASPECT:"{http://www.alfresco.org/model/knowledgebase/1.0}article"'
      + ' AND NOT TYPE:"{http://www.alfresco.org/model/content/1.0}thumbnail"'
      + ' AND NOT TYPE:"{http://www.alfresco.org/model/content/1.0}folder"';

   // if you have a siteId, append it into the query
   if (siteId != null)
   {
      alfQuery += ' AND PATH:"' + SITES_SPACE_QNAME_PATH + '/cm:' + siteId;
      alfQuery += '/cm:documentLibrary//*"';
   }

   // Perform fts-alfresco language query for articles
   var queryDef = {
      query: alfQuery,
      language: "fts-alfresco",
      page: {maxItems: maxResults},
      templates: []
   };

   // Get article nodes
   var nodes = search.query(queryDef),
      articles = [],
      item;

   // Turn nodes into article objects
   for (var i = 0, j = nodes.length; i < j; i++)
   {
      // Create core object
      node = nodes[i];
      item =
      {
         nodeRef: node.nodeRef.toString(),
         type: node.typeShort,
         name: node.name,
         title: node.properties["cm:title"],
         description: node.properties["cm:description"],
         modifiedOn: node.properties["cm:modified"],
         modifiedByUser: node.properties["cm:modifier"],
```

```
         createdOn: node.properties["cm:created"],
         createdByUser: node.properties["cm:creator"],
         author: node.properties["cm:author"],
         nodeDBID: node.properties["sys:node-dbid"],
         properties: {}
      };

      // Calculate display names for users
      var person = people.getPerson(item.modifiedByUser);
      item.modifiedBy = (person != null ? (person.properties.firstName + " " +
                        person.properties.lastName) : item.modifiedByUser);
      person = people.getPerson(item.createdByUser);
      item.createdBy = (person != null ? (person.properties.firstName + " " +
                       person.properties.lastName) : item.createdByUser);

      // Add the Article namespace properties
      for (var k in node.properties)
      {
         if (k.match("^{http://www.alfresco.org/model/knowledgebase/1.0}") ==
             "{http://www.alfresco.org/model/knowledgebase/1.0}")
         {
            item.properties["kb_" + k.split('}')[1]] = node.properties[k];
         }
      }
      articles.push(item);
   }

   return articles;
}

/**
 * The WebScript bootstrap method
 *
 * @method main
 */
function main()
{
   // Gather webscript parameters
   var siteId = url.templateArgs.site;
   var maxResults = (args.maxResults !== null) ? parseInt(args.maxResults) :
                    DEFAULT_MAX_RESULTS;

   // Perform search
   var articles = doSearch(siteId, maxResults);

   // Generate model from results
   model.data = {
      items: articles
   };
}

main();
```

Code snippet extension\templates\webscripts\org\alfresco\knowledgebase\kb-search.get.js

Available for download on Wrox.com

Knowledge Base–search Web script JSON template

```
<#escape x as jsonUtils.encodeJSONString(x)>
{
   "items":
   [
   <#list data.items as item>
      {
         "nodeRef": "${item.nodeRef}",
         "type": "${item.type}",
         "name": "${item.name}",
         "title": "${item.title!''}",
         "description": "${item.description!''}",
         "modifiedOn": "${xmldate(item.modifiedOn)}",
         "modifiedByUser": "${item.modifiedByUser}",
         "modifiedBy": "${item.modifiedBy}",
         "createdOn": "${xmldate(item.createdOn)}",
         "createdByUser": "${item.createdByUser}",
         "createdBy": "${item.createdBy}",
         "author": "${item.author!''}",
         "nodeDBID": "${item.nodeDBID}",
         "properties":
         {
         <#assign first=true>
         <#list item.properties?keys as k>
         <#if item.properties[k]??>
            <#if !first>,<#else><#assign first=false></#if>"${k}":
            <#assign prop = item.properties[k]>
            <#if prop?is_date>
               "${xmldate(prop)}"
            <#elseif prop?is_boolean>
               ${prop?string("true", "false")}
            <#elseif prop?is_enumerable>
              [<#list prop as p>"${p}"<#if p_has_next>,</#if></#list>]
            <#elseif prop?is_number>${prop?c}
            <#else>"${prop}"
            </#if>
         </#if>
         </#list>
         }
      }
      <#if item_has_next>,</#if>
   </#list>
   ]
}
</#escape>
```

Code snippet extension\templates\webscripts\org\alfresco\knowledgebase\kb-search.get.json.ftl

15

Custom Knowledge Base: Basic Share Customizations

WHAT'S IN THIS CHAPTER?

- Adding a custom dashlet to Alfresco Share
- Defining new pages for Alfresco Share sites
- Adding new types of sites to Alfresco Share

This chapter guides you through the process of extending Alfresco Share to implement a custom dashlet and a custom page. It walks you through the configuration of each of these into an Alfresco Share project site. It also looks at how you can define new site presets and make them available to your users.

This chapter builds on the foundation reading from Chapter 14. The Alfresco Share customizations that you are going to build will interact with the Knowledge Base repository work from the previous chapter. If you have not worked through the previous chapter, please take time to do so.

This chapter is structured to provide the following sections:

- **Overview** — A high-level explanation of the concepts and application extension points that you will use in the example. You don't have to type in any of the code in this section — it is simply provided to help guide along the conversation.
- **Installing the Code** — A step-by-step guide to the approach you will need to take in order to install all of the sample code on your own Alfresco installation.
- **Putting It into Action** — A walkthrough of your new extensions. Try them out and see what they do!

At the end of this chapter you will find the source code for the samples. This is only provided for reference. To install, you should download the source files from the book's page at `www.wrox.com` and follow the instructions provided in the section titled "Installing the Code."

OVERVIEW

In the previous chapter, you worked on the repository-side pieces required to provide a Knowledge Base content model and services. You provided a RESTful interface in the form of a Web script so that external applications could retrieve information from your Knowledge Base.

In this chapter, you'll look at one such external application in the form of Alfresco Share. You will explore Alfresco Share and look at how you can extend it to introduce Knowledge Base functionality into collaborative projects. You will build the following:

- A Knowledge Base dashlet
- A Knowledge Base page
- A Knowledge Base site type (a preset)

This section provides an overview of Alfresco Share and covers what each of these things is. You'll go through them one at a time. There will be some code snippets at times to make the reading a little easier. However, you don't have to type in any code in this section. Just read and enjoy!

Sites

Alfresco Share allows users to discover, join, and participate in collaborative *sites* for content projects. An Alfresco Share site consists of content, users, and tasks around a project or team objective. Sites provide a dynamic place where people can collaborate with the help of productivity tools built around their project.

Sites are preconfigured with applications properly scoped to the project being worked on. They often include things such as a team blog, a project wiki, a team calendar, a document library, discussion boards, and membership management. These applications can be enabled or disabled as the site manager sees fit.

Alfresco Share provides a friendly user interface that makes it very easy for users to discover existing sites or to create new sites. In fact, behind the scenes, sites are actually *site spaces* in the Alfresco repository. You looked at spaces in the previous chapter. Every interaction with Alfresco Share is actually against a space or a content item in the Alfresco repository.

The repository site spaces are located under the following path:

/Company Home/Sites

For example, if you create a site called My First Site and give it the URL name of *first*, you will find that you have a space under the Sites folder with the following path:

/Company Home/Sites/first

Each site you create consists of a top-level space with subspaces dedicated for the purposes of the applications configured for the site. The applications use these subfolders to save application-specific content.

In most cases, an application uses a single subspace. In addition, in most cases, an application also uses a single *site page* for all of its functionality. A site can have many pages; they will appear in a tabbed page navigation component along the top of the application (see Figure 15-1).

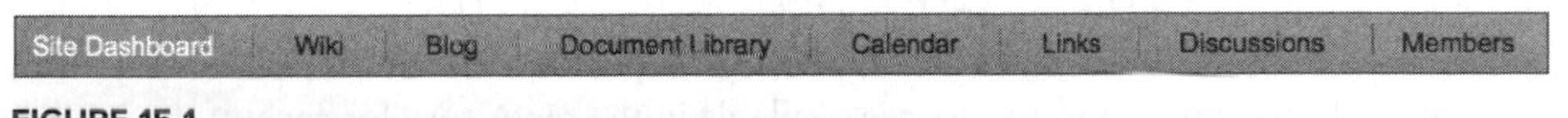

FIGURE 15-1

As you can see, the site dashboard is only one of many pages available to the site. It is one of two mandatory pages. The other mandatory page is Members. The rest of the pages are entirely optional.

You can configure which pages should be included in the site by clicking the More menu located on the right-hand side of the application and selecting Customize Site (see Figure 15-2).

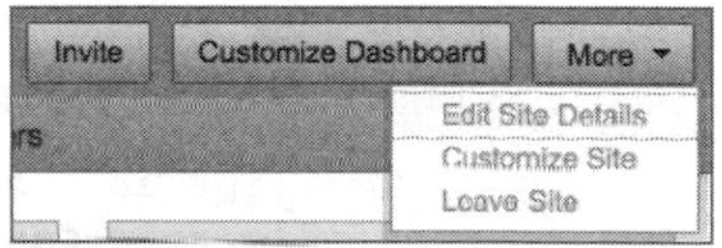

FIGURE 15-2

After you click Customize Site, you will be taken to a window where you can select from available application pages (see Figure 15-3). You can add pages to your site or remove existing pages from your site.

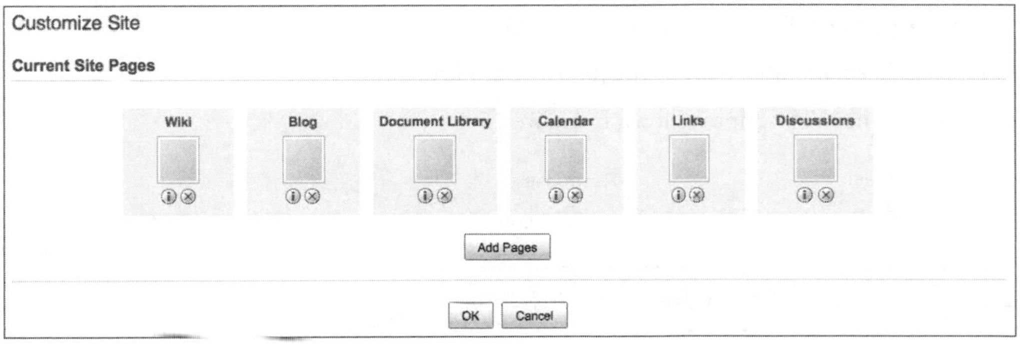

FIGURE 15-3

Shown in Figure 15-3 are the default site pages provided with Alfresco Share for the Collaboration Site type. If you create a site using the Create Site dialog, Collaboration Site is the default type of site available to you.

Alfresco Share lets you define new site pages as well as new types of sites. By defining new site pages, you empower site managers to include new and interesting applications in their projects. By defining entirely new types of sites, you enable users to spin up project spaces that have prewired site configurations, pages, and business logic.

Custom Dashlet

When users arrive to a site, they are initially greeted by the site dashboard. The site dashboard provides a place where managers can place one or more *dashlets*. A dashlet offers a quick view into the content or activities of the site. The Site Activities dashlet, for example, provides a quick glance into the activities of the site and allows for simple sorting right there on the Site Dashboard page. You can use the out-of-the-box dashlets or you can add your own custom dashlets.

Later in this chapter, you will add a custom Knowledge Base dashlet. The Knowledge Base dashlet is a read-only view into the Knowledge Base that provides a quick glance into the population of the Knowledge Base. It shows how many articles are available in the repository for each of the available status values: *draft*, *pending approval*, *current*, and *archived*.

A dashlet consists of a Spring Web script. For it to appear as an option on the Alfresco Share site dashboard configuration screen, it must have its `family` element set to `site-dashlet` in its Web script descriptor:

```
<webscript>
   <shortname>Knowledge Base</shortname>
   <description>A summary of all knowledge base articles</description>
   <family>site-dashlet</family>
   <url>/components/dashlets/knowledgebase</url>
</webscript>
```

A simple and typical approach to building a dashlet is to include a scriptable controller and a view template file. Bind these to the `GET` method and HTML format by naming them as shown here:

- **JavaScript controller** — knowledgebase.get.js
- **FreeMarker template** — knowledgebase.get.html.ftl

The invocation of the Web script is shown in Figure 15-4.

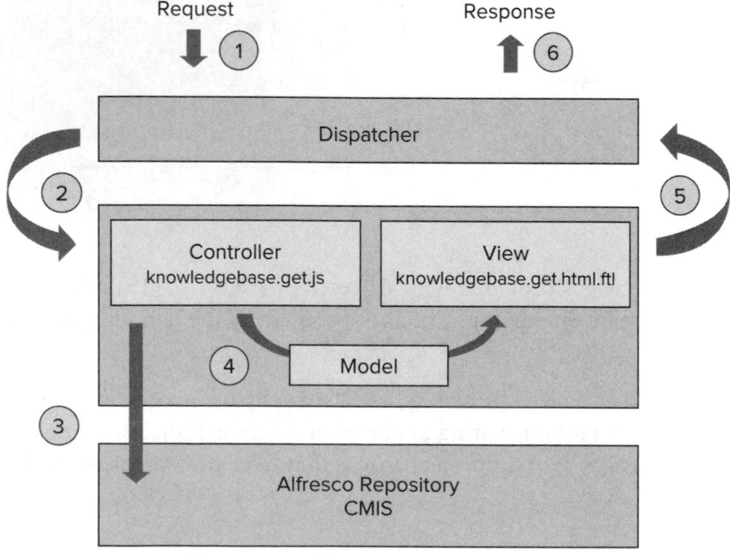

FIGURE 15-4

Here is what happens:

1. The request for the dashlet arrives to the Web script dispatcher.
2. The dispatcher calls the JavaScript controller (if available).
3. The controller opens up a connection to the Alfresco repository and uses either a RESTful interface or the CMIS interface to retrieve XML or JSON as pure data.
4. The controller populates the model with the data needed to render.
5. The dispatcher calls the view to render HTML markup.
6. The dispatcher hands the markup back to the requester.

In this case, the requester is the Alfresco Share page renderer itself. The dashlet renders into the site dashboard page at the exact location where the site manager has instructed it to appear.

Browser Dependencies

The design provided thus far for your dashlet is sufficient for simple dashlets with minimal browser dependencies. Good HTML design practices suggest that your dashlet can render HTML-compliant markup and allow the overall Alfresco Share framework to assert the proper CSS used to decorate your dashlet.

However, if your dashlet wants to use CSS includes or browser-side JavaScript, your dashlet will need to inform the Web framework to inject specific dependencies into the HTML `<head>` tag.

Spring Surf lets your Web scripts declare these kinds of dependencies. All you need to do is add a template with the name knowledgebase.get.head.ftl. The special .head naming convention indicates to Surf that this template should be executed ahead of the Web script's view template. Its output will be stitched into the XHTML compliant `<head>` tag.

This HEAD generation template has full access to the model generated by the scriptable controller. Thus, the `<head>` tag for your Web script can be dynamic and based on the model established by the controller.

Internationalization (I18N)

You can improve on your design once more by ensuring that all markup generated by your dashlet supports internationalization. Internationalization (often abbreviated I18N) means that your dashlet is mindful of the current user's language and locale settings. For example, the dashlet should render in Spanish for Spanish speakers and in French for French speakers.

Your dashlet produces a response from two different sources:

- The content of one or more Knowledge Base articles. This is the pure data received in the JSON response from the Alfresco repository.
- Additional content and markup generated by the dashlet itself.

You are in good shape with respect to the former. The Alfresco repository provides all the facilities necessary to have your content model leverage multiple languages. Alfresco provides multilingual support for all of its content objects. In fact, you can manage all of this right inside of Alfresco Explorer.

The Knowledge Base article you defined in your content model is already I18N enabled. The repository Web script (`kb-search`) introduced in the previous chapter will hand back a pure data version of this article. This Web script can handle any locale-specific selection for you.

Therefore, you should turn your attention to the content and markup generated by the dashlet itself. This consists of two kinds of things: HTML markup and human-readable text. In general, HTML markup is not a concern. The intention behind HTML is that it should work the same across different countries and different browsers. The same is not true for human-readable text. This can be vastly different. For example, Chinese has little in common with Dutch – at least as it appears on the screen (inspired linguists may disagree).

The solution is to use a message bundle to store keys or identifiers that your dashlet will look up in order to determine the human-readable text to use when generating a response for a given locale. The Web script runtime will automatically locate the bundle and make it available to your dashlet.

You simply name this file knowledgebase.get.properties and define within it any key/value pairs that you like. It might look like this:

```
header.knowledgebase=Knowledge Base
label.all=Total number of articles
label.drafts=Drafts
label.pendingApprovals=Pending for approval
label.current=Current
label.archived=Archived
error.call=An error occured when getting the knowledge base summary
```

This is the default bundle that will be used if the locale cannot be determined or if there is no matching bundle for the current locale. You can add locale-specific bundles as well. For example, you might add a file named knowledgebase.get.properties.es_BO to support Spanish in Bolivia or knowledgebase.get.properties.fr_BE to support French in Belgium. You can access these values in your Web script using code like this:

```
${msg("header.knowledgebase")}
```

This will pull the value of header.knowledgebase from the bundle appropriate to the current locale. In Bolivian Spanish, it might print out "Base de Conocimiento." In Belgian French, it might print out "Base de Connaissance." And by default, it would just print out "Knowledge Base."

It is important to keep in mind that the dialects of French, Spanish, Chinese, English, and other languages can vary widely from country to country (or sometimes even within a country). For example, Spanish in Bolivia can be quite different than Spanish in Spain. You should try to support the range of dialects for all the locales you seek to serve. By following this pattern, you can build dashlets that work across many different locales without duplicating code. This also helps design for the future by giving you an easy way to support additional locales should the need arise.

Custom Site Page

Alfresco Share comes with several site pages available out of the box. When Alfresco Share starts up, it looks to its own configuration file to determine which site pages have been set up and how to identify them.

The following configuration is an example of what is defined for Alfresco Share in a default installation:

```
<config evaluator="string-compare" condition="SitePages">
   <pages>
      <page id="calendar">calendar</page>
      <page id="wiki-page">wiki-page?title=Main_Page</page>
      <page id="documentlibrary">documentlibrary</page>
      <page id="discussions-topiclist">discussions-topiclist</page>
      <page id="blog-postlist">blog-postlist</page>
      <page id="links">links</page>
      <page id="tasks">tasks</page>
   </pages>
</config>
```

Each `<page>` element has an `id` that defines the ID of the page in Spring Surf. The value of the `<page>` element provides information that will be used by the Spring Surf components on the page to look up the content of the page.

You can define your own custom site page by simply developing a Spring Surf page and then adding it to the Alfresco Share configuration previously shown. The inner workings of Spring Surf are covered in Chapter 12.

Building a new site page for Alfresco Share is easier than building a page from scratch because you can reuse much of the application user interface that was already provided for you. For example, the template for your Knowledge Base page is shown in Figure 15-5.

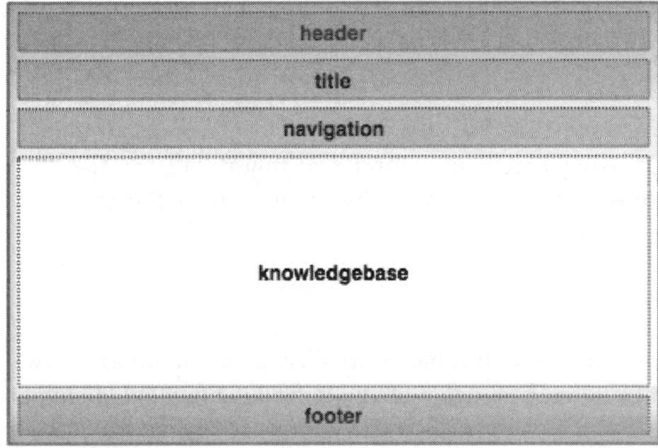

FIGURE 15-5

In Figure 15-5, the template consists of five regions: header, title, navigation, knowledgebase, and footer. Four of these regions already have components defined that you can reuse. Alfresco Share provides them for you out of the box. They are the very same ones that every other page uses.

Thus, you can inherit a consistent look and feel with the rest of the application quickly by simply reusing the header, the title section, the navigation controls, and the footer. That leaves the knowledgebase region in the middle. You'd like to put something there.

A Knowledge Base Component

To add something to the knowledgebase region of the page, you need to build a Surf component and bind it to the region. Then it will render in that spot. You do this by writing a Web script. Web scripts consist of a few simple files on disk that implement things like scriptable controllers and template views. Alfresco Share picks them up without the need for a server restart or recompilation.

Most of the effort involved in building a site page is actually that of building Web scripts. A simple site page will have a single Web script. More complex pages (for example, the Document Library page) may have many Web scripts on a single page participating together.

Every Web script has a *Web script descriptor* file that follows a prescribed naming convention. For your Knowledge Base component, you might call this file knowledgebase.get.desc.xml. The Web script descriptor informs the Web script dispatcher of some basic properties about the Web script. It describes the URL to which the Web script will be bound.

```
<webscript>
   <shortname>knowledgebase</shortname>
   <description>Knowledge Base Component</description>
   <url>/components/knowledgebase</url>
</webscript>
```

In Figure 15-4, you see that the dispatcher allows you to define a *scriptable controller* that will handle the request and begin populating the model using server-side JavaScript. You'll use this for your Knowledge Base component and you might call the file knowledgebase.get.js. This controller will do all of the data operations; it will call out to Alfresco using CMIS and retrieve Knowledge Base articles and populate the model with results.

The dispatcher then lets you define a *template view* that uses the values in your model to generate markup for the body of the Web script using FreeMarker and you might call the file knowledgebase.get.html.ftl. This will generate the HTML markup that constitutes what the end user sees rendered into the knowledgebase region of the page.

Browser Dependencies

A Web script essentially only needs a descriptor file, a scriptable controller, and a template view. However, you can go a little further and employ some best practices by defining a few extra elements.

First, your Web script that fits nicely inside the page may need to define browser-side dependencies for JavaScript or CSS. These dependencies are generally part of the HTML `<head>` tag. You can add an additional template file responsible for injecting these dependencies into the proper place in the total page markup that renders back to the browser.

This file might be called knowledgebase.get.head.ftl. This would get picked up by the Surf engine and recognized as defining things that you would like to go into the HTML <head> tag. You could set it to contain the following:

```
<#include "../component.head.inc">

<!-- Knowledge Base-->
<@link rel="stylesheet" type="text/css"
 href="${page.url.context}-extension/components/knowledgebase/knowledgebase.css" />
<@script type="text/javascript"
 src="${page.url.context}-extension/components/knowledgebase/knowledgebase.js">
</@script>

<!-- Tag Library -->
<@link rel="stylesheet" type="text/css"
 href="${page.url.context}/modules/taglibrary/taglibrary.css" />
<@script type="text/javascript"
 src="${page.url.context}/modules/taglibrary/taglibrary.js">
</@script>
```

Once that file is in place, Surf will include your HTML HEAD markup in the FreeMarker `${head}` variable, which is injected into the <head> tag of the overall HTML received by the browser.

This HEAD generation template has full access to the model generated by the scriptable controller. Thus, the <head> tag for your Web script can be dynamic and based on the model established by the controller.

Internationalization (I18N) and Configuration

It is good practice to design your site's page components so that they are enabled to work for multiple locales. As with custom dashlets, you can use message bundles to enable internationalization of your Web script. You might add another file named knowledgebase.get.properties.

This properties file defines the key/value pairs that should be consulted when the Web script needs to render in the default locale. It should contain key/value pairs similar to those shown here:

```
title.current=Current articles
title.drafts=Draft articles
title.pendingApprovals=Articles pending for approval
title.archived=Archived articles
```

You could provide additional message bundles for different locales. For example, if you wanted to support Dutch in the Netherlands, you could add the extension `nl-NL` to the file.

It is also good practice to design your Web script to use a configuration file so you can modify runtime information without needing to change the source code itself. Web script configuration files sit right alongside your scriptable controllers and view templates. Their contents are available to your Web script when it executes.

A Web script configuration file consists of XML from which your Web script can draw properties and values. You will use one of these with the Web script for your custom page component. By convention, it would be called knowledgebase.get.config.xml and look like this:

```
<knowledgebase>
   <serviceFormat>json</serviceFormat>
   <!--<serviceFormat>cmis</serviceFormat>-->
</knowledgebase>
```

This configuration file provides information to the Web script's scriptable controller about how to access the Alfresco repository service. It can talk to the Alfresco repository using either `json` or `cmis`. If you configure it to use JSON, the Web script will call over to the custom `kb-search` Web script that you wrote in the previous chapter. On the other hand, if you configure it to use CMIS (Content Management Interoperability Services), the Web script will call over using the CMIS open-standard APIs!

By default, things are set up to use your custom Web script (the JSON option). However, if you are on a CMIS 1.0–compatible version of Alfresco, you can simply elect to use the CMIS APIs. If you do that, you don't even need the `kb-search` repository Web script! Aren't you glad you waited until this chapter to learn that?

Alfresco Share Configuration

Once you have built your page, all you have to do is declare it as available to Alfresco Share through the Alfresco Share configuration file. You can use a configuration similar to what is shown here:

```
<config evaluator="string-compare" condition="SitePages">
   <pages>
      <page id="calendar">calendar</page>
      <page id="wiki-page">wiki-page?title=Main_Page</page>
      <page id="documentlibrary">documentlibrary</page>
      <page id="discussions-topiclist">discussions-topiclist</page>
      <page id="blog-postlist">blog-postlist</page>
      <page id="links">links</page>
      <page id="tasks">tasks</page>
      <page id="knowledgebase">knowledgebase</page>
   </pages>
</config>
```

The new line is highlighted in bold. That's all there is to it.

Custom Site Preset

Alfresco Share provides a Create Site dialog that you can use to quickly configure and create a new site. It's easy to access – you just click Create Site in the Sites dashlet on your user dashboard.

This wizard provides a form where you set up the new site's properties. It also provides a drop-down list where you can select the kind of site you would like to create. It makes available all the types of sites that are registered through configuration. If you're daring and want to see what this looks like, you can glance ahead to Figure 15-7.

By default, there is only one type of site available in this menu. It is called a Collaboration Site (see Figure 15-6). When you create a site of this type, Alfresco Share automatically creates your site space and preconfigures your site with pages and site-dashboard components.

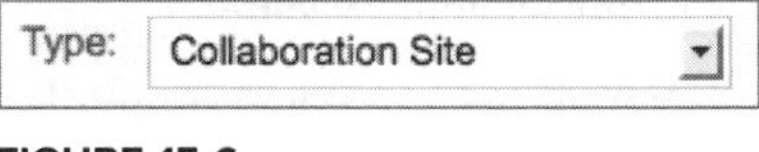

FIGURE 15-6

You can configure the default options for the Collaboration Site through Alfresco Share's configuration files. You can also introduce new types of sites. You do this by modifying a configuration file called presets.xml. This file defines site presets.

A *site preset* is a type of site. This file defines one or more site presets that describe preconfigured sets of pages, dashlets, components, and templates. These elements are bundled together with an ID. You just add your own custom site presets into this file.

As an example, you can create an additional site preset that defines a Knowledge Base site. This site is for Knowledge Base – article contributors and consumers. Therefore, you can tweak things so that the default pages and default dashlets on the site dashboard are more meaningful to that audience.

You modify the presets.xml file to include your custom site preset definition as shown here:

```
<pages>
   <page id="site/${siteid}/dashboard">
      <title>Knowledge Base Site Dashboard</title>
      <title-id>page.kbSiteDashboard.title</title-id>
      <description>Knowledge Base site's dashboard page</description>
      <description-id>page.kbSiteDashboard.description</description-id>
      <template-instance>dashboard-3-columns</template-instance>
      <authentication>user</authentication>
      <properties>
         <sitePages>[{"pageId":"knowledgebase"}, {"pageId":"documentlibrary"},
                     {"pageId":"links"}, {"pageId":"discussions-topiclist"}]
         </sitePages>
      </properties>
   </page>
</pages>
```

This defines a site preset with four site pages: your custom Knowledge Base page, the Document Library page, the Links page, and the Discussions page. You specify that your Knowledge Base site dashboard requires authentication and that it should default to a three-column layout.

The next step is to adjust the Create Site dialog's drop-down control so that your new type of site appears as an option. The Create Site dialog populates that drop-down control by making a callback to a Web script on the Alfresco Share server.

This Web script can be adjusted so that your Knowledge Base site is available as one of the options. You'll do this later on, so don't worry about how it looks yet. Rather, take a look at how the adjusted scriptable controller appears:

```
var sitePresets = [
 {id: "site-dashboard", name: msg.get("title.collaborationSite")},
 {id: "kb-site-dashboard", name: msg.get("title.kbSite")}
];
model.sitePresets = sitePresets;
```

You simply add the line shown in bold. Notice that this now hands back `kb-site-dashboard` as an option. It also uses your resource bundles for I18N support in the Create Site dialog.

Dashboard Configuration

A preset allows you to define a fixed set of pages that should be available to the site upon creation. However, it also lets you preconfigure the site dashboard that will be created for the site.

A preset can include descriptions of components that should be bound into the dashboard. These descriptions specify the URL of the dashlet's Web script as well as the column and row into which to place the dashlet.

The configuration appears something like this:

```
<preset id="kb-site-dashboard">
    <components>
        ...
        <!-- dashboard components -->
        <component>
            <scope>page</scope>
            <region-id>component-1-1</region-id>
            <source-id>site/${siteid}/dashboard</source-id>
            <url>/components/dashlets/site-welcome</url>
        </component>
        <component>
            <scope>page</scope>
            <region-id>component-2-1</region-id>
            <source-id>site/${siteid}/dashboard</source-id>
            <url>/components/dashlets/activityfeed</url>
        </component>
        ...
    </components>
</preset>
```

This is just a snippet. You may have many more components defined. Notice that each component can specify the row and the column where it is to appear on the dashboard. Your preset can therefore completely set up the default layout of the site dashboard as well as all of the default dashlet bindings. The end of the chapter shows a full view of how the additional Alfresco Share preset XML appears.

Internationalization (I18N)

As before, you want to follow best practices in building your site so that you can quickly provision it for many different countries and languages. In this case, you need to provide a message bundle for the Alfresco Share configuration. To do so, you need to wire in your own message bundle to Alfresco Share.

You can define a Spring bean that overrides Alfresco Share's default message bundle values so it includes your custom bundle.

```
<?xml version='1.0' encoding='UTF-8'?>
<!DOCTYPE beans PUBLIC '-//SPRING//DTD BEAN//EN'
   'http://www.springframework.org/dtd/spring-beans.dtd'>

<beans>

   <bean id="webscripts.resources"
         class="org.alfresco.i18n.ResourceBundleBootstrapComponent">
```

```
        <property name="resourceBundles">
           <list>
              <value>alfresco.messages.webscripts</value>
              <value>alfresco.messages.slingshot</value>
              <value>alfresco.web-extension.messages.kbsite</value>
           </list>
        </property>
     </bean>

  </beans>
```

This Spring bean adds in support for an additional message bundle called `kbsite.properties` located under web-extension/messages. This is shown in bold in the previous code. In this message bundle, you might define the following key/value pairs:

```
page.kbSiteDashboard.title=Knowledge Base Site Dashboard
page.kbSiteDashboard.description=Knowledge Base site's dashboard page
title.kbSite=Knowledge Base Site
```

Notice that these are the same keys that the preset configuration and drop-down list Web script were looking for. That's all there is to it. You can now fully internationalize your new site preset. You can provide bundles so that the Create Site dialog works for languages such as Spanish or Mandarin Chinese.

INSTALLING THE CODE

This section provides step-by-step instructions for installing this chapter's code into your Alfresco installation. It assumes that you have downloaded the sample source code from `www.wrox.com`. This is available as a ZIP compressed file.

Inside of the ZIP file, you will find the following folder structure:

```
/chapter15
      /extension
      /scripts
      install_chapter_15.bat
      readme.txt
```

If you have performed a default installation on Windows under the C:\Alfresco directory, you can run the install_chapter_15.bat file to quickly install all of this chapter's sample code in one step! If you elect to do so, you can skip ahead to the section titled "Putting It into Action."

Otherwise, follow the manual installation instructions provided here. The sample files are assumed to have been extracted into a location referred to as *<sampleLocation>*. Bear in mind that the path references in this section use a Windows file convention. If you are using a non-Windows box (such as a Linux distribution), you will need to adjust the file paths accordingly.

Please read through the readme.txt file for last-minute updates and tips on installing the sample code.

The code provided in this chapter builds on what was developed in the previous chapter. It assumes that you have completed and installed the sample code from Chapter 14. Please make sure you have completed the sample code installation from Chapter 14 before continuing.

Stopping the Alfresco Server

Before doing anything else, you should stop the Alfresco server. You can do this either from a command line or through the Windows Start menu (if you used the Windows Installer).

From the command line, type the following:

```
cd <installLocation>
alf_stop.bat
```

This shuts down Alfresco and returns you to the command prompt.

Adding the Custom Dashlet

Next you'll add the custom Knowledge Base dashlet to Alfresco Share. This makes the dashlet available for you to plug into a site dashboard.

From the following directory:

- *<sampleLocation>*\chapter15\web-extension\site-webscripts\org\alfresco\components\dashlets

copy the following files:

- knowledgebase.get.desc.xml
- knowledgebase.get.head.ftl
- knowledgebase.get.html.ftl
- knowledgebase.get.js
- knowledgebase.get.properties
- knowledgebase.get.config.xml

to:

- *<installLocation>*\tomcat\shared\classes\alfresco\web-extension\site-webscripts\org\alfresco\components\dashlets

Adding the Custom Site Page

These instructions walk you through the process of installing the custom site page. This involves adding the Web script for your custom page as well as the Surf objects for the page, template instance, and components.

Adding the Web Script

To begin, you'll introduce the Web script that provides most of the functionality for your new site page. This Web script is included in the site page as part of the Surf page rendering process.

From the following directory:

- *<sampleLocation>*\chapter15\web-extension\site-webscripts\org\alfresco\components\knowledgebase copy the following files:

- knowledgebase.get.desc.xml
- knowledgebase.get.head.ftl
- knowledgebase.get.html.ftl
- knowledgebase.get.js
- knowledgebase.get.properties
- knowledgebase.get.config.xml

to:

- <*installLocation*>\tomcat\shared\classes\alfresco\web-extension\site-webscripts\org\alfresco\components\knowledgebase

This puts the Web script descriptor, scriptable controller, template view, and html `<head>` renderer into place. It also sets up the configuration file and the message bundle to provide I18N support.

Adding the Surf Page

You can now define the Surf page that will plug into your site. The page has the ID *knowledgebase* and is defined in a single file.

From the following directory:

- <*sampleLocation*>\chapter15\web-extension\site-data\pages

copy the following file:

- knowledgebase.xml

to:

- <*installLocation*>\tomcat\shared\classes\alfresco\web-extension\site-data\pages

Adding the Surf Template Instance

Add the Surf template instance now. The template instance provides additional configuration that the FreeMarker file may use while rendering.

From the following directory:

- <*sampleLocation*>\chapter15\web-extension\site-data\template-instances

copy the following file:

- knowledgebase.xml

to:

- <*installLocation*>\tomcat\shared\classes\alfresco\web-extension\site-data\template-instances

Adding the FreeMarker Template

Now you'll add the FreeMarker template file. This file converts the page model into markup for the browser to consume.

From the following directory:

- <*sampleLocation*>\chapter15\web-extension\templates\org\alfresco

copy the following file:

- knowledgebase.ftl

to:

- <*installLocation*>\tomcat\shared\classes\alfresco\web-extension\templates\org\alfresco

Adding the Surf Component Bindings

For your new site page to work, the only remaining thing to do is bind the Web scripts into the template regions.

There are five regions in total. One is in the global scope and the other four are in the template scope. The globally scoped region will be resolved for you by Spring Surf. You just need to define the other four.

Of the other four, you can reuse existing Alfresco Share Web scripts for three of them. Your new Web script is then bound in as the new element. You bind it to the knowledgebase region.

From the following directory:

- <*sampleLocation*>\chapter15\web-extension\site-data\components

copy the following files:

- template.navigation.knowledgebase.xml
- template.title.knowledgebase.xml
- template.toolbar.knowledgebase.xml
- template.knowledgebase.knowledgebase.xml

to:

- <*installLocation*>\tomcat\shared\classes\alfresco\web-extension\site-data\components

Configuring Your Site Page for Alfresco Share

Now that the site page is defined, all you have to do is configure it to be available as a selectable option. Site managers should be able to see the site page as one of several available pages they may elect to include on their site dashboard.

From the following directory:

- <*sampleLocation*>\chapter15\web-extension

copy the following file:

- share-config-custom.xml

to:

- <*installLocation*>\tomcat\shared\classes\alfresco\web-extension

Adding the Common Library

The knowledgebase.lib.js file contains helper methods for performing Knowledge Base searches using JSON as well as using CMIS. This file is used by the custom dashlet as well as the custom page component Web scripts.

From the following location:

➤ <*sampleLocation*>\chapter15\web-extension\site-webscripts\org\alfresco\components\knowledgebase

copy the following file:

➤ knowledgebase.lib.js

to:

➤ <*installLocation*>\tomcat\shared\classes\alfresco\web-extension\site-webscripts\org\alfresco\components\knowledgebase

Configuring a Custom Site Preset

These instructions walk you through the process of setting up the new site preset. This involves adding the preset, making it available from the Create Site Dialog, and adding message bundles for I18N support.

Adding the Preset

The first thing you need to do is to add the additional preset definition to the presets.xml file. The sample code provided with this book has already done this for you. The code to insert is provided toward the end of the chapter.

From the following location:

➤ <*sampleLocation*>\chapter15\web-extension\site-data\presets

copy the following file:

➤ presets.xml

to:

➤ <*installLocation*>\tomcat\shared\classes\alfresco\web-extension\site-data\presets

Overriding the Create Site Dialog Drop-Down List

You override the scriptable controller for the `create-site` Web script by simply copying in a new JavaScript file that gets picked up instead of the out-of-the-box one.

From the following location:

➤ <*sampleLocation*>\chapter15\web-extension\site-webscripts\org\alfresco\modules

copy the following file:

➤ create-site.get.js

to:

- <*installLocation*>\tomcat\shared\classes\alfresco\web-extension\site-webscripts\org\alfresco\modules

Adding Your Custom Message-Bundle

Your custom message bundle defines text values for the default locale. If you want to provide additional bundles for other locales, you just need to assign the correct suffix extensions.

From the following location:

- <*sampleLocation*>\chapter15\web-extension\messages

copy the following file:

- kbsite.properties

to:

- <*installLocation*>\tomcat\shared\classes\alfresco\web-extension\messages

Overriding the Message-Bundle Bootstrap Component

To include your own custom message bundle along with the Alfresco Share message bundles so that you can fully support I18N with your new site preset, you need to override the Spring bean responsible for doing so.

From the following location:

- <*sampleLocation*>\chapter15\web-extension

copy the following file:

- custom-slingshot-application-context.xml

to:

- <*installLocation*>\tomcat\shared\classes\alfresco\web-extension

Adding Files to the Tomcat ROOT Web Application

Both the custom dashlet and the custom page component have browser-side dependencies. These files need to be resolvable by the browser. One option is to modify the share.war file, but a better option is to simply place them in an alternate Web application.

In this case, you've elected to place them into the ROOT Web application under Tomcat. This section will walk you through how to set this up.

Adding the web.xml File

The web.xml file is a required file for the ROOT Web application. If it already exists in your Tomcat server, you can skip to the next step. If it doesn't exist, you may have to create the following directory structures yourself.

From the following location:

- *<sampleLocation>*\chapter15\ROOT\WEB-INF

copy the following file:

- web.xml

to:

- *<installLocation>*\tomcat\webapps\ROOT\WEB-INF

Adding the Custom Dashlet Dependencies

The custom dashlet has a single CSS file dependency.

From the following location:

- *<sampleLocation>*\chapter15\ROOT\share-extension\components\dashlets

copy the following file:

- knowledgebase.css

to:

- *<installLocation>*\tomcat\webapps\ROOT\share-extension\components\dashlets

Adding the Custom Page Component Dependencies

The custom page component has CSS and JS dependencies.

From the following location:

- *<sampleLocation>*\chapter15\ROOT\share-extension\components\knowledgebase

copy the following files:

- knowledgebase.css
- knowledgebase.js

to:

- *<installLocation>*\tomcat\webapps\ROOT\share-extension\components\knowledgebase

PUTTING IT INTO ACTION

If you have followed the instructions, you should be ready to put things into action.

Starting the Alfresco Server

You can start up the Alfresco server either from a command prompt or through the Windows Start menu (if you used the Windows Installer).

From the command line, type the following:

```
cd <installLocation>
alf_start.bat
```

This starts up Alfresco and returns you to the command prompt.

Creating a New Alfresco Share Site

You'll begin by creating a simple Collaboration Site in Alfresco Share and configuring it to use your new site page.

1. Open a browser and go to Alfresco Share. You can access Alfresco Share using the following URL:

   `http://localhost:8080/share`

2. Log in to Alfresco Share. You can log in using the administrator account. The administrator has a user name of `admin` and a password of `admin`.

   Once you log in, you will see the user dashboard.

3. To create a new site, click on the arrow next to Sites at the top of the page, and then click Create Site in the drop-down list (see Figure 15-7).

   FIGURE 15-7

   This brings up the Create Site dialog.

4. In the Create Site dialog, do the following (see Figure 15-8):

   a. In the Name field, give your site a name, such as *My First Project*.

   b. In the URL Name field, type **first**.

   c. You can leave the Description field blank.

   d. In the Type list, select Collaboration Site.

5. Click OK to create the site.

FIGURE 15-8

Since you were the one to create the site, you are automatically designated as the site manager. This means that you can customize and tweak the site as you see fit. You can set up the site dashboard and invite new participants to the site. You can specify their roles and rights.

Adding the Custom Dashlet to Your Site

Now that you are feeling high and mighty as the site manager, you'll set about making the custom Knowledge Base dashlet available to your users. You will add the dashlet to the site dashboard so that all users who arrive to your site will have a quick view into what is happening in the Knowledge Base.

Along the top of the page, you should see a blue site bar that indicates the name of your site on the left side and provides a few interesting buttons along the right side. This is depicted in Figure 15-9.

FIGURE 15-9

1. Click Customize Dashboard to begin tweaking the site dashboard that your users will see. This will take you to a page where you can see a list of all of the dashlets configured for the site dashboard.
2. Scroll down to the section on dashlets and click Add Dashlets to see a list of available dashlets, including the Knowledge Base dashlet (see Figure 15-10).

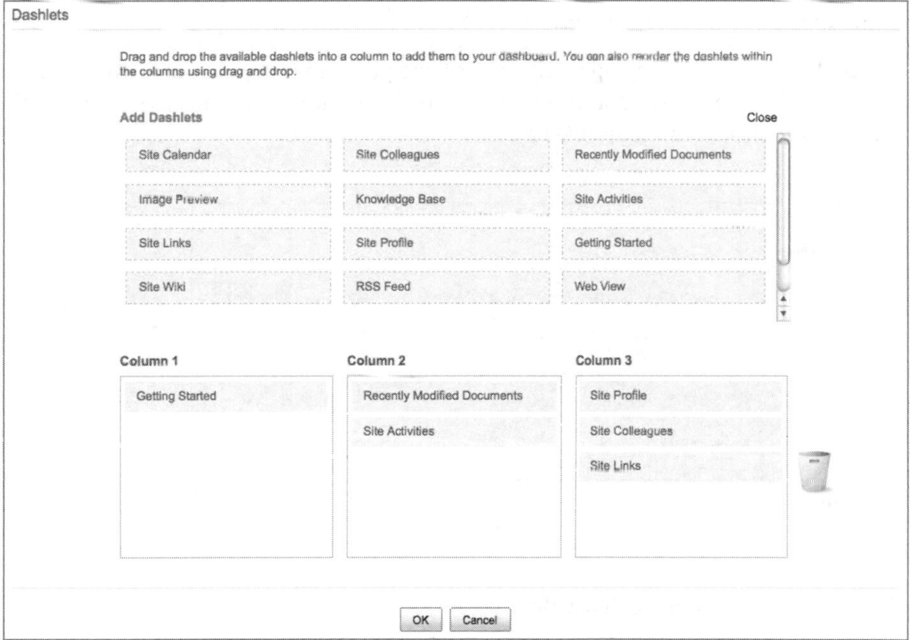

FIGURE 15-10

3. Click the Knowledge Base dashlet to select it, and then drag and drop it into one of the three columns on the bottom part of the window.

   You can place the dashlet wherever you like.

4. Once you have placed the dashlet into the site dashboard configuration, click OK to save your changes.

   You are returned to the site dashboard displaying your Knowledge Base dashlet. It will appear on the page in the location that you specified. It will display as shown in Figure 15-11.

You may wonder why your Knowledge Base doesn't have any content in it. Why don't you see the Knowledge Base articles from the previous chapter? That's because those articles were created in a space under Company Home. The dashlet is clever and is looking for Knowledge Base articles that are specifically located in this Alfresco Share site. You haven't created any yet.

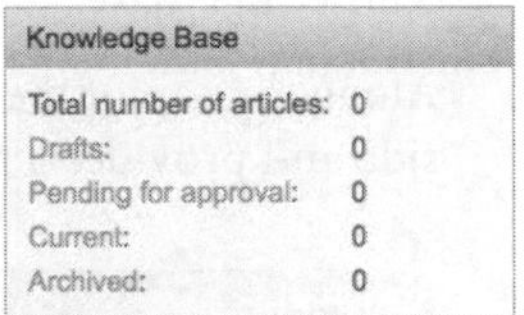

FIGURE 15-11

Adding the Custom Page to Your Site

As the much-esteemed site manager, you can configure additional pages for your site. You can also remove pages that you don't want or need. Follow these steps to add to your site the custom page that you created.

1. In the blue site bar along the top of the page, click the More menu, and then click Customize Site in the drop-down list.

   This takes you to a page where you will see a listing of all of the pages that currently make up your site.

2. Click Add Pages to bring up a selection of site pages that are available and are not currently being used by your site. You should see your Knowledge Base page listed among the available options (as shown in Figure 15-12).

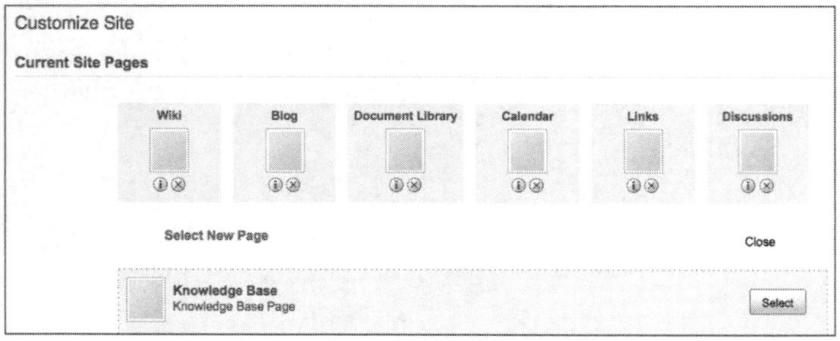

FIGURE 15-12

3. Click Select for the Knowledge Base page.

4. Click OK on the bottom of the page.

   You are taken back to the site dashboard, where you should see the Knowledge Base page in the navigation region of the application (see Figure 15-13).

FIGURE 15-13

5. Click the Knowledge Base page in the navigation menu. This will render your custom Knowledge Base page! See Figure 15-14 for an example of what it looks like.

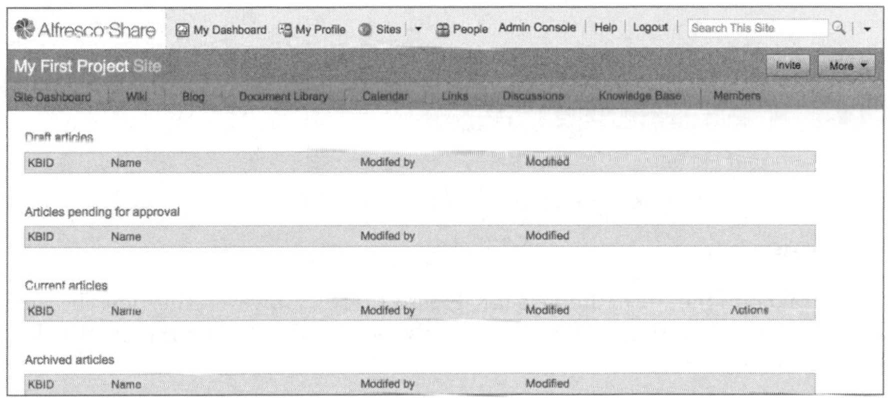

FIGURE 15-14

Congratulations! You have created a brand new site page and it has been added to your site. It reuses much of the Alfresco Share user interface and looks consistent with the rest of the application. In the middle of the page is your custom Web script.

Creating a Knowledge Base Site

Now try out your new site preset. You will create a new Knowledge Base Share site.

1. At the top of the page, click the arrow next to Sites, then click Create Site in the drop-down list.

   This brings up the Create Site Dialog. You saw this dialog before. You used it to create a Collaboration site. This time around, you're going to create a Knowledge Base site.

2. In the Create Site dialog, do the following (as shown in Figure 15-15):

   a. In the Name field, type *My Second Project*.

   b. In the URL Name field, type *second*.

   c. Leave the Description field blank.

   d. In the Type list, select Knowledge Base Site.

3. Click OK to create the site.

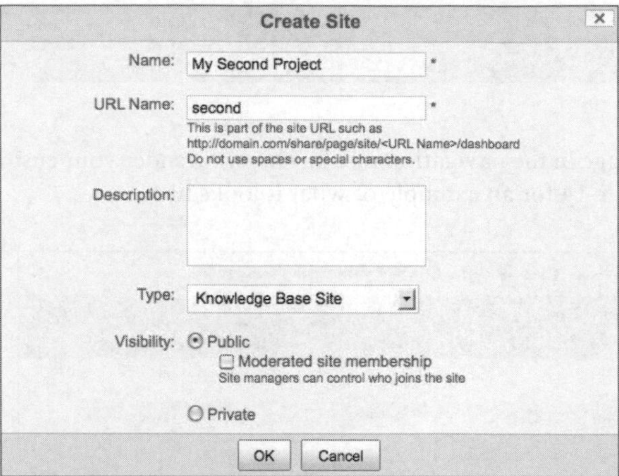

FIGURE 15-15

You are taken to the site dashboard (see Figure 15-16). However, this time the site dashboard should look a little different. You should only see four dashlets on the site dashboard and a limited number of pages.

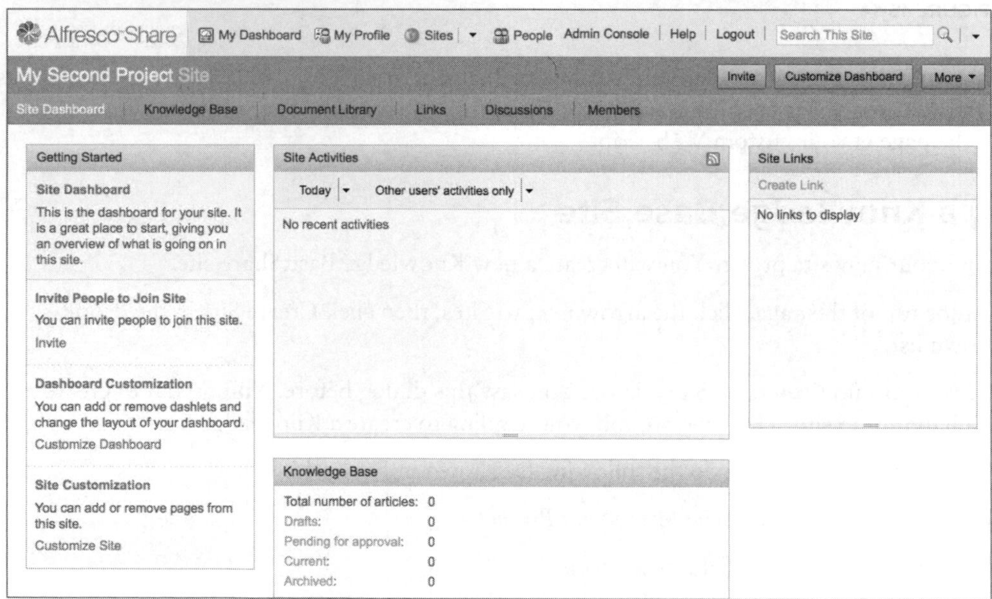

FIGURE 15-16

Recall that when you defined the additional preset within presets.xml, you constrained the number of dashlets to four. These were the Getting Started dashlet, the Site Activities dashlet, the Knowledge Base dashlet, and the Site Links dashlet.

You also limited the number of pages to four. These were the Knowledge Base page, the Document Library page, the Links page, and the Discussions page. The Site Dashboard and Members pages are mandatory.

Clicking on the Document Library

You're just about done. There is just one thing left to do. Click on the Document Library tab in the menu bar. The only reason you need to do this is to ensure that the document library services initialize for your site. This helps to make sure your site space contains a subfolder named *documentLibrary*. You'll need that in the next chapter!

Feel free to click around and try out your Alfresco Share extensions. In the next chapter, you'll begin creating content and using these extensions. You'll also add a few more tweaks and goodies to your Alfresco Share site.

SAMPLE CODE

This section provides sample code used in this chapter. This code is also available from `www.wrox.com`. This is available as a ZIP compressed file. The paths to source files mentioned in this section are relative to the root of the ZIP file.

Alfresco Share – Custom Dashlet

This section describes the files required to implement the custom Knowledge Base dashlet for Alfresco Share.

Web Script

The following files should be placed into this directory:

<installLocation>\tomcat\shared\classes\alfresco\web-extension\site-webscripts\org\alfresco\components\dashlets

Available for download on Wrox.com

Defines the Knowledge Base dashlet's Web script Implementation

```
<webscript>
   <shortname>Knowledge Base</shortname>
   <description>A summary of all Knowledge Base articles</description>
   <family>site-dashlet</family>
   <url>/components/dashlets/knowledgebase</url>
</webscript>
```

Code snippet web-extension\site-webscripts\org\alfresco\components\dashlets\knowledgebase.get.desc.xml

Available for download on Wrox.com

Defines the Knowledge Base dashlet's Web script HEAD markup

```
<#include "../component.head.inc">

<@link rel="stylesheet" type="text/css"
      href="${page.url.context}-extension/components/dashlets/knowledgebase.css"
/>
```

Code snippet web-extension\site-webscripts\org\alfresco\components\dashlets\knowledgebase.get.head.ftl

Available for download on Wrox.com

Defines the Knowledge Base dashlet's Web script controller

```
<import resource="classpath:alfresco/web-extension/site-webscripts/org/alfresco/ \
                components/knowledgebase/knowledgebase.lib.js">

/**
 * Gathers information on all knowledgebase articles within the site.
 *
 * @method main
 */
function main()
{
   var knowledgeBaseConfig = new XML(config.script);
   var site = page.url.templateArgs.site;
   var serviceFormat = knowledgeBaseConfig.serviceFormat ?
                       knowledgeBaseConfig.serviceFormat : "json";
   var maxResults = args.maxResults ? parseInt(args.maxResults) : 50;
   var articles;

   // Search for all knowledge base articles in the site
   // The service either returns an Array of results (can be empty)
   // or an integer status code
   if (serviceFormat == "json")
   {
      articles = jsonSeachKnowledgeBaseArticles(site, maxResults);
   }
   else if (serviceFormat == "cmis")
   {
      articles = cmisSeachKnowledgeBaseArticles(site, maxResults);
   }

   if (articles instanceof Array)
   {
      // Group articles and prepare model
      var articleGroups = groupArticlesByStatus(articles);
      model.all = articles.length;
      model.drafts = articleGroups["Draft"] ? articleGroups["Draft"].length : 0;
      model.pendingApprovals = articleGroups["Pending Approval"] ?
```

```
                                    articleGroups["Pending Approval"].length : 0;
        model.current = articleGroups["Current"] ? articleGroups["Current"].length:0;
        model.archived = articleGroups["Archived"] ?
                                articleGroups["Archived"].length : 0;
    }
    else
    {
        // An error code was returned
        model.error = articles;
    }
}

main();
```

Code snippet web-extension\site-webscripts\org\alfresco\components\dashlets\knowledgebase.get.js

Defines the Knowledge Base dashlet's Web script view

```
<div class="dashlet knowledgebase">
   <div class="title">${msg("header.knowledgebase")}</div>
   <div class="body">
      <div class="msg">
<#if (error?exists)>
         <div>${msg("error.call")}</div>
<#else>
         <table>
            <tr>
               <td>${msg("label.all")}:</td>
               <td>${all}</td>
            </tr>
            <tr>
               <td><a href="${url.context}/page/site/${page.url.
               templateArgs.site!""}/documentlibrary?filter=
               tag&filterData=draft#" class="theme-color-1">
               ${msg("label.drafts")}</a>:</td>
               <td>${drafts}</td>
            </tr>
            <tr>
               <td><a href="${url.context}/page/site/${page.url.
               templateArgs.site!""}/documentlibrary?filter=
               tag&filterData=pending#" class="theme-color-1">
               ${msg("label.pendingApprovals")}</a>:</td>
               <td>${pendingApprovals}</td>
            </tr>
            <tr>
               <td><a href="${url.context}/page/site/${page.url.
               templateArgs.site!""}/documentlibrary?filter=
               tag&filterData=current#" class="theme-color-1">
               ${msg("label.current")}</a>:</td>
```

```
                <td>${current}</td>
            </td>
            <tr>
                <td><a href="${url.context}/page/site/${page.url.
                templateArgs.site!""}/documentlibrary?filter=
                tag&filterData=archived#" class="theme-color-1">
                ${msg("label.archived")}</a>:</td>
                <td>${archived}</td>
            </td>
        </table>
</#if>
        </div>
    </div>
</div>
```

Code snippet web-extension\site-webscripts\org\alfresco\components\dashlets\knowledgebase.get.html.ftl

Available for download on Wrox.com

Defines the Knowledge Base dashlet's default properties bundle

```
header.knowledgebase=Knowledge Base
label.all=Total number of articles
label.drafts=Drafts
label.pendingApprovals=Pending for approval
label.current=Current
label.archived=Archived
error.call=An error occured when getting the knowledge base summary
```

Code snippet web-extension\site-webscripts\org\alfresco\components\dashlets\knowledgebase.get.properties

Available for download on Wrox.com

Defines the Knowledge Base dashlet's configuration

```
<knowledgebase>
   <serviceFormat>json</serviceFormat>
   <!--<serviceFormat>cmis</serviceFormat>-->
</knowledgebase>
```

Code snippet web-extension\site-webscripts\org\alfresco\components\dashlets\knowledgebase.get.config.xml

Alfresco Share – Custom Page

This section describes the files required to implement the custom Knowledge Base page for Alfresco Share.

Surf Object — Page

The following file should be placed into this directory:

<*installLocation*>\tomcat\shared\classes\alfresco\web-extension\site-data\pages

Available for download on Wrox.com

Defines the Knowledge Base page

```
<?xml version='1.0' encoding='UTF-8'?>
<page>
   <id>knowledgebase</id>
   <page-type>knowledgebase</page-type>
   <title>Knowledge Base</title>
   <title-id>page.knowledgebase.title</title-id>
   <description>Knowledge Base Page</description>
   <description-id>page.knowledgebase.description</description-id>
   <template-instance>knowledgebase</template-instance>
   <authentication>user</authentication>
</page>
```

Code snippet web-extension\site-data\pages\knowledgebase.xml

Surf Object — Template Instance

The following file should be placed into this directory:

<installLocation>\tomcat\shared\classes\alfresco\web-extension\site-data\template-instances

Available for download on Wrox.com

Defines the Knowledge Base template instance

```
<?xml version='1.0' encoding='UTF-8'?>
<template-instance>
   <template-type>org/alfresco/knowledgebase</template-type>
</template-instance>
```

Code snippet web-extension\site-data\template-instances\knowledgebase.xml

Surf Objects — Components

The following files should be placed into this directory:

<installLocation>\tomcat\shared\classes\alfresco\web-extension\site-data\components

Available for download on Wrox.com

Binds the custom Knowledge Base Web script to the Knowledge Base region

```
<?xml version='1.0' encoding='UTF-8'?>
<component>
   <scope>template</scope>
   <region-id>knowledgebase</region-id>
   <source-id>knowledgebase</source-id>
   <url>/components/knowledgebase</url>
   <properties>
      <maxResults>25</maxResults>
   </properties>
</component>
```

web-extension\site-data\components\template.knowledgebase.knowledgebase.xml

Binds the stock navigation Web script to the navigation region

```
<?xml version='1.0' encoding='UTF-8'?>
<component>
   <scope>template</scope>
   <region-id>navigation</region-id>
   <source-id>knowledgebase</source-id>
   <url>/components/navigation/collaboration-navigation</url>
</component>
```

Code snippet web-extension\site-data\components\template.navigation.knowledgebase.xml

Binds the stock title Web script to the title region

```
<?xml version='1.0' encoding='UTF-8'?>
<component>
   <scope>template</scope>
   <region-id>title</region-id>
   <source-id>knowledgebase</source-id>
   <url>/components/title/collaboration-title</url>
</component>
```

Code snippet web-extension\site-data\components\template.title.knowledgebase.xml

Binds the stock toolbar Web script to the toolbar region

```
<?xml version='1.0' encoding='UTF-8'?>
<component>
   <scope>template</scope>
   <region-id>toolbar</region-id>
   <source-id>knowledgebase</source-id>
   <url>/components/knowledgebase/collaboration-toolbar</url>
</component>
```

Code snippet web-extension\site-data\components\template.toolbar.knowledgebase.xml

Template

Template files should be placed into this directory:

<*installLocation*>\tomcat\shared\classes\alfresco\web-extension\templates\org\alfresco

Defines the Knowledge Base page template

```
<#include "include/alfresco-template.ftl" />

<@templateHeader/>

<@templateBody>
```

```
    <div id="hd">
       <@region id="header" scope="global" protected=true />
       <@region id="title" scope="template" protected=true />
       <@region id="navigation" scope="template" protected=true />
    </div>
    <div id="bd">
       <div>
          <div id="yui-main">
             <div id="divknowledgebaseList">
                <@region id="knowledgebase" scope="template" />
             </div>
          </div>
       </div>
    </div>
</@>

<@templateFooter>
    <div id="ft">
       <@region id="footer" scope="global" protected=true />
    </div>
</@>
```

Code snippet web-extension\templates\org\alfresco\knowledgebase.ftl

Web Script

Web script files should be placed into this directory:

<installLocation>\tomcat\shared\classes\alfresco\web-extension\site-webscripts

The Knowledge Base Web script descriptor

```
<webscript>
   <shortname>knowledgebase</shortname>
   <description>Knowledge Base Component</description>
   <url>/components/knowledgebase</url>
</webscript>
```

Code snippet web-extension\site-webscripts\org\alfresco\components\knowledgebase\knowledgebase.get.desc.xml

The Knowledge Base Web script configuration

```
<knowledgebase>
   <serviceFormat>json</serviceFormat>
   <!--<serviceFormat>cmis</serviceFormat>-->
</knowledgebase>
```

Code snippet web-extension\site-webscripts\org\alfresco\components\knowledgebase\knowledgebase.get.config.xml

Available for download on Wrox.com

The Knowledge Base Web script HEAD markup generator

```
<#include "../component.head.inc">

<!-- Knowledge Base-->

<@link rel="stylesheet" type="text/css"
 href="${page.url.context}-extension/components/knowledgebase/
  knowledgebase.css" />
<@script type="text/javascript"
src="${page.url.context}-extension/components/knowledgebase/knowledgebase.js">
</@script>

<!-- Tag Library -->

<@link rel="stylesheet" type="text/css"
 href="${page.url.context}/modules/taglibrary/taglibrary.css" />
<@script type="text/javascript"
 src="${page.url.context}/modules/taglibrary/taglibrary.js"></@script>
```

Code snippet web-extension\site-webscripts\org\alfresco\components\knowledgebase\knowledgebase.get.head.ftl

Available for download on Wrox.com

Defines the Knowledge Base Web script view

```
<#macro dateFormat date>${date?string("EEE d MMM yyyy HH:mm:ss")}</#macro>
<#macro printArticles articles type buttons>
   <div class="title">${msg("title." + type)}</div>
   <table>
      <thead class="theme-bg-color-3">
         <tr>
            <th class="kbid">${msg("header.kbid")}</th>
            <th class="name">${msg("header.name")}</th>
            <th class="modified-by">${msg("header.modifiedBy")}</th>
            <th class="modified-date">${msg("header.modifiedDate")}</th>
            <th class="actions"><#if buttons?size &gt; 0>
            ${msg("header.actions")}</#if> </th>
         </tr>
      </thead>
      <tbody id="${el}-${type}-tbody">
         <#if articles?is_number>
            <tr>
               <td colspan="5">${msg("article.error")}</td>
            </tr>
         <#else>
            <#list articles as article>
               <tr>
                  <td class="kbid">${article.nodeDBID!""}</td>
                  <td class="name"><a href="${url.context}/page/site/
```

```
                    ${page.url.templateArgs.site!""}/document-
                   details?nodeRef=${article.nodeRef}">
                   ${article.name!msg("label.articleNameNotFound")}</a></td>
                    <td class="modified-by"><a href="${url.context}
                   /page/user/${article.modifiedByUser}/profile">
                   ${article.modifiedBy!""}</a></td>
                    <td class="modified-date">${article.modifiedOn!""}</td>
                    <td class="actions"><#list buttons as button>
                    <button class="archive" value="${article.nodeRef}">
                    ${msg("button." + button)}</button></#list></td>
                 </tr>
              </#list>
           </#if>
        </tbody>
     </table>
</#macro>
<#assign el=args.htmlid>
<script type="text/javascript">//<![CDATA[
   new Alfresco.kb.KnowledgeBase("${el}").setOptions(
   {
      siteId: "${page.url.templateArgs.site!""}"
   }).setMessages(
      ${messages}
   );
//]]></script>

<div id="${el}-body" class="knowledgebase">
   <#-- Print all article types -->
   <@printArticles articles=drafts           type="drafts"           buttons=[] />
   <@printArticles articles=pendingApprovals type="pendingApprovals" buttons=[] />
   <@printArticles articles=current          type="current"          buttons=
   ["archive"] />
   <@printArticles articles=archived         type="archived"         buttons=[] />
</div>
```

Code snippet web-extension\site-webscripts\org\alfresco\components\knowledgebase\knowledgebase.get.html.ftl

Available for download on Wrox.com

Defines the Knowledge Base Web script controller

```
<import resource="classpath:alfresco/web-extension/site-webscripts/org/alfresco/
                  components/knowledgebase/knowledgebase.lib.js">

/**
 * Loads Knowledge Base articles from the server and groups them by status
 *
 * @method main
 */
function main()
{
```

```
   // Set input input paramaters
   var knowledgeBaseConfig =  new XML(config.script);
   var site = page.url.templateArgs.site;
   var serviceFormat = knowledgeBaseConfig.serviceFormat ?
                       knowledgeBaseConfig.serviceFormat : "json";
   var maxResults = args.maxResults ? parseInt(args.maxResults) : 50;
   var articles;

   // Load articles from server with configured service format
   if (serviceFormat == "json")
   {
      articles = jsonSeachKnowledgeBaseArticles(site, maxResults);
   }
   else if (serviceFormat == "cmis")
   {
      articles = cmisSeachKnowledgeBaseArticles(site, maxResults);
   }

   if (articles instanceof Array)
   {
      // Group articles by status and prepare model
      var articleGroups = groupArticlesByStatus(articles);
      model.drafts = articleGroups["Draft"] ? articleGroups["Draft"] : [];
      model.pendingApprovals = articleGroups["Pending Approval"] ?
                               articleGroups["Pending Approval"] : [];
      model.current = articleGroups["Current"] ? articleGroups["Current"] : [];
      model.archived = articleGroups["Archived"] ? articleGroups["Archived"] : []
   }
   else
   {
      // An error code was returned
      model.error = articles;
   }
}

// Start webscript
main();
```

Code snippet web-extension\site-webscripts\org\alfresco\components\knowledgebase\knowledgebase.get.js

Available for download on Wrox.com

Defines the Knowledge Base Web script

```
title.current=Current articles
title.drafts=Draft articles
title.pendingApprovals=Articles pending for approval
title.archived=Archived articles

header.kbid=KBID
header.name=Name
header.modifiedBy=Modifed by
```

```
header.modifiedDate=Modified
header.actions=Actions

button.archive=Archive

label.articleNameNotFound=Name not found!
label.searchError=Could not get knowledgebase articles from the server

message.archiveError=Could not archive article
```

Code snippet web-extension\site-webscripts\org\alfresco\components\knowledgebase\knowledgebase.get.properties

Alfresco Share – Custom Site Preset

This section describes the files required to implement the custom Knowledge Base page for Alfresco Share.

Share Object — Preset

The following file fragment should be included into the existing presets.xml file in this directory. You will need to copy this file out of the share.war file or locate it in the sample files ZIP distribution.

<installLocation>\tomcat\shared\classes\alfresco\web-extension\site data\presets

Additional configuration for the presets.xml file

```
<preset id="kb-site-dashboard">
   <components>
      <!-- title -->
      <component>
         <scope>page</scope>
         <region-id>title</region-id>
         <source-id>site/${siteid}/dashboard</source-id>
         <url>/components/title/collaboration-title</url>
      </component>
      <!-- navigation -->
      <component>
         <scope>page</scope>
         <region-id>navigation</region-id>
         <source-id>site/${siteid}/dashboard</source-id>
         <url>/components/navigation/collaboration-navigation</url>
      </component>
      <!-- dashboard components -->
      <component>
         <scope>page</scope>
         <region-id>component-1-1</region-id>
         <source-id>site/${siteid}/dashboard</source-id>
         <url>/components/dashlets/site-welcome</url>
      </component>
      <component>
         <scope>page</scope>
```

```
            <region-id>component-2-1</region-id>
            <source-id>site/${siteid}/dashboard</source-id>
            <url>/components/dashlets/activityfeed</url>
        </component>
        <component>
            <scope>page</scope>
            <region-id>component-2-2</region-id>
            <source-id>site/${siteid}/dashboard</source-id>
            <url>/components/dashlets/knowledgebase</url>
        </component>
        <component>
            <scope>page</scope>
            <region-id>component-3-1</region-id>
            <source-id>site/${siteid}/dashboard</source-id>
            <url>/components/dashlets/site-links</url>
        </component>
    </components>
    <pages>
        <page id="site/${siteid}/dashboard">
            <title>Knowledge Base Site Dashboard</title>
            <title-id>page.kbSiteDashboard.title</title-id>
            <description>Knowledge Base site's dashboard page</description>
            <description-id>page.kbSiteDashboard.description</description-id>
            <template-instance>dashboard-3-columns</template-instance>
            <authentication>user</authentication>
            <properties>
                <sitePages>
                    [{"pageId":"knowledgebase"}, {"pageId":"documentlibrary"},
                     {"pageId":"links"},{"pageId":"discussions-topiclist"}]
                </sitePages>
            </properties>
        </page>
    </pages>
</preset>
```

Code snippet web-extension\site-data\presets\presets.xml (additional fragment)

Share Module – Site Creation

The following file should be placed into this directory:

<installLocation>\tomcat\shared\classes\alfresco\web-extension\site-webscripts\org\alfresco\modules\

Available for download on Wrox.com

Override for the Create Site Web script controller

```
var sitePresets = [
   {id: "site-dashboard", name: msg.get("title.collaborationSite")},
   {id: "kb-site-dashboard", name: msg.get("title.kbSite")}
];
model.sitePresets = sitePresets;
```

Code snippet web-extension\site-webscripts\org\alfresco\modules\create-site.get.js

Alfresco Share – Common Library

The following file is a common server-side JavaScript library that is used by both the custom dashlet and the custom page. It should be placed in the following location:

> <*installLocation*>\tomcat\shared\classes\alfresco\web-extension\site-webscripts\org\alfresco\components\knowledgebase

Defines common JavaScript functions for the Knowledge Base

```
/**
 * CMIS Version
 *
 * Performs a CMIS search
 *
 * @method cmisSeachKnowledgeBaseArticles
 * @param site {string} The site to search in
 * @param pageSize {int} The maximum number of articles to return
 */
function cmisSeachKnowledgeBaseArticles(site, pageSize)
{
   // Get the nodeRef for the sites documentLibrary
   var connector = remote.connect("alfresco"),
       result = connector.get("/slingshot/doclib/container/" +
       stringUtils.urlEncodeComponent(site) + "/documentLibrary"),
       data = eval('(' + result + ')'),
       container = data.container;
       docLibNodeRef = container ? container.nodeRef : null;

   // Do search limited to the site's document library
   var query = "<?xml version=\"1.0\" encoding=\"UTF-8\" standalone=\"yes\" ?>" +
               "<query xmlns:cmis=\"http://www.cmis.org/2008/05\">" +
               "   <statement>" +
               "      select d.*, s.* " +
               "      from cmis:document as d " +
               "       join kb:status as s on s.cmis:objectid = d.cmis:objectid " +
               "      where in_tree('" + docLibNodeRef + "')" +
               "      and d.cmis:objecttypeid &lt;&gt; 'D:cm:thumbnail'" +
               "   </statement>" +
               "   <pageSize>" + pageSize + "</pageSize>" +
               "</query>";
   result = connector.post("/cmis/queries", query, "application/cmisquery+xml");
   var feed = atom.toFeed(result.response),
       entries = feed.entries,
       entriesLength = entries.size(),
       entryEl = null,
       objEl,
       propertiesEl,
       propertiesList,
       propertyEl,
       articles = [],
       article;
```

```
    // Convert to object format similar to the json response
    for (var ei = 0; ei < entriesLength; ei++)
    {
       entryEl = entries.get(ei);
       article = {
          properties: {}
       };
       objEl = getElementByTagName(entryEl.getExtensions(), "object");
       propertiesEl = getElementByTagName(objEl.getElements(), "properties");
       propertiesList = propertiesEl.getElements();
       for (var pi = 0, pl = propertiesList.size(); pi < pl; pi++)
       {
          propertyEl = propertiesList.get(pi);
          if (propertyEl.getAttributeValue("propertyDefinitionId") == "s.kb:status")
          {
             article.properties["kb_status"] = propertyEl.firstChild.text;
          }
          else if (propertyEl.getAttributeValue("propertyDefinitionId") ==
                   "d.cmis:name")
          {
             article.name = propertyEl.firstChild.text;
          }
          else if (propertyEl.getAttributeValue("propertyDefinitionId") ==
                   "d.cmis:lastModifiedBy")
          {
             article.modifiedByUser = propertyEl.firstChild.text;
             article.modifiedBy = article.modifiedByUser;
          }
          else if (propertyEl.getAttributeValue("propertyDefinitionId") ==
                   "d.cmis:lastModificationDate")
          {
             article.modifiedOn = propertyEl.firstChild.text;
          }
          else if (propertyEl.getAttributeValue("propertyDefinitionId") ==
                   "d.cmis:objectId")
          {
             article.nodeRef = propertyEl.firstChild.text;
          }
       }
       articles.push(article);
    }
    return articles;
 }

 /**
  * Helper method that returns elements (org.apache.abdera.model.Element)
  * in the list (java.util.List) having an element tag name matching elTagName
  *
  * @method getElementByTagName
  * @param list {string} (mandatory) The list to look for elements in
  * @param elTagName {string} (optional) The tagName to look for
```

```
 * @return {array|object} An element in the list matching elTagName
 * @private
 */

function getElementByTagName(list, elTagName)
{
   var el;
   for (var i = 0, l = list.size(); i < l; i++)
   {
      el = list.get(i);
      if (el.QName.localPart == elTagName)
      {
         return el;
      }
   }
   return null;
}

/**
 * JSON version.
 *
 * Returns person display name string as returned to the user.
 * Caches the person full name to avoid repeatedly querying the repository.
 *
 * @method jsonSeachKnowledgeBaseArticles
 * @param siteId {string} (mandatory) The site id
 * @param maxResults {int} (optional) The maximum number of results to return
 * @return {array|int} The found knowledgebase articles or integer status
   code on error
 */
function jsonSeachKnowledgeBaseArticles(siteId, maxResults)
{
   // Prepare the webscript url
   var url = "/slingshot/knowledgebase/search/site/" +
   stringUtils.urlEncode(siteId) +
   (maxResults ? ("?maxResults=" + maxResults) : "")

   // Call server webscript
   var connector = remote.connect("alfresco");
   result = connector.get(url);

   if (result.status == 200)
   {
      // Return knowledgebase articles
      return eval('(' + result + ')').items;
   }
   else
   {
      // Return error code to indicate error
      return result.status;
   }
}
```

```
/**
 * Takes the articles and groups them by status.
 *
 * @method groupArticlesByStatus
 * @return {object} An object using statuses as keys and arrays of articles
   as values
 */

function groupArticlesByStatus(articles)
{
   var articleGroups = {},
       status,
       article;
   for (var i = 0, l = articles.length; i < l; i++)
   {
      article = articles[i];
      status = article.properties ? article.properties["kb_status"] : null;
      if (status)
      {
         if (articleGroups[status] === undefined)
         {
            articleGroups[status] = [];
         }
         articleGroups[status].push(article);
      }
   }
   return articleGroups;
}
```

Code snippet web-extension\site-webscripts\org\alfresco\components\knowledgebase\knowledgebase.lib.js

Alfresco Share – Configuration Files

The following configuration files should be placed into this directory:

<*installLocation*>\tomcat\shared\classes\alfresco\web-extension

Available for download on Wrox.com

Custom Alfresco Share configuration file

```
<alfresco-config>

   <!-- Add a custom page type -->
   <config evaluator="string-compare" condition="SitePages" replace="true">
      <pages>
         <page id="calendar">calendar</page>
         <page id="wiki-page">wiki-page?title=Main_Page</page>
         <page id="documentlibrary">documentlibrary</page>
         <page id="discussions-topiclist">discussions-topiclist</page>
         <page id="blog-postlist">blog-postlist</page>
         <page id="links">links</page>
```

```
            <page id="tasks">tasks</page>
            <page id="knowledgebase">knowledgebase</page>
         </pages>
      </config>

   </alfresco-config>
```

Code snippet web-extension\share-config-custom.xml

Available for download on Wrox.com

Defines custom Spring beans or Spring bean overrides for Alfresco Share

```
<?xml version='1.0' encoding='UTF-8'?>
<!DOCTYPE beans PUBLIC '-//SPRING//DTD BEAN//EN' 'http://www.springframework.org/
dtd/spring-beans.dtd'>

<beans>

   <bean id="webscripts.resources"
         class="org.alfresco.i18n.ResourceBundleBootstrapComponent">
      <property name="resourceBundles">
         <list>
            <value>alfresco.messages.webscripts</value>
            <value>alfresco.messages.slingshot</value>
            <value>alfresco.web-extension.messages.kbsite</value>
         </list>
      </property>
   </bean>

</beans>
```

Code snippet web-extension\custom-slingshot-application-context.xml

Alfresco Share – Message Bundle

The following message bundle should be placed here:

<installLocation>\tomcat\shared\classes\alfresco\web-extension\messages

Available for download on Wrox.com

Defines custom message bundle elements for Alfresco Share

```
page.kbSiteDashboard.title=Knowledge Base Site Dashboard
page.kbSiteDashboard.description=Knowledge Base site's dashboard page

# Customise site
page.knowledgebase.title=Knowledge Base
page.knowledgebase.description=Displays the Knowledge Base content

# Create site preset
title.kbSite=Knowledge Base Site
```

Code snippet web-extension\messages\kbsite.properties

Tomcat ROOT Web Application Files

The following files are used by the custom dashlet and custom page implementations provided in these samples. They are not part of the core Alfresco Share Web application. Rather than modify the Alfresco Share Web application itself, they are copied into a separate ROOT Web application in Tomcat.

Custom Dashlet — CSS

The following file should be copied into your Tomcat ROOT Web application directory at the following location:

<*installLocation*>\tomcat\webapps\ROOT\share-extension\components\dashlets

CSS for the Knowledge Base custom page

```
.knowledgebase.dashlet .body .msg
{
   padding: 0.5em;
}

.knowledgebase.dashlet .body table td
{
   padding: 0.15em 0.5em 0.15em 0.25em;
}
```

Code snippet ROOT\share-extension\components\dashlets\knowledgebase.css

Custom Page – CSS and JavaScript

The following files should be copied into your Tomcat ROOT Web application directory at the following location:

<*installLocation*>\tomcat\webapps\ROOT\share-extension\components\knowledgebase

CSS for the Knowledge Base custom page

```
.knowledgebase
{
   padding: 1em;
}

.knowledgebase .title
{
   line-height: 2.5em;
   color: #008000;
   font-size: 108%;
}

.knowledgebase table
{
   margin-bottom: 2em;
   width: 70em;
```

```
   border: 1px solid #C0C0C0;
}

.knowledgebase caption
{
   padding: 0.5em;
   font-size: 1.23%;
}

.knowledgebase tbody
{
   border-top: 1px solid #C0C0C0;
}

.knowledgebase th,
.knowledgebase td
{
   padding: 0.25em;
}

.knowledgebase table th.kbid
{
   width: 10%;
}

.knowledgebase table .name
{
   width: 30%;
}

.knowledgebase table .modified-by
{
   width: 20%;
}

.knowledgebase table .modified-date
{
   width: 20%;
}

.knowledgebase table .actions
{
   width: 15%;
   text-align: center;
}

.knowledgebase table .actions .yui-button button
{
   line-height: 1;
   min-height: 1em;
   padding: 0 3px;
}
```

Code snippet ROOT\share-extension\components\knowledgebase\knowledgebase.css

Available for download on Wrox.com

Browser-side JavaScript for the Knowledge Base custom page

```
/**
 * Alfresco Knowledge Base namespace.
 *
 * @namespace Alfresco
 * @class Alfresco.kb
 */
Alfresco.kb = Alfresco.kb || {};

/**
 * Knowledge Base component.
 *
 * Lists all knowledge base articles and gives the possibility to archive the
 * current ones.
 *
 * @namespace Alfresco
 * @class Alfresco.kb.KnowledgeBase
 */
(function()
{
   /**
    * YUI Library aliases
    */
   var Dom = YAHOO.util.Dom,
       Event = YAHOO.util.Event;

   /**
    * Dashboard KnowledgeBase constructor.
    *
    * @param {String} htmlId The HTML id of the parent element
    * @return {Alfresco.KnowledgeBase} The new component instance
    * @constructor
    */
   Alfresco.kb.KnowledgeBase = function KB_constructor(htmlId)
   {
      Alfresco.kb.KnowledgeBase.superclass.constructor.call(this,
         "Alfresco.kb.KnowledgeBase", htmlId, ["button"]);
      return this;
   };

   YAHOO.extend(Alfresco.kb.KnowledgeBase, Alfresco.component.Base,
   {
      /**
       * Object container for initialization options
       *
       * @property options
       * @type object
       */
      options:
      {
         /**
          * Current siteId.
          *
```

```
     * @property siteId
     * @type string
     */
    siteId: "",

    /**
     * ContainerId representing root container
     *
     * @property containerId
     * @type string
     * @default "documentLibrary"
     */
    containerId: "documentLibrary"
},

/**
 * Fired by YUI when parent element is available for scripting
 *
 * @method onReady
 */
onReady: function KB_onReady()
{
    var el = Dom.get(this.id)
    var archiveButtons = Dom.getElementsByClassName("archive",
    "button", el);
    for (var i = 0, l = archiveButtons.length; i < l; i++)
    {
        Alfresco.util.createYUIButton(this, null, this.onArchiveButtonClick,
            {}, archiveButtons[i]);
    }
},

/**
 * Fired when the user clicks the Cancel button.
 * Takes the user back to the details edit page without saving anything.
 *
 * @method onArchiveButtonClick
 * @param p_oEvent {object} a "click" event
 */
onArchiveButtonClick: function KB_onArchiveButtonClick(p_oEvent, p_oButton)
{
    // Disable buttons to avoid double submits
    var buttonSpanEl = p_oButton.get("element");
    p_oButton.set("disabled", true);

    // Prepare archive webscript url
    var url = YAHOO.lang.substitute(Alfresco.constants.PROXY_URI_RELATIVE +
        "/slingshot/doclib/action/archive/site/{siteId}/{containerId}",
    {
        siteId: this.options.siteId,
        containerId: this.options.containerId
    });
```

```
            // Request article to be archived
            Alfresco.util.Ajax.jsonPost(
            {
               url: url,
               dataObj:
               {
                  nodeRefs: [ p_oButton.get("value") ]
               },
               successCallback:
               {
                  fn: function(response)
                  {
                     // Remove button from row and move row to archive table
                     var trEl = buttonSpanEl.parentNode.parentNode;
                     buttonSpanEl.parentNode.removeChild(buttonSpanEl);
                     Dom.get(this.id + "-archived-tbody").appendChild(trEl);
                  },
                  scope: this
               },
               failureMessage: this.msg("message.archiveError")
            });
         }
      });
   })();
```

Code snippet ROOT\share-extension\components\knowledgebase\knowledgebase.js

16

Custom Knowledge Base: Advanced Share Customizations

WHAT'S IN THIS CHAPTER?

- Customizing the document library
- Using a custom workflow in Alfresco Share
- Configuring a custom form for Alfresco Share
- Customizing metadata with the Alfresco Forms engine

This chapter walks you through the process of adding advanced customizations to Alfresco Share and the Alfresco repository. These customizations include the addition of archiving logic based on the Alfresco repository rules you created in Chapter 14. You will further customize the Alfresco Share interface by introducing new actions and workflows to the document library. Finally, you will look at how you can introduce new custom forms based on the Alfresco Forms Service.

This chapter builds on the foundation work from Chapter 14 as well as the Alfresco Share customizations from Chapter 15. The sample code in this chapter builds on top of the sample code from the two previous chapters. Thus, if you haven't worked through the previous two chapters, please take the time to do so.

This chapter is structured to provide the following sections:

- **Overview** — A high-level explanation of the concepts and application extension points that you will use in the example. You don't have to type in any of the code in this section; it is simply provided to help guide along the conversation.

- **Installing the Code** — A step-by-step guide to the approach you will need to take in order to install all of the sample code on your own Alfresco installation.
- **Putting It into Action** — A walkthrough of your new extensions. Try them out and see what they do!

At the end of this chapter you will find the source code for the samples. This is only provided for reference. To install, you should download the source files from the book's page at `www.wrox.com` and follow the instructions provided in the section titled "Installing the Code."

OVERVIEW

In Chapter 14, you looked at customizing the Alfresco repository to provide Knowledge Base services in the form of a Web script. In Chapter 15, you looked at extension points within Alfresco Share and explored ways that you can introduce Knowledge Base functionality into your collaboration sites.

In this chapter, you'll step it up a notch by introducing more advanced customizations to both the Alfresco repository and to Alfresco Share. You'll focus on the document library and look at how you can extend it to offer the following:

- Support for the `kb:article` aspect
- A new action for archiving a Knowledge Base article
- A new workflow for approving Knowledge Base articles

In addition, you'll use the Alfresco Forms engine to customize the look and feel of the content entry and editing screens for your Knowledge Base articles. Alfresco Share includes the Forms engine by default.

This section provides an overview of Alfresco Share and covers what each of these things are. You'll go through them one at a time. There will be some code snippets at times to make the reading a little easier. However, you don't have to type in any code in this section. Just read and enjoy!

Alfresco Share Document Library

The document library is one of the default site pages that is included with Alfresco Share collaboration sites. You saw this in the previous chapter. The document library appears in the navigation menu as Document Library (as shown in Figure 16-1).

FIGURE 16-1

The document library is a common point of extension for most customers and community members building a solution on top of Alfresco Share. It is the workhorse for most of the document-level collaboration inside of an Alfresco Share site. It features a number of configuration options and is scripted on top of Spring Surf. You can extend the document library without the need for Java development or compilation.

The functionality for the document library lives in two places (see Figure 16-2):

- Alfresco Share
- Alfresco repository

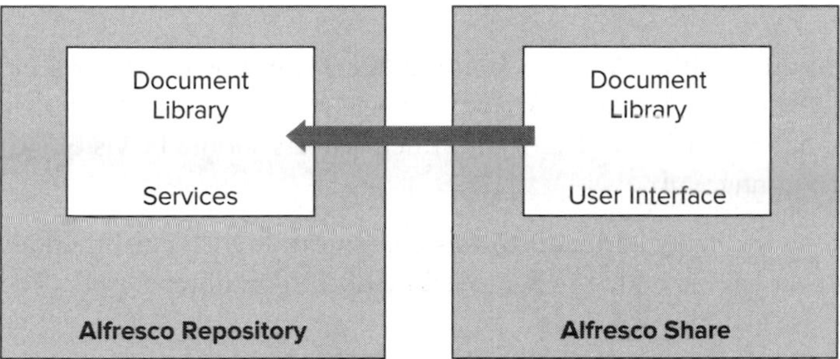

FIGURE 16-2

Alfresco Share contains the document library's user interface elements. This includes things like the buttons, theme elements, and images. This often consists of files like browser-side JavaScript, CSS, or static files like JPGs.

The Alfresco repository contains the services that the document library depends upon. All the data operations occur in the services within the Alfresco repository. The Alfresco repository receives the instructions, performs the task, and then hands back a response (usually in the form of JSON or XML).

The document library provides configuration options in both locations. You can apply some configuration settings within the services to tweak the kinds of data that is sent "over the wire" to Alfresco Share. You can then tweak Alfresco Share itself to adjust how things are presented.

Aspects

The document library provides a user interface for setting aspects onto your documents. It gives you a list of available aspects to pick from. The list is generated within the document library services.

You can add your `kb:article` aspect to this list by configuring the document library services responsible for handing back document library aspects. This is implemented as a single Web script. As you might suspect, it hands back a JSON string that lists all of the aspect information for a given document. The JSON string looks like this:

```
{
   "current": ["cm:auditable", "sys:referenceable", "cm:titled",
               "cm:author","app:inlineeditable"],
   "visible": ["cm:generalclassifiable","cm:complianceable","cm:dublincore",
               "cm:effectivity","cm:summarizable","cm:versionable",
               "cm:templatable","cm:emailed","emailserver:aliasable",
               "cm:taggable"],
   "addable": [],
   "removeable": []
}
```

If you're not an expert on JSON, fear not. It's pretty straight forward. The JSON lists out four properties – `current`, `visible`, `addable`, and `removeable`. Each property has an array of aspects. The *current* property contains the array of all of the aspects that are currently applied to the document. The *visible* property contains the array of all of the aspects potentially available for the current document. The `addable` and `removeable` properties contain the arrays of aspects that can be added to or removed from the current document.

The document library uses this information within Alfresco Share to figure out how to render a meaningful user interface to the end user. All of this comes back from a single repository-side Web script. This Web script looks to a single configuration file to determine which aspects should be visible to the end user. This file is called aspects.get.config.xml.

You can make your `kb:article` aspect visible by adding it to this configuration file. You could also specify whether your `kb:article` aspect can be added or removed by document library users. The configuration is essentially as simple as the following code.

```
<aspects>
   <visible>
      ...
      <aspect name="{http://www.alfresco.org/model/knowledgebase/1.0}article" />
      ...
   </visible>
</aspects>
```

A full configuration example is provided at the end of this chapter. However, this is the general idea. This simple configuration adjustment enables the document library to work with your Knowledge Base article aspect.

Actions

The document library also provides a user interface that lets you run repository actions against your documents. The actions appear on the right-hand side of the document list page. Clicking on an action tells Alfresco Share to fire into the appropriate action handler within the document library services.

A Web script within Alfresco Share generates the list of actions. This Web script is configuration-driven just like the previous one. This means that you can adjust the list of actions through configuration without having to do any coding.

Suppose you wanted to add an action to the right-hand side of the document library. It's easy enough to do. You could adjust the Web script configuration file to appear something like this:

```
<documentList>
   <actionSets>
      <actionSet id="empty"></actionSet>
      <actionSet id="document">
         ...
         <action id="onActionArchive" type="action-link" permission=""
                 label="actions.document.archive" />
         ...
      </actionSet>
```

```
        <actionSet id="locked">...</actionSet>
        <actionSet id="lockOwner">...</actionSet>
        <actionSet id="workingCopyOwner">...</actionSet>
        <actionSet id="folder">...</actionSet>
        <actionSet id="link">...</actionSet>
    </actionSets>
</documentList>
```

This configuration file lets you describe actions that are to be available for documents in various states. For example, you can define which actions should be available for documents that are locked. Or you can define which actions should be available for folders.

The new configuration for the new action is shown in bold. This describes a new action with the ID `onActionArchive`. It is to be made available when documents are selected in the document library.

You then need to define a JavaScript function that is responsible for handling this action within the browser. When you click on the new action, Alfresco Share will look for a browser-side JavaScript method named `onActionArchive` to handle the click. You need to supply a browser-side JavaScript file that defines this click handler.

The actions-common.get.head.ftl file defines what should appear in the `HEAD` of the HTML markup for the document list. You can modify this file to include your own `<script>` tag to pull in browser-side JavaScript. In the example that you'll install, you will have this file pull in JavaScript from the knowledgebase-action.js file.

The knowledgebase-action.js file defines the function that handles the click. It uses the Alfresco Share client-side API to call back to the Alfresco Share server with a proxy request. The proxy request asks Alfresco Share to call over to the Alfresco repository on behalf of the user. In other words, Alfresco Share will call over to the Alfresco repository and access the document library services on your behalf.

You might choose to have your JavaScript function make a proxy request over to one of the out-of-the-box document library Web scripts. Or you may choose to write your own Alfresco repository Web script as an action handler. It is completely up to you.

In the case of knowledgebase-action.js, the function asks Alfresco Share to invoke a custom action handler. You add the action handler to the document library services by defining a new Web script in the repository. This Web script responds to the `POST` method. It is written in the style of the Alfresco Share repository Web scripts and uses a library that allows it to handle one document or multiple documents at once.

The Web script considers the incoming document nodes. If they are valid, the script sets the `kb:status` property of the documents to the value of *Archived*. This indicates an *Archived* lifecycle state in your Knowledge Base.

Workflow

Alfresco Share lets you configure the workflows that can be launched from within the document library. As before, the document library uses a Web script to determine which workflows should be shown to the end user for selection. There is a single Web script file that you can tweak:

/org/alfresco/modules/documentlibrary/workflow.get.html.ftl

You can edit the file and modify its contents to include the following fragment:

```
<div class="field">
   <select id="${el}-type" name="type" tabindex="0">
      <option value="wf:review" selected="selected">Review &amp; Approve</option>
      <option value="wf:articleapproval">KB Article Review &amp; Approve</option>
      <option value="wf:adhoc">Adhoc Task</option>
   </select>
</div>
```

The section shown in bold is new. By adding that in, the selector for the document library will let you choose the `wf:articleapproval` workflow. This ID matches the ID of the workflow declared in the kb-approval-process-definition.xml file that defines your workflow. Alfresco Share will then make the `wf:articleapproval` workflow available to your users.

Forms in Alfresco Share

Alfresco Share allows you to define and customize interactive forms for use in creating, displaying, and editing your content objects (see Figure 16-3). It does this by packaging the Alfresco Forms engine for you. It is delivered as part of Alfresco Share and includes everything you need.

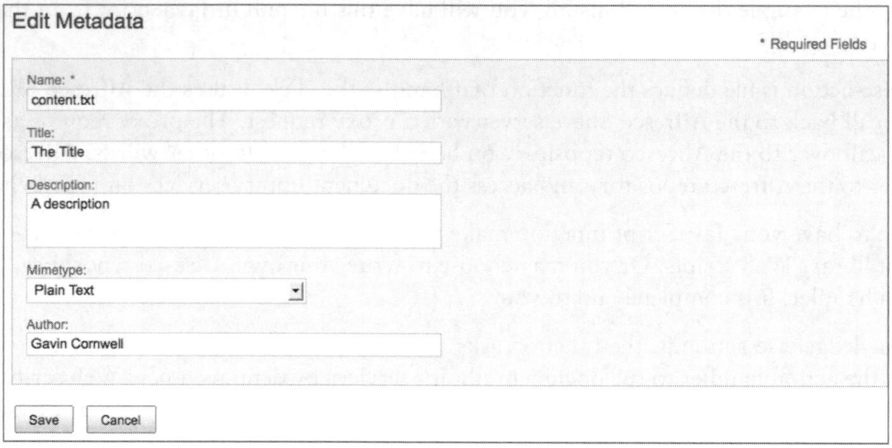

FIGURE 16-3

The Alfresco Forms engine provides a configuration-driven approach to building and delivering role-based interactive forms. Using simple XML configuration, you can define new forms or interfaces for your content metadata. You can also plug in validation logic and browser-side assertions.

For example, you could define a simple view-form for content consumers. This form would just show the basic properties that most people are interested in when they casually glance at a document. You then also define an edit-form for content editors. This form would be editable and would show additional properties that are of interest only to the editors.

One example you could keep in mind is the `kb:status` property from your Knowledge Base content model. This property is an internal property that indicates the lifecycle state of the document.

Consumers may be interested to see it. However, editors shouldn't be allowed to edit it. In fact, the value of the `kb:status` property should be entirely managed by the rules and workflow in your Knowledge Base space.

The Alfresco Forms engine draws its configuration from the Alfresco configuration service, which means that your XML configuration is able to use inheritance and extension patterns. It is also based on Spring and makes available many options for advanced users, including the ability to plug in custom generator and persistence classes. These let you adapt the Forms engine to custom schema types within Alfresco or within external third-party systems.

Alfresco Share Configuration

You define forms within the share-config-custom.xml file. Within this file, you can override everything from a form definition for a particular content type to all aspects of the form presentation system. The configuration file specification follows. There's a lot that you can do!

```
<config>
   <forms>
      <default-controls>
         <type name="type" template="path">
            <control-param name="name">value</control-param>
         </type>
      </default-controls>
      <constraint-handlers>
         <constraint type="id" validation-handler="function" [message-id="key"]
            [message="string"] [event="string"] />
      </constraint-handlers>
      <dependencies>
         <js src="path" />
         <css src="path" />
      </dependencies>
   </forms>
</config>

<config evaluator="node-type" condition="type">
   <forms>
      <form [id="string"] [submission-url="url"]>
         <view-form template="path" />
         <edit-form template="path" />
         <create-form template="path" />
         <field-visibility>
            <show id="string" [for-mode="view|edit|create"] [force="boolean"] />
            <hide id="string" [for-mode="view|edit|create"] />
         </field-visibility>
         <appearance>
            <set id="string" appearance="fieldset|panel" [parent="string"]
                 [label="string"] [label-id="key"] [template="path"] />
            <field id="string" [label-id="key"] [label="string"] [description-
                   id="key"] [description="string"]
                  [read-only="boolean"] [mandatory="boolean"] [set="string"]>
               <control [template="path"]>
                  <control-param name="name">value</control-param>
               </control>
```

```
                <constraint-handlers>
                    <constraint type="id" validation-handler="function" [message-
                                id="string"] [message="string"] [event="string"] />
                </constraint-handlers>
            </field>
        </appearance>
    </form>
  </forms>
</config>
```

Imagine that the Forms engine is asked to render an edit-form for your Knowledge Base article. It begins by looking for a configuration block that is appropriate for your article. This configuration block defines the template to use for the form as well as all of the controls.

In your Knowledge Base content model, you allowed any kind of content to be an article. In fact, you explicitly sought to use aspects so as to make things more flexible. Thus, you can provide your form for `cm:content`. This is the base content type within Alfresco.

The configuration block might look like this:

```
<config evaluator="node-type" condition="cm:content">
   <forms>
      <default-controls>
         <type name="text"
               template="/org/alfresco/components/form/controls/textfield.ftl" />
      </default-controls>
      <form>
         <edit-form template="/2-column-edit-form.ftl" />
         <field-visibility>
            <show id="kb:articletype" />
            <show id="kb:status" for-mode="view" />
         </field-visibility>
         <appearance>
            <field id="kb:articletype" label="Article Type"
                   description="Knowledge Base Article Type" />
            <field id="kb:status" label="Status" description="Approval Status" />
         </appearance>
      </form>
   </forms>
</config>
```

When the Forms engine is asked to render an edit-form for a content object of type `cm:content`, it will gather together all of the configuration blocks and will include yours. Your configuration block instructs the Forms engine to do the following:

- It overrides the form template to use the FreeMarker template file described by the path /2-column-edit-form.ftl.
- It specifies that the `kb:articletype` field should be visible.
- It specifies that the `kb:status` field should be visible only when the view-form is being shown.
- It specifies that the `kb:articletype` field should have the label "Article Type" and the description "Knowledge Base Article Type."
- It specifies that the `kb:status` field should have the label "Status" and the description "Approval Status."

The Forms engine will look to the `<edit-form>` element's template attribute to determine which FreeMarker file to use for the form layout. If this isn't provided, it will use the default form layout.

The Forms engine then begins to walk through the properties of the content object. For each property, it must determine which *control* to use as well as look to the configuration to inform the control about what appearance settings to use.

Consider the `kb:status` property of type `d:text`. The Forms engine has to figure out what kind of control to render to the screen for this field. The Forms engine has a number of default controls set up out of the box for the Data Dictionary types (such as `d:text`).

However, you can also override the default controls as shown in the previous `<default-controls>` element. You've indicated that text fields should use a specific FreeMarker template. This overrides the out-of-the-box settings. You can also provide form specific overrides for the view-form if you wish.

The Forms engine renders all of the controls onto the screen by invoking FreeMarker for all of the individual controls. The FreeMarker files are located in the share.war file but you can also override them or implement your own by placing your templates under the /web-extension/templates directory.

This is just an example of what you can do with the Forms engine. As you can see from the full configuration settings, you can also do things like indicate browser-side constraints. You'll install a Forms configuration file as part of the sample file installation process.

INSTALLING THE CODE

This section provides step-by-step instructions for installing this chapter's code into your Alfresco installation. It assumes that you have downloaded the sample source code from `www.wrox.com`. This is available as a ZIP compressed file.

Inside of the ZIP file, you will find the following folder structure:

```
/chapter16
      /extension
      /web-extension
      /ROOT
      install_chapter_16.bat
      readme.txt
```

If you've performed a default installation on Windows under the C:\Alfresco directory, you can run the install_chapter_16.bat file to quickly install all of this chapter's sample code in one step! If you elect to do so, you can skip ahead to the section titled "Putting It into Action."

Otherwise follow the manual installation instructions provided here. The sample files are assumed to have been extracted into a location referred to as *<sampleLocation>*. Bear in mind that the path references in this section use a Windows file convention. If you are using a non-Windows box (such as a Linux distribution), you will need to adjust the file paths accordingly.

Please read through the readme.txt file for last-minute updates and tips on installing the sample code.

The code provided in this chapter builds on what was developed in the previous two chapters. It assumes that you have completed and installed the sample code from Chapters 14 and 15. Please make sure you have completed the sample code installation from Chapters 14 and 15 before continuing.

Stopping the Alfresco Server

Before doing anything else, you should stop the Alfresco server. You can do this either from a command line or through the Windows Start menu (if you used the Windows Installer).

From the command line, type the following:

```
cd <installLocation>
alf_stop.bat
```

This shuts down Alfresco and returns you to the command prompt.

Document Library Services

The following steps involve customizations to the document library services in the Alfresco repository.

Adding the Custom Workflow

Begin by adding a custom workflow to your Alfresco repository. A custom workflow comprises a process definition file and a workflow bootstrap file. The latter consists of a Spring bean that informs the Alfresco repository of the new workflow process definition.

From the following directory:

- *<sampleLocation>*\chapter16\extension

copy the following files:

- kb-approval-process-definition.xml
- kb-workflow-context.xml

to:

- *<installLocation>*\tomcat\shared\classes\alfresco\extension

Adding the Archive Action Handler

Now you'll introduce a custom Web script that will act as an HTTP `POST` handler for your Archive action.

From the following directory:

- *<sampleLocation>*\chapter16\extension\templates\webscripts\org\alfresco\slingshot\documentlibrary\action

copy the following files:

- archive.post.desc.xml
- archive.post.json.js
- archive.post.json.ftl

to:

- *<installLocation>*\tomcat\shared\classes\alfresco\extension\templates\webscripts\org\alfresco\slingshot\documentlibrary\action

Setting Up the kb: article Aspect

At this point, you will inform the document library to make your custom `kb:article` aspect visible.

From the following directory:

- *<sampleLocation>*\chapter16\extension\templates\webscripts\org\alfresco\slingshot\documentlibrary

copy the following file:

- aspects.get.config.xml

to:

- *<installLocation>*\tomcat\shared\classes\alfresco\extension\templates\webscripts\org\alfresco\slingshot\documentlibrary

Alfresco Share

The following steps involve customizations to Alfresco Share.

Adding the Archive Action to the Document Library

The Document Library page in Alfresco Share features a list of actions along the right-hand side. You would like to add a new Archive action to this list.

When users click the Archive action, an HTTP POST should be performed to the Alfresco repository server. The Web script on that side will put your content into an *Archived* state.

From the following directory:

- *<sampleLocation>*\chapter16\web-extension\site-webscripts\org\alfresco\components\documentlibrary

copy the following files:

- actions-common.get.head.ftl
- documentlist.get.config.xml

to:

- *<installLocation>*\tomcat\shared\classes\alfresco\web-extension\site-webscripts\org\alfresco\components\documentlibrary

Configuring Alfresco Share to Show Your Custom Workflow

Earlier, you defined your new custom workflow process and bootstrapped it into the Alfresco repository. You would now like to configure Alfresco Share so that your workflow process appears for end users. You will enable end users to select your workflow and launch it.

From the following directory:

- *<sampleLocation>*\chapter16\web-extension\site-webscripts\org\alfresco\modules\documentlibrary copy the following file:

- workflow.get.html.ftl

to:

- *<installLocation>*\tomcat\shared\classes\alfresco\web-extension\site-webscripts\org\alfresco\modules\documentlibrary

Configuring the Alfresco Share Form for kb:article Objects

Alfresco Share comes out of the box with the ability to render metadata forms for viewing and editing content objects. All you need to do is provide the form definitions and associate them to your `kb:article` aspect. You can do all of this within the Alfresco Share configuration file.

From the following directory:

- *<sampleLocation>*\chapter16\web-extension

copy the following file:

- share-config-custom.xml

to:

<installLocation>\tomcat\shared\classes\alfresco\web-extension

If you worked through Chapter 15, then you will need to overwrite a file with the same name.

Adding the Alfresco Share Form Template

You will also need to copy in the template for your form.

From the following directory:

- *<sampleLocation>*\chapter16\web-extension\site-webscripts

copy the following file:

- 2-column-edit-form.ftl

to:

<installLocation>\tomcat\shared\classes\alfresco\web-extension\site-webscripts

Adding Your Custom Message Bundle

Your custom message bundle defines text values for the default locale. If you want to provide additional bundles for other locales, you just need to assign the correct suffix extensions.

From the following location:

- *<sampleLocation>*\chapter16\web-extension\messages

copy the following file:

- kbsite.properties

to:

➤ <*installLocation*>\tomcat\shared\classes\alfresco\web-extension\messages

If you worked through Chapter 15, then you will need to overwrite a file with the same name.

Overriding the Message Bundle Bootstrap Component

To include your own custom message bundle along with the Alfresco Share message bundles so that you can fully support I18N with your new site preset, you need to override the Spring bean responsible for doing so.

From the following location:

➤ <*sampleLocation*>\chapter16\web-extension

copy the following file:

➤ custom-slingshot-application-context.xml

to:

➤ <*installLocation*>\tomcat\shared\classes\alfresco\web-extension

If you worked through Chapter 15, then you will need to overwrite a file with the same name.

Adding Files to the Tomcat ROOT Web Application

The customizations in this section have dependencies that need to be resolvable by the browser. One option is to modify the share.war file but a better option is to simply place them in an alternate Web application.

In this case, you've elected to place them into the ROOT Web application under Tomcat. This section will walk you through how to set this up.

Adding the web.xml File

The web.xml file is a required file for the ROOT Web application. If it already exists in your Tomcat server, you can skip to the next step. If it doesn't exist, you may have to create the following directory structures by hand.

From the following location:

➤ <*sampleLocation*>\chapter16\ROOT\WEB-INF

copy the following file:

➤ web.xml

to:

➤ <*installLocation*>\tomcat\webapps\ROOT\WEB-INF

Adding the Document Library Dependencies

From the following location:

➤ <*sampleLocation*>\chapter16\ROOT\share-extension\components\documentlibrary copy the following files:

- knowledgebase-actions.js
- knowledgebase-documentlist.css

to:

- *<installLocation>*\tomcat\webapps\ROOT\share-extension\components\documentlibrary

Adding the Knowledge Base Article Image

From the following location:

- *<sampleLocation>*\chapter16\ROOT\share-extension\components\documentlibrary\images

copy the following file:

- kbarchive-16.png

to:

- *<installLocation>*\tomcat\webapps\ROOT\share-extension\components\documentlibrary\images

PUTTING IT INTO ACTION

If you have followed the instructions, you should be ready to try things out.

Restarting the Alfresco Server

If your Alfresco server is already running, you should stop it, either from a command prompt or from the Windows Start menu (if you used the Windows Installer).

From the command line, type the following:

```
cd <installLocation>
alf_stop.bat
```

You should then start up Alfresco once again. You can it start up either from a command prompt or from the Windows Start menu (if you used the Windows Installer).

From the command line, type the following:

```
cd <installLocation>
alf_start.bat
```

This starts up Alfresco and returns you to the command prompt.

Setting Up a Knowledge Base

In Chapter 15, you created a custom Knowledge Base Site preset for Alfresco Share and used this to build a new site. You called this site *My Second Project* and gave it the short name of *second*.

Now you'll go into Alfresco Explorer and add a Knowledge Base space to this site's document library. Follow these instructions:

1. Open a browser and go to Alfresco Explorer. You can access Alfresco Explorer using the following URL:

   `http://localhost:8080/alfresco`

2. Click the Login link at the top of the page to log in to Alfresco Explorer.

   You can use the administrator account with the user name `admin` and password `admin`. Your user dashboard will display once you log in.

3. Click the Company Home link at the top left of the page. This takes you to the root space of the repository.

   On the left-hand side of the page you will see a Navigator view of the repository.

4. Click the arrow next to the Sites space to reveal the subspaces inside.

5. Click the arrow next to the subspace named *second*. This will expand the subspace and you should see a few folders underneath it. It should appear similar to Figure 16-4.

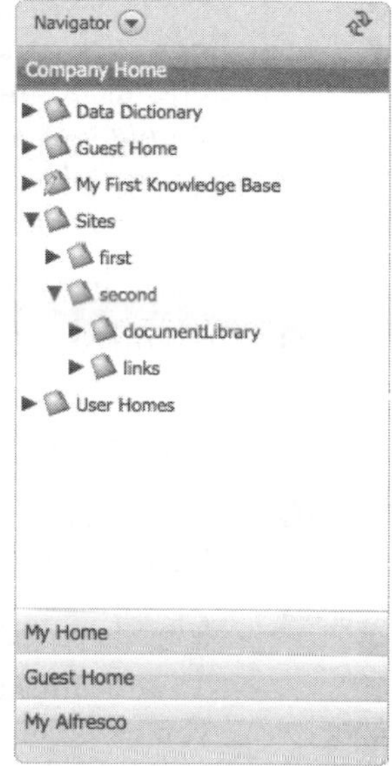

FIGURE 16-4

6. Click on the space named *documentLibrary* in the left-hand Navigator's subspaces. This will take you into the document library for the *My Second Project* site. It should look a little like what is shown in Figure 16-5.

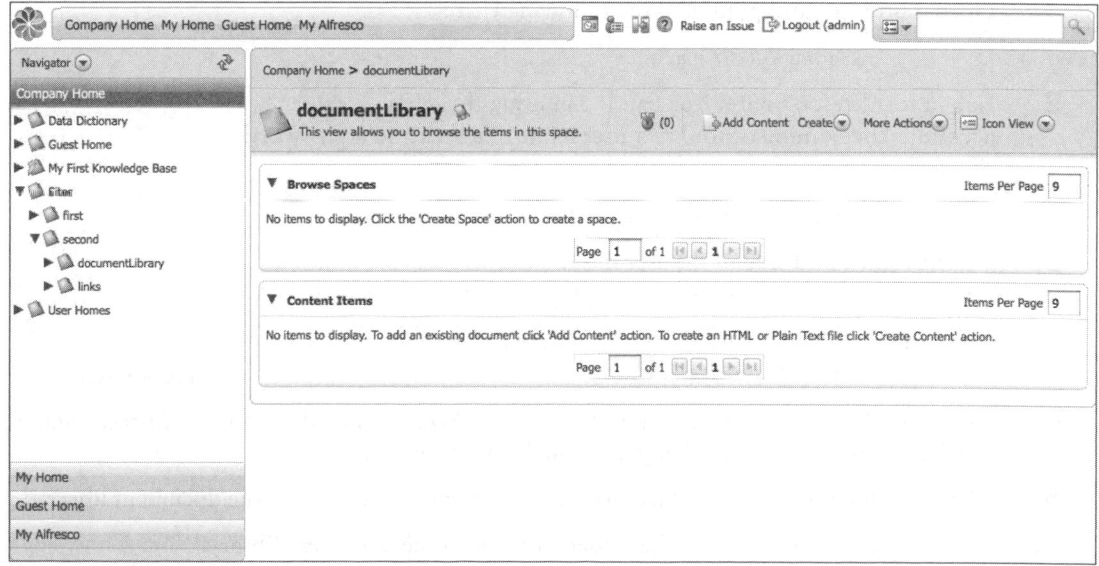

FIGURE 16-5

If you don't see a space named documentLibrary *in your site space, then you skipped a step in Chapter 15! Actually, it's not so bad – you probably only skipped the very last step. In your Knowledge Base site within Alfresco Share, you need to first click on the Document Library tab in the navigation menu. Otherwise, the* documentLibrary *folder will not appear. If you're caught in this conundrum, you should take a slight detour into Alfresco Share and follow the steps prescribed in Chapter 15.*

7. Click the Create menu and select Advanced Space Wizard from the list.
8. On the Step One - Starting Space page, choose the Using a Template option and click Next.
9. On the next page, Step Two – Space Options, select Knowledge Base Project from the drop-down list and click Next.
10. Give your new Knowledge Base the name *Knowledge Base* and leave the description field blank.
11. Click Create Space to create the space.

    The document library now has a Knowledge Base space under it. This includes all of the rules you set up in Chapter 14.

Browsing to the Knowledge Base

Now that your Knowledge Base is properly situated inside of the document library, you can set about adding some content to it. To do so, you'll use Alfresco Share. You'll also check out some of the customizations you added.

1. Open a browser and point it to the following URL:

   `http://localhost:8080/share`

2. Log in to Alfresco Share. You can log in using the administrator account. The administrator has a user name of `admin` and a password of `admin`.

   Once you log in, you will see the user dashboard.

3. On the right-hand side of the user dashboard, you will see a dashlet that lists all of your sites, as shown in Figure 16-6.

   You can see all of the sites that you have created during the course of building out this sample application.

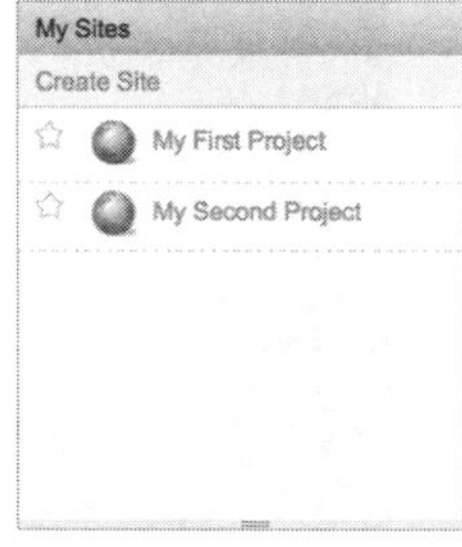

FIGURE 16-6

4. Click the My Second Project link in this dashlet. You will be taken into the Alfresco Share site. This is the second site that you created in Chapter 15.
5. Click the Document Library link along the site menu to navigate to the document library.
6. Click Show Folders to reveal the folders that are in the document library. Your Knowledge Base space displays!
7. Click on the Knowledge Base space to navigate into it.

Inside the Knowledge Base space, you should see an Archived folder. This is because you used your Knowledge Base space template to stamp out the structure and rules. The Knowledge Base space is preconfigured for you.

Adding a Document to the Knowledge Base

Now you'll add a document to the Knowledge Base. It really doesn't matter what document you add. You might pick from a handy file on your desktop, perhaps a Word document, or a photo of your family. Anything will work just fine.

If you're really hard up for material, there is some sample content included along with the ZIP file. Assume that you wish to upload the following file:

chapter16\samplecontent\sample.doc

Please proceed with the following steps:

1. Click the Upload button under the navigation menu (see Figure 16-7).

FIGURE 16-7

   You will then be presented with a window to help coordinate your upload. This window will let you upload many files at once, if you choose. However, in this case you will just focus on uploading a single file.

2. Click the button along the top to select files to upload. You will be presented with a file picker. Pick the sample.doc file as described above or pick one of your own files.
3. Once your files are selected, click the Upload Files button to send your files to the document library (see Figure 16-8).

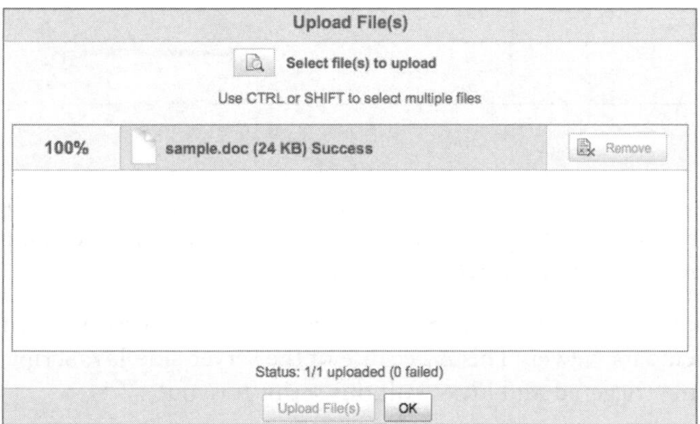

FIGURE 16-8

   Of course, this assumes you used the sample.doc file for this upload. If you used a different file, you will see its name shown in the image.

4. Click OK to close the Upload Files dialog.

   You should now see your content appear in the document library along with a thumbnail icon that identifies the document's content (as shown in Figure 16-9).

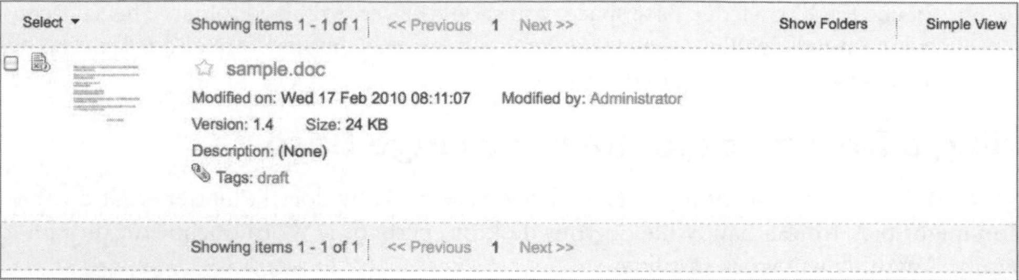

FIGURE 16-9

5. Click on the document to bring up the document details and preview (see Figure 16-10).

   On the left-hand side, you will see a Flash preview of the document you uploaded. The rest of the page shows details about the document.

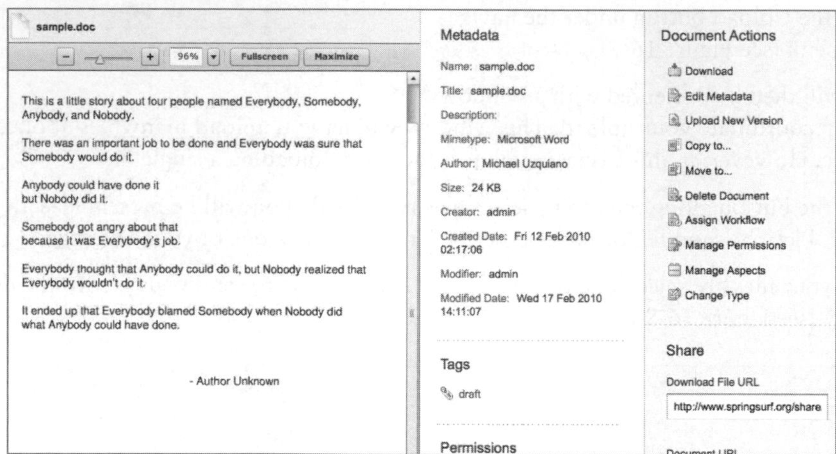

FIGURE 16-10

Notice that the document was automatically marked with the `kb:article` aspect. Why? Because you uploaded it into the Knowledge Base! You defined a rule for the Knowledge Base (the first of three) that automatically marked any content placed into it with the `kb:article` aspect.

Pretty cool. You may also notice that content has also been tagged with the Alfresco Tagging service. It has tags that show up in the metadata viewer. This is because of the server-side JavaScript file that you uploaded in Chapter 14. The rule triggered and kicked off this script for you!

Editing the Document Metadata Using a Form

Along the right-hand side of the page, you will see a list of actions you can perform against this document (appropriately shown in a section titled Document Actions).

1. Click the Edit Metadata link to bring up a form that will let you edit the metadata for your content object (see Figure 16-11).

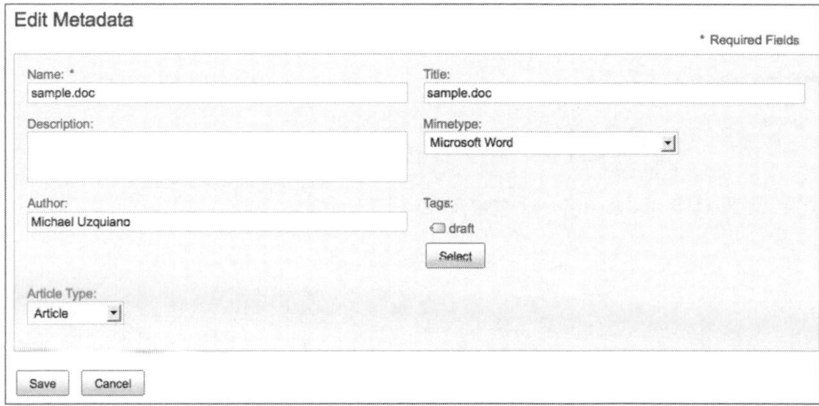

FIGURE 16-11

This metadata editor appears and uses the Forms configuration that you provided for Alfresco Share. The form displayed uses the template and settings that you provided for the edit-form portion of your configuration block.

2. If you wish to make a change, go ahead and then click Save. The Forms engine will map your values back onto the object and save it.

   Notice that the form does not display the `kb:status` field. You specifically indicated in your form configuration that you didn't want this field to be shown for the edit-form. That way, editors can't change the article's lifecycle without first having it pass through a formal approval process.

Requesting Approval for Your Document

When you added the Knowledge Base article, it was automatically assigned a lifecycle state of *Draft* as per the rules on your Knowledge Base space. In order to approve this Knowledge Base article, you need to have it participate in a workflow process and be formally approved.

The workflow process that you bootstrapped into the repository will do this for you. All you need to do is assign the Knowledge Base article to the workflow and let the workflow engine take over. It will pass the article to someone for approval. If they approve it, the article will have its lifecycle state switched to *Current*.

When the article's lifecycle state switches to Current, it will have its `kb:status` field updated. This update will trigger the rules on your Knowledge Base space to automatically invoke the Tagging Service. Rules help to keep your Knowledge Base nice and consistent.

Therefore, submit your Knowledge Base article for approval. You'll do this by assigning a workflow to it. Along the right-hand side of the page, you'll see another action titled Assign Workflow. You can use this action to launch a workflow for this document.

1. Click the Assign Workflow link to bring up the workflow assignment window. It appears much like Figure 16-12.

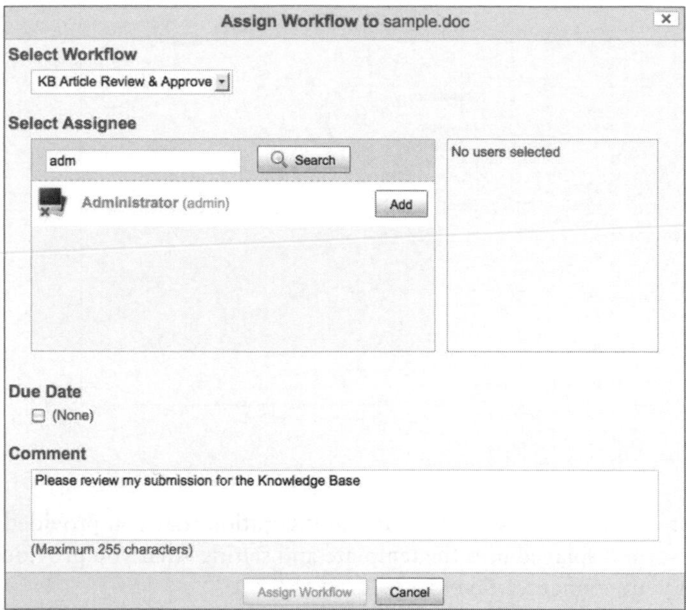

FIGURE 16-12

Your custom workflow is available as one of the options you can select under Select Workflow. It is titled KB Article Review & Approve. This is the workflow process definition that you bootstrapped into your Alfresco repository. You then configured it to appear as an available option for Alfresco Share.

2. Select the KB Article Review & Approve workflow.

   You then need to assign someone to act as the approver of the workflow. You should simply assign yourself (Administrator) for the purposes of this example. As shown in Figure 16-12, the Administrator user was assigned as the recipient of the workflow.

   The KB Article Review & Approve workflow is a simple example that allows you to pick who you wish to have approve the Knowledge Base article. In practice, you would constrain this set to one or more in a group of knowledge experts.

3. Fill in a comment for the workflow. If a comment is not provided, the workflow cannot be assigned. Any comment will do!

4. Click Assign Workflow to assign the workflow to the document. This formally puts into motion the request for your Knowledge Base article to be approved.

After you click on Assign Workflow, you will be taken back to the metadata view of the Knowledge Base article. If you refresh the page, you'll notice that the article's tags have already been updated. It used to have a Draft tag and now it has Pending Approval.

Approving the Document

Wouldn't it be a wonderful thing if you could approve all of your own requests? Imagine the efficiency gains you would achieve in expense reports alone! Well, for the purposes of this chapter, you'll do exactly that. You'll approve your own Knowledge Base article.

1. Click the My Dashboard link at the top of the page. This will take you back to your user dashboard.

   You will see a dashlet on your user dashboard called My Tasks. By default it is positioned along the right-hand side below the Sites dashlet. This dashlet shows you all of the tasks that have landed in your to-do list. This includes in-flight workflows. The dashlet will appear much like you see in Figure 16-13.

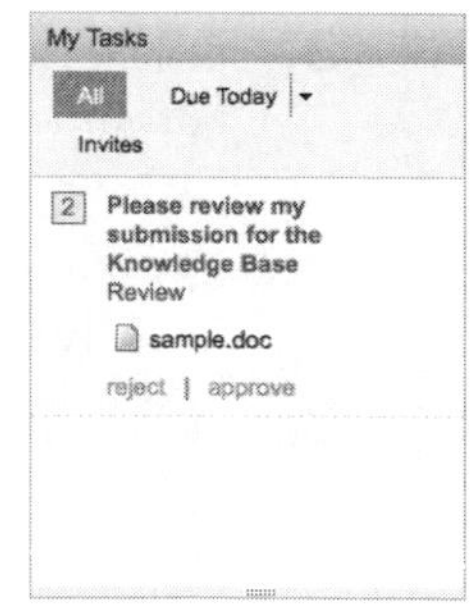

FIGURE 16-13

2. In My Tasks, click on Approve to approve the Knowledge Base article. The dashlet will refresh and indicate that your workflow has successfully approved the Knowledge Base article.

3. Click on Task Done to complete the task.

4. Click on My Second Project in the My Sites dashlet (see Figure 16-6) to verify that the Knowledge Base article has successfully transitioned out of Pending Approval and into the Current lifecycle state.

   Notice that the Knowledge Base dashlet you built in Chapter 15 now reflects that your site's Knowledge Base has one article and that this article is in the Approved state (see Figure 16-14).

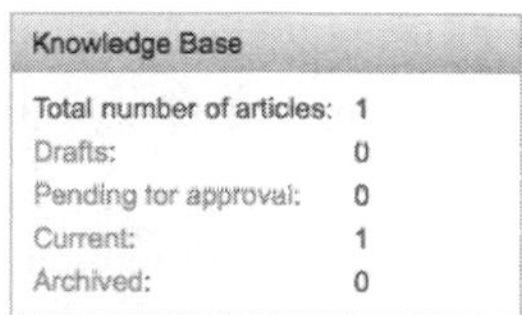

FIGURE 16-14

Archiving the Document

The last thing you need to do is to try out your custom Archive action. You configured Alfresco Share to provide an Archive action for documents. You should now be able to trigger this action and archive your document.

Archiving allows you to complete the content lifecycle for documents. Documents that are Current will eventually need to be replaced as new information or better content becomes available. You will want to archive your Current documents prior to replacing them so that they are backed up. At some point in the future, when you're sure that you won't need these documents any more, you may choose to delete them.

Please perform the following:

1. Click on the Document Library page in the navigation menu. This will take you into the document library for the site.

2. Click on the Knowledge Base folder. This will take you into the Knowledge Base space.

If the Knowledge Base folder doesn't appear, try clicking the Show Folders button.

From the document list, you will see a list of action commands along the right side, with three visible choices: Download, Edit Metadata, and Upload New Version.

3. Click the More . . . link to summon a drop-down list of additional available actions (see Figure 16-15).

   At the bottom, you will see your Archive action.

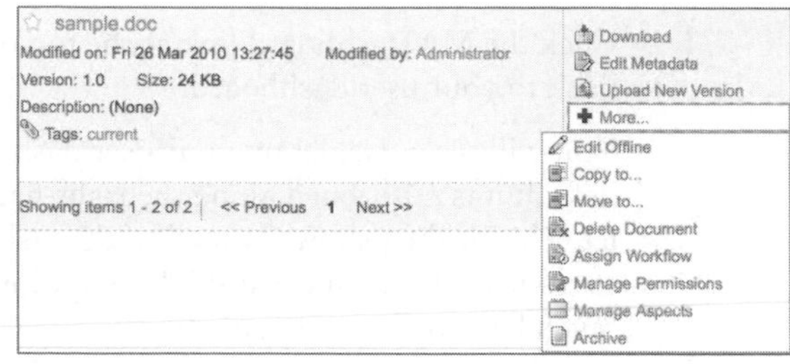

FIGURE 16-15

4. Click the Archive action to archive the document. Doing so will invoke your browser-side JavaScript function that makes a proxy request back to the Alfresco Share server. Alfresco Share will then invoke the appropriate HTTP POST handler on the document library services in the Alfresco repository.

   You added the custom HTTP POST handler as part of your customization to the document library services. This handler will set the `kb:status` property of your document to the value Archived. It will also save the document.

   Once the document is saved, the second of your three rules on the document library space will trigger. It will trigger because the Update event of the document will have been raised because the document was saved. The rule executes and the document is moved to the Archived folder.

5. Click on the Knowledge Base page in the navigation menu to see your article in the Custom Site Page that you built in Chapter 15 (see Figure 16-16).

Congratulations! You have completed the sample application.

Draft articles

KBID	Name	Modifed by	Modified

Articles pending for approval

KBID	Name	Modifed by	Modified

Current articles

KBID	Name	Modifed by	Modified	Actions

Archived articles

KBID	Name	Modifed by	Modified
798	sample.doc	Administrator	2010-03-26T13:31:23.434-05:00

FIGURE 16-16

SAMPLE CODE

This chapter's sample code is provided in this section. This code is also available from `www.wrox.com`.

Alfresco Repository

The following describes configuration of the Alfresco repository.

Custom Workflow

The following files should be placed into this directory:

<*installLocation*>\tomcat\shared\classes\alfresco\extension

Defines a custom Knowledge Base – article approval workflow

```
<?xml version="1.0" encoding="UTF-8"?>
<process-definition xmlns="urn:jbpm.org:jpdl-3.1" name="wf:articleapproval">

   <swimlane name="initiator" />

   <start-state name="start">
      <task name="wf:submitReviewTask" swimlane="initiator" />
         <event type="node-leave">

            <!-- Call script once the package exists i.e. on node-leave -->
            <action class="org.alfresco.repo.workflow.jbpm.AlfrescoJavaScript">

               <!-- Check you have a document attached to the package -->
               <!-- Apply the KB Aspect (kb:status) if not set already. -->
               <!-- Note: The default kb:status property is draft -->
                  <script>
                var l = bpm_package.children.length;
                if (l > 0)
                {
                          for (var i = 0, child = null; l > i; i++)
                          {
                            child = bpm_package.children[i];
                      if (!child.hasAspect("kb:status"))
                      {
                         child.addAspect("kb:status");
                         child.save();
                      }
                          }
                }
                else
                {
                   if (logger.isLoggingEnabled())
                   {
                      logger.log("Error: Package has no content. Length: " +
                         bpm_package.children.length + " Package: " + bpm_package);
                   }
                }
                </script>
            </action>
         </event>
      <transition name="" to="review" />
   </start-state>

   <swimlane name="reviewer">
       <assignment actor-id="#{bpm_assignee.properties['cm:userName']}" />
   </swimlane>
```

```
<task-node name="review">
   <!-- Update the status to In Review when you enter this task -->
   <event type="node-enter">
      <action class="org.alfresco.repo.workflow.jbpm.AlfrescoJavaScript">
         <script>
            for (var i = 0, child = null,
                 l = bpm_package.children.length; l > i; i++)
            {
               child = bpm_package.children[i];
               child.properties["kb:status"] = "Pending Approval";
               child.save();
            }
         </script>
      </action>
   </event>

   <task name="wf:reviewTask" swimlane="reviewer">
      <event type="task-create">
         <script>
            if (bpm_workflowDueDate != void)
            {
               taskInstance.dueDate = bpm_workflowDueDate;
            }
            if (bpm_workflowPriority != void)
            {
               taskInstance.priority = bpm_workflowPriority;
            }
          </script>
       </event>
   </task>
   <transition name="reject" to="rejected" />
   <transition name="approve" to="approved"/>
</task-node>

<task-node name="rejected">
   <!-- Update the status to Draft when you enter this task -->
   <event type="node-enter">
      <action class="org.alfresco.repo.workflow.jbpm.AlfrescoJavaScript">
         <script>
            for (var i = 0, child = null,
                 l = bpm_package.children.length; l > i; i++)
            {
               child = bpm_package.children[i];
               child.properties["kb:status"] = "Draft";
               child.save();
            }
         </script>
      </action>
   </event>
   <task name="wf:rejectedTask" swimlane="initiator" />
   <transition name="" to="end" />
</task-node>

<task-node name="approved">
```

```
    <!-- Update the status to Approved when you enter this task -->
    <event type="node-enter">
       <action class="org.alfresco.repo.workflow.jbpm.AlfrescoJavaScript">
          <script>
             for (var i = 0, child = null,
                  l = bpm_package.children.length; l > i; i++)
             {
                child = bpm_package.children[i];
                child.properies["kb:status"] = "Current";
                child.save();
             }
          </script>
       </action>
    </event>

    <task name="wf:approvedTask" swimlane="initiator" />
    <transition name="" to="end" />
 </task-node>

 <end-state name="end" />

 <event type="process-end">
    <!-- Update the status to Approved when you enter this task -->
    <action class="org.alfresco.repo.workflow.jbpm.AlfrescoJavaScript">
       <script>
          if (cancelled)
          {
             for (var i = 0, child = null,
                  l = bpm_package.children.length; l > i; i++)
             {
                child = bpm_package.children[i];
                if (child.hasAspect("kb:status"))
                {
                   child.properties["kb:status"] = "Draft";
                   child.save();
                }
                if (logger.isLoggingEnabled())
                {
                   logger.log("Workflow cancelled, status reset to Draft");
                }
             }
          }
          if (logger.isLoggingEnabled())
          {
             logger.log("Workflow completed");
          }
       </script>
    </action>
 </event>

</process-definition>
```

Code snippet extension\kb-approval-process-definition.xml

Available for download on Wrox.com

Bootstraps the custom workflow into the Alfresco repository

```
<?xml version='1.0' encoding='UTF-8'?>
<!DOCTYPE beans PUBLIC '-//SPRING//DTD BEAN//EN'
   'http://www.springframework.org/dtd/spring-beans.dtd'>
<beans>

   <bean id="parallel.workflowBootstrap" parent="workflowDeployer">
      <property name="workflowDefinitions">
         <list>
            <props>
               <prop key="engineId">jbpm</prop>
               <prop key="location">
                  alfresco/extension/kb-approval-process-definition.xml
               </prop>
               <prop key="mimetype">text/xml</prop>
               <prop key="redeploy">false</prop>
            </props>
         </list>
      </property>
   </bean>

</beans>
```

Code snippet extension\kb-workflow-context.xml

Archive Web Script (POST Handler)

The following files should be placed into this directory:

> <*installLocation*>\tomcat\shared\classes\alfresco\extension\templates\webscripts\org\alfresco\slingshot\documentlibrary\action

Available for download on Wrox.com

Defines the POST action handler Web script for the document library services

```
<webscript>
   <shortname>Archive</shortname>
   <description>
      Document List Action - Archive Knowledge Base articles
   </description>
   <url>/slingshot/doclib/action/archive/site/{site}/{container}</url>
   <format default="json">argument</format>
   <authentication>user</authentication>
   <transaction>required</transaction>
</webscript>
```

Code snippet extension\templates\webscripts\org\alfresco\slingshot\documentlibrary\action\archive.post.desc.xml

Available for download on Wrox.com

Scriptable controller for the POST action handler Web script

```
<import resource="classpath:/alfresco/templates/webscripts/org/alfresco/slingshot \
                  /documentlibrary/action/action.lib.js">

/**
 * Archive multiple files action
 * @method POST
 */

/**
 * Entrypoint required by action.lib.js
 *
 * @method runAction
 * @param p_params {object} Object literal containing files array
 * @return {object|null} object representation of action results
 */
function runAction(p_params)
{
   var results = [];
   var files = p_params.files;
   var file, fileNode, result, nodeRef;

   // Must have array of files
   if (!files || files.length == 0)
   {
      status.setCode(status.STATUS_BAD_REQUEST, "No files.");
      return;
   }

   for (file in files)
   {
      nodeRef = files[file];
      result =
      {
         nodeRef: nodeRef,
         action: "archiveFile",
         success: false
      }

      try
      {
         fileNode = search.findNode(nodeRef);
         if (fileNode === null)
         {
            result.id = file;
            result.nodeRef = nodeRef;
            result.success = false;
         }
         else
         {
            if (fileNode.properties["kb:status"] != "Current")
            {
```

```
               // Only knowledge base articles with staus "Current" may be archived
               status.setCode(status.STATUS_BAD_REQUEST, "No Current");
               return;
            }
            else
            {
               result.id = fileNode.name;
               result.type = fileNode.isContainer ? "folder" : "document";
               result.nodeRef = nodeRef;

               // set the kb:status property to "Archived"
               fileNode.properties["kb:status"] = "Archived";
               fileNode.save();

               result.success = (result.nodeRef !== null);
            }
         }
      }
      catch (e)
      {
         result.id = file;
         result.nodeRef = nodeRef;
         result.success = false;
      }

      results.push(result);
   }

   return results;
}

/* Bootstrap action script */
main();
```

Code snippet extension\templates\webscripts\org\alfresco\slingshot\documentlibrary\action\archive.post.json.js

Available for download on Wrox.com

Template view for the POST action handler Web script

```
<#import "action.lib.ftl" as actionLib />
<@actionLib.resultsJSON results=results />
```

Code snippet extension\templates\webscripts\org\alfresco\slingshot\documentlibrary\action\archive.post.json.ftl

Document Library Services

This file should be placed in the following location:

<installLocation>\tomcat\shared\classes\alfresco\extension\templates\webscripts\org\alfresco\slingshot\documentlibrary

Available for download on Wrox.com

Defines the availability of aspects within the document library

```
<aspects>
 <visible>
  <aspect name="{http://www.alfresco.org/model/content/1.0}generalclassifiable" />
  <aspect name="{http://www.alfresco.org/model/content/1.0}complianceable" />
  <aspect name="{http://www.alfresco.org/model/content/1.0}dublincore" />
  <aspect name="{http://www.alfresco.org/model/content/1.0}effectivity" />
  <aspect name="{http://www.alfresco.org/model/content/1.0}summarizable" />
  <aspect name="{http://www.alfresco.org/model/content/1.0}versionable" />
  <aspect name="{http://www.alfresco.org/model/content/1.0}templatable" />
  <aspect name="{http://www.alfresco.org/model/content/1.0}emailed" />
  <aspect name="{http://www.alfresco.org/model/emailserver/1.0}aliasable" />
  <aspect name="{http://www.alfresco.org/model/content/1.0}taggable" />
  <aspect name="{http://www.alfresco.org/model/knowledgebase/1.0}article" />
 </visible>

 <!-- Aspects that a user can add. Same as "visible" if left empty -->
 <addable>
 </addable>

 <!-- Aspects that a user can remove. Same as "visible" if left empty -->
 <removeable>
 </removeable>
</aspects>
```

Code snippet extension\templates\webscripts\org\alfresco\slingshot\documentlibrary\aspects.get.config.xml

Alfresco Share

The following describes configuration of Alfresco Share.

Configuration Files

The following file should be placed in this location:

> *<installLocation>*\tomcat\shared\classes\web-extension

Available for download on Wrox.com

Custom Alfresco Share configuration file

```
<alfresco-config>
   <!-- Put Share Client in debug mode -->
   <!--
      <config replace="true">
         <flags>
            <client-debug>true</client-debug>
            <client-debug-autologging>true</client-debug-autologging>
         </flags>
```

```
   </config>
-->

<!-- Add a custom page type -->
<config evaluator="string-compare" condition="SitePages" replace="true">
   <pages>
      <page id="calendar">calendar</page>
      <page id="wiki-page">wiki-page?title=Main_Page</page>
      <page id="documentlibrary">documentlibrary</page>
      <page id="discussions-topiclist">discussions-topiclist</page>
      <page id="blog-postlist">blog-postlist</page>
      <page id="links">links</page>
      <page id="tasks">tasks</page>
      <page id="knowledgebase">knowledgebase</page>
   </pages>
</config>

<!-- Specify another theme as the default theme -->
<config evaluator="string-compare" condition="WebFramework">
   <web-framework>
      <application-defaults>
         <theme>default</theme>
      </application-defaults>
   </web-framework>
</config>

<!-- Form definition for cm:content -->
<config evaluator="node-type" condition="cm:content">
   <forms>
      <form>

         <!-- 2 column template -->
         <edit-form template="/2-column-edit-form.ftl" />

         <field-visibility>

            <show id="sys:node-dbid" for-mode="view" />

            <show id="kb:articletype" />

            <show id="kb:status" for-mode="view" />

         </field-visibility>

         <appearance>
            <field id="sys:node-dbid" label="KBID"
                   description="Knowledge Base ID" />
            <field id="kb:articletype" label="Article Type"
                   description="Knowledge Base Article Type" />
            <field id="kb:status" label="Status"
                   description="Approval Status" />
         </appearance>
```

```
            </form>
        </forms>
    </config>

</alfresco-config>
```

Code snippet web-extension\share-config-custom.xml

Form Template

The following file should be placed in this location:

<installLocation>\tomcat\shared\classes\web-extension\site-webscripts

Available for download on Wrox.com

A two-column edit-form for metadata in Alfresco Share

```
<#import "/org/alfresco/components/form/form.lib.ftl" as formLib />

<#if error?exists>
   <div class="error">${error}</div>
<#elseif form?exists>

   <#assign formId=args.htmlid + "-form">
   <#assign formUI><#if args.formUI??>${args.formUI}<#else>true</#if></#assign>

   <#if formUI == "true">
      <@formLib.renderFormsRuntime formId=formId />
   </#if>

   <div id="${formId}-container" class="form-container">

      <#if form.showCaption?exists && form.showCaption>
         <div id="${formId}-caption" class="caption">
         <span class="mandatory-indicator">*</span>
         ${msg("form.required.fields")}</div>
      </#if>

      <#if form.mode != "view">
         <form id="${formId}" method="${form.method}" accept-charset=
         "utf-8" enctype="${form.enctype}" action="${form.submissionUrl}">
      </#if>

      <div id="${formId}-fields" class="form-fields">
        <#list form.structure as item>
            <#if item.kind == "set">
               <@renderSetWithColumns set=item />
            <#else>
               <@formLib.renderField field=form.fields[item.id] />
            </#if>
         </#list>
      </div>
```

```
         <#if form.mode != "view">
            <@formLib.renderFormButtons formId=formId />
            </form>
         </#if>

      </div>
   </#if>

   <#macro renderSetWithColumns set>
      <#if set.appearance?exists>
         <#if set.appearance == "fieldset">
            <fieldset><legend>${set.label}</legend>
         <#elseif set.appearance == "panel">
            <div class="form-panel">
               <div class="form-panel-heading">${set.label}</div>
               <div class="form-panel-body">
         </#if>
      </#if>

      <#list set.children as item>
         <#if item.kind == "set">
            <@renderSetWithColumns set=item />
         <#else>
            <#if (item_index % 2) == 0>
            <div class="yui-g"><div class="yui-u first">
            <#else>
            <div class="yui-u">
            </#if>
            <@formLib.renderField field=form.fields[item.id] />
            </div>
            <#if ((item_index % 2) != 0) || !item_has_next></div></#if>
         </#if>
      </#list>

      <#if set.appearance?exists>
         <#if set.appearance == "fieldset">
            </fieldset>
         <#elseif set.appearance == "panel">
               </div>
            </div>
         </#if>
      </#if>
   </#macro>
```

Code snippet web-extension\site-webscripts\2-column-edit-form.ftl

Document Library – HEAD Override

The following file should be placed in this location:

> <*installLocation*>\tomcat\shared\classes\web-extension\site-webscripts\org\alfresco\components\documentlibrary

Available for download on Wrox.com

Customization that includes additional JS reference

```
<#include "../component.head.inc">

<!-- Actions -->
<@script type="text/javascript" src="${page.url.context}/components/
documentlibrary/actions.js"></@script>

<!-- Simple Dialog -->
<@script type="text/javascript" src="${page.url.context}/
modules/simple-dialog.js"></@script>

<!-- Copy-To -->
<@link rel="stylesheet" type="text/css" href="${page.url.context}/
modules/documentlibrary/copy-to.css" />
<@script type="text/javascript" src="${page.url.context}/
modules/documentlibrary/copy-to.js"></@script>

<!-- Move-To -->
<@link rel="stylesheet" type="text/css" href="${page.url.context}/
modules/documentlibrary/move-to.css" />
<@script type="text/javascript" src="${page.url.context}/
modules/documentlibrary/move-to.js"></@script>

<!-- Details -->
<@link rel="stylesheet" type="text/css" href="${page.url.context}/
modules/documentlibrary/details.css" />
<@script type="text/javascript" src="${page.url.context}/
modules/documentlibrary/details.js"></@script>

<!-- Tag Library -->
<@link rel="stylesheet" type="text/css" href="${page.url.context}/
modules/taglibrary/taglibrary.css" />
<@script type="text/javascript" src="${page.url.context}/
modules/taglibrary/taglibrary.js"></@script>

<!-- Assign Workflow -->
<@link rel="stylesheet" type="text/css" href="${page.url.context}/
modules/documentlibrary/workflow.css" />
<@script type="text/javascript" src="${page.url.context}/
modules/documentlibrary/workflow.js"></@script>

<!-- People Finder Assets (req'd by Assign Workflow)  -->
<@link rel="stylesheet" type="text/css" href="${page.url.context}/
components/people-finder/people-finder.css" />
<@script type="text/javascript" src="${page.url.context}/
components/people-finder/people-finder.js"></@script>

<!-- Manage Permissions -->
<@link rel="stylesheet" type="text/css" href="${page.url.context}/
modules/documentlibrary/permissions.css" />
<@script type="text/javascript" src="${page.url.context}/
modules/documentlibrary/permissions.js"></@script>
```

```
<!-- Manage Aspects -->
<@link rel="stylesheet" type="text/css" href="${page.url.context}/
modules/documentlibrary/aspects.css" />
<@script type="text/javascript" src="${page.url.context}/
modules/documentlibrary/aspects.js"></@script>

<!-- KB Archive Action -->
<script type="text/javascript" src="${page.url.context}-extension/
components/documentlibrary/knowledgebase-actions.js"></script>
```

Code snippet web-extension\site-webscripts\org\alfresco\components\documentlibrary\actions-common.get.head.ftl

Document Library – Action List

This file should be placed in the following location:

> *<installLocation>*\tomcat\shared\classes\web-extension\site-webscripts\org\alfresco\components\documentlibrary

Includes additional archive action for documents

```
<documentList>

   <actionSets>

      <actionSet id="empty"></actionSet>

      <actionSet id="document">
         <action id="onActionDownload" type="simple-link"
                 href="{downloadUrl}" label="actions.document.download" />
         <action id="onActionDetails" type="action-link" permission="edit"
                 label="actions.document.edit-metadata" />
         <action id="onActionUploadNewVersion" type="action-link"
                 label="actions.document.upload-new-version" />
         <action id="onActionEditOnline" type="action-link"
                 permission="edit,online-edit"
                 label="actions.document.edit-online" />
         <action id="onActionEditOffline" type="action-link"
                 permission="edit" label="actions.document.edit-offline" />
         <action id="onActionCopyTo" type="action-link"
                 label="actions.document.copy-to" />
         <action id="onActionMoveTo" type="action-link" permission="delete"
                 label="actions.document.move-to" />
         <action id="onActionDelete" type="action-link" permission="delete"
                 label="actions.document.delete" />
         <action id="onActionAssignWorkflow" type="action-link"
                 label="actions.document.assign-workflow" />
         <action id="onActionManagePermissions" type="action-link"
                 permission="permissions"
                 label="actions.document.manage-permissions" />
         <action id="onActionManageAspects" type="action-link" permission="edit"
```

```
                label="actions.document.manage-aspects" />
            <action id="onActionArchive" type="action-link" permission=""
                label="actions.document.archive" />
        </actionSet>

        <actionSet id="locked">
            <action id="onActionDownload" href="{downloadUrl}" type="simple-link"
                label="actions.document.download" />
        </actionSet>

        <actionSet id="lockOwner">
            <action id="onActionDownload" href="{downloadUrl}" type="simple-link"
                label="actions.document.download-original" />
        </actionSet>

        <actionSet id="workingCopyOwner">
            <action id="onActionUploadNewVersion" type="action-link"
                label="actions.document.upload-new-version" />
            <action id="onActionDownload" href="{downloadUrl}" type="simple-link"
                label="actions.document.download-again" />
            <action id="onActionCancelEditing" type="action-link"
                label="actions.document.cancel-editing" />
        </actionSet>

        <actionSet id="folder">
            <action id="onActionDetails" permission="edit" type="action-link"
                label="actions.folder.edit-metadata" />
            <action id="onActionMetadata" type="simple-link" href="{folderDetailsUrl}"
                label="actions.folder.view-metadata" />
            <action id="onActionCopyTo" type="action-link"
                label="actions.folder.copy-to" />
            <action id="onActionMoveTo" permission="delete" type="action-link"
                label="actions.folder.move-to" />
            <action id="onActionDelete" permission="delete" type="action-link"
                label="actions.folder.delete" />
            <action id="onActionManagePermissions" permission="permissions"
                type="action-link" label="actions.folder.manage-permissions" />
            <action id="onActionManageAspects" type="action-link" permission="edit"
                label="actions.folder.manage-aspects" />
        </actionSet>

        <actionSet id="link">
            <action id="onActionDelete" permission="delete" type="action-link"
                label="actions.link.delete" />
        </actionSet>

    </actionSets>

</documentList>
```

Code snippet web-extension\site-webscripts\org\alfresco\components\documentlibrary\documentlist.get.config.xml

Workflow

The following file should be placed in this location:

> *<installLocation>*\tomcat\shared\classes\web-extension\site-webscripts\org\alfresco \modules\documentlibrary

Available for download on Wrox.com

Includes additional reference to custom workflow

```
<#assign el=args.htmlid>
<script type="text/javascript">//<![CDATA[
 Alfresco.util.ComponentManager.get("${el}").setMessages(${messages});
//]]></script>
<div id="${el}-dialog" class="workflow">
<div id="${el}-title" class="hd"></div>
<div class="bd">
<form id="${el}-form" action="" method="post">
<input type="hidden" name="date" id="${el}-date" value="" />
<div class="yui-g">
<h2>${msg("header.type")}</h2>
</div>
<div class="field">
<select id="${el}-type" name="type" tabindex="0">
<option value="wf:review" selected="selected">Review &amp; Approve</option>
<option value="wf:articleapproval">KB Article Review &amp; Approve</option>
<option value="wf:adhoc">Adhoc Task</option>
</select>
</div>
<div class="yui-g">
<h2>${msg("header.people")}</h2>
</div>
<div class="yui-ge field">
<div class="yui-u first">
<div id="${el}-peoplefinder"></div>
</div>
<div class="yui-u">
<div id="${el}-peopleselected" class="people-selected"></div>
</div>
</div>
<div class="yui-g">
<h2>${msg("header.date")}</h2>
</div>
<div class="field">
<input id="${el}-dueDate-checkbox" name="-" type="checkbox" value=
"${msg("label.due-date.none")}" tabindex="0"/> 
<span id="${el}-dueDate"><label for="${el}-dueDate-checkbox">
${msg("label.due-date.none")}</label></span>
</div>
<div id="${el}-calendarOverlay" class="calendar-overlay">
<div class="bd">
<div id="${el}-calendar" class="calendar"></div>
</div>
</div>
```

```
<div class="yui-g">
<h2>${msg("header.comment")}</h2>
</div>
<div class="field">
<textarea id="${el}-comment" name="description" rows="3" tabindex="0"></textarea>
<span>${msg("label.comment.max-length")}</span>
</div>
<div class="bdft">
<input type="button" id="${el}-ok" value="${msg("button.assign")}" tabindex="0" />
<input type="button" id="${el}-cancel" value=
"${msg("button.cancel")}" tabindex="0" />
</div>
</form>
</div>
</div>
```

Code snippet web-extension\site-webscripts\org\alfresco\modules\documentlibrary\workflow.get.html.ftl

Tomcat ROOT Web Application Files

The following files are used by the customizations provided in this chapter. They are not part of the core Alfresco Share Web application. Rather than modify the Alfresco Share Web application itself, we elected to copy them into a separate ROOT Web application in Tomcat.

Document Library – Browser Dependencies

The following files should be copied into your Tomcat ROOT Web application at the following location:

<*installLocation*>\tomcat\webapps\ROOT\share-extension\components\documentlibrary

Available for download on Wrox.com

Defines a browser-side event handler for the Archive action in Alfresco Share

```
/**
 * DocumentList "Archive" action
 *
 * @namespace Alfresco
 * @class Alfresco.DocumentList
 */
(function()
{
 /**
* Backup single document.
*
* @method onActionBackup
* @param file {object} Object literal representing one or more file(s) or
  folder(s) to be actioned
*/
```

```
 Alfresco.doclib.Actions.prototype.onActionArchive =
 function DL_onActionArchive(file)
 {
this.modules.actions.genericAction(
{
 success:
 {
event:
{
 name: "metadataRefresh"
},
message: this.msg("message.archive.success", file.displayName)
 },
 failure:
 {
message: this.msg("message.archive.failure", file.displayName)
 },
 webscript:
 {
name: "archive/site/{site}/{container}",
method: Alfresco.util.Ajax.POST
 },
 params:
 {
site: this.options.siteId,
container: this.options.containerId
 },
 config:
 {
requestContentType: Alfresco.util.Ajax.JSON,
dataObj:
{
 nodeRefs: [file.nodeRef]
}
 }
});
 };
})();
```

Code snippet ROOT\share-extension\components\documentlibrary\knowledgebase-actions.js

Available for download on Wrox.com

Includes additional custom CSS used by the document library

```
.doclist .onActionArchive a
{
 background-image: url(images/kbarchive-16.png);
}
```

Code snippet ROOT\share-extension\components\documentlibrary\knowledgebase-documentlist.css

17

Integrating with Other Applications

WHAT'S IN THIS CHAPTER?

- Understanding why applications use content management over a file system or database
- Examining options for integrating Alfresco with your application
- Investigating patterns of integrating content management into an application
- Integrating with Alfresco

The Alfresco system is both an application and a platform to build content applications or provide content capabilities to other applications. As an application, it can become a component of a much larger application or even become a framework for new applications. With Alfresco Share, you have seen how you can use and extend Share to create collaborative applications. Much of the work of creating menus, pages, and layout are already done and adding your components can become a matter of configuration.

However, just like database management systems and their use in many different types of applications for managing and manipulating data, a content management system like Alfresco can provide powerful application features for various applications and Web sites that would otherwise need to be built from scratch. Some examples of capabilities that can be added to otherwise–non-content applications include:

- **Presenting relevant content and images** — An application that is just data or short strings can potentially be deadly dull. You can enhance data with explanatory text or images that provide context. Data enhanced with analysis in the form of content becomes a much more useful business tool.
- **Adding collaboration** — Even a very data-intensive application can benefit from providing users the ability to discuss and resolve issues around data in a collaborative environment.

By providing social capabilities around the data, such as blogs, users can provide updates and news around changes in data, and allow others to track these changes through news feeds.

- **Archiving reports and data** — Enterprise Resource Planning (ERP) and Customer Relationship Management (CRM) systems like SAP and Oracle Applications have included integrations with Enterprise Content Management (ECM) systems for many years to archive reports and audit trails.
- **Content for portals** — A portal without content, news, and information may still be an important source of data and reports; however, without content, a portal can be an uninteresting destination and can cause users to miss out on some important information. This is why you rarely see a portal without some sort of content management. Many portals may include a basic content management capability, but these often lack some of even the most basic capabilities of a purpose-built content management system.
- **Document-enabling a Web site** — Documents, such as reports, plans, and policies, can enhance a Web site and the services it provides its users. Integrating browsing and search capabilities similar to those of Alfresco Share can allow users to access information that may not be easily presented in a purely HTML format.
- **Document scanning** — Some applications, such as legal and accounting applications, require the capture of paper documents that may be related to the data in the system. Some examples include contracts, receipts, invoices, and purchase orders that are the source for the numbers in the system and may be required for auditing purposes.
- **Publishing and reports** — Some applications may generate documents as part of their functionality, such as generating contracts or financial reports. The application may have the data, but managing the descriptive content and images that are part of these documents may require more effort than the core data functionality of the application.
- **Microsoft Office integration** — Generating and then managing office documents, such as spreadsheets and Word reports, can be much easier if these are integrated with Microsoft Office. More importantly, if a user needs to change the default output, managing the document after it has been generated can be done much more easily through a content management system than on a file system that may not have security and version controls in place.
- **Social networking applications** — You are likely familiar with the pictures and micro-blogs of social networking systems like Facebook, but documents and other content, such as more elaborate blogs, can be a useful and compelling point of discussion and social networking. Your site or internal social network can provide content, such as resumes or even presentations, as in the Web 2.0 sites SlideShare (`www.slideshare.com`) and Scribd (`www.scribd.com`), along with collaboration and social tagging.

WHY INTEGRATE CONTENT MANAGEMENT INTO APPLICATIONS?

Patterns of integrating content management systems have developed over the last 20 years based upon requirements of enterprise systems and applications to use, capture, and manage content. Generally, these have only been used in high-value applications where the investment in the application could justify the cost and complexity of integrating an ECM system, such as integrations with ERP systems. Often, smaller and lower-value applications built these patterns as an extension of the application, using a database system and file system for storing the content.

With the emergence of open source and both the commoditization and standardization of content management, applications and sophisticated Web sites no longer need to add this functionality themselves, but can use the capabilities of content management systems. Alfresco provides the following capabilities:

- Capture content as the output of an application or transactional information that results from the application for retention, archival, and future use. This includes managing the lifecycle of this content as well as providing the process to turn this content into an official record.
- Search and retrieve application-specific and contextually relevant content based upon metadata, categories, or full text within content in order to provide the application with content that can assist the user in their task or to provide context that may not be easily encoded in the application.
- Organize, categorize, and browse application content, such as instructions, notes, shared tips, diagrams, photos, or maps, using a clear hierarchy of information, a standardized categorization scheme, user-contributed tags, or all of the above.
- Generate context-specific lists and catalogs of content using sophisticated queries based upon metadata, category, or full-text content.
- View and access content in its original application or transform it into Web-friendly formats, such as Flash, HTML, or text. Provide previews and thumbnail images of content to allow the user to decide whether they want to download content before doing so.
- Control and version application-specific content along with workflow-based review and approval to ensure accuracy, currency, and timeliness of critical instructions, information, and updates.
- Compose and publish Web pages, documents, or articles that include images, diagrams, or other content. Manage the linkages, associations, and dependencies between content components.

Why Not Just Use a File System or a Database?

So why wouldn't you just implement this functionality in a relational database or store this content on a file system and use normal file system tools and file interfaces to manage this content? This is probably the approach that most applications have taken and most often the reason is cost. ECM systems can be extremely expensive. Some large commercial systems have even used source code–control systems to manage their content. Still, even if the cost were zero, either a file system or a database would be many developers' default choice for managing any information, including content.

There are many reasons for using a content management system rather than a database or file system. File systems are generally the most primitive and least controlled ways to handle content. There is usually no context or metadata other than the file's name, application type, and location in a folder hierarchy. This often leads to context being encoded in the folder name and hierarchy. Content in this structure is not queryable; thus, paths need to be hardcoded, even if they are relative paths. In addition, large amounts of content and large numbers of files become as unmanageable as any departmental shared drive. Normally, the only control over content is through permissions or a read-only bit. There is no review and approval of the content, no versioning, no recovery, and no guarantee that the content has not been tampered with. Such a foundation for content would never survive an audit and can irritate users even more than bugs in an application.

Relational databases provide an easy default choice for application developers, particularly since most applications already have a database. Binary large objects, or *blobs*, were introduced into relational databases to store content for applications. Treated like any other data, they use the same programming interfaces as the data in an application and they can take advantage of services provided by the database, such as backup and replication. However, since content is generally not a core competence of the database vendors, some of the trade-offs made for fast and general purpose handling of data have meant that databases are often not a good choice for managing content.

One of the primary reasons is the same as why many content systems have chosen not to store content in the database. Database caches are designed to handle small pages of data rather than large, unstructured streams of data that can quickly overwhelm database caches. Also, the clear separation between the database interface and where the blob is stored means that content must be copied to perform reads, writes, and selective writing into random accessed portions of the content. Due to how the blobs are stored in the database and the need to locate them near the other columns in the row, there are usually limitations on the size and number of the blobs in order to control effective use of storage and performance. These limitations have meant that content applications built upon a pure database interface tend to be less scalable and poorer-performing than content management systems, except where the content is smaller and usage is more constrained.

Scalability and size limitations ignore the additional domain model and logic that have been implemented on top of the relational systems by content management systems. Virtually every content management system is built upon a relational database to manage metadata and associations, although they tend to store the actual body of the content as files for performance. The domain model of Alfresco and other content management systems have pre-defined models of frequently used objects such as content types, content properties, folders, versions, and associations, as well as tools to extend these models with application-specific domain models that reuse core model definitions.

In addition, content management systems like Alfresco provide a number of services in managing, controlling, searching, and retrieving content beyond the simple insert, update, and delete functions of a database. Content management systems provide:

- Version control and locking
- Lifecycle and retention management
- Transformation
- Metadata extraction
- Hierarchical navigation
- Classification and tagging
- Query facilities that combine relational, full-text, and hierarchical searching
- Business process services for human-based review and approval

- Access to functions through file and mail services
- Audit trails and compliance checks
- Fine-grained permission controls

If any of these services is of use to the application or for the control and guarantees of the content used in an application, then these would have to be re-implemented on top of a relational database. In effect, these services are provided out of the box for an application to use and can use the same database as the application.

APPLICATION INTEGRATION OPTIONS

To support the previously mentioned use cases where applications need content services, Alfresco provides a number of different programmatic ways to access the content management capabilities of the system. In some cases, the application doesn't even need to be aware that it is accessing Alfresco. By supporting a number of standards-based protocols, applications and application development environments can use tools already available to it to access, update, and search content.

Although Alfresco is built using the Java programming language, the system can be used by most of the popular programming languages. Either through the direct embedding of the language environment, as you have already seen with JavaScript and FreeMarker, or through REST-based or SOAP-based protocols, many of the popular development languages can access Alfresco. Content Management Interoperability Services (CMIS) will probably broaden the number of languages significantly.

Some applications can integrate with Alfresco by using their normal means of accessing information without having to change at all. The file system emulation of Alfresco allows ordinary document production tools to access and store documents via their normal Open and Save dialogs. Mail-based systems can access Alfresco using widely adopted mail protocols. Feed readers can use the feed and search interfaces of Alfresco as a normal source of feeds. Automatic metadata extraction and folder-based rules can solve many of the problems of capturing metadata as content is entered into the system.

Alfresco enables you to use the tools that are easiest to get your application up and going as quickly as possible, where the repository takes care of handling metadata, workflow, lifecycles, location, and search access. The tool you use depends on the level of control your application needs over metadata, context, and business processes, as well as the tools your application or your development environment provide for handling content. The following sections offer some guidelines on how and where you might use these various integration points as part of your application.

CMIS

The OASIS Technical Committee developing the CMIS specification identified a set of use cases that CMIS would target. Aimed at avoiding scope creep and making it practical to get interoperability across a wide variety of systems, it nevertheless surfaces a wide range of capabilities in the Alfresco repository. Alfresco's support for CMIS has already been covered previously; however, using CMIS should be considered in general whenever your application needs programmatic access to the content repository. You should especially consider CMIS if you intend to port your application to other content management systems.

Web Scripts

There is a number of existing Web scripts, which have already been described, that provide a great deal of functionality in Alfresco. However, if you wish to perform an operation in Alfresco that is not covered by a Web script or you wish to perform several operations and minimize network communication, then you can create your own Web scripts. This can increase the performance of your application and push the logic down to the Alfresco repository, where it can be reused.

File-Based Access

If metadata is not important to your application or processing of content and metadata can be handled with rules and actions, then file-based access may be an easier route to integration with Alfresco. With the CIFS, WebDAV, NFS, and FTP file system emulation, storing and accessing content to and from Alfresco may already be supported by your application through standard file interfaces. Applications that create content can store content in Alfresco and it is now available for other applications and Web sites to access. Applications that access files through Open dialogs or through programmatic file interfaces can navigate folder hierarchies and the content seamlessly.

Although the content appears to be a file, the application is not directly accessing the content. Rather, it uses Alfresco APIs, so all the controls and services are in place. File access is simply an emulation of files and its access and storage would be no different than through APIs directly.

By storing content using file system emulation, logic for processing content (for example, archiving, applying workflows and retention policies, and extracting metadata) can be performed with rules. Applied at the folder or space level, these rules are initiated when the file is stored; therefore, the application integrating with Alfresco does not need to be modified to use Alfresco. All the business logic can be stored in the Alfresco repository.

OpenSearch and Feeds

Some applications, Web sites, and portals may use standard Web-based technology to access external information using feeds (such as RSS or Atom subscription protocols) or queries using OpenSearch. Alfresco provides out-of-the-box RSS feeds to observe the contents of an individual folder or space, as well as activities related to a user or Share site. The Alfresco system also implements OpenSearch, which is a standard query protocol supported by many Web sites, such as Yahoo!, Google, and Amazon.

If an application is designed to use either feeds or OpenSearch, then the application can access Alfresco using the feed or search address. The results return descriptive information about the content return and a URL pointing directly to the content.

If more specialized information is required or you would rather point to the properties page in Share or Explorer, then you can create new RSS feeds or OpenSearch APIs as fairly simple Web scripts. See the actual RSS feed and OpenSearch templates in the Data Dictionary as a reference for how to build your own.

Java Applications

If a repository is single-purpose and performance is most important, then you may want to access the Alfresco core API directly. This requires your application to reside on the same application server as the

Alfresco system. A Java application can access all the base APIs and Web scripts with minimal context switch.

PHP Applications

PHP applications can access Alfresco through CMIS, through Web scripts as a RESTful interface, or directly from the same application server as Alfresco. Alfresco has an optional extension that includes the Quercus PHP interpreter in a Tomcat server. The Quercus PHP interpreter is capable of running popular PHP applications, such as Joomla!, Drupal, WordPress, and MediaWiki. With the Quercus integration with Alfresco, these applications are capable of accessing the Alfresco system, as are other PHP applications. The most popular way of accessing Alfresco is remotely through CMIS.

.NET Applications

Integrating Alfresco applications with .NET applications is very similar to integrations with Java applications through remote interfaces such as Web scripts or CMIS. With Microsoft's support of CMIS in SharePoint, there will likely be more tools to support using CMIS to integrate other CMSs, such as Alfresco. Either the SOAP or Atom Publishing interfaces can be used. All patterns of integration can be supported.

Surf Components

Surf components are designed to work with other Web frameworks, such as Spring Webflow or Spring MVC. Surf components can save a lot of work in reimplementing user interface portions of your application or Web site if they replicate functionality that you were intending to build in a different Web framework, such as a browser or viewer.

Authentication and Directory Services

In order to interoperate between an application and Alfresco, it is important to consistently authenticate users to ensure secure access to either system. In addition, both systems need a consistent understanding of the identity of the user, so sharing a common directory service is also important. Alfresco synchronizes and uses standard LDAP and Active Directory services for authentication and directory services. The security systems are open as well to adapt to other systems. Alfresco also integrates with a few single sign-on technologies to provide a seamless navigation between Alfresco and another Web application.

PATTERNS OF CONTENT MANAGEMENT INTEGRATION

When applications use the value of a content management system like Alfresco, they use common patterns in the way that they access this information. These patterns have developed as a result of the way users interact with systems that they use on a day-to-day basis. File systems and the standard Open/Save/Save As dialogs provide a common mental model for how they find and share information. Google has standardized the way users tend to look for information and how they express queries. Transactional systems, with their tabular presentation of information, set users' expectations of how they filter and sort information. Online commerce and Web 2.0 sites have influenced users in how to access and share large amounts of information and have set the bar in responsiveness of the applications. There are some common office practices that are modeled in applications as their real-world counterparts, such as review and approval.

Based upon users' expectations from other systems and developers' own usage of database systems, applications and Web sites have integrated content management in common patterns that are similar to file systems, physical paper handling and storage systems, online commerce and news sites, and popular search and retrieval tools. The following shows some of the most common patterns of content management integration.

Content Service Mappers

Not all integrations work exclusively with Alfresco APIs. Sometimes there are standardized interfaces, which are Service Provider Interfaces to which a content management system provides an implementation. These are often protocol-based services to provide language neutrality and to naturally balance the load between the application and the CMS. Services typically include authentication, query, folder navigation, CRUD (Create, Read, Update, Delete) operations, content transfer, and versioning. These services are abstract and mapped onto the Alfresco native APIs.

Some of the patterns you will see in this chapter are implemented using a Content Service Mapper to access Alfresco from other applications (see Figure 17-1). Most patterns are similar between Content Service Mappers and are generally determined by commonality between the ECM systems they are accessing. As a result, these Content Service Mappers often implement a lowest common denominator of functionality.

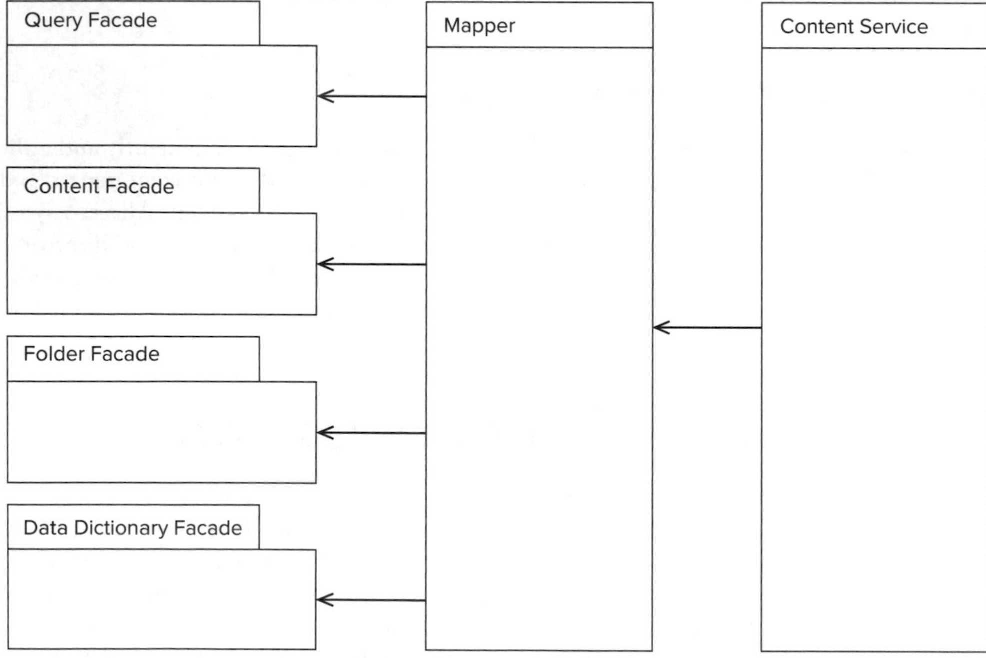

FIGURE 17-1

Using a Content Service Mapper

A content service accesses the content management system through either a remote protocol or through direct calls. In most cases, the access is remote to allow for reuse of the repository by other applications and to simplify the administration of applications without dependencies on the ECM system. The most common protocols are based on SOAP or RESTful Web services, such as AtomPub. However, some applications will mandate other Remote Procedure Call interfaces.

A Content Service Mapper then translates the calls into the appropriate mapping in the ECM system. The most common areas of mapping are Data Dictionary for determining what content types are available in the system, content access to map metadata and content streams, folder navigation to map Folder/Space hierarchies, and query interfaces to provide query and retrieval functionality. Query mapping can potentially be complex, such as XML query mapping against an SQL-based system. These mappings are implemented as Facades on the underlying ECM system.

Many systems provide kits for implementing a Content Service Mapper. Much of the framework may be already implemented in Java or C, leaving only the mapping functionality of the Facades to be implemented.

When to Use It

Content Service Mappers are used when an application connects to more than one CMS and the developer wishes to isolate the porting of the application to a separate layer. Some examples of Content Service Mapper interfaces that are specified by other applications include SAP ArchiveLink for archiving reports and accessing attached image files, IBM/Lotus's Quickr Services for ECM, and OASIS CMIS as a general-purpose connector for many different types of applications. The Alfresco IMAP protocol mapping is an unusual Content Service Mapper in that it maps content services to an email domain model.

You can also define and build a Content Service Mapper if something like CMIS is overkill for your needs or you need functionality or protocol not covered by CMIS. For example, some applications use JSON for remote access of objects and these applications may need the CMS to comply with this pattern. Some systems provide aspects and since CMIS does not support aspects, it may be necessary to provide a separate Content Service Mapper. If an application needs only to access well-structured content as simple objects, a simple Content Service Mapper may be a simpler, higher-performance alternative.

Example

The Alfresco ECM Services for IBM Lotus Quickr are an example of a Content Service Mapper that provides content services on top of Alfresco and maps them to a service interface that Lotus Quickr is expecting in the Quickr application. The Content Service Mapper allows Quickr to navigate the Alfresco repository, store and retrieve content from Quickr into Alfresco, and manipulate metadata in the content objects from Quickr.

In order to provide the mapping to Quickr, IBM has provided a guide of the services required to access an ECM system like Alfresco or IBM FileNet. This interface required implementing a combination of SOAP for content transfer and AtomPub services for metadata manipulation. Details can be found at `www.ibm.com/developerworks/lotus/library/quickr-web-services/`. IBM provides a WSDL for the SOAP interfaces and can generate the abstract implementations of the WSDL.

In the case of the SOAP interfaces, the Alfresco Content Mapper for Quickr used the same Web services infrastructure as the Alfresco CMIS Web services. The AtomPub interface used Web scripts implemented in Java for performance reasons. Both implementations used the Alfresco Java Foundation API.

The following example shows one portion of the implementation that lists children of a document as a feed. Notice that the Mapper is primarily handling the translation of terminology and the mechanics of accessing the objects. The concepts are roughly the same between Quickr and Alfresco. A collection is an artifact of AtomPub rather than Quickr, but the notions of folders, content, and children are the same in both systems.

```
publicclass AlfrescoAtomBasedFeedServiceImpl implements AtomBasedFeedService
{

  private NodeService nodeService;

  private PersonService personService;

  public Feed getListDocuments(String id)
  {
    NodeRef storeRef = newNodeRef(id);

    // <feed>
    Feed feed = newFOMFeed();

    feed.setBaseUri("/library/" + id + "/");

    // <generator>
    feed.setGenerator("", "1.0", "Teamspace Documents");

    // <id>
    feed.setId("urn:lsid:ibm.com:td:" + id);

    // <link>
    feed.addLink("feed", "self");
    feed.addLink("http://quickr.acme.com/wps/mypoc?uri=dm:" + id
            + "&verb=view", "alternate");
    feed.addLink("feed?pagesize=2&page=3", "next");
    feed.addLink("feed?pagesize=2&page=1", "previous");

    String contentName = (String) nodeService.getProperty(storeRef,
              ContentModel.PROP_NAME);

    // <collection>
    feed.setCollection(new FOMCollection(contentName, "feed",
              new String[] { "*/*" }));

    String authorName = (String) nodeService.getProperty(storeRef,
                        ContentModel.PROP_AUTHOR);
    String email = (String) nodeService.getProperty(
                          personService.getPerson(authorName),
                          ContentModel.PROP_EMAIL);
    String userName = (String) nodeService.getProperty(
                          personService.getPerson(authorName),
                          ContentModel.PROP_USERNAME);
```

```
// feed.addAuthor(createPerson(storeRef));

// <author>
feed.addAuthor(authorName, email, "uid=" + userName + ",o=acme");

// <title>
feed.setTitle(contentName);

// <updated>
feed.setUpdated((Date) nodeService.getProperty(storeRef,
                                ContentModel.PROP_MODIFIED));

// add<entry>
for (ChildAssociationRef childAssoc : nodeService.getChildAssocs(storeRef))
{
   NodeRef childRef = childAssoc.getChildRef();
   String childName = (String) nodeService.getProperty(childRef,
                                     ContentModel.PROP_NAME);

   Entry entry = newFOMEntry();

   // <id>
   entry.setId("urn:lsid:ibm.com:td:" + childRef.getId());

   // <link>
   entry.addLink("document/" + childRef.getId() + "/entry", "self");
   entry.addLink("http://quickr.acme.com/wps/mypoc?uri=dm:" + childRef.getId()
     + "&verb=view", "alternate");
   entry.addLink("document/" + childRef.getId() + "/entry", "edit");
   if (nodeService.getProperty(childRef, ContentModel.PROP_CONTENT) != null)
   {
     entry.addLink("document/" + childRef.getId() + "/entry", "edit-media");
     entry.addLink("document/" + childRef.getId() + "/entry", "enclosure",
           (String) nodeService.getProperty(childRef,
     ContentModel.PROP_CONTENT), childName, "en",
           (Long) nodeService.getProperty(childAssoc.getChildRef(),
     ContentModel.PROP_SIZE_CURRENT));

     // <category>
     entry.addCategory("tag:ibm.com,2006:td/type", "document", "document");
   }
   else
   {
     // <category>
     entry.addCategory("tag:ibm.com,2006:td/type", "folder", "folder");
   }

   authorName = (String) nodeService.getProperty(childRef,
     ContentModel.PROP_AUTHOR);
   email = (String) nodeService.getProperty(
     personService.getPerson(authorName),
     ContentModel.PROP_EMAIL);
   userName = (String) nodeService.getProperty(
     personService.getPerson(authorName),
```

```
          ContentModel.PROP_USERNAME);

        // <author>
        entry.addAuthor(authorName, email, "uid=" + userName + ",o=acme");

        // <title>
        entry.setTitle(childName);

        // <published>
        entry.setPublished((Date) nodeService.getProperty(childRef,
          ContentModel.PROP_CREATED));

        // <updated>
        entry.setUpdated((Date) nodeService.getProperty(childRef,
          ContentModel.PROP_MODIFIED));

        return feed;
    }
```

This example implements a small but important portion of the Quickr API as a Content Mapper Service. This is the service to get a list of documents that may be used in a portlet or document browser. The service, implemented as an Atom-based feed, references a space node by ID and returns the metadata associated with the space. It then iterates through the children of the node through the child associations. If the child is a document, it provides a link to the content. If it is a folder, it provides a link to the space representing that folder. This is likely to be a common pattern in many Content Mappers.

Property View

A Property view (see Figure 17-2) is a building block of any Alfresco or any other content management application. A Property view presents information about a content object based on the content object's ID. Usually there will be additional actions that can be performed on the object, such as Download, Check Out/In, Edit using WebDAV, Invoke Workflow, and others. The actions will be determined based on the context of the content object in the application and whether the Property view is read-only or editable. An integrated viewer using a Flash viewer or an in-line editor can make for a more streamlined experience for the user.

Using a Property View

The Property view uses a Web Script Controller to fetch the content object using either CMIS or Web scripts. The Property view accesses the properties needed for the view. If the view is dynamic, then it may use the Data Dictionary or introspection to find out what properties are appropriate for the object fetched. A Property view can be read-only or bi-modal, allowing for editing of properties if appropriate for the application.

The view then constructs an HTML page with the properties and any actions that are appropriate for the object. If the view is read-only, then the Property view is generally very simple, adding only basic controls to download content. However, you can add other controls that are relevant to the application, such as e-commerce or process-related actions. On an OK or Cancel action, control is returned to the Browser or Query view that invoked the Property view and returned to the original context.

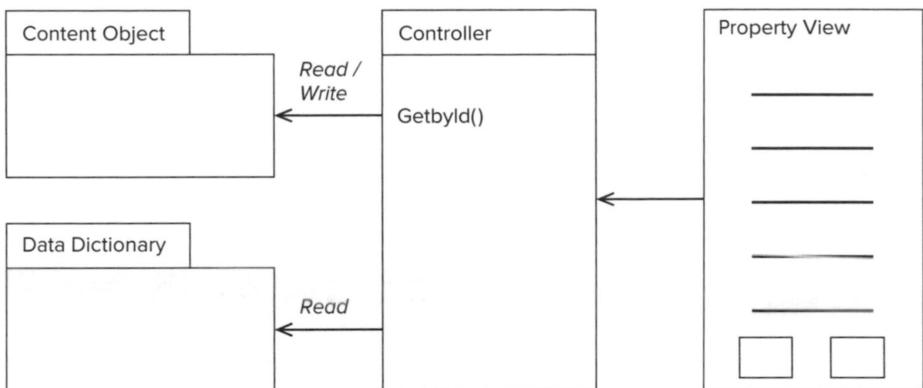

FIGURE 17-2

It is possible to add a Flash-based viewer, such as the one found in Alfresco Share. An example will be provided with the online reference.

If the view is editable, then a more sophisticated controller needs to be built, such as the one used in Alfresco Share. It may be best under those circumstances to direct control to the Property view in Share. If it is important for the Edit view, then the developer can create a special purpose fixed form, use the Data Dictionary to construct a dynamic form, or use the Forms Service from Alfresco Share. Details on the Forms Service can be found on the Alfresco wiki.

When to Use It

A Property view is generally used with either a Browser view or a Query view and invoked by an action on the line item of either. The Property view can be used to view basic properties on content or can be specialized for different types and aspects. Property views can also be specialized based on the nature of the content. For example, if a content object is used to present a product for sale, such as in a catalog, then the Property view can be used to display the content, such as a photo, and provide actions for purchasing the item. A Property view can also be used for very specialized content types, such as high-resolution photos, providing different thumbnail views and exposure information for digital assets in a Digital Asset Management catalog.

Example: Confluence

Confluence is an enterprise wiki from Atlassian used in many development shops. An integration of Confluence with Alfresco was created using CMIS by Alfresco and SourceSense. The project can be found at `http://code.google.com/p/confluence-alfresco`.

The following are some examples of a Property view created to work with the wiki built by Sourcesense. In this case, the view is constructed in Java using the wiki syntax for the wiki to render. It uses the Apache Abdera AtomPub toolkit and the Abdera extensions for CMIS to access the CMIS AtomPub protocol.

```
  private String renderEntry(Entry entry) {
StringBuilder out = new StringBuilder();
out.append("||Property||Value||\n");
```

```
        ExtensibleElement cmisObject = entry.getExtension(CMISConstants.OBJECT);
        if (cmisObject != null) {
          ExtensibleElement cmisProperties =
            cmisObject.getExtension(CMISConstants.PROPERTIES);
          if (cmisProperties != null) {
            List<Element> cmisProps = cmisProperties.getElements();
            for (Element prop : cmisProps) {

              System.err.println(prop.getQName());

              if (!CMISConstants.CMIS_NS_URI.equals(prop.getQName().getNamespaceURI())){
                continue;
              }
              String name = prop.getAttributeValue(CMISConstants.NAME);
              if (name == null) {
                continue;
              }
              Element cmisValue =
                ((ExtensibleElement)prop).getExtension(CMISConstants.VALUE);
              if (cmisValue != null) {
                String value = cmisValue.getText();
                if (CMISConstants.PROPERTY_BOOLEAN.equals(prop.getQName()))
                  value = "true".equalsIgnoreCase(value) ? "(/)" : "(x)";
                else if (CMISConstants.PROPERTY_URI.equals(prop.getQName()))
                  value = "[LINK|" + value + "]";
                out.append("|");
                out.append(name);
                out.append("|");
                out.append(value);
                out.append("|\n");
              }
            }
          }
        }
        return out.toString();
      }
```

This code snippet is part of a macro extension added into the Confluence wiki engine to iterate to present the properties of a document. In this case, it uses CMIS to fetch the object. The string `out` is used to construct a wiki fragment using wiki syntax. The list of elements `cmisProps` is used to iterate through the properties and present them as a set of attribute value pairs in a wiki-formatted table. The vertical bar is used to separate columns in the table with the property name as one column and the property value as another. The string that is composed is then sent to the wiki formatting engine for presentation when the macro is called.

Article

An article pattern (see Figure 17-3) is a single content object used in relation to the context of the application or Web site to present relevant and rich information to the user. For example, the information presented may be a featured document, an explanatory piece of text, or a deeper description of a category of information. A physical article in a magazine is a good analog of a single content object or document used by the application or Web site to showcase new information or provide a deeper understanding of a piece of information.

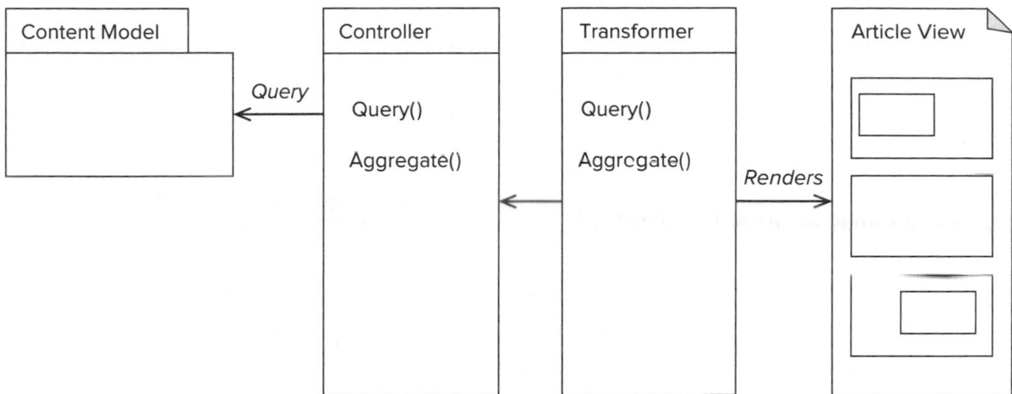

FIGURE 17-3

User-generated content, such as a blog, is a good example of an article and a content repository is a good place to store this content. A photo article may consist of something as simple as an image and a caption, or a title, image, and caption. A photo article can also contain multiple images, which is usually driven by a top article that determines the order of the photos.

Compound documents are a special case of article, which may be assembled from other related objects to create the composed or compound document. Using associations to create compound documents in a related document management application is best for identifying the associated objects.

Using the Article Pattern

The article is retrieved from the repository with, usually, a singleton query. This allows the article to be identified logically based upon context and to change which content will change. For instance, a tip of the day can be identified as the latest tip of the day. Avoid hard-coding any identifiers.

Set up a query with a predicate that identifies the appropriate content object. It is not necessary to retrieve any properties other than the identifier since you will have the object available for any properties. CMIS provides all the required functionality to implement access to an article and the result will be portable. However, using Web scripts can be equally effective. Fetch the content object and any properties you wish to display. The title of the article may be derived from the title property.

Stream the article into your user interface, usually as text or HTML. If it is XML, then you will need to either load the payload as into a DOM object or render using an XSLT transformation. Alternatively, if there is a Flash-based preview available (such as those built into Share), derived from Office documents or PDF, you could embed the Flash content along with a Flash viewer as Share does.

If the article is a compound object, then the application walks the associations including sub-components and any in-line images. The simplest way to assemble the content is to walk the tree depth-first and make sure that embedded objects are presented as valid HTML.

When to Use It

Use the article pattern when a single piece of content is required in a well-known position of the application. The following examples indicate where an article may be useful:

- **Introduction** — As you enter the application, view a new section of the application, or walk through a wizard, an introductory article can provide context for the user as to what will happen when they use that part of the application. A banner or introductory article can also present a more professional appearance for the user. In addition to being only text, these can include video in the form of an embedded Flash object.
- **Application assistant** — Instructions or help can aid a complex part of an application. This content can be presented as in-line instructions, pop-up help, or an aid. These can also be presented where you anticipate the user will need help, such as with a tip of the day.
- **Related information** — If the user wishes to go beyond this portion of the application, see related information, or be presented with news related to the context of the application, then an article is a better way to provide a richer set of description and guidance than with a simple list of URLs.

Example

The Home Page of this Surf site includes a static HTML file that is created using the article.xsd Web form in the Surf Framework. This creates the file latestNews.html within the repository to ROOT/content/news, which is then deployed to ROOT/content/news. The Surf Web application then includes latestNews.html at request time, as seen in Figure 17-4.

FIGURE 17-4

The HTML include import is done by the Surf component; however, before this will function, you need to configure Surf (using Spring) to look into the deploy directory for the static content and Web scripts. For example, you can create a Web extension configuration bean as follows:

```
<!-- Local Store Abstract  -->
<bean id="webframework.localstore"
      class="org.alfresco.web.scripts.LocalFileSystemStore"
      abstract="true" init-method="init">
  <property name="root">
    <value>/surf-sample/sample/deploy</value>
  </property>
</bean>
<!-- Web Scripts: Local Store -->
<bean id="webframework.localstore.webscripts"
      parent="webframework.localstore">
  <property name="path">
    <value>alfresco/site-webscripts</value>
  </property>
</bean>
```

Once this is configured, components can access static content. The component that is used on the home page is site-data/components/page.main.index.xml and looks like this:

```
<?xml version='1.0' encoding='UTF-8'?>
  <component>
    <scope>page</scope>
    <region-id>main</region-id>
    <source-id>index</source-id>
    <component-type-id>/component/common/include</component-type-id>
    <properties>
      <container>div</container>
    </properties>
    <resources>
      <resource id="source" type="webapp">/content/news/latestNews.html</resource>
    </resources>
  </component>
```

You can see that you are using one of the Web scripts that comes bundled with Surf, which is referenced by /component/common/include. The resource ID is then passed in (that is, the HTML fragment).

Query View

A Query view (see Figure 17-5) is a general-purpose pattern that generates very application-specific views for accessing sets of content and presenting a consistent set of metadata about that set. Like most ECM systems, Alfresco provides query facilities that are based on SQL. In particular, Alfresco has been careful to follow the CMIS-query language specification that is based on SQL 92 with extensions to support querying within folders and adding full-text expressions for searching within the text of the content. The view is constructed from the query model and presented to the user for further action, either within the application or by handing control to one of the Alfresco applications, such as Share.

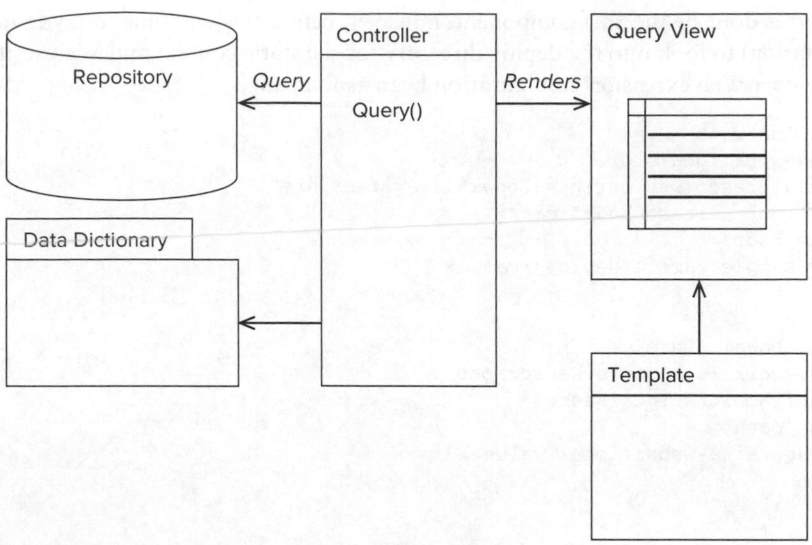

FIGURE 17-5

Using a Query View

A Query view can be used to provide a flat set of content filtered on a specific folder, metadata (such as a project name or author), the text within the content (such as all documents containing the word "Aspirin"), or any combination preceding. The qualification can be as expressive as SQL. The target list can contain any property that is common to the object types or aspects listed in the FROM clause. The qualification can be either hard-coded in the application or captured from a form in the application. For instance, a form can capture a project to be searched.

The query in the Query view can be constructed using the CMIS query specification and sent through either CMIS or Web scripts. The query is executed in the repository, which then formats the query results as a flat tuple set with the properties requested by the query. Normally, the content ID is returned so that the content can be retrieved or some other action can be taken on the content. Alfresco can also provide specialized properties specifically for applications and user interfaces, such as icon types. CMIS allows rendition types to be added to queries to present thumbnails with the results. This enables the application to provide visual indicators as well as data indicators of what content information is being returned.

The view in the Query view then constructs a Web page with the information retrieved and constructs a set of links for further action. The view is normally built using a templating language geared toward constructing Web pages or Web page fragments, such as FreeMarker, PHP, or JSP. The view may be part of a wider Web framework, such as a portal, Share, or a Surf application. The view will normally present the results in a tabular view with standard metadata, such as name, title, author, and creation date. If a thumbnail rendition is selected, then the thumbnail will normally be of a size that fits neatly into a row associated with a content object. If there are a lot of nodes, it is the responsibility of the view to handle pagination of results sets.

The links constructed by the view are normally URLs linking to the content itself; another page of the application that provides more context or information; the property sheet of the content object in Share where the content preview, metadata, and actions can be found; or another part of the application that may show a more application-specific view of the content properties and actions. If a link to the content needs to be fast, then this may be a direct, read-only link to the content from the content store. If the content needs to be editable, then it is best to use a WebDAV link using the WebDAV protocol. CMIS will construct a direct, read-only link and is portable. An application can construct a link to the Share application by pointing to the right site path and appending the path to the content in the document library. Specialized content views can be constructed for simpler viewing, annotating for linking to other application objects.

When to Use It

A Query view is used when a logical set of content is needed for an application and the content is very commonly used. Use a Query view to assemble content related to a particular topic or subject by using keyword-based properties, tags, or categories provided by Alfresco. Also use this view to assemble process or project information. In this case, status information captured by Alfresco or the application can be used to filter the appropriate information. Workflow status can also be useful in the query. Content that might be of interest to the end user can be assembled by querying for content that has the user as an author or is waiting on that user for action in a workflow.

A Query view allows the content view to be very specific to the application by filtering out irrelevant content across the repository. Unlike a browser or folder view, only relevant information is displayed, making for a much easier user experience.

Example: Drupal and OpenSearch

In this example, Drupal already uses OpenSearch as a mechanism to search other content sources, and integrating Alfresco OpenSearch is an easier route to integrating search. This Drupal module successfully mixes CMIS AtomPub for deeper object inspection and creation of content, but is able to simply add Alfresco as another search source. To download the source code and view additional information, visit `http://drupal.org/project/cmis_alfresco`.

The following is an implementation in the Drupal Content Construction Kit (CCK): `http://drupal.org/node/101723`.

```
/**
 * Keyword based search
 *
 * @param $keyword
 * @param $p
 */
function cmis_alfresco_opensearch_view($keyword = NULL, $p = 1) {
  module_load_include('utils.inc', 'cmis_alfresco');

  // Add opensearch form
  $contents = drupal_get_form('cmis_alfresco_opensearch_form', NULL);

  if ($keyword) {
    $result = cmis_alfresco_invoke_service('/api/search/keyword.atom?q='.
```

```
        urlencode($keyword) .'&p='. $p);
    if (false != $result) {

      // Process the returned XML
      $xml = cmis_alfresco_utils_get_CMIS_xml($result);
      // Set up results list
      $contents .= theme('cmis_alfresco_opensearch_results',
           $xml->xpath('//D:entry'));

      // Set up pager
      $opensearch = $xml->children(cmis_alfresco_utils_ns('opensearch'));
      $total_items = (int) $opensearch->totalResults;
      $items_per_page = (int) $opensearch->itemsPerPage;

      if (fmod($total_items, $items_per_page) == 0) {
        $last_page_number = floor($total_items / $items_per_page);
      }
      else {
        $last_page_number = floor($total_items / $items_per_page) + 1;
      }

      // Add pagination bar
      $contents .= theme('cmis_alfresco_pager', 'cmis/opensearch/'. $keyword .'/',
           $last_page_number);
      }
      else {
        $contents .= 'Error';
      }
    }

    return $contents;
  }
```

The actual Query view is implemented through the Drupal CCK, which ties the OpenSearch query view to a theme.

```
/**
 * Implementation of hook_theme()
 *
 */
function cmis_alfresco_theme() {
  return array(
    'cmis_alfresco_opensearch_results' => array('arguments' => array('entries')),
    'cmis_alfresco_pager' => array('arguments' => array('base_search_url',
    'last_page_number'))
  );
}

function theme_cmis_alfresco_opensearch_results($entries) {
  if (empty($entries)) {
    return '<div class="empty-search">There are no results for your search.</div>';
  }

  module_load_include('utils.inc', 'cmis_alfresco');
```

```
  foreach ($entries as $entry) {
    $summary = $entry->summary;
    $score = $entry->children(cmis_alfresco_utils_ns('relevance'))->score;
    $updated = date_create($entry->updated);
    $updatedStr = date_format($updated, 'n/j/Y g:i A');
    $alfIcon = $entry->icon;
    $documentLink = l($entry->title, 'cmis/get',
           array('query' => array('id' => $entry->id)));

    $rows[] = array('<img src="'. $alfIcon .'" />'. $documentLink,
           $entry->author->name, $updatedStr, $score);
  }

  $contents .= theme('table', $header, $rows);

  return $contents;
}

function theme_cmis_alfresco_pager($base_search_url, $last_page_number) {
  $contents .= '<div class="pagination">';
  $contents .= l('first', $base_search_url .'1');

  for ($counter = 1; $counter <= $last_page_number; $counter++) {
    if ($p!= $counter) {
        $contents .= ' '. l($counter, $base_search_url . $counter);
    }
    else {
      $contents .= ' '. $counter;
    }
  }

  $contents .=  ' '. l('last', $base_search_url . $last_page_number);
  $contents .= '</div>';

  return $contents;
}
```

Where needed, Drupal can also use the CMIS query interface.

```
/**
 * Implementation of cmisapi_query method
 *
 * @param $repositoryId
 * @param $statement
 * @param $searchAllVersions
 * @param $includeAllAllowableActions
 * @param $includeRelationships
 * @param $maxItems
 * @param $skipCount
 * @return array
 */
function cmis_alfresco_cmisapi_query($repositoryId, $statement,
               $searchAllVersions = FALSE, $includeAllAllowableActions = FALSE,
               $includeRelationships = NULL, $maxItems = 0, $skipCount = 0)
{
  module_load_include('utils.inc', 'cmis_alfresco');
```

```
    $postvars = '<?xml version="1.0" encoding="UTF-8" standalone="yes" ?>'.
        '<query xmlns="'. cmis_alfresco_utils_ns('cmis') .'">'.
          '<statement>'. $statement .'</statement>'.
          '<searchAllVersions>'. ($searchAllVersions?'true':'false') .
          '</searchAllVersions>'.
          '<maxItems>'. $maxItems .'</maxItems>'.
          '<skipCount>'. $skipCount .'</skipCount>'.
          '<returnAllowableActions>'. ($includeAllAllowableActions?'true':'false') .
          '</returnAllowableActions>'.
        '</query>';

    $header[] = 'Content-type: application/cmisquery+xml';
    $header[] = 'Content-length: '. strlen($postvars);
    $header[] = 'MIME-Version: 1.0';

    $response = cmis_alfresco_invoke_service('/api/query', $header, 'CUSTOM-POST',
        $postvars);
    if (false != $response) {
      return _cmis_alfresco_getEntries(cmis_alfresco_utils_get_CMIS_xml($response,
            '//D:entry'));
    }

    return FALSE;
  }
```

Here the function is constructing a CMIS query by composing the XML to wrap around the query passed as the variable `$statement`. The query is then posted to the CMIS query service in Alfresco.

Browser View

A Browser view generates a File System Explorer–like view on top of the repository (see Figure 17-6). The user drills down a hierarchical view of the repository folder structure. The view then guides the user to the next level of the hierarchy. Normally, this tree structure is exposed in a single view that expands as a tree. However, it may also be presented as a single level at a time with a breadcrumb trail showing the user's current location. Browsers are useful for general purpose browsing of a repository to allow the user to explore the structure of the repository.

Browsers can also take the form of dialogs similar to Open File dialogs. These can be used for finding and selecting content for articles within the application, or attachments to attach content to business objects in the application.

Using a Browser View

A Browser view typically begins with a starting folder, which can be the root folder, the user's home folder, or another folder that has a semantic context, such as a project or team folder. From this starting point, a model is constructed that traverses all the children in that folder. This can be done through either Web scripts or CMIS.

Alternatively, a Browser view can navigate a category structure. Since there is no standardized structure of categories within CMIS, it is best to use Web scripts to navigate the hierarchy. A parent-child hierarchy is very similar to a folder-child hierarchy.

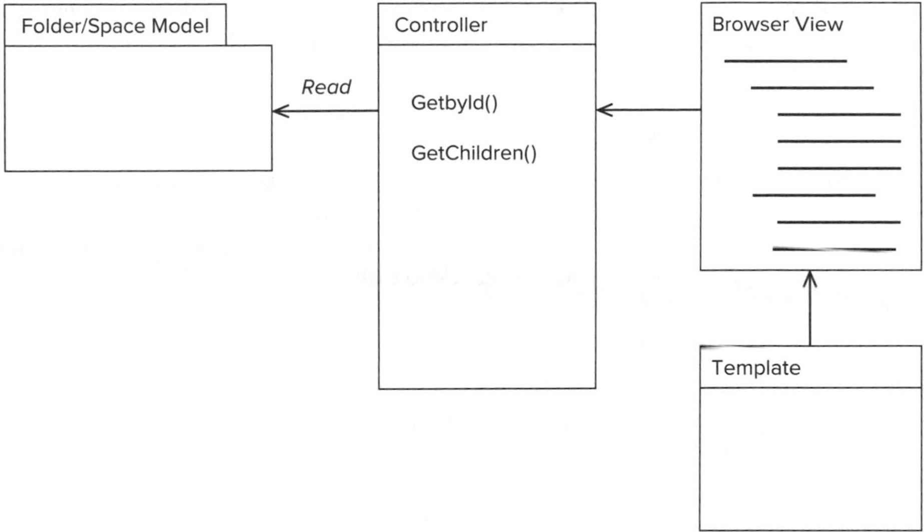

FIGURE 17-6

A view constructs a page or page component with the Container object and its immediate children, usually starting with the children that are themselves Containers. Unlike the Query view, which presents a normalized view of the result set, a Browser view usually constructs a Property view that is specific to the type of the child. For instance, folders would be presented as leading to a new level, documents might have document-oriented information and actions, and Web pages may have their URLs listed. Normally all the information required is immediately available as part of the child object.

When a child is clicked, the view will recurse to the next level, either refreshing the view to the next level or expanding an indented or accordion view of the next level. The navigation tree of Container nodes may be displayed in a separate view. For a simpler view, particularly in more limited portal environments, a flat structure is more often used but should contain a breadcrumb trail above the list of children. This trail prevents the user from getting lost and enables a quick return to previous levels. The easiest way to maintain a consistent breadcrumb that is compatible with the Back button of a browser is to walk the primary ancestor path of a node.

As with the Query view, the Browser view constructs the actions for the user to take as a set of URL links behind the metadata that is presented by the view. As with the Query view, this can take the form of accessing the content directly or leading to a specialized property page. Browsers generally replace Share or Explorer, so are less likely to point to those applications for property sheets.

When to Use It

Browsers are useful for general-purpose content management and document management applications where Share and Explorer are not appropriate for portability or platform reasons. Browsers are particularly useful where folders are a logical organizer of information. They do not replace, but can supplement, Query views. Folder structures often mimic organization, team, project, and record hierarchies, so browsers are useful for navigating these structures. Collaboration sites may organize their content in such structures and provide a Browser view.

Some of the first general-purpose tools built using CMIS were browsers using the Browser view. These browsers were designed to exercise the CMIS interface and provide value-added viewing and exploration on top of these views.

Example: Drupal Repository Browser

In the following Drupal integration example, the CCK is used again and provides the presentation layer functionality. The Browser Controller uses CMIS to get the children of the current node based upon which level you are browsing. In the Drupal example, it starts with the Company Home Page. Following are some of the helper methods for accessing CMIS calls.

```
/**
 * Implementation of cmisapi_getRepositoryInfo method
 *
 */
function cmis_alfresco_cmisapi_getRepositoryInfo() {
  static $repository_info;

  if (empty($repository_info)) {
    module_load_include('utils.inc', 'cmis_alfresco');

    $response = cmis_alfresco_invoke_service('/api/repository');
    $xml = cmis_alfresco_utils_get_CMIS_xml($response);

    if ($xml) {
      $cmis = $xml->workspace->children(cmis_alfresco_utils_ns('cmis'));
      $repository_info = $cmis->repositoryInfo;
    }
  }
return $repository_info;
}

/**
 * Implementation of cmisapi_getChildren method
 *
 * @param $repositoryId
 * @param $folderId
 */
function cmis_alfresco_cmisapi_getChildren($repositoryId, $folderId) {
  module_load_include('utils.inc', 'cmis_alfresco');

  $folderId = cmis_alfresco_objectId($folderId);
  if ($folderId['noderef_url']) {
    $url = '/api/node/'. $folderId['noderef_url'];
  }
  else {
    $url = $folderId['url'];
  }

  $response = cmis_alfresco_invoke_service($url .'/children');
  if (false != $response) {
    return _cmis_alfresco_getEntries(cmis_alfresco_utils_get_CMIS_xml($response,
        '//D:entry'));
  }
```

```
return FALSE;
}

/**
 * Implementation of cmisapi_getObjectParents method
 *
 * @param $repositoryId
 * @param $folderId
 */
function cmis_alfresco_cmisapi_getObjectParents($repositoryId, $folderId) {
  module_load_include('utils.inc', 'cmis_alfresco');

  $folderId = cmis_alfresco_objectId($folderId);
  if ($folderId['noderef_url']) {
    $url = '/api/node/'. $folderId['noderef_url'];
  }
  else {
    $url = $folderId['url'];
  }

  $response = cmis_alfresco_invoke_service($url .'/parent');
  if (false != $response) {
    return _cmis_alfresco_getEntries(cmis_alfresco_utils_get_CMIS_xml($response,
    '//D:entry'));
  }

return FALSE;
}

/**
 * Implementation of cmisapi_getProperties method
 *
 * @param $repositoryId
 * @param $objectId
 */
function cmis_alfresco_cmisapi_getProperties($repositoryId, $objectId) {
  module_load_include('utils.inc', 'cmis_alfresco');
  $objectId = cmis_alfresco_objectId($objectId);

  if ($response =cmis_alfresco_invoke_service(
          '/api/node/'.$objectId['noderef_url'])) {
    if ($entries = _cmis_alfresco_getEntries(
            cmis_alfresco_utils_get_CMIS_xml($response, '//D:entry'))) {
      return $entries[0];
    }
  }

  watchdog('cmis_alfresco_cmisapi_getProperties', 'Unknown objectId "@objectId"',
            array('@objectId' => $objectId));
return FALSE;
}

/**
 * Implemetation of cmisapi_getContentStream method
```

```
 *
 * @param $repositoryId
 * @param $objectId
 */
function cmis_alfresco_cmisapi_getContentStream($repositoryId, $objectId) {
module_load_include('utils.inc', 'cmis_alfresco');

  $objectId = cmis_alfresco_objectId($objectId);
return cmis_alfresco_invoke_service(
'/api/node/content/'. $objectId['noderef_url']);
}
```

The following Drupal module processes the XML entries that return from the CMIS AtomPub call. There is no standard Atom entry processing in Drupal.

```
/**
 * Process CMIS XML.
 *
 * @param $xml CMIS response XML.
 * @param $xpath xpath expression.
 */
function cmis_alfresco_utils_get_CMIS_xml($xml, $xpath = NULL) {
  try {
    $cmis_service = new SimpleXMLElement($xml);
  }
  catch (Exception $e) {
    cmis_error_handler('cmis_alfresco_utils_get_CMIS_xml', $e);
    throw new CMISException(t('Unable to process xml.'));
  }

  foreach (cmis_alfresco_utils_get_namespaces() as $ns => $namespace) {
    $cmis_service->registerXPathNamespace($ns, $namespace);
  }

  if ($xpath) {
    return $cmis_service->xpath($xpath);
  }

  return $cmis_service;
}

/**
 * Utility function for returning CMIS objects from cmis response
 * (ie. getChildren, query, getDescendants)
 *
 * @param $entries
 * @return array
 */
function _cmis_alfresco_getEntries($entries) {
  $result = array();
  foreach ($entries as $entry) {
    $cmis_object = _cmis_alfresco_utils_entry($entry);
    $cmis_object->properties = array();
    $cmis_element = $entry->children(cmis_alfresco_utils_ns('cmis'));
```

```
    foreach (_cmis_alfresco_utils_known_property_types() as $type) {
      $property_tag = 'property'. $type;
      foreach ($cmis_element->object->properties->$property_tag as $property) {
        $attrs = $property->attributes(cmis_alfresco_utils_ns('cmis'));
        $cmis_object->properties[(string) $attrs->name] =
              cmis_alfresco_utils_cast($property->value, $type);
      }
    }

    $cmis_object->type = $cmis_object->properties['BaseType'];

    if ($cmis_object->type == 'document') {
      $cmis_object->size = $cmis_object->properties['ContentStreamLength'];
      $cmis_object->contentMimeType =
          $cmis_object->properties['ContentStreamMimeType'];
      $cmis_object->versionSeriesCheckedOutBy =
           $cmis_object->properties['VersionSeriesCheckedOutBy'];
    }

    $result[] = $cmis_object;
  }

return $result;
}

/**
 * Utility function for returning a common entry object from a feed entry
 *
 * @param $xml_element
 * @return stdClass
 */
function _cmis_alfresco_utils_entry($xml_element) {
  $entry = new stdClass();

  $tmp_objectId = cmis_alfresco_objectId((string) $xml_element->id);
  $entry->id = $tmp_objectId['noderef'];

  $entry->title = (string) $xml_element->title;
  $entry->summary = (string) $xml_element->summary;
  $entry->updated = date_create($xml_element->updated);
  $entry->author = (string) $xml_element->author->name;

return $entry;
}

/**
 * Utility function form casting cmis properties
 *
 * @param $value
 * @param $type
 * @return mixed
 */
function _cmis_alfresco_utils_cast($value, $type) {
  $return = NULL;
```

```
  switch ($type) {
  case 'Integer':
    $return = (int) $value;
    break;
  case 'Boolean':
    $return = (bool) $value;
    break;
  case 'String':
  case 'Id':
    $return = (string) $value;
    break;
  case 'DateTime':
    $return = date_create((string) $value);
    break;
  default:
    $return = $value;
  }

return $return;
}

/**
 * Utility function for encoding cmis properties
 *
 * @param $propertyCollection
 * @return string
 */
function _cmis_alfresco_utils_properties_to_xml($propertyCollection = array()) {
  $properties_xml = '';

  foreach ($propertyCollection as $key => $value) {
    $property_type = gettype($value);

    switch ($property_type) {
    case 'integer':
    case 'boolean':
    case 'string':
      $properties_xml .= '<cmis:property'. ucfirst($property_type)
          .'cmis:name="'. $key .'">';
      $properties_xml .= '<cmis:value>'. $value .'</cmis:value>';
      $properties_xml .= '</cmis:property'. ucfirst($property_type) .'>';
      break;
    default:
      watchdog('_cmis_alfresco_utils_properties_to_xml',
          'Unable to map property "@property" of type "@property_type" '.
          'for destination object "@objectId"',
          array('@property' => $key, '@property_type' => $property_type,
              '@objectId' => $objectId), WATCHDOG_ERROR);

      drupal_set_message(t(
          'Unable to map property "@property" of type "@property_type" for ' .
          'destination object "@objectId"',
          array('@property' => $key, '@property_type' => $property_type,
             '@objectId' => $objectId)), 'error');
```

```
        }
      }

    return $properties_xml;
    }
```

These calls, in turn, are used to hook into the CCK, which has predefined templates for presenting forms and tabular information of similar types. Reusing work to integrate other hierarchical browsers, tabular results, and metadata forms, this Drupal integration provides the following hook points.

```
<?php
// $Id: cmis_alfresco_field.module,v 1.2 2009/09/09 16:51:41 cbalan Exp $

/**
 * Implementation of hook_field_settings
 *
 * @param $op - operation
 * @param $field - field begin operated on
 * @return - form or settings array dependent on operation
 */
function cmis_alfresco_field_field_settings($op, $field) {
  switch ($op) {
  case 'form':
    $form['root_directory'] = array(
        '#title' => t('Root Directory'),
        '#description' => t('Root Directory for Alfresco nodes'),
        '#type' => 'textfield',
        '#autocomplete_path' => 'cmis/autocomplete',
        '#default_value' => '/Company Home',
      );
    return $form;

  case 'save':
    $settings = array('root_directory');
    return $settings;

  case 'database columns':
    $columns = array(
      'path' => array('type' => 'varchar', 'length' => 255, 'not null' => FALSE),
    );
    return $columns;
  }
}

/**
 *
 * @param $op - operation
 * @param $node - node
 * @param $field - field settings
 * @param $items - field value(s)
 * @param $teaser - boolean for whether or not we're displaying a teaser
 * @param $page - boolean for whether or not we're displaying a page
 * @return unknown_type
 */
```

```
function cmis_alfresco_field_field($op, &$node, $field, &$items, $teaser, $page) {
  switch ($op) {
  case 'validate':
    foreach ($items as $i) {
      if (empty($i)) {
        form_set_error('', 'The field cannot be empty');
      }
    }
  return $items;
  break;
  }
}

/**
 * Implementation of hook_widget_info
 *
 * @return array defining the widget
 */
function cmis_alfresco_field_widget_info() {
  return array(
    'cmis_alfresco_field_widget' => array(
       'label' => t('Alfresco browser'),
       'field types' => array('cmis_alfresco_field'),
       'multiple values' => CONTENT_HANDLE_CORE,
       'callbacks' => array('default value' => CONTENT_CALLBACK_CUSTOM),
       'description' => t('Click to browse the Alfresco repository and ' .
            'select an Alfresco node to associate with this Drupal node.' )
    )
  );
}

/**
 * Implementation of hook_elements()
 *
 * @return array elements to be processed by FAPI
 */
function cmis_alfresco_field_elements() {
  return array(
    'cmis_alfresco_field_widget' => array(
      '#input' => TRUE,
      '#process' => array('cmis_alfresco_field_widget_process')
  )
  );
}

/**
 * Implementation of hook_process()
 *
 * @param $element - the form element array
 * @param $edit -
 * @param $form_state - form state array
 * @param $form - form array
 * @return array - form element
 */
```

```
function cmis_alfresco_field_widget_process($element, $edit, $form_state, $form) {
  $defaults = $element['#value'];
  if (!is_array($defaults)) {
    $defaults = unserialize($defaults);
  }

  $element['path'] = array(
    '#type' => 'textfield',
    '#default_value' => $defaults['path'],
    '#autocomplete_path' => 'cmis/autocomplete',
  );

return $element;
}

/**
 * Implementation of hook_widget()
 *
 * @param $form - form array
 * @param $form_state - form state array
 * @param $field - field array
 * @param $items - field values
 * @param $delta - id of the field (if there is more than one in the form)
 * @return form element array
 */
function cmis_alfresco_field_widget(& $form, & $form_state, $field, $items,
                $delta = 0) {
  $element = array(
    '#type' => $field['widget']['type'],
    '#default_value' => isset($items[$delta]) ? $items[$delta] : ''
  );

return $element;
}

/**
 * Implementation of hook_field_formatter_info
 *
 * @return array
 */
function cmis_alfresco_field_field_formatter_info() {
  return array(
    'default' => array(
       'label' => t('Alfresco browser'),
       'field types' => array('alfresco_cmis_field')
    )
  );
}

/**
 * Implementation of hook_theme()
 *
 * @return array of theme functions
 */
```

```
function cmis_alfresco_field_theme() {
  return array(
    'cmis_alfresco_field_widget' => array('arguments' => array('element')),
    'cmis_alfresco_field_formatter_default' =>
         array('arguments' => array('element' => NULL))
  );
}

/**
 * Function to theme the widget form
 * @param $element
 * @return string - themed output of the widget
 */
function theme_cmis_alfresco_field_widget(&$element) {
return theme('form_element', $element, $element['#children']);
}

function theme_cmis_alfresco_field_formatter_default($element = NULL) {
if (empty( $element['#item'])) {
return '';
  }

return print_r($element, TRUE);
}
?>
```

The most important part of the previous example is the first section, which gets the repository information, enumerates through children in a folder, and gets the properties of an entry. The sections that follow are common for browser-style interfaces that present a user interface. The second section handles the mechanics of manipulating the Atom feed generated by CMIS, as well as the feed to CMIS. In this case, neither Drupal nor PHP has a native library for handling Atom and its data types, but the functions presented can be reused for these purposes and are not specific to Alfresco. Finally, the hook functions in the last section are needed to integrate the browser with the CCK, but are similar to other Drupal theme extensions using CCK.

Librarian

A Librarian (see Figure 17-7) is a specialized browser that controls the content in a hierarchical view. Because the primary context in which content normally lives within an Alfresco repository is the folder/space hierarchy, the Browser view is the natural place to put library type controls. Library services describe the Check Out and Check In services originally designed for engineering document control, but has been extended to document management and Web content management. It provides the tools to edit the content with integration to the appropriate authoring application, which may or may not be available within the browser, depending upon the MIME type of the content. It also provides a view to explore the version history of a content object.

Using a Librarian

A Librarian provides the hierarchical browsing experience of a browser, while adding the ability to check out a content object for revision. It also provides a property sheet for metadata entry and update, an interface to add or replace the content file, and a form to check in the content object. In addition, there is a Query view for exploring and accessing the version history of a content object.

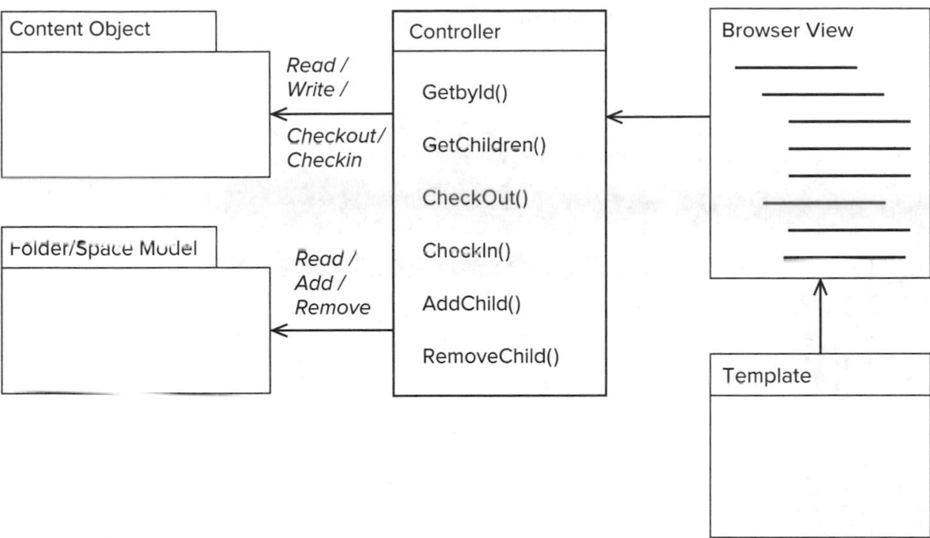

FIGURE 17-7

The Librarian view presents specific actions for the content Check Out and Check In. It must also present a property sheet to edit the content object properties with whichever properties should be editable, as well as those properties that are mandatory. This information is available from the Data Dictionary, which is accessible through Web scripts and CMIS if the Librarian dynamically generates the forms for different types.

The Librarian view provides the interfaces for adding or replacing content. If the MIME type of the content is text, HTML, or even some types of XML, it may be possible to provide an editing tool within the browser application. More complex AJAX applications can be used to manipulate even more complex document types, such as graphical drawings and Office documents. In most cases beyond basic text and HTML, the Librarian will be responsible for launching the correct application or will use the MIME type for the browser to launch the correct application. Using WebDAV to edit the document makes it possible for the application to replace the content in the repository; the repository then controls versioning and user permissions.

When to Use It

A Librarian is useful for applications that provide general or special purpose controls of large amounts of content. A general purpose document management tool that is independent of an underlying repository usually implements a Librarian. Image-scanning and -management tools are also Librarians. Applications that manage special purpose libraries, such as research libraries, reference materials, or policy libraries, are vertical examples of libraries. However, these are often best handled with something like the Alfresco Share application or a general-purpose CMIS library tool extended with domain-specific pages or forms.

Example

CMIS Spaces, from Integrated Semantics, is a CMIS-based Librarian that uses Adobe Flex for the user interface (see Figure 17-8). Flex provides a very rich browser experience with all the functionality of a thick client. CMIS Spaces can be distinguished from a browser in that it provides library services for uploading and updating content as well as manipulating metadata.

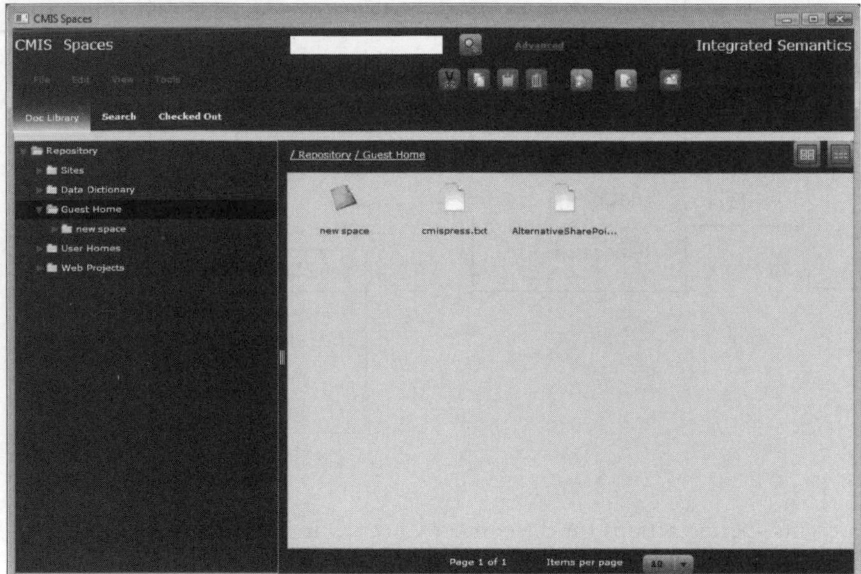

FIGURE 17-8

CMIS Spaces provides Rich Internet Application (RIA) clients for Flex and AIR (the Adobe client-based runtime) Flex and Internet browser (such as Microsoft IE or Mozilla Firefox). CMIS Spaces uses the UI-independent ActionScript (Adobe's JavaScript-like script-based process language) and APIs for both CMIS AtomPub REST and CMIS Web services (SOAP). It uses a number of other open source projects, such as Cairngorm, Presentation Model pattern, and Spring ActionScript.

CMIS Spaces' Flex+AIR configuration also can handle the headers and delete/put HTTP verbs for AtomPub updating. For Flex+Browser AtomPub updating, CMIS Spaces can be configured to use sockets (as 3httpclientlib).

Catalog View

A Catalog view (see Figure 17-9) is either a Query view or a specialized Browser view to present a list of items to act upon, such as purchasing the item being presented. A Catalog view may make extensive use of images. The number of items may determine whether to use a Query view, a Browser view, or both. The List view of the catalog will present information specific to what the content is describing rather than the content object itself. Likewise, a detail or Property Sheet view will present metadata and actions relevant to the subject of the content rather than the content. For instance, a catalog of products may have a set of images, but present information and metadata about the product rather than the actual photo. However, a catalog can still present photos and articles and be content-specific since that may be the subject matter of the catalog.

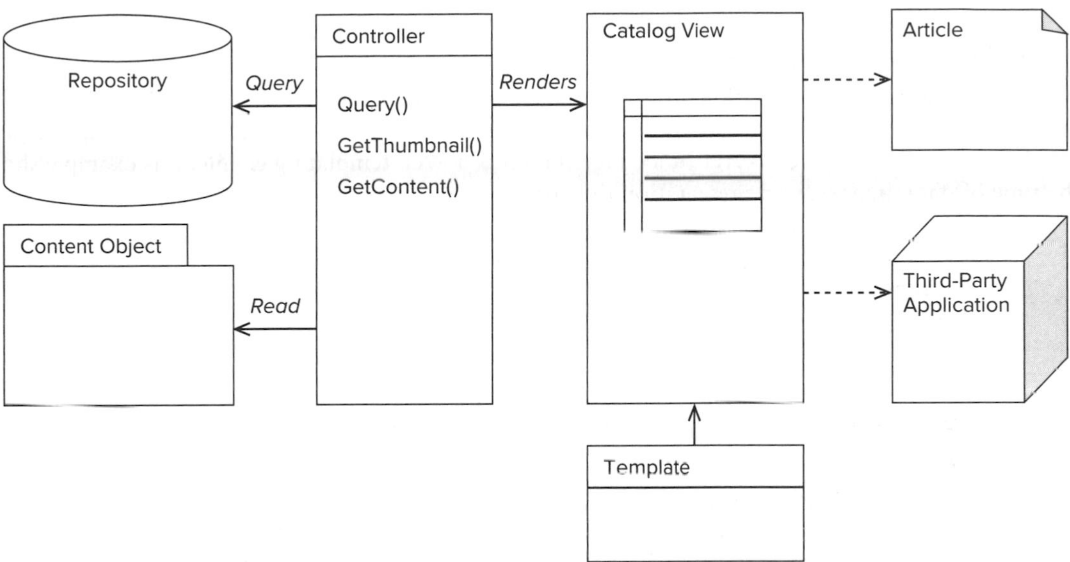

FIGURE 17-9

Using a Catalog View

A Catalog view uses a Query view either when there are relatively few items or when a categorization is not appropriate, often because there are too many categories. A catalog of articles is a relatively simple example of a catalog and doesn't really require much structure if there are a dozen or so articles. If there are tens of thousands of items that are not easily accessible through a category structure, then queries may be the easier way to access the catalog item. In such a circumstance, additional Query views may be used to show recently added items.

A Catalog view uses a Browser view when there is a moderate number of items and is easily browsed and accessed through a folder or category hierarchy. Using the native folder system in a subset of folders is usually the best way to manage the catalog for presenting catalog items through a Browser view. Even in this case, it is usually best to provide a Query view to find the catalog items.

The view generated for either the Query view or the Browser view may be presented differently than in the normal views. If the catalog is more visual because the content is an image or a thumbnail is more important than the metadata, then the view may generate more of a "Light Box" view that adds as many images as possible on a page or page component. Otherwise, a standard Browser view list would be more appropriate.

The property sheet should present the actions that are appropriate for the purpose of the catalog, such as download or purchase. Metadata should be kept to a minimum, such as name, description, and date added or available.

When to Use It

Catalogs are useful for presenting lists of articles or images that can be used for business purposes. Catalogs can enhance applications by presenting lists of content that might be helpful in using the application.

Example: Image Gallery in Share

An image gallery, in this case of photos or graphics, is a good example of a catalog. The image gallery available with Alfresco Share is an example of how you can build a similar catalog-type interface using FreeMarker with the Alfresco API. Since FreeMarker is a Web templating engine, this example shows the type of data, images, and presentation that are required.

```
<#macro detailsUrl image label>
  <a href="${url.context}/page/site/${page.url.templateArgs.site}\
/document-details?nodeRef=${image.nodeRef}" class="theme-color1">${label}
  </a>
</#macro>
<script type="text/javascript">//<![CDATA[
  new Alfresco.ImageSummary("${args.htmlid}");
  new Alfresco.widget.DashletResizer("${args.htmlid}", "${instance.object.id}");
//]]></script>
<div class="dashlet">
  <div class="title">${msg("header.title")}</div>
  <div id="${args.htmlid}-list" class="body scrollableList"
        <#if args.height??>style="height: ${args.height}px;"</#if>>
    <#if images.message?exists>
      <div class="detail-list-item first-item last-item">
        <div class="error">${images.message}</div>
      </div>
    <#elseif images.items?size == 0>
      <div class="detail-list-item first-item last-item">
        <span>${msg("label.noitems")}</span>
      </div>
    <#else>
      <#assign detailsmsg = msg("label.viewdetails")>
      <#list images.items as image>
        <#assign nodeRefUrl=image.nodeRef?replace('://','/')>
        <div class="images">
          <div class="item">
            <div class="thumbnail">
              <a href="${url.context}/proxy/alfresco/api/node/content/\
${nodeRefUrl}/${image.name?url}"
                  rel="lightbox"
                  title="${image.title?html} -
                  ${msg("text.modified-by", image.modifier)}
                  ${image.modifiedOn?datetime(
                    "dd MMM yyyy HH:mm:ss 'GMT'Z '('zzz')'")
                  ?string("dd MMM, yyyy HH:mm:ss")}">
                <img src="${url.context}/proxy/alfresco/api/node/\
${nodeRefUrl}/content/thumbnails/doclib?c=force"/>
              </a>
            </div>
            <div class="details">
```

```
                    <@detailsUrl image detailsmsg />
                  </div>
                </div>
                </div>
              </#list>
            </#if>
          </div>
      </div>
```

In this example, the `#list` directive of FreeMarker is used to iterate through the items in a space that is dedicated to images. A thumbnail generated by the Thumbnail service is accessed from the repository and placed next to the metadata. Within a catalog, thumbnails are a good way to present images, products, or media for detailed access and actions, such as download or purchase.

Attachment

An attachment (see Figure 17-10) is a document logically attached to a business object in an application, such as an invoice, a contract, or a quality-control report. The attachment is important in the process in which the business object is involved, providing documentation such as transactional information or quality data. The attachment may be added outside the application, such as in Alfresco Share with a Share extension, or it may be added by the application, either by adding the content directly or using a browser to find existing content. The attachment is generally available when users access or browse the business object.

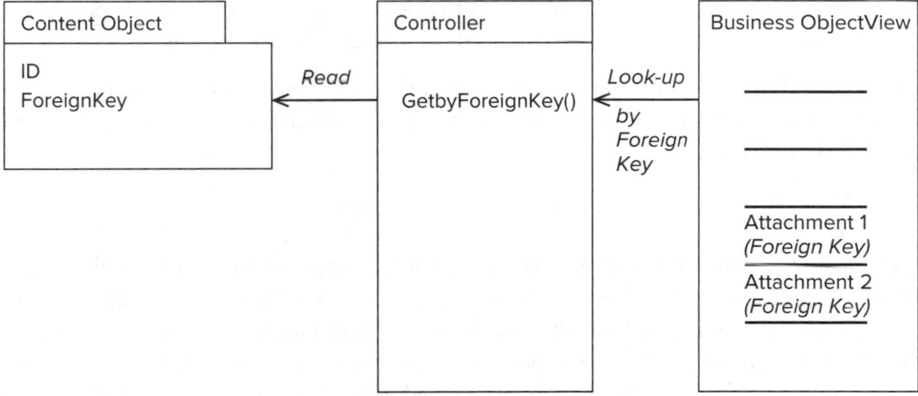

FIGURE 17-10

Using an Attachment

In the design of the attachment, you must first determine how the content will be associated with the business object. If the sole purpose of the document is to act as an attachment to one and only one business object, then it is best to have a foreign key (`http://en.wikipedia.org/wiki/foreign_key`) as part of an Alfresco type or aspect. If the application is responsible for managing the relationship, such as in SAP, then it is still a good idea to have a foreign key to provide a backward reference for access to the business object. If there is more than one business object associated with a document or the document is used for other purposes, you can either use an aspect with a repeating foreign key or use an association in Alfresco. If you are using CMIS, then you must use a foreign key in a type or association.

The attachment first needs to exist in the Alfresco repository. If the application either creates or captures the document that will become the attachment, then the application stores the document in the repository. Applications generally place the content in well-known locations or create the folders/spaces in which to place the content in order to simplify the user's interaction with the application.

If the attachment already exists in Alfresco, then you can add it either in Alfresco Share or using a browser in the application. In Share, you can create a special property sheet associated with an application-specific aspect that allows you to choose a foreign key to associate with the document by querying the applications database for a list of foreign keys. If the application adds the attachment, then the application can present a browser to choose the document to attach.

If the application provides an interface to add an attachment, then it must also provide an interface to remove an attachment.

When the user navigates to a Business Object in the application, the application provides links to the attachment. Normally this would open the attachment either *in situ* or in a separate window.

When to Use It

Many ERP and CRM applications already provide interfaces to attach content from content management systems or archives. Alfresco makes a good alternative to other systems for this purpose. If an application drives a business process with a requirement to document data (such as invoices or receipts) being entered into a business object, the application needs an object, like an attachment.

If there are reference materials that can help explain a set of data or some other context and the users are capable of adding this content, then an attachment is a good mechanism for allowing users to generate and attach this content.

Example

The SAP ArchiveLink integration created by CTAC, a system integrator in Germany, implements the Content Services Mapping protocol to allow access of SAP systems to external ECM systems. On top of the ArchiveLink protocol, SAP implements the Archive and Query pattern to store and find content in the underlying ECM system. The Attachment pattern is associated with individual business objects in SAP to access the content. Although the metadata is stored in SAP, a copy is made in Alfresco by the CTAC system, as seen in Figure 17-11. The content is accessed from the attachments through the ArchiveLink protocol.

Annotation

An annotation (see Figure 17-12) is a piece of user-generated content that annotates an object (usually a document, Web page, or article) with information or comments regarding that object. Annotations themselves can be annotated, leading to a threaded trail of discussion. Annotations provide the end user with the opportunity to comment on the quality, intent, or accuracy of the document, which improves the document. Thus, annotations are a good way to capture user-generated content for a Web site or Web 2.0 application.

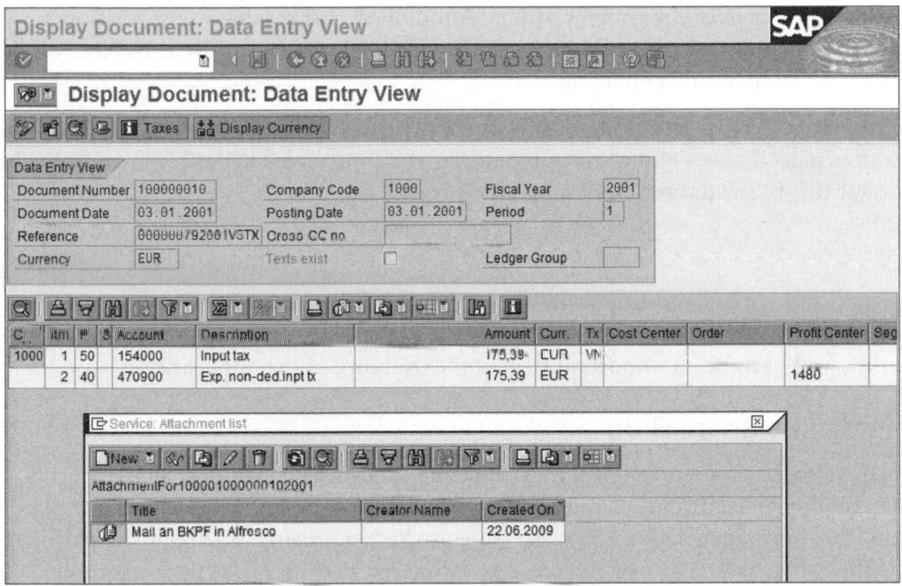

FIGURE 17-11

Annotations can be put in the context of a specific location on a page or can trail the document at the end, appearing to be part of the metadata of the document. Threaded annotation discussions are best kept separate from the content. However, an annotation placed *in situ* in the document must be done in conjunction with either a desktop-based or rich client-based editor, such as those associated with PDF or Computer Aided Design (CAD) tools.

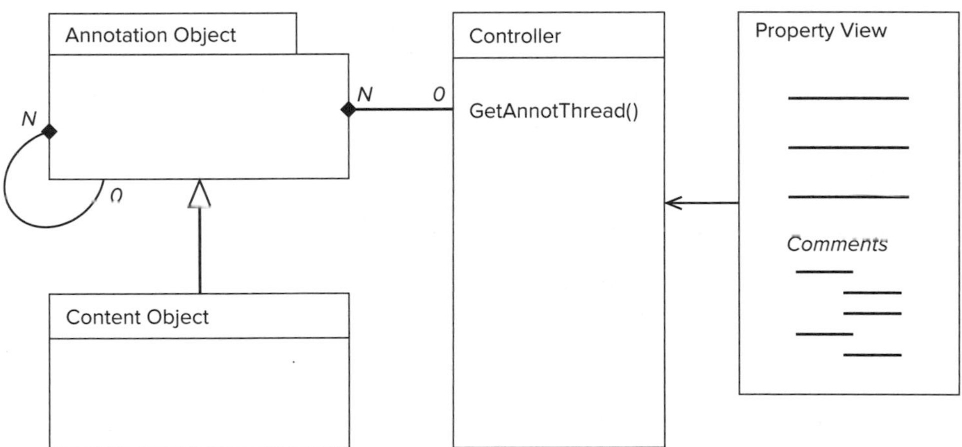

FIGURE 17-12

Using an Annotation

The application presents a simple form to capture the comment about the content. This is usually done in the Property view. This form is normally either plain text or restricted HTML limited to only basic formatting. The application creates the content as type Annotation and creates an association between the annotation and the document. If the annotation is threaded, an association is also made to the annotation to which this annotation is referring.

Once stored, the Property view regenerates the form view or uses AJAX to append the new annotation. The new annotation is placed at the end of the annotations if the preferred order is chronological or after the annotation if this is an annotation of an annotation.

When to Use It

Annotations are important for collaborative applications as they provide an important part of the feedback loop on the quality of content and presentation of a document or article. They are also useful for engaging the user, and become an important part of the usability of the application.

Example: Comments in a Share Blog

The following is an example of annotations with comments in a blog in Alfresco Share. In this case, these are the comments at the end of the blog and are handled by the FreeMarker template comments.get.html.ftl. This is included in the same page as the blogs using Surf regions. This lists the comments attached to a blog. Most of the setup is for layout within Surf, but the core of the functionality is at the end.

```
<script type="text/javascript">//
<![CDATA[
  new Alfresco.CommentList("${args.htmlid}").setOptions({
    siteId: "${page.url.templateArgs.site!""}",
    containerId: "${template.properties.container!"blog"}",
    height: ${args.editorHeight!180},
    width: ${args.editorWidth!700},
    editorConfig: {
      height: ${args.editorHeight!180},
      width: ${args.editorWidth!700},
      theme: 'advanced',
      theme_advanced_buttons1:
      "bold,italic,underline,|,bullist,numlist,|,\
forecolor,backcolor,|,undo,redo,removeformat",
      theme_advanced_toolbar_location: "top",
      theme_advanced_toolbar_align: "left",
      theme_advanced_statusbar_location: "bottom",
      theme_advanced_resizing: true,
      theme_advanced_buttons2: null,
      theme_advanced_buttons3: null,
      theme_advanced_path: false,
      language: '${locale?substring(0, 2)}'
      }
    }).setMessages(${messages});
//]]>
</script>
<div id="${args.htmlid}-body" class="comment-list" style="display:none;">
  <div class="postlist-infobar">
    <div id="${args.htmlid}-title" class="commentsListTitle"></div>
    <div id="${args.htmlid}-paginator" class="paginator"></div>
  </div>
```

```
    <div class="clear"></div>
    <div id="${args.htmlid}-comments"></div>
  </div>
```

There is a link in the Comments section that invokes the Web script implemented by createcomment.get.html.ftl. This presents a special view to capture the comment and add it to the repository.

```
<script type="text/javascript">//<![CDATA[
  new Alfresco.CreateComment("${args.htmlid}").setOptions(
  {
    siteId: "${page.url.templateArgs.site!""}",
    containerId: "${template.properties.container!"blog"}",
    height: ${args.editorHeight!250},
    width: ${args.editorWidth!538},
    editorConfig : {
      height: ${args.editorHeight!250},
      width: ${args.editorWidth!538},
      theme: 'advanced',
      theme_advanced_buttons1:
      "bold,italic,underline,|,bullist,numlist,|,\
forecolor,backcolor,|,undo,redo,removeformat",
      theme_advanced_toolbar_location: "top",
      theme_advanced_toolbar_align: "left",
      theme_advanced_statusbar_location: "bottom",
      theme_advanced_resizing: true,
      theme_advanced_buttons2: null,
      theme_advanced_buttons3: null,
      theme_advanced_path: false,
      language: '${locale?substring(0, 2)}'
    }
   }).setMessages(${messages});
//]]></script>

<div id="${args.htmlid}-form-container" class="addCommentForm hidden">
  <div class="commentFormTitle">
    <label for="${htmlid}-content">${msg("addComment")}:</label>
  </div>
  <div class="editComment">
    <form id="${htmlid}-form" method="post" action="">
      <div>
        <input type="hidden" id="${args.htmlid}-nodeRef" name="nodeRef" value="" />
        <input type="hidden" id="${args.htmlid}-site" name="site" value="" />
        <input type="hidden" id="${args.htmlid}-container" name="container"
             value="" />
        <input type="hidden" id="${args.htmlid}-itemTitle" name="itemTitle"
             value="" />
        <input type="hidden" id="${args.htmlid}-page" name="page" value="" />



        <input type="hidden" id="${args.htmlid}-pageParams"
             name="pageParams" value=""/>

        <textarea id="${htmlid}-content" rows="8" cols="80" name="content">
```

```
          </textarea>
        </div>
        <div class="commentFormAction">
          <input type="submit" id="${htmlid}-submit" value="${msg('postComment')}"/>
        </div>
      </form>
    </div>
  </div>
```

The code here is the presentation layer using Surf to present a list of comments and then to capture a comment from a user. There are calls to set up the theme for the forms, but the main part in both is to use div classes to set up the presentation of the list or form. In the first part, Surf is used to present the list of comments associated with `htmlid` of the object to which the comments are attached. In the second part, a comment is captured using an HTML form and posted to the object identified by `htmlid`.

Archive

An Archive (see Figure 17-13) is a repository for the long-term storage and control of information that must be retained for operational or regulatory reasons. Typical uses for an archive are to store reports, scanned documents, or electronic documents that are no longer used, but which the organization wishes to retain for possible future use. Records are a special case of Archive in which the documents and content stored in the archive are managed according to official rules of retention, lifecycle, and/or review process.

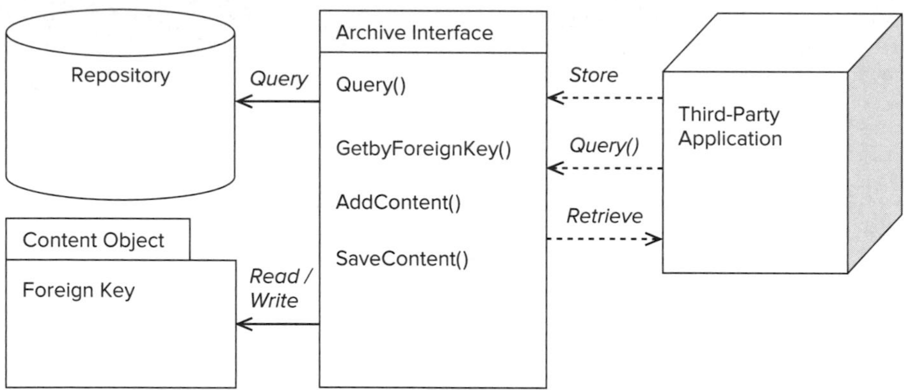

FIGURE 17-13

Using an Archive

An archive is usually a section of an Alfresco repository that has a separate folder/space structure specifically for the documents stored in the archive. An archive will specify permission controls on who can add, modify, or delete documents. An archive also provides lifecycles on change of state and location.

The Alfresco Records Management module provides even more sophisticated controls over security and retention. File plans are associated with folders, which can determine how long records will be retained and what happens to the record after retention: is it destroyed or transferred, how often must it be reviewed, and what events change the state of the record? If the application chooses to use the Records Management option, it should either be responsible for filing the records and adding all mandatory information, or it should direct the user or records manager to the Records Management application to process the record.

Most applications integrating an archive are using it to store captured or generated information from the application. The application may also use the archive to store attachments that are part of a business process. Therefore, an archive usually works in cooperation with attachments. There is usually enough information in the application to allow the application to decide where to store the information in the archive. In addition, the application should be responsible for generating the foreign key to allow retrieval and association of the document in the archive.

Since many applications use the file system to store their output, then using the CIFS, NFS, or WebDAV interface may be an alternative way to store and access the documents in the archive. Most email clients support IMAP, so Alfresco's IMAP interface is capable of acting as an archive for email as well. This can be a very simple way to integrate content into a repository, although it will not be able to capture as much metadata as a direct connection. For email, there may be enough information in the From, To, and Subject fields to extract and classify emails going into an archive. The application would be dependent upon rules, actions, and metadata extraction to fill in default information. By associating a workflow with a folder through a rule, Alfresco could forward the document for further metadata entry.

A separate Query view may be generated to present an application specific view were the documents in the archive based upon context in the application. For instance, if an application was archiving reports based upon a specific portion of that application, then the application would provide a view of those reports that may be independent of where they are stored. It may also provide context, status, and process information that are specific to that application. Alternatively, an application could use a URL link to a specialized Share view or portlet.

Because an archive is used for long-term storage, a separate content store may be used for a Hierarchical Storage Management system or secondary storage. This can be controlled by the application by applying a special aspect that determines into which store the content will go.

When to Use It

Scanning applications commonly use archives. Paper documents are scanned to simplify their retrieval and use in electronic business processes. Scans are also stored to ensure the documents' long-term retention. Very simple scanning interfaces can use the file system emulation to store content in the archive. More sophisticated scanning applications, such as Kofax, use repository-specific release scripts that capture and load metadata into the archive.

Enterprise Resource Planning and Customer Relationship Management applications, such as SAP and Oracle, use Service Provider Interfaces (SPI) for storing reports and archiving data. SAP's ArchiveLink interface was one of the first of its kind to standardize and certify interfaces for archiving. Similar applications that are very process- and report-heavy are also good candidates for an archive.

General clearing and retention of documents and emails are other good uses for an archive. Email clients can use an archive with the IMAP protocol to drag and drop or use email rules to archive old emails. By presenting the archive as a shared drive, it is easy to move content and still make it accessible.

Records in either governmental or regulatory use can also use an archive with the Records Management module. Documents, reports, and scanned documents all represent potential records in an archive backed by the Records repository.

Example: Kofax Release Script

Micro Strategies, Inc. (`www.microstrategies.com`) has created a Kofax release script that is a standard way to integrate to the Kofax scanning system (`www.kofax.com`). Kofax is a high-end, high-volume image-scanning system that works with multiple content repositories, and a release script is the standard way to capture metadata and store the content and metadata into a content repository.

In this instance, the release script is written in C# and .NET to integrate with the Kofax client and uses Web scripts to access the Alfresco repository. This file, AlfrescoRelease.cs, uploads the images as documents and hooks into standard Kofax integration points.

```
/// <summary>
/// The Release URL for Alfresco: This is the URL used to post documents
/// to Alfresco.
/// It uses a ticket for authentication. For example:
/// <code>
/// /service/kofax/release?alf_ticket={0}
/// </code>
/// </summary>
public string ReleaseURL
{
  get { return releaseURL; }
  set { releaseURL = value; }
}

/// <summary>
/// Releases documents to Alfresco: Retrieves all document and metadata information
/// from Kofax and inserts it into Alfresco.
/// </summary>
/// <returns>A KfxReturnValue object detailing if the release was successful
/// </returns>
public KfxReturnValue release()
{
  try
  {
    int uniqueDocumentID = this.releaseData.UniqueDocumentID;
    CustomProperties properties = this.releaseData.CustomProperties;
    initializeCustomProperties(properties);
    initializeWorkingFolders(uniqueDocumentID);

    string response = uploadDocuments();

    //Process Result
    if (response.StartsWith("ERROR"))
    {
      logger.Error(response);
      this.releaseData.SendMessage(response, 9999,
          KfxInfoReturnValue.KFX_REL_DOC_ERROR);
      error.LogError(response, "Alfresco.Kofax.Release.WebScripts.Release",
          response, true, true, "");
```

```
            return KfxReturnValue.KFX_REL_ERROR;
          }
          else
          {
            WebStatus status = new WebStatus(response);
            int code = status.Code;
            string description = status.Description;
            string message = status.Message;
            string statusName = status.Name;

            if (message.StartsWith("ERROR"))
            {
              logger.Error(response);
              this.releaseData.SendMessage(message, 9999,
                  KfxInfoReturnValue.KFX_REL_DOC_ERROR);
              error.LogError(message, "Alfresco.Kofax.Release.WebScripts.Release",
                  response, true, true, "");
              return KfxReturnValue.KFX_REL_ERROR;
            }
          }
        }
      }

      /// <summary>
      /// Uploads the documents.
      /// </summary>
      /// <returns></returns>

      private string uploadDocuments()
      {
        //Upload Documents
        string kofaxPDFFileName = this.releaseData.KofaxPDFFileName;

        string ticket = AlfrescoTicketHelper.getTicket(url + String.Format(loginURL,
            customUsername, customPassword));

        WebUpload release = new WebUpload(url + String.Format(releaseURL, ticket));
        release.addField("contentType", contentType);
        release.addField("overwrite", overwrite);
        release.addField("uploaddirectory", defaultFolder);
        if ((dynamicFolder != null) && (!dynamicFolder.Equals("")))
          release.addField("dynamicuploaddirectory", dynamicFolder);
        foreach (Value oVal in this.releaseData.Values)
        {
          string destination = oVal.Destination;
          string source = oVal.SourceName;
          string value = oVal.Value;

          if (source.Equals("Image"))
          {
            releaseData.ImageFiles.Copy(imageDirectory, 0);

            //rename move all docs to the primary release dir
            FileInfo[] files = imageDirectoryInfo.GetFiles();
```

```
            foreach (FileInfo file in files)
            {
              release.addFile(destination, file.FullName, "image/tiff");
            }
          }
        ]
      ]
```

This module posts the documents scanned in Kofax to Alfresco using a ticket for authentication. It collects the documents and metadata from Kofax and provides this information as part of the post. It then uploads the document as a stream.

To help the release script, Kofax has created the following C# module, WebUpload.cs, to access the Web scripts that provide the functionality in the Alfresco server needed to process the documents.

```
namespace Alfresco.Kofax.Release.WebScripts
{
  public class WebUpload
  {
    private string boundary;
    private HttpWebRequest httpWebRequest;
    private Stream requestStream;
    private FileStream fileStream;
    private Hashtable fields;
    private static readonly ILog logger = LogManager.GetLogger(typeof(WebUpload));

    public WebUpload(string url)
    {
      // Create a boundary
      boundary = "----------------------------" + DateTime.Now.Ticks.ToString("x");

      // Create the web request
      httpWebRequest = (HttpWebRequest)WebRequest.Create(url);
      httpWebRequest.ContentType = "multipart/form-data; boundary=" + boundary;
      httpWebRequest.Method = "POST";
      httpWebRequest.KeepAlive = true;
      fields = new Hashtable();
    }

    public string upload()
    {
      string responseString = "";
      try
      {
        //Add Fields to Stream - Content should already be added.
        addFieldsToStream();

        // Get the boundary in bytes
        byte[] boundarybytes = System.Text.Encoding.ASCII
                .GetBytes("\r\n--" + boundary + "--\r\n");

        // Write out the trailing boundary
        requestStream.Write(boundarybytes, 0, boundarybytes.Length);
```

```
            // Close the request and file stream
            requestStream.Close();
            fileStream.Close();

            WebResponse webResponse = httpWebRequest.GetResponse();
            Stream responseStream = webResponse.GetResponseStream();
            StreamReader responseReader = new StreamReader(responseStream);
            responseString = responseReader.ReadToEnd();

            // Close response object.
            webResponse.Close();
          }
          catch (WebException e)
          {
            if (e.Status == WebExceptionStatus.ProtocolError)
            {
              HttpWebResponse response = ((HttpWebResponse)e.Response);
              string text;
              try
              {
                using (Stream stream = response.GetResponseStream())
                            {
                using (StreamReader reader = new StreamReader(stream))
                              {
                text = reader.ReadToEnd();
                responseString = "ERROR: " + text;
                logger.Error(text);
              }
            }
          }
          catch (WebException ex)
          {
            logger.Error(ex.Message);
            responseString = "ERROR: " + ex.Message;
          }
        }

        return responseString;
      }

      public void addFile(string formFileName, string file, string mimeType)
      {
        // Get the boundary in bytes
        byte[] boundarybytes = System.Text.Encoding.ASCII.GetBytes("\r\n--"
              + boundary + "\r\n");

        // Get the header for the file upload
        string headerTemplate = "Content-Disposition: form-data;\
    name=\"{0}\";filename=\"{1}\"\r\n Content-Type: " + mimeType + "\r\n\r\n";

        // Add the filename to the header
        string header = string.Format(headerTemplate, formFileName, file);

        //convert the header to a byte array
```

```
    byte[] headerbytes = System.Text.Encoding.UTF8.GetBytes(header);

    // Get the output stream
    requestStream = httpWebRequest.GetRequestStream();

    // Write out the starting boundary
    requestStream.Write(boundarybytes, 0, boundarybytes.Length);

    // Write the header including the filename.
    requestStream.Write(headerbytes, 0, headerbytes.Length);

    // Open up a filestream
    fileStream = new FileStream(file, FileMode.Open, FileAccess.Read);

    // Use 4096 for the buffer
    byte[] buffer = new byte[4096];

    int bytesRead = 0;
    // Loop through whole file uploading parts in a stream.
    while ((bytesRead = fileStream.Read(buffer, 0, buffer.Length)) != 0)
    {
      requestStream.Write(buffer, 0, bytesRead);
      requestStream.Flush();
    }
  }

  private void addFieldsToStream()
  {
    // Loop through all items of a Hashtable
    IDictionaryEnumerator item = fields.GetEnumerator();
    while (item.MoveNext())
    {
      addFieldToStream(item.Key.ToString(), item.Value.ToString());
    }
  }

  public void addField(string formFieldName, string value)
  {
    fields.Add(formFieldName, value);
  }

  private void addFieldToStream(string formFieldName, string value)
  {
    // Get the boundary in bytes
    byte[] boundarybytes = System.Text.Encoding.ASCII
            .GetBytes("\r\n--" + boundary + "\r\n");

    // Get the header for the file upload
    string headerTemplate = "Content-Disposition: form-data; name=\"{0}\"\r\n\r\n";

    // Add the filename to the header
    string header = string.Format(headerTemplate, formFieldName);

    //convert the header to a byte array
```

```
        byte[] headerbytes = System.Text.Encoding.UTF8.GetBytes(header);
        byte[] valuebytes = System.Text.Encoding.UTF8.GetBytes(value);

        // Get the output stream
        requestStream = httpWebRequest.GetRequestStream();

        // Write out the starting boundary
        requestStream.Write(boundarybytes, 0, boundarybytes.Length);

        // Write the header
        requestStream.Write(headerbytes, 0, headerbytes.Length);

        // Write the value
        requestStream.Write(valuebytes, 0, valuebytes.Length);
    }
}
```

These helper methods provide the tools for the .NET release script to add the metadata and file binaries to the HTTP request that interacts with the Web script. These are used in the preceding release script example and can be valuable for any .NET application accessing a Web script.

Project Space

A Project Space (see Figure 17-14) is a place for users of an application to share ideas, comments, documents, emails, and other information. If a business application is very data-centric, then it will generally not have a good place to store unstructured information as the users of the application develop changes to configuration or structured information that may go into the application. Given a certain context and structure, a Project Space can enhance a data-centric business application to take advantage of collaboration between users of the application. Share, in turn, can access information through a view presented by the business application.

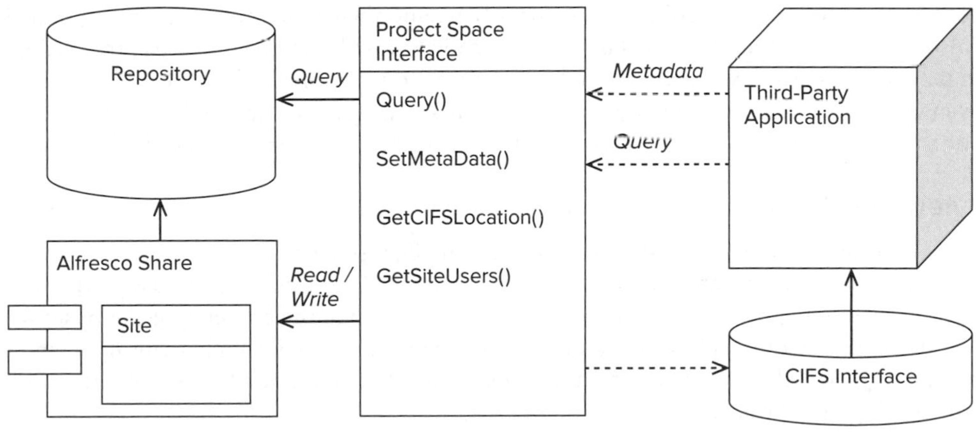

FIGURE 17-14

Using a Project Space

This is really a cooperation of two applications: the business application and Alfresco Share. The business application interacts with Share through an interface similar to an archive to store and retrieve information. This can either be through a file emulation interface, such as CIFS, NFS, or FTP, or through an API. This is where the business application deposits information that might be useful for the collaboration, such as reports or analysis.

To capture the results of the project, it is best to provide a view on the business application to the users of the Project Space. This is best provided with a Page Component for Alfresco Share that may simply expose an iFrame, or through a Share dashlet, which again can be an iFrame. A button or interface on or near this view can be used to capture the action taken in the business system to record the results.

When to Use It

In Customer Relationship Management or Bid Management systems, large teams may collaborate in the creation of offerings and terms for customers. A Project Space provides a space for them to discuss and decide on approaches and iterate on the offerings or contracts. The document management system provides the tools for creation, management, reuse, and delivery of the output, while the CRM system takes the result as an attachment, thus enhancing the sales process.

Configuration of complex data or structures in a business application, such as an ERP or CRM system, can be difficult to track. By turning the process into a recipe upon which other people collaborate, it is possible to walk through the scenarios of what changes in the configuration would mean and then take action. If the change in configuration is not complete, then the team can collaborate on new configurations. Alfresco Share would allow them to document changes, discuss the possible outcomes, and act. The view from the business application would allow the configuration to take place.

Review and Approval Workflow

A Review and Approval workflow (see Figure 17-15) is similar to a Project Space but the purpose is more focused on tracking the review of critical documents in a review process. The workflow takes an artifact and delivers it to key responsible people for review, and then either approval or rejection. The workflow also provides an audit trail of the decisions made. As with the Project Space, the business application may lack a workflow capability and a repository to track the artifacts of the business process. A Review and Approval workflow demonstrates that key documents and deliverables have been signed off by those responsible for the end result, either for regulatory or operational efficiency reasons.

Using a Review and Approval Workflow

A workflow is built using jBPM either in XML or using the Eclipse-based workflow design tool for jBPM. One or more workflows can be made available for usage. The easiest way to assign the workflows is to use a rule in a space in an archive dedicated to processing the contents of the business application. Alternatively, the application can initiate the workflow using a Web script upon entry in the archive. Using the Attachment pattern, the content can be added to the business object and then the workflow is initiated on that document.

The workflow then manages the process of Review and Approval. The content is delivered to the end user via email. The user can then track items that need action through the Alfresco clients or via a portlet. The Alfresco system can also be configured to send reminders if necessary.

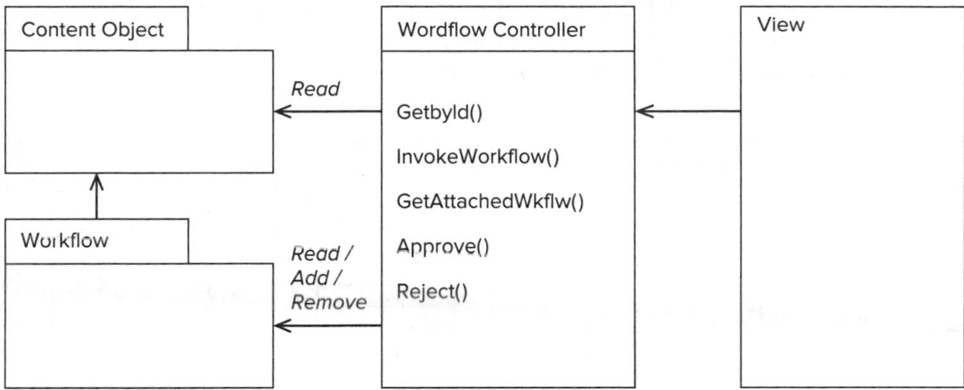

FIGURE 17-15

Status can be tracked using an aspect. This aspect should have the status and the identifier of the workflow to allow action on that workflow if necessary. This status can be inspected by the application to indicate whether the document is ready for use or not and whether it has been processed and edited properly. The attachment can then indicate the current status of its associated workflow through that aspect so that the status persists beyond the life of the workflow. Status can also be tracked using a Query view that queries the status of currently active documents for review.

When to Use It

When an application must provide documentation that procedures and policies are being followed, a Review and Approval workflow can demonstrate that the appropriate reviews have been taken by those responsible. This is often required for compliance with regulatory authorities, such as for Sarbanes-Oxley, and for industry certification such as ISO 9000.

Example: Kofax

In the Kofax example provided earlier, Micro Strategies used the rules and actions capabilities of Alfresco. As part of the repository setup, the spaces that the images are stored in are assigned a workflow for any new images coming in. As soon as the images are added, the rule associated with new items assigns a quality control workflow that puts the image through a workflow and assigns the image to the appropriate person. No coding was necessary.

Feed

Some applications can access or track content using RSS feeds (see Figure 17-16). Some examples are mail clients, feed readers, or portals that have feed readers built in. With these feed readers, the application can track changes or actions that a user needs to take in a workflow. In addition, feeds are a good way to track the changes in a repository that, in turn, can be a good way to track what is happening in the business if you are tracking business-critical documents or Web pages.

Using a Feed

A feed can be implemented as a simple Query view implemented as a Web script that is rendered as an RSS feed using an RSS template. There are default feeds defined in Alfresco Share and Explorer, so these do not need to be coded if the default feeds suit your purpose. The links from the feed can be directed either to the content directly or to the Properties page in Alfresco Share. The Web script can also render the Activities feed to track changes across multiple sites.

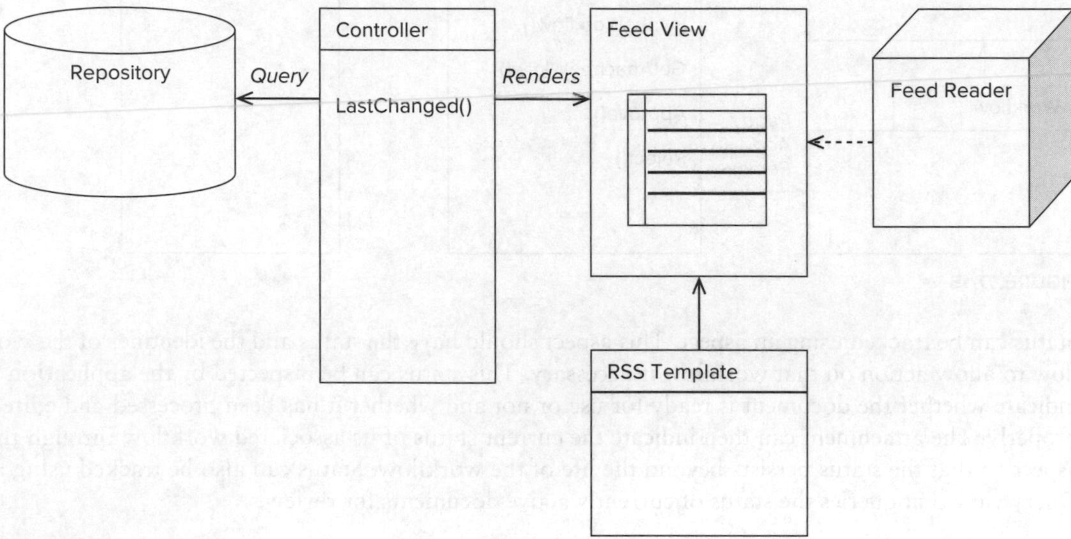

FIGURE 17-16

When to Use It

Use a feed to track process changes or changes in business-critical information in a repository. Workflow changes are tracked well if they are delivered to a favorite feed reader. Also, feeds can be an easy way to integrate into a portal.

Example: Activities Atom Feed

The following is an example of an Atom subscription feed implemented using the FreeMarker API. Specifically, this is getting the activities associated with a site and returning the latest updates as an Atom feed.

```
<#assign mode = args.mode!"">
<#if mode = "user">
  <#assign title=msg("atom.title.user", user.fullName?xml)>
<#else>
  <#assign title=msg("atom.title.site", args["site"]?xml)>
</#if>
<#assign genericTitle=msg("title.generic")>
<?xml version="1.0" encoding="UTF-8"?>
  <feed xmlns="http://www.w3.org/2005/Atom">
    <generator version="1.0">Alfresco (1.0)</generator>
    <link rel="self" href="${absurl(url.full)?xml}" />
    <id>${absurl(url.full)?xml}</id>
    <title>${title?xml}</title>
    <#if activities?exists && activities?size &gt; 0>
```

```
          <updated>${activities[0].date.isoDate}</updated>
          <#list activities as activity>
            <#assign userLink="
              <a href=\"${absurl(activity.userProfile)}\">
                    ${activity.fullName?html}</a>">
            <#assign itemLink="
              <a href=\"${absurl(activity.itemPage)}\">
                    ${activity.title?html}</a>">
            <#assign siteLink="
              <a href=\"${absurl(activity.sitePage)}\">
                    ${activity.siteId?html}</a>">
            <entry xmlns='http://www.w3.org/2005/Atom'>
              <#assign detail = msg(activity.type, activity.title?xml,
                    activity.fullName?xml,activity.custom0, activity.custom1)>
              <#if mode="user" && !activity.suppressSite>
                <#assign detail=msg("in.site", detail, activity.siteId?xml)></#if>
              <title><![CDATA[${detail?xml}]]></title>
              <link rel="alternate" type="text/html"
                          href="${absurl(activity.itemPage)}" />
              <id>${activity.id}</id>
              <updated>${activity.date.isoDate}</updated>
              <#assign detailHTML = msg(activity.type, itemLink, userLink,
                          activity.custom0, activity.custom1)>
              <#if mode = "user" && !activity.suppressSite>
                <#assign detailHTML = msg("in.site", detailHTML, siteLink)></#if>
              <summary type="html">
                <![CDATA[${msg(detailHTML)}]]>
              </summary>
              <author>
                <name>${activity.fullName?xml}</name>
                <uri>${absurl(activity.userProfile)?xml}</uri>
              </author>
            </entry>
          </#list>
        </#if>
      </feed>
    </xml>
```

The `#list` directive in FreeMarker is used to iterate through the activities of the site. FreeMarker has access to the activities as a collection and this script accesses each activity and formats the information specified by the Atom subscription specification, including name, author, and date.

Portlet View

Many Alfresco installations use Alfresco in conjunction with portals, such as Liferay. Portals provide a page view composed of individual windows called portlets (see Figure 17-17), which aggregate and assemble information according to the user's preference. Content from content management systems is often some of the most important information that comes through a portal in the form of corporate news, key business decisions, changes in plans or products, or policies and procedures.

A portlet consists of specialized Query views or Browser views. The portlets are designed to work with JSR-168 or JSR-286–compatible portals. The presentation technology is either Web scripts or Surf. Depending on how they are rendered, they can also be used as Google Gadgets, which is a similar technology. The Portlet views can be used for tracking workflow tasks, currently checked-out documents, activities from Share sites, or documents of interest to the user based upon topic or keyword. A Portlet view can also present a Browser view for navigating a repository from the portal.

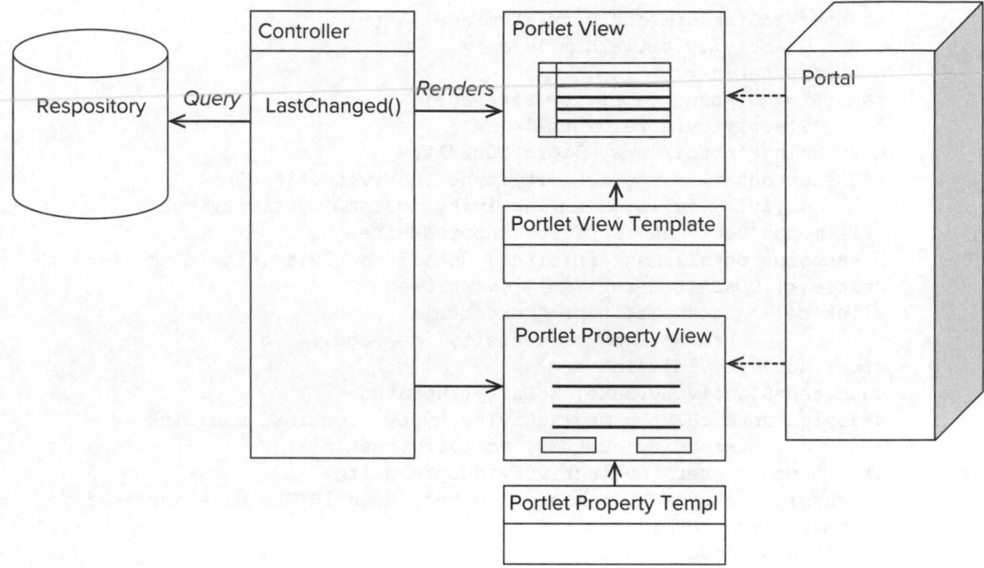

FIGURE 17-17

Using a Portlet View

A Portlet view wraps a Query view or a Browser view within a JSR-168 container. This container persists preferences and can provide configuration information for the portlet, as well as authentication and personalization. The portlet redirects a request to a Web script, which in turn renders a Query view as a JSR-168 portlet. The actions rendered by the Query view should be consistent with a portlet. For example, when a view accesses a content and details page, this should be handled in a portal-friendly way.

A Property view in a portal should be its own portlet, allowing the user to navigate correctly through the portal. In this case, the Property view should appear as a portlet, providing details of an object that would have been clicked through from a Query view or Browser view.

When to Use It

Portals are useful when integrating information from many sources, particularly across the enterprise. When you wish to present more than just content from Alfresco, such as news feeds, general information (for example, weather), information from other enterprise applications, or analytical dashboards, then a portal can be a good choice for accessing Alfresco as well. Liferay is the most common open source portal used with Alfresco. However, other portals have also been used, such as IBM WebSphere, Oracle/BEA WebLogic, and Microsoft SharePoint.

Example: Liferay and CMIS

The following is an example of a portlet designed to work in the Liferay portal using CMIS to access the repository. It uses a basic XML parser to handle the AtomPub protocol for accessing CMIS.

```
package training;

import java.io.IOException;
import java.io.PrintWriter;
import java.io.Writer;

import javax.portlet.ActionRequest;
import javax.portlet.ActionResponse;
import javax.portlet.GenericPortlet;
import javax.portlet.PortletException;
import javax.portlet.PortletSecurityException;
import javax.portlet.PortletSession;
import javax.portlet.PortletURL;
import javax.portlet.RenderRequest;
import javax.portlet.RenderResponse;
import javax.xml.parsers.DocumentBuilderFactory;

import org.apache.commons.httpclient.Credentials;
import org.apache.commons.httpclient.HttpClient;
import org.apache.commons.httpclient.UsernamePasswordCredentials;
import org.apache.commons.httpclient.auth.AuthScope;
import org.apache.commons.httpclient.methods.GetMethod;
import org.w3c.dom.Document;
import org.w3c.dom.Element;
import org.w3c.dom.NodeList;

public class AlfrescoTrainingPortlet extends GenericPortlet {

  @Override
  protected void doView(RenderRequest request, RenderResponse response)
     throws PortletException, IOException
  {

    response.setContentType("text/html");

    HttpClient client = new HttpClient();
    client.getParams().setAuthenticationPreemptive(true);
    Credentials defaultcreds = new UsernamePasswordCredentials("admin", "admin");
    client.getState().setCredentials(AuthScope.ANY, defaultcreds);
    String url;

    String objectIdParam = (String)    request.getPortletSession()
            .getAttribute("objectId", PortletSession.PORTLET_SCOPE);
    if (objectIdParam == null) {
      url = http://localhost:8080/alfresco/s/api/path/workspace/SpacesStore/"+
              "Company%20Home/children";
    } else {
      url = "http://localhost:8080/alfresco/s/api/node/workspace/SpacesStore/" +
            objectIdParam + "/children";
    }
```

```
    GetMethod method = new GetMethod(url);
    client.executeMethod(method);
    PortletURL actionURL = response.createActionURL();

    PrintWriter writer = response.getWriter();
    try {
      Document dom = DocumentBuilderFactory.newInstance().newDocumentBuilder()
            .parse(method.getResponseBodyAsStream());
      NodeList list = dom.getElementsByTagName("cmis:propertyId");
      int len = list.getLength();
      for (int i = 0; i < len; i++) {
        Element element = (Element) list.item(i);
        String propertyName = element.getAttribute("cmis:name");
        String objectId = null;
        if (propertyName.equals("ObjectId")) {
          objectId = element.getElementsByTagName("cmis:value")
                .item(0).getTextContent();
          objectId = objectId.replaceAll("workspace://SpacesStore/", "");
          writer.println("<p>" + objectId);
        }
        if (objectId == null) {
          continue;
        }
        NodeList stringList = ((Element) element.getParentNode())
              .getElementsByTagName("cmis:propertyString");
        int stringSize = stringList.getLength();
        for (int j = 0; j < stringSize; j++) {
          Element strElem = ((Element) stringList.item(j));
          String strName = strElem.getAttribute("cmis:name");
          if (strName.equals("Name")) {
            actionURL.setParameter("objectId", objectId);
            writer.println("<a href='" + actionURL.toString() + "'>"
                  + strElem.getTextContent() + "</a>");
            break;
          }
        }
      }
    } catch (Exception exc) {
     exc.printStackTrace();
    }
  }

  @Override
  public void processAction(ActionRequest request, ActionResponse response)
      throws PortletException, PortletSecurityException, IOException
  {
    String objectId = request.getParameter("objectId");
    if (objectId != null) {
      request.getPortletSession().setAttribute("objectId", objectId,
              PortletSession.PORTLET_SCOPE);
    }
  }
}
```

This class, specialized from GenericPortlet, uses the method `doView()` to actually create the Portlet view. It is using CMIS `getChildren()` to get the children of the folder browsed, initially the Company Home Page at the top of the repository. It constructs a Browser view specialized for a portlet and creates links for the next level of browsing. It also iterates through all the properties to display their values in the portlet.

EXAMPLE INTEGRATIONS

You have already seen a number of systems that have integrated with Alfresco. Many of these use CMIS because of the opportunity to make them work with other ECM systems. However, Alfresco is often the starting point for these integrations because of the open source implementation available as a community download and because of the growing community of CMIS developers around Alfresco.

Following are examples of some of the most popular or requested integrations.

Joomla and Drupal

Joomla and Drupal represent the most popular PHP-based content management systems and a significant percentage of LAMP (Linux Apache MySQL PHP) implementations. Neither system has focused on repository or document capabilities, so Alfresco as an open source content repository represents a popular way of managing documents or other controlled content. Also, because content is stored in a MySQL database, Alfresco becomes a scalable way of storing information.

Integrations are available from both communities (see Figures 17-18 and 17-19) and focus on the Browser and Search patterns.

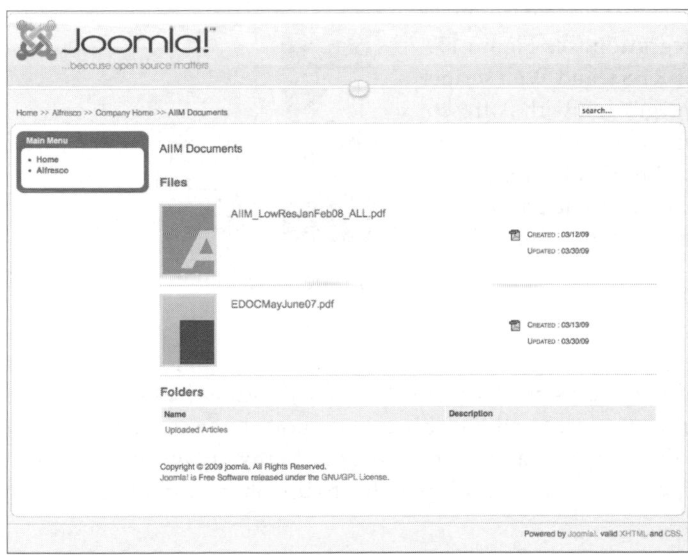

FIGURE 17-18

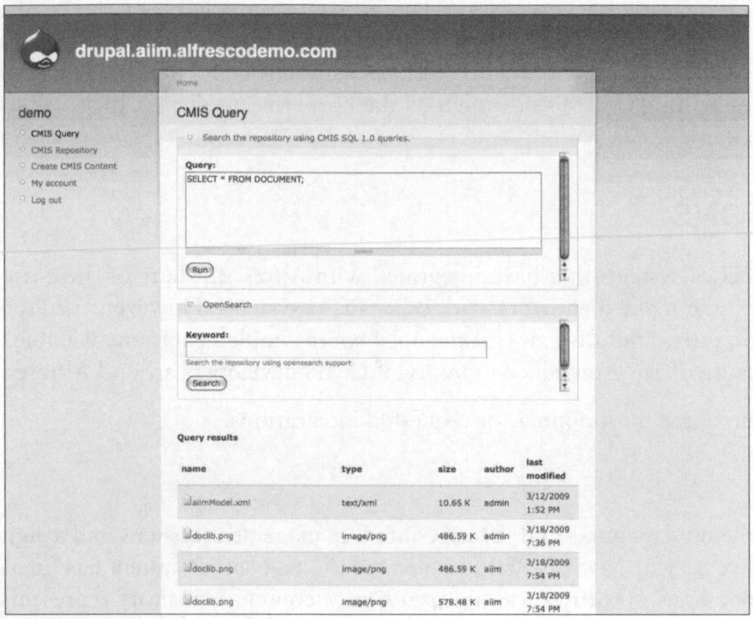

FIGURE 17-19

Confluence

Confluence is a popular wiki from Atlassian often used in development and increasingly used in enterprise environments. Based upon Java, the Confluence integration (see Figure 17-20) fits neatly with Alfresco and uses REST and Web scripts to integrate, as well as CMIS. The integration with Alfresco consists primarily of macros that can be used in wiki pages to access documents or other content in the Alfresco repository. These macros implement either the browser pattern or the query pattern, allowing the wiki page author to put a CMIS query in the page.

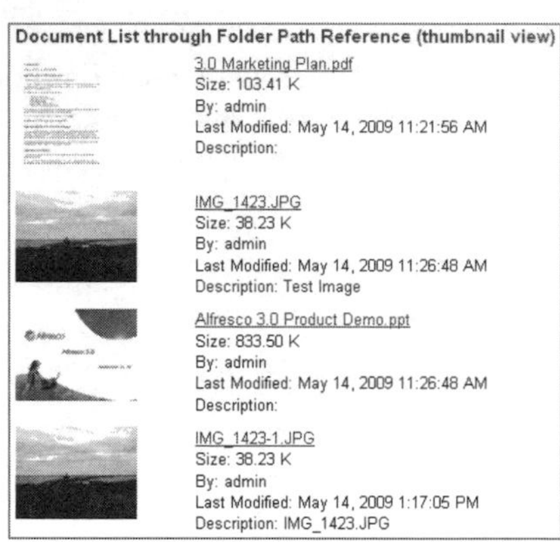

FIGURE 17-20

Liferay Portal

Alfresco integrates with a number of portals, particularly JSR-168 and JSR-286–based portals, but Liferay is probably the most popular open source and possibly general portal integrated with Alfresco. Integration with Alfresco consists of single sign-on and a set of portlets. Many organizations write their own portlets with Alfresco; however, with Alfresco 3.3 it is possible to use Share portlets and the Share document library as portlets as well.

SAP

Alfresco is used in several SAP installations, as seen in Figure 17-21, using the archive pattern and the SAP ArchiveLink protocol. Thus the ArchiveLink and SAP implement the Content Service Mapping pattern for ArchiveLink and Archive patterns inside the SAP system. This allows the linkage of content to SAP business objects and to archive reports. In addition, ArchiveLink supports the Attachment pattern to attach scanned images, perhaps with Kofax, and attaching those images to a business object.

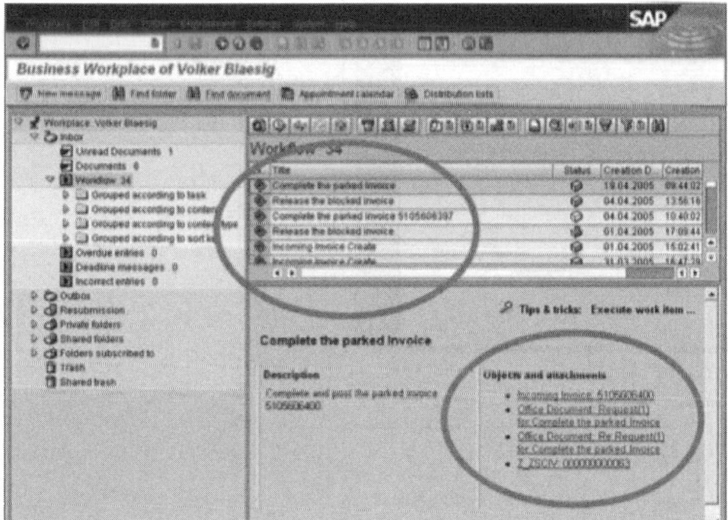

FIGURE 17-21

Kofax Image Scanning

The Kofax integration was built by Micro Strategies and integrates Alfresco through release scripts. These release scripts implement the archive pattern by storing content and metadata in Alfresco, and implement the workflow pattern by presenting quality control workflows inside the Alfresco system. Images are scanned locally and the user is presented with metadata to capture. Users can access and process images through the Web, as seen in Figure 17-22.

Microsoft SharePoint

CMIS-based Web parts can integrate Microsoft SharePoint with Alfresco. Some prototype Web parts were demonstrated during the CMIS Technical Committee face-to-face meetings. It is likely that CMIS-based Web parts will be available with the official release of SharePoint 2010 and the official version of CMIS 1.0 by OASIS. These Web parts would implement the Portlet, Browser, and Search patterns.

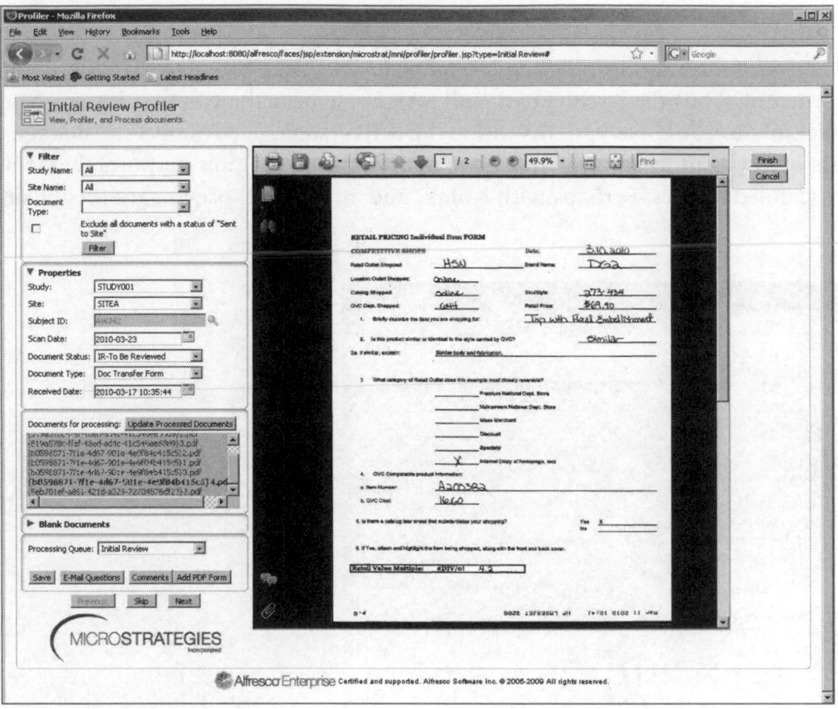

FIGURE 17-22

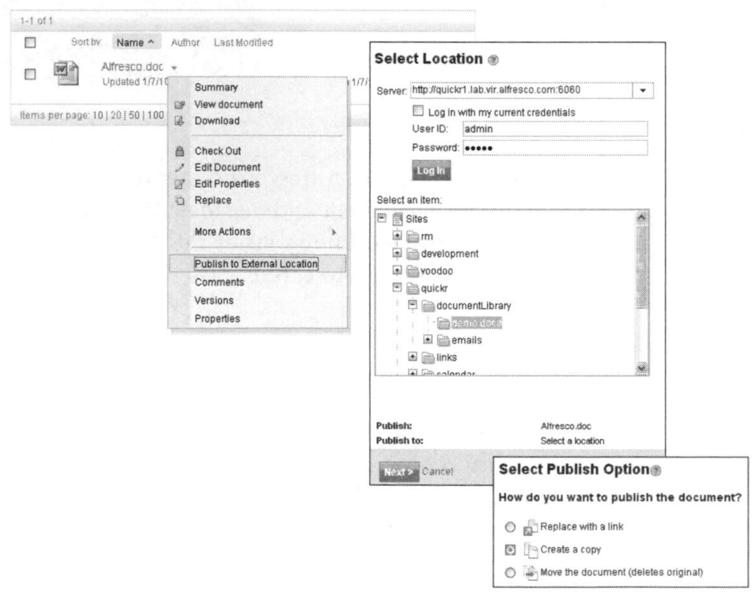

FIGURE 17-23

Lotus Quickr

IBM Lotus Quickr and Connections access content services through ECM Services for Quickr, an abstract interface to ECM systems. Alfresco ECM Services for Quickr provides this interface as an extension to the Alfresco system using a combination of AtomPub and Web services calls. Alfresco Services for Quickr implements the Content Service Mapping pattern to allow access to Alfresco; the Archive pattern for storing transient content in Quickr into Alfresco; the Attachment pattern by having a link in Quickr to access the content; and, finally, the Browser pattern to navigate the Alfresco repository. This provides to Quickr users lightweight ECM and archiving services that can run on the same machine as the Quickr system (see Figure 17-23).

Email Clients

Integrating email clients such as Microsoft Outlook, Lotus Notes, or Apple Mail can be done through the Alfresco IMAP protocol, as seen in Figure 17-24. The IMAP protocol itself implements the Content Services Mapping pattern by mapping browsing calls to mail folders and individual content items to mail with the content presented as attachments. In addition, this can implement the Archive pattern in that email may be archived by drag and drop or by archiving to what appear to be mail folders.

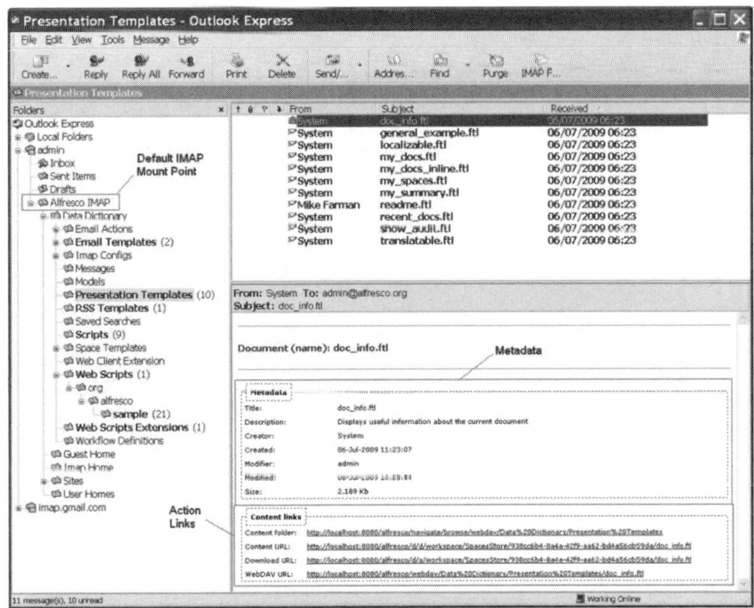

FIGURE 17-24

INDEX

The prefix "ON" before a page number indicates that the entry can be found in the online appendices.

A

D

E

F

G

H

N

O

P

S

T

U

X

Z